Flex 3 in Action

Flex 3 in Action

TARIQ AHMED

with JON HIRSCHI
and FAISAL ABID

MANNING

Greenwich
(74° w. long.)

For online information and ordering of this and other Manning books, please visit www.manning.com. The publisher offers discounts on this book when ordered in quantity. For more information, please contact:

Special Sales Department
Manning Publications Co.
Sound View Court 3B   Fax: (609) 877-8256
Greenwich, CT 06830   Email: orders@manning.com

♾ Recognizing the importance of preserving what has been written, it is Manning's policy to have the books we publish printed on acid-free paper, and we exert our best efforts to that end. Recognizing also our responsibility to conserve the resources of our planet, Manning books are printed on paper that is at least 15% recycled and processed elemental chlorine-free

Manning Publications Co.
Sound View Court 3B
Greenwich, CT 06830

Development Editor: Tom Cirtin
Copyeditor: Tiffany Taylor
Typesetter: Tony Roberts
Cover designer: Leslie Haimes

ISBN: 9781933988740
Printed in the United States of America
2 3 4 5 6 7 8 9 10 – MAL – 15 14 13 12 11 10 09

brief contents

contents

foreword

The ability to create Rich Internet Applications (RIAs) has been around much longer than the term itself; since version 8, the Flash Platform has been a viable RIA platform. But it was initially geared toward designers using the environment from a creative perspective, which wasn't ideal for those coming from a pure development background.

If you were a Flash application developer, major hurdles still remained in your way. Delivering feature-laden rich applications in a productive and timely manner was difficult because you had to do most of the work yourself.

The challenge became clear and simple: provide a pure development environment that leveraged the ubiquity and capabilities of Flash yet catered directly to developers and their systems-development lifecycle. Give developers tools to be productive, and give them a framework that did most of the hard work for them so that they could focus their efforts on application logic. The solution to this challenge was Flex.

Flex has been on quite a journey since its release in March 2004 by Macromedia. That first version was followed by the more widely distributed version 1.5 later that year. Flex started as a server product and was billed as a way for developers to create applications on the Flash Platform.

This opened up a whole new world and helped light the fire for RIAs. As Flex-based RIAs began to gain traction, it proved that a demand existed for RIAs and that the general premise for the technological approach was sound. The next step would be to bring RIAs to the masses.

Now under the Adobe brand, the product made a huge jump with the release of Flex 2 in June 2006. Performance was greatly improved as a result of a language overhaul (ActionScript 3) and a major update to the Flash Player (V9).

The tooling switched to the Eclipse platform, which gave it instant credibility with programmers. Flex 2 saw the split of basic compilation and server-side data management. We also saw the first release of the free SDK for compiling Flex apps outside of the IDE. The server-side component evolved into Flex Data Services, now known as LiveCycle Data Services, which enabled real-time data sharing.

These changes helped legitimize the idea of RIAs by proving a desktop experience was possible inside of the browser. At this point, what RIAs needed most was community support.

Tariq saw the need for community support and was there from the very start. He began by creating the first portal and community dedicated to Flex—also known as Community Flex (CFLEX.Net).

CFLEX.Net aggregated tips, tricks, blog posts, events, and technical articles about how to get started with this new framework. Tariq was instrumental in contributing content to the early Flex community, and I owe many of my Flex skills to him.

Early on, Tariq grasped the importance of data services and how real-time data can help complete a Rich Internet Application. He's built everything from internal business-facing Flex applications to great consumer applications. He's seen and used everything the platform has to offer, which is one of many reasons he's an ideal author for a Flex book. I think it's long overdue that this recognized expert's work be bound and made portable.

The release of Flex 3 brings us to a new and exciting stage in the framework and the technology. Adobe open-sourced much of the Flex platform in an effort to be as transparent as possible and to incorporate valuable feedback (not to mention great code) from the community.

With the release of the Adobe AIR, developers can now use Flex to deploy desktop applications as well as browser-based applications.

Adobe has long been known for its great design tools. Flex 3 is the first release that allows designers using those tools to seamlessly collaborate with developers to create great-looking Flex applications. Numerous productivity enhancements in the framework and Flex Builder also make it easier for new developers to get started and scale their applications.

Regardless of your development background or experience with Flex, you'll find *Flex 3 In Action* to be an invaluable guide. There is something for everyone in this book. Tariq and his coauthors Jon and Faisal provide a must-have for any Flex library. This is to be expected from the star who has provided the Flex community with the must-have resource we all know and love, CFLEX.Net.

RYAN STEWART
Platform Evangelist
Adobe Systems, Inc.

preface

For years I had been searching for a way to provide users with a better online experience. It took time before Google wowed everyone with the innovative Google Maps site, so for a long time users didn't know how much better things could be.

Through the years of using the web for document distribution, users' expectations devolved from the power of native desktop applications to the anemic ability of HTML applications. That's not a knock against HTML and the web—the web is perfect for what it does, which is deliver platform-neutral documents. Developers and companies focused on the web's ability to give them time-to-market rapid application development; and users accepted whatever was in front of them because, hey, that's how web applications are. Right?

It bothered me that with every click, a back-end system executed a lot of code to result in minimal UI changes. Even worse was the constant bombardment of database servers. For a technologist, the quick remedy to this is simple: slap in more memory, load up on virtual machines, scale out horizontally with low-cost commodity servers, and call it a day. But I'm talking about the cost to the user. On their end, they were experiencing that annoying click 'n' wait feeling that was common for web applications. In addition, UIs were limited. Sure, you could use JavaScript; but you could only go so far before you needed advanced skills. From an ROI perspective, it generally wasn't worth it.

At the time, Java Applets and Flash were available, and they seemed to offer the potential to achieve what I was looking for. But Applets failed as a solution; they were bloated, slow, and inconsistent across platforms. Flash was promising, but trying to produce enterprise business applications in a designer's environment proved to be more challenging than it was worth.

During my time in the Knowledge Management department at eBay, this challenge came up again. I needed a way to abstract the complexity of the data and make it simple for users to work in a visual environment.

Along came Flex in 2004 (V1 initially, and V1.5 shortly after that). I was able to make a business case for using it and our team delivered experiences at an entirely new level. At this point, I knew Flex would be big. It delivered the desktop power users needed while maintaining the development velocity that software teams require to survive.

As a believer in Flex, I made it a personal mission to help grow the Flex community. I created CFLEX.Net (www.cflex.net), believing that the bigger the community, the more it will reinvest in itself through knowledge and code sharing, and in this way continue to boost the technology's adoption rate. If there's a strong support network, you take less of a risk in bringing a new technology into your organization.

For the early adopters of Flex, the learning curve was rough because only a limited number of books and other reading material was available. That changed with the release of Flex 2, when the number of resources dramatically increased.

I left eBay in late 2005 to join Amcom Computer Services and build and manage a team of developers. As with any new technology, experts in the field are hard to come by, so your best bet is to grow the skill. While training developers on Flex, I found that the current set of books didn't map to how they think, and that obvious challenges were never addressed.

In continuing my mission of growing the community, I set out to write this book, hoping it would help solve the learning challenges that everyday developers face. Instead of grouping topics based on feature categories, the book is structured according to the natural progression of creating an application. I focused on maximum simplicity by not introducing anything you don't need to know until it was needed and by using small code examples that are easy to absorb. I also found that people learn best when they're able to relate new things to things they already know; so whenever possible, I use analogies to how you would do things in another technology.

My hope is that if I can provide you with a solid foundation of understanding, the Flex community will expand as a result, as you too will be able to share your knowledge and experience with those around you.

Now is the time to get into Flex. The community continues to grow, more and more third-party vendors are coming out with Flex-related technologies, and Flex user groups are popping up all over the place.

The RIA space is heating up quickly as other vendors scramble to catch up, but Adobe continues to prove it's a few steps ahead. We're in for some exciting times! HTML web applications will always have a place; but it's time to take your skills to another level, because the industry is moving forward with or without you.

Sit down, buckle up, and strap in for the ride!

TARIQ AHMED

acknowledgments

This has been a long and amazing journey from the initial concept to the final printed book. At first, I didn't think being the lead author would be possible considering the demands of work, responsibilities on the home front, and my other activities in the Flex community. Writing this book helped me achieve new levels of planning and organization, purely because it was the only way I could allocate the required time. And then I needed to learn how to maintain a high degree of focus in order to make efficient use of that time.

Although most developers want to believe that choices related to technology are premised on purity, capability, and supremacy, the reality is that in the end it boils down to business—and technology as a tool to help businesses achieve their goals. In this book I try to keep this perspective in mind, because a well-rounded view will help you be successful. I've learned about this perspective—and so much more—from my manager and mentor Steve McClary, president of Amcom Computer Services.

This book was made possible—and better—by contributions from Jon Hirschi and Faisal Abid. Jon demystifies Events, shows us how to exchange data from back-end systems, and provides an in-depth lowdown on Pop-Ups and View States. Faisal covers application architecture topics with Objects and Classes, and Reusability. Faisal also gives a quick glimpse into taking your Flex applications beyond the browser by using Adobe's Integrated Runtime (AIR). I also have to thank Abdul Qabiz for giving us a huge head start with View States, and Frank Krul for his technical expertise.

Of course, the crew at Manning are the silent heroes here. Since this was my first foray into the realm of book writing, I didn't know what to expect. The folks at Manning make being an author as easy as possible. With their open and collaborative approach, they guided me along this long journey; their professionalism and willingness to help made the process smooth and easy. They also made the experience a personal one—and that meant a lot to me. There are a lot of people to thank at Manning, starting with publisher Marjan Bace, assistants Christina Rudloff and Megan Yockey, and review editor Karen Tegtmeyer, but special kudos to my editors, Michael Stephens and Tom Cirtin, and to the production team for the book: Dianne Russell, Tiffany Taylor, Elizabeth Martin, Tony Roberts, Leslie Haimes, and Mary Piergies.

I am grateful to the reviewers who took time to read the manuscript at different points in its development and to provide valuable feedback: Christophe Bunn, Ken Brueck, Rick Evans, Charlie Griefer, Andrew Grothe, Jon Messer, Doug Warren, and John Wilker. Special thanks to the two reviewers who did a technical proofread of the chapters during production, Billy Blackerby and Robert Glover, and to Ryan Stewart of Adobe Systems who agreed to write the foreword.

Most importantly I thank my wife Juliana and my daughter Zafira for being supportive of this project. Although I was physically around most of the time, I was often in another dimension, mentally. I know it was hard for them, and I want to thank them with all my heart for giving me the opportunity to achieve this goal.

To everyone mentioned above, thank you for believing in me!

about this book

Flex is an event-driven, object-oriented application framework and programming language that lets you build compelling and fluid Rich Internet Applications (RIAs) that run in the Adobe Flash environment.

Historically, the priority in web application development has been feature velocity and time to market, at the cost of usability to the end user. Flex lets you maintain that centrally deployed rapid-turnaround model, but it gives you the power to achieve usability at the same time.

Someone coming into Flex faces unique challenges. First, many developers aren't used to an event-driven technology. They can understand it at a high level, but don't truly *get it* for a long time. Until that happens, you can't use the technology to its full capability; and, more important, you won't be able to work as productively.

The second challenge stems from the fact that many developers have been working in their current technology stack for many years. Because people go with what they know, they tend to copy what they did in HTML over into Flex. That will work, but you're limiting yourself creatively.

The third challenge is the complexity that comes as a result of Flex's power. It's not complicated *per se,* but a lot of web-application technologies are procedural and non-event-driven. The learning curve starts off slowly as you see the basic examples; but the moment you try to go one step further, it suddenly *feels* a lot harder.

Flex 3 in Action addresses these challenges and uses them as an underlying premise; it's what makes the book unique. With the first challenge, the book emphasizes the event-driven nature of Flex by periodically reminding you how to leverage the event objects. We also help you catch on more quickly by showing many ways of doing the same thing along with the advantages and disadvantages of each.

Addressing the second challenge, we don't negate your existing skills and we understand that you're probably coming from another web technology. We came from there, too, and we know the mental leap it takes to break out of a mold you're accustomed to. The book continuously provides suggestions how you can harness the power of a particular feature.

As far as the third challenge—complexity—is concerned, the mission of the book is to enable you to become an effective Flex developer in a short time. We do this through a combination of techniques that include using small examples you can relate to. We also leverage your existing skills by relating how you used to do things in other technologies with how you do them in Flex. The chapters are ordered in a logical progression of how you would go about building an application, starting with the easy stuff and ramping up your skills along the way.

You're in good hands, and we'll be your guide as you take your skills and career to the next level. The one thing we haven't figured out is how to deal with all the fanfare that you'll get from appreciative users—you'll have to figure that out on your own!

Roadmap

Chapter 1 introduces Flex. It defines the problem and the approach Flex takes to solving it. Playing off that, we give you the business case that you'll need to make in order to sell Flex to your department, customer, or clients. We describe how Flex works at a high level along with the concept of events, and where Flex sits in the overall suite of Adobe products.

Chapter 2 gets you started with building applications in Flex by introducing the toolset, environment, and languages. Events are fleshed out a bit more to ensure that your understanding continues to grow.

Chapter 3 is about Flex's core language: ActionScript. This powerful ECMAScript-compliant, object-oriented language is what makes Flex possible. The chapter reviews data types, operators, loops, conditionals, and so on. You won't get far without ActionScript, so it's worth learning about it early on.

Chapter 4 addresses the layout of an application. It covers how you position display objects, as well as use containers to group visual objects together.

Chapter 5 begins by teaching you how to capture user input via forms. Flex has form inputs similar to those in HTML, but it also has a number of inputs that move beyond how they are captured in HTML.

Chapter 6 continues the topics from chapter 5 by discussing how Flex's validators are used to validate user input. From a usability perspective, validating up front saves the user time and grief.

Chapter 7 flips things around by using formatters to format raw information (now that you have it). Often used alongside validators, formatters address the headache of having to format things yourself.

Chapter 8 explores the workhorse of Flex: list-based components. Lists are data-driven components that automatically build their display based on the data that they're pointed at.

Chapter 9 continues the topic of lists and focuses on how to customize them, from quick 'n' dirty approaches to using full-blown item renderers for customized display. Chapter 9 also introduces editors, which allow for inline editing.

Chapter 10 goes all out on events. By this point, we'll have introduced how to use events in a minimal way; but this chapter takes it to the next level by going deep into how they work.

Chapter 11 shows you how to add navigation to your application so you can give your users the ability to switch between features.

Chapter 12 covers the use of pop-up windows as an extension to application navigation. It describes how your application can communicate with the pop-up by sending information back and forth.

Chapter 13 explores the subject of application flow and discusses a unique Flex feature known as view states. This mechanism can save you a lot of time by configuring the different views in your application; you can then switch from one view to another easily.

Chapter 14 begins the subject of working with data, particularly with getting data to and from your application from a back-end service. This includes connecting to servers that support Flex's native binary protocol (AMF), XML over HTTP, and web services.

Chapter 15 dives into working with XML. XML is a ubiquitous language; but Flex is the first to support the E4X syntax, which lets you work with XML as if it were a native Flex object.

Chapter 16 covers objects and classes. Flex is an object-oriented language, after all. And although the comfort factor of sticking to its tag-based MXML language is nice, being aware of how ActionScript objects are created and used only adds to your powers.

Chapter 17 goes into detail about custom components, which is an area in which you'll spend a lot of your development time. Custom components are your primary vehicle to break your application into small, manageable, reusable pieces.

Chapter 18 wraps up application structure with an overview of Flex's reusability features such as sharing custom components across multiple projects and compiling shared libraries of functionality.

Chapter 19 begins the subject of customizing the experience. This topic includes using Flex's version of CSS styles, skinning, and themes. Images and fonts are also covered.

Chapter 20 dives into one of Flex's coolest features: effects. Effects add that "wow" factor to your application, and we also show how they can assist you in increasing usability.

Chapter 21 finishes our discussion of customization by showing you in detail how to use the drag-and-drop feature. This is a crowd favorite, but from the usability perspective you can save your users a few clicks by speeding up the workflow.

Chapter 22 is about charting. We review the various types of charts and give you advice about when to use each type. We also discuss the parts that make up a chart and how to customize it.

Chapter 23 covers testing and debugging. At this point, you're wrapping up the project and entering the QA cycle. Knowing how to debug applications and how to isolate issues is key. Flex comes with a number of built-in features, but we also review third-party tools.

Chapter 24 wraps up the project with the final steps. These involve adding print capabilities to your application, using wrappers to load your application, and developing a release plan to deploy a production build of the software.

Following chapter 24 is a listing of developer resources, discussion forums, open source initiatives, the Flex ecosystem, and user groups in North America and internationally.

Code downloads and conventions

This book contains numerous examples of Flex, ActionScript, and XML code. All code examples can be found at the book's website: http://www.flexinaction.com as well as at the publisher's website: http://www.manning.com/ahmed or http://www.manning.com/Flex3inAction.

The following conventions are used throughout the book:

- *Italic* typeface is used to introduce new terms.
- `Courier/Fixed-Width` typeface is used on code samples, as well as elements, attributes/properties, function names, and class names. MXML components, when used by name, won't use this typeface in text unless they're referenced as part of an actual code snippet.
- ***`Bold and Italic face Courier/Fixed-Width`*** typeface is used to highlight portions within code.
- Code annotations accompany many segments of code. Certain annotations are marked with bullets such as ❶. These annotations have further explanations that follow the code.
- The > symbol is used to indicate menu items that should be selected in sequence.
- Code-line continuations use the ➥ symbol.

Author Online

Purchase of *Flex 3 in Action* includes free access to a private web forum run by Manning Publications where you can make comments about the book, ask technical questions, and receive help from the authors and from other users. To access the forum and subscribe to it, point your web browser to www.manning.com/Flex3inAction. This page provides information on how to get on the forum once you're registered, what kind of help is available, and the rules of conduct on the forum.

Manning's commitment to our readers is to provide a venue where a meaningful dialogue between individual readers and between readers and the authors can take place. It isn't a commitment to any specific amount of participation on the part of the authors, whose contributions to the book's forum remain voluntary (and unpaid). We suggest you try asking the authors some challenging questions, lest their interests stray!

The Author Online forum and the archives of previous discussions will be accessible from the publisher's website as long as the book is in print.

About the authors

TARIQ AHMED is an accomplished web-application pioneer, having introduced next-generation web technologies to companies such as Bell Canada and Reuters. He and Jon Hirschi were first to introduce eBay to Adobe Flex; it later proliferated to other teams. As an Adobe Flex Community Expert, Tariq has been evangelizing the technology and supporting the community through various projects and is well known for his Community Flex (CFLEX.Net) site. Tariq is currently the manager of product development at Amcom Technology, located in the San Francisco Bay area.

JON HIRSCHI has been innovating with Flex since its first version. As an Adobe Flex Community Expert, he's been sharing his expert-level knowledge through his personal blog, technology magazine articles, and user groups. Jon was involved not only in the introduction of Flex at eBay, but also in its continuance via a cutting-edge command center that allows eBay to manage its servers. Jon is currently the manager of technology at Kadoink Inc., located in the San Francisco Bay area.

FAISAL ABID is a software engineering student in Toronto, Canada, and runs his own RIA consulting company G-uniX Technologies. He's written RIA solutions for various clients, including internet startups Buzzspot and RazorCom. Faisal's community involvement includes numerous articles for magazines, and he is known for his experiments with technology.

About the title

By combining introductions, overviews, and how-to examples, the *In Action* books are designed to help learning and remembering. According to research in cognitive science, the things people remember are things they discover during self-motivated exploration.

Although no one at Manning is a cognitive scientist, we are convinced that for learning to become permanent it must pass through stages of exploration, play, and, interestingly, retelling of what is being learned. People understand and remember new things, which is to say they master them, only after actively exploring them. Humans learn *in action*. An essential part of an *In Action* guide is that it's example-driven. It encourages the reader to try things out, to play with new code, and explore new ideas.

There is another, more mundane, reason for the title of this book: our readers are busy. They use books to do a job or solve a problem. They need books that allow them to jump in and jump out easily and learn just what they want, just when they want it. They need books that aid them *in action*. The books in this series are designed for such readers.

About the cover illustration

The illustration on the cover of *Flex 3 in Action* bears the caption "An Armenian" and is taken from a collection of costumes of the Ottoman Empire published on January 1, 1802, by William Miller of Old Bond Street, London. The title page is missing from the collection and we have been unable to track it down to date. The book's table of contents identifies the figures in both English and French, and each illustration also bears the names of two artists who worked on it, both of whom would no doubt be surprised to find their art gracing the front cover of a computer programming book...two hundred years later.

The collection was purchased by a Manning editor at an antiquarian flea market in the "Garage" on West 26th Street in Manhattan. The seller was an American based in Ankara, Turkey, and the transaction took place just as he was packing up his stand for the day. The Manning editor did not have on his person the substantial amount of cash that was required for the purchase and a credit card and check were both politely turned down. With the seller flying back to Ankara that evening the situation was getting hopeless. What was the solution? It turned out to be nothing more than an old-fashioned verbal agreement sealed with a handshake. The seller simply proposed that the money be transferred to him by wire and the editor walked out with the bank information on a piece of paper and the portfolio of images under his arm. Needless to say, we transferred the funds the next day, and we remain grateful and impressed by this unknown person's trust in one of us. It recalls something that might have happened a long time ago.

The pictures from the Ottoman collection, like the other illustrations that appear on our covers, bring to life the richness and variety of dress customs of two centuries ago. They recall the sense of isolation and distance of that period—and of every other historic period except our own hyperkinetic present.

Dress codes have changed since then and the diversity by region, so rich at the time, has faded away. It is now often hard to tell the inhabitant of one continent from another. Perhaps, trying to view it optimistically, we have traded a cultural and visual diversity for a more varied personal life. Or a more varied and interesting intellectual and technical life.

We at Manning celebrate the inventiveness, the initiative, and, yes, the fun of the computer business with book covers based on the rich diversity of regional life of two centuries ago, brought back to life by the pictures from this collection.

Part 1

Application basics

Your journey into Flex is about to begin. This part of the book is focused on getting you ramped up with the basics of making Flex applications.

Before the coding starts, we'll present a high-level overview of what Flex is, from its languages to its ecosystem, and how the parts fit together. Building on what you learn, you'll set up your development environment so you can create and build Flex applications.

With the ability to compile and run Flex applications, the coding (a.k.a. the good stuff) begins with an overview of ActionScript—the core language of Flex. Progressively, you'll put together all the building blocks that make up the essence of every application from layout, to building and validating forms, to formatting data, to displaying lists of information.

1 Introduction to Flex

This chapter covers:

- Solving problems with Flex
- Using RIAs and RWAs
- Comparing Flex to the competition
- Learning the Flex ecosystem

This chapter makes the case why Flex is a great addition to your personal skill set or your organization. With buzzwords flying all over, a nonstop stream of websites with missing vowels in their names, and the Web 2.0 space on fire, a hodgepodge of technologies leaves the common developer caught in the middle. It is vital to be able to defend the decision to move forward with Flex to both customers and management.

In this chapter, we'll talk about challenges that a web developer faces and how to solve them using Flex by Adobe. We'll also get into the mechanics of a Flex application and discuss the ecosystem as a whole.

1.1 Why are web applications so prolific?

Web applications are so prolific because the strength of the web is also its weakness. The original intent of the web was to be a lightweight information distribution system: a simple way to post documents on a server and retrieve them just as easily.

This key advantage is so compelling that by using it to make dynamic pages (web applications), it renders desktop applications old school (figure 1.1).

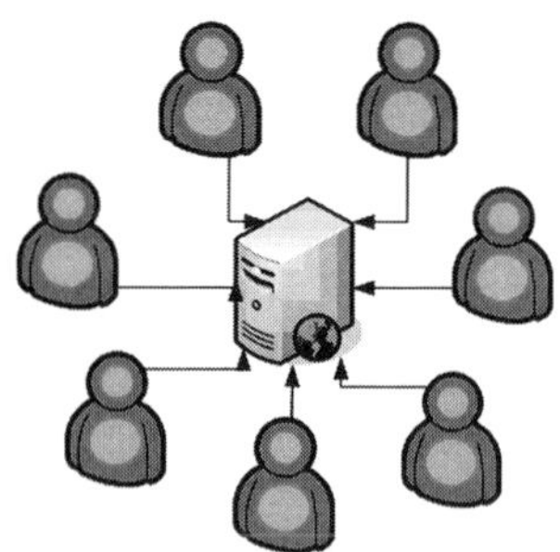

Figure 1.1 The great web advantage—centralized deployment

Yes, desktop applications are rich and robust; you can do anything the OS permits. But their deployment model is a borderline nightmare. The logistical complications of trying to get thousands, if not hundreds of thousands, of clients to run the precise version of your software at the exact same time are immense. Figure 1.2 shows a typical pop-up window nagging the user to upgrade an application.

Often, you need to provide support to handle multiple versions of desktop clients connecting to your back-end infrastructure. To cope, the only feasible option is to group large collections of enhancements and fixes into massive releases. And that's not taking into consideration how exponentially more complicated it becomes if you're supporting multiple platforms.

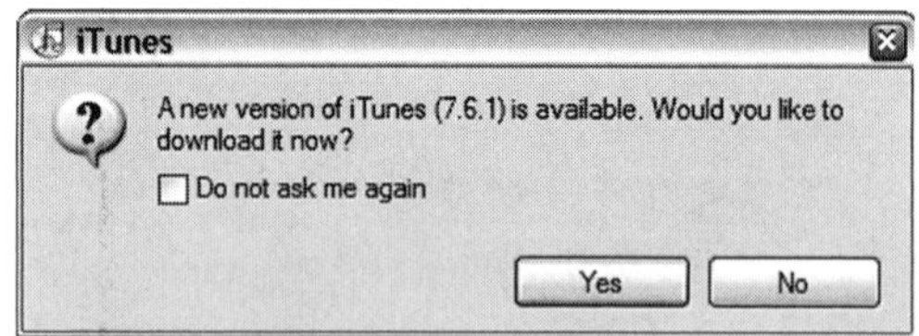

Figure 1.2 What if you had to respond to this once a week? Or daily? You'd stop using it.

Of course, with the web, you can release enhancements and fixes as fast as you can code them. Your releases are usually as simple as pushing out the new database changes and copying over the latest set of files. Bingo! Now all your users can take advantage of the latest and greatest updates transparently.

1.2 Prolific, but at a price

Seems like a no-brainer right? If you're already a web developer, you bask in this great advantage—yet at what price?

As you know, technologies quickly become obsolete, yet the centralized deployment model of web applications is so effective that we've continued to use its HTML-based language since its last revision in 1999. Isn't that embarrassing?

Perhaps you may not think of yourself as a hardcore ColdFusion developer using the Model-Glue framework, or a Java developer using Enterprise JavaBeans (EJBs) and Struts. But during all this time, one critical element was overlooked: the user experience (figure 1.3). Users willingly gave up usability for the ubiquity of web applications. Ultimately, we trained ourselves and the users to accept it.

Throw in JavaScript that manipulates Cascading Style Sheets (CSS) visibility properties, and hope that it solves the problem. But it doesn't. The core of the usability problem lies in the historical roots of the web—its structure has been built around what was intended to be a documentation-distribution mechanism.

As a developer, you exert a significant amount of effort to restore some semblance of usability by transferring as much application logic as possible to the front-end (client side) to mimic a client (desktop-like) experience. Much of that effort is spent fighting the nature of the platform.

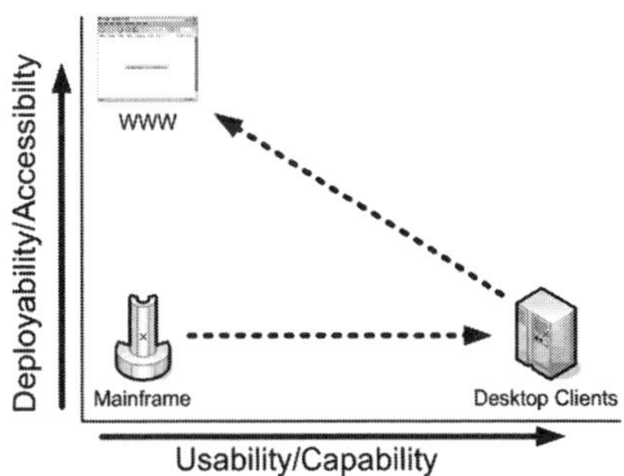

Figure 1.3 We took a great step backward in terms of usability for the sake of deployability.

Mind you, the web was supposed to be platform-agnostic. Yet, ironically, the more you push logic to the client side, the more you struggle with browser incompatibilities. This is where rich internet applications (RIAs) come into play.

1.3 The RIA solution

In this data-centric society, users and businesses depend on being able to work with information efficiently. Users simply want information quickly and easily. Businesses, from a customer-retention perspective, want to provide a better user experience than the competition, and need the technology to ensure the workforce is functioning productively.

In a sense, you now have a paradox: users wanting a pleasant experience and businesses trying to achieve high-feature velocity and operational efficiency. This is the case with traditional technologies and the divide upon which RIAs capitalize.

1.3.1 They all want it all

Users want to be able to access their data from whatever computer they're on. They also want to be able to do such trivial things as dragging and dropping. They want a rich, fluid graphical experience that incorporates sound and video. But they *don't* want to be constantly nagged to download the latest version.

Developers and software teams want it all too. Time-to-market is of high strategic value, whereas software development and maintenance is enormously expensive. Not being able to guarantee that all users are on the same version at the very same time introduces a high degree of overhead. Developers want to create software quickly and not worry about how to make it work on various platforms. They want the process of pushing out updates to be easy and fast.

Figure 1.4 summarizes who wins—and who loses—in each scenario.

But with problems or challenges come opportunity, and this is the opportunity that RIAs seize by providing the best of both worlds.

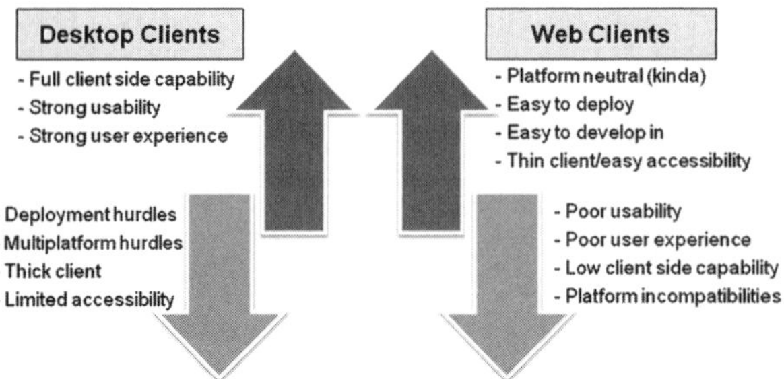

Figure 1.4 Pros and cons of desktop and web clients—choose the lesser of the evils.

1.3.2 RIAs to the rescue

RIAs solve this problem by incorporating the best of both worlds. RIAs are a technology that gives businesses-feature velocity and rapid deployment through the centralized internet deployment model, while providing users a desktop-like experience (figure 1.5).

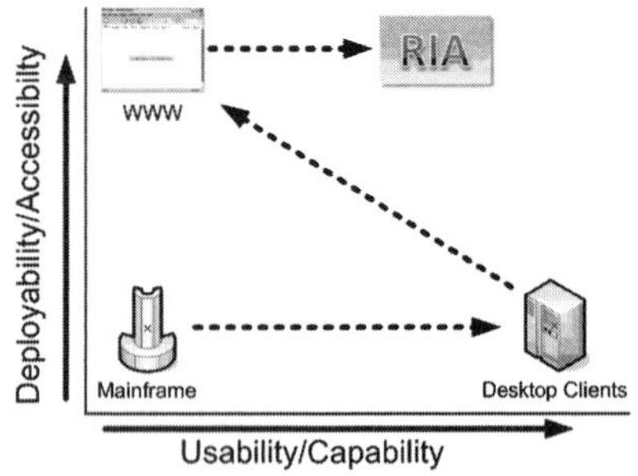

Figure 1.5 RIAs add the best of both worlds

RIAs bring back usability by enabling developers to give their users a compelling and fluid experience with that feeling of a live application (versus completely reloading a page every time you click something). That's the core ingredient to providing users a sense of engagement.

At the same time, the deployment and accessibility model remains the same—users can load these applications from any machine and all be running the same version. The best part is true platform neutrality; the same application yields the same look and feel regardless of environment.

1.3.3 How RIAs do it

RIAs are able to accomplish this primarily through the use of a browser plug-in that acts as a local runtime engine. With a runtime engine available for various browsers and operating systems, you're able to achieve platform neutrality.

Since it is a plug-in it can piggyback onto the browser. Using the browser as a delivery mechanism gives the plug-in the high degree of deployability that web applications enjoy.

1.4 The RIA contenders

The RIA space is hot right now, and contenders are standing in their respective corners of the ring. In one corner, you have the front-runner, Flex by Adobe; and in another corner is the top contender, Silverlight by Microsoft. Sun is also trying to capture a piece of the prize with the new kid on the block, JavaFX.

Here's a brief summary of the major RIA contenders.

1.4.1 Flex by Adobe

First out of the blocks, Adobe has maintained a fierce pace in expanding this platform. With Flex 3, Adobe made the framework open source; the software development kit (SDK) has been free since Flex 2, and the price point for the optional IDE is attractive.

Flex has the following things going for it:

- It leverages the nearly ubiquitous Flash Player, which has a 98% penetration level (trying to find a computer that doesn't have Flash is very challenging).
- The huge Flash community and its knowledge.
- Tight integration with other Adobe products from designer (Photoshop, Fireworks, and so on), to developer, to server (ColdFusion, media streaming, and so forth).
- A four-year head start.
- Open source framework.
- Free SDK.

On the downside:

- Although Flex's printing abilities are satisfactory, there is a lot of room for improvement (particularly with respect to report-style printing).
- Because the technology is still relatively new, the size of the community (an estimated 150,000 developers) is relatively small compared to .NET and Java.
- RIA applications are launched from a browser plug-in, so the application exists within the instance of that plug-in. This means pop-up windows aren't able to exist outside of the window in which the main Flex application is located (figure 1.6). Although Flex offers ways around this limitation (using third-party tools) it is not native to the platform.

Figure 1.6 Pop-up windows can't easily live in a window outside the instance of the Flash Player that's executing the Flex application.

1.4.2 Silverlight by Microsoft

Microsoft isn't well known for being an early innovator, seemingly preferring to invest enormous amounts of capital to dominate only after others have invented market spaces.

Silverlight doesn't yet have a spectrum of supporting products. But from the design perspective, Microsoft has a product called Expression Studio; from the platform perspective, it has some of the bases covered by supporting Windows and Apple OSs, as well as browsers such as Internet Explorer, Firefox, Safari, and Opera.

Microsoft is moving quickly with Silverlight 1.0, which was released in September 2007 (2.0 is already in beta). Version 2.0 continues to focus on fundamentals, which are features such as layout and data service components that Flex has incorporated since its earliest versions.

Adobe recognizes that an end-to-end systems development lifecycle exists. The life of a Flex application doesn't necessarily start when the Flex developer starts coding—it starts with the designers and the folks on user-experience teams who are mocking up the experience from its inception by using tools such as Fireworks, Photoshop, and Flash. The workflow is seamless; each type of user can work within his realm and collaborate easily with whoever is next in line both upstream and downstream.

The biggest thing that Silverlight has going for it is that users are able to leverage the existing .NET framework, components, and language. This will be a natural draw to those who are already in that development camp.

1.4.3 JavaFX by Sun Microsystems

At this time, JavaFX amounts to nothing more than an announcement.

If we were to speculate, we'd need to look back into Sun's history to postulate what to expect. For a company that generates $13 billion in revenue per year, it is well known for only two things: Java and its servers.

Sun had the opportunity to be the RIA leader with Java but failed to capitalize on it, rendering JavaFX pretty much a second attempt. Sun is also engaged in a strategic partnership with Laszlo Systems, which may help the company catch up.

Sun is a company that creates technologies for technologists, who in turn make solutions for technologists. The company's vision and spectrum are specific, focusing less on the average user as part of a usability case story.

Existing tools from Sun are functional and utilitarian and assume a certain level of subject-matter expertise. Creativity and design are definitely not Sun's strengths. In order for the company to succeed, it will need to take measures to compensate for its weaknesses. For example, having strong support for integration with the top tools in each industry—such as Photoshop for design—will get Sun past some early adoption hurdles.

Sun's biggest advantage will be the sheer size of the Java development community, with users who tend to be loyal to their platform.

Sun's biggest mistake would be to copy what Flex and Silverlight can do without offering any unique advantages or capabilities, thus relegating itself to being a "me-too" technology.

1.5 Flex vs. web applications

Management, clients, and adjacent team members may challenge you with a pure web approach—the argument being that we're talking about two different things: Flex (RIAs) versus rich web applications (RWAs).

These terms were concocted by vendors to market their wares, so there are no official definitions. We use RWA to define an HTML-based web application that uses advanced JavaScript toolkits and the AJAX technique of transferring data using XML.

Many people categorize RWAs as RIAs, but there are significant differences. The discussion that follows explains those dissimilarities.

1.5.1 Web applications are based on documents

Web applications are based on the eight-year-old HTML 4.01 specification, which was optimized for documentation distribution. Look at some of the terminology surrounding the web and web applications:

- Web pages
- Bookmarks
- Home pages
- Search engines with index pages

A web application is like a choose-your-own adventure book. Do you ever bookmark what you're doing in Photoshop or SQL Server Enterprise Manager? Would you index the Microsoft Project executable? These are all live applications; of course you wouldn't.

Another thing to look at is the rendering engine of web applications, the browser.

1.5.2 The role of browsers as transfer stations and document renderers

Although Flex applications are typically invoked using a browser, the browser serves merely as a transfer mechanism, accessing and downloading whatever is behind a URL.

To showcase the difference, look at the Flex-based mind mapping tool from Mindomo (figure 1.7), and you'll see an example of an application that is live and very rich. A browser serves two high-level purposes: to access and transfer data and information, and to render HTML documents. You also use the browser to load your Flex applications. But just because it is in a web browser doesn't make it a web application.

Flex applications truly are rich *internet* applications; they're platform-agnostic, internet-deployed thin clients. Flex supports multiple transfer protocols such as text/XML, web services, RTMP/Messaging, and the binary format known as Action Message Format (AMF). It also has a robust charting engine, can stream video natively, and do much more.

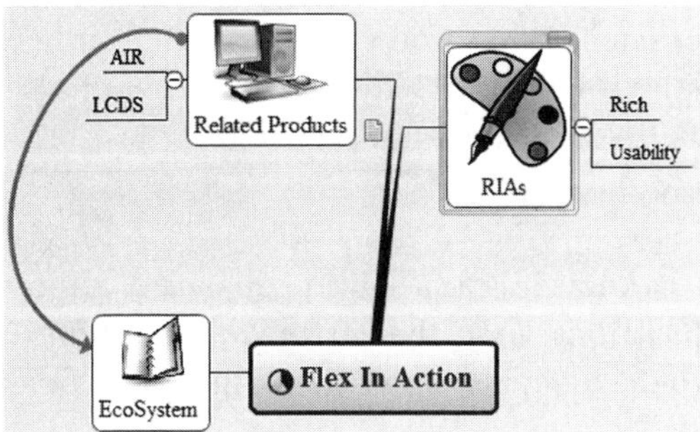

Figure 1.7 Mindomo's mind mapping tool allows users to visualize thoughts, and teams to collaborate over concepts in a highly visual environment using Flex. Visit http://www.mindomo.com.

Its data services capabilities allow you to create multiuser-aware, stateful (versus the web's stateless) applications where changes are pushed to the client (versus web applications that require constant polling to refresh), and paging of record sets (for better performance, if you're working with 1,000 records, you can specify only 50 be sent at one time over the network).

Some would argue they've seen RWAs that are RIA-like with cool-looking UI widgets and effects. But is it a platform on which you can expand?

1.5.3 RWAs—the last stand

Impressive results have been achieved using extremely advanced JavaScript and Dynamic HTML (DHTML) techniques in combination with the browser's `XMLHTTPRequest` function. But in the end, it is a last great effort to squeeze every possible ounce of application usability from a document platform.

It works fairly well and is a good option for making web applications more usable, or what we'll call RWAs.

AJAX is limited by almost decade-old technologies of HTML and JavaScript. And although the W3C has had plans for ages to advance them, don't count on anything new happening soon. AJAX applications have been stuck with the same set since the dawn of web applications. Worse still, you can't extend AJAX to create your own custom set.

With Flex, you can extend any existing component—a form component or something else—and give it additional abilities. Or you can start with something completely fresh. For example, both HTML and Flex provide a check box component that you can use to flag an on or off state. What if you want a three-state check box? Figure 1.8 shows how Microsoft Excel supports the expanded check box component to indicate that the current selection in this case has cells that are already merged.

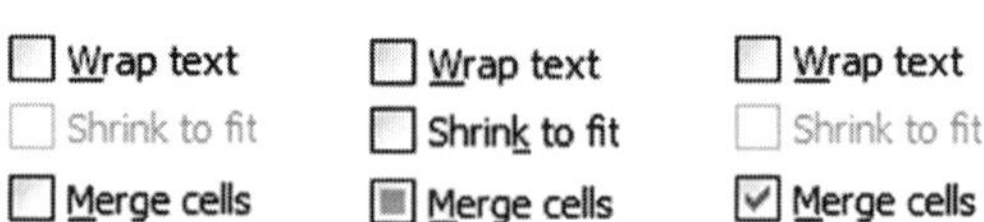

Figure 1.8 In Flex, you can make a three-state `ComboBox` just like that of Microsoft Excel. In HTML, the option to extend components isn't available.

In HTML you can fake it using a graphic, but you're not providing a true form field with properties and values JavaScript can use to evaluate the selection. And because it is a hack, any CSS styles you have for check boxes won't be applied.

As we mentioned earlier, impressive innovations have resulted from this last-hurrah squeeze, but they've come at a price that is incurred by platform inconsistencies.

1.5.4 Cross-platform issues

If you've worked with JavaScript, you know it is a massive headache to support multiple browsers. Every browser has variations, such that if you utilize advanced AJAX/JavaScript techniques, the result would require a significantly increased quality-assurance cycle (figure 1.9).

This deficiency alone severely impairs the ability of a business or customer to achieve the desired return on investment (ROI); the biggest single cost of systems development is developer time.

Admittedly, JavaScript UI frameworks such as jQuery and Adobe's Spry do a lot of the work to shield developers from these challenges, but the requirement to test isn't eliminated, especially if you do any custom development.

Because of the ubiquitous Flash Player, Flex abstracts platform specifics so you as the developer need to focus on only one platform—the Flash Player runtime known as the ActionScript Virtual Machine (AVM). If it works on one, it works on all, and the experience is the same.

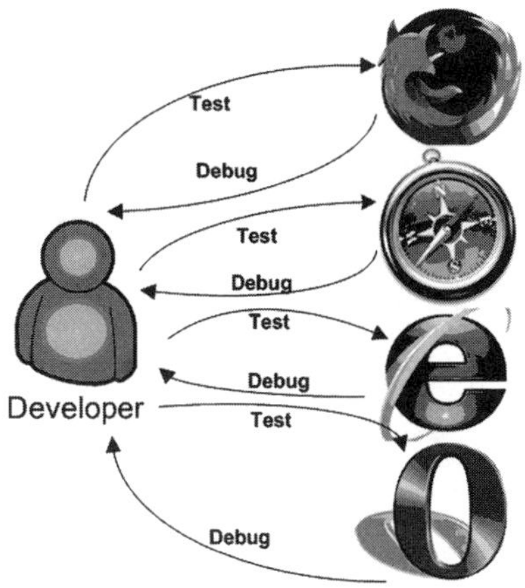

Figure 1.9 Don't forget to factor in the development costs of supporting multiple browsers when using supposedly free JavaScript/AJAX implementations.

The argument so far has been that of development logistics and technical capability, but a rich technology should be...well, rich!

1.5.5 *Where's the richness?*

To be considered an RIA technology, you need to satisfy the *R* in RIA: *rich*! What's so rich about JavaScript/AJAX and HTML? '

- Can it play sound files natively?
- Can it stream video natively?
- Can it interact with video devices such as a webcam?
- Does it provide drag and drop natively?

If you were making a monitoring tool for your network operations center staff, wouldn't it be nice if the application sounded a different alert depending on the severity of the event that triggered it? Or how about an industrial-strength, enterprise-class collaboration tool that supported voice chat and video conferencing?

1.5.6 *AJAX communication limits*

AJAX supports just one thing: text over HTTP. Traditionally that text has been in the form of XML, and the more recent trend is to use JSON to reduce client-side processing. In either case both are inefficient for transferring large amounts of information due to the verbose amount of text.

Try transferring 5,000 records using `XMLHTTPRequest`, then parsing them in JavaScript. That's exactly what Adobe's technical evangelist James Ward did, and you can see the results posted on his blog (http://www.jamesward.org/wordpress/2007/04/30/ajax-and-flex-data-loading-benchmarks/).

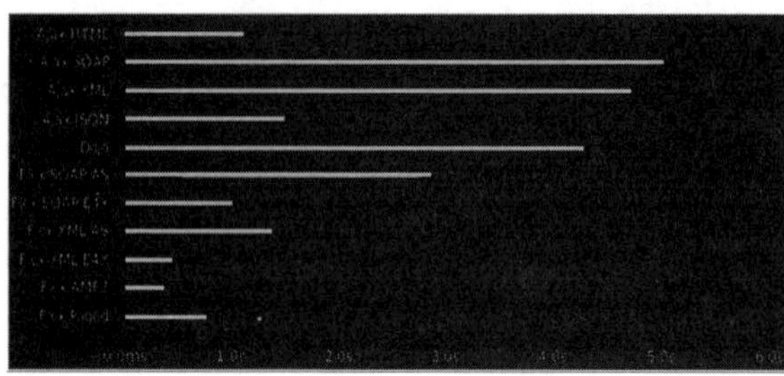

Figure 1.10 The speed of Flex's binary protocols versus the verbose approaches of AJAX

In figure 1.10, you can see how Flex—using its binary format, AMF3, versus XML or SOAP in AJAX—is up to 10 times faster. There are two reasons for this. First, as just mentioned, XML is verbose, which results in quite a bit of overhead in the message payload. Second, JavaScript is an interpreted language, whereas Flex is compiled to platform-neutral byte code.

Beyond speed, Flex's compact binary format offers other advantages. Less overhead means less demand on resources such as memory and network utilization.

NOTE Keep in mind that Flex and Flash do support simple transfer of textual data over HTTP and SOAP web services.

AMF3 provides a clear advantage, particularly for large-scale applications or applications that need to exchange large volumes of data.

AMF3—THE SECRET WEAPON

The secret weapon behind AMF3 is its protocol—something AJAX doesn't have. It allows you to utilize Real Time Messaging Protocol (RTMP), which uses a publish-subscribe model instead of a request-receive approach that is common with the web and most network applications.

This lets the client application register its specific interests and maintains an active connection with the server. When something new falls within the criteria specified, the server pushes this new item to the client. This is more efficient than what is required for an AJAX client. With AJAX, the client would need to repeatedly poll for new information, even if nothing had changed on the server.

A classic example that uses RTMP and a push model is a stock-price-tracking tool that only transmits changes to the price of a specific stock, and only if that stock exhibits activity.

Again, this efficiency can have a substantial payoff on a large scale. Imagine if you had hundreds of thousands of users. Would you want them polling every 5 seconds, constantly querying your database, when most often there was nothing new to be transmitted?

1.5.7 Apples and oranges

The fact that JavaScript and HTML haven't had to evolve for many years is a true testament to their longevity. They have stood the test of time and will continue to thrive in some form or another for decades to come. This is because the web is great at what is does—distributing platform-neutral documents.

Web applications will have their place too, but the trend is clear that users are demanding more. True RIA technologies will take over where web applications leave off.

In the RIA space, Flex is the front-runner and continues to maintain its lead. Compared to RWAs, it has a catalog of distinct advantages. You should feel confident in moving forward with Flex and endorsing it to management and clients—at least from a high-level perspective. Let's continue your understanding by going one level deeper.

1.6 Becoming acquainted with Flex

Flex is a programmatic way (you use code) to make RIAs leverage the Flash platform. Flash, of course, is famous for interactive banner ads, cool animated portions of web pages, and interactive marketing experiences, which are often used for promotional sites.

Flex has a head start with its ability to leverage the widely recognized and mature technology of Flash Player in addition to taking advantage of its widespread deployment. But it doesn't lock you out of the HTML world; you can have Flex interacting with web applications using JavaScript, while at the same time being a part of the large Adobe technology ecosystem.

1.6.1 Taking advantage of Adobe Flash

At the heart of Flex execution is Adobe Flash Player. This incredibly powerful, fast, lightweight, and platform-agnostic runtime engine is based on an object-oriented (OO) language called ActionScript. The experience is the same for Mac users as it is for Windows users—or users of any platform, for that matter (smart phones, PDAs, and so on).

The Flash Player on which Flex applications execute is capable of processing large amounts of data and has robust 2D graphical-rendering abilities, multithreaded processing, and support for various communication protocols. Flash puts the rich in RIA by supporting multimedia formats such as streaming video, images, and audio.

The end result is the ability to provide a rich desktop-like experience that allows developers to be innovative and creative. It also lets you present unique approaches to optimize the workflow for the end user.

WHY NOT DO IT IN FLASH?

Savvy Flash developers were making RIAs before Flex existed. But those coming from the development world and trying to get into Flash found it difficult to adopt the Flash mindset. Because Flash's roots are in animation (figure 1.11), its environment is based on timelines, layers, frames, frames per second, and so on. It is somewhat strange for someone with a development background based in lines of code to think of an application being a movie.

Even for seasoned Flash veterans, the cost of developing applications purely in Flash is significantly more than in other development environments (mostly due to the intensive work required to deal with change).

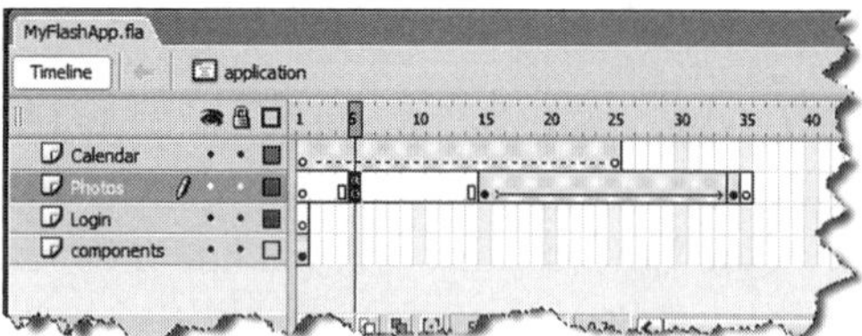

Figure 1.11 Flash has always been capable of making RIAs, but can you imagine coding based on time?

Although Flash and Flex can function as standalone applications, they can also interact with web applications by using JavaScript as a bridge between them.

1.6.2 *Flex and JavaScript can play together*

If you've been developing HTML-based web applications and using JavaScript, as you get into Flex you'll notice that its ActionScript language looks incredibly similar.

That's because JavaScript and ActionScript are based on the ECMAScript standard. If you've used JavaScript extensively, you'll find comfort in familiarity. One interesting tidbit is that Flex's ActionScript was the first production language to adopt the current ECMAScript 4 standard.

In working with Flex you are not locked into technology silos. That is, it doesn't have to be all Flex or bust. Although RIAs and RWAs are different, Flex allows you to operate between technologies. To do this, Flex employs a feature called the External API, which enables JavaScript applications to communicate with Flex applications.

In the context of AJAX, Flex has an additional feature called the Flex-AJAX Bridge (a.k.a. FABridge) that makes it easy to integrate AJAX and Flex applications. If you have a significant investment in an existing AJAX application, but would like to leverage Flex's capabilities, you can use Flex to generate interactive charts from your AJAX application.

Figure 1.12 shows the Nitobi business intelligence reporting tool, which is a hybrid application of web and Flex technologies working in harmony.

The harmony doesn't stop there; because Flex is made by Adobe, it also fits into a larger encompassing suite of technologies.

Figure 1.12 Business intelligence and reporting tools company Nitobi uses FABridge to leverage Flex's charting engine from within its AJAX application.

1.6.3 The Flex ecosystem

The amazing technology built into Flex is not its only major advantage. Because it is part of a set of technologies from Adobe, your organization can achieve a smooth workflow from designer to developer to deployment. Figure 1.13 shows where Flex sits in relation to the entire graphics suite landscape.

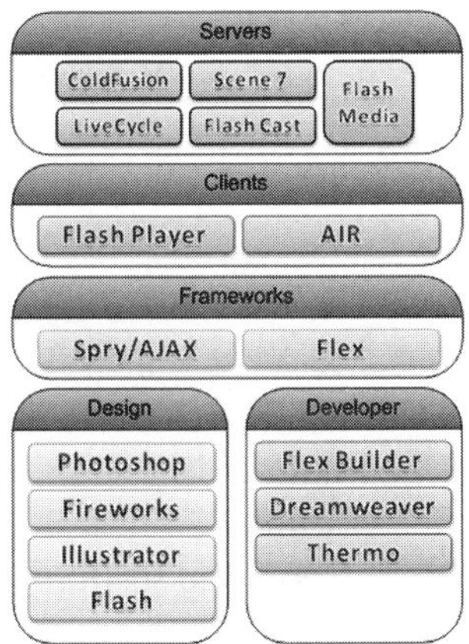

Figure 1.13 Flex is part of a big technology stack.

In the land of regular web development, a lot of time is wasted bouncing between designers and developers. As you may know, designers use tools such as Photoshop to design what the application is like, and developers laboriously slice up the images and generate CSS.

But in the Flex ecosystem, designers can export themes (skins), and developers can import them without tightly coupling the application to the design. And it keeps getting better. Thermo, a product that hasn't yet been released, will allow you to create a design and automatically generate the Flex code to make it work.

Another client technology that has garnered a lot of press and is directly related to Flex is AIR, which allows your Flex applications to run as native desktop applications.

A BLURB ON AIR

AIR (formerly known as Apollo) stands for Adobe Integrated Runtime. AIR allows you to go one step further by transforming your Flex RIAs into what we call rich desktop applications (RDAs). Although there's no official term for it, this type of technology is also known as a *hybrid desktop internet application.*

Because Flex is launched via the browser, for security reasons it is limited in its ability to do certain things such as accessing data on hard drives or interacting with peripherals like scanners. AIR liberates Flex applications from the browser and lets them execute directly on the desktop (figure 1.14), giving you the full desktop experience. With AIR, you can perform functions such as:

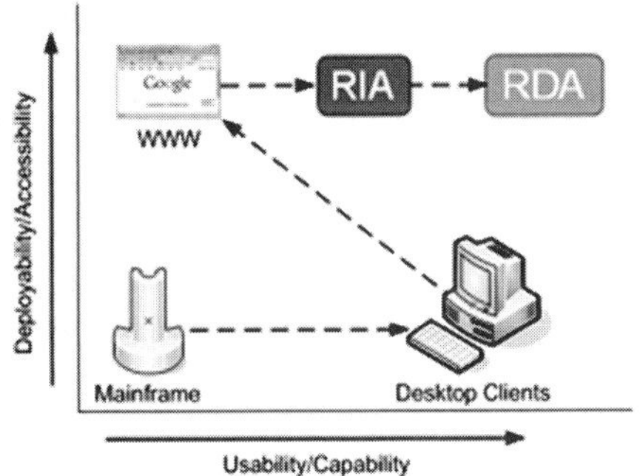

Figure 1.14 RDAs go that extra mile by achieving the desktop experience that RIAs are not able to reach. RDAs exist outside of the browser, and like a desktop application have access to the operating system's clipboard, and local file system.

- Access cut-and-paste information from the operating system's clipboard
- Drag and drop from the desktop into the application
- Create borderless applications that do not require the square frame of a browser around them

AIR provides additional capabilities:

- Built-in database server
- Transparent and automatic software updates to ensure everyone is using the same version
- Built-in HTML rendering engine

It is a revolutionary platform. If you decide you want to take your Flex applications beyond the browser, check out Manning Publications's *Adobe AIR in Action* (Joey Lott, Kathryn Rotondo, Sam Ahn, and Ashley Atkins, 2007; ISBN: 1933988487).

A BLURB ON BLAZEDS

BlazeDS is a trimmed-down version of LiveCycle Data Services (LCDS) from Adobe. It is a middle-tier server component that acts as a middleman between back-end components and services (other server technologies like Java and .NET), as well as connectors to database servers and messaging technologies such as Java Message Service (JMS).

Its capabilities include:

- Transferring back-end data to the Flex client using the binary AMF3 protocol.
- High-performance data transfer.
- Real-time data push using HTTP and AMF3. (It can notify your Flex application about new data, instead of your Flex application polling for new information.)
- Publish/subscribe messaging. (Through a technique known as long polling, RTMP is only available in the LCDS product.
- Recordset paging with a database. (It can stream 50 database records at a time, or do the last/next 10 records from a query.)
- Data synchronization. (If your Flex application modifies data on the client side, it can automatically notify BlazeDS to update the corresponding record in the database in real time.)
- The best part is that it is free! As another piece of Adobe's open source software, this technology is available and can be distributed under the LGPL v3 license.

1.6.4 How Flex works

At the heart of Flex is a free SDK that provides the framework for making Flex applications. In a nutshell, it is all the out-of-the-box libraries and the compiler.

On top of that is the Eclipse-based IDE named Flex Builder. Instead of using the Flash editor to make Flash applications, you use Flex Builder.

Flex comprises two programming languages:

- The XML-based MXML tag language. (No one knows what MXML stands for, but two popular assumptions are Macromedia XML and Magic XML.)
- The ActionScript scripting language.

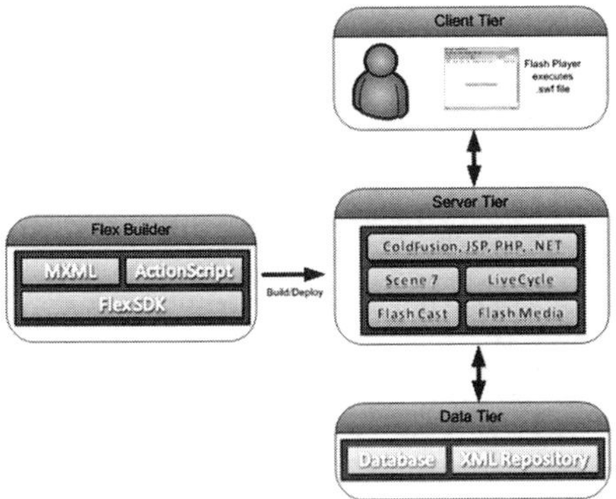

Figure 1.15 Use Flex Builder to compile your application, and then deploy it to a server.

When developing in Flex, you use both: MXML for primary layout of the application core (the visual components) and ActionScript to script out all the logic needed to drive your application.

Although it is not particularly pertinent to our discussion at the moment, MXML is compiled behind the scenes into ActionScript. This means you can make a full-fledged Flex application using only ActionScript. (That's what it ends up being anyway.)

TIP New users struggle to determine when to use ActionScript and when to use MXML. A simple rule of thumb is to pretend HTML is like MXML, which allows you to visually lay out how you want your application to initially appear. Then, think of ActionScript as JavaScript—it adds the brains to your application. As you become comfortable with it, you'll find you can make entire applications using nothing but ActionScript.

Using the two languages, you create your application by compiling it into a single executable file that is then deployed onto a web server (figure 1.15). Listing 1.1 has a simple example of how these two languages are related.

Listing 1.1 Example of a simple application

```
<mx:Application xmlns:mx="http://www.adobe.com/2006/mxml">
  <mx:Script>
    <![CDATA[
     import mx.controls.Alert;
     public function handleEvent():void
     {
       mx.controls.Alert.show("Event handled");
     }
    ]]>
  </mx:Script>
  <mx:Button label="Click on me" click="handleEvent()"/>
</mx:Application>
```

❶ ActionScript used for scripting out logic

❷ MXML used to lay out componentss

Even if you've never seen Flex code, this sample may feel somewhat familiar. One reason is the tag-based MXML language ❷ is a derivative of XML. Another reason is that the script logic ❶ is similar to JavaScript.

Let's look at the typical lifecycle of the development process.

THE DEVELOPMENT LIFE CYCLE

This is what the Systems Development Life Cycle (SDLC) of a typical Flex application looks like:

1 Using Flex Builder or the SDK, build in your local development environment by writing MXML and ActionScript code.
2 When testing, use Flex Builder or the SDK to compile your code. Doing so generates the main output .swf file (often pronounced *swiff* file).
3 Use the browser to launch this file, thus invoking the Flash Player plug-in. Your application begins to execute.
4 A Flex application typically interacts with a server tier to exchange data.
5 When the application is ready to be released, the .swf (and any accompanying files, such as images) is published to your production web server, where it is available to be invoked by your users via a URL.

For those who work with application servers like ColdFusion and PHP, note you're not pushing the source files to production, but rather a compiled application (similar to Java's .class files, but a Flex application also contains all the libraries needed for the application to work).

1.6.5 *Events, events, events*

It is all about events. Flex is an event-driven environment, which may be a big departure from what you're used to.

In traditional web development technologies, an event represents an action such as a user clicking a link or a submit button. The server responds, executing whatever function is required—in this case, displaying a web page or sending field data.

If you've been developing web applications, you've undoubtedly created JavaScript that responds to certain user gestures such as highlighting an item on a page by changing the background color of the item as the user moves the mouse over it (figure 1.16).

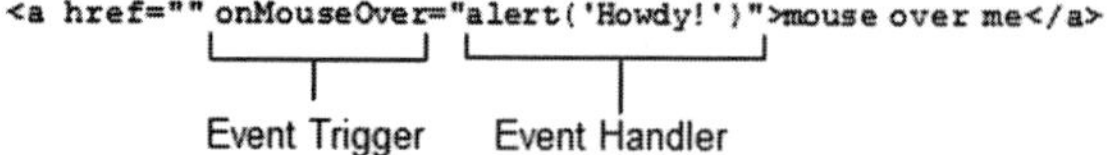

Figure 1.16 Flex, like JavaScript, uses events that consist of triggers and handlers.

That's an event! But that term isn't used as much in traditional web applications because the majority of the application resides on the back end. As in the JavaScript example we just described, Flex is a client-side technology, meaning all the action occurs on the user's side.

A Flex application is driven entirely through events; something causes something to occur, and something else handles it when it occurs. The two main pieces of an event-driven application are:

- *Event triggers*—Triggers cause events: the user moving the mouse over a button, the application loading, data coming back from a web service, and so on.
- *Event handlers*—Handlers respond to events: invoking a function that changes display characteristics, committing an input form, and so on; handlers are where the logic is.

Coming from a traditional web technology, you won't be used to thinking like this. We'll gradually introduce how events are used, but you'll need to let go of the web application notion of generating pages. With Flex, the application is already loaded; all you're doing is capturing events and responding accordingly.

1.7 What's new in Flex 3

Since its inception, Flex technology has been evolving at an incredibly rapid pace. The product started as a pure server-side technology, modeling the conventions of most server-based web application technologies.

Flex 2 was a major overhaul of the language. Adobe split it into two portions: the client portion consists of the application framework and tools to compile a Flex application; the server portion is the data bridge. This has evolved into LCDS/BlazeDS. The Flex 2 overhaul also involved a technology rewrite—a one-time hit to provide an industrial-strength platform that could grow well into the future.

Flex 3 comes with a lot of new, key features, including:

- *The profiler*—Allows you to see how your application is consuming CPU and memory, and where that consumption occurs.
- *Refactoring*—Makes it easy to rename almost anything, such as functions, variables, and classes.
- *Wizards*—A number of step-by-step wizards to help you get a head start with hooking into back-end application servers, along with generating the code to do so.
- *Design to developer flow*—Makes it easier for designers to work on the graphical aspect of the application without developers needing to spend a lot of time converting those designs into technical implementation.
- *Charting enhancement*—Supports what Adobe calls a data-oriented implementation. This gives you a lot of fine-grained control over what and how information is presented, including user interactions with data points.
- *Persistent Framework Cache (PFC)*—Enables you to cache the Flex application framework on the client side so your application is much smaller (because it doesn't need to embed all that overhead).
- *DataGrid component*—Displays tabular data and is quite popular. The Advanced DataGrid provides additional abilities such as multicolumn sorting and column spanning.

The Adobe ecosystem moved forward in parallel with the open sourcing of the Flex framework and BlazeDS products. Adobe AIR was also released at around the same time.

1.8 Summary

You've seen that historically, usability has been sacrificed for the sake of rapid deployment and a semi-neutral platform, but it came at the cost of the user experience. Amazingly, users (including ourselves) became accustomed to it. When it came to web applications, we assumed that being limited was normal.

It was just a matter of time in our information-crazed lives until the cost of this sacrifice began to outweigh the benefits. Users were suffering, and businesses were paying the price in productivity and efficiency.

RIAs demonstrate that we can achieve the best of both worlds. On the development side, a centralized deployment model on a platform-neutral environment means enhancements can be made quickly. On the user side, we can provide a desktop-like experience, allowing for fluid and engaging experiences from any device that can access the application.

Flex entered this RIA scene, leveraging its ubiquitous cross-platform Flash Player by creating a programmatic way to make a Flash application. This programmatic approach uses Flex's core languages: the XML templating language (MXML) and its scripting language (ActionScript).

Now in its third major version, Flex maintains a lead in the RIA space, although Microsoft is working hard to catch up. But what Microsoft doesn't have is Flex's ecosystem—a large technology environment that encompasses the end-to-end workflow of software development. From designer to developer to deployment, Adobe offers the environments and tools for each phase of the game.

In the next chapter, we'll explain how to set up your development environment, become familiar with the language reference, and begin to learn how to make Flex applications.

2 Getting started

This chapter covers:

- Touring the Flex tools
- Creating your first Flex application
- Understanding how MXML works
- Fitting ActionScript into the picture

To begin coding in Flex, you first need to set up a working environment. Flex comes with a free open source SDK that allows you to get started and create Flex applications, but serious developers prefer to use the Eclipse-based Flex Builder IDE.

We'll show you how to make the most of a limited budget by taking advantage of open source tools, and we'll spend a good part of this chapter going over the features of Flex Builder. Later, we'll present how to begin producing Flex applications.

As a Flex developer you're likely to spend most of your time in the Flex Builder tool. Before we jump in, you may want to ask yourself: can I get away with developing in Flex for free?

2.1 Flex on the cheap

With Flex's free and open source SDK, there's nothing to stand in your way toward making Flex RIAs. The SDK includes the compiler to convert source code into Flash .swf files, as well as the Flex framework to handle the guts of an application, and the core components, including visual components such as buttons.

Our goal is to make Flex simple and easy to get into, and the way we can do that is by filtering out the facets that are seldom used, thus keeping you focused on the areas that will make a difference in your ability to be a successful Flex developer.

When taking the SDK route, keeping things simple may be easier said than done as using the SDK is more complicated and involves more work than using Flex Builder. At the same time if you are learning Flex on your own dime, perhaps to expand your skill set, or to sell Flex to your organization (which hasn't yet bestowed its financial support), it is worth gaining insight into this free option.

NOTE Flex Builder is available as a 60-day free trial which would allow you to conduct an evaluation to determine if it provides enough value to justify the price.

The purpose of this section is to give you a sense of what's involved in working with the SDK, from which point you can determine if it is an approach you want to pursue. If you decide to go the SDK route, here is what your game plan is going to look like:

- *Set up a compile environment*—You can build applications via a command line interface (an MS-DOS window, for example) by downloading the free SDK.
- *Set up an editing environment*—A simple text editor can be used, but you'll want an environment that maximizes productivity.

The first order of business is to prepare an environment that will allow you to convert your source code into a compiled application.

2.1.1 Setting up the compile environment

The Flex SDK comes in the form of a zip file that you download from an Adobe website. Download and deploy the files, then configure your command line environment.

1. The compiler needs the Java Runtime Environment (JRE version 1.4.2_06 or later). If you don't have this, you can obtain it at http://www.java.com/en/download/manual.jsp.
2. Navigate to the Flex SDK page on the Adobe website at http://www.adobe.com/go/flex3_sdk. Near the bottom of the page you'll find an option to download the free SDK (approximately 80 MB).
3. Next, unzip the .sdk file to a location of your choice. You may want to keep things simple and keep it near the root level (for example, c:\flex in Windows).
4. If you have the current version of the Flash Player on your desktop, uninstall it before proceeding any further.

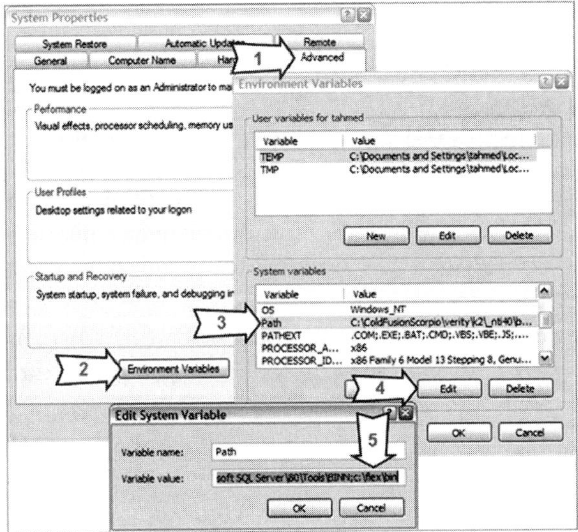

Figure 2.1 Follow these steps to add the SDK bin directory to your path in Windows.

5 Install the debug version of Flash Player. You'll find it in the runtimes/player folder. For you Windows folks there are two main files:
   - Install Flash Player 9 ActiveX.exe is the debug player for Internet Explorer.
   - Install Flash Player 9 Plugin.exe is the debug player for other browsers such as Firefox.

6 Add the bin folder to your path so you don't need to provide the full path (figure 2.1).
   - In Windows XP, go to Control Panel > System > Advanced
   - Click Environment Variables
   - Edit the Path System variable
   - Append installfolder\bin to the end of the path (c:\flex in our example).

7 Verify it works.
   - Create a directory where you want to store your Flex projects, for example, c:\apps
   - Create a directory called HelloWorld within c:\apps
   - Create a text file inside c:\apps\HelloWorld\ called HelloWorld.mxml. (You can use Notepad to do this.)
   - Type the following code in the HelloWorld.mxml file:

```
<?xml version="1.0"?>
<mx:Application xmlns:mx="http://www.adobe.com/2006/mxml"/>
```

   - Open a command line interface. In Windows, select Start > Run > cmd. Macintosh and Linux users will need to open a shell.
   - Enter the following command: `mxmlc.exe HelloWorld.mxml`
   - If all goes well, you should see something similar to that of figure 2.2.

Figure 2.2 Testing to ensure you can compile a Flex application

You should now have a new file called HelloWorld.swf in the same folder where HelloWorld.mxml is located. Double-click the new file, but don't be alarmed if it doesn't look like much. All it should do is display a bluish-gray background. The goal at this point is to verify the compiler executes properly.

Now that we know you're able to compile Flex applications, we can assume the SDK is properly installed. The next order of business is to set up an efficient way to work on the code.

2.1.2 Setting up the editing environment

Unless you're a huge fan of VI in Linux or Notepad in Windows, you'll want the best code editor that absolutely *no* money can buy. For Flex we recommend going with the popular Eclipse editor. You can find it at http://www.eclipse.org/.

Eclipse is an open source plug-in—based editor and IDE framework, meaning it does a good job of code editing but allows third parties to extend its capabilities through modules. The commercial Flex IDE (Flex Builder) is based on Eclipse; if you decide to purchase Flex Builder, you can download the Eclipse plug-in, adding its features to what you've already built.

APTANA STUDIO

Next, you'll want to get Aptana Studio, which comes in both commercial and freeware varieties. The free version is known as the Community Edition and can be downloaded at http://www.aptana.com/studio/.

This Eclipse plug-in has a number of features you can read about on the Aptana website, but in particular the components that'll come in handy for you as you edit code are:

- Adobe AIR Development
- AJAX Libraries
- HTML/CSS/JavaScript Development

NOTE The commercial version of Eclipse (Professional Edition) is $99. It adds features such as enhanced XML editing and JavaScript Serialized Object Notation (JSON) support.

With the SDK and the ability to compile a Flex application squared away, you can now edit code in a more fluid manner. The final task is to automate the process of building the applications so they are not as command-line intensive.

2.1.3 *Next steps (if you're still interested)*

You are now at a point at which you have enough information to determine if you like the free approach, or find it is too much of a hassle. If you're comfortable with it, you'll want to look at the following steps:

- Learning all the parameters that can be sent to the compiler. Refer to the MXMLC documentation online at http://livedocs.adobe.com/flex/3/html/compilers_13.html.
- Creating wrapper files (HTML files that launch your Flex application). See chapter 24 for more information on wrapper files.
- Using build scripts such as .bat files in Windows, or shell scripts in Linux and Mac OS X, to make it easier for you to perform compiling. For an example of shell scripts, look in the *installfolder*/samples folder for some Flex applications and their build scripts.
- You have to hand it to the open source community; if you've encountered a common challenge, the odds are someone has created a tool to deal with it.

One particular challenge is automating repetitive tasks, and there's a neat tool out there that can help—appropriately named *Another Neat Tool*.

ANOTHER NEAT TOOL (ANT) + FLEX ANT TASKS

Coders who come from languages such as C++ or Java are aware of the `make` utility, which is a ubiquitous scripting tool for building applications. But as venerable and popular as `make` is, it is cumbersome to create and maintain its configuration files. This is a common problem with shell scripting because you use commands that are specific to the OS on which it runs.

Born out of the Apache software project, Ant is a free and open source tool that makes scripting builds much easier. As a Java-based application that uses XML configuration files, it is platform-neutral, while at the same time fairly easy to learn and use.

Adobe has contributed a free-to-use Ant-based build mechanism called Flex Ant Tasks, and it comes standard with the SDK. You'll find it under the *installroot/*ant folder of the SDK.

You won't need either Ant or Flex Ant Tasks to get started making Flex applications, but it is something to be aware of down the line. For more information on Ant visit http://ant.apache.org.

If you want to look at Ant in more depth, there's a great book on this technology by Steve Loughran and Erik Hatcher (Manning Publications) titled *Ant in Action* (ISBN: 1-932394-80-X). This book can teach you how to get ramped up with Ant and maximize its strengths.

THINGS TO CONSIDER

- Note the Flex SDK doesn't come with everything that Flex Builder Professional has, but it does include:
- Automated testing framework
- Memory/Performance profiler (for identifying resource bottlenecks)

- Certain components, such as the charting and the `AdvancedDataGrid` component (the code will work, but a watermark image is layered over it)

If you want to become serious about Flex, it would definitely be worth the investment to purchase the Flex Builder project. Flex Builder will save you time immediately, and that time savings will in turn yield an instant ROI.

With features such as tag completion, code hinting, built-in API reference manual, automatic importing of libraries, wizards, visual layout and styling, and automatic builds, Flex Builder is a lifesaver. In the game of software development, the number one cost is resource time—or more accurately, developers.

2.2 Get serious with Flex Builder

Flex Builder is a feature-rich IDE for designing, developing, testing, and building Flex applications. If you've skipped the previous section because you know you don't want to take that path, we briefly remind you that Flex Builder is based on the open source IDE framework and editor Eclipse (http://www.eclipse.org), and adds onto it as an Eclipse plug-in (so you can download Flex Builder as a plug-in to an existing Eclipse install, or download Flex Builder and Eclipse as a single install).

But how much is this all going to cost? Flex 3 prices have dropped substantially, making the entry point easier than ever before. Shop around for the best deal.

2.2.1 Product and pricing matrix

Flex Builder is available in multiple versions at varying price points (see table 2.1). What you see online are the manufacturer's suggested retail prices. Purchasing from a value-added reseller may save you a couple of bucks and if you work for an organization that has prenegotiated discounts with Adobe you might be entitled to a better deal. If you're pitching Flex to a customer or to your company, it might help seal the deal by keeping the proposed capital expenditures down.

Table 2.1 Flex Builder and SDK pricing

Version	Price	Extras
SDK	$0	N/A
Standard	$250	Step-through debugger, code hinting/completion, code coloring, CSS editing, integrated API Reference, visual layout designer, data. integration wizards, Creative Suite 3-skin importing, automatic compiling, and so on. You can still create charts, but there'll be a watermark image in them.
Professional	$699	Standard version features, plus memory and performance monitoring/profiling, automated testing framework, and advanced components such as charts and `AdvancedDataGrid`.
Education Professional	$0	Free for students and faculty.

Is it worth paying for these tools? The answer is another question: what is the value of your time? If every hour you or your company saves is worth $50, by investing in Flex Builder you'll have recovered the cost in less than a week; if you're using the professional version, in as little as 14 hours.

If you're learning Flex for personal interests and don't have any intention of applying it to a live project, there may not be an immediate value in purchasing the standard or professional versions. You'll want to employ the Flex-on-the-cheap approach as described earlier.

Otherwise, there's no question that you or your organization will benefit from having the proper tool to do the job efficiently and productively.

TIP If you find management is still hesitant because of the price, create a proof-of-concept interactive reporting dashboard that makes use of the `Charts` component. If it is one thing management finds irresistible, it is reporting and business intelligence.

If you want to explore Flex Builder 3 without risk, a 60-day trial version is available. That should be a sufficient amount of time to give it a good test run.

2.2.2 Getting Flex Builder

Flex Builder comes in two flavors: standalone and as a separate plug-in.

The standalone version is comprised of Eclipse and the plug-in, which are installed as a single product out of the box. The plug-in version is useful for those who already have Eclipse for other programming languages and want to add Flex development as part of their environment. In either case you can add more third-party plug-ins as you progress with your development experience.

If you don't have Flex Builder installed, download it by going to http://www.adobe.com/go/flex_trial. If you install it without entering a serial number, you can use it for 60 days, after which time you'll need the serial number to continue.

With installation complete, you can launch the application and you're good to go! Next, we'll cover the features of Flex Builder.

2.3 Exploring Flex Builder

Flex Builder works on the basis of projects, which are collections of folders, files, and settings. Projects can be created, closed, imported, and exported (figure 2.3).

This is a different concept compared to other editors (for example, Dreamweaver) that use a full-file browser approach in which you navigate through file folders residing anywhere across your file system and network.

In Flex Builder, projects are made up of *assets* which are the types of files nested within folders, usually located under the main project folder (though you can also link to folders in other locations).

Using figure 2.3 as a reference, let's take a look at the basic Flex Builder layout.

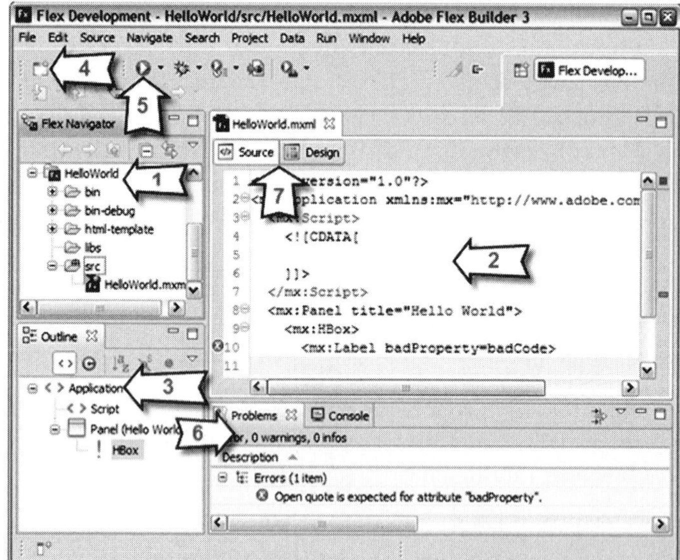

Figure 2.3 The major work areas and windows of the Flex Builder basic layout

NAVIGATOR (1)

This lists all your projects and the assets within each. Unlike a standard file browser, it only shows files within a configured project. You can't navigate across the entire file system with this window.

An important feature to note here is you can configure the properties of your project by right-clicking on the top-level project folder.

SOURCE CODE EDITOR (2)

This is where all the action happens. The source code editor is where you write your code. It boasts nifty features such as color-coding the text and *code hinting*. Code hinting is similar to an auto-complete feature because it attempts to anticipate what you want to type based on what you have already input. It then displays a list of possible match options from which you can select the remaining syntax. This helps speed up development, as you don't need to remember exact syntax.

APPLICATION OUTLINE VIEW (3)

This is a different kind of navigator that dynamically builds a map of your application. It comes in handy when your application becomes large and you need to see how the pieces fit together. Selection of any of the items within the outline view is mirrored in the source code editor, which will jump to the corresponding item.

THE WIZARDS (4)

This feature of Flex becomes incredibly useful when kick-starting projects from scratch. Not only does it help those who are new to Flex get set up quickly, it also comes in handy to the advanced Flex developer who wants to get going fast. Right out of the box, wizards, whose purposes range from creating an ActionScript class to generating a Flex CSS file, are available. But its most common use is to create Flex projects and custom Flex components.

APPLICATION LAUNCHER (5)

This button launches your application. Part of that process involves compiling any code you've written (if necessary), copying the latest compiled code to the output folder, and launching the application to the configured URL.

BOTTOM PANE (6)

The bottom pane displays either the problems or console views. The problems view (the default) works hand-in-hand with the editor view by pointing out any issues it encounters as you code (figure 2.4). It displays any errors found in your application, along with the file and associated line number in which the error occurred.

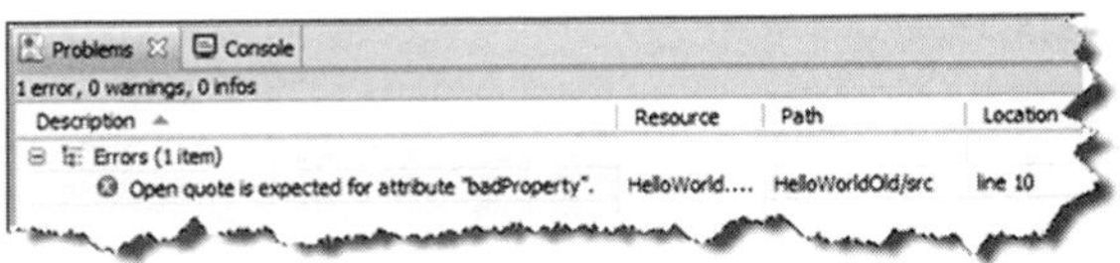

Figure 2.4 The problems view alerts you to issues within your code, and where they are located.

The console view is used when testing your application. It displays warnings, alerts, and any other messages you specify, then saves them to a file called the *trace log*. (Chapter 23 goes deeper into how to use the trace log.)

SOURCE AND DESIGN VIEW (7)

These two tabs let you switch between the source code editor and the interactive design view. The design view presents a WYSIWYG display of your application and certain visual elements while allowing you to control various properties of these visual elements such as color, transparency, size, and positioning.

2.4 Views and perspectives

We described a couple of views previously, and you'll notice Flex Builder is split into various sections, or panes. Each pane contains views; collections of views are called *perspectives*.

2.4.1 Out-of-the-box perspectives

During the course of developing a Flex application, there are three major modes in which you'll normally work: developing, debugging, and profiling (testing/tuning). Perspectives are collections of views and panes that Flex supplies out-of-the-box and are optimized for each of the major stages.

DEVELOPMENT PERSPECTIVE

The development perspective is a collection of views optimized for core development work: outline, problems, console, and navigator views.

DEBUGGING PERSPECTIVE

This perspective contains a collection of panes and views to help with debugging. Flex Builder will automatically switch to this perspective when you enter debugging mode (see chapter 23 for more information). The debugging perspective adds views that let you monitor the values of variables you're tracking, as well as the ability to control the execution of the application (pause, cancel, execute code line-by-line, and so on).

PROFILING PERSPECTIVE

The profiling perspective is similar to the debugging perspective in that it helps you isolate issues. This perspective leverages Flex's memory profiler capabilities by presenting information that allows you to track memory and performance usage. This information includes a memory usage chart, a list of functions that are being called, how often they're called, and how much time is spent inside each function.

2.4.2 Switching perspectives

You can change your perspective at anytime by clicking Window > Perspective to present a list of the available perspectives, as shown in figure 2.5.

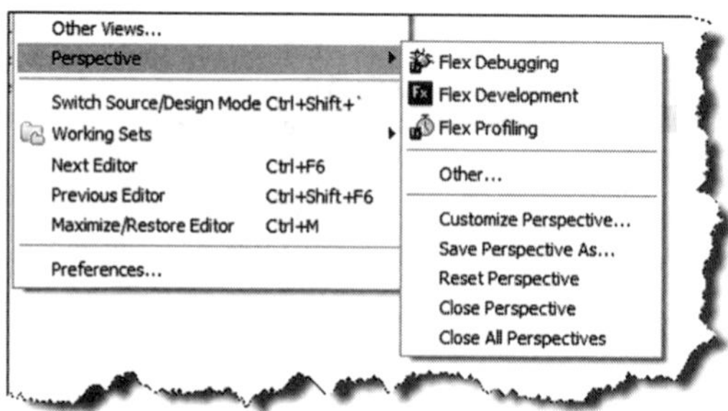

Figure 2.5 Flex Builder comes configured with three perspectives, but you can always add your own.

Over time you may find that you prefer a certain layout, or require certain views, depending on the task at hand. The cool thing is Flex offers you a way to customize your own perspectives.

2.4.3 Customizing perspectives

You can add and move views around the various panes then save the arrangement (along with any number of layouts) as a custom perspective.

MODIFY THE LAYOUT.

Let's try modifying the layout. Follow the steps below to get a feel for it:

1. Click and hold the mouse button on the Console tab, and drag the tab around the window.
2. You'll see a gray outline appear in different locations as you move around (figure 2.6), indicating a potential place to drop the view.
3. Release the mouse button, and voila!a

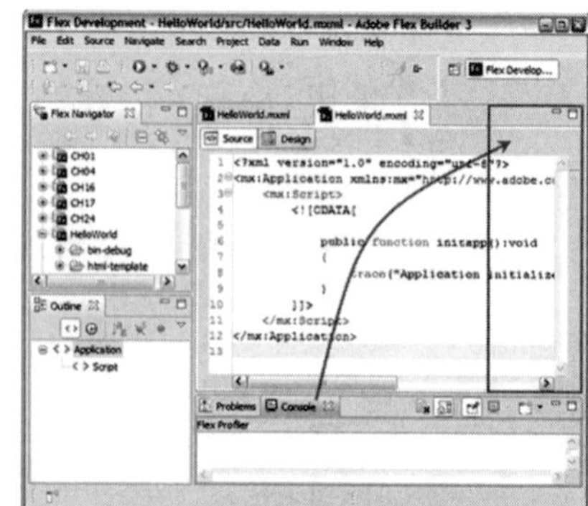

Figure 2.6 You can click and hold the mouse button to reposition a view.

Rearranging the existing layout is a breeze, but you may want to display more information by adding views to the layout.

ADD A VIEW TO THE LAYOUT.

You can add new views to a perspective by following these steps:

1. Click Window at the top of Flex Builder. A number of views will appear (figure 2.7) such as the flex properties view; if you select other views you'll see the full list (figure 2.8).
2. Select any one of these views and it will appear inside the Flex Builder window.
3. Refer to the previous instructions to reposition the layout as needed.

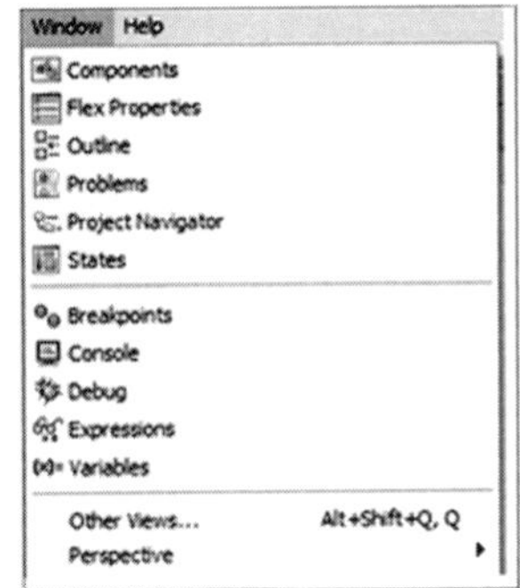

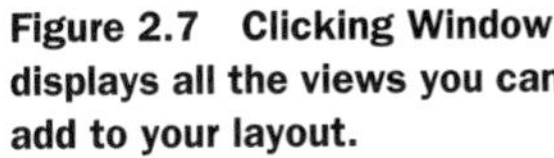

Figure 2.7 Clicking Window displays all the views you can add to your layout.

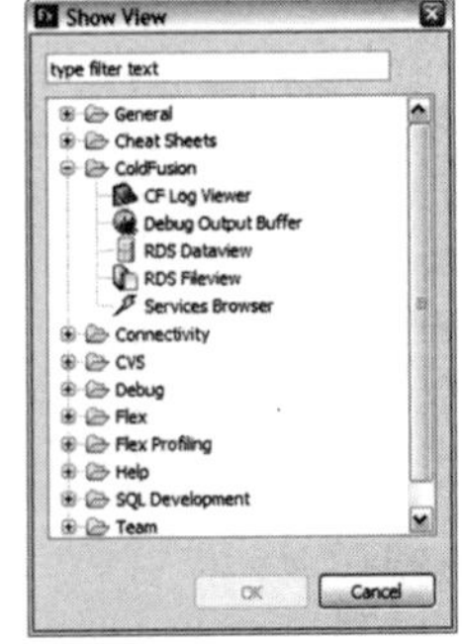

Figure 2.8 Clicking other views shows you the gamut of available views.

Be sure to check out the other views option to display all the available choices. For example, if you're a ColdFusion developer you might want to make use of the ColdFusion-specific views.

2.5 *Our first project—Hello World!*

As described earlier in the chapter, Flex applications are based on projects. When you're in development mode, almost everything you do is contained within a project.

A project in Flex Builder is a collection of all the source code files, assets (images, mp3 files, and so on), and configuration settings. Let's get started creating our first project.

2.5.1 *Create the project*

Flex Builder comes with a collection of handy wizards that methodically steps you through the processes. In particular, there's a new Flex Project wizard that guides you through selecting the name of your project, where to store files, and even which back-end server technology is to be used by the application. We'll make use of this wizard right away by performing the following steps:

Figure 2.9 Click the wizard icon to launch the Flex Project wizard.

1. Invoke the wizard selector

   In Flex Builder, click the top left button to launch Flex Builder's wizard (figure 2.9).
2. Select the Flex Project wizard

   Select Flex > Flex Project wizard (figure 2.10) then click the Next button.
3. Name the project

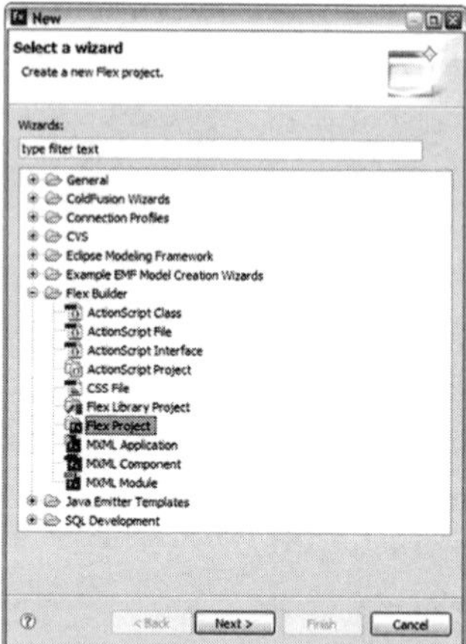

Figure 2.10 The wizard presents guides to step you through the setup for your new project.

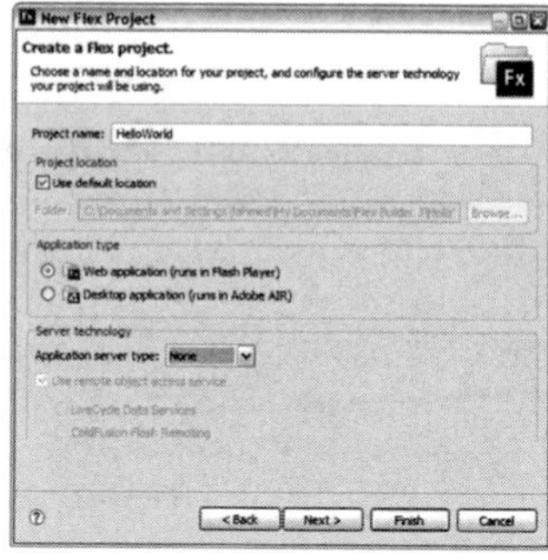

Figure 2.11 The Create a Flex project wizard.

You'll be prompted to provide a project name and application server type (figure 2.11). The project name can be anything you want, but let's call this one HelloWorld, and select None for the application server type. Click Next to continue.

NOTE In chapter 14, we'll talk about how to use the application server type feature. This Flex Builder option saves steps, and makes it easier to connect to a back-end system that supports Flash's binary communication protocol (AMF). Currently, the New Flex Project wizard supports ColdFusion, ASP.Net, Java 2 Platform, Enterprise Edition (J2EE), and PHP. We won't be using any of these protocols just yet, so select None for now.

4 Configure the output directory

This step allows you to select where you want the output directory to be created (figure 2.12).

By default, it is located within your main project folder, but it can be located elsewhere if that is more convenient.

Flex Builder will publish the compiled debug version (necessary for testing) of your application to the specified folder. Chapter 24 covers the process of creating production builds in more detail.

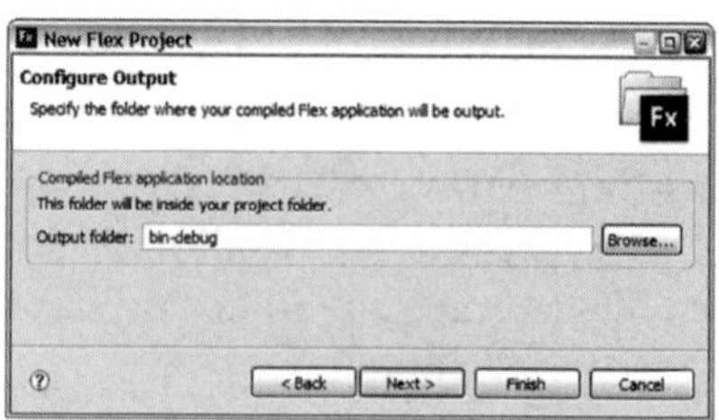

Figure 2.12 The specified output directory in which a debug version of your application is built and deployed.

TIP You're more than welcome to use a location of your choosing. This will likely be the norm as you become more comfortable with Flex Builder and standardize the location of projects within your organization.

5 Complete the creation process

By default, the name you choose for your project is used as the name of your application's root folder, and the name of the main Flex application file.

Click the Finish button at the bottom of the wizard window as shown in figure 2.13. Flex Builder will now initialize your project.

Figure 2.13 The final step lets you choose options such as which file in your project you want to serve as the main file of your

In this example, your project will reside in a folder called HelloWorld, and the main file will be called HelloWorld.mxml.

The project is now set up and ready for you to begin entering code.

2.5.2 *Entering code*

After you click Finish, Flex Builder will automatically open the main project file, HelloWorld.mxml, and will look like that of listing 2.1.

Listing 2.1 A very rudimentary application

```
<?xml version="1.0" encoding="utf-8"?>
<mx:Application xmlns:mx="http://www.adobe.com/2006/mxml"
   layout="absolute">
</mx:Application>
```

Listing 2.1 shows the basic shell of an application that uses the MXML language to house the main elements of your application. This is good enough for now as all we want to do is verify that we can compile and execute the project.

2.5.3 *Compile and run*

Compiling and running a Flex project is as easy as a mouse click. On the Flex Builder toolbar, locate the green button with a right arrow (▶). Click the button; a new browser window should appear pointing to the file HelloWorld.html. You'll be looking at a blank page, but you have officially made your first Flex application!

This HTML page is just a wrapper to invoke your Flex application. It includes additional JavaScript to perform Flash Player version checking, and set up the client-side environment in which your Flex application will run.

2.5.4 *Making it real*

In true Hello World! fashion, let's make one quick modification to the source code by going back to Flex Builder and adding in the extra line (in bold) in listing 2.2.

Listing 2.2 Hello World!

```
<?xml version="1.0" encoding="utf-8"?>
<mx:Application xmlns:mx="http://www.adobe.com/2006/mxml"
   layout="absolute">
  <mx:Button label="Hello World!" fontSize="40"/>
</mx:Application>
```

Now, give it a run and see what happens. You should see something similar to that in figure 2.14.

Figure 2.14 Your first Flex application! Congratulations, you are now a Flex developer.

That wasn't too bad, was it? What you added was a button (no surprise there). Anything you can add via MXML is categorized as a *component*. Visual components such as buttons are also known as *controls*. Flex comes with a lot of components, but if you can't find what you want among them, you can make your own as well (which is what chapter 17 is all about).

In this example, we added our button programmatically, but Flex Builder has a design side to it as well, which can help in prototyping and creating proof-of-concepts quickly.

2.6 Using design mode

Flex Builder has an interesting feature called design mode that lets you visually create your application (see figure 2.3, item #7 to enable). Design mode allows you to drag and drop visual components into the application, position them, and tweak their properties (such as the background color).

Going back to the Hello World! example, click the Design mode button. This time you should notice a couple more views on the right side of the window, titled states and Flex properties.

TIP A component is a reusable object you can invoke in your MXML. It is a way of making code reusable, similar to a Java class or a ColdFusion component (CFC). Components that are visual in nature are also known as controls.

Let's add more to our application. Start off by locating the Components view, which should be displayed on the bottom left of Flex Builder (figure 2.15). If you expand the tree, you'll see a catalog of all available components. Let's throw in a `Panel` component—you can keep doing this for as long as you want to continue laying out your application.

With your components placed, we will shift our focus to Flex properties. Selecting one component in the design mode displays all of that component's properties, which you can then edit in the Flex Properties view.

This can be used to change visual characteristics of the component such as color, transparency, and positioning. In its standard view, only a few characteristics are pre-

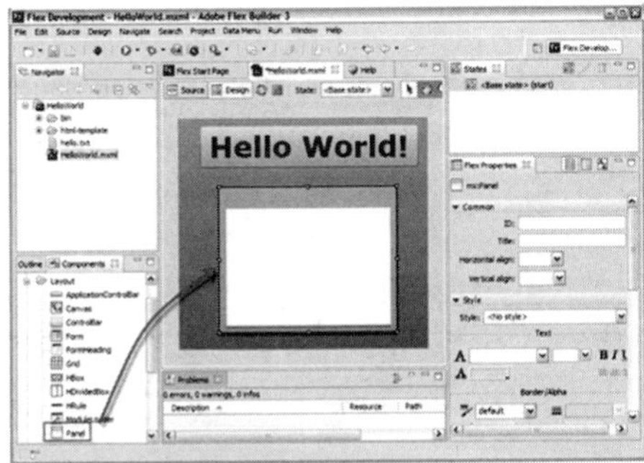

Figure 2.15 Flex Builder's Design view allows you to visually lay out your application.

sented, but if you click the Category tab (figure 2.16) you'll gain access to every property available.

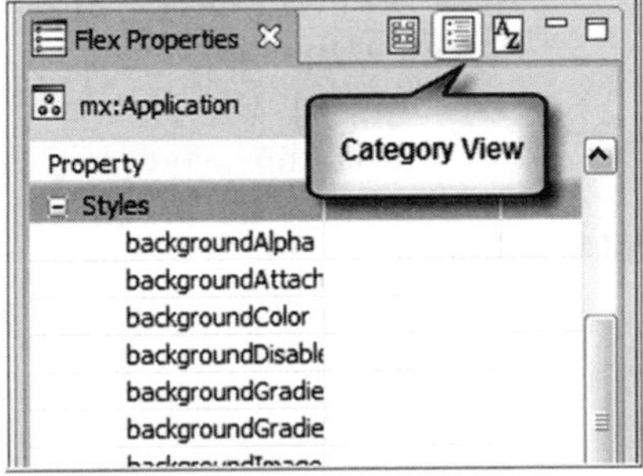

Figure 2.16 Use the Category view within the Flex Properties view to see all the component properties you can manipulate.

The biggest benefit of this graphical ability to design and build an application is that of creating proof-of-concept (POC). It is a great time saver when working with customers and end users to interactively model how the application should appear before you begin coding, as everyone is in sync with your ultimate goals.

In the lifecycle of software development, usually simple wire-frame mockups are provided as POCs, which don't furnish the user with a feel for what the application is going to look like. And to put together a more lifelike POC requires investing a significant amount of time. Flex Builder gives you the best of both worlds with the ability to create lifelike POCs in a minimal amount of time.

Although it is possible to build small applications entirely in design mode, its primary usefulness is in creating POCs, laying out your initial application, and adjusting visual properties to see how they will appear.

When you start working on real projects, the reality is you'll likely be doing straight-up coding as you would with any other language.

Flex Builder gives you powerful wizards to create projects, it has capabilities for mocking up layouts, and, as with any good integrated development environment, it has built-in help to make your coding experience all the more efficient.

2.7 Built-in help

Flex is an object-oriented language. In chapter 16 we delve into what object-oriented programming (OOP) is all about. But don't worry, leading up to that we'll progressively increase your understanding of its concepts as you work through the chapters.

An important factor in your ability to be productive as a Flex developer is how well you can leverage the Flex API help reference. We'll explore this in the following section.

2.7.1 Object-oriented languages and their APIs

One characteristic of object-oriented languages is they tend to require the use of an API Reference moreso than non-OO languages. This is because non-OO languages have variable types and functions that are independent of one another. For example, with ColdFusion the `cfquery` tag returns a query structure that has some properties—end of story.

In object-oriented languages land, you have objects, which contain functions (known as methods) and properties combined. You can keep extending one object from another, with each extension inheriting everything from the last (for example, animal > dog > pit bull).

What does all this have to do with help? Because you're dealing with so many objects, you'll find yourself needing to refer to the API Reference more frequently than in a non-OO language.

Throughout this book we periodically show you where in the API Reference you can go to find answers.

The more you become comfortable with the API Reference, the more efficient you'll become at coding in Flex.

2.7.2 Accessing the API Reference

Because you're just starting out, the API Reference isn't of much value yet. The only thing you need to do is make a mental note of how to access it as needed.

DYNAMIC HELP

The easiest way to use the API Reference is through Flex Builder's automatic Dynamic Help feature. To demonstrate how this works, try out the following:

1. From the Flex Builder toolbar, select Help > Dynamic Help.
2. In the code editor, click anywhere within the `<mx:Button>` line of code to position the cursor on that line.
3. A new pane appears (figure 2.17) on the right-hand side. In the very first section are links to the API.
4. In this case a link to `mx.controls.Button` is displayed, which is the formal location and definition of the button. Click it to see what the API Reference looks like for this component.

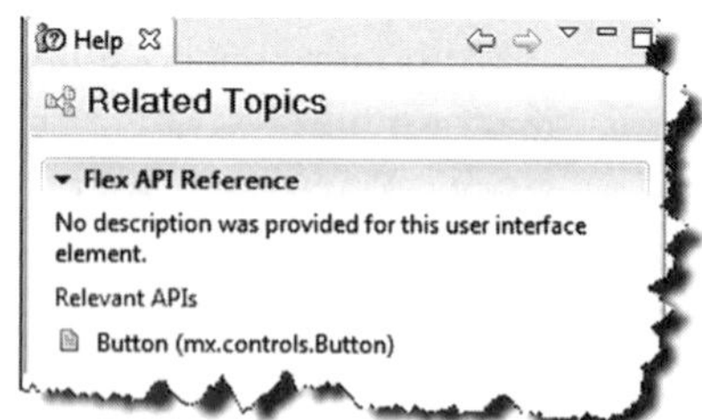

Figure 2.17 Dynamic Help automatically presents a link to the API Reference depending on where in your application

Having a live document search ready when you need it—and displaying relevant information—can help save time, and isn't something too many IDEs can boast about. This isn't the only type of help available either. There's an awesome shortcut you'll want to memorize that brings up the API Reference immediately.

SHIFT+F2 HELP

Similar to the Dynamic Help approach, if you don't have the search pane already displayed, or you want to maintain what's currently shown under Dynamic Help, you can pull up the API Reference quickly using a hot key combination by following the steps below:

1 In the Code Editor, click anywhere within the line of code that contains the `<mx:Button>`.
2 Press Shift+F2.
3 The API Reference for the button will appear.

It will take some time to develop the habit of using this key combination, but once you do, you'll be using it constantly.

At this juncture, all you've done is display the API Reference. Now you need to understand what you're looking at.

2.7.3 Perusing API Reference

Let's look at the elements of an API Reference page. Having accessed the reference page of the button component using either Dynamic Help or the Shift+F2 technique, you should see something similar to figure 2.18.

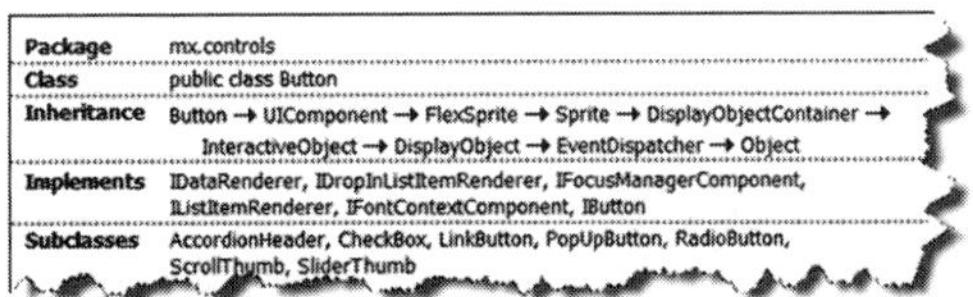

Package	mx.controls
Class	public class Button
Inheritance	Button → UIComponent → FlexSprite → Sprite → DisplayObjectContainer → InteractiveObject → DisplayObject → EventDispatcher → Object
Implements	IDataRenderer, IDropInListItemRenderer, IFocusManagerComponent, IListItemRenderer, IFontContextComponent, IButton
Subclasses	AccordionHeader, CheckBox, LinkButton, PopUpButton, RadioButton, ScrollThumb, SliderThumb

Figure 2.18 The first section of an API Reference page describes the world around a particular object.

Using the term object in a generic sense (versus the object-oriented nomenclature), here are brief descriptions of the five categories shown in figure 2.18:

- *Package*—Indicates to what directory the object belongs.
- *Class*—The particular object the API Reference page is describing.
- *Inheritance*—Who are the parents of this object? A child will generally inherit the properties and functions of its ancestors. This is important to know, as being aware of what a parent object can do gives you insight as to what the child object can do as well.
- *Implements*—The lists of items here are called interfaces. These are like contracts to which the object agrees to adhere. Specifically, it will implement the properties and functions/methods the interface demands.
- *Subclasses*—These are children of the object. Meaning anything this object can do, the children can do as well.

The next portion of the API Reference page (not shown in figure 2.18) contains all the important pieces of information to which a Flex developer would regularly refer in order to manipulate an object or component. Following is a summary of those sections:

- *Properties*—Values you can retrieve and potentially set, such as width and height.
- *Methods*—Supporting functions, such as those that cause a component to redraw itself.

- *Events*—Actions to which objects will react (such as being clicked), that trigger the execution of specific instructions whenever the event occurs.
- *Styles*—Similar to CSS styles in HTML, these are stylesheet references.
- *Effects*—Used in conjunction with events to specify effects to be played. For example, if the mouse rolls over an object, you can specify a glowing effect to highlight that object.

Every API Reference page is going to look like this, and some even include examples of how to use an object or component. The key here is, once you get used to parsing the information and isolating the portion you need, you'll be able to flip back and forth between coding and the API Reference effortlessly.

2.8 MXML and ActionScript in a nutshell

Flex is based on MXML and ActionScript. As a result, when first learning Flex, it is often confusing deciding when to use one or the other, and new developers often ask themselves if they should be following some established best practice.

Let's start by taking a closer look at these two languages and explore this question a bit further.

2.8.1 The structure of MXML

In the previous example, you wrote a Flex application using pure MXML. MXML is a tag-based coding system derived from XML. Because of this heritage, it follows all the rules and conventions of XML, most notably:

- XML files, and therefore MXML files, require the XML declaration, which defines the version and character encoding.

```
<?xml version="1.0" encoding="utf-8"?>
```

- XML files must have a top-level root tag (and corresponding closing tag at the end of the file).
- The language is case sensitive.
- Tags must have an opening and closing tag.
- For example, `<myTag>…</myTag>`
- You can also use the shorthand version of `<myTag/>`
- Tags must be nested properly.
- HTML is rather relaxed about this, but XML is very strict and won't allow for such shenanigans.
- valid: `<a><b>…</b></a>`
- invalid: `<a><b>…</a></b>`
- Attribute values must be quoted.
- For example, `<tag attribute="value">`
- White space counts; HTML ignores consecutive repeating spaces, counting them as one.

If you've done a lot of work with XML, we're not breaking any new ground here. If you haven't, most of these conventions will feel like those rules that nag as an HTML developer.

NOTE Flex Builder automatically indicates any violations of XML rules, and won't let you compile until you've resolved any outstanding issues.

What it really boils down to is keeping things clean, consistent, and structured.

2.8.2 How MXML and ActionScript relate

One point that puzzles some is why is Flex made up of two languages in the first place? Think of it this way; as a web developer you use HTML to describe your visual elements, such as tables, form inputs, and images. But these elements carry no functionality on the client side until you add JavaScript (to execute form validation, for instance).

It is the same in Flex. You use MXML to lay down your basic visual elements, as well as to define some nonvisual pieces, such as formatters and validators, and to access data services (we'll get into those a bit later).

TIP Think of the relationship of MXML to ActionScript as similar to that of HTML to JavaScript.

In Flex you use ActionScript when you need to add functionality, decision making, interactivity, and business logic. As an example, let's go back to your Hello World! Flex project. But now we'll use ActionScript to modify it to appear as in listing 2.3.

Listing 2.3 Using ActionScript and MXML together

```
<?xml version="1.0" encoding="utf-8"?>
<mx:Application xmlns:mx="http://www.adobe.com/2006/mxml"
  ➥layout="absolute">
 <mx:Button label="Marco" fontSize="40"
  click="mx.controls.Alert.show('Polo')"/>
</mx:Application>
```

When you run the code in listing 2.3 and click the button labeled Marco, a pop-up alert will display (figure 2.19).

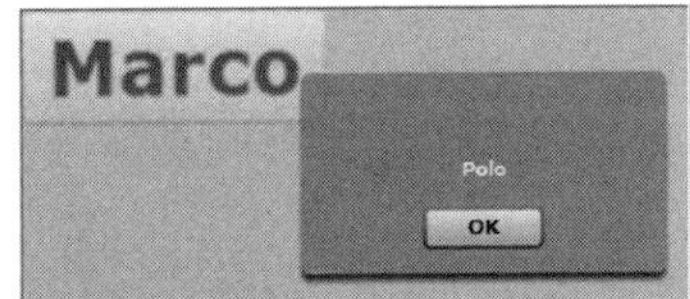

Figure 2.19 ActionScript allows you to script in the logic and flow of your application.

If you approach this with the mindset that Flex is to ActionScript as HTML is to JavaScript, it will make it easier to understand.

One mental hurdle web developers face comes as a result of having limited experience using client-side logic such as JavaScript. Traditional web technologies and web document models are such that most of the application logic resides on the server.

For example, ColdFusion folks are accustomed to using a tag-based language not only for the HTML, but also for the logic:

```
<cfif itsAllGood>
  <b>It's all good</b>
</cfif>
```

The natural instinct when in Flex, therefore, is to code as in the following snippet:

```
<mx:if>…</mx:if>
```

Keep in mind the Flex to ActionScript/HTML to JavaScript model and you'll be in good shape going forward. If ActionScript is to JavaScript, and JavaScript has events, you'd be correct in assuming that ActionScript also supports some kind of an event mechanism.

2.8.3 Events are handled by ActionScript

Flex is an event-driven application, which means everything occurs as a result of something happening. This is very common with client-side technologies such as Flex. First you have something that triggers the event then something that handles the event.

The device that handles the event is called (not surprisingly) an event handler, and is implemented in ActionScript. If you refer to listing 2.3, you'll see that ActionScript was executed when the mouse button triggered the `click` event.

```
<mx:Button label="Marco" fontSize="40" click="mx.con-
  trols.Alert.show('Polo')"/>
```

In the previous example, the specific event handler we wanted, `mx.controls.Alert.show('Polo')`, appears between quotation marks, but you can put any ActionScript event mechanism between them. Usually you call an event handler function to process all the logic you want executed when the event occurs.

ALMOST THE SAME AS IN JAVASCRIPT

This isn't any different than execution in JavaScript. JavaScript is used heavily to handle mouse-button and mouse-over events. For example, you may need to validate data entered into a form before you send it to a server for processing.

Consider how this is done in the code presented in listing 2.4.

Listing 2.4 JavaScript, like ActionScript, is event-driven

```
<script language="JavaScript">
  img_over =new Image(); img_over.src ="over.gif";
  img_off=new Image();  img_off.src="off.gif";

  function handleOver()
  {
    document.myImg.src=img_over.src;        ❶
  }

  function handleOut()
  {
    document.myImg.src=img_off.src;         ❷
  }
</script>
```

```
<a href="#" onMouseOver="handleOver();" onMouseOut="handleOut();">
  <img name=myImg src="off.gif">
</a>
```

This is the classic mouse-over technique commonly used in JavaScript. You can see it makes use of two key events:

- `onMouseOver`—Caused by the mouse moving over a target ❶
- `onMouseOut`—Caused by the mouse moving off a target ❷

If you look at this from the JavaScript perspective you should feel right at home with the similarities. The comparison takes a bit of a departure though, as Flex has an event object as well.

ALMOST THE SAME, BUT ACTIONSCRIPT HAS AN EVENT OBJECT

JavaScript events are almost the same, but not quite. The main difference is ActionScript events also make available an event object.

All events are rooted from a generic top-level event object, and events add extra details through inheritance. What's cool about this is it allows you to easily write event handlers that are highly reusable as they can obtain the event's details through the event object. This includes information such as:

- Where the event came from
- Reference to the data
- Type of event (for example, a click versus a mouse over)

To give you an idea of how that works, let's take a look at listing 2.5.

Listing 2.5 Using the event object makes event handlers more generic

```
<?xml version="1.0" encoding="utf-8"?>
<mx:Application xmlns:mx="http://www.adobe.com/2006/mxml"
    backgroundColor="white">
<mx:Script>
  <![CDATA[
    import mx.controls.Alert;
    public function clickHandler(clickEvent:Event):void      <- Accepts an event object
    {
  Alert.show("Event Type:" + clickEvent.type +                <- Displays the type of event
            " came from:" + clickEvent.currentTarget.id);     <- References properties from where the event came
    }
  ]]>
</mx:Script>
<mx:Button label="Handle Click" id="myButton"
        click="clickHandler(event)"/>                         <- Triggers the event
</mx:Application>
```

Listing 2.5 demonstrates an event handler function being invoked when the user clicks his mouse button. When the mouse click occurs, an event object is created and passed along to the event handler (figure 2.20).

The event handler function has no idea who called it, but by using the event object it can find out any of the properties of the component that triggered the event, as well as what type of event it is.

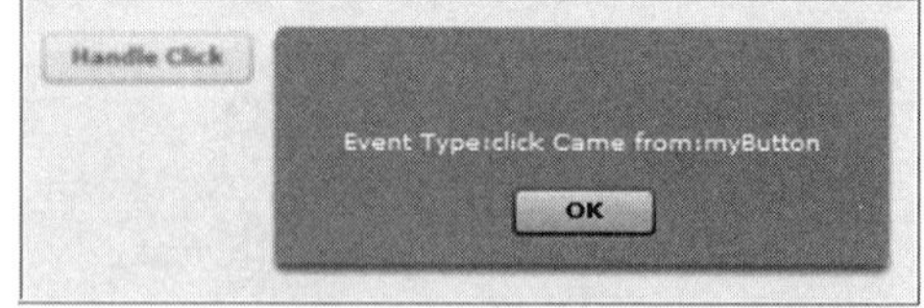

Figure 2.20 Using the event object, a handler can access details such as from where the event came.

This is extremely handy when you want to make an event handler reusable, as the handler doesn't need to know any specifics about how to access the related components.

2.9 Summary

We've covered a lot of ground over the last two chapters, and things are going to ramp up quickly as we jump into more code. Before we do that, let's review a few things.

To those who may challenge your decision to use Flex due to cost, you can counter with the fact that the Flex SDK is free, and by using the free Eclipse IDE and plug-ins you can get quite far in creating complete Flex applications. From a productivity perspective, the ROI realized by upgrading to Flex Builder (which is based on the Eclipse IDE) is easily justified and highly recommended.

Flex Builder's interface can be completely customized by the use of views, panes, and perspectives. Although there are default perspectives, you can alter the layout, add from the extensive catalog of views, and save them as new perspectives. This gives you a lot of freedom to customize how you work within the IDE.

Flex Builder comes with a catalog of wizards you can use to help perform all kinds of tasks, including creating a new project. The New Project wizard will assist you in defining the main folder, its source directory, and where you want the compiled application to reside.

Flex is an object-oriented language, and because of that you'll need to become comfortable with the API Reference, more so than you would with a procedural language. This is because objects inherit from one another and contain built-in properties and functions. Knowing what an object's parents and children are let you know their capabilities. Use the dynamic help and Shift+F2 features to assist you in that goal.

ActionScript is to MXML as JavaScript is to HTML. Use MXML to lay out your components then add ActionScript for all the business logic. ActionScript and JavaScript are very similar; they're both derived from the same scripting standard called ECMAScript, they both are client-side technologies, and they're both based on an event-driven model.

One key difference is ActionScript creates an event object that an event handler can use to access almost everything it needs without needing to know about the actual source of the event.

In the next chapter, we'll jump right into ActionScript so we can add applicable logic going forward.

Working with ActionScript

3

This chapter covers:

- Comments
- Variable types
- Operators
- Loops
- Conditions
- Arrays
- Functions

In chapter 2 we introduced ActionScript, but what exactly can you do with it? As you'll soon see, quite a bit.

ActionScript is an extremely powerful object-oriented language about which you can dedicate entire books. In this chapter we'll focus on ActionScript's core concepts; obviously you will need to be familiar with them before we get to the more powerful aspects of Flex itself. Speaking of which, you're probably anxious to get back into Flex, but tackling some ActionScript fundamentals will allow us to pick up the pace and move further forward.

A fundamental concept in any programming language is that of comments, so we'll begin our discussion with how Flex supports documenting your code.

3.1 Comments

A basic construct of any programming language is the ability to document the mechanics of an application from within the code itself. You will learn to do this through the use of comments.

From the perspective of implementation, a comment is a sequence of delimited text that is ignored by the Flex compiler. Flex's ActionScript language supports two popular formats: inline comments with regular code, and block style with multiline comments.

3.1.1 Inline comments

The first comment type is the inline style which you invoke using double-forward slashes:

```
// one comment
var i:int;
var x:int; // another comment
```

As you can see, comments can exist on their own line, or inline, alongside code. Using inline comments has limitations; the compiler recognizes the text following double-forward slashes as a comment only until the end of the current line. A line return signals the end of the comment and the resumption of programmatic code.

3.1.2 Block comments

If you want to provide a much larger description using free-form text, you can use a multiline comment instead. Begin a multiline comment by typing a forward slash and asterisk (`/*`), and close it with the inversion (`*/`):

```
/*
  here is a chunk
  of text
*/
```

Commenting code serves two major purposes: it helps describe how the code works, and it assists in testing and debugging. With respect to documenting the code, it makes sense to use comments not only to be meaningful to other programmers, but to help keep track of what you've done for your own benefit. For debugging, you can temporarily comment out blocks of code to perform testing and diagnostics during the development process.

Let's move to variables, which allow you to gather and store information.

3.2 Variables

Variables of course, are the basic building block of any programming language. They contain data you use to keep track of information, maintain the state of your application, and enable the user to manage data.

Although variables are common in all languages, their implementation varies from language to language. ActionScript may be a considerable departure from that with which you're currently familiar. ActionScript is based on a standard called ECMAScript, which is the same standard on which JavaScript is based (though ActionScript follows a more recent version of ECMAScript).

3.2.1 Variable names

Variables have names and, as you may expect, there are rules to follow when creating them. Variable names may contain only letters, numbers, underscores, and the dollar sign. You can use any combination of those characters as long as the name doesn't begin with a number.

3.2.2 Strict data typing

Unlike JavaScript and ColdFusion, ActionScript uses *strict data typing*. This means when you declare a variable of a certain type, the value you assign it must be the same or a compatible type. Look at the following code snippet:

```
var myVar:Number;
myVar = "test"; //would result in an error
```

This code is invalid because you're trying to assign text to a variable that is expecting a numeric value.

3.2.3 Static vs. dynamic type checking

Flex checks for type mismatches using two approaches known as *static* and *dynamic* type checking. Static type checking is performed during compile time with the compiler ensuring the rules of typing are being maintained. Programmers coming from Java and C++ will be accustomed to this method.

ActionScript can also perform dynamic type checking. With dynamic type checking, Flash Player examines your variable types during application execution. Of course, there are pros and cons to both approaches. One benefit of dynamic type checking is it makes development more convenient as you can quickly prototype applications without coping with compiler warnings and errors.

By default, static is the mode that's used when compiling your application. You can change this via the enable strict type checking option found under Project > Properties > Flex Compiler setting.

Keep in mind that even if you turn static mode off, during the execution of your application the Flash Player still performs type checking; disabling static mode simply skips the compile-time check.

Although it can be less of a nuisance to avoid compile-time checking, I recommend you save yourself some grief and leave static mode on. In the long run you'll be better off looking into whatever the compiler is complaining about.

3.2.4 Primitive and complex data types

There are two classifications of data types: primitive and complex. As its name implies, primitive data types are low-level, rudimentary bits of data such as numbers and letters. Complex data types are pretty much anything else, such as objects, pointers, and structures.

In chapter 16, we'll go into classes and OOP in greater depth, but let me mention that object-oriented languages typically envelop primitive data types with an object-oriented wrapper to provide a more robust, or flexible version, of the primitive.

PRIMITIVE DATA TYPES

A primitive data type typically involves lower overhead (memory and processing power) than its complex data type counterparts. But in ActionScript, everything is an object, so technically there's not much of a difference.

For the most part that difference equates to a simplified syntax in your code, which ultimately translates into a convenience advantage for you. From a runtime perspective, the Flash Player does treat primitives differently compared to other objects, and doesn't employ as much of the object management needed for a complex data type, which results in a slight performance advantage. Table 3.1 lists the primitive data types.

Table 3.1 ActionScript and Flex primitive variable types

Data Type	Description
`Boolean" \t` "*See also* variable"	Stores the values of true or false. Used as a flag.
`int" \t` "See also variable"	An integer field that stores whole numbers. Good for loop counters. Data is stored as a 32-bit value.
`uint`	Unsigned integer, similar to `int`, but they can only store nonnegative numbers such as RGB values for colors. Data is stored as a 32-bit value.
`Number`	A more generic numeric data type that is more flexible and robust. Required if you want to store floats (decimal values). Data is stored as a 64-bit value.
`String`	A sequence of characters. Used to store text.

When do you use an `int` and when do you use a `Number`? In many cases they are interchangeable, but there is a difference.

INTS VS. NUMBERS

There has been debate in blogs and discussion forums over which data types have a performance advantage. You would think that as a result of not carrying decimal precision, `int`s would have a speed advantage over `Number`. With Flash Player, in most cases, `Number`s have the advantage. Flash Player uses `Number` internally to store all numeric data. Therefore, when you use an `int`, some behind-the-scenes effort is required to convert it to a `Number`. This extra effort potentially eliminates any performance advantage the `int` may have enjoyed.

In reality, performance shouldn't be the only reason why you choose one data type over the other; the difference is miniscule, and that's when you're looping through hundreds of thousands of numerical manipulations. Rather, your decision should be based on code maintainability—if you need an integer (such as a loop counter), using an `int` communicates the intended purpose to others who may be involved in maintaining your code.

COMPLEX DATA TYPES

There is no absolute list of complex data types. In addition to the primitives, Flex and ActionScript 3 come with a massive collection of complex data types (otherwise known as classes).

Flex employs a concept called *core classes*. Normally to use a class you have to import it into your application so that the compiler knows where to find the class you're referring to. But with a core class these are objects that are ready for use. They don't need to be explicitly imported in order to use them; at the same time you don't need to call the object's constructor (a function that initializes the object).

TIP Most object-oriented languages support a constructor function that is executed automatically whenever the object is created. It gives the object the opportunity to configure itself before being used.

Core classes let you generate code such as the following:

```
var myString:String = "hello";
```

Conversely, if `String` weren't part of the core, you would need to create it explicitly using its constructor:

```
var myString:String = new String("hello");
```

In the preceding line, you can use both methods with a `String` because it is a core class.

All the primitive data types are part of the core set. Also included as part of the core classes are the complex data types listed in table 3.2.

Table 3.2 Complex data types that are part of the core classes

Data Type	Description
`Object`	The grandfather of all objects, this is the object from which all others are derived and inherit their attributes. Its default value is null.
`Array`	A collection of objects sequenced one after another, and numerically indexed. For example, instead of having a separate variable for each address on your street, you could have a single address array that stores each individual address.
`Date`	As the name implies, this object stores date-related information. `Date` provides a number of functions for handling and converting to and from local or daylight savings, and GMT/UTC time.
`Error`	Used for handling exceptions and managing unexpected conditions you would prefer to handle more gracefully.
`Function`	Otherwise known as the method to a class.

Table 3.2 Complex data types that are part of the core classes *(continued)*

Data Type	Description
`RegExp`	Regular expressions—a sublanguage for string parsing and pattern matching.
`XML`	Used to work with a set of XML data that contains a single root node.
`XMLList`	Similar to XML, but designed to handle multiple sets of top-level nodes.

That sums up variables, but there are some final rules related to special data types.

SPECIAL DATA TYPES

These are data types from which you can't create variables. In essence, they're reserved words and values. It is also worth noting that you shouldn't try to make a variable using any of the special data type names. Table 3.3 provides a list of the special data types along with their descriptions.

Table 3.3 Special data types

Data Type	Description
`*`	An optional method to indicate to the compiler you will set the variable's data type later.
`void`	Used in function declarations to indicate the function isn't returning any data.
`undefined`	Works hand-in-hand with void. The value of void is undefined.
`null`	Used by complex data types and `Strings` to indicate they currently have no associated value.
`NaN`	Not a number. Used by the `Number` data type to indicate it is currently not assigned to a numerical value.

To summarize, ActionScript variables are case sensitive, and you need to be sure their assigned values agree, or are compatible with their data types. ActionScript includes both primitive and complex types; all primitive types and some complex types are a part of a collection of core classes.

Often when working with arrays you'll want to process the collection of values using a loop. We'll take a look at that next.

3.3 Loops

Loops are another fundamental construct all languages provide, in one variation or another. From a conceptual point of view, loops iterate over a range of numbers, or a collection of items until a specified condition is no longer true.

In this section, we'll explore the types of loops ActionScript supports and how to use them, starting with the `for` loop.

3.3.1 For (starting value; valid condition; increment)

The standard for loop, common in most languages, lets you specify a starting value, stipulate the valid condition in which the loop will continue to iterate, and increment the starting value in accordance with what you specify:

```
for(var x:int=1;x<=10;x++)
  trace(x);
```

In this example, trace() outputs to a log file. The loop assigns the variable x a value of one. It then performs its iteration, incrementing the x variable by one with each pass, until the variable's value equals 10. This type of loop comes in handy when you know how many times you need to perform a function, such as the number of items in an array.

3.3.2 For (property names in array/object)

If you have an array or an object, the for..in loop lets you iterate over all the items contained within that array or object by property name. This comes in handy when you're working with XML and XMLList objects.

```
var myArray:Array  = ["alpha","beta","chi"];
for(var i:String in myArray) {
  trace(i);
}
```

There's a catch—we're looping over property names, and in an array the property name is the array's index. This means the output for the previous example would be:

```
0
1
2
```

In this case, the first index of an array would be 0.

Because we're getting the index, we can obtain the values through the following:

```
var myArray:Array  = ["alpha","beta","chi"];
for(var i:String in myArray) {
  trace(myArray[i]);
}
```

The variable i is the zero-based index number of the items contained within myArray. When i is 0, it would get the first item in myArray.

Output:

```
alpha
beta
chi
```

Why is the variable i a String and not an int? In most cases, you would receive an error if you tried using int because the for..in loop is returning property names, which are `Strings`. (In the second example, the Flash player is able to auto-convert to a number, as the index of an array is a number.)

The case for objects is similar; unlike arrays (which contain a sequence of items), objects simply have properties, or attributes.

```
var myObject:Object = {firstName:'Jeff', lastName:'Smith'};
for(var i:String in myObject) {
  trace("Property: " + i + "=" + myObject[i]);
}
```

TIP For you ColdFusion users, `myObject[i]` is similar to accessing a key in a structure as an associative array.

Output:

```
Property:firstName=Jeff
Property:lastName=Smith
```

This kind of loop has a variety of ways it can be used. If you simply want the value of each item, you'll find the `for each..in` loop easier to use.

3.3.3 For each (item in array/object)

The `for each..in` loop iterates over arrays and objects, but instead of property names, it tests for the property's value.

```
var myObject:Object = {firstName:'Jeff', lastName:'Smith'};
for each(var i:String in myObject) {
  trace(i);
}
```

Output:

```
Jeff
Smith
```

This type of loop is a simplified version of the `for..in` loop. `for` loops work great when used against known quantities like arrays and objects, but when you want to keep looping until a condition is met you'll need the `while` loop.

3.3.4 While (condition)

The `while` loop continues iterating until the specified condition is no longer true.

```
var x:int = 0;
while(x<5)
{
  trace('x is now ' + x);
  x=x+1;
}
```

Output:

```
x is now 0
x is now 1
```

```
x is now 2
x is now 3
x is now 4
```

Note that the `while` loop checks the condition at the start of the loop; if the condition isn't true upon the loop's initiation, no iterations will be performed.

3.3.5 Do while (condition)

The `do while` loop is the same as a `while` loop, with the subtle, but important, difference of the test condition being evaluated at the end of the loop, instead of the beginning. This comes in handy if you need to run through a section of code at least once, regardless of the test condition's status. Use the `while` loop if you need to verify the condition is valid before engaging the loop.

```
var x:int = 5;
do
{
  trace('x is now ' + x);
  x=x+1;
} while(x<5);
```

Output:

```
x is now 5
```

The various types of loops provide you with all the control you will need to iterate over a known set of quantities, or while a condition is valid. The next building block to look at is adding conditional logic.

3.4 Conditional statements (if statements and switches)

Conditional statements are a fundamental piece of programming. ActionScript implements two forms of them, the `if` and `switch` statements, just like most languages. Note the particular syntax here as ActionScript provides the same constructs as any other language and nothing more in this case.

3.4.1 If..else

When you need to check if a condition has been met, such as whether the user has provided a password, `if..else` statements are your primary mechanism for doing so.

Here's a simple exercise to see how `if..else` works:

- Load your `HelloWorld` project
- Change the code to that presented in listing 3.1
- Test if the `if..else` statement is doing its job by entering any password in the text input box generated by your code (figure 3.1) then trying it without a password.

Listing 3.1 Using an if..else conditional statement to do a password check

```
<?xml version="1.0" encoding="utf-8"?>
<mx:Application xmlns:mx="http://www.adobe.com/2006/mxml"
   ➥layout="horizontal">
  <mx:Script>
    <![CDATA[
      public function checkPassword():void
      {
        if(password.text.length < 1)
          mx.controls.Alert.show("Missing Password!");
        else
      mx.controls.Alert.show("Looks Good!");
      }
    ]]>
  </mx:Script>
  <mx:TextInput id="password"/>
  <mx:Button label="Check Password" click="checkPassword()"/>
</mx:Application>
```

Curly braces are optional around the Alert code, but are not used in this case as there's only one line of code after `if` and `else`.

Figure 3.1 shows a simple text input box with a submit button created by the new code in listing 3.1.
Running our example with and without text generates the appropriate alerts, as shown in figures 3.2 and 3.3.

Figure 3.1 Simple password checking application verifies a password has been entered.

When working with `if` statements, you don't necessarily need the `else` branch. In the previous example, if you want to pop the Missing Password! alert (but not display the Looks Good! message), you could use the `if` branch and omit the `else` section altogether.

```
public function checkPassword():void
{
if(password.text.length < 1)
mx.controls.Alert.show("Missing Password!");
}
```

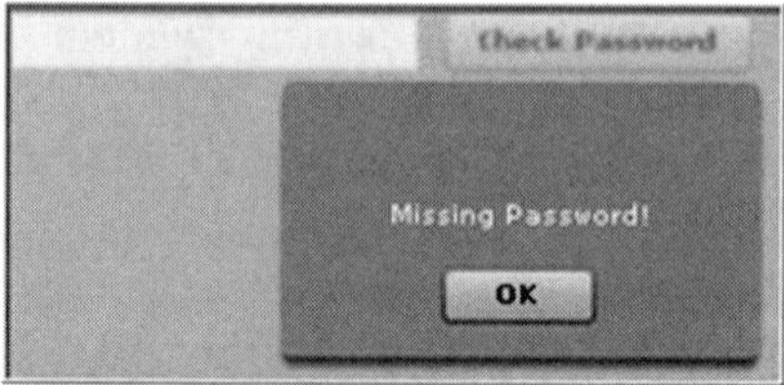

Figure 3.2 An Alert pop-up window appears when the `if` statement tests true for an empty password field.

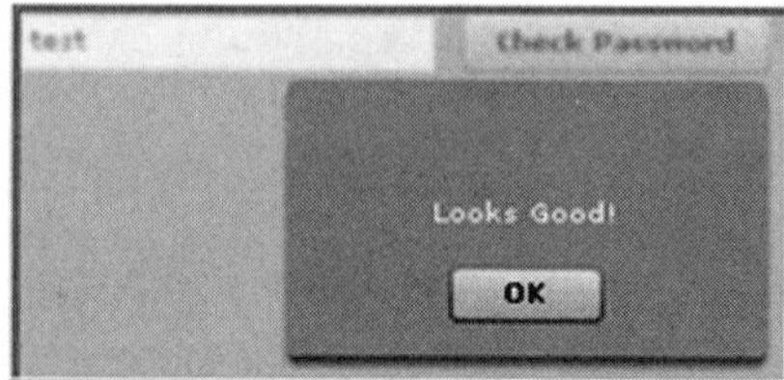

Figure 3.3 When the `if` statement tests false, the `else` branch of the statement is used, which displays a different message.

If you need to continue checking more conditions after the current condition has failed, you'll want to use the `else if` command. Let's assume you want to test for a missing password as one condition, check for a password containing too few characters as another, and allow anything other than the first two conditions as a third. Each condition will display the appropriate message to the user. Listing 3.2 shows how to configure the code.

Listing 3.2 Nesting multiple conditional statements

```
if(password.text.length < 1)
mx.controls.Alert.show("Missing Password!");
else if (password.text.length < 5)
mx.controls.Alert.show("Not Enough Characters!");
else
mx.controls.Alert.show("Looks Good!");
```

You can continue adding as many `else ifs` as needed, but this can become unwieldy if there are many conditions to check. This is where the `switch` statement makes a better alternative.

3.4.2 Switch

If you need to evaluate many conditions, it is often easier to use a `switch` statement instead of repeated `else if` commands. Listing 3.3 shows a `switch` statement evaluating a number of possible values.

Listing 3.3 Using a switch statement makes managing many conditions easy

```
<?xml version="1.0" encoding="utf-8"?>
<mx:Application xmlns:mx="http://www.adobe.com/2006/mxml"
            layout="horizontal">
  <mx:Script>
    <![CDATA[
      public function moodCheck():void
      {
        switch(myMood.text)
        {
          case 'happy':
            mx.controls.Alert.show("Life is good isn't it?");
            break;                                   <- Ends the case block
          case 'sad':
            mx.controls.Alert.show("Some Prozac will cheer you up!");
            break;
          default:                                   <- A catch all for conditions that don't match any of the above
            mx.controls.Alert.show("Neither here nor there eh?");
        }
      }
    ]]>
  </mx:Script>
  <mx:TextInput id="myMood"/>
  <mx:Button label="Check your mood" click="moodCheck()"/>
</mx:Application>
```

Using a `switch` statement makes the code naturally easier to read by grouping each condition in a `case` block, but there are a couple of unique syntax characteristics you'll want to keep in mind when using it:

- Don't wrap `case` blocks in curly braces.
- The end of each section requires a `break` statement.
- Instead of the `case` keyword, you can use `default` to catch anything that doesn't match any of the above.

To summarize, `if`, `else`, and `switch` statements are the basic way to add conditional logic to your application. Switching gears (get it?), we're going to cover another of the important fundamentals: arrays.

3.5 Arrays

An array is a variable that can store multiple values. For example, if you owned three houses and wanted to store information about the tenants living in each one, you could create one variable per occupant:

```
House1="John Doe";
House2="Michael Dorsay";
House3="Herald McGee";
```

The problem here is this pseudocode isn't scalable. With this approach you're required to know in advance how many variables you'll need (which isn't realistic in most real-world scenarios). If you were coding for hundreds (or thousands) of houses, it would require maintaining a lot of overhead.

An array is perfect for handling just these kinds of situations:

```
HouseArray[1]="John Doe"
HouseArray[2]="Michael Dorsay"
HouseArray[3]="Herald McGee"
```

ActionScript supports three main types of arrays:

- *Indexed*—Use a number as a key for each value. This is useful when the values you need to store are based on some kind of sequence. For example, it would lend itself well to a queue of tasks that need to be executed in sequential steps, one-by-one.
- *Associative*—Use any kind of a key (usually a string) to associate values to the key. Associative arrays are useful when you want to make some kind of lookup mechanism. For example, you could use Social Security numbers as a key to store the name and details of the person associated with a specific number.
- *Multidimensional*—Arrays of arrays. Multidimensional arrays are useful when you need to use a combination of keys to store and retrieve information. Each dimension can be a mix of indexed and associative arrays. For example, you could use a two-dimensional array to store a grid of colors, using one dimension for the *x*-coordinate and the second for the *y*-coordinate.

Let's take a closer look at how indexed and associative arrays work (keep in mind a multidimensional array is just a combination of these).

3.5.1 *Indexed arrays*

This is the array that usually comes to mind. Indexed arrays store, and allow access to data, through a numerical index. To create one, you declare it as follows:

```
var houseArray:Array = new Array();
```

When you declare an array in this fashion, it contains no items, but you can add an extra parameter with which you can assign it an initial value.

```
var houseArray:Array = new Array(3);
```

Typically, in programmer's parlance, to load items into an array, you *push* and *unshift* them. To retrieve items, you *pop*, and *shift* them off. To make life a bit easier, there's a multifunctional mechanism called a *splice* that lets you do both.

TIP The index of the first item in an indexed array is 0—not 1, as would be your natural inclination to think.

Here are the common array functions you can use:

- `push()`—Appends the item onto the end of the array.

```
houseArray.push("John Doe");
houseArray.push("Michael Dorsay");
```

- `unshift()`—Inserts the item onto the front of the array.

```
houseArray.unshift("Herald McGee");
houseArray.unshift("Jon Hirschi");
```

- `pop()`—Takes an item off the end of the array.

```
houseArray.pop();
```

- `shift()`—Takes an item off the front of the array.

```
houseArray.shift();
```

- `splice()`—Remove items from a position, and optionally insert new items. The first line adds an item in the second position. The next line takes out the second item.

```
houseArray.splice(1,0,"Tariq Ahmed");
houseArray.splice(1,1);
```

Most of these functions are self-explanatory, except the `splice()` function, which needs further explanation.

A CLOSER LOOKED AT SPLICE()

Let's talk a little bit more about the `splice()` function by looking at its parameters:

- *Parameter 1*—The index position in the array at which you want to start. Because the first item in an indexed array is 0, 1 would be the second item.
- *Parameter 2*—The amount of items you want to take off, starting at the position defined in parameter 1. If you set this to 0, no items will be removed.
- *Parameter 3*—Insert new items into the array starting at the position specified by parameter 1. This is done after items are removed (if any) as indicated in parameter 2.

Here's a brief example; starting at the fourth position, take out two items, and add three more:

```
houseArray.splice(3,2,"Ryan Stewart","Matt Chotin","Jeff Dougherty");
```

Although arrays are common in all languages, the `splice()` function is unique to ActionScript's implementation of this data type. Some languages also provide a shorthand way to initialize arrays. ActionScript provides a shorthand method as well, and we'll show you what it is.

SHORTHAND INITIALIZATION OF ARRAYS

You can take advantage of shorthand notation to initialize your arrays and set their starting values:

```
var houseArray:Array = new ["John Doe","Michael Dorsay","Herald McGee"];
```

In the previous code snippet, the square brackets indicate an array. The items contained in the array are separated by commas.

Now that you have a populated array, you'll want to be able to loop through it.

LOOPING THROUGH ARRAYS

To benefit from the full potential of arrays you'll want to loop through their range of index values. The key to accomplishing that is the array's `length` property, which indicates how many items are contained within.

NOTE The `trace()` function is a simple logging mechanism for printing text to the Flash Player's log file. We'll begin using it here as part of our demonstrations, but for more detailed information on the `trace()` function, see chapter 23.

When we talked about `for` loops we mentioned they are commonly used with arrays. Taking a look at listing 3.4, let's review a `for` loop used to iterate over each item in an array.

Listing 3.4 Looping through an array

```
var myFriendsArray:Array = ["John Doe","Marco Polo","Warren Jones"];
for (var i:int=0;i<myFriendsArray.length;i++)     <-- Determine array size
{
 trace(myFriendsArray[i]);     <-- Output to the log file
}
```

Listing 3.4 demonstrates how the array's length property is used to evaluate how many items it contains while progressively looping over each item.

You're not restricted to using numbers as a key to each item in the array. Another option is using a string for the key instead.

3.5.2 *Associative arrays*

The mechanics of an associative array are a little different in that you deal with keys instead of indices. For ColdFusion folks, you'll find comfort here, as the mechanism is exactly the same as ColdFusion's associative arrays (using a Struct).

As with indexed arrays, you create an associative array using the same method:

```
var carManufacturersByModel:Array = new Array();
```

But going forward, instead of pushing and popping, you simply assign values based on a textual string as shown here:

```
carManufacturersByModel["xA"] = "Scion";
carManufacturersByModel["Viper"] = "Dodge";
carManufacturersByModel["is350"] = "Lexus";
```

Then, to retrieve the value associated with the key, you simply access it using the key:

```
trace(carManufacturersByModel["xA"]);       Output: Scion
trace(carManufacturersByModel["Viper"]);    Output: Dodge
trace(carManufacturersByModel["is350"]);    Output: Lexus
```

Ultimately, you want to loop through all the items in the associative array, and to do this you typically would use the reliable `for..in` loop.

```
for (var key:String in carManufacturersByModel)
{
  trace("Key:"+key);
  trace("Value:"+carManufacturersByModel[key]);
}
```

Output:

```
Key:Viper
Value:Dodge
Key:is350
Value:Lexus
Key:xA
Value:Scion
```

Alternatively, if you want the values themselves and are not interested in the corresponding keys, you can use the `for each..in` loop as this snippet demonstrates:

```
for each (var manufacturer:String in carManufacturersByModel)
{
  trace(manufacturer);
}
```

Notice the output in this case displays only the values of the items:

```
Lexus
Scion
Dodge
```

Do you sense something a little odd with this output? The order displayed (Lexus, Scion, Dodge) isn't the order in which the items were originally added (Scion, Dodge, Lexus). You'll need to keep in mind that items stored in an associative array are stored in an nonordered fashion—there's no predictability, so don't count on an order.

There is an alternate way to do all this by using the grandfather of all objects: the object! Instead of creating an instance of an array, you can create an instance of an object:

```
var carManufacturersByModel:Object = new Object();
```

For all intents and purposes, there is not much difference except using an object lets you use the shorthand ability to populate the array upon initialization.

```
var carManufacturersByModel:Object =
  {xA:"Scion",Viper:"Dodge",is350:"Lexus"};
```

One bit of syntax to which new ActionScript users will need to adapt, is using a colon for value assignment (`is350:"Lexus"`). Don't worry, you'll get used to it. The last aspect of the associative array we'll cover is its support for dot notation.

DOT NOTATION

A nifty characteristic of associative arrays is you can use a feature known as dot notation to access items within the array. It is another way of doing the same thing as the colon, but if you're accustomed to a particular coding style, you may prefer this format:

```
trace(carManufacturersByModel.xA);
trace(carManufacturersByModel.Viper);
trace(carManufacturersByModel.is350);
```

Something to keep in mind if you use this style of notation; ActionScript variables cannot contain spaces, so although it is perfectly valid to use it in a key, you would generate errors if you then tried to access it using dot notation.

```
carManufacturersByModel["Land Cruiser"]="Toyota";
trace(carManufacturersByModel.Land Cruiser);
```

Error!

Dot notation in general is the preferred syntax to use by most Flex developers—it is faster to type, and easier to read. On the topic of syntax, there are number of other tidbits regarding the ActionScript language that we'll examine next.

3.6 ActionScript tidbits

Every language supports certain characteristics, shortcuts, and nuances. In this section we'll briefly go over a collection of tidbits you'll want to know about when working with ActionScript, starting with curly braces.

3.6.1 Braces

When writing code blocks for scripts, such as functions, loops, `switch`es, and `if` statements, you use curly braces to indicate to Flex all the code that falls under the switch control of those statements—*unless* the instruction after the statement is comprised of only one line.

Let's take a look at some examples as shown in listing 3.5.

Listing 3.5 Examples of when curly braces are required or optional

```
for each (var manufacturer:String in carManufacturersByModel)
{
  trace(manufacturer);
}

for each (var manufacturer:String in carManufacturersByModel)
  trace(manufacturer);

while(x<5)
{
  trace('x is now' + x);
  x=x+1;
}

if(x==5)
  trace(x);
else

{
  x=0;
  trace(x);
}
```

Annotations: Braces optionally used (first for each); Skip the braces (second for each); Braces are require (while); Braces not needed (if/else); Braces are used (else block).

These curly brace rules are the same as those prescribed by JavaScript, so you'll enjoy a bit of familiarity in that respect. You can skip the braces if there is only one line of code or only one line of code after the `for...each` statement. Braces are required if there is more than one line. Some people like using the curly braces even when it is not required. This is mostly a matter of personal preference, and as there's no industry-adopted standard, feel free to use whatever approach you're most comfortable with.

3.6.2 Logical operators and shortcuts

Logical operators are special characters, or sets of characters, that have some kind of operational meaning to the compiler. Let's take a look at what these are, and how to use them.

++ AND —

To increase or decrease a number, the ++ and -- operators are quick and direct to the point, as the following code snippet demonstrates:

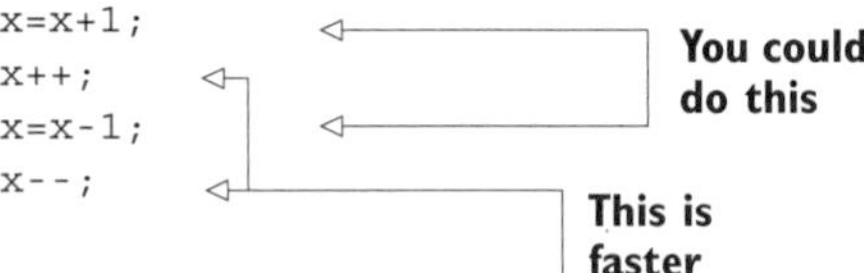

These two operators work on both side of a variable; when it is on the left side, ActionScript will adjust the variable first before using its value in the rest of the statement, otherwise it executes the statement as is, then applies the operator.

```
var x:int=0;
trace(x++);      // Outputs 0; increases the value!
trace(x);        // Outputs 1

var y:int=0;
trace(++y);      // Increases value; outputs 1
```

Comparative operators, use to compare values, are similar to logical operators.

BASIC COMPARATIVE OPERATORS

When conducting a comparison for test purposes—in an `if` or `while` statement—there are several operators you can use to evaluate one value against another. Table 3.4 presents each operator and what it does.

Table 3.4 Operators for conducting comparisons

Operator	Description	Example
==	Determines if one value is equal to another	`if(x==y) trace("X and Y are the same");`
!=	Determines if one value is not equal to another	`if(x!=y) trace("X is not equal to Y");`
<	Determines if one value is less than another	`if(x<y)trace ("X is less than Y");`
<=	Determines if one value is less than, or equal to another	`if(x<=y) trace("X is less than or the same as Y");`
>	Determines if one value is greater than another	`if(x>y) trace ("X is greater than Y");`
>=	Determines if one value is greater than, or equal to another	`If(x>=y) trace ("X is greater than or equal to Y");`
!	The `not` operator takes the inverse of the value	`var x:Boolean=false;` `if(!x)trace ("x is not true");`

Lastly, we have mathematical operators for performing computations.

MATHEMATICAL OPERATORS

When you need to manipulate numbers, create algorithms, or develop formulas, a group of mathematical operators are available to assist you. Table 3.5 lists these operators and their descriptions.

Let's review the different kinds of operators; logical operators can act as short cuts, comparative operators evaluate one item against another, and mathematical operators perform numerical manipulation.

Table 3.5 Mathematical operators

Operator	Description	Example
`*`	Multiplication	`z = x * y;`
`/`	Division	`z = x/y;`

`%`	Modulus, the remainder of the first number divided by the second.	`trace(9 % 3); // output 0`
		`trace(7 % 3); // output 1`

`+`	Adds one value to another. Note: This operator can be used with `Strings`. When used with `Strings`, the + operator joins text together.	`var z:int = 4 + 2; // z is 6`
		`var x:String="good"+"bye"; // x is "goodbye"`

`-`	Subtraction	`var z= x-y;`

The elements of code in which you would normally contain all this logic are typically functions. Next, we'll look at what functions are and how operators work within them.

3.7 Sneak peek at functions, classes, and packages

When creating your applications, you'll eventually start splitting up your logic into smaller modules for reusability and maintenance. Chapters 17 and 18 will go much deeper into that subject, but for now let's take a peek at what this is all about.

A function is a way to encapsulate blocks of logic in such a way that the logic can be reused in a modular fashion by other elements, within your application. Functions can even be used by elements in other applications.

Recall from chapter 2, when you used the code repeated below in listing 3.6, you were invoking a function of the `Alert` class called `show()`.

Listing 3.6 Making note of a function used in the chapter 2

```
<?xml version="1.0" encoding="utf-8"?>
<mx:Application xmlns:mx="http://www.adobe.com/2006/mxml"
   layout="absolute">
  <mx:Button label="Marco" fontSize="40"
         click="mx.controls.Alert.show('Polo')"/>
</mx:Application>
```

To make functions reusable, they accept input parameters; in this example a single text parameter with the value `Polo` was passed along in `mx.controls.Alert.show`. The item `mx.control.Alert` itself is called a *class*, which is a self-contained collection of functions and variables. Instances of classes are usually referred to as an object.

NOTE Functions are also referred to as methods.

Again, referring to listing 3.6, we're using the function `show()` of the `Alert` class, which is part of a package called `mx.controls`. A *package* is a collection of classes. Does ActionScript let you make functions on our own? It does indeed, and we're about to learn how.

3.7.1 *Your own functions*

Declaring a function is easy, and looks something like the illustration in figure 3.4:

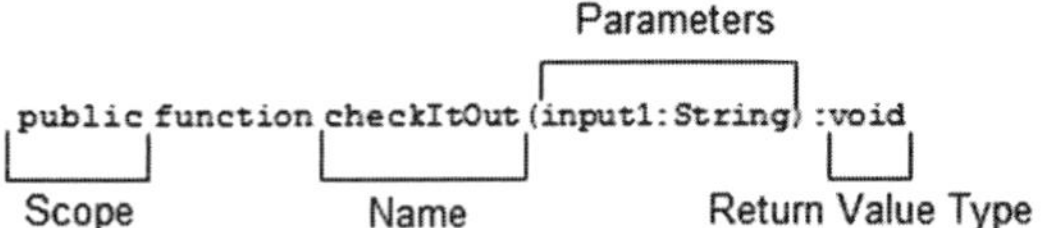

Figure 3.4 This is what a function looks like in ActionScript.

The first keyword (`public`) in figure 3.4 declares the *scope* of the function, which identifies who can access it. *Who*, in this context, is other code from within the same class/component (let's just say object for now), or code making use of the function from outside the class/component. Table 3.6 lists the available scopes.

Table 3.6 Available scopes you'll encounter when working with functions

Scope	Description
Public	Your object, and anyone calling your object can access the function.
Private	Only your object can access the function.
Protected	Only your object, and children of your object, can access the function.

The second keyword (`function`), informs `ActionScript` you're declaring a function.

The third keyword is your function's name. It can be anything, as long as it doesn't start with a number, doesn't contain spaces, and doesn't contain non-alphanumeric characters (except the underscore (_) character).

The fourth keyword (between the parentheses) is a set of *typed parameters*. Earlier in this chapter, we discussed data typing, and this is an example of where that applies. What this means is you need to declare all the input parameters you're going to allow, and what kind of variables you expect them to be (for instance, `ints`, `Strings`, and so on).

The fifth keyword is the *return type*, which notifies anyone calling your function what kind of variable you're going to send back—for example, a `Number`, `Object`, or `Boolean`. In this case, nothing is being returned, so we used the keyword `void`.

Let's put this all together and make our own function.

CREATING OUR OWN FUNCTION

Using what we've learned about functions let's put it into action by creating our own as shown in listing 3.7.

Listing 3.7 Creating our first function

```
<?xml version="1.0" encoding="utf-8"?>
<mx:Application xmlns:mx="http://www.adobe.com/2006/mxml"
  ➥layout="horizontal">
  <mx:Script>
    <![CDATA[
      public function displayMe(input1:String):void
      {
        mx.controls.Alert.show(input1);
      }
    ]]>
  </mx:Script>
  <mx:TextInput id="thisTextInput" text=""try this"/>
  <mx:Button label="Display It" click="displayMe(thisTextInput.text)"/>
</mx:Application>
```

After compiling and running the example, you'll see something similar to figure 3.5. Enter some text and click the Display It button. The text just entered will be passed along to a function.

Now, let's learn what happened in more detail. You created an input box in which you can type text. When you click the Display It button, you are telling Flex to invoke our function named `displayMe()`, which captures the text entered into the input box as a variable, and assigns that variable the name, `thisTextInput`, using the `id` property.

Figure 3.5 User-entered text is passed along to a function

Our function, which takes a single argument (the text from the input box), passes it along to `Alert`'s `show()` function. In all this code, you likely noticed something new—the cryptic-looking `<![CDATA[ ... ]]>`.

CDATA

Since Flex MXML files are XML-compliant, we are obliged to follow the rules of XML. `CDATA` instructs Flex Builder (and its compiler) to take the content within the square brackets ([]) as is and not try to process it as XML code.

In this case, we technically didn't need to use `CDATA`, as we wouldn't have broken any rules with the contents of our variable. But, it won't take long before you find yourself handling data that uses the less than (<) or greater than (>) operator, and without that CDATA directive, Flex will think you're opening or closing an MXML tag.

It is always best practice to wrap a block of `ActionScript` within a `CDATA` directive.

One tedious aspect of working with functions is the amount of text used to call them from their packages. Fortunately, there's a way to ease that burden by importing the entire package.

IMPORTING PACKAGES

Let's assume you plan on expanding listing 3.7 and need to keep using the `Alert.show()` function. You can make life easier by making the package that contains

Alert.show() available throughout the span of your application. To do this, you can do what's known as an import. This way you don't need to repeatedly type the entire code block every time you use Alert.show().

The next code demonstrates how efficient importing can be:

```
import mx.controls.Alert;
public function displayMe(input1:String):void
{
  Alert.show(input1);
}
```

NOTE When you perform an import, whatever you imported is only available for that module (basically per MXML file or ActionScript class). With each module you would import the statement again, as necessary. This doesn't cost overhead, as Flex is merely pointing to the functionality, not making copies every time you invoke it.

The last piece to demonstrate is returning a value from the function to whatever invoked it.

RETURNING A VALUE

Taking things a bit further, let's return a data type. You'll notice in listing 3.8 the function has been updated from void to String, meaning this function is declaring it will return a text string.

Listing 3.8 Creating a function that returns a value of data type String

```
<?xml version="1.0" encoding="utf-8"?>
<mx:Application xmlns:mx="http://www.adobe.com/2006/mxml"
   ➥layout="horizontal">
  <mx:Script>
    <![CDATA[
      import mx.controls.Alert;
      public function textMerge(input1:String,input2:String):String
      {
        var x:String = input1 + input2;
        return x;
      }
]]>
  </mx:Script>
  <mx:TextInput id="value1"/>
  <mx:Label text="and"/>
  <mx:TextInput id="value2"/>
  <mx:Button label="Join The Two"
          click="Alert.show(textMerge(value1.text,value2.text))"/>
</mx:Application>
```

Here, we have functions calling functions:

- When you click the button, Alert.show() calls textMerge(), passing the values of the two text inputs.
- textMerge() in turn, joins the two Strings together and returns the result to Alert.show(), which then displays the result (figure 3.6).

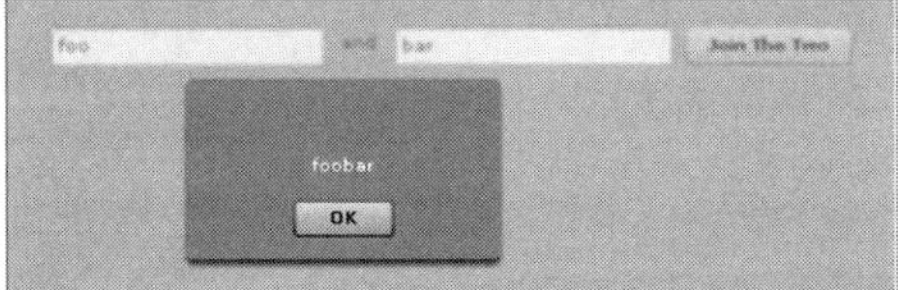

Figure 3.6 This function takes two separate pieces of text, and returns them combined into one.

In all these examples, we've shown ActionScript inside MXML, similar to how JavaScript can be embedded within an HTML file. But this is just an option; the other option is separating it into individual files.

3.7.2 *Separating ActionScript to individual files*

Your ActionScript doesn't need to reside in your MXML files; you can split it into its own files. This makes it easier to maintain your code as your applications grow in size, as well as making your functions more reusable by allowing multiple applications to source-in their logic.

To do this, pull out any ActionScript into a file, and save it with a `.as` extension as demonstrated in listing 3.9.

Listing 3.9 `myFunctions.as`—ActionScript saved separately

```
public function textMerge(input1:String,input2:String):String
{
  var x:String = input1 + input2;
  return x;
}
```

In your main MXML file, you can source it back in as presented in listing 3.10.

Listing 3.10 Main MXML file sources the `myFunctions.as` file

```
<?xml version="1.0" encoding="utf-8"?>
<mx:Application xmlns:mx="http://www.adobe.com/2006/mxml"
    layout="horizontal">
  <mx:Script source="myFunctions.as"/>     ❸
  <mx:Script>
    <![CDATA[
      import mx.controls.Alert;     ❷
    ]]>
  </mx:Script>
  <mx:TextInput id="value1"/>
  <mx:Label text="and"/>
  <mx:TextInput id="value2"/>
  <mx:Button label="Join The Two"
          click="Alert.show(textMerge(value1.text,value2.text))"/>     ❶
</mx:Application>
```

Note that because the `Button` is calling `Alert.show()` ❶, we have to import the library ❷ in this same file; meaning that if you moved that `import` statement to the `myFunctions.as` ❸ file it wouldn't be visible in the main MXML file ❶. The import only has relevance for anything within the file that does the import.

We have only one more feature to cover, called data binding (or just binding for short) before we wrap up this chapter.

3.8 Simple data binding

ActionScript includes a feature that lets one item listen to the value of another. This is called binding. Not only does it help reduce the amount of code you need to write, it also assists on making your applications more scalable by being able to easily abstract where information comes from, or who is interested in it.

Let's take an example using the visual `TextInput` component in which you want to take its value and display it somewhere else. In this case, we'll use the `Label` component. From what we've learned so far, we could do it as is shown in listing 3.11.

Listing 3.11 You can manually copy values from one place to another

```
<?xml version="1.0" encoding="utf-8"?>
<mx:Application xmlns:mx="http://www.adobe.com/2006/mxml"
          layout="horizontal">
<mx:TextInput id="myTextInput"/>
<mx:Button label="Copy:" click="myText.text=myTextInput.text"/>
<mx:Text id="myText"/>

</mx:Application>
```

Listing 3.11 uses ActionScript to copy the `text` property of the `TextInput` component to the `text` property of the `Text` component (figure 3.7).

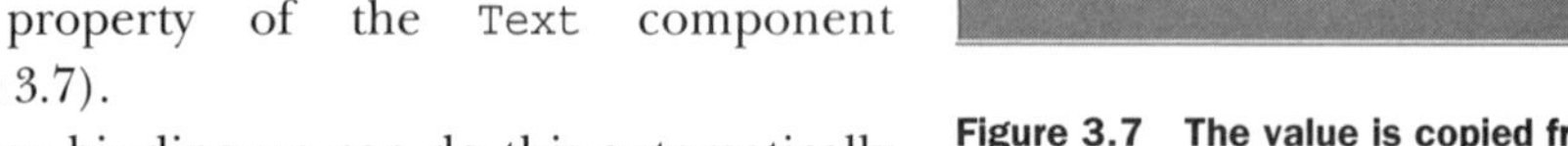

Figure 3.7 The value is copied from one variable to another.

Using binding we can do this automatically as demonstrated in listing 3.12.

Listing 3.12 Using binding, you can do an automatic copy to a target

```
<?xml version="1.0" encoding="utf-8"?>
<mx:Application xmlns:mx="http://www.adobe.com/2006/mxml"
          layout="horizontal">
  <mx:TextInput id="myTextInput"/>
  <mx:Text id="myText" text="{myTextInput.text}"/>
</mx:Application>
```

This would give you the dynamic implementation demonstrated in figure 3.8.

Figure 3.8 Values are captured in real time using binding.

As you type in the text box, the characters are appearing in real time to the right of the input box because we've instructed the text property of `Text` to listen to the text property of `TextInput`.

3.8.1 Once again, it is about events

To give you insight as to what's going on behind the scenes, Flex makes heavy use of the concept of events (see chapter 10). Events can be subscribed to by what is called a listener, which listens to events as they're dispatched. In the previous example, myText.text is subscribed as a listener (by using the curly braces {}) to myText-Input.text.

3.8.2 Bidirectional binding

You can even perform bidirectional binding by instructing components to listen to each other. Let's create two `TextInput` components that listen to each other's `text` property (listing 3.13).

Listing 3.13 Bidirectional binding allows two components to listen to each other

```
<?xml version="1.0" encoding="utf-8"?>
<mx:Application xmlns:mx="http://www.adobe.com/2006/mxml"
  ➥ layout="horizontal">
<mx:TextInput id="myTextInput1" text="{myTextInput2.text}"/>
<mx:TextInput id="myTextInput2" text="{myTextInput1.text}"/>
</mx:Application>
```

As you type in one box, the other box automatically updates (figure 3.9). You can do all this with your own variables as well, by using the keyword `[Bindable]`.

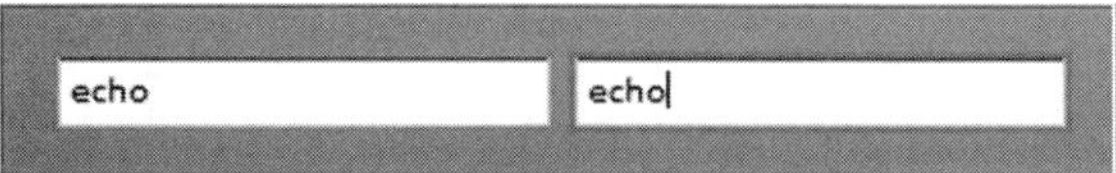

Figure 3.9 You type in one box and the other box automatically updates.

By default, Flex doesn't assume everything is bindable—you need to explicitly instruct it as to what is and what isn't bindable. Listing 3.14 explicitly authorizes `String` to be bindable.

Listing 3.14 Making your own bindable variable

```
<?xml version="1.0" encoding="utf-8"?>
<mx:Application xmlns:mx="http://www.adobe.com/2006/mxml"
   layout="horizontal">
  <mx:Script>
   <![CDATA[
    [Bindable]
    public var s:String="";
   ]]>
  </mx:Script>
  <mx:TextInput id="myTextInput1"/>
  <mx:Button label="Update my variable" click="s=myTextInput1.text"/>
  <mx:Text id="myText" text="{s}"/>
</mx:Application>
```

When you type data into `TextInput`, and click the Update my variable button, the value will be copied to the `String` variable. The `Text` component then displays the value of that `String` automatically. You might end up with something like figure 3.10.

Figure 3.10 Text is copied to a bindable variable, which is then displayed.

In a real-world application you would have numerous components that are using binding to listen to a variety of variables you configure and manage throughout the life of your application. The components react as the data changes, but are not concerned with the source of that data and information. A common scenario for this is retrieving data from some external source and storing the results locally in bound variables; visual components listening to those variables would display the information.

3.9 Summary

That was a lot of material to cover, and you should give yourself a pat on the back for powering through it. A lot of it is reference in nature and thus, you don't need to memorize it.

Construct-wise, many of the concepts are the same in ActionScript as they are in any other language, particularly when it comes to evaluating data, looping over information, and working with arrays.

Syntax-wise, ActionScript may vary considerably depending on what other languages you're accustomed to, but it should look familiar enough as ActionScript follows the ECMAScript standard, as does JavaScript (except ActionScript follows the most recent version).

One neat feature of Flex is data binding, which makes it easy to assign one variable to another, and have those values automatically stay synchronized. This comes in handy as you don't need to write all the code necessary to copy values throughout your application.

Now that we have covered ActionScript, we can move forward into the features of Flex. In the next chapter we'll learn how to use the layout feature.

4 Layout and containers

This chapter covers:

- Absolute and automatic layout
- Constraints-based layout
- Variable and fixed sizing
- Containers
- Dynamic layout with `Repeaters`

Now that you have been introduced to ActionScript, and can manipulate visual effects, let the fun continue! In this chapter we'll talk about the visual building blocks and the types of containers you can use to quickly create layouts in a Flex application.

Containers are the foundation on which all your visual components rely. They make it easy for you to group and position collections of visual components. Layout is hosted within these containers, but is limited to a specific set of components within a given container. Often referred to as child objects of the host container, these components can be anything from buttons, tables, graphics, and even other containers.

It might make it easier to think of a container as a box. You can place items within the box (including other boxes) and define where they are to be placed, with positioning specific to each item.

4.1 Absolute layout

Absolute layout is a composition mode in which you control the exact position and size of elements you place within the container.

Containers implement positioning based on a two-dimensional coordinate grid. The top-left corner of any container represents the home coordinates of 0,0. Any item placed in the container is positioned in the grid relative to this point.

One of the benefits of using absolute layout in a container is it gives you fine-grained control of how objects are located and sized. Another benefit is Flex (technically the Flash Player) doesn't need to burn processing power calculating how items should look. Instead it uses the coordinates and dimensions you provided for the individual items. Using absolute layout is optional for each container you create. This means you can choose to use this method in one container, but not others.

A drawback to absolute layout is there's a chance two items on the screen could be inadvertently positioned on the same real estate and overlap. If your container is hosting a set of static components (that is, previously created items, versus those dynamically generated on the fly) this shouldn't be a problem.

Let's get started by taking a look at a container with which you're already familiar—the Application container. Using the `layout` property (shown in bold) you can tell Flex you want to work in absolute layout mode (listing 4.1).

Listing 4.1 In absolute layout, the container doesn't waste effort arranging its children

```
<?xml version="1.0" encoding="utf-8"?>
<mx:Application xmlns:mx="http://www.adobe.com/2006/mxml"
            layout="absolute">
  <mx:Button label="Button 1"/>
  <mx:Button label="This is Button 2"/>
</mx:Application>
```

Run the application and look at the results in figure 4.1. Because we didn't explicitly specify coordinates, each button defaults to positioning itself at the top-left corner of the container (coordinates 0,0), resulting in the buttons overlapping one another.

Figure 4.1 The result of omitting coordinates when laying out items in absolute layout. These buttons overlap.

By explicitly providing values to the Button's x and y properties, this situation is easily resolved. As shown in figure 4.2, adjusting the x property on Button 2 shifts that button to the right. The following snippet shows how to make the adjustment:

```
<mx:Button label="This is Button 2" x="85"/>
```

As figure 4.2 demonstrates, specifically defining the coordinate fixes the problem nicely. We can shift the button down by providing a value to the y property:

Figure 4.2 Overlapping is fixed in absolute layout by explicitly defining a position.

```
<mx:Button label="This is Button 2"
  y="30"/>
```

You can also use both properties at the same time:

```
<mx:Button label="Button 1" x="120" y="50" />
<mx:Button label="This is Button 2" x="100" y="80"/>
```

In this case, we apply coordinates to both buttons to position them in the center of the container, as shown in figure 4.3.

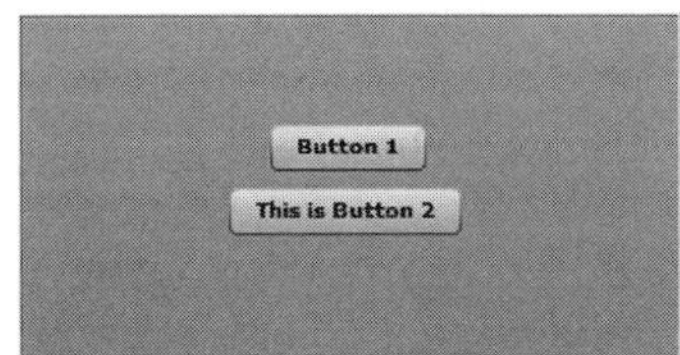

Figure 4.3 Using the x and y properties, these buttons were positioned on a more granular level.

If you're coming from many years in the HTML world, you'll want to train yourself to be aware of the more creative things you can do in Flex. For instance, in HTML if you caused an overlap such as we saw in figure 4.1, it would generally be considered a bug. The majority of web developers use HTML tables to lay out pages which prevents overlapping from occurring. In Flex we can use overlap to our advantage.

It is up to your imagination; there's nothing to say that overlapping is bad, and you may very well want to use the effect as part of your design. For example, as figure 4.4 demonstrates, you could have folder icons positioned slightly offset over each other to represent a folder structure, or depth.

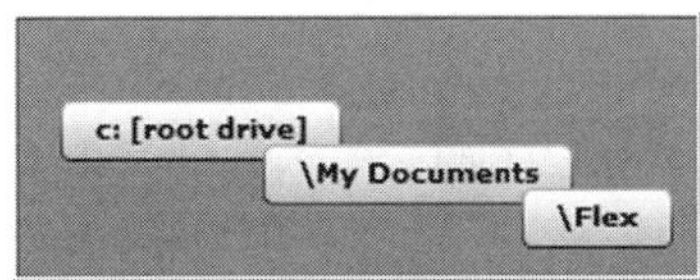

Figure 4.4 Programmatically you can use absolute layout in innovative

Another cool aspect of absolute positioning is the x and y properties can also take negative values. This allows you to move an item out of the visual range, or screen of the container, hiding it until you're ready to display it. Let's try out this effect in listing 4.2.

Listing 4.2 Using a negative value in the x property to hide a component off screen

```
<?xml version="1.0" encoding="utf-8"?>
<mx:Application xmlns:mx="http://www.adobe.com/2006/mxml"
            layout="absolute">
  <mx:Button id="button1" label="Show the other button" x="120" y="50"
              click="button2.x=170;"/>
  <mx:Button id="button2" label="Hello!" x="-100" y="80"/>
</mx:Application>
```

ActionScript responds

The x parameter is manipulated

Figure 4.5 shows how the button labeled Hello!—originally positioned out of view—appears after clicking Show the other button. By manipulating these positioning properties you can make UIs interactive.

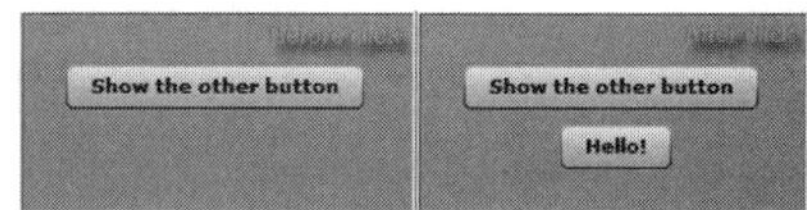

Figure 4.5 The second button is always there. It is out of view until a change in its horizontal coordinate brings it in view.

TIP The `id` attribute allows you to uniquely name an instance of a component (much the same as with HTML and JavaScript), which you can later use to access and manipulate the component's properties and functions.

Absolute layout requires many assumptions regarding positioning. Alternatively, you can use the constraint approach, which determines positioning relative to certain anchor points.

4.2 Constraint-based layout

If supplying exact coordinates is impractical for your application you can use a variation on absolute layout known as constraint-based layout. Instead of specifying `x` and `y` coordinates to position components relative to the container's top-left corner, constraint-based layout has you position items relative to the edges of the container, or its center.

The advantage of this method is you can configure components to maintain a relative position within the container, even if the user resizes their window. For example, if you define a button to be 5 pixels from the bottom-right of your window, a user could later change the dimensions of that window, but the button would remain 5 pixels from the resized bottom and right edges.

To achieve the same results using fixed coordinates would require a considerable amount of coding in ActionScript to perform the calculations, and update the component's `x` and `y` values in response to any changes in window size.

4.2.1 Basic constraints

Using the constraint-based approach, you only need to tell Flex you want your button to maintain a position 5 pixels from the bottom right of the window. Flex handles all the behind-the-scenes work to hold that position for you. Table 4.1 describes all the properties you can use with constraints.

Table 4.1 Constraint-based properties

Property	Type	Description
`top`	`Number`	The number of pixels between the top edge of the container and the top edge of the component.
`bottom`	`Number`	The number of pixels between the bottom edge of the container and the bottom edge of the component.
`left`	`Number`	The number of pixels between the left edge of the container and the left edge of the component.

Table 4.1 Constraint-based properties *(continued)*

Property	Type	Description
`right`	`Number`	The number of pixels between the right edge of the container and the right edge of the component.
`horizontalCenter`	`Number`	The number of horizontal pixels between the center of the container and the center of the component. Note: use of this property excludes the use of the top or bottom attributes.
`verticalCenter`	`Number`	The number of vertical pixels between the center of the container and the center of the component. Note: use of this property excludes the use of the left or bottom attributes.

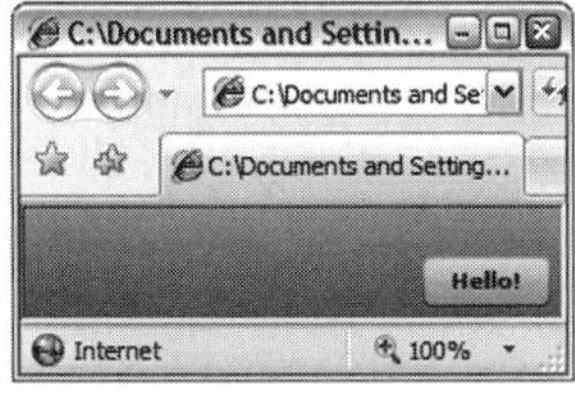

Figure 4.6 Using constraint-based layout, this button is positioned relative to the bottom-right of the page.

Let's apply some of the properties listed in Table 4.1 to the previous scenario. Listing 4.3 illustrates how to anchor a button to the bottom-right corner of the page, and figure 4.6 shows the results.

Listing 4.3 Positioning a button 5 pixels from the bottom-right corner of a window

```
<?xml version="1.0" encoding="utf-8"?>
<mx:Application xmlns:mx="http://www.adobe.com/2006/mxml"
            layout="absolute">
  <mx:Button label="Hello!" bottom="5" right="5"/>
</mx:Application>
```

As you can see in figure 4.6, regardless of window size or shape, the button maintains its position relative to the bottom-right corner of the page. If this weren't convenient enough, Flex Builder includes a feature that allows you to easily configure your components (figure 4.7):

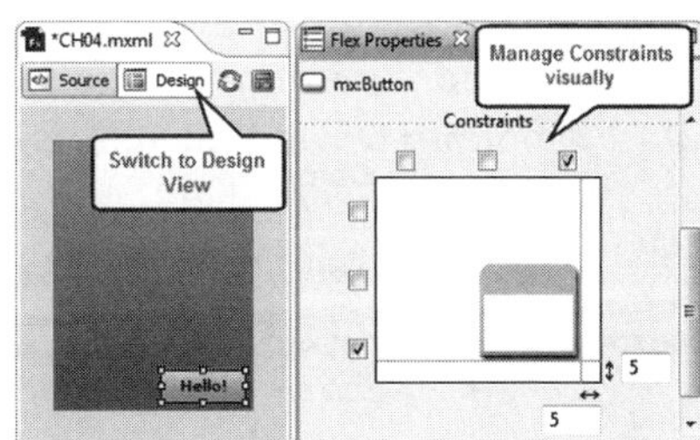

Figure 4.7 Design View in Flex Builder allows you to control constraints interactively.

1. In Flex Builder, click the Design View button to switch into Flex's visual mode.
2. Click your `Button` component.

3 In the Flex Properties window, scroll down to the Layout section.
4 Notice the check boxes along the top and left side of the layout window. You should see check marks in the furthest right and bottom check boxes.
5 Click the check boxes at random to see the effect each has on your button's position within the window.

For example, if you want your button to appear in the center of the page, you would click the center check boxes as shown in figure 4.8.

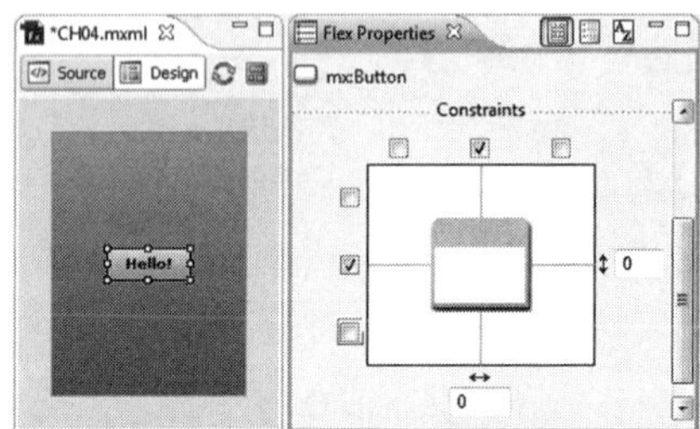

Figure 4.8 Constraints can be used to position objects relative to the center, as well as the edges of the window.

NOTE Because Flash has its ancestry in an animation tool, the term *stage* is often used instead of page. Flex developers come in two varieties: traditional programmers, and Flash developers and designers. You'll notice in discussion forums and blog postings, the folks that come from the Flash world tend to use the term stage. When you hear the phrase centered on stage, it means an item is centered in a container or page.

When you want to fix the exact position of a component within a container—no matter the browser dimensions—use absolute layout. When you want a component to be able to move relative to a window's changing dimensions, but stay within a specified distance of a browser's edge (or center), use constraint-based layout to handle this automatically.

If you find you prefer constraints, but need more precise control, Enhanced constraints can offer you extended flexibility.

4.2.2 Enhanced constraints

Enhanced constraints, (new in Flex 3) take the concept of constraints one step further by allowing you to arbitrarily create hidden horizontal and vertical guidelines against which you can position components. These guidelines are known respectively as constraint rows and constraint columns. Guidelines expand your positioning options beyond the limits of the basic constraint-based layout, with which you can only designate the edges or center of the container as anchor points.

Constraint rows and constraint columns can be governed by three methods:

- *Fixed*—The position is determined by an absolute number (in pixels).
- *Relative*—The position is determined by a percentage, relative to the size of the container.
- *Content-Sized*—Similar to relative constraint, with the exception that the position is based on the content (scaling up and down to accommodate the content), whereas a relative constraint is based on the size of the container.

Two tags are used to implement constraint guides, <mx:ConstraintColumn> (table 4.2) and <mx:ConstraintRow> (table 4.3), which support the following properties.

Table 4.2 `ConstraintColumn` properties

Property	Type	Description
`id`	`String`	A unique identifier (name) for the constraint column.
`width`	`Number`	Optional. Determines the width of a column. This can be a fixed number, or a percentage of the total width of the container. If this value is unspecified it will auto-resize based on the size of your item.
`minWidth`	`Number`	Optional. Specifies the minimum width of a column.
`maxWidth`	`Number`	Optional. Specifies them maximum width of a column.

Table 4.3 `ConstraintRow` properties

Property	Type	Description
`id`	`String`	A unique identifier (name) for the constraint row.
`height`	`Number`	Optional. Determines the height of a row This can be a fixed number, or a percentage of the total height of the container. If this value is unspecified it will auto-resize based on the size of your item.
`minHeight`	`Number`	Optional. Specifies the minimum height of a row.
`maxHeight`	`Number`	Optional. Specifies the maximum height of a row.

Enhanced constraint properties can be a little confusing at first. Instead of explaining all the rules and describing how Flex applies these properties, we'll first work through a couple of examples to help you understand them more clearly.

TIP Because you're assuming layout control with constraints, they're almost exclusively used with the Canvas container.

The easiest way to remember how Enhanced constraints work is to view them as a mechanism for splitting the container into sections. Let's look at examples how we can do this.

2-COLUMN FIXED SLICE

Let's start by slicing a container into two sections. We'll use the <mx:ConstraintColumn> tag to create two columns, as shown in listing 4.4.

Listing 4.4 Using two constraint columns to align a pair of buttons

```
<?xml version="1.0" encoding="utf-8"?>
<mx:Application xmlns:mx="http://www.adobe.com/2006/mxml"
  backgroundColor="white">
```

```
  <mx:Canvas width="100%" height="100%">
    <mx:constraintColumns>
      <mx:ConstraintColumn id="col1" width="200"/>
      <mx:ConstraintColumn id="col2" width="50" />
    </mx:constraintColumns>
    <mx:Button label="Button 1" left="col1:0"/>
    <mx:Button label="Button 2" left="col2:0"/>
  </mx:Canvas>
</mx:Application>
```

Listing 4.4 produces two buttons: Button 1 is 200 pixels from the first constraint column; Button 2 is 50 pixels further right than Button 1 (figure 4.9).

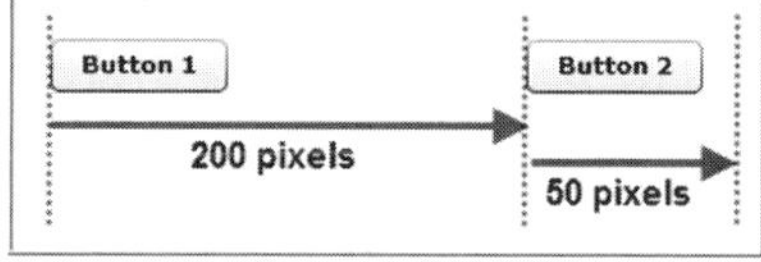

Figure 4.9 These buttons are aligned against named constraints.

Here are a couple of items to note:

- We're telling each button's left constraint property to base itself on the `ConstraintColumn` position.
- The first portion of the syntax, `col1:0`, specifies the `ConstraintColumn` identified as col1 as the `ConstraintColumn` we want to use, and the second portion instructs the button to offset 0 pixels in from that `ConstraintColumn`—meaning, no offset.

This example is fairly straightforward, and is similar to creating a guide in a graphical tool to which you can align objects.

2-COLUMN FIXED SLICE WITH BOTH LEFT AND RIGHT CONSTRAINTS

Next, we're going to make the width of a button scale to the width of the column in which it is placed. We accomplish this by specifying the right property constraint, while still using the original `ConstraintColumn`:

```
<mx:Button label="Button 1" left="col1:0" right="col1:0"/>
<mx:Button label="Button 2" left="col2:0" right="col2:0"/>
```

As figure 4.10 shows, the left property is set so the button will line up against the left side of the `ConstraintColumn`. Likewise, the button's right side will line up against the right side of the `ConstraintColumn`.

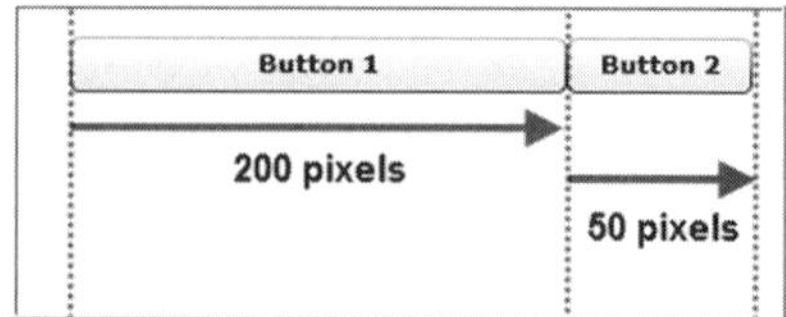

Figure 4.10 These buttons are both configured to stretch their left and right edges to the constraints.

That wasn't too much of a stretch from the previous example (bad joke). Let's make things more interesting by adding rows.

2-ROW MIXED SLICE WITH BOTH TOP AND BOTTOM CONSTRAINTS

You can construct your page vertically in a similar manner using a row-based approach. In listing 4.5, we will position a pair of buttons, one above the other, using both a relative and a fixed `ConstraintRow`.

Listing 4.5 Create a relative- and a fixed-size constraint row

```
<?xml version="1.0" encoding="utf-8"?>
<mx:Application xmlns:mx="http://www.adobe.com/2006/mxml"
   backgroundColor="white">
  <mx:Canvas width="100%" height="100%">
    <mx:constraintRows>
      <mx:ConstraintRow id="row1" height="50%"/>      <- A relative size
      <mx:ConstraintRow id="row2" height="100"/>      <- A fixed size
    </mx:constraintRows>
    <mx:Button label="Button 1" top="row1:0" bottom="row1:0"/>
    <mx:Button label="Button 2" top="row2:0" bottom="row2:0"/>
  </mx:Canvas>
</mx:Application>
```

This method affords you the ability to mix and match absolute and relative sizing approaches. Figure 4.11 illustrates the results of using the two together, and highlights the following:

- Button 1 scales to 50% of the canvas height as the user resizes the browser.
- Button 2 always remains 100 pixels in height, and begins vertically wherever Button 1 ends.

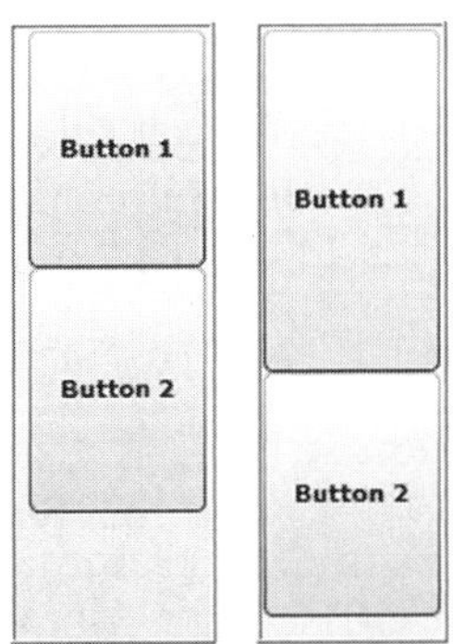

Figure 4.11 Button 1 changes in size as its constraint row is set to relative versus Button 2, which is set to a fixed

To this point, we've presented separate column and row examples, now let's combine them in a new exercise.

2 ROWS + 2 COLUMNS WITH OFFSETS

If your application requires it, you can combine constraint rows and constraint columns. In listing 4.6, we're going to do just that, but in addition, we're going to make use of the offset parameter to see how it functions.

Listing 4.6 Create both constraint columns and rows

```
<?xml version="1.0" encoding="utf-8"?>
<mx:Application xmlns:mx="http://www.adobe.com/2006/mxml"
            backgroundColor="white">
  <mx:Canvas width="100%" height="100%">
    <mx:constraintColumns>
      <mx:ConstraintColumn id="col1" width="100"/>
    </mx:constraintColumns>
    <mx:constraintRows>
      <mx:ConstraintRow id="row1" height="50"/>
      <mx:ConstraintRow id="row2" height="50"/>
    </mx:constraintRows>
    <mx:Button label="Button 1" left="col1:0" right="col1:0"
                        top="row1:0" bottom="row1:0"/>
    <mx:Button label="Button 2" left="col1:10" right="col1:10"
                        top="row2:0" bottom="row2:0"/>
  </mx:Canvas>
</mx:Application>
```

Figure 4.12 displays how your buttons will appear when you run listing 4.6. By now, you've noticed you have a lot of creative freedom to mix and match these constraints to generate and control a variety of visual effects.

Looking at figure 4.12, we have specified a value in the offset parameter for Button 2 that results in the button being squeezed 10 pixels from the right and left side of the column.

Realistically, this is about as complicated a use of constraints you are likely to see, although you can continue to design even more creative implementations if you'd like. The last approach we'll look at is content-sized constraints.

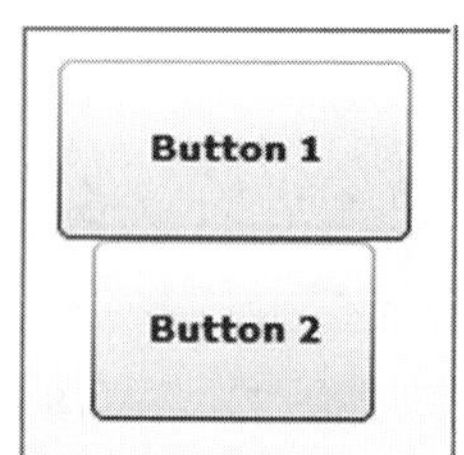

Figure 4.12 These buttons are positioned using both column and row constraints.

USING CONTENT-SIZED CONSTRAINTS

Content-sized constraints are enabled automatically by not supplying values to a constraint's height and width properties. Flex will scale all items to the column width or row height, which themselves will be based on the largest item in your container. Listing 4.7 shows how this is done.

Listing 4.7 Using content-sized constraints

```
<?xml version="1.0" encoding="utf-8"?>
<mx:Application xmlns:mx="http://www.adobe.com/2006/mxml"
   backgroundColor="white">
  <mx:Canvas width="100%" height="100%">
    <mx:constraintColumns>
      <mx:ConstraintColumn id="col1"/>
      <mx:ConstraintColumn id="col2"/>
    </mx:constraintColumns>
    <mx:constraintRows>
      <mx:ConstraintRow id="row1" height="50"/>
      <mx:ConstraintRow id="row2" height="30"/>
    </mx:constraintRows>
    <mx:Button label="Button 1" left="col1:0" top="row1:0" width="200"  />
    <mx:Button label="Button 2" left="col1:0" top="row2:0"/>
    <mx:Button label="Button 3" left="col2:0"/>
  </mx:Canvas>
</mx:Application>
```

This produces results similar to the HTML table trick of setting the column width to zero, which causes the column to shrink to the minimum size needed to accommodate an image. The difference is, with Flex it is not a hack; you're in complete control, as figure 4.13 illustrates.

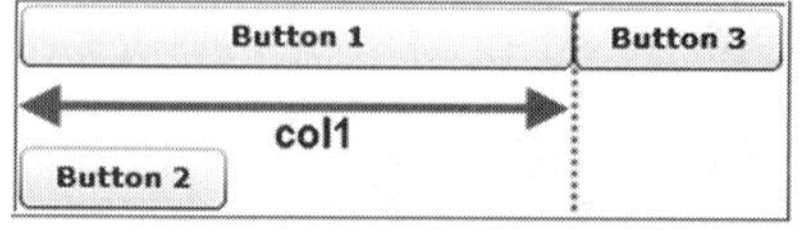

Figure 4.13 In a content-sized constraint, the column stretches to the size of the largest component within it.

Buttons 1 and 2 use the same `ConstraintColumn`, but because Button 1 is the largest component in the container, the `ConstraintColumn` defaults to its width.

YOU GET THE IDEA

The best thing you can do is experiment on your own. With so many constraint combinations available, it would take a separate chapter to cover them all. Give random combinations a try and see where they lead. There is yet one more feature to point out: you can manipulate constraint properties using ActionScript. For instance, you can change the size of your elements based on user interactions or a specific chain of events. (In chapter 13 we'll talk about how to use view states to achieve this efficiently.)

As powerful as constraints are, more work on your part is required to ensure your application has the look you want. If you don't particularly care about exact positioning, you always have the option of automatic layout.

4.3 Automatic layout

Automatic layout is a considerable departure from absolute layout, in which you explicitly determine the location and layout of elements within a container. With automatic layout, you're directing the container to position elements for you. You can choose between two layout modes: vertical or horizontal—also known as the *direction*. The container places child objects, one after another, based on the selected direction (listing 4.8).

Listing 4.8 Automatic horizontal layout used to place two buttons side-by-side

```
<?xml version="1.0" encoding="utf-8"?>
<mx:Application xmlns:mx="http://www.adobe.com/2006/mxml"
  ➥layout="horizontal">
<mx:Button label="One"/>
<mx:Button label="Two"/>
</mx:Application>
```

Figures 4.14 and 4.15 show the difference between the container-controlled horizontal and vertical layout modes. In figure 4.14, the container positions the buttons side-by-side because the layout mode in listing 4.8 is set to `horizontal`. Try changing the layout property to vertical to see how the container responds (figure 4.15).

Figure 4.14 The application container automatically places these buttons side-by-side (horizontally).

This is obviously much easier than manually positioning components. Another option is `Spacer`. You can liken `Spacer` to an empty HTML column (`<td width="100%"></td>`), or, the HTML `spacer.gif` trick, which was used for some time to distribute elements evenly. Table 4.4 shows `Spacer`'s properties and their descriptions.

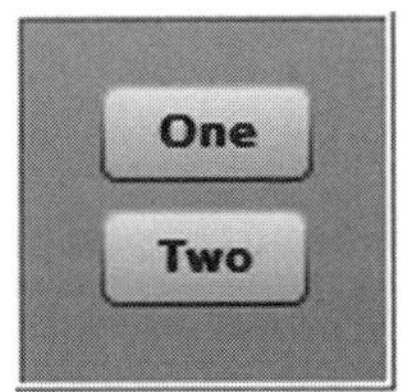

Figure 4.15 When the layout property is set to vertical, the buttons are placed one above the other.

Table 4.4 `Spacer` properties

Value	Type	Description
`width`	`Number`	Determines how much space to use horizontally. Accepts absolute numbers and percentages.
`height`	`Number`	Determines how much space to use vertically. Accepts absolute numbers and percentages.
`maxWidth`	`Number`	Specifies the maximum allowed width of the `Spacer`. Accepts absolute numbers and percentages.
`maxHeight`	`Number`	Specifies the maximum allowed height of the `Spacer`. Accepts absolute numbers and percentages.
`minWidth`	`Number`	Specifies the minimum required width of the `Spacer`. Accepts absolute numbers and percentages.
`minHeight`	`Number`	Specifies the minimum required height of the `Spacer`. Accepts absolute numbers and percentages.

In listing 4.9, we instruct `Spacer` to use 100% of the available space, which for the example, we'll define as 300 pixels.

Listing 4.9 Use a `Spacer` to push two buttons apart

```
<?xml version="1.0" encoding="utf-8"?>
<mx:Application xmlns:mx="http://www.adobe.com/2006/mxml"
                layout="horizontal">
  <mx:Button label="One"/>
  <mx:Spacer width="100%" maxWidth="300"/>
  <mx:Button label="Two"/>
</mx:Application>
```

Figure 4.16 illustrates how `Spacer` pushes the buttons apart by applying whatever space is available between elements (in this case, just two buttons).

Figure 4.16 These buttons were pushed to the edge using `Spacer`.

In automatic layout you can use as many `Spacers` as you need to achieve the look you want. Listing 4.10, shows how to evenly space three buttons, at the same time configuring a 10-pixel offset from the side of the container.

Listing 4.10 Multiple `Spacers` can be used to evenly distribute several components

```
<?xml version="1.0" encoding="utf-8"?>
<mx:Application xmlns:mx="http://www.adobe.com/2006/mxml"
                layout="horizontal">
  <mx:Spacer width="10"/>
  <mx:Button label="One"/>
  <mx:Spacer width="50%"/>
  <mx:Button label="Two"/>
```

```
  <mx:Spacer width="50%"/>
  <mx:Button label="Three"/>
  <mx:Spacer width="10"/>
</mx:Application>
```

By adding multiple Spacers (figure 4.17) you can evenly distribute components using relative-based (percentage) sizing.

Figure 4.17 Showing two equal spaces between, and a specifically defined offset at each end sets these buttons in their place.

Whether you use automatic or absolute layout for your project, components themselves are capable of controlling their own size.

4.4 Variable and fixed sizing

Similar to HTML, but far beyond what HTML supports, all Flex visual components support variable and fixed sizing.

This is made possible by the width and height properties which accept not only fixed values to define the element size in absolute numbers (in pixels), but also percentages that scale your item relative to the size of its host container. .

4.4.1 Variable sizing

To demonstrate variable sizing, let's again use our workhorse Button component. If you want a button to scale proportionally but not exceed 80% of the width of the host container, you can simply use the code:

```
<mx:Button label="Hello!" width="80%"/>
```

This results in a button that spans 80% of the browser window's width as shown in figure 4.18.

Figure 4.18 Scaled to 80%, this button will consume 80% of the page width as the page changes in size.

You can apply this technique to the vertical axis as well, or both height and width properties at the same time:

```
<mx:Button label="Hello!" width="80%"
  ➥height="80%"/>
```

If you want your button centered on the page, set horizontalCenter="0" and verticalCenter="0".

That takes care of variable sizing. Now, let's look at its counterpart—fixed sizing.

4.4.2 Fixed Sizing

Fixed sizing isn't much of a departure from variable sizing. You use the same parameters, except instead of specifying percentages you use whole numbers to specify the dimensions of your component (in pixels).

To make our button 120 pixels wide, and 80 pixels high you would use:

```
<mx:Button label="Hello!" width="120" height="80"/>
```

There's not much more to say about fixed sizing; it is extremely simple! Now that we can control the size and positioning of components, and are familiar with the principles behind automatic layout, we'll explore the containers that utilize these features.

4.5 Containers

Containers provide your application a visual structure by providing *frames* in which to house your display components. Flex comes with a variety of containers, and each provides unique characteristics. Their purpose is universal—to help you lay out your components visually rather than programmatically.

4.5.1 Application container

The Application container we've been using all along is indeed special. All Flex programs have an Application container, but because your application itself is rooted within it, you can only use one container of this type for each application you create. From a layout perspective, the `layout` property (table 4.5) gives you the options of automatic or manual positioning.

Table 4.5 The `layout` property accepts three values.

Value	Description
`absolute`	Instructs the container to be use absolute positioning mode in which you explicitly position each child component
`horizontal`	Instructs the container to automatically lay out its child components horizontally
`vertical`	Instructs the container to automatically lay out its child components vertically

Adding these values into code would look like this:

```
<mx:Application xmlns:mx="http://www.adobe.com/2006/mxml"
   ➥layout="absolute">

<mx:Application xmlns:mx="http://www.adobe.com/2006/mxml"
   ➥layout="vertical">

<mx:Application xmlns:mx="http://www.adobe.com/2006/mxml"
   ➥layout="horizontal">
```

Another unique characteristic of the root container is the *preloader* which is the progress bar you see when launching a Flex application. You can turn the preloader off by inserting the following code:

```
<mx:Application xmlns:mx="http://www.adobe.com/2006/mxml"
   usePreloader="false">
```

Because this is the top-level object of your application, you can use it to house global variables and functions, allowing you to access them from anywhere within your application.

Custom components is a subject we'll take up in detail in chapter 17, but briefly, custom components are a means to modularize your code. Listing 4.11 demonstrates how to invoke a custom component.

Listing 4.11 Invoking a custom component

```
<?xml version="1.0" encoding="utf-8"?>
<mx:Application xmlns:mx="http://www.adobe.com/2006/mxml" xmlns:local="*">
  <mx:Script>
    public var myString:String = "hello!";     <-- The message
  </mx:Script>
  <local:customComponent/>
</mx:Application>
```

You also have a publicly accessible variable (meaning anyone or anything can access it) in your main application file that carries a message. You can use a custom component in a file we'll call customComponent.mxml, to access that variable (listing 4.12).

Listing 4.12 customComponent.mxml—accessing the application's variables

```
<?xml version="1.0" encoding="utf-8"?>
<mx:Canvas xmlns:mx="http://www.adobe.com/2006/mxml">
<mx:Button label="{mx.core.Application.application.myString}"/>
</mx:Canvas>
```

After running the application you should end up with a button that says hello!. You have many types of containers in your file but you'll have only one Application container. For simplicity, the next core container we'll look at will be the Canvas container.

4.5.2 Canvas container

Canvas containers are the most basic types of container, but they're lightweight and not very robust. Although you get a performance boost using it, the tradeoff is in functionality. The performance boost comes from sacrificing the ability to automatically lay out any visual components within it. It assumes you will do this manually using the absolute or constraint-based layout options described earlier in this chapter.

If you are expecting to use specific sizing, or plan on containing something so simple that it doesn't requires automatic layout, you could take advantage of the enhanced performance afforded by using the Canvas container.

The previous example demonstrated this perfectly. A Canvas container was used as a custom component which was embedded as part of a larger piece. One thing to remember is if you have multiple items inside the Canvas container, make sure you have set their positioning carefully, otherwise, they'll overlap. Listing 4.13 presents multiple Canvas containers used to group components.

Listing 4.13 Multiple Canvas containers used to group components

```
<?xml version="1.0" encoding="utf-8"?>
<mx:Application xmlns:mx="http://www.adobe.com/2006/mxml"
         layout="vertical" >
```

```
  <mx:Canvas width="200">
    <mx:Text text="A"/><mx:Button label="B" x="20" y="0"/>
  </mx:Canvas>
  <mx:Canvas width="200">
    <mx:Text text="C"/><mx:Button label="D" x="20" y="0"/>
  </mx:Canvas>
</mx:Application>
```

Some interesting points to note at this juncture. We have two Canvases which are being automatically positioned (figure 4.19) as a result of the `layout="vertical"` property of the `Application` tag. Both buttons are using the same x and y properties, but because they're relative to the top left corners of the parent container (versus the coordinates of the screen or application), they display in different positions.

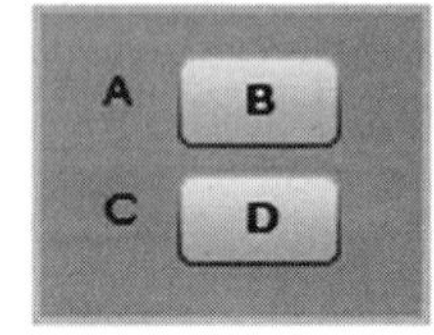

Figure 4.19 Multiple Canvases were used to group these components.

In figure 4.19 we see the two Canvases are stacked as a result of the automatic layout feature of the Application container. Within each Canvas, the position is manually controlled.

If automatic layout is what you want, the Box containers are designed to do just that.

4.5.3 Box, HBox, and VBox containers

Using combinations of Box containers will give you quite a bit of flexibility in arranging components in your application. These are particularly handy when you're supporting a variable-width application—such as when you intend the user to change the size of the window—and you want Flex to calculate the best way to handle the layout.

A Box is a square container that by default lays out its child objects vertically (listing 4.14).

Listing 4.14 The Box container is used to automatically lay out components vertically

```
<?xml version="1.0" encoding="utf-8"?>
<mx:Application xmlns:mx="http://www.adobe.com/2006/mxml" >
  <mx:Box>
    <mx:Button label="A"/><mx:Button label="B"/>
  </mx:Box>
</mx:Application>
```

The code in listing 4.14 produces two button components that will be stacked one above the other (figure 4.20). You can change the direction of the layout using the `direction="horizontal"` attribute, but there is a more direct way to do this by instead using the HBox (Horizontal Box) and VBox (Vertical Box) containers.

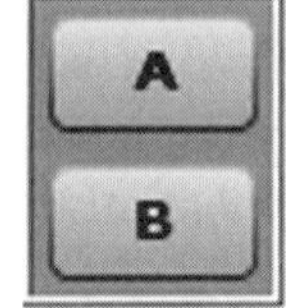

Figure 4.20 The Box container works automatically to handle the layout.

You can nest boxes to achieve a more desired effect, as shown in listing 4.15.

Listing 4.15 Using nested boxes for more complex layout

```
<?xml version="1.0" encoding="utf-8"?>
<mx:Application xmlns:mx="http://www.adobe.com/2006/mxml" >
  <mx:VBox>
    <mx:HBox>
      <mx:Text text="Button"/> <mx:Button label="A"/>
    </mx:HBox>
    <mx:HBox>
      <mx:Text text="Button"/> <mx:Button label="B"/>
    </mx:HBox>
  </mx:VBox>
</mx:Application>
```

After compiling the application, you'll see a table-like structure of text and buttons as shown in figure 4.21.

A bit of caution—don't go too crazy nesting as you'll start taking a performance hit if you nest too deeply. This is due to the complex negotiation that goes on between components and all their child objects as Flex, through Flash Player, calculates how and where elements are going to be positioned on the screen. The rule of thumb here is, if you need to nest—go for it. But if you have other options available, definitely consider using them first.

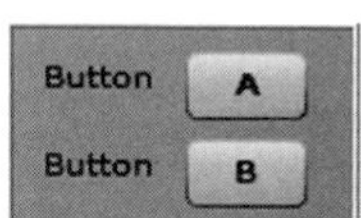

Figure 4.21 Nested boxes can lay out components horizontally and vertically.

4.5.4 *Panel container*

Definitely a crowd favorite, the Panel container is used as a top-level container for the entire application (although you can have panels inside of panels). What's neat about this container is it adds a title and status bar to the top of the window, and by default draws a border around its child objects.

Vertical placement is the default layout behavior for Panel containers, but as shown in listing 4.16, you can use the layout property to change this to horizontal or absolute.

Listing 4.16 Using the layout property to change how components lay out

```
<?xml version="1.0" encoding="utf-8"?>
<mx:Application xmlns:mx="http://www.adobe.com/2006/mxml">
<mx:Panel title="My Application" status="Welcome"
       width="200" layout="horizontal">
<mx:Text text="Button"/> <mx:Button label="B"/>
</mx:Panel>
</mx:Application>
```

Note how the `layout` property is set to `horizontal`, causing the `Text` and `Button` components in figure 4.22 to position themselves side-by-side.

In addition to the cool border around it, and the title area at the top, Panel containers can also support features such as a `ControlBar`.

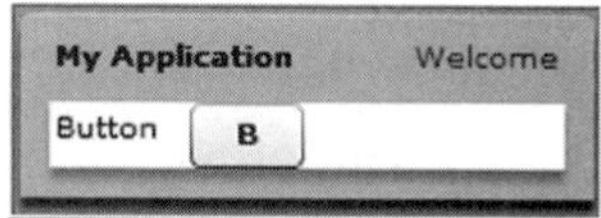

Figure 4.22 Using horizontal layout, these components were placed side-by-side.

4.5.5 *ApplicationControlBar and ControlBar containers*

These containers are unique in that you don't use them by themselves. As their name implies, they add a control bar area to your application. Let's take a look.

The `ApplicationControlBar` container creates an area that's common with Windows applications, in which functions such as file, edit, and view are grouped. To use this container, you combine it with the Application container as presented in listing 4.17.

Listing 4.17 The `ApplicationControlBar` provides easy access to functionality

```
<?xml version="1.0" encoding="utf-8"?>
<mx:Application xmlns:mx="http://www.adobe.com/2006/mxml">
  <mx:ApplicationControlBar width="300">
    <mx:Button label="Back"/>
    <mx:Button label="Forward"/>
    <mx:TextInput width="60"/><mx:Button label="Search"/>
  </mx:ApplicationControlBar>
</mx:Application>
```

Similarly, the `ControlBar` container can be paired with a Panel or a `TitleWindow` (more commonly known as a pop-up window). Take a look at listing 4.18 which adds a `ControlBar` to a panel.

Listing 4.18 Panels can also make use of the `ControlBar`

```
<?xml version="1.0" encoding="utf-8"?>
<mx:Application xmlns:mx="http://www.adobe.com/2006/mxml">
<mx:Panel title="My Application" layout="vertical" width="300">
<mx:Text text="What's your email?"/>
<mx:TextInput/>
<mx:ControlBar>
<mx:Button label="Cancel"/>
<mx:Button label="Save"/>
</mx:ControlBar>
</mx:Panel>
</mx:Application>
```

By combining the two, you end up with a layout such as illustrated in figure 4.23.

This is a convenient way to add flow, as well as access to application-wide functionality.

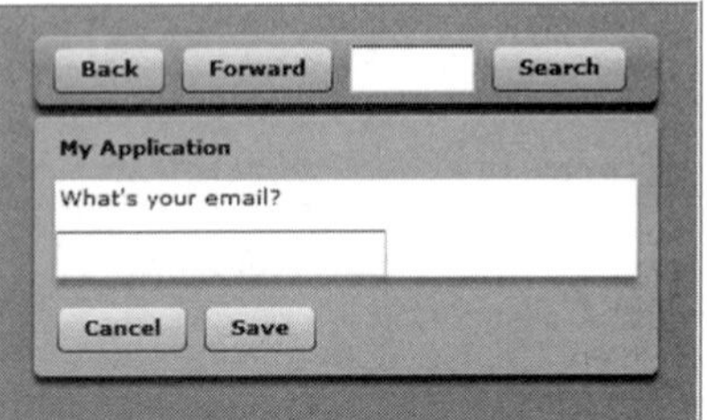

Figure 4.23 The `ApplicationControlBar` used at the top; the panel has a `ControlBar` too.

4.5.6 *DividedBox, HDividedBox, and VDividedBox containers*

This group of containers can be considered the big brothers to the Box. They provide an extra bit of juice with their ability to split the box with a divider bar that can be repositioned. This is similar to HTML Frames where frame resizing was enabled.

Just like Box, DividedBox supports both horizontal and vertical (default) layout using the direction attribute. For a direct route you can use HDividedBox (horizontal layout) or VDividedBox (vertical layout).

Using the mouse pointer, you can click the divider's hotspot to resize the pane. This option permits users to customize their viewing space. In addition, you can nest them for some interesting and useful layouts.

In listing 4.19, a number of DividedBoxes are used to split portions of the application.

Listing 4.19 Using divided boxes to allow the user to resize portions of the screen

```
<?xml version="1.0" encoding="utf-8"?>
<mx:Application xmlns:mx="http://www.adobe.com/2006/mxml">
  <mx:Panel title="Reports Dashboard" width="300">
    <mx:DividedBox direction="horizontal" width="100%">
      <mx:VBox backgroundColor="#eeeeee" height="100%">
        <mx:Text text="Categories" fontWeight="bold"/>
        <mx:Button label="Finance" width="100%"/>
        <mx:Button label="Operations" width="100%"/>
        <mx:Button label="I.T" width="100%"/>

        <mx:Button label="Support" width="100%"/>
        <mx:Button label="Network" width="100%"/>
      </mx:VBox>
      <mx:VDividedBox width="50%" height="100%">
        <mx:VBox backgroundColor="#eeeeee" width="100%" >
          <mx:Text text="Finance Reports" fontWeight="bold"/>
          <mx:Text text="2008 Q1 Sales"/>
          <mx:Text text="2008 Q2 Sales"/>
        </mx:VBox>
        <mx:VBox backgroundColor="#eeeeee" width="100%" >
          <mx:Text text="2008 Q1 Sales" fontWeight="bold"/>
          <mx:Text text="North America: $2,832,132"/>
          <mx:Text text="Europe: $1,912,382"/>
          <mx:Text text="Asia: $3,112,987"/>
        </mx:VBox>
      </mx:VDividedBox>
    </mx:DividedBox>
  </mx:Panel>
</mx:Application>
```

This type of container is particularly useful when setting up drill-down displays, such as dashboards.

If you have a lot of information to present in any of these divided sections (figure 4.24), this convenient mechanism allows the user to adjust how each section of real estate is allocated, giving the opportunity to adjust the view to see more of what's important.

Working with forms is always an aspect to any application, and there is a container for that too.

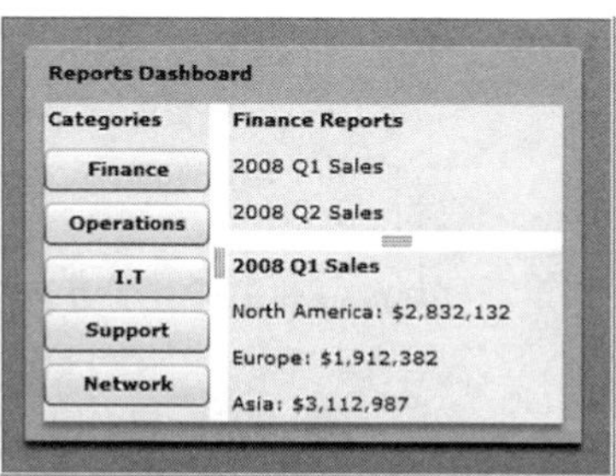

Figure 4.24 Divided boxes allow the user to customize the dimensions of the application.

4.5.7 Form container

The purpose of the Form container is to make it easy to lay out a form in your application. The Form container is similar to creating forms in HTML, but in Flex the Form container has mechanisms to place labels beside each of your form input fields. Unlike HTML, which requires form elements to be contained within an HTML form tag, the Flex Form container is purely for lay out and it is not necessary to have form items within the container.

The Form container is one of a collection of three tags:

- `Form`—The main container
- `FormHeader`—An optional component for adding section headers
- `FormItem`—A component that lets you associate text with each form input field

Putting these together, listing 4.20 builds a form to capture user input.

Listing 4.20 Making use of form-related containers

```
<?xml version="1.0" encoding="utf-8"?>
<mx:Application xmlns:mx="http://www.adobe.com/2006/mxml">
  <mx:Form>
    <mx:FormHeading label="Contact Info"/>
    <mx:FormItem label="First Name">
      <mx:TextInput/>
    </mx:FormItem>
    <mx:FormItem label="Last Name">
      <mx:TextInput/>
    </mx:FormItem>
  </mx:Form>
</mx:Application>
```

Figure 4.25 shows a basic login window, such as you can see in many applications. The form-related containers make it easy to create the pattern of field label and field input.

If you need more flexibility then the two column approach of a form, check out the Grid container.

Figure 4.25 Form containers make it easy to lay out input components and give each component a label.

4.5.8 Grid container

The Grid container is very similar to an HTML table in that there is a top-level `grid` tag to signal the start of the grid, a `GridRow` tag for entering rows, and a `GridItemtag` for entering data into each cell. Let's make use of the Grid container to build an MP3 player control panel (listing 4.21).

Listing 4.21 Making use of the Grid container

```
<?xml version="1.0" encoding="utf-8"?>
<mx:Application xmlns:mx="http://www.adobe.com/2006/mxml">
  <mx:Grid>
```

```
    <mx:GridRow>                          <-- Create the
      <mx:GridItem>                           first row
        <mx:Button label="Rewind"/>
      </mx:GridItem>
      <mx:GridItem>
        <mx:Button label="Play"/>
      </mx:GridItem>
      <mx:GridItem>
        <mx:Button label="Forward"/>
      </mx:GridItem>
    </mx:GridRow>                           Create the
    <mx:GridRow>                        <-- second row
      <mx:GridItem colSpan="3">
        <mx:Button label="STOP" width="100%"/>
      </mx:GridItem>
    </mx:GridRow>
  </mx:Grid>
</mx:Application>
```

If you want a row to span more than one column (figure 4.26), you can use the `rowSpan` attribute on any `GridItem`.

Now that we're familiar with the Grid container, let's talk about another container that supports table-like approach to layout: the Tile container.

Figure 4.26 Control panel showing the layout abilities of the Grid container, which produces results similar to HTML tables.

4.5.9 *Tile container*

Tile containers are similar to a Grid, except there's no row or column spanning allowed. Tile containers lay out child objects within cells, or tiles, that metaphorically speaking is very similar to laying out tiles on a floor. Of particular strength, the Tile container will create tiles as necessary when you have a dynamic number of items you want to display, such as a collection of image thumbnails.

NOTE When driven by data the Tile container will create and remove tiles as the data changes.

As with other containers, it supports the `direction` property. The default is horizontal but it also accepts vertical. The purpose of this property is to instruct the Tile container to generate each new tile in a specified direction until it runs out of space, at which point it will begin a new row or column.

Let's take a look at an example that uses the Tile container to display a list of weather icons (listing 4.22).

Listing 4.22 The Tile container is used to automatically lay out weather icons

```
<?xml version="1.0" encoding="utf-8"?>
<mx:Application xmlns:mx="http://www.adobe.com/2006/mxml">
  <mx:Tile direction="horizontal" >
```

```
        <mx:Image source="heavyrain.png"/>
        <mx:Image source="partlycloudy.png"/>
        <mx:Image source="sunny.png"/>
        <mx:Image source="thunder.png"/>
        <mx:Image source="cloudy.png"/>
        <mx:Image source="drizzle.png"/>
        <mx:Image source="snow.png"/>
        <mx:Image source="clearnight.png"/>
    </mx:Tile>
</mx:Application>
```

Run the application and you can see, as shown in figure 4.27, we have a number of weather icons presented in a grid-like display. Nifty!

The Tile container is useful when you have an unknown number of items that you want to display in a catalog format. Another way to achieve the same effect is by using a `Repeater` component.

Figure 4.27 The Tile container lays out its child objects in a tile pattern.

4.6 Dynamic layout with Repeaters

When you have a static number of items to display, presentation is easy. But what if this amount is dynamic? This is when the use of a `Repeater` can help.

A `Repeater` is a nonvisual component that iterates over a collection of information, creating components on the fly as it moves along. One of the most common uses for this type of functionality is dynamic forms, or catalog-like interfaces. In such scenarios, a database is queried to retrieve a list of context-relevant information, upon which a UI is generated.

4.6.1 dataProvider sneak peek

A `dataProvider` represents a source of data; it is a reference (similar to a pointer) to where a source of information may be found. We'll discuss `dataProviders` in more detail in chapter 8, but we need to briefly introduce them here, as they are used to drive `Repeaters`, and therefore relevant to the examples that follow.

The type of data a `dataProvider` represents is similar in nature to an array. Although Flex does have arrays, it utilizes what are known as collections for `dataProviders`. Put bluntly, a collection is an array on steroids, and a lot more built-in capabilities such as sorting and filtering.

TIP For you ColdFusion folks, think of a collection as similar to an array of structures. Java folks might view it similar to an `ArrayList` of `Hashmaps`.

You can give a `dataProvider` a plain array and it will work fine, because Flex will wrap a collection around the array behind the scenes. Using the previous tile example, in listing 4.23 let's make a collection out of our list of weather icons using a type of collection called an `ArrayCollection`.

Listing 4.23 image file names are contained inside an `ArrayCollection` variable

```
<?xml version="1.0" encoding="utf-8"?>
<mx:Application xmlns:mx="http://www.adobe.com/2006/mxml" xmlns:local="*">
<mx:Script>
  <![CDATA[
    import mx.collections.ArrayCollection;
    [Bindable]
    public var images:ArrayCollection =          <-- Configure images
       new ArrayCollection(                          in a variable
             [
              {source:"heavyrain.png"},
              {source:"partlycloudy.png"},
              {source:"sunny.png"},
              {source:"thunder.png"},
              {source:"cloudy.png"},
              {source:"drizzle.png"},
              {source:"snow.png"},
              {source:"clearnight.png"}
             ]
            );
]]>
</mx:Script>
</mx:Application>
```

The following is a description of the configurations in listing 4.23:

- The collection's library is imported, enabling us to use it.
- An instance of an `ArrayCollection` (a type of collection) is created.
- The code, `[Bindable]`, informs anyone binding to the variable when changes occur—when changes do occur, the variable prompts whoever is binding to it to respond appropriately, such as updating the display.
- An `ArrayCollection` was created using shorthand array notation.
- Square [ ] brackets are used to indicate an array.
- Braces { } are used to indicate an object.

Consequently, we're passing an array of objects. In the real world, we might have queried a database to get this information, and the `ArrayCollection` would be the query result.

Now that we've established where the data is coming from, the next step is to know what properties and events are available to connect us into the `Repeater`.

4.6.2 *Properties and events of a Repeater*

In order to make effective use of a `Repeater` we need to know what properties exist, and how they can be applied. Table 4.6 lists these properties, the most important of which is `dataProvider`, used to target a source from which to retrieve data.

Table 4.6 Properties of the `Repeater`

Property	Type	Description
`id`	`String`	The identifier of the `Repeater`
`dataProvider`	`Object`	A reference to the data to iterate.
`startingIndex`	`Number`	The index at which to start the loop. Defaults to 0.
`count`	`Number`	Sets the number of loops to conduct. Defaults to the size of the `dataProvider`.
`currentIndex`	`Number`	Stores the current position in the loop (starting at 0) you can use to check where in the loop you currently are. This is a read-only property.
`currentItem`	`Object`	A reference to the object to which `currentIndex` is pointing.
`recycleChildren`	`Boolean`	A performance setting that allows Flex to reuse Child components if possible. Allowed values are `true` (default) or `false`.

Table 4.7 lists a group of events we can use to execute code through the `Repeater`.

Table 4.7 Repeater-based events

Event	Description
`repeat`	Occurs after each iteration of a loop
`repeatStart`	Occurs as the Repeater is about to begin looping
`repeatEnd`	Occurs after the last iteration is complete

If you make use of events you would need to evaluate properties such as `currentIndex` and `currentItem` to learn the status of the properties. We'll show you an example later in this chapter.

4.6.3 *Creating the Repeater*

The next thing we need to do is create a `Repeater` using the <mx:Repeater> tag, and specify the `dataProvider` we want it to use. Listing 4.24 shows what this would look like.

Listing 4.24 An `ArrayCollection` will feed the `Repeater's dataProvider`

```
<mx:Tile direction="horizontal" >
  <mx:Repeater id="myRepeater" dataProvider="{images}">

  </mx:Repeater>
</mx:Tile>
```

The Repeater is inside Tile because we want it to create child objects inside the Tile by looping over the ArrayCollection. Adding what you've learned about a Repeater's properties, the last piece is to add the component that we want created with each iteration—for this example, an Image component. Using the currentItem property we can use the binding mechanism of Flex to get the current image at any point in time:

```
<mx:Image source="{myRepeater.currentItem.source}"/>
```

Let's put this all together in listing 4.25 and see what the code looks like.

Listing 4.25 Using images, loop and create image components

```
<?xml version="1.0" encoding="utf-8"?>
<mx:Application xmlns:mx="http://www.adobe.com/2006/mxml" xmlns:local="*">
  <mx:Script>
    <![CDATA[
      import mx.collections.ArrayCollection;
      [Bindable]
      public var images:ArrayCollection =
           new ArrayCollection([
                   {source:"heavyrain.png"},{source:"partlycloudy.png"},
                   {source:"sunny.png"},{source:"thunder.png"},
                   {source:"cloudy.png"},{source:"drizzle.png"},
                   {source:"snow.png"},{source:"clearnight.png"}]);
    ]]>l
  </mx:Script>
  <mx:Tile direction="horizontal" >
    <mx:Repeater id="myRepeater" dataProvider="{images}">
      <mx:Image source="{myRepeater.currentItem.source}"/>
    </mx:Repeater>
  </mx:Tile>
</mx:Application>
```

Store all the filenames

Create images

To no surprise, the output in figure 4.28 is exactly the same visually as before (figure 4.27), except you can now add or remove items to the ArrayCollection, without needing to change the code that handles the output.

Think of a Repeater as a loop statement that iterates over an array. The item in the array to which the iteration is currently pointing is accessible via the Repeater's currentItem and currentIndex properties.

Generating the display is the major goal of a Repeater, but with Flex there are always events available to react when certain triggers occur.

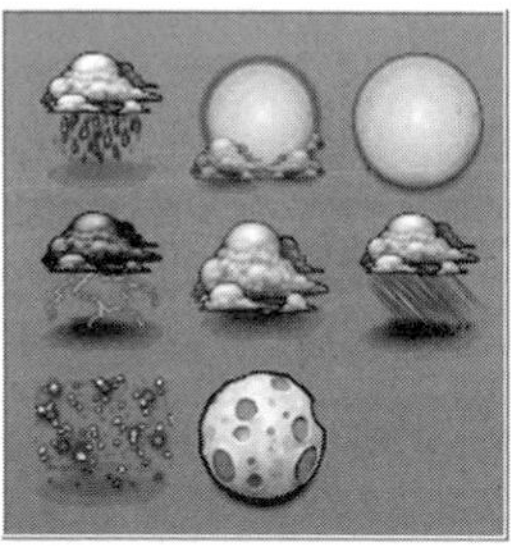

Figure 4.28 Using a Repeater, these Image components were created on the fly using an ArrayCollection variable.

4.6.4 *Working with Repeater events*

You can easily tie into the events of a Repeater by specifying what ActionScript you want to execute. In the Repeater, we're going to specify a couple of event handlers to invoke when these events occur:

```
<mx:Repeater id="myRepeater" dataProvider="{images}"
        repeatStart="handleRepeatStart()"
        repeat="handleRepeat()"
        repeatEnd="handleRepeatEnd()">
```

The code for these event handlers looks along the lines of listing 4.26.

Listing 4.26 Collection of functions to handle `Repeater` events

```
public function handleRepeatStart():void
{
 mx.controls.Alert.show("Repeater starting!");
}

public function handleRepeat():void
{
  trace("Currently on index:" + myRepeater.currentIndex);
  trace("Image is:" + myRepeater.currentItem.source);
}

public function handleRepeatEnd():void
{
 mx.controls.Alert.show("Repeater finished!");
}
```

If you were to run this script, you would see two pop-up alerts for the start and end events, and your output log (listing 4.27) would have a line item for each image.

Listing 4.27 The output from the `Repeater` events per listing 4.26

```
Currently on index:0
Image is:heavyrain.png
Currently on index:1
Image is:partlycloudy.png
Currently on index:2
Image is:sunny.png
Currently on index:3
Image is:thunder.png
Currently on index:4
Image is:cloudy.png
Currently on index:5
Image is:drizzle.png
Currently on index:6
Image is:snow.png
Currently on index:7
Image is:clearnight.png
```

NOTE For more information on how to configure logging, see chapter 23.

`Repeater`s are a handy way of generating components from a collection of variable data.

4.7 Summary

Flex's display is predicated on the concept of layout. You have the option of choosing the simple approach—absolute layout, wherein you control the coordinates of each component. Or, you can choose a variation of that, the constraint-based layouts, which let you specify the position of elements relative to locations on the window itself, such as its edges, or the center point.

Because the browser window dimensions can vary, you can use automatic layout to let Flex do the calculations to position all the components. And it is not an all or nothing-at-all proposition; using containers you can mix and match your use of automatic and absolute layout.

Flex comes with a number of containers, each of which provides a unique approach to layout and UI positioning.

But what if the components don't exist initially? If you need to make components on the fly based on a set of data, you can use a `Repeater` to generate those for you.

The Form container in Flex is nothing more than a standard container, but in the next chapter, we'll go into how to actually create forms and capture user input.

5 Displaying forms and capturing user input

This chapter covers:

- Creating forms in Flex
- Using input components (controls)
- Capturing user input

Let's put our newly acquired understanding of layout and ActionScript to work and apply it to a fundamental operation of any application—capturing user input.

As mentioned in chapter 4, even though Flex offers a `Form` component, its use is optional and you'll find it functions best as a layout tool. In the land of Flex you are equipped with control components (usually referred to as controls) that display information and accept user input. Alongside controls are events and event handlers that recognize and respond to user actions, such as clicking a mouse.

When event handler functions run, they access data from whatever source they've been instructed; there's no master `Form` tag that contains all the inputs as in HTML.

NOTE Say goodbye to the notion of HTML `Forms`. The optional `<Form>` tag in Flex does nothing more than lay out UI components called controls.

Remember, you're not restricted to the set of controls that come with Flex. Unlike HTML, which limits your UI controls to the HTML specification and browser implementation, Flex encourages you to extend an existing control to add more functionality, or create your own, completely new, UI controls from scratch.

One of the teaching approaches this book employs is to show many ways of doing the same thing. From example to example, we'll use an idea from the previous one, but then change a portion of it to demonstrate an alternative. The alternatives aren't necessarily any better, they're just different, but more importantly help you to think with the ActionScript mentality.

A core piece to that understanding is the invaluable `id` attribute, a handle to an MXML component that allows you to access the values contained by the `id` attribute.

5.1 The id attribute

You were first introduced to the `id` attribute in chapter 2, but it is worth taking the time to review and expand what you learned. The `id` attribute can be used on any component and you can access it the same as you would any other variable. It gives you a mechanism to uniquely name any instances of a component, which allows you to refer to the component explicitly using its unique identifier.

HTML `Form` tags also have `id` attributes that are similar in their role and use. Unlike HTML, MXML does not require you to use functions like JavaScript's `getElementByID()` to access an `id`.

When it comes to building `Forms`, the `id` property will be the key to retrieving the values from target components.

5.2 Text controls

The basic purpose for the UI of any application is to display text. Flex provides a variety of components that allow you to capture and display textual information. Table 5.1 presents these controls and their descriptions.

Table 5.1 Text controls for displaying and capturing text

Control	Description
`Text`	A simple control that displays textual information. Its goal is to appear as if the text is embedded in the application, and not some arbitrary visual element floating around the window. This means it has no scrollbars (other components enable scrollbars if they run out of space), it is borderless, and the background is transparent (by default). Textual data stored by `Text` can always wrap, and it supports HTML text.
`Label`	The same as `Text`, except the textual data it contains doesn't wrap. Common uses for this include the title to a section of your application, or the label of an input field.
`TextInput`	Presents a single-line text entry field. This control is similar to the `<input type="text">` tag in HTML.

Table 5.1 Text controls for displaying and capturing text *(continued)*

Control	Description
`TextArea`	Presents a multiple-row text entry field. Similar to the `<textarea>` tag in HTML.
`RichTextEditor`	As the name implies, a robust editor that allows the user to format their text. This includes parameters like color, font, and text size. HTML does not offer a similar feature to `RichTextEditor` natively.

Listing 5.1 demonstrates each of these in a single application in which we'll put together our first form. Our form will employ a `Panel` component to automatically lay out all the controls.

Listing 5.1 This code makes use of all of the text-based control components

```
<?xml version="1.0"?>
<mx:Application xmlns:mx="http://www.adobe.com/2006/mxml">
  <mx:Script>
    public function showMsg(msg:String):void
    {
      mx.controls.Alert.show(msg);
    }
  </mx:Script>

  <mx:Panel title="Profile" width="400" height="400">

  <mx:Label text="Enter your name" fontWeight="bold" />

 <mx:TextInput id="yourName"
              width="250" valueCommit="showMsg(yourName.text)"/>

 <mx:Text text="Profile Summary"/>

 <mx:TextArea id="aboutYou" textAlign="center" width="250"
             valueCommit="showMsg(aboutYou.text)"/>

<mx:Label text="Enter your profile" fontWeight="bold" color="#ff0000"/>
 <mx:RichTextEditor id="rte" height="150"
                  valueCommit="showMsg(rte.text)"/>
  </mx:Panel>

</mx:Application>
```

Display a pop-up window with the message

Pass the component's text value to showMsg

Try compiling and running the application and you'll see a display similar to figure 5.1.

Now let's look at what we've created and how it works. The `Label` component is used to display a descriptive label above each input control. To give you a sense of what `Label` can do we've modified some of its styling properties. When a user enters a value and *commits* it—for example, by clicking Enter or Tab, or an element such as a Submit button—Flex will recognize this event and run the `showMsg()` function as instructed.

These text fields can be used to capture a broad range of data. You could even use them to capture a date. This would likely be your natural inclination when coming from an HTML background because there isn't a native date `Form` input available. A better choice would be to use Flex's `Date` controls.

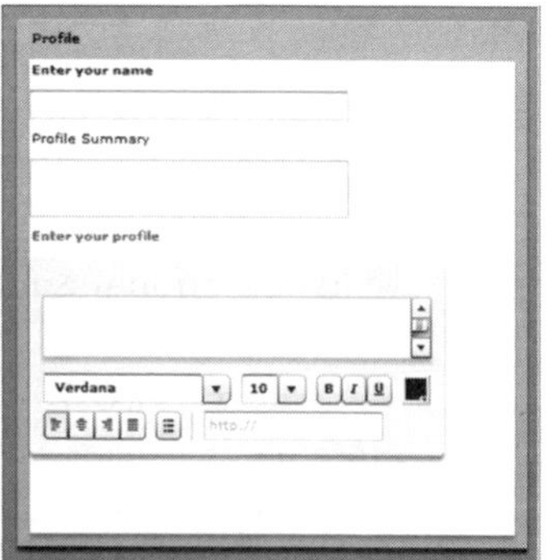

Figure 5.1 A form constructed using Flex's text-based components.

5.3 Date controls

When using HTML, a common technique to capture date-related input is to use the form's `<input type="text">` tag, paired with a calendar image displayed directly after the tag. When invoked, a calendar appears in a pop-up window. When a user selects a date from the calendar, a bit of JavaScript is executed to copy the selected value to the input field.

Fortunately, there's an easier way to capture calendar-related data in Flex, which offers two date-based fields (listing 5.2).

Table 5.2 Date-based controls

Control	Description
`DateChooser`	Displays a small calendar similar to most HTML-based calendar selection widgets. A noteworthy feature is you can control the display of ranges of dates, as well as determine which ranges are selectable. This is quite useful if you wanted to block out dates, such as holidays.
`DateField`	The input control that appears similar to the `<input type="text">` tag/calendar image combination used in HTML. It allows the user to enter a date, or, if the icon is selected, it displays the `DateChooser` control.

The code in listing 5.2 demonstrates how to use both of these components.

Listing 5.2 Flex's two date-based components used to capture date information

```
<?xml version="1.0"?>
<mx:Application xmlns:mx="http://www.adobe.com/2006/mxml">
  <mx:Script>
    public function showMsg(msg:String):void
    {
    mx.controls.Alert.show(msg);
    }
  </mx:Script>
  <mx:Panel title="Profile" width="400" height="400">
  <mx:DateField text="12/05/2008" id="thisDateField"
           change="showMsg(thisDateField.selectedDate.toString())"/>
<mx:DateChooser maxYear="2010" minYear="2006"
 selectedDate="{new Date(2008,10, 15)}"
              id="thisDateChooser"
```

Set limits on the range of years

Default the date

Access the instance of the component

Default selectedDate

```
        change="showMsg(thisDateChooser.selectedDate.toString())"/>
    </mx:Panel>
</mx:Application>
```

Triggers calling showMsg()

Notice how the id property's set value is used to access the value of that component? The intention was merely to show you how the id property could be used; later in the chapter we'll show alternative ways to accomplish the same thing.

Did you also notice how the change event is used instead of valueCommit? The difference between these two specific events is valueCommit is triggered when the user performs an action that indicates she's completed setting the value (for example, pressing the Enter key). The change event responds as the value changes, so feedback occurs in real time with each keystroke.

Compile and run the application and you'll see the result of Flex's two date-based components illustrated in figure 5.2.

Figure 5.2 Flex's two date-based components displayed together.

NOTE Why can't you default the date on the DateChooser to a simple text representation of a date?

If you pull up the Flex API Reference for this object you'll see that selectedDate expects a Date object—in our example we're creating one on the fly, and inline. The DateField also supports this attribute.

Just as date-based controls can be used more effectively to acquire calendar data than a text input box, Flex also has controls that are specific to capturing numeric values.

5.4 Numeric controls

Numeric controls are a great example of how the benefits of Flex move beyond HTML. Nothing similar to Numeric controls exists in the land of traditional web applications.

The user input controls presented in table 5.3 allow you to capture numeric data from the user. As you would expect, they can be used for the more obvious tasks—such as obtaining someone's age—but you can also use them to resize an image in real time, or to filter a set of data.

Table 5.3 Controls used for capturing numeric values

Control	Description
NumericStepper	A simple control that lets the user increment and decrement values. You can specify the minimum and maximum allowed values, as well as the unit size of the increment/decrement step.

Table 5.3 Controls used for capturing numeric values *(continued)*

Control	Description
`HSlider`	Allows the user to slide what's known as a *thumb* horizontally along a track. You can control the minimum and maximum allowed values, `snapInterval` increments (positions on the slide to which the thumb will snap), and visible increments (called ticks). You also have the option to set up more than one thumb if you want to allow the user to specify multiple values (for example, a range).
`VSlider`	Identical to the `HSlider`, except the orientation of the track is vertical.

Let's put these controls to work in listing 5.3 and capture some numbers.

Listing 5.3 Using Flex's `Numeric` input controls to capture values

```
<?xml version="1.0"?>
<mx:Application xmlns:mx="http://www.adobe.com/2006/mxml">
  <mx:Script>
    public function showMsg(msg:String):void
    {
      mx.controls.Alert.show(msg);
    }
  </mx:Script>

  <mx:Panel title="Profile" width="360" height="240" layout="horizontal">
    <mx:VBox>
      <mx:Text fontWeight="bold" text="How many kids do you have?"/>

      <mx:NumericStepper id="kids"
                minimum="0" maximum="15"          Age range between 0 and 15
                stepSize="1"                      Increment/decrement by 1
                change="showMsg(kids.value.toString())"/>

        <mx:Text fontWeight="bold" text="How long is your commute (mins)?"/>

      <mx:HSlider id="commuteTimeRange" minimum="0" maximum="180"
           snapInterval="5"      ❶
           tickInterval="15"     ❷
           labels="[0 mins,180 mins]"     ❸
           thumbCount="2"                 2 thumb sliders
           change="showMsg(commuteTimeRange.values.toString())" />

</mx:VBox>
<mx:VBox>
      <mx:Text fontWeight="bold" text="How tall are you (cm)?"/>
      <mx:VSlider id="yourHeight" minimum="0" maximum="300"
              tickInterval="50" snapInterval="1"     ❹
              labels="[0,50,100,150,200,250,300]"    ❺
                 change="showMsg(yourHeight.values.toString())"/>
    </mx:VBox>
  </mx:Panel>
</mx:Application>
```

We can select in units of 5 ❶ and display markers every 15 units ❷. The display is two evenly spaced labels (one at each end) ❸. In the vertical slider ❹, the markers are further apart than in the horizontal slider. Finally, we display seven evenly spaced labels ❺.

After compiling and running the application, you'll see the results shown in figure 5.3. This is a collection of user input controls that you certainly have never seen in HTML—they're not even that common among desktop applications.

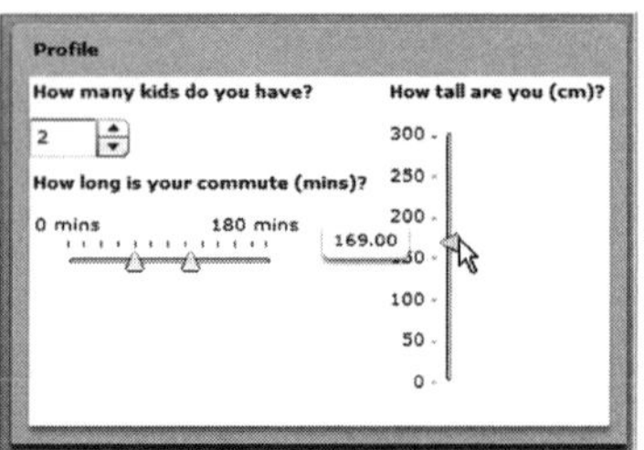

Figure 5.3 Flex's numeric-based components offer a unique way to capture values.

Many developers fail to take full advantage of these components, usually because they come from an HTML background and are not used to this level of utility. This is unfortunate, because you can use numeric-based components in ways more creative than simply capturing a value. You can use that value to provide real-time control to your end user. As another example, if you're designing a dashboard, you can have the display change in real time as the user moves a slider back and forth—effectively filtering data in and out.

5.5 Buttons

A whole section on buttons? When it comes to Flex, the answer is a resounding, yes! Flex goes beyond the plain old button offered by HTML and adds a collection of interesting options (see table 5.4). Buttons are one of stalwarts of GUIs, but they can be a bit boring. Flex takes them to a higher level with a number of variations.

Table 5.4 Flex offers an expanded range of button components

Control	Description
`Button`	The standard, all-purpose button for accepting a mouse click interaction. Flex buttons have built-in support that let you easily add an image into the button. In HTML you can use an image to create a `psuedo-Text+Image` button, but your text will be static. With Flex, the text remains dynamic.
`ButtonBar`	Dynamically generates a series of buttons based on an array. You could do the same thing by dynamically generating `Buttons` on your own, but not only is a `ButtonBar` easier to implement, it adds some flair by rounding the edges of the outer most buttons to lend the appearance of a single Menu bar, split into sections.
`LinkButton`	Flex's version of an HTML link. If you pull up the class reference for this object (in the Flex API Reference) you'll see it is a descendent of the `Button`, but styled and extended to behave like an HTML link by having a transparent background and no border.
`LinkBar`	Similar to the relationship between a `Button` and a `ButtonBar`, the `LinkBar` is an easy way to create a series of `LinkButtons`.

Table 5.4 Flex offers an expanded range of button components *(continued)*

Control	Description
ToggleButtonBar	Nearly identical to a ButtonBar, except it persists the selection—if you press one of the buttons it stays down (and highlighted) until you change to another button. Think of it as a radio button with a label inside.
PopUpButton	A dual-button that combines the functionality of two buttons—the left side acts like a normal Button; the right side invokes another UI object (anything derived from the UIComponent object). This is typically used to create a multiselection Button that looks as if it is a Button and a ComboBox merged into one.
PopUpMenuButton	A descendent of the PopUpButton, it is geared to specifically create a drop-down menu.

Listing 5.4 presents a look at how to invoke all these button choices.

Listing 5.4 A collection of Button-based components in action

```
<?xml version="1.0"?>
<mx:Application xmlns:mx="http://www.adobe.com/2006/mxml">
  <mx:Script>
    <![CDATA[
      public function showMsg(msg:String):void
      {
        mx.controls.Alert.show('You just clicked on ' + msg);
      }
    ]]>
  </mx:Script>
  <mx:Panel title="Profile" width="360" height="240" layout="vertical">

    <mx:VBox>

      <mx:Button id="thisBtn" label="Button" click="showMsg('button')"/>

      <mx:LinkButton id="thisLinkBtn" label="LinkButton"
               click="showMsg('linkbutton')"/>

    </mx:VBox>

    <mx:VBox>

      <mx:ButtonBar id="thisBtnBar"
              dataProvider="{['One','Two','Three']}"
              itemClick="showMsg(event.label)" />

      <mx:LinkBar id="thisLinkBar"
            dataProvider="{['One','Two','Three']}"
            itemClick="showMsg(event.label)" />

      <mx:ToggleButtonBar id="thisToggleBar"
                  dataProvider="{['One','Two','Three']}"
                  itemClick="showMsg(event.label)"/>

    </mx:VBox>
  </mx:Panel>
</mx:Appliclation>
```

dataProvider populates the display of components

Being an OOP language Flex tends to build upon itself, using some components as a foundation then creating variants on top of those. The Button family demonstrates this strategy quite well.

5.5.1 Bars of Buttons

ButtonBar, LinkBar, and ToggleButtonBar are such close siblings that from a mechanical perspective, aside from minor presentation differences, they're the same thing (see figure 5.4). More important is their use of dataProvider, which is a property that accepts array-like data to generate its display (see chapter 4 for a discussion on the Repeater and its dataProvider property).

As with many applications, Flex makes arrays available, but you can also take advantage of its more powerful cousin, ArrayCollection. In the following example, we used ActionScript shorthand to create a hard-coded array on the fly. An alternative method would be to create an ArrayCollection variable, and assign that variable to the dataProvideras follows:

```
<mx:Script>
  import mx.collections.ArrayCollection;
  [Bindable]
  public var arData:ArrayCollection = new
                ArrayCollection(['One','Two','Three']);
</mx:Script>
<mx:ButtonBar id="thisBtnBar" dataProvider="{arData}" />
```

The benefit of creating an ArrayCollection variable is the ability to decouple the logic it contains from the component that displays it. You can read in configuration data and populate variables accordingly.

NOTE What is the difference between click and itemClick? Not much. Flex applications are event-driven, and triggers cause an event to occur. Different components respond to all kinds of events. click refers to the mouse button being pressed (the trigger) on a Button component; itemClick is used to capture the selection from a list of items.

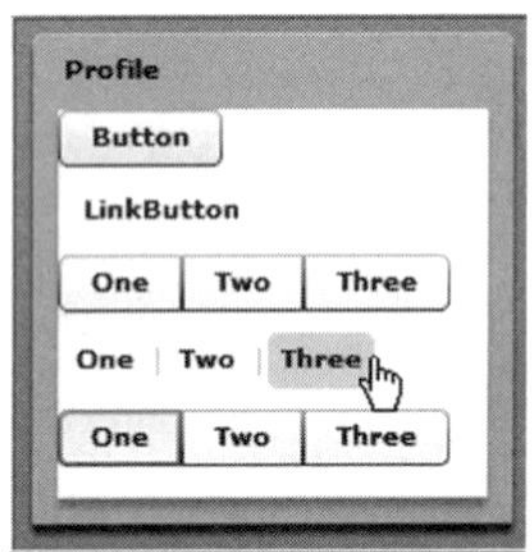

Figure 5.4 Flex has a number of Button-based components at your disposal.

The previous examples have covered all of the buttons, except two: the PopUpButton and the PopUpMenuButton. As self-explanatory as they appear, in order for you to make proper use of them, some more explanation will be required.

5.5.2 The PopUpButton and PopUpMenuButton

We're not playing favorites by giving these two controls special attention. They're considered special cases, and as such, they do need a more thorough explanation.

Listing 5.5 illustrates a PopUpMenuButton in action.

Listing 5.5 Example of how to use a PopUpMenuButton

```
<?xml version="1.0"?>
<mx:Application xmlns:mx="http://www.adobe.com/2006/mxml">

  <mx:Script>
   public function showMsg(msg:String):void
   {
     mx.controls.Alert.show('You just clicked on ' + msg);
   }
  </mx:Script>

  <mx:Panel width="100" height="100">
    <mx:PopUpMenuButton id="menuBtn"
      dataProvider="{['One','Two','Three']}"
      click="showMsg('left side')"
      itemClick="showMsg('right side with ' + event.label)"/>
  </mx:Panel>
</mx:Application>
```

Notice that this example makes use of both the click and itemClick events. When you click the right secondary Button (figure 5.5), a drop-down menu will appear, prompting you to select an item. When a selection is made, the itemClick event will be triggered. But if you click the left side of the primary Button, the itemClick and click events will fire, one after the other.

This is useful when you need to differentiate between these two user interactions. For example, let's assume the drop-down menu defined in listing 5.5 contained a list of credit card brands (for example, Visa, MasterCard, and American Express). When the user changes the selection (itemClick) the credit card type is stored to a variable, but when the primary Button (click) is clicked, Flex will submit the Form.

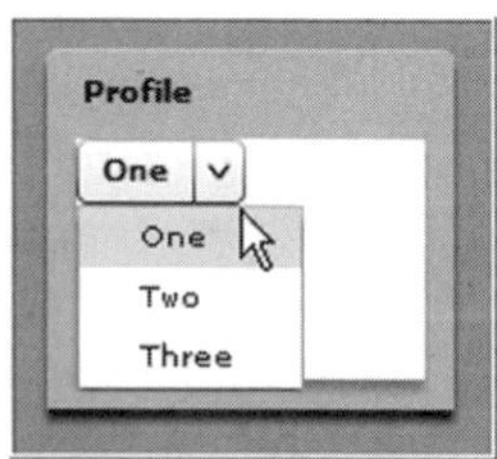

Figure 5.5 PopUpMenuButton **is similar to a** Button **and a** ComboBox **wrapped into one.**

Let's move on to the father of PopUpMenuButton: the PopUpButton. The PopUpButton can perform the same tasks as PopUpMenuButton but possesses broader capabilities, which, naturally takes more code to implement.

PopUpMenuButton uses an element called Menu to generate the drop-down (another standard object with Flex). But Menu is the only thing PopUpMenuButton can display.

PopUpButton can display a greater variety of elements but it doesn't default to any one in particular. This means it is considerably more flexible, but you do need to explicitly specify what PopUpButton is going to show.

To produce the same result as listing 5.5 using PopUpButton, the code would look like that in listing 5.6.

Listing 5.6 Using PopUpButton to display an optional menu

```
<?xml version="1.0"?>
<mx:Application xmlns:mx="http://www.adobe.com/2006/mxml">
  <mx:Script>
```

```
import mx.events.*;
import mx.controls.Menu;

public var menuItems:Object =
[{label:'One'},{label:'Two'},{label:'Three'}];
public var thisMenu:Menu = Menu.createMenu(null,menuItems,false);

public function handleItemClick(event:MenuEvent):void
{
   menuBtn.label = event.label;
}
</mx:Script>l

<mx:Panel width="100" height="100">
<mx:PopUpButton id="menuBtn"
 creationComplete="thisMenu.addEventListener('itemClick',handleItemClick)
 ;"
 popUp="{thisMenu}"/>
</mx:Panel>
</mx:Application>
```

Create a variable with array-like menu values

Populate a Menu object

Call an item when the menu item is clicked

Set the text label on the button

Here are three points to note about listing 5.6:

- In most examples, the variable containing the information to be populated is an array. In the previous example, we used an object. If you recall from chapter 3, there's not much difference between them. In this context you could have declared `menuItems` an array instead of an object and it would have worked as well.
- `We've introduced creationComplete`. This event instructs `PopUpButton` to call extra code when its creation is finished.
- This extra code tells our `Menu` object (`thisMenu`) to listen for the `itemClick` event, and if that occurs, to call our event handler (`handleItemClick`) to manage it.

That seems like a lot more work, so why bother? Taking a look at figure 5.6, the `Button` and drop-down menu appear nearly the same as those produced by `PopUpMenuButton` demonstrated earlier. Is it worth the effort? Yes. Unlike with `PopUpMenuButton`, the label in the `Button` doesn't default to the first item in the list.

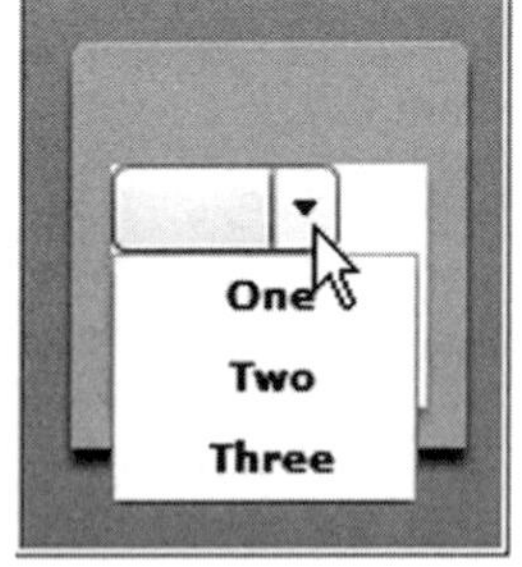

Figure 5.6 A `PopUpButton` can behave similar to a `PopUpMenuButton`, but provides more control. The trade-off: it takes more work to set up.

The main difference between using `PopUpButton` and `PopUpMenuButton` is with `PopUpButton` you're not restricted to using it for menus, you can make use of any visual element to interact with the user. If all you want is the drop-down menu effect, go with the `PopUpMenuButton`. If you need more control over the options you want to present the user, leverage the flexibility of `PopUpButton`.

Along with buttons, the other common user input paradigm (in both desktop and web applications) is a `picklist`, which provides a selection list from which the user can choose one or more items.

5.6 Picklist controls

Picklists are controls that represent everything else—they present lists of options from which you can choose, and we've listed them in table 5.5.

Table 5.5 Flex's picklist controls

Control	Description
`CheckBox`	The generic `CheckBox` control (identical in behavior to an HTML `CheckBox`). It is a descendent of the `Button`, except it is designed specifically for the purpose of being checked and unchecked. The most common use for a `CheckBox` is to provide a series of options from which the user can check (select) one or more of those options.
`RadioButton`	Similar to the `CheckBox`, except when grouped as a range of choices, the user can select only one. The `RadioButton` is also a descendent of `Button`.
`ComboBox`	This drop-down menu control displays the currently selected option, but when clicked drops a display list of options from which to choose. `ComboBox` is the same as a `<select>` box in HTML, except unlike its HTML equivalent, you can allow the user to free-form edit the selected text. Although it appears to be based on `Button`, it is not a descendent.
`ColorPicker`	A sibling to `ComboBox`. It drops down a color menu allowing the user to select from a color palette. You could use this to allow users to customize their desktop, or as part of the application workflow (for example, a color selector with which visitors to an automobile manufacturer's website can view a vehicle's color options in real time).

To get an idea of what these look like in action we assembled a program fashioned on the concept of a user profile form (listing 5.7).

Listing 5.7 Examples of picklist controls

```
<?xml version="1.0"?>
<mx:Application xmlns:mx="http://www.adobe.com/2006/mxml">

  <mx:Script>
    public function showMsg(msg:String):void
    {
      mx.controls.Alert.show(msg);
    }
  </mx:Script>

  <mx:Panel width="400" height="150" title="Profile">

  <mx:HBox>
    <mx:Label text="Your hobbies:"/>
    <mx:CheckBox id="cbVideoGames" label="Video Games"
          click="showMsg('Video Games is ' + cbVideoGames.selected)"/>   ❶
    <mx:CheckBox id="cbFishing" label="Fishing"
          click="showMsg('Fishing is ' + cbFishing.selected)"/>
  </mx:HBox>
```

```
<mx:HBox>
  <mx:Label text="Do you like spam:"/>
  <mx:RadioButtonGroup id="Spam"
               itemClick="showMsg('User picked ' +
               event.currentTarget.selectedValue)"/>
<mx:RadioButton id="rbYes" value="Yes" groupName="Spam"
            click="showMsg('Yes')" label="Yes"/>
  <mx:RadioButton id="rbNo" value="No" groupName="Spam"
            click="showMsg('No')" label="No"/>
</mx:HBox>

<mx:HBox>
  <mx:Label text="Favorite car maker:"/>
  <mx:ComboBox id="combo"
          change="showMsg('Favorite car is ' +
          event.currentTarget.selectedItem)">
    <mx:Array>
      <mx:String>Ferrari</mx:String>
      <mx:String>Porsche</mx:String>
      <mx:String>Hyundai</mx:String>
    </mx:Array>
  </mx:ComboBox>

  <mx:Label text="With the color of:"/>
  <mx:ColorPicker id="clr"
        change="showMsg('Color ' +
              event.currentTarget.selectedColor)"/>
 </mx:HBox>

</mx:Panel>

</mx:Application>
```

❷ (RadioButton group)

Show changes in value

Inline data to populate the ComboBox

Display the color

We present two CheckBoxes and display their value when clicked ❶. In our next step ❷ we create two grouped RadioButtons, which triggers two pop-up windows. First click on the RadioButton will fire, followed by itemClick. RadioButtonGroup is optional—use it when you need to call a single function regardless of RadioButton.

After compiling and running the application you'll see something similar to that of figure 5.7 which contains various questions using these picklist controls.

In comparing these components to their HTML forms equivalents, there's not much of a departure in their general behavior—although the color picker stands apart as something completely different.

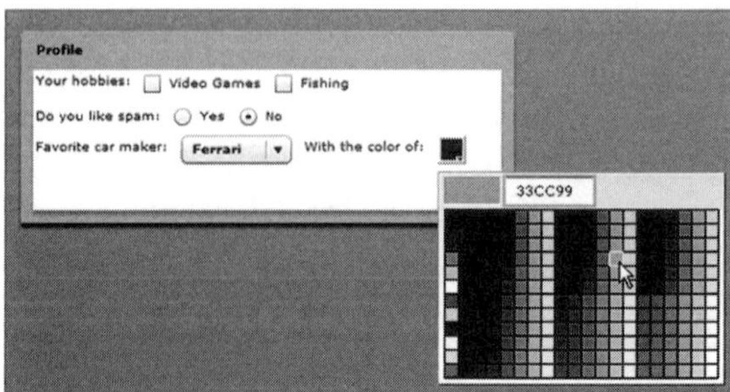

Figure 5.7 Take your pick! Picklist controls allow users to choose from a range of options.

NOTE The term picklist isn't an official term associated with Flex, it is something we use as a category for these particular controls.

Now having covered all of the user input components (controls) along with usage examples, we need to take a deeper look at what your options are when interacting with the user, and accessing any values they have input.

5.7 Accessing the control's value

As with any programming language, there are many ways to carry out the same task. In the previous examples, the most straightforward techniques were used to make it easy to see what's going on in the background. Be aware that for each of these examples, there are other (and perhaps better) ways to execute them.

5.7.1 Passing values to a function

The previous examples contain many instances of passing values to a function. Although my intention was to keep the examples streamlined and easy to understand, passing values to independent functions is a good technique to employ, as you relieve the logic that processes data from needing to know where the data came from.

This will allow you to reuse that function and to change the implementation—for example, switching from a `RadioButton` to a `CheckBox`) doesn't faze the function at all. This is what you observed with the `showMsg` function:

```
public function showMsg(msg:String):void
{
  mx.controls.Alert.show(msg);
}
```

When we call a function to which we pass the value, it is in response to a trigger that caused the event to occur. Each event has an event object to go along with it, which, by means of the `currentTarget` property, contains all kinds of goodies, including where the event came from.

This is what we're doing in the following code as we use `currentTarget` (in this case a reference to the `RadioButtonGroup`) to extract the `selectedValue` of the `RadioButtonGroup`.

```
<mx:RadioButtonGroup
  itemClick="showMsg(event.currentTarget.selectedValue)"/>
```

But if we assign that control an `id`, we can reference it using that instead:

```
<mx:RadioButtonGroup id="Spam"
  itemClick="showMsg(Spam.selectedValue.toString())"/>
```

Passing simple values is common in any language, but Flex, which is event–based, provides an opportunity to tap into the event itself.

5.7.2 Passing events to a function

An inverse approach is to put more responsibility on the function by increasing its awareness of the data's origin.

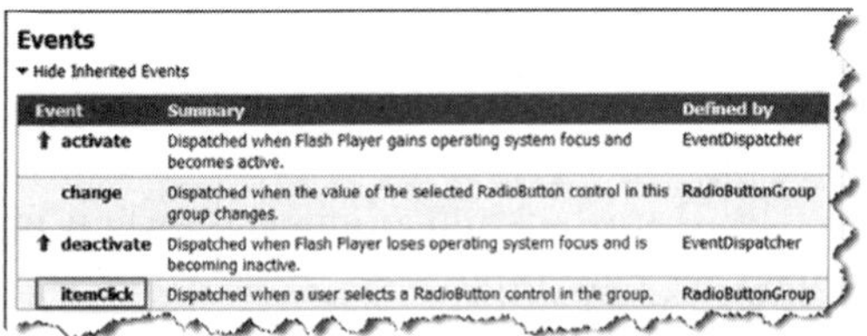
Events

▾ Hide Inherited Events

Event	Summary	Defined by
↑ activate	Dispatched when Flash Player gains operating system focus and becomes active.	EventDispatcher
change	Dispatched when the value of the selected RadioButton control in this group changes.	RadioButtonGroup
↑ deactivate	Dispatched when Flash Player loses operating system focus and is becoming inactive.	EventDispatcher
itemClick	Dispatched when a user selects a RadioButton control in the group.	RadioButtonGroup

Figure 5.8 To learn more about a particular event, such as which class to import, select the event from the events list in the API Reference for a given component.

To do that, we can pass the entire event object as shown in listing 5.8.

Listing 5.8 When the user clicks a control, you can pass the entire event object

```
<mx:Script>
import mx.events.ItemClickEvent;   <-- ❶ Import the event class
public function showMsg(anEvent:ItemClickEvent):void
{
  mx.controls.Alert.show(anEvent.currentTarget.selectedValue);
}
</mx:Script>
<mx:RadioButtonGroup id="Spam" itemClick="showMsg(event)"/>
```

As you can see, it is more involved, but it does simplify matters for the control that invokes the function. It only needs to pass the event object; the event handler function can independently process the event in whatever fashion is required. The key aspect to note is you'll need to know the type of event that's being passed and execute an import of the class ❶.

You can determine this by displaying the component or control's class reference in the Flex API Reference (see chapter 2).

TIP The quickest way to access the Flex API class reference (in this case to show the definition of the control) is to click the control in question then press Shift+F2.

For example, in listing 5.8, we can determine the event was an `itemClickEvent` object by following these steps:

1. In your code, click `RadioButtonGroup` then press Shift+F2. The API Reference for this component will display.
2. We're using events, so scroll down to the events section.
3. Select `itemClick` from the list (see figure 5.8).
4. The API Reference for the event itself will appear. The class will be listed under the event object type area (see figure 5.9). In this example it shows we need the `mx.events.ItemClickEvent` class.

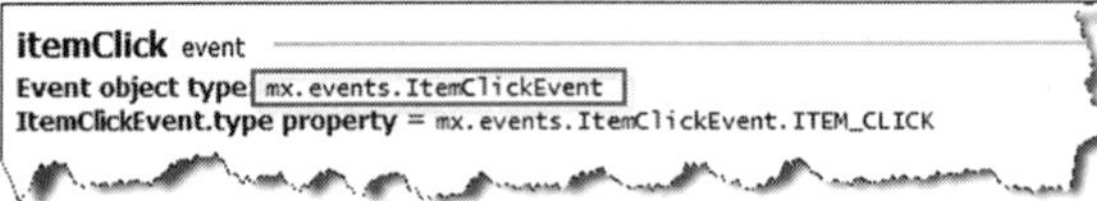
itemClick event

Event object type `mx.events.ItemClickEvent`

ItemClickEvent.type property = `mx.events.ItemClickEvent.ITEM_CLICK`

Figure 5.9 When looking at an event in the API Reference, look at the object type to determine which class to import.

Initially, this approach takes the most amount of work to implement, but if you wanted a really fast route, your function can directly access properties of the components to retrieve the values.

5.7.3 Accessing properties directly

Finally, the most tightly coupled approach. This requires your function to have very specific knowledge of what it is accessing. This, of course, limits your function's reusability. Worse case, if the property it is accessing changes, the code could break down.

On the flip side, it is a very convenient approach that doesn't require passing any data (listing 5.9).

Listing 5.9 This function accesses the value of the component directly

```
<mx:Script>
 public function showMsg():void
 {
  mx.controls.Alert.show(Spam.selectedValue.toString());
 }
</mx:Script>
<mx:RadioButtonGroup id="Spam" itemClick="showMsg()"/>
```

In this scenario, you can respond to an event on the input control if you want, but since you're accessing the value of the control directly you can access it at any time, such as when a submit `Button` is pressed.

You can also use this technique in combination with any of the others previously mentioned. In listing 5.10 an event handler is used to validate the input value using a highly decoupled function that doesn't know where the value came from, at the same time the submit `Button` is clicked on another function used to explicitly access a particular instance of the `TextInput`.

Listing 5.10 Combining techniques to access values of a control

```
<?xml version="1.0"?>
<mx:Application xmlns:mx="http://www.adobe.com/2006/mxml">
  <mx:Script>
    <![CDATA[
      import mx.controls.Alert;
      public function checkValue(inputValue:String):void    <-- Receives the control's value as a passed parameter
      {
        if(inputValue.length < 5)
          Alert.show("Are you sure there's not that much new?");
      }
      public function submitClicked():void    <-- Accesses the control's value directly
      {
        Alert.show("User says:" + whatsnew.text + " is new.");
      }
    ]]>
  </mx:Script>
  <mx:Panel title="Profile" width="400" height="400">
    <mx:Label text="What's new?"/>
```

```
    <mx:TextInput valueCommit="checkValue(event.currentTarget.text)"
            id="whatsnew"/>
    <mx:Button label="Submit" click="submitClicked()"/>
  </mx:Panel>
</mx:Application>
```

TIP Notice that `<![CDATA[ ... ]]>` was used inside the `<mx:Script>` block. This is because we're using a less than (<) character in ActionScript. In order to keep the examples short we've been omitting this declaration, but it is always a good idea to declare it in your ActionScript blocks (refer to chapter 3 for a refresher).

Clearly, there's quite a bit of flexibility, but the question is which technique is the way to go?

5.7.4 Which approach to use?

Although purists may be adamant about how to implement functions that need to work with the values of controls, there's no hard and fast rule as to which approach works best. And as with any other programming language, the more time you invest upfront making your code reusable and easier to maintain, the less it will cost you in the long run.

In the end, there is no wrong way. It is a matter of evaluating factors, such as the size of the application, its life expectancy, and other issues. For example, if the goal of the application is to be a quick, one-off project, or proof of concept, it may not warrant investing a lot of time concerning yourself with reusability issues.

5.8 Summary

Flex comes with a number of interface components known as controls. Some controls have equivalents in HTML, and many go far beyond their HTML equivalents.

For example, the `ColorPicker`, `Sliders`, and sheer variety of `Buttons` offer tremendous freedom to be creative when building interfaces and forms.

Keep in mind, unlike HTML, where a `Form` encapsulates a collection of form inputs, in Flex a form does nothing more than help lay out components. Those components don't necessarily need to be inside a `<mx:Form>` container.

There are a number of ways you can retrieve the value of user selections; you can do it in real time by leveraging events, or you can access the value as needed by using the `id` property of the component.

Capturing user input is one thing, but what about validating it? For instance, you may need to build an application that requires a user to enter a password made up of at least five characters. In the next chapter we'll take a look at how Flex validators can be used to undertake this, and much more.

6 Validating user input

This chapter covers:

- Validation versus enforcement
- Pass-through validation
- Committed-value validation
- Scripted and real-time validation

Conducting client-side validation is a key strength of Flex. From a usability point-of-view you want your application to do as much prevalidation as possible. This helps to avoid aggravating situations in which a user spends a fair amount of time filling out a large form then clicks the submit button, only to find something is wrong with the input.

This is exactly the sort of thing that prevents an application from being fluid. In the HTML environment you have JavaScript to handle some data validation. How many times have you filled out a form, only to find out the password you provided doesn't comply?

Wouldn't it be nice to have all the validation done prior to submitting a form to avoid wasting time? Flex to the rescue! Flex provides a real-time validation mechanism that unobtrusively accomplishes that goal.

In this chapter, we'll look at how Flex handles validation, and the different types of validators—including those which. verify the proper formatting of phone numbers and structure of email addresses)—it makes available. Finally, we'll put them to use, employing several different approaches.

First let's get a sense of how Flex differs from other applications in its approach to validation.

6.1 Overview of validation

Have you ever tried entering a comment on a blog engine that uses the captcha antispam mechanism? Captcha works by intentionally distorting text characters and mixing some graphical noise in the background making it almost impossible for a machine to decipher. Only human intellect can make sense of the image and read the characters. See figure 6.1.

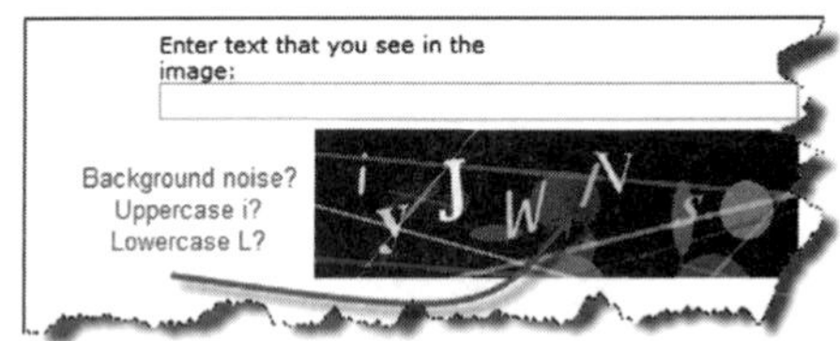

Figure 6.1 HTML-based input validation has its limits as this captcha image demonstrates how annoying this can be to users.

After you enter your comment in the blog, the application challenges you to correctly enter the letters embedded in the image. This becomes frustrating to the user as they feel they're repeating unnecessary steps and the validation takes time.

If you were to validate the user's input as she provides it, it presents immediate feedback that guides the user as to what your application is expecting. With HTML-based applications JavaScript is commonly used to provide this feedback to some degree of success; the drawback is that often the burden is on the developer to build the logic for validating the input itself and communicating problems to the user.

Flex makes validating easy with built-in components to do the hard work for you, and offers a number of approaches to invoke them. The following list explains common ways to validate user input:

- **Real-Time validation**—With every keystroke or mouse interaction the application checks to see the data is input as expected, or required.
- **Committed-Value validation**—Similar to real time, except instead of evaluating every keystroke, the application waits until the user has filled out the field completely and commits his entry (for example, by pressing Enter, or Tab to change fields).
- **Pass-Through validation**—Usually the result of hitting a submit button, this type of validation passes through all the form inputs to make sure everything is validated at once.
- **Scripted validation**—Using ActionScript you can dynamically create validators, and even reuse the same validator on multiple elements.

In all of these cases you're controlling when the validation occurs. If you're not in compliance, Flex highlights the field (in an unobtrusive way) and displays a friendly mouse-over message indicating what the problem is (figure 6.2).

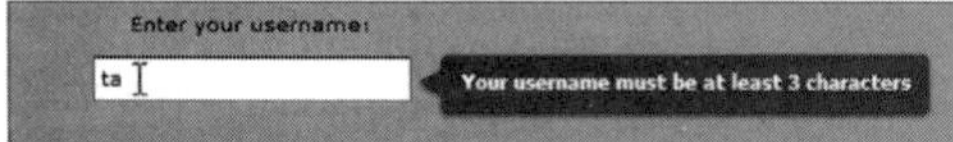

Figure 6.2 How Flex implements validation by alerting the user in a friendly manner.

Keep in mind that we're not talking about automatic enforcement. Validation is about alerting both the user and the developer that certain criteria haven't been met. The developer needs to determine how to enforce the validation by prompting the user as to what needs to be done to comply with the application's requirements.

Now, let's take a look at what Flex has to offer with its built-in validators..

6.2 Built-in validators

Flex comes with a number of built-in validators. Each is a descendent of the parent, validator class, so it carries a common set of properties, methods, and events.

The Flex team at Adobe extended the validator class to create preassembled validators that accommodate frequent validation scenarios. Each carries additional and unique properties relevant to its context.

Table 6.1 lists Flex's validators, and describes what is unique about each. Keep in mind each of them has the same capability as the parent (validator).

6.2.1 Validator

The father of them all, this serves predominantly as a template for all other derived validators. As the validator component is rudimentary, its only purpose and capability is to check if the user provided a value to a given control (for example, a form input) to which the validator is targeted.

Before we can use the validator component, let's take a look at its properties as shown in table 6.1.

Table 6.1 Key properties and functions of the validator component

Property	Type	Description
`enabled`	`Boolean`	`true` or `false`. Allows you to toggle whether or not validation is active.
`required`	`Boolean`	`true` or `false`. Is this a field in which the user is required to provide input?
`requiredFieldError`	`String`	If `required` is `true`, this is the message that is displayed to the user. If unspecified, it defaults to a general message.
`source`	`Object`	The object (for example, a `TextInput`) that you want to validate against.
`property`	`String`	The property (for example, the text property of the `TextInput`) of the source object that is checked to validate if the value provided is compliant.

Table 6.1 Key properties and functions of the validator component *(continued)*

Property	Type	Description
`listener`	`Object`	By default this is what the `source` is set to. When the property of the `source` doesn't validate, Flex will highlight the source object, but if you want a different object highlighted you can use the `listener`.
`valid`	`Function`	The name of a function you want to call if validation passes.
`invalid`	`Function`	The name of a function you want to call if validation fails.
`trigger`	`Object`	By default this is what the `source` is set to. It's the name of the object that will cause the `trigger` to occur (such as a Submit button).
`triggerEvent`	`String`	The name of the event that we want to cause validation to execute based on the trigger (for example, a Submit button's `click` event). By default it will look for the `valueCommit` event (which is usually caused by the user moving to another field by pressing the Tab key or clicking elsewhere).

Listing 6.1 shows an example of the validator component in action in its most basic form.

Listing 6.1 A basic validator in action

```
<?xml version="1.0" encoding="utf-8"?>
<mx:Application xmlns:mx="http://www.adobe.com/2006/mxml">
   <mx:Validator source="{username}" property="text" required="true" />
   <mx:Text text="Enter your username:"/>
   <mx:TextInput id="username" />
</mx:Application>
```

Listen for valueCommit events

After compiling and running the code you'll see an application similar to figure 6.3; click the input field where it asks you to enter your username.

Figure 6.3 The validator component highlights a field with a message when validation fails.

Notice that as you move your mouse over the field, the focus changes. In addition, the field border will turn red and a message pop-up should appear informing the user the field is required.

The following is a summary of what happened:

- A change of focus—which occurs by moving from one UI piece to another (whether by mouse click, the Tab key, or the Enter key)—generally causes an input control to commit its value.
- Whatever is in the text field becomes committed—in this case, the text field was empty.

- The `triggerEvent` default is `valueCommit`. The validator is set to watch for the `valueCommit` event on the `text` property.
- When the `text` property of `TextInput` is empty it causes the validation to fail, and highlights the field in red.

Because all validators inherit from the parent validator class, they all make use of this process. The difference is they can each be configured to validate based on different criteria.

For example, the `StringValidator` can evaluate the number of characters entered versus the validator's simple `Boolean` (true/false) check.

6.2.2 *StringValidator*

This is a general purpose validator, which does all that its father (the validator) does, but adds the ability to check if a `String` is too short or too long. Table 6.2 shows the additional properties that a `StringValidator` provides beyond that of the validator component.

Table 6.2 Additional properties of the `StringValidator`

Property	Type	Description
`minLength`	`Number`	The minimum number of characters required. If not set, the field is ignored.
`tooShortError`	`String`	A custom message displayed if the input string contains fewer characters than is specified in `minLength`. Optional. If not set it will default to a standard too short message.
`maxLength`	`Number`	The maximum number of characters allowed. If not set, the field is ignored.
`tooLongError`	`String`	A custom message displayed if the input string contains more characters than is specified in `maxLength`.

In listing 6.2 the `StringValidator` is used to check that the input text contains at least 3 characters, but no more than 20.

Listing 6.2 Using `StringValidator` to check if the character count is within range

```
<?xml version="1.0" encoding="utf-8"?>
<mx:Application xmlns:mx="http://www.adobe.com/2006/mxml">
   <mx:StringValidator
   source="{username}" property="text"
   minLength="3" maxLength="20"
   trigger="{submitButton}" triggerEvent="click"     <- Used to trigger validation
   tooShortError="Your username must be at least 3 characters"
   tooLongError="As if you'll remember that long of a username"
   />
   <mx:Text text="Enter your username:"/>
   <mx:TextInput id="username" />
   <mx:Button label="Submit" id="submitButton"/>
</mx:Application>
```

In figure 6.4 we use the button click to trigger the validation.

You'll notice two things were done differently:

Figure 6.4 This `StringValidator` warns the user that the minimum required number of characters has not been entered into the field.

- By default the validator (in the generic sense) is going to listen for the triggering event to occur on the component it's validating (normally it would look for the user to commit the value in the `TextInput`). This was overridden by setting the `trigger` property to point to the button instead.
- By default, the triggering event is the `valueCommit` event. But as we're using a button we want the validator to watch for the button's `click` event, rather than pressing the Enter or Tab keys.

Using validators is pretty straightforward without a whole lot of pizzazz. They're utility-oriented, and have a narrow purpose making them an easy-to-use mechanism.

Knowing there are string-based validators you would be correct in assuming there is also a counterpart number-based validator.

6.2.3 *NumberValidator*

As its name implies, the `NumberValidator` caters to evaluating numerical information. It's so versatile that you can test to verify the input value is neither too big nor too small, or perhaps that it should be an integer only, or that it doesn't contain negative numbers. The `NumberValidator` is also smart enough to recognize the separation between numbers in the thousands (for instance, 23,543,121.72). Table 6.3 lists the available properties of the `NumberValidator`.

Table 6.3 Properties that are specific to the `NumberValidator`

Property	Type	Description
`allowNegative`	`Boolean`	Are you allowing negative values? Defaults to `true`.
`negativeError`	`String`	A custom message alerting the user she has input a negative value when `allowNegative` is set to `false`. If not set this field will default to a standard message.
`domain`	`String`	`real` or `int`. Defaults to `real`. When set to `real` the values entered may be decimals.
`integerError`	`String`	A custom message alerting the user she input a decimal when `domain` is set to `int`. If not set this field will default to a standard message.

Table 6.3 Properties that are specific to the `NumberValidator` *(continued)*

Property	Type	Description
`decimalSeparator`	`String`	A non-numerical character that indicates the decimal point. This gives you the option to localize your input fields to an intended audience (for example, Europeans use a comma for the decimal separator). Defaults to a period (`.`) if not set.
`decimalPointCountError`	`String`	A customer message alerting the user he has input a number with more than one decimal point. If not set this field will default to a standard message.
`minValue`	`Number`	The minimum value required. If not set, the field is ignored.
`lowerThanMinError`	`String`	A custom message alerting the user he has input a value lower than that specified in `minValue`. Optional. If not set it will default to a standard too-low message.
`maxValue`	`Number`	The maximum value allowed. If not set, the field is ignored.
`exceedsMaxError`	`String`	A custom message alerting the user she has input a value greater than that specified in `maxValue`. Optional. If not set it will default to a standard too great message.
`precision`	`Number`	Determines how many digits to the right of the decimal point are permitted. Setting this to –1 will ignore the parameter, which is the default.
`precisionError`	`String`	A custom message alerting the user he has input more digits to the right of the decimal point than was specified in the precision parameter. Optional. If not set it will default to a standard message regarding this error.
`thousandsSeparator`	`String`	The specified character to indicate thousands separation. Default is a comma.
`separationError`	`String`	A custom message alerting the user he has used a different character to indicate thousands separation. Optional. If not set it will default to a standard message regarding this error.

With all the properties that are available, this is a very flexible validator. In listing 6.3 we put it to work by making sure the value of the number entered by a user falls within the range of 5 and 110, and the number is an integer.

Listing 6.3 NumberValidator used to check a value and if the number is an integer

```
<?xml version="1.0" encoding="utf-8"?>
<mx:Application xmlns:mx="http://www.adobe.com/2006/mxml">
  <mx:NumberValidator
    source="{age}" property="text" allowNegative="false"
    negativeError="I highly doubt you're that young!"
    minValue="5" maxValue="110" domain="int"
    trigger="{submitButton}" triggerEvent="click"/>
    <mx:Text text="Enter your age:"/>
    <mx:TextInput id="age" />
    <mx:Button label="Submit" id="submitButton"/>
</mx:Application>
```

Figure 6.5 shows the results of entering a negative number; you should get a warning that the input provided is unacceptable.

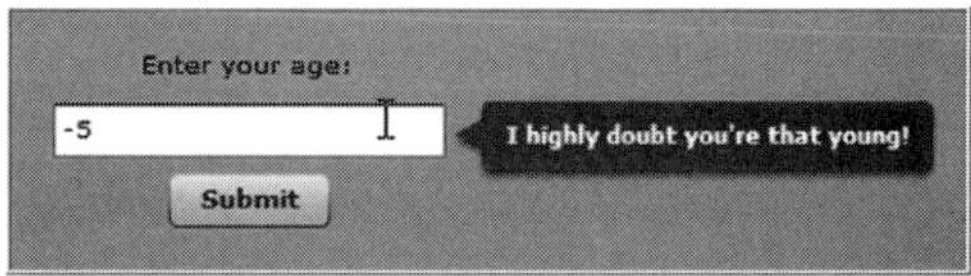

Figure 6.5 NumberValidator used to check if a user has typed in a realistic age.

The allowNegative attribute is redundant in the previous example. You can use it with no adverse effects; it would only indicate to the user (as shown in figure 6.5) that a negative number is not allowed. Because we defined a minimum value, the user would have already been warned.

We have shown you how to validate strings and numbers. The next most popular components to validate are dates.

6.2.4 DateValidator

You guessed it! This helps you work with entries designed to receive calendar data. A neat feature of the DateValidator is it accepts three separate input controls that store the year, month, and day (unlike other validators in which you target a single source).

You have the option of using the standard single source (for example, a TextInput) that will store the number in the format 08/21/85. Table 6.4 lists the properties of a DateValidator when using the single-source approach. If you do want the date captured in separate fields, look at table 6.5 which lists the additional required properties.

Table 6.4 Basic properties of a DateValidator

Property	Type	Description
allowedFormatChars	String	A series of characters allowed in the date to separate day, month, and year. For example, / . will allow for "12/31/2008" and "12.31.2008". Defaults to /\- ..
invalidCharError	String	The message displayed when characters in the date don't match those specified in allowedFormatChars.

Table 6.4 Basic properties of a `DateValidator` *(continued)*

Property	Type	Description
`inputFormat`	`String`	A `String` defining the date format, or the order in which day, month, and year will appear. For example, "mm/dd/yyyy", "yyyy/mm/dd", and so on. The enforcement of delineation is still determined by `allowedFormatChars`.
`formatError`	`String`	The message displayed when the date entered doesn't match the format allowed by `inputFormat`.
`validateAsString`	`Boolean`	`true` or `false`. Treat the source as a free-form text field? This defaults to `true`. If set to `false` it assumes the source property is a `Date` object (a `DateField` control).

If you choose to store your date in three separate fields, table 6.5 presents the ad ditional properties you'll need to validate them as a whole.

Table 6.5 Multifield `DateValidator` properties

Property	Type	Description
`daySource`	`Object`	The object (the name specified in the `id` property of a `TextInput` control) against which you want to validate the day.
`dayProperty`	`String`	The property (the `text` property of the `TextInput`) of the `daySource` object that is checked to validate if the value provided is compliant. Defaults to the `text` property.
`dayListener`	`Object`	By default this is what the `daySource` is set to. When the `dayProperty` of the `daySource` doesn't validate, Flex will highlight the `daySource` object, but if you want a different object highlighted you can use the `dayListener`.
`wrongDayError`	`String`	The message displayed when the number entered for the day isn't a day in the given month. Optional. If not set will display a default message.
`monthSource`	`Object`	The object (the name specified in the `id` property of a `TextInput` control) against which you want to validate the month.
`monthProperty`	`String`	The property (the `text` property of the `TextInput`) of the `monthSource` object that is checked to validate if the value provided is compliant. Defaults to the `text` property.
`monthListener`	`Object`	By default this is what the `monthSource` is set to. When the `monthProperty` of the `monthSource` doesn't validate, Flex will highlight the `monthSource` object, but if you want a different object highlighted you can use the `monthListener`.

Table 6.5 Multifield `DateValidator` properties *(continued)*

Property	Type	Description
`wrongMonthError`	`String`	The message displayed when the number entered isn't between 1 and 12. Optional. If not set will display a default message.
`yearSource`	`Object`	The object (for example, the name specified in the `id` property of a `TextInput` control) that you want to validate the year against.
`yearProperty`	`String`	The property (the text property of the `TextInput`) of the `yearSource` object that is checked to validate if the value provided is compliant. Defaults to the `text` property.
`yearListener`	`Object`	By default this is what the `yearSource` is set to. When the `yearProperty` of the `yearSource` doesn't validate, Flex will highlight the `yearSource` object. If you want a different object highlighted you can use the `yearListener`.
`wrongYearError`	`String`	The message displayed when the number entered isn't between 0 and 9999. Optional. If not set will display a default message.

To demonstrate using a single source `DateValidator`, listing 6.4 checks a `TextInput` to see if what's been entered is a valid date.

Listing 6.4 Using the `DateValidator` to validate a single source input

```
<?xml version="1.0" encoding="utf-8"?>
<mx:Application xmlns:mx="http://www.adobe.com/2006/mxml">
   <mx:DateValidator
     source="{birthday}" property="text" inputFormat="mm/dd/yyyy"
     allowedFormatChars="/"
     trigger="{submitButton}" triggerEvent="click"/>
   <mx:Text text="Enter your birth date:"/>
   <mx:TextInput id="birthday" />
   <mx:Button label="Submit" id="submitButton"/>
</mx:Application>
```

In figure 6.6 you can see the `DateValidator` responds because December does not have 39 days. It even points out to the user where the error lies. We take this example a bit further in listing 6.5 by splitting the date into separate fields using the advanced properties.

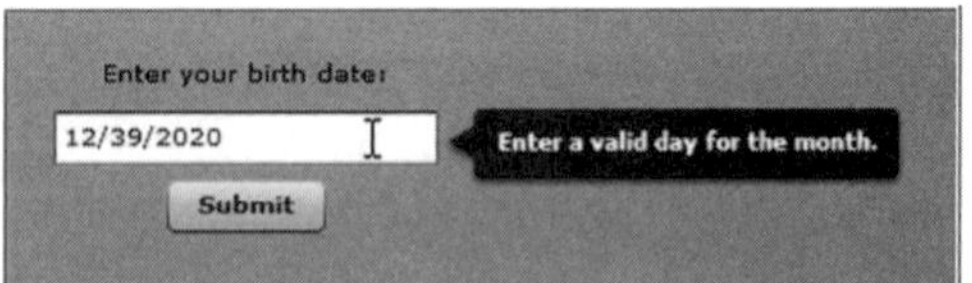

Figure 6.6 `DateValidator` doesn't like the date entered.

Listing 6.5 Advanced properties example

```
<?xml version="1.0" encoding="utf-8"?>
<mx:Application xmlns:mx="http://www.adobe.com/2006/mxml"
   layout="horizontal">
   <mx:DateValidator
```

```
    monthSource="{month}" monthProperty="value"
    daySource="{day}" dayProperty="value"
    yearSource="{year}" yearProperty="text"
    trigger="{submitButton}" triggerEvent="click"/>
  <mx:Text text="Month:"/>
  <mx:NumericStepper id="month" />
  <mx:Text text="Day:"/>
  <mx:NumericStepper id="day" />1
  <mx:Text text="Year:"/>
  <mx:TextInput id="year"/>
  <mx:Button label="Submit" id="submitButton"/>
</mx:Application>
```

Identifying a date split across multiple inputs

Let's put this to the test by entering all three sections—the day, month, and year—of the date. This time, enter a bogus date as shown in figure 6.7. A pop-up will prompt you to fix the problem.

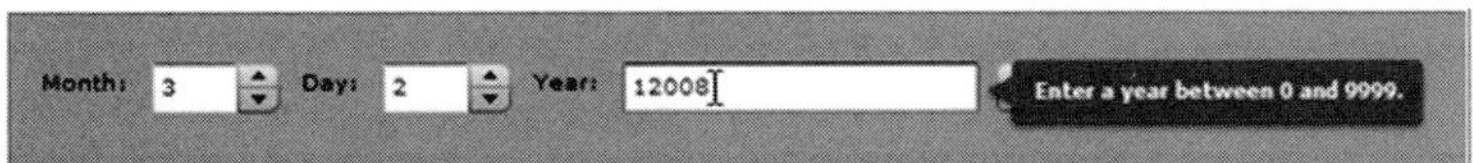

Figure 6.7 A `DateValidator` can be used to validate the separate form inputs that make up the complete date.

The `DateValidator` is a convenient way to validate single text date entries, or dates that are captured in separate fields.

TIP In a real world application, you'd want to use the `DateField` or `DateChooser` controls to capture a date from the user.

Now that we've covered the basic validators, we'll look at other common use cases, starting with email validation.

6.2.5 *EmailValidator*

Verifying email addresses is a staple of any registration feature of an application, and often postvalidation is done on the server side. The `EmailValidator` is fairly thorough in its verification and checks everything from making sure you have an @ sign to verifying there is a proper domain suffix.

The only properties you can configure are error messages. The reason for this is simple: an email is an email wherever you go, with a standardized naming structure and limited variations to that structure, so there's not much you would need to prepare for to capture an address. Table 6.6 shows the properties that are unique to the `EmailValidator`.

Table 6.6 Properties of the `EmailValidator`

Property	Type	Description
`invalidCharError`	`String`	Allows you to specify an alert message to display if an email address contains an invalid character, such as a space. If not set, it will default to a standard message.
`invalidDomainError`	`String`	Allows you to specify the message to display when the domain doesn't appear correct. If not set, it will default to a standard message.
`invalidIPDomainError`	`String`	Similar to `invalidDomainError`, but used when there is an error in the IP address. If not set, it will default to a standard message.
`invalidPeriodsInDomainError`	`String`	Allows you to specify the message to display when there are periods in incorrect places within the address, (usually caused by having more than one side-by-side). If not set, it will default to a standard message.
`missingAtSignError`	`String`	Allows you to specify the message to display when the @ character is missing from the address. If not set, it will default to a standard message.
`missingPeriodInDomainError`	`String`	Allows you to specify the message to display if there is no period in the domain name. If not set, it will default to a standard message.
`missingUserName`	`String`	Allows you to specify the message to display if the user didn't specify the username portion of the email address (the part to the left of the @ sign). If not set, it will default to a standard message.
`tooManyAtSignsError`	`String`	Allows you to specify the message to display if more than one @ sign is present in the address. If not set, it will default to a standard message.

Putting this to work, listing 6.6 uses an `EmailValidator` to check if an email address is formatted properly (no spaces, special characters, missing characters, and so on).

Listing 6.6 Verifying that what is entered is a properly structured email address

```
<?xml version="1.0" encoding="utf-8"?>
<mx:Application xmlns:mx="http://www.adobe.com/2006/mxml"
  layout="horizontal">
  <mx:EmailValidator source="{email}" property="text"
   invalidCharError="You've got some funky characters in that Email"
   trigger="{submitButton}" triggerEvent="click"/>
  <mx:Text text="Email:"/>
  <mx:TextInput id="email"/>
  <mx:Button label="Submit" id="submitButton"/>
</mx:Application>
```

Custom warning message (annotation for the `invalidCharError` line)

After compiling and running the application, try entering an email address with some invalid characters and you should see the error message shown in figure 6.8.

Figure 6.8 The `EmailValidator` flags this address, because there is an invalid space character within it.

Prevalidating an email address in real time isn't something that's done too often in the web development world. The more complex the validation, the more developers are going to defer validating to the back-end's server-side technology.

Email prevalidation is conducted infrequently in HTML+JavaScript, but what is even more rare is validating a credit card number on the fly.

6.2.6 *CreditCardValidator*

Now we're getting into some interesting validators that you don't come across in too many programming languages. In this case we're talking about the `CreditCardValidator` which uses the *Luhn mod10* algorithm to verify if the number and credit card type supplied by the user are a match.

This validator requires two input sources:

- Credit card type (Flex supports American Express, Diners Club, Discover, MasterCard, and Visa)
- Credit card number

Table 6.7 presents the `CreditCardValidator` properties.

Table 6.7 `CreditCardValidator` properties

Property	Type	Description
`allowedFormatChars`	`String`	Characters allowed in the credit card number to use as formatting separators. Defaults to a space and dash (`-`).
`cardNumberSource`	`Object`	The object that contains the credit card number (the `id` of a `TextInput`).
`cardNumberProperty`	`Object`	The property of the `cardNumberSource` that contains the actual value of the credit card number (the `text` property of a `TextInput`).
`cardNumberListener`	`Object`	The object that will receive the result of the validation. Defaults to whatever the `cardNumberSource` is.
`cardTypeSource`	`Object`	The object that contains the credit card type (the `id` of a **`TextInput`**).
`cardTypeProperty`	`Object`	The property of the `cardTypeSource` that contains the actual value of the credit card type (the `text` property of a `TextInput`).
`cardTypeListener`	`Object`	The object that will receive the result of the validation. Defaults to whatever the `cardTypeSource` is.

Table 6.7 `CreditCardValidator` properties *(continued)*

Property	Type	Description
`invalidCharError`	`String`	Allows you to specify the message displayed when the credit card contains invalid characters. If not set, it will default to a standard message.
`invalidNumberError`	`String`	The most common message likely to be encountered. This will occur when the credit card number doesn't match the credit card type. If not set, it will default to a standard message.
`noNumError`	`String`	Allows you to specify the message displayed if the credit card number is blank. If not set, it will default to a standard message.
`noTypeError`	`String`	Allows you to specify the message displayed if the credit card type is not specified. If not set, it will default to a standard message.
`wrongLengthError`	`String`	Allows you to specify the message displayed if the number of digits input doesn't match the given credit card type. If not set, it will default to a standard message.
`wrongTypeError`	`String`	Allows you to specify the message displayed if the credit card type is unknown. If not set, it will default to a standard message.

In listing 6.7, instead of hard-coding many of the properties, we're going to allow the user to select the credit card type. Then, using data binding, update the appropriate property on the `CreditCardValidator`.

Listing 6.7 Using data binding to know which type of credit card to validate

```
<?xml version="1.0" encoding="utf-8"?>
<mx:Application xmlns:mx="http://www.adobe.com/2006/mxml"
   layout="horizontal">
  <mx:CreditCardValidator
    cardNumberSource="{cardNumber}" cardNumberProperty="text"
    cardTypeSource="{cardType}"  cardTypeProperty="selectedItem"
    trigger="{submitButton}" triggerEvent="click"/>
    <mx:ComboBox id="cardType">
      <mx:dataProvider>
      <mx:String>American Express</mx:String>
      <mx:String>Visa</mx:String>
  <mx:String>Diners Club</mx:String>
  <mx:String>Discover</mx:String>
  <mx:String>MasterCard</mx:String>
    </mx:dataProvider>
    </mx:ComboBox>
    <mx:Text text="Card Number:"/>
    <mx:TextInput id="cardNumber"/>
    <mx:Button label="Submit" id="submitButton"/>
</mx:Application>
```

Changes are passed to validator

Card type set dynamically using binding (annotation on `cardTypeSource` line)

Figure 6.9 `CreditCardValidator` **used to pair-up a credit card type and credit card number.**

Let's test this by running the application and inserting four blocks of four digits to represent a credit card number. Unless you actually typed a valid Visa number, you'll get a warning similar to that of figure 6.9.

While we're on the subject of online transactions, what about validating currencies? If your system accepts international orders, the next step would be to verify the value of currency conversions.

6.2.7 *CurrencyValidator*

If you've written applications for the international market you understand the extra effort involved to encompass the many different ways in which people around the world express the same thing.

The `CurrencyValidator` provides some relief as it's designed to help you validate an expression containing currency. It is very similar to the `NumberValidator` because it allows you to check for decimal point precision, minimum and maximum values, decimal separator, and so on. Table 6.8 describes all the available properties for `CurrencyValidator`.

Table 6.8 Properties available to the `CurrencyValidator`

Property	Type	Description
`allowNegative`	`Boolean`	Are you allowing negative values? Defaults to `true`.
`negativeError`	`String`	Allows you to specify a custom message to display if the user enters a negative value when `allowNegative` is set to `false`. If not set, this field will default to a standard error message.
`decimalSeparator`	`String`	A non-numerical character that indicates the decimal point. Defaults to a period (`.`) if not set.
`decimalPointCountError`	`String`	Allows you to specify a custom message to display if a number with more than one decimal point has been entered. If not set, this field will default to a standard message.
`minValue`	`Number`	The minimum required value. If not set, the field is ignored.
`lowerThanMinError`	`String`	Allows you to specify a custom message to display if a value lower than that specified in `minValue` has been entered. Optional. If not set it will default to a standard error message.

Table 6.8 Properties available to the `CurrencyValidator` *(continued)*

Property	Type	Description
`maxValue`	`Number`	The maximum allowed value. If not set, the field is ignored.
`exceedsMaxError`	`String`	Allows you to specify a custom message to display if a value greater than that specified in `maxValue` has been entered. This property is optional. If not set it will default to a standard error message.
`Precision`	`Number`	Determines how many digits to the right of the decimal point are allowed. Setting this to –1 will ignore the parameter, which is the default.
`precisionError`	`String`	Allows you to specify a custom message to display if there are more digits to the right of the decimal point than allowed by the precision parameter. This property is optional. If not set it will default to a standard error message.
`thousandsSeparator`	`String`	The character specified as the thousands separator. Defaults to a comma (`,`).
`separationError`	`String`	Allows you to specify a custom message to display if an invalid thousands separator is used. This property is optional. If not set it will default to a standard error message.
`alignSymbol`	`String`	Specifies the location of the currency symbol (`left` or `right`). Defaults to `left`.
`currencySymbol`	`String`	Specifies the current symbol being used. Defaults to `$`.
`currencySymbolError`	`String`	Allows you to specify a custom message to display if the currency symbol doesn't match what is defined in `currencySymbol`.
`invalidCharError`	`String`	Allows you to specify a custom message to display if an unexpected character is encountered. This property is optional. If not set it will default to a standard error message..
`invalidFormatCharsError`	`String`	Allows you to specify a custom message to display if the format of the currency doesn't match what has been defined (for example, invalid thousands separation). This property is optional. If not set it will default to a standard error message.

In listing 6.8, we'll use a `CurrencyValidator` to verify numbers only have 2 decimal places.

Listing 6.8 Using a `CurrencyValidator` to make sure money values are correct

```
<?xml version="1.0" encoding="utf-8"?>
<mx:Application xmlns:mx="http://www.adobe.com/2006/mxml">
  <mx:CurrencyValidator
   source="{income}" property="text" allowNegative="false"
   negativeError="You pay your employer?"
   precision="2" precisionError="Just 2 decimals please."     <-- Only accept 2 decimals places
   trigger="{submitButton}" triggerEvent="click"  />
  <mx:Text text="How much do you make?"/>
  <mx:TextInput id="income" />
  <mx:Button label="Submit" id="submitButton"/>
</mx:Application>
```

In figure 6.10 we see there's a problem with the amount of money entered in response to the prompt (although you may feel the error is that you don't make enough money). In this scenario the validation failed because the user entered three digits to the right of the decimal point, triggering our custom error message to pop up.

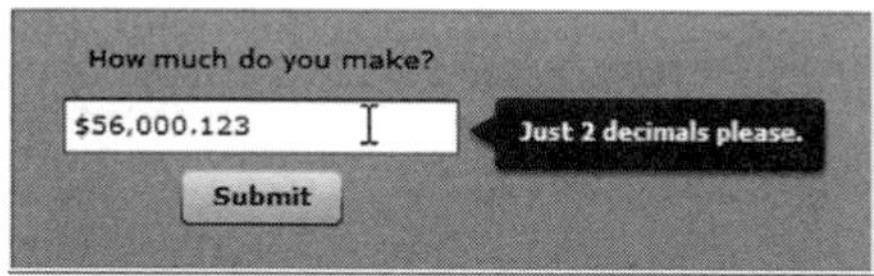

Figure 6.10 This example fails validation as the `CurrencyValidator` is configured to check for 2 decimal places only.

Similar to the `CurrencyValidator`'s role in international trade, `PhoneNumberValidator` facilitates global communication by validating international telephone numbers.

6.2.8 *PhoneNumberValidator*

This is a simple validator indeed—you either type in a proper number or you don't. It can recognize numbers originating internationally, as well as in North America.

You only need to look for two things: the number must contain at least ten digits, and any formatting characters you use must be valid. Table 6.9 lists the properties that `PhoneNumberValidator` supports.

Table 6.9 Properties of `PhoneNumberValidator`

Property	Type	Description
`allowedFormatChars`	`String`	Specifies the permitted characters with which to format the number. Defaults to `()- .+`.
`invalidCharError`	`String`	Allows you to specify a custom message to display if the number contains a character outside those listed in `allowedFormatChars`. If not set this field will default to a standard error message.
`wrongLengthError`	`String`	Allows you to specify a custom message to display if the phone number isn't at least ten digits in length. If not set, a default error message will be displayed.

In listing 6.9 we present a simple example that checks to see if the number entered validates a typical phone number.

Listing 6.9 Checking if the phone number entered is a valid format

```
<?xml version="1.0" encoding="utf-8"?>
<mx:Application xmlns:mx="http://www.adobe.com/2006/mxml">
   <mx:PhoneNumberValidator
     source="{phone}" property="text"
     trigger="{submitButton}" triggerEvent="click" />
   <mx:Text text="What number can we reach you at?"/>
   <mx:TextInput id="phone" />
   <mx:Button label="Submit" id="submitButton"/>
</mx:Application>
```

Compile and run the application, but in this case, enter both valid and invalid phone numbers to observe how the validator interprets your input, as shown in figure 6.11.

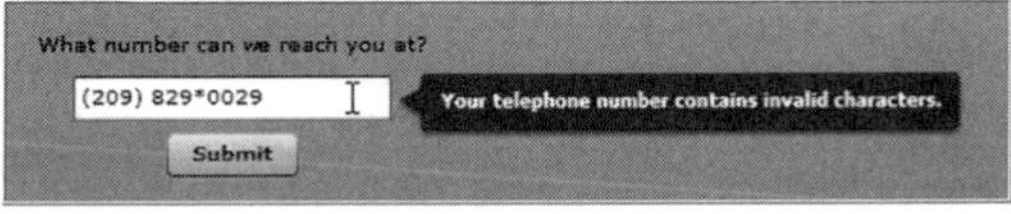

Figure 6.11 The PhoneNumberValidator is used to verify only properly formatted phone numbers pass validation.

Trying to write your own phone number validator would be quite cumbersome, if for no other reason than there are so many ways phone numbers are structured. But if you ever come across a situation in which you need to check something these validators don't support, there's always the general, all-purpose, regular expression validator at your disposal.

6.2.9 RegExpValidator

RegEx (regular expressions) goes back decades, and still its simple yet powerful language has almost no limits. The validator in this case compares a RegEx expression against a value to determine if a match has been found (and therefore is valid).

Taking a look at table 6.10 we find this validator is driven by a few properties that break into the regular expression itself, and the messages you can display if a match isn't found.

Table 6.10 Properties of the RegExpValidator

Property	Type	Description
expression	String	A RegEx pattern against which to match.
flags	String	Corresponding optional RegEx flags. g is a global search in that it will try to find all occurrences. i tells the validator to ignore a case. The m flag for multiline tells the validator to apply the ^ and $ RegEx expression to test on every line (at the start and end, as opposed to treating the value as one continuous String).
noExpressionError	String	The message displayed when the expression attribute is empty.
noMatchError	String	The message to display when the value doesn't match the RegEx expression.

For example, if you want to validate the user entered a Social Security number (SSN), we can test if the text entered matches the SSN pattern using a `RegEx` pattern as shown in listing 6.10.

Listing 6.10 `RegExpValidator` matches text against a `RegEx` pattern

```
<?xml version="1.0" encoding="utf-8"?>
<mx:Application xmlns:mx="http://www.adobe.com/2006/mxml">
  <mx:RegExpValidator source="{ssn}" property="text" flags="gmi"
    expression="\d\{3\}.\d\{2\}.\d\{4\}"
    noMatchError="Your SSN is unrecognized."
    trigger="{submitButton}" triggerEvent="click"/>
  <mx:Text text="Social Security Number:"/>
  <mx:TextInput id="ssn" />
  <mx:Button label="Submit" id="submitButton"/>
</mx:Application>
```

SSN RegEx pattern

Looking at figure 6.12, we can see the result is like any other validator, except behind the scene, the `RegExpValidator` works a little differently. This is because regular expressions are rooted in pattern matching (versus validation). You can use this ability to see how many hits were successful matches of that pattern, and where they're located in the `String`.

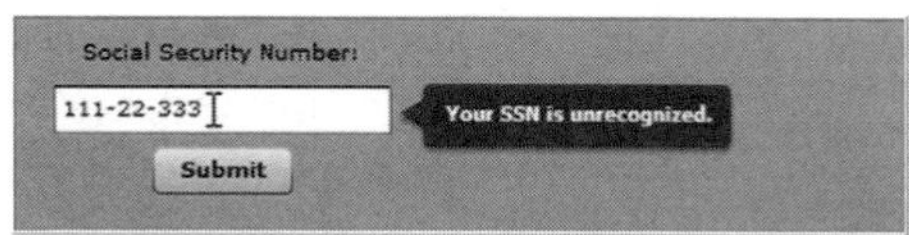

Figure 6.12 A regular expression used to validate an SSN.

You then need to employ a little ActionScript to create a validation event handler as listing 6.11 demonstrates.

Listing 6.11 Using `RegExpValidator` to find all the matches on the pattern

```
<?xml version="1.0" encoding="utf-8"?>
<mx:Application xmlns:mx="http://www.adobe.com/2006/mxml">
  <mx:Script>
    <![CDATA[
      import mx.events.ValidationResultEvent;
      import mx.validators.RegExpValidationResult;
      import mx.controls.Alert;
      private function handleValidation(event:ValidationResultEvent):void
      {
        var oneResult:RegExpValidationResult;
        for (var i:int = 0; i < event.results.length; i++)

        {
         oneResult = event.results[i];
         Alert.show("Found a match at Index:" + oneResult.matchedIndex +
               "\nOn the characters of:" + oneResult.matchedString
               ,"RegEx Results",Alert.NONMODAL);
        }
      }
    ]]>
  </mx:Script>
```

Import necessary libraries

Evaluate each match

Loop over each pattern match

Temporary variable used for convenience

Display information about the match

```
  <mx:RegExpValidator source="{test}" property="text" flags="gmi" 1
                valid="handleValidation(event)"
                expression="m[ai]n" noMatchError="I don't like it!"
                trigger="{submitButton}" triggerEvent="click"/>
    <mx:Text text="Try me:"/>
  <mx:TextInput id="test" />
  <mx:Button label="Submit" id="submitButton"/>
</mx:Application>
```

In the previous example, a couple of valid pattern matches are returned (figure 6.13), then using ActionScript we loop through all the matches.

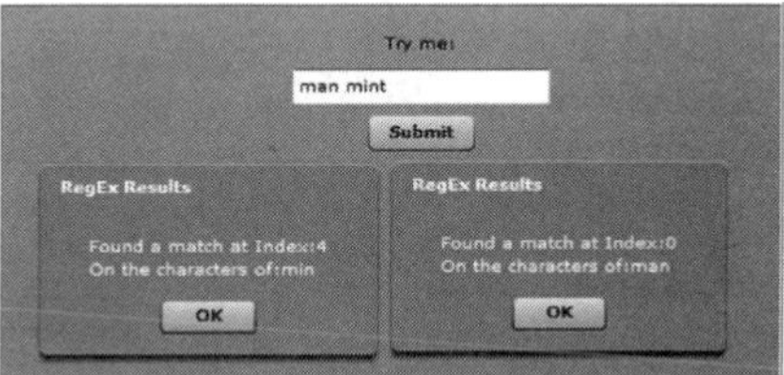

Figure 6.13 The submitted text pattern results in two matches found by the regular expression.

Regular expressions are so powerful that if you could only have one validator, `RegExpValidator` could be used to replace almost the entire set of validators offered by Flex. Although, that would require everyone to be a `RegEx` guru—which is probably not a career objective for many.

6.2.10 *SocialSecurityValidator*

In the previous example, we used a `RegExpValidator` to validate an SSN, but lo and behold, Flex happens to have a validator specifically crafted for the numerical identifier.

Operationally, this is a straightforward validator which expects a series of digits and a separator in the format of "xxx-xx-xxxx." In addition, the `SocialSecurityValidator` lets you specify the delimiter character (a dash or space by default), and it adheres to the SSN rule that the first 3 digits cannot be "000" (table 6.11).

Table 6.11 Properties of the `SocialSecurityValidator`

Property	Type	Description
`allowedFormatChars`	`String`	Valid characters that can be used as the separator for each block of digits. Defaults to allow either a space or a dash (-).
`invalidCharError`	`String`	Allows you to specify a custom message to display when a character other than what was specified in `allowedFormatChars` is used. Defaults to a standard error message if nothing is specified.
`wrongFormatError`	`String`	Allows you to specify a custom message to display if the input doesn't match 9 digits or the xxx-xx-xxxx format. If not specified, a standard error message will be displayed.
`zeroStartError`	`String`	Allows you to specify a custom message to display if an SSN starts with three zeros. If nothing is specified, a default error message will be displayed.

Compare listing 6.11, which used a regular expression, to listing 6.12, which uses the SocialSecurityValidator.

Listing 6.12 SocialSecurityValidator alerts user if SSN improperly formatted

```
<?xml version="1.0" encoding="utf-8"?>
<mx:Application xmlns:mx="http://www.adobe.com/2006/mxml">
  <mx:SocialSecurityValidator
     source="{ssn}" property="text"
     trigger="{submitButton}" triggerEvent="click" />
  <mx:Text text="Try me:"/>
  <mx:TextInput id="ssn" />
  <mx:Button label="Submit" id="submitButton"/>
</mx:Application>
```

After you compile and run the application, any input that doesn't match the expected SSN pattern will trigger an error message as shown in figure 6.14.

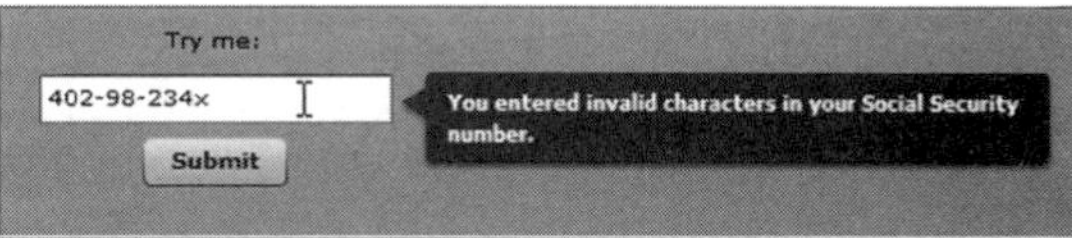

Figure 6.14 Busted! The SocialSecurityValidator detected the value entered isn't a valid SSN.

6.2.11 ZipCodeValidator

Last but not least, the ZipCodeValidator. It's a simple convenience validator that lets you check if a U.S. ZIP Code, or a Canadian postal code has been properly entered. For ZIP Codes, it accepts either the 5-digit format, or the 5+4 format (table 6.12).

Table 6.12 Properties of the ZipCodeValidator

Property	Type	Description
domain	String	Specifies to look for either US Only or US or Canada. Defaults to US Only.
allowedFormatChars	String	Valid characters allowed as the separator for each block of digits in the ZIP. Defaults to allow either a space or a dash (-).
invalidCharError	String	Allows you to specify a custom message to display if a character other than those specified in allowedFormatChars was used. Defaults to a standard error message if nothing is specified.
invalidDomainError	String	Allows you to specify a custom message to display if the domain is set to a value other than those allowed. If nothing is specified, a standard error message will be displayed.
wrongCAFormatError	String	Allows you to specify a custom message to display if a Canadian postal code isn't formatted correctly. If nothing is specified, a default error message will be displayed.
wrongLengthError	String	Allows you to specify a custom message to display if the number of characters entered doesn't match the requirement for the domain.

Table 6.12 Properties of the `ZipCodeValidator` *(continued)*

Property	Type	Description
`wrongUSFormatError`	`String`	Allows you to specify a custom message to display if the U.S. ZIP Code isn't formatted correctly. If nothing is specified, a default error message will be displayed.

Listing 6.13 shows how a `ZipCodeValidator` is used to check if the user input matches the ZIP Code format.

Listing 6.13 Trying out the `ZipCodeValidator` to test for U.S ZIP Codes

```
<?xml version="1.0" encoding="utf-8"?>
<mx:Application xmlns:mx="http://www.adobe.com/2006/mxml">
  <mx:ZipCodeValidator
    source="{zipcode}" property="text" domain="US Only"
    trigger="{submitButton}" triggerEvent="click"  />
  <mx:Text text="What's your Zip Code (U.S Only)?"/>
  <mx:TextInput id="zipcode" />
  <mx:Button label="Submit" id="submitButton"/>
</mx:Application>
```

This is another validator with which you'll want to experiment. Entering an invalid ZIP Code causes a warning to appear, such as illustrated in figure 6.15. Here, a Canadian postal code is entered when only U.S. ZIP Codes are permitted.

Figure 6.15 The `ZipCodeValidator` has been configured to check only for ZIP Codes, so this Canadian postal code fails.

Because the `ZipCodeValidator` has been configured to validate for ZIP Codes only, entering a Canadian postal code won't work (though the validator is capable of accepting both via the domain property).

That wraps up all of the available out-of-the-box Flex validators. Next we'll look at the different approaches toward employing validation.

6.3 Real-time validation

To validate in real time, or to put it another way, to catch input mistakes as they happen, requires that you "listen" for each change that occurs when data is input.

To do that, we want to monitor the `change` trigger event as illustrated in listing 6.14.

Listing 6.14 Using the `change` event we can validate in real time

```
<?xml version="1.0" encoding="utf-8"?>
<mx:Application xmlns:mx="http://www.adobe.com/2006/mxml">
  <mx:StringValidator source="{address}" minLength="5" property="text"
                trigger="{address}"
```

```
                triggerEvent="change"/>
  <mx:Text text="What's your address?"/>
  <mx:TextInput id="address"  />
</mx:Application>
```

Use change event to trigger validation

In listing 6.14, the moment the user starts typing, the field will turn red until the minimum required number of characters (five) has been entered. It's an effective way to keep the user typing until the minimum requirement has been met, but it might also be annoying. To avoid leaving a bad taste in the user's mouth, it may be more appropriate to validate when the user commits the value.

6.4 Committed value validation

This is a slight variation on real-time validation using `change`—instead of validating on every keystroke, you might prefer to validate as the user commits their value. This can occur when the Tab, Enter, or any of the arrow keys are pressed, or the mouse is clicked on another component.

In order to do this we need to change the `triggerEvent` from `change` to `valueCommit`:

```
<mx:StringValidator source="{address}" minLength="5" property="text"
        trigger="{address}" triggerEvent="valueCommit"/>
```

It adds a nice flavor of interactivity, but there may be cases where you want to delay validation yet further until a few fields are filled out. This is when you want to use pass-through validation.

6.5 Pass-through validation

Pass-through validation is the more passive approach in which you delay conducting the validation of inputs. In many web applications it's fairly common to let the user fill out the entire form, and validate before committing any values to a database.

The Submit button is the usual paradigm in such a case, and to make that happen we change the trigger and `triggerEvent` attributes so they don't default to wherever the `source` is pointed, but instead to the click event of a button instance.

In an actual form, you would have many inputs that would have their validators engage on that button click.

Listing 6.15 demonstrates how multiple validators are set up to check various `TextInput` fields, but notice how they're all configured to listen for the `click` event from the submit button.

Listing 6.15 Using a submit button to validate form fields

```
<?xml version="1.0" encoding="utf-8"?>
<mx:Application xmlns:mx="http://www.adobe.com/2006/mxml">
  <mx:StringValidator source="{username}" property="text"
      minLength="6" trigger="{submitButton}" triggerEvent="click"/>

  <mx:EmailValidator source="{email}" property="text"
      trigger="{submitButton}" triggerEvent="click"/>
```

Validators are set up for the form fields

Validate on the button click

```
    <mx:Text text="Email:"/>
    <mx:TextInput id="email"/>                       Input form fields
                                                     have validators
    <mx:Text text="Enter your username:"/>
    <mx:TextInput id="username" />

    <mx:Button label="Submit" id="submitButton"/>
  </mx:Application>
```

This and the previous examples make use of automatic events, meaning they respond without manual assistance at the triggering of the event. But you can validate a value whenever you want using scripted validation.

6.6 Scripted validation

All the validators presented thus far have an ActionScript equivalent to provide maximum convenience and control.

You would typically use the ActionScript version when you want to reuse the same validator to check many values. Those values don't need to be user input controls; you can use them to validate anything.

Listing 6.16 Using ActionScript to validate values at will

```
<?xml version="1.0" encoding="utf-8"?>
<mx:Application xmlns:mx="http://www.adobe.com/2006/mxml">
  <mx:Script>
    <![CDATA[
      import mx.validators.EmailValidator;           Import the
      import mx.validators.StringValidator;          ActionScript
      import mx.controls.Alert;                      classes we need
      import mx.events.ValidationResultEvent;

      public var emailVal:EmailValidator = new EmailValidator();       ❶
      public var stringVal:StringValidator = new StringValidator();
      public function validateForm():void    ❷
      {
        var valResult:ValidationResultEvent;
        stringVal.source = username;
        stringVal.property = "text";
        stringVal.minLength=6;
                                              ❸
        emailVal.source = email;
        emailVal.property = "text";

    valResult = emailVal.validate();    ❹
    if(valResult.type == "invalid")
    {
      Alert.show("Please fix your Email address.");
        }
    else
    {
      valResult = stringVal.validate();    ❺
      if(valResult.type == "invalid")
      {
        Alert.show("Please fix your Username.");
```

```
        }
      }
    }
  ]]>
  </mx:Script>

  <mx:Text text="Email:"/>
  <mx:TextInput id="email"/>

  <mx:Text text="Enter your username:"/>
  <mx:TextInput id="username" />

  <mx:Button label="Submit" id="submitButton" click="validateForm()"/>
</mx:Application>
```

In listing 6.16, we have two validators ❶ aimed at the two `TextInputs` ❸. When the submit button is pressed, the `validateForm()` function is invoked ❷. The email address is validated first; ❹ if it's okay, `validateForm()` moves to the next input field to check the username ❺.

We've covered the types of validators and how they can be utilized, but we have a couple of parting tips to share before we wrap up this chapter.

6.7 Validation tidbits

For the most part, validation is clear-cut, but there are a few more items to cover to round out your understanding of how validators work.

6.7.1 Does a validator always check all criteria?

What if the user types in something that fails to meet more than one of the requirements. Will all of the error messages show? No. Flex runs through its laundry list, checking one thing after another and then the moment one of the tests fail, it stops on that issue.

6.7.2 Validating what was entered vs. criteria matching

To best understand validators, keep in mind that although they can be used to verify values entered are of type—for example, what was entered is a date, or a credit card number, or telephone number—they can also be used for the more important task of determining if the value matches certain criteria, such as checking to ensure a date entered by the user is within a certain time frame.

6.7.3 Controlling what triggers validation

To keep things simple we labeled some high-level approaches to validation (for instance, real-time validation), but using the `trigger` and `triggerEvent` properties you can cause validation to initiate off any event you want.

In our examples, we used the `id` of a button for the `trigger`, and its corresponding `click triggerEvent`.

How do you know what events are available for you to use? In Flex Builder you can view components in which you're interested via the API Reference which can be accessed by clicking Help > Search, or click the component and Shift+F2.

TIP Another approach is to allocate an area within your Flex Builder workspace for a dynamic help view (see chapter 2), which will automatically display the reference.

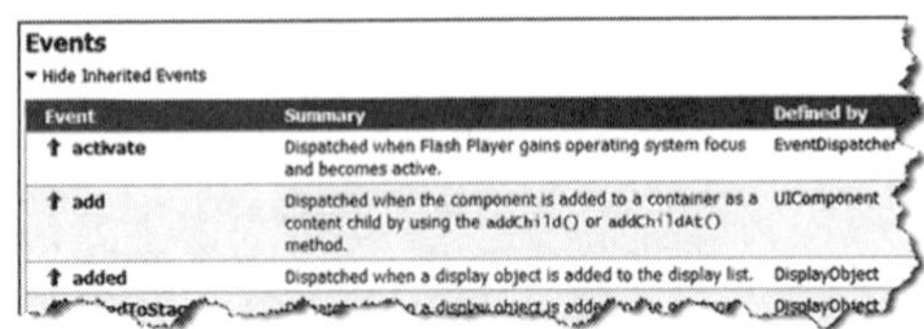

Figure 6.16 Use the API Reference to learn which events are available to use as a `triggerEvent`.

Scroll down to the section titled events. Anything you see listed (figure 6.16) is fair game. For example, you could save the user a click by using the button's `mouseOver` event as a trigger.

6.8 Summary

Validation is a valuable mechanism for providing a positive experience to your users by minimizing the amount of back-and-forth activity between their client device and a server. By validating on the client side, you add usability by reducing the time it takes to fill out a form. There's also something in it for you and your back-end systems, as you'll be relieving some of the server's workload by providing data that has been prevalidated on the front-end.

Flex comes with an impressive collection of out-of-the-box validators that range from basic text and numerical validators, to more specialized ones that can validate SSNs and phone numbers. If none of those match your needs, you have the regular expression validator that can be used to not only match a pattern, but all occurrences of that pattern in the text.

You can employ validation in different ways: in real time to check every keystroke as they're entered, as soon as the user has committed the value, or you can wait to validate all your fields at one time by triggering off the click of a submit button.

To be certain, you don't have to limit yourself to automatic events, such as clicks. You can use ActionScript to programmatically create a validator on the fly and test it against some specified data.

Having validated your fields a common thing to do then is format it nicely. In the next chapter we take a look at how this can be done using Flex's formatters.

7 Formatting data

This chapter covers:

- Formatting raw data with Flex's built-in formatters
- Types of formatters
- Real-time formatting and scripted formatting
- Dealing with formatting errors

Formatters are a class of objects which take raw data and transform it into a presentable visual format. From a usage perspective, they're comparable to validators in that similar mechanisms are employed to implement them. Formatters can be configured to function in two modes:

- *Real-time*—Formatting is conducted on the fly automatically via data binding.
- *Scripted*—Using ActionScript you can create instances of formatters explicitly when needed and process the data accordingly.

The most important thing to know is formatters are incredibly easy to use. Raw data is fed in and structured, legible content is delivered back. In this chapter we'll show you how to use the built-in formatters that come with Flex, and all the ways they can be applied.

NOTE Formatters only work with raw, unformatted data. If you use a formatter on a user-editable field, be sure any formatting code is removed from the input before attempting to process it again.

Formatters can function independently and can be used across a range of scenarios. One of their more common uses is retrieving data from a server (a database for instance) and presenting it in an organized, readable fashion. Of course, this is usually done over the internet, but we don't want to waste a lot of time in this chapter dealing with connectivity issues, so to keep things simple we'll use static XML to simulate this data.

Let's start with the built-in formatters.

7.1 Built-in formatters

Flex provides a number of built-in formatters that get you going quickly. Each is a descendent from the parent formatter class, and, by default, carries a common set of attributes, functions, and events.

As they did with validators, Adobe's Flex team extended the formatter class to create specialized tools that address common, but specific formatting scenarios through their context-relevant properties.

In the next section we'll list all the formatters, and their unique characteristics. Note that each can do what the parent (formatter) can do.

7.1.1 Formatter

Formatter is a parent object, and serves as a template for its family of more specialized formatters. As a base class, its utility is limited, but as shown in table 7.1, it does define one key function.

Table 7.1 The key function of all formatters.

Function	Description
`format`	Takes in an object that needs to be formatted and returns a `String` with the result.

Formatter also has an important property (table 7.2) that's used to determine the source of a format problem.

Table 7.2 The key property of all formatters.

Property	Type	Description
`error`	`String`	Use this property when trying to isolate a format problem. You'll know an error has occurred when the `format()` function returns an empty `String`.

Other formatters may have additional configuration properties, but the usage is the same.

7.1.2 NumberFormatter

No doubt, the most popular formatter is `NumberFormatter`, which handles numerical presentation details, such as decimal point precision and designating the character to use for thousands separation.

TIP ColdFusion provides a similar `NumberFormat()` function.

Table 7.3 presents a list of the additional properties included as part of NumberFormatter.

Table 7.3 Additional properties of NumberFormatter.

Property	Type	Description
`decimalSeparatorFrom`	`String`	Specifies the character to be used as the decimal separator for the input data. The default is a period (`.`).
`decimalSeparatorTo`	`String`	Specifies the character to be used as the decimal separator for the formatted result. The default is a period (`.`).
`precision`	`Number`	Sets the level of precision (number of decimal places) to be presented in the formatted result. The default setting (`-1`), instructs the formatter to ignore this property and use the same precision as was used for the input .
`rounding`	`String`	Allows you to round off a decimal result. Available options are `up`, `down`, and `nearest`. The default value is `none`. Using *nearest*, the formatter will round up or down to the next full integer (whole number) based on which is closer.
`thousandsSeparatorFrom`	`String`	Specifies the character to be used as the thousands separator for the input data. The default is a comma (`,`).
`thousandsSeparatorTo`	`String`	Specifies the character to be used as the thousands separator for the formatted result. The default is a comma (`,`).
`useNegativeSign`	`Boolean`	`true` (default) or `false`. When `true`, a minus sign is used to indicate a negative value. `false` specifies the number will be displayed within parentheses (accounting style).
`useThousandsSeparator`	`Boolean`	`true` (default) or `false`. Determines if a thousands separator is to be used at all. If `true`, the thousands separator will be included in the output, represented by the character specified in the `thousandsSeparatorTo` property?

Let's create our first example by using the NumberFormatter to take in a raw number with four decimals, and reformat it to display only two decimal accuracy (figure 7.1). Listing 7.1 shows how this is done.

Weight 32.56lbs

Figure 7.1 NumberFormatter used to format this price.

Listing 7.1 Using a NumberFormatter to format a number to two decimal places

```
<?xml version="1.0"?>
<mx:Application xmlns:mx="http://www.adobe.com/2006/mxml"
  backgroundColor="white">
  <mx:XML id="myData">
    <root>
      <forsale>
        <item name="weight" value="32.5698" />     <- Raw data
      </forsale>
    </root>
  </mx:XML>
  <mx:NumberFormatter id="fmtNumber" precision="2"/>     <- Define a NumberFormatter
  <mx:Label
    text="Weight {fmtNumber.format(myData.forsale.item.@value)}lbs"/>   <- Format the raw
</mx:Application>
```

Notice the number (32.5698) was truncated, but recall from table 7.3 we can use the rounding property to round off that return value. The absence of the rounding property in listing 7.1 results in the default of no rounding. If you want the output to round up, you would override the default as follows:

```
<mx:NumberFormatter id="fmtNumber" precision="2" rounding="up"/>
```

NumberFormatter has a few additional error messages (beyond that of the generic formatter) that are specific to its context. These messages are listed in table 7.4.

Table 7.4 Error messages of NumberFormatter

Error Message	Description
Invalid Value	The value provided doesn't match what the formatter was expecting. For example, non-numeric characters were provided.
Invalid Format	A combination of parameters doesn't make sense. This can be the result of incorrect property settings, such as specifying an unsupported value for rounding.

These error messages appear in the error property of NumberFormatter, which in this case would be fmtNumber.error.

Now that we've looked at NumberFormatter, you may already be visualizing how you could use it to process dollar amounts (or any other denomination). And while you could ostensibly use it for monetary presentation, you'll find that NumberFormatter has a close sibling known as CurrencyFormatter that specializes in performing just such tasks.

7.1.3 CurrencyFormatter

Given raw numerical information, CurrencyFormatter will organize the data to present it in a recognizable monetary expression by inserting a predefined currency symbol and thousands separators, if needed.

TIP For you ColdFusion folks this is similar to DollarFormat().

CurrencyFormatter supports all the same properties as the NumberFormatter, but includes two additional currency-specific attributes, as shown in table 7.5.

Table 7.5 CurrencyFormatter's two additional properties

Property	Type	Description
alignSymbol	String	Instructs where in the output string to place the currency symbol. Options are left (default) or right.
currencySymbol	String	Specifies which currency symbol to use in the output string. The default symbol is the dollar sign ($).

Putting the CurrencyFormatter to work, we find it is nearly the same as the NumberFormatter (listing 7.2), but it automatically adds the currency symbol as shown in figure 7.2.

Laptop Price $599.99

Figure 7.2 CurrencyFormatter automatically adds the currency symbol for you.

Listing 7.2 CurrencyFormatter used to display a price

```
<?xml version="1.0"?>
<mx:Application xmlns:mx="http://www.adobe.com/2006/mxml">
  <mx:XML id="myData">
    <root>
      <forsale>
        <item name="Laptop" price="599.99" />
      </forsale>
    </root>
  </mx:XML>
  <mx:CurrencyFormatter id="fmtCurrency" precision="2"/>
  <mx:Label text="Laptop Price
    {fmtCurrency.format(myData.forsale.item.@price)}"/>
</mx:Application>
```

CurrencyFormatter also shares the same error messages with its sibling NumberFormatter. Refer to table 7.4 to review those messages.

Moving away from numbers, formatting dates is a ubiquitous requirement in almost all applications. Next, we'll take a look at how to work with them using DateFormatter.

7.1.4 DateFormatter

`DateFormatter` is probably the most heavily used of all formatters. As its name implies, it provides control over how dates appears in your output. Table 7.6 presents the key property this formatter supports (in addition to the properties it inherits from the main `Formatter` class.

Table 7.6 Additional properties of `DateFormatter`

Property	Type	Description
`formatString`	`String`	A pattern mask to apply to the date.

That's it! One property that makes use of a *pattern mask*, a sequence of characters that instructs the formatter of the order in which the parts of the date are presented and how to separate each of those parts. The pattern mask, `formatString`, can take a multitude of combinations, and table 7.7 presents a summary of the characters you can use in it.

Table 7.7 Formatting characters used in `DateFormatter's formatString` property

Character	Description/Examples
`Y`	Year: `YY`—Two-digit year. Example: 08 `YYYY`—Four-digit year. Example: 2008
`M`	Month: `M`—One-digit minimum. Example: 8 and 12 `MM`—Two-digit minimum. Example: 08 and 12 `MMM`—Three-character month. Example: Aug and Dec `MMMM`—Full month name. Example: August and December
`D`	Day of Month: `D`—One-digit minimum. Example: 6 and 22 `DD`—Two-digit minimum. Example: 06 and 22
`E`	Day of Week (0 = Sunday): `E`— One-digit. Example: 0 `EE`—Padded with a zero. Example: 00 `EEE`—Three-character name. Example: Sun `EEEE`—Full name. Example: Sunday
`A`	AM/PM
`J`	Hour of the day in 24-hour format, where 0 is the first hour: `J`—One-digit minimum. Example: 4 and 18 `JJ`—Two-digit minimum. Example: 04 and 18
`H`	Hour of the day in 24-hour format, where 1 is the first hour: `H`—One-digit minimum. Example: 4 and 12 `HH`—Two-digit minimum. Example: 04 and 12

Table 7.7 Formatting characters used in `DateFormatter's formatString` property *(continued)*

Character	Description/Examples
`K`	Hour of the day in 12-hour-format, where 0 is the first hour: `K`—One-digit minimum. Example: 0 and 11 `KK`—Two-digit minimum. Example: 00 and 11
`L`	Hour of the day in 12-hour format, where 1 is the first hour: `L`—One-digit minimum. Example: 1 and 12 `LL`—Two-digit minimum. Example: 01 and 12
`N`	Minute: `N`—One-digit minimum. Example: 5 and 55 `NN`—Two-digit minimum. Example: 05 and 55
`S`	Second. `S`—One-digit minimum. Example: 2 and 56 `SS`—Two-digit minimum. Example: 02 and 56
`Misc Format Characters`	Nested between any of the other `DateFormatter` properties, you can specify any other characters you wish to use in your presentation. Common characters are commas, dashes, forward slashes, and spaces.

As with other formatters, this includes error messages as shown in table 7.8.

Table 7.8 Error messages of `DateFormatter`

Error Message	Description
`Invalid Value`	`DateFormatter` didn't recognize the data as a date. It accepts either a `Date` object, or a **`String`** object that contains a date.
`Invalid Format`	A noncompliant format was entered into `formatString`.

Although `DateFormatter's format()` function can take the date as a string, it can also take an actual date object as demonstrated in listing 7.3.

Listing 7.3 `DateFormatter` can format strings with dates and date objects

```
<?xml version="1.0"?>
<mx:Application xmlns:mx="http://www.adobe.com/2006/mxml">
  <mx:Script>
    <![CDATA[
      [Bindable]
      public var sDate:String = "12/01/08 12:42";
      [Bindable]
      public var dDate:Date = new Date("12/01/08 12:42");
    ]]>
  </mx:Script>
```

Date represented as a String to be formatted (annotation: `sDate`)

Date object to be formatted (annotation: `dDate`)

```
<mx:DateFormatter id="fmtDate" formatString="MM.DD.YY"/>

<mx:Label text="Formatting the Date as a String:
        {fmtDate.format(sDate)}" />
<mx:Label text="Formatting the Date as a Date object:
        {fmtDate.format(dDate)}" />
</mx:Application>
```

A single DateFormatter used in both cases

The formatter in this example isn't directly bound to any specific variable—an instance is created and it is reused as necessary to format both `String` and `Date` objects.

Formatting the Date as a String: 12.01.08

Formatting the Date as a Date Object: 12.01.08

Figure 7.3 A single `DateFormatter` is used to format both `Strings` and `Date` objects.

USING XML WITH THE DATEFORMATTER

Listing 7.3 used variables as the data to format, but to apply the same approach to XML data doesn't return the expected results, as listing 7.4 shows.

Listing 7.4 You would think this works, but it doesn't

```
<mx:XML id="myData">
  <root>
    <info>
      <item lastvisit="12/01/08 12:42"/>
    </info>
  </root>
</mx:XML>

<mx:DateFormatter id="fmtDate" formatString="MM.DD.YY"/>
<mx:Label text="{fmtDate.format(new String(myData.info.item.@lastvisit))}"
    />
```

This doesn't work because Flex internally transforms XML into a collection of high-level objects—neither specifically a `Date` nor a `String` (which is what the format function expects).

But, this is a simple fix by wrapping a `String` around the variable as follows:

```
<mx:Label text="Last {fmtDate.format(String(myData.info.item.@lastvisit))}"
    />
```

This technique is known as *casting*, which lets you convert (cast) one type of data into another.

You'll be using the `DateFormatter` quite a bit in your Flex applications. The main thing to remember is this formatter is slightly different in that it can accept not only a textual `String`, but also a `Date` object.

Another aspect that makes the `DateFormatter` somewhat special is its `formatString` property, which offers significant control in how the date is displayed. This property is shared by `PhoneFormatter`, which we'll explore next.

7.1.5 PhoneFormatter

`PhoneFormatter` is particularly useful if you're storing phone numbers—in a database, for example—in plain digits only, but want to present them in commonly recognized forms.

In terms of its behavior, it is very similar to `DateFormatter` in that you have a `formatString` to specify the display pattern to apply to the number, and its `format()` function accepts two types of objects: a `String` and a `Number`.

Table 7.9 contains a list of the available properties supported by `PhoneFormatter`.

Table 7.9 Properties of `PhoneFormatter`

Property	Type	Description
`formatString`	`String`	A pattern to apply the phone number.
`areaCode`	`Number`	Allows you to specify an area code if a 10-digit phone number is entered. If set to `-1`, this property will be ignored. The default value is `-1`.
`areaCodeFormat`	`String`	Defines how the area should be presented. Defaults to (###).
`validPatternChars`	`String`	A list of valid characters allowed in the `formatString`. The pound sign (#), is used to indicate placement of a digit. Defaults characters are + ( ) # -.

`PhoneFormatter` properties supply a broad range of formatting flexibility. Between the default characters and those you can define explicitly you can create virtually any pattern for your output. Table 7.10 presents a few examples.

Table 7.10 Examples of patterns that can be used for the `formatString` property

Pattern	Input Data	Result
###-###-####	2099109872	209-910-9872
(###)-###-####	2099109872	(209)-910-9872
###.###.####	2099109872	209.910.9872
#-###-###-####	12099109872	1-209-910-9872
+##-########	6569362267	+65-69362267

Listing 7.5 shows a `PhoneFormatter` being used to display raw phone number digits in a common pattern. Figure 7.4 illustrates the formatted results.

Contact Phone: (201) 667-9872

Figure 7.4 A nicely formatted phone number thanks to the `PhoneFormatter`.

Listing 7.5 `PhoneFormatter` used to format raw, unformatted phone digits

```
<?xml version="1.0"?>
<mx:Application xmlns:mx="http://www.adobe.com/2006/mxml">
  <mx:XML id="myData">
    <root>
```

```
      <contactlist>
        <item name="contact" phone="2016679872" />
      </contactlist>
    </root>
  </mx:XML>
  <mx:PhoneFormatter id="fmtNumber" formatString="(###) ###-####"/>
  <mx:Label text="Contact Phone:
         {fmtNumber.format(myData.contactlist.item.@phone)}"/>
</mx:Application>
```

If you encounter any problems, be sure to refer to the `error` property of the `PhoneFormatter` to see if an issue occurred. If there is an error, it'll be one of those in table 7.11.

Table 7.11 Error messages of the `PhoneFormatter`

Error Message	Description
`Invalid Value`	This formatter accepts either a `String` or a `Number`, anything else will result in this error. In the case of a `String`, the number of characters has to match the number of characters in the `formatString`, otherwise you'll get this error.
`Invalid Format`	Indicates an error in `formatString`. This could be caused by either invalid input characters, or the area code doesn't contain three digits.

One important rule to which you need to adhere; `PhoneFormatter` expects the number of digits in your input data to match the number of pound signs you specify in the `formatString`.

7.1.6 *ZipCodeFormatter*

The `ZipCodeFormatter` is useful when formatting U.S ZIP Codes or Canadian postal codes. Although there's not a lot of formatting involved with ZIP Codes, it does give you some added convenience when dealing with 5+4 ZIP Codes, as well as when you want to separate each three-part block of the Canadian postal code.

Table 7.12 lists the properties available in `ZipCodeFormatter`.

Table 7.12 The main property of `ZipCodeFormatter`

Property	Type	Description
`formatString`	`String`	The pattern mask to apply to the ZIP or Canadian postal code. The mask you apply must be a known pattern for ZIP or postal code representation. Defaults to `#####`.

For U.S. ZIP Codes you must indicate either five pound symbols (#), or nine. Canadian postal codes must always have six.

If you defined a nine-digit format but only five digits are input, `0000` will be displayed for the additional four digits of the 5+4 portion of the ZIP Code. Conversely, if your input data contains nine digits but `ZipCodeFormatter` is expecting only five, the additional four digits of the 5+4 portion of the ZIP Code will be ignored.

Let's use the now-familiar `formatString` in listing 7.6 to format a ZIP Code with the 5+4 format. After running the example you should see something similar to figure 7.5.

ZIP Code 95376-3233

Figure 7.5 ZIP Code formatted using the `ZipCodeFormatter`.

Listing 7.6 Using the `ZipCodeFormatter` to format a 5+4 ZIP Code

```
<?xml version="1.0"?>
<mx:Application xmlns:mx="http://www.adobe.com/2006/mxml">
  <mx:XML id="myData">
    <root>
      <contacts>
        <item name="John Doe" zipcode="953763233"/>
      </contacts>
    </root>
  </mx:XML>
  <mx:ZipCodeFormatter id="fmtZip" formatString="#####-####"/>
  <mx:Label text="Zip Code
        {fmtZip.format(myData.contacts.item.@zipcode)}"/>
</mx:Application>
```

Any errors encountered are usually related to a mismatch between the amount of characters entered as input and the number of characters expected by `ZipCodeFormatter`. Table 7.13 lists those errors and their message descriptions.

Table 7.13 Error messages for the `ZipCodeFormatter`

Error Message	Description
`Invalid Value`	This can occur if the input value doesn't match the number of digits `ZipCodeFormatter` expects. In a U.S. ZIP Code only numbers are allowed, and in the case of a Canadian postal code it must have 6 six characters.
`Invalid Format`	Indicates an error in `formatString`. This could be caused by an invalid input character, or the pattern itself isn't a recognized format.

If the `ZipCodeFormatter`, or any of the other formatters we've just seen, don't meet your needs, you can always take advantage of the general purpose `SwitchSymbolFormatter`.

7.1.7 *SwitchSymbolFormatter*

`SwitchSymbolFormatter` is a generic, catch-all device for presenting data that doesn't fall neatly into Flex's predefined formatters. It stands apart from the other formatters in that it has no contextual understanding of the type of data it is manipulating, making its use somewhat limited.

This formatter is for those who want to get into advanced Flex development and create their own custom formatter (by extending it and adding additional logic, see chapter 17 for more on that). The `SwitchSymbolFormatter` is the foundation to do that.

Because of this, an MXML component version doesn't exist; but for fun we can make use of it anyway by using the ActionScript version. See table 7.14 for a list of available functions you can use.

Table 7.14 Functions of the `SwitchSymbolFormatter`

Function	Description
`SwitchSymbolFormatter`	The constructor (default function). It accepts a character value which indicates the character you're using as a placeholder for digits. Defaults to the pound symbol (#).
`formatValue`	Takes a combination of a format `String`, and a reference to a `Source` object that contains text to format. The format `String` is anything you want, but for each digit in the `Source` object there has to be a corresponding pound symbol (#), unless you specify a different digit-indicator.

It is hard to visualize what this formatter does until you see it in action. Take a look at listing 7.7, which uses a `SwitchSymbolFormatter` to process and format raw data.

Listing 7.7 Formats an eight-digit number to be split by a dash

```
<?xml version="1.0"?>
<mx:Application xmlns:mx="http://www.adobe.com/2006/mxml">
  <mx:Script>
  <![CDATA[
    import mx.formatters.SwitchSymbolFormatter;        <- We need to import the class
    public var fmtSymbol:SwitchSymbolFormatter =
                              new SwitchSymbolFormatter("#");   <- Create an instance of the formatter

    public function formatMe(rawData:String):String
    {
      return fmtSymbol.formatValue("####-####",rawData);   <- Format raw data on demand
    }
  ]]>
  </mx:Script>
  <mx:XML id="myData">
    <root>
      <workorders>
          <item name="Fix something" id="99818382" />    <- The raw data
      </workorders>
    </root>
  </mx:XML>
  <mx:Label text="Work Order: {formatMe(myData.workorders.item.@id)}"/>   <- Formatting function called to format the data
</mx:Application>
```

Because this is a high-level formatter, `SwitchSymbolFormatter` has no unique error messages.

Now let's explore different ways we can leverage the formatters we've seen so far.

Work Order: 9981-8382

Figure 7.6 The eight-digit number was formatted using a `SwitchSymbolFormatter`.

7.2 Real-time formatting

This isn't the official term for it, but it is the approach we've been using for all of the examples in this chapter thus far (except for the `SwitchSymbolFormatter`), in which the formatter's `format()` function have been invoked on the fly.

For example, this snippet will format phone numbers in real time:

```
<mx:PhoneFormatter id="fmtPhone" formatString="###-###-####"/>
<mx:Label text="Contact Phone: {fmtNumber.format("1112223333")}"/>
```

It is nothing fancy, but it is easy to use and gets the job done, but the limitation is there isn't any kind of specific business logic embedded within it. If you wanted to add custom logic as part of the process, you'll need to move on to scripted formatting.

7.3 Scripted formatting

Whether you call it scripted, or dynamic formatting, this approach involves using ActionScript to process input on a more granular level.

Although there are many variations to this approach, they all involve using a function to handle the formatting.

7.3.1 Using a function with a formatter component

In this variation we pass the value that we need to format, and receive back the formatted result from the function. The function itself makes use of an MXML formatter component that has been previously created.

Because the formatter is not tightly coupled to, or aware of, the source of the information, this approach is practical in that it makes your function more reusable. At the same time it is still fairly easy to use.

In listing 7.8 a function is invoked when formatting is necessary. It contains some custom logic to change the `formatString` on the fly.

Listing 7.8 Using ActionScript with a static formatter to format if and when needed

```
<?xml version="1.0"?>
<mx:Application xmlns:mx="http://www.adobe.com/2006/mxml">
  <mx:Script>
    <![CDATA[
      [Bindable]
      public var rawPhone:String = "2223333";        Raw data

      public function formatThis(plainText:String):String
      {
//We can add some extra business logic if we want.
//For example, changing the formatString on the fly
```

```
//depending on the size of the text.
      if(plainText.length == 7)
        fmtPhone.formatString = "###-####";
      else
        fmtPhone.formatString = "###-###-####";

      return(fmtPhone.format(plainText));
    }
  ]]>
  </mx:Script>
  <mx:PhoneFormatter id="fmtPhone"/>
  <mx:Label text="{formatThis(rawPhone)}"/>     ❶
</mx:Application>
```

Add extra business logic if we want.

From the perspective of the code that needs something to be formatted, this approach is nearly as easy as the real-time formatting method. It calls the format function, `formatThis()` ❶ as needed. But you're able to isolate your reusable logic into a function.

One limitation to this approach is you need to know what kind of formatter you're going to use at the outset. Although you could create an MXML instance of each type of formatter and access each accordingly, it would probably be easier to use the ActionScript version of a formatter to create an instance as needed.

7.3.2 *Using a function with a formatter class*

Each formatter has an ActionScript class equivalent. This affords you the option of not requiring an MXML component to be packaged along with it. This makes it easier to create a totally self-contained function that doesn't rely on the user ensuring an MXML formatter component exists (listing 7.9).

Listing 7.9 Create an instance of a `PhoneFormatter` on the fly using ActionScript

```
<?xml version="1.0"?>
<mx:Application xmlns:mx="http://www.adobe.com/2006/mxml">
  <mx:Script>
   <![CDATA[
      //import the formatters we want to use
    import mx.formatters.*

    [Bindable]
    public var rawPhone:String = "2223333";

    public function formatThis(plainText:String):String
    {
      var fmtPhone:PhoneFormatter = new PhoneFormatter();
      if(plainText.length == 7)
        fmtPhone.formatString = "###-####";
      else
        fmtPhone.formatString = "###-###-####";

      return(fmtPhone.format(plainText));
    }
]]>
  </mx:Script>
```

```
  <mx:Label text="{formatThis(rawPhone)}"/>
</mx:Application>
```

In the previous listing, we create a `PhoneFormatter` object on the fly every time the function is called. This new formatter would then be deleted when the function completes execution. With this approach there is a bit of extra overhead, so if you knew a particular formatter will be used often, it might be better to declare it once outside of the function as demonstrated in the following:

```
import mx.formatters.*
public var fmtPhone:PhoneFormatter = new PhoneFormatter();
```

The drawback here is the formatter would exist, whether you're using it or not.

Being modular, you can continue expanding this reusability. For example, you could pass `formatString` along with the `String` to be formatted (listing 7.10).

Listing 7.10 This custom formatting function also accepts a formatting pattern

```
<?xml version="1.0"?>
<mx:Application xmlns:mx="http://www.adobe.com/2006/mxml">
  <mx:Script>
    <![CDATA[
      import mx.formatters.*
      public var fmtZip:ZipCodeFormatter = new ZipCodeFormatter();

      public function formatThis(plainText:String,formatString:String):String
      {
        fmtZip.formatString = formatString;
        return(fmtZip.format(plainText));
      }
    ]]>
  </mx:Script>
  <mx:Label text="U.S Zip Code: {formatThis('95376','#####')}"/>
  <mx:Label text="Canadian Postal Code: {formatThis('K1E2X5','### ###')}"/>
</mx:Application>
```

As the output in figure 7.7 shows, using the ActionScript approach affords you extensive flexibility. You can continue innovating this way indefinitely. For example, you could invoke a different kind of formatter depending on the data type—you get the idea.

U.S ZIP Code: 95376

Canadian Postal Code: K1E 2X5

Figure 7.7 Using ActionScript, a single function was used to create a `ZipCodeFormatter` where the formatting `String` was passed as a parameter.

The last thing we need to discuss is how to deal with the possible errors you may encounter when working with formatters.

7.4 Working with formatting errors

Another benefit of using the scripted approach, is you have an opportunity to address problems. As described previously, the formatters have an `error` property, which you can use as an alert that a problem has occurred.

If all goes well the `error` property is blank, but if an issue is encountered it will be presented as an error code (either `Invalid value`, or `Invalid format`). When this occurs, the formatted value will also be set to blank as shown in listing 7.11.

Listing 7.11 Use the error property to check if a problem occurred during formatting

```
<?xml version="1.0"?>
<mx:Application xmlns:mx="http://www.adobe.com/2006/mxml">
  <mx:Script>
    <![CDATA[
      import mx.formatters.*
      public function formatThis(plainText:String):String
      {
        var fmtPhone:PhoneFormatter = new PhoneFormatter();
        var formattedString = fmtPhone.format(plainText);
        if(fmtPhone.error == "Invalid value")
        {
          mx.controls.Alert.show('The value you entered is invalid.');
        }
        else if(fmtPhone.error == "Invalid format")
        {
          mx.controls.Alert.show('The value you entered is invalid.');
        }
        return(formattedString);
      }
    ]]>
  </mx:Script>
  <mx:Label text="{formatThis('222')}"/>
</mx:Application>
```

Check the error (annotates the `if(fmtPhone.error == "Invalid value")` line)

Return an empty String if a problem occurred (annotates the `return(formattedString);` line)

When working with formatters it is always a good idea to check that `error` property soon after you invoke the `format()` function, as it gives you a chance to deal with any issues that may have occurred.

7.5 Summary

Formatters are similar to validators, with the two often being used hand-in-hand to first validate data, then format any output to be displayed.

Flex comes with a number of predefined formatters that can make your development chores easier. These Flex formatters have been specifically designed to handle data that typically comes from a back-end system, such as a database, but likely isn't in a presentable format for the user to comfortably view.

Making use of formatters can be done in a number of ways, from real-time formatting that uses a static formatter, to ActionScript-based approaches that give you the flexibility to inject custom logic.

Don't forget to check the `error` property though, as you can't guarantee that the formatter was able to successfully work with the data.

In the next chapter we move onto lists, which are a major workhorse of Flex applications. Often these lists are used to display the data results from a back-end system, and as you will see, formatters and lists are often used in conjunction with each another to carry out that task.

8 DataGrids, lists, and trees

This chapter covers:

- Using List-based components to display flat data
- Using List-based components to display hierarchical data
- Handling user interactions with List-based components
- Retrieving selected items from List-based components

`List`-based components are a powerful part of your RIA arsenal, and some consider them the workhorse of an application.

`Lists` handle the bulk of the work involved with receiving and displaying data and provide many of the conveniences users have come to expect, such as sortable columns and word wrapping.

8.1 List genealogy

As discussed in chapter 2, Flex is an object-oriented language and framework, and it is important to at least be aware of how objects are related. Any element derived

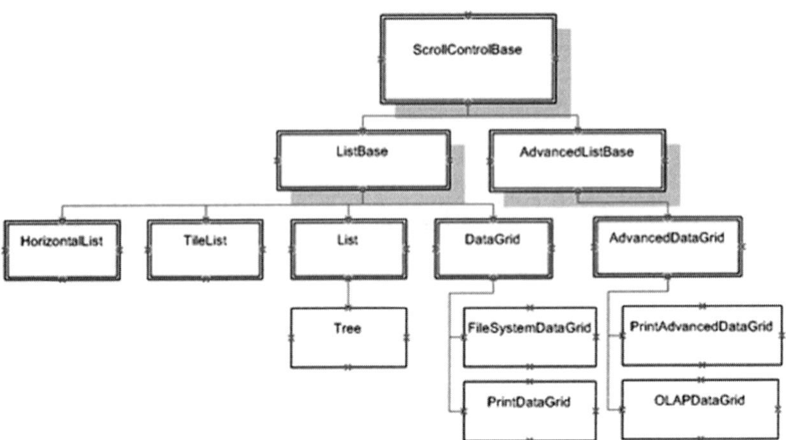

Figure 8.1 The `List`-based family of components, and how they're related

from another element inherits all of the parent element's features.

When it comes to `Lists` (Flex `List` components, not categorical lists), the top dogs are the `ListBase` and `AdvancedListBase` objects. You don't use either directly; instead, they act as a foundation for `List` objects created from them.

`ListBase` and `AdvancedListBase` provide support for attributes such as width and height, how many rows are to be displayed, and basic display of information. They also support actions such as event triggers (for example, an item being selected). The diagram in figure 8.1 demonstrates these relationships.

Looking at figure 8.1, you can see that whatever the `List` component is capable of doing, so too is the `Tree` component, through inheritance. They're all based on a master parent, so you can leverage a core list of properties.

8.1.1 ListBase and AdvancedListBase's properties

Because all `List` or `Tree` components are derived in some shape or form from `ListBase` and `AdvancedListBase`, at a minimum each will include the properties of those objects. That's quite a few properties to cover all at once, so we'll save some for later. For now, let's look at the basics, which are listed in table 8.1.

Table 8.1 Common properties that all `List`-based components support

Property	Type	Description
`columnCount`	Number	Number of columns to be displayed.
`columnWidth`	Number	Width of the columns.
`dataProvider`	Object	Object containing the data to be displayed.
`iconField`	String	Fieldname, if any, that contains a reference to an icon. By default `Lists` look for a field called icon and use it if available.

Table 8.1 Common properties that all `List`-based components support *(continued)*

Property	Type	Description
`iconFunction`	Function	Optional function name you'd like to run for each icon. This can be used for formatting the icon.
`labelField`	String	Field name that contains a value to be displayed in the column.
`labelFunction`	Function	Optional function name you can call for each record. The function determines how the label is formatted and displayed.
`lockedColumnCount`	Number	Number of columns that always remains in view as the user scrolls horizontally. Used by `DataGrid` and `AdvancedDataGrid`.
`lockedRowCount`	Number	Similar to `lockedColumnCount`, but applies to rows. Lets you specify how many rows at the top of a table are always in view as the user scrolls vertically.
`rowCount`	Number	Number of rows to display.
`rowHeight`	Number	Height of each row in pixels.
`selectable`	Boolean	Value that indicates whether you're allowing items to be selected by the user. Options are `true` (default) and `false`.
`selectedIndex`	Number	Row that has been selected (if any), if the component is selectable.
`selectedIndices`	Array	Array of all the selected indices; used when multiple selection is allowed.
`selectedItem`	Object	Link to the item that is currently selected. You can use this to access all the values pertaining to that row.
`selectedItems`	Array	Array of `selectedItems` for use when multiple selections are allowed.
`variableRowHeight`	Boolean	Value indicating whether each row can dynamically adjust its height to fit the content. Set this to `true` if you're allowing `wordWrap`. Options are `true` and `false` (default).
`wordWrap`	Boolean	Value indicating whether word wrapping is turned on. Options are `true` and `false` (default).

The list of properties is lengthy, but considering that `List`-based components are the visual workhorse of a Flex application, they must include enough configurable and flexible options to carry out their tasks.

Keep in mind that Flex is an event-driven environment, so knowing which events are available is just as important.

8.1.2 ListBase events

Just as a `ListBase` passes a minimum set of properties to its child objects, it also passes any supported events (see table 8.2). You can specify a function name or any Action-

Script code you'd like to run when that event occurs.

Table 8.2 Events that are common to `List`-based components

Property	Type	Description
`change`	Event	Triggers when the user selects a new row
`dataChange`	Event	Triggers when the data changes
`itemClick`	Event	Triggers when a user clicks a column
`itemDoubleClick`	Event	Triggers when a user double-clicks a column
`itemRollOut`	Event	Triggers when the user moves the mouse off an item
`itemRollOver`	Event	Triggers when the user moves the mouse over an item

Later in this chapter, we'll explain how to use these events; basically, they follow the standard event-trigger and event-handler paradigm.

`List`-based components would be boring if you didn't populate them with something. Let's look at where that data comes from and how you get it into a component.

8.2 The dataProvider and collections

You saw the `dataProvider` in action in chapter 5. Let's talk about it a bit more.

Most components that display a series of items are powered by a `dataProvider`, sometimes referred to as a *data-driven control*. Essentially, the procedure is as simple as giving the component the name of a variable that holds the data you want to present.

You can do this many ways. Let's look at how you can feed the `dataProvider` information.

8.2.1 Feeding the dataProvider

Variables can be in the form of lower-level objects, including an array, an `XML` object, or an `XMLList` object. But the object of choice to feed a `dataProvider` is a collection. If you elect not to use a collection, the component will automatically wrap a collection around the lower-level object anyway.

Think of a collection as a high-powered array that has built-in sorting and filtering capabilities (just for starters). It also provides a universal plug-and-play interface to any object that has a `dataProvider` by abstracting the complexities of the data-interaction process.

Another key advantage of a collection is that if its status changes, it automatically informs whoever is using it of the change and about the need to refresh the display. To do this, the collection broadcasts an event indicating what has changed. Anything that is listening for that event will respond accordingly.

The low-level objects don't support this automatic change notification; if they're altered, anything using them (to drive a display, for instance) won't be aware that a change has occurred.

8.2.2 *Types of collections*

The different types of collections all support a common set of base capabilities, which each type extends further with context-specific features:

- `ArrayCollection`—The celebrity of collections. `ArrayCollection` is based on an `Array`.
- `XMLListCollection`—A wrapper around XML and `XMLList` objects that adds the standard collection features.
- `GroupingCollection`—Used explicitly by the `AdvancedDataGrid` to group data together.

These collections are used to drive anything that supports the `dataProvider`, of which `List`-based components are a key user.

8.2.3 *Users of collections*

`List`-based components are the prime users of collections, but collections aren't limited to `Lists`. Table 8.3 lists other components fueled by their `dataProvider`.

Table 8.3 Components that can use a collection for their `dataProvider`

`AdvancedDataGrid`	`Menu`
`ButtonBar`	`MenuBar`
`Charting components including`	`OLAPDataGrid`
`Legends`	`PopUpMenuButton`
`ColorPicker`	`Repeater`
`ComboBox`	`TabBar`
`DataGrid`	`TileList`
`Datefield`	`ToggleButtonBar`
`HorizontalList`	`Tree`
`LinkBar`	
`List`	

You now know the benefits of collections and that these advanced array-like objects can be used as the `dataProvider` for many data-driven components. Next, you'll learn how to use them.

8.3 *Initializing collections*

You can use two methods to initialize a collection. The first is the MXML approach via the associated tag, shown in listing 8.1.

Listing 8.1 Initializing an `ArrayCollection` using MXML with embedded data

```
<mx:ArrayCollection id="myAC">
  <mx:Object label="Jon Hirschi" data="jhirschi"/>
  <mx:Object label="Tariq Ahmed" data="tahmed"/>
  <mx:Object label="Frank Krul" data="fkrul"/>
</mx:ArrayCollection>
```

Alternatively, you can initialize a collection purely in ActionScript by importing the class, then declaring a variable instance, as shown in listing 8.2.

Listing 8.2 This `ArrayCollection` is initialized using pure ActionScript

```
<mx:Script>
  <![CDATA[
    import mx.collections.ArrayCollection;
    public var myAC:ArrayCollection = new ArrayCollection([
      {label:"Jon Hirschi", data:"jhirschi"},
      {label:"Tariq Ahmed", data:"tahmed"},
      {label:"Frank Krul", data:"fkrul"}
    ]);
  ]]>
</mx:Script>
```

Import class so Flex knows which ArrayCollection is being referenced

NOTE Why does the ActionScript version need to be imported, but the MXML version doesn't? Look at the `<mx:Application>` tag and notice the syntax `xmlns:mx="..."`. That's MXML's way of doing something similar to the ActionScript import. We'll explain in detail how this works in chapter 17.

Let's quickly parse the ActionScript version:

- Start by assigning the variable (`myAC`) to a new instance of an `ArrayCollection`.
- The `ArrayCollection`'s *constructor* (the function that executes when an object is created) accepts an array of information to use for initial population.
- The square brackets `[ ]` are a shorthand notation for creating an array (see chapter 3), which is what that constructor expects.
- The curly braces `{ }` are a shorthand notation for creating an object. In listing 8.2, you're creating an array of objects, where each object contains two fields (`label` and `data`).
- You can have as many fields as you want.

NOTE You can assign your fields any names you desire, but by default components that use a `dataProvider` assume the field containing the display value is called `label` and the field containing data is called `data`. In the interest of convenience, it is nice to take advantage of these defaults; but if your fields are named something else, it is easy to instruct the components what field names they need to find.

In this example, the data is hardcoded into the initialization. In most real cases, you'll probably need to dynamically populate the collection after it is initialized.

8.4 Populating collections

Usually, `List`-based components are populated dynamically by pulling in data from some middle-tier application server (for example, from ColdFusion, returning a query).

In chapter 14, we'll explain that process in detail; in a nutshell, you retrieve XML data over an HTTP connection, or call a WebService function, or use a RemoteObject

(Flex's binary data-transfer mechanism), to pull in the data—for example, from ColdFusion, LCDS, AMFPHP in PHP, and so on. When that data is returned, you convert it to a collection for which your `List`-based component is listening, whereupon it displays the information accordingly.

At this point, let's keep it simple and use static mechanisms to populate your collections. In the following sections, we'll show you a few techniques.

8.4.1 List

The `List` is a lightweight component for displaying a listing of information. It is a single-column approach to presenting information.

INVOKING A LIST

You can create and populate a `List` component many ways. Let's start with listing 8.3, which demonstrates the simplest method.

Listing 8.3 Using a `List` component to display a single column of names

```
<?xml version="1.0" encoding="utf-8"?>
<mx:Application xmlns:mx="http://www.adobe.com/2006/mxml">
  <mx:List id="myFriends">
    <mx:String>Tom Ortega</mx:String>
    <mx:String>Ryan Stewart</mx:String>
    <mx:String>Abdul Qabiz</mx:String>
  </mx:List>
</mx:Application>
```

If you compile and run the application you'll see a `List` component similar to that in figure 8.2, which contains a single column list of names. Note that there's no column header and that mousing over any of the items causes the background color to change automatically.

Pretty easy, right? This example uses a shorthand approach to populate the `List`'s `dataProvider`; you'd use this approach only if you wanted to hardcode the display (which is fine for making proof-of-concepts).

Figure 8.2 A `List` component used to display names

Realistically, you wouldn't couple the data so tightly to your code. You want to separate them so your `List` component is told where to look for the information but not how that information is populated. This way, if you need to change how your collection is managed, your `List` isn't affected.

Using only MXML, let's update the example to separate the data into an `ArrayCollection`, then use that to feed the `List`'s `dataProvider`; see listing 8.4.

Listing 8.4 Using an `ArrayCollection` to drive the display of a `List` component

```
<?xml version="1.0" encoding="utf-8"?>
<mx:Application xmlns:mx="http://www.adobe.com/2006/mxml">
```

```
  <mx:ArrayCollection id="myAC">
    <mx:Object label="Tom Ortega"/>
    <mx:Object label="Ryan Stewart"/>
    <mx:Object label="Abdul Qabiz"/>
  </mx:ArrayCollection>
  <mx:List id="myFriends" dataProvider="{myAC}"/>
</mx:Application>
```

Uses binding to link dataProvider to ArrayCollection

Why does this example use an array of `<mx:Object>`s when the original `List` example used `<mx:String>`? You could use the following approach:

```
<mx:String>Tom Ortega</mx:String>
```

But a `String` holds only that one value, and in a real application you'll most likely be working with multiple fields.

Another option is shown in listing 8.5, which uses the ActionScript class of `ArrayCollection` to populate it with a group of objects.

Listing 8.5 Populating the `List` using ActionScript

```
<?xml version="1.0" encoding="utf-8"?>
<mx:Application xmlns:mx="http://www.adobe.com/2006/mxml">
<mx:Script>
  <![CDATA[
  import mx.collections.ArrayCollection;
  [Bindable]
  public var myAC:ArrayCollection  = new ArrayCollection([
                              {label:"Jon Hirschi"},
                              {label:"Tariq Ahmed"},
                              {label:"Frank Krul"}
                              ]);
  ]]>
  </mx:Script>
  <mx:List id="myFriends" dataProvider="{myAC}"/>
</mx:Application>
```

That's straightforward. But unless your data will always have a field called `label`, you need a way to identify that `label` more uniquely.

SPECIFYING A LABEL

In the real world, your data will probably be representative of the columns of the database in which it is stored. With all these columns being returned, you need to tell the `List` which field to use as the display, by specifying the `labelField`.

Listing 8.6 takes the previous example one step further by incorporating this concept and informing the `List` which column to display via the `labelField`.

Listing 8.6 Using the `labelField` to tell the `List` which column to present

```
<?xml version="1.0" encoding="utf-8"?>
<mx:Application xmlns:mx="http://www.adobe.com/2006/mxml">
<mx:Script>
 <![CDATA[
  import mx.collections.ArrayCollection;
```

```
  [Bindable]
  public var myAC:ArrayCollection  = new ArrayCollection([
       {name:"Jon Hirschi", email:"j_hirschi@domain.com",
                 url:"http://www.flexablecoder.com"},
       {name:"Tariq Ahmed", email:"t_ahmed@domain.com",
                 url:"http://www.dopejam.com"},
       {name:"Frank Krul", email:"f_krul@domain.com", url:""}
  ]);
 ]]>
</mx:Script>
<mx:List id="myFriends" dataProvider="{myAC}" labelField="name"/>
</mx:Application>
```

Now you know how to invoke the `List` component, populate it with a collection, and specify which column in the collection is to be used for display purposes. At this point, the `List` displays in a vertical format; but if you want to view it in a horizontal orientation?

8.4.2 HorizontalList

The default layout orientation for a `List` component is vertical (the content displays from top to bottom). If you're the type of person who likes to be accurate, you can refer to this as a *vertical list.* As luck would have it, the vertical list has a counterpart, known as the `HorizontalList`; it functions exactly like the default `List`, except that its orientation is ... horizontal.

Revisiting listing 8.6, let's change the `List` to a `HorizontalList` (listing 8.7) and see how it affects the output.

Listing 8.7 Switching from `List` to `HorizontalList`

```
<?xml version="1.0" encoding="utf-8"?>
<mx:Application xmlns:mx="http://www.adobe.com/2006/mxml">
<mx:Script>
 <![CDATA[
  import mx.collections.ArrayCollection;
  public var myAC:ArrayCollection  = new ArrayCollection([
       {name:"Jon Hirschi", email:"j_hirschi@domain.com",
                 url:"http://www.flexablecoder.com"},
       {name:"Tariq Ahmed", email:"t_ahmed@domain.com",
                 url:"http://www.dopejam.com"},
       {name:"Frank Krul", email:"f_krul@domain.com", url:""}
  ]);
 ]]>
</mx:Script>
<mx:HorizontalList id="myFriends" dataProvider="{myAC}" labelField="name"/>
x:Application>
```

After compiling and running the application (figure 8.3), you can see that `HorizontalList` is identical to `List`—except it does its job sideways.

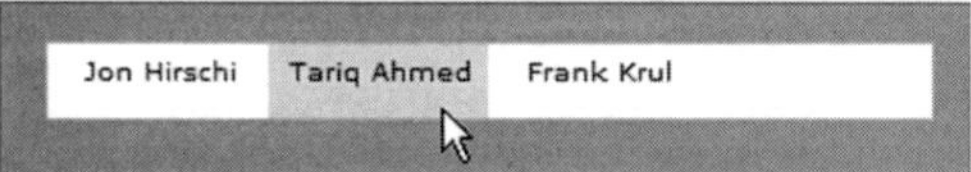

Figure 8.3 The `HorizontalList` is identical to the `List`, except it presents a horizontal layout.

A common use of this component is to present images side by side in applications such as product selectors or thumbnails in a photo viewer.

8.4.3 TileList

`TileList` is similar in concept to its sibling, `List`, but instead of a single column it creates a grid of equal-sized *tiles* that contain your display items. There are no column headers, nor anything to sort. `TileList` comes in handy if you want to display a visual catalog.

DIRECTIONS

`TileList` populates and displays its contents either horizontally (the default) or vertically. The primary difference between the two is how scrollbars are used:

- *Horizontal direction*—Horizontal direction builds from left to right, adding new rows as needed. If the grid is made up of more rows than can be displayed in a single view, a vertical scrollbar appears.
- *Vertical direction*—Vertical direction builds top to bottom, creating new columns as needed. If the grid contains more columns than can be displayed on the screen, a horizontal scrollbar appears.

If you want to control the number of columns or rows, check out the `columnCount` and `rowCount` properties, respectively.

INVOKING A TILELIST

Let's take our trusty `List` example and modify it from a `List` to a `TileList` (listing 8.8) to see how the data is presented now.

Listing 8.8 Using a `TileList`

```
<?xml version="1.0"?>
<mx:Application xmlns:mx="http://www.adobe.com/2006/mxml">
<mx:Script>
 <![CDATA[
  import mx.collections.ArrayCollection;
  [Bindable]
  public var myAC:ArrayCollection  = new ArrayCollection([
       {name:"Jon Hirschi", email:"j_hirschi@domain.com",
                url:"http://www.flexablecoder.com"},
       {name:"Tariq Ahmed", email:"t_ahmed@domain.com",
                url:"http://www.dopejam.com"},
       {name:"Frank Krul", email:"f_krul@domain.com", url:""}
  ]);
 ]]>
</mx:Script>
<mx:TileList id="myFriends" dataProvider="{myAC}" labelField="name"/>
</mx:Application>
```

Compile and run the application, and you'll see the `ArrayCollection` laid out as shown in figure 8.4.

As you can see, by default TileList lays out items left to right. To control that behavior, add the direction property, and set it to vertical (see figure 8.5)

```
<mx:TileList id="myFriends"
   direction="vertical" dataProvider="{myAC}"
   labelField="name"/>
```

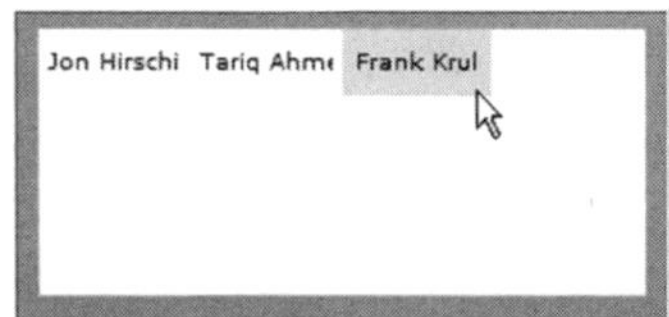

Figure 8.4 This `TileList` defaults to a horizontal direction. It adds one item after another until the end of the row, where it begins a new line.

You'll notice in both figures 8.4 and 8.5 that some of the text is cut off. This happens because the default width of the column isn't sufficient to accommodate the data you're displaying. This is easily corrected by setting the columnWidth property to a value that fits your longest item.

TILELIST VS. TILE

Hold it! Isn't this exactly like the Tile component you saw in chapter 4? Yes, it is similar; but there are basic tradeoffs to consider.

Using a TileList consumes less memory and produces a faster initial response, although it only renders the viewable portion of the data. As you scroll to bring more items into view, they must be rendered on the fly, increasing the lag time between scroll movement and a repainted window. The benefit is that from a memory perspective, the TileList is generating the minimum amount of objects needed to display on screen (versus generating all of them, regardless of whether they're on the screen). The drawback can be usability if the contents of the TileList are complex and numerous, which makes the application feel sluggish.

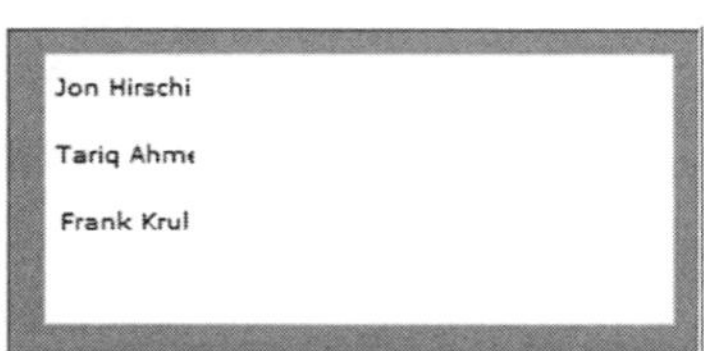

Figure 8.5 Setting the `direction` property to `vertical` instructs the `TileList` to display in a column-by-column format.

Conversely, a Tile renders everything in it all at once, whether or not it is immediately visible to the user. Rendering a lot of items can add significantly to the amount of time the user must wait for the initial window to display. On the plus side, once the render is complete, scrolling occurs with little or no lag time. Keep in mind this increase in usability comes at a considerable cost in memory.

As a general guideline, TileList is usually the better way to go.

8.4.4 DataGrid

Everyone's favorite display component, the DataGrid, is your go-to component when you need to display tabular information such as the results of a database query. Most web developers have flocked to this component to substitute for HTML-like tables. Technically, the Grid component is closer to an HTML table, but the DataGrid makes life so easy, it is addictive.

TIP In the Flex community, the DataGrid component is often referred to as *DG*.

DataGrid offers features such as sortable columns and user-interchangeable columns—the user can arrange the order of columns. It is similar to the List component but includes multiple-column formatting and column headers.

TIP For you ColdFusion folks, the CFGRID tag, using the Flash format, is based on Flex's DataGrid.

Everything we discussed about the List also applies to the DataGrid. Table 8.4 lists a couple of additional properties DataGrid supports that are specific to its multicolumn nature.

Table 8.4 Additional properties of the DataGrid component

Property	Type	Description
resizeableColumns	Boolean	Determines whether the user is allowed to resize the column. Applies to all columns. Options are true (default) and false.
sortableColumns	Boolean	Determines whether the user is allowed to sort the columns. Applies to all columns. Options are true (default) and false.

INVOKING A DATAGRID

Referring to the genealogy tree of List-based components, the DataGrid is a close sibling to List. As demonstrated in listing 8.9, invoking a DataGrid is similar to invoking a List.

Listing 8.9 Invoking a DataGrid, which is similar to invoking a List

```
<?xml version="1.0"?>
<mx:Application xmlns:mx="http://www.adobe.com/2006/mxml">
  <mx:DataGrid id="dg" width="500" height="200" >
    <mx:Object name="Tariq Ahmed" email="t_ahmed@domain.com"/>
    <mx:Object name="Jon Hirschi" email="j_hirschi@domain.com"/>
    <mx:Object name="Frank Krul" email="f_krul@domain.com"/>
  </mx:DataGrid>
</mx:Application>
```

The output of listing 8.9 (shown in figure 8.6) illustrates differences that should stand out when compared to previous examples. For starters, a DataGrid includes a header row, and is made up of multiple columns.

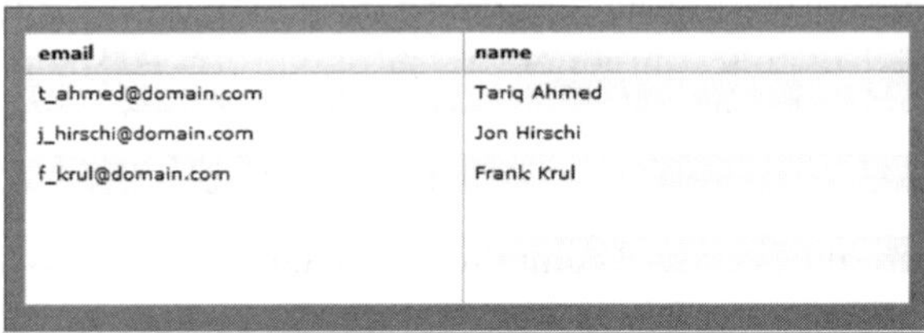

Figure 8.6 The first look at a DataGrid reveals a sortable header row and resizable columns.

Try the DataGrid's user-friendly features. Click the column titles to sort a column; click and hold the divider line between the columns and move it left and right to resize them; finally, try clicking and holding a column title and dragging to change its position.

As with a List, your dataProvider is populated externally (refer to section 8.2). Borrowing from the previous ActionScript example, you bind your dataProvider to a variable that contains the information (see listing 8.10).

Listing 8.10 Using an ArrayCollection to feed the DataGrid's dataProvider

```
<?xml version="1.0"?>
<mx:Application xmlns:mx="http://www.adobe.com/2006/mxml">
<mx:Script>
 <![CDATA[
  import mx.collections.ArrayCollection;
  [Bindable]
  public var MyAC:ArrayCollection  = new ArrayCollection([
  {name:"Jon Hirschi", email:"j_hirschi@domain.com"},
  {name:"Tariq Ahmed", email:"t_ahmed@domain.com"},
  {name:"Frank Krul",  email:"f_krul@domain.com"}
  ]);
 ]]>
</mx:Script>
<mx:DataGrid id="dg" width="500" height="150" dataProvider="{myAC}" >
  <mx:columns>
    <mx:DataGridColumn dataField="name"
                 headerText="Contact Name" width="300" />
    <mx:DataGridColumn dataField="email"
                 headerText="E-Mail" width="200"/>
  </mx:columns>
</mx:DataGrid>
</mx:Application>
```

To support and control the DataGrid's extra display capabilities, you can use yet another set of properties. In particular, you can control the ability to sort.

CONTROLLING SORTABILITY

sortableColumns is the main switch that allows you to enable or disable column sorting for the entire DataGrid. To disable sorting, set sortableColumns to false. To enable or disable sorting on a per-column basis, set the sortable property on DataGridColumn to true or false as needed.

SPECIFYING COLUMN TITLES WITH DATAGRIDCOLUMN

The DataGrid is a bright individual; without much information, it can glean the field-names as the titles for the columns.

But as demanding coders, we always want more—and in this case, we want to be able to control a lot more. To grant that control, Flex provides a tag called the DataGridColumn that works in conjunction with DataGrid.

You can use the DataGridColumn tag to control attributes such as these:

- Column width

- Column header or title
- Word-wrapping within a column
- Enabling inline editing
- Instructions for handling mouse clicks in a column

Let's give DataGridColumn a try by using it to label each column's header in a more human-consumable manner; see listing 8.11.

Listing 8.11 With `DataGridColumn` you can control attributes such as column titles

```
<?xml version="1.0"?>
<mx:Application xmlns:mx="http://www.adobe.com/2006/mxml">
  <mx:DataGrid id="dg" width="500" height="150" >
    <mx:columns>
      <mx:DataGridColumn dataField="name"
                   headerText="Contact Name" width="300"/>
      <mx:DataGridColumn dataField="email"
                   headerText="E-Mail" width="200"/>
    </mx:columns>
    <mx:Object name="Tariq Ahmed" email="t_ahmed@domain.com"/>
    <mx:Object name="Jon Hirschi" email="j_hirschi@domain.com"/>
    <mx:Object name="Frank Krul" email="f_krul@domain.com"/>
  </mx:DataGrid>
</mx:Application>
```

Defines title and width for each column

Figure 8.7 shows the results. Mission accomplished—and you use only two of the many properties DataGridColumn supports. To see the full range, check out table 8.5.

Contact Name	E-Mail
Tariq Ahmed	t_ahmed@domain.com
Jon Hirschi	j_hirschi@domain.com
Frank Krul	f_krul@domain.com

Figure 8.7 Using the `DataGridColumn`, each column now has a specified title and width.

Table 8.5 Properties of the `DataGridColumn`

Property	Type	Description
`dataField`	String	Which field in your dataset is represented by the selected column.
`headerText`	String	Column title.
`headerWordWrap`	Special	Permits word wrapping for a column title. Options are `true` (word wrap enabled) and `false` (disabled). If no value is entered, defaults to the `wordWrap` property setting in the `DataGrid` component.
`labelFunction`	Function	If a function name is specified, passes the raw data to the function and displays the text that comes back. Useful for formatting raw data.

Table 8.5 Properties of the `DataGridColumn` *(continued)*

Property	Type	Description
`minWidth`	Number	Minimum width of a column.
`resizeable`	Boolean	Value that specifies whether the user is permitted to resize columns. Options are `true` (default) and `false`.
`sortable`	Boolean	Value that specifies whether the user is permitted to sort a column. Options are `true` (default) and `false`.
`sortCompareFunction`	Function	Adds the custom logic necessary to enable `DataGrid` to sort columns based on specified criteria such as numbers, dates, and so on. By default, the `DataGrid` uses a basic string comparison.
`sortDescending`	Boolean	Default sort order. Options are `true` (descending) and `false` (default, ascending).
`visible`	Boolean	Value that specifies whether the column is displayed. Options are `true` (default) and `false`.
`width`	Number	Width of the column. Can be given as a fixed number (in pixels) or a percentage of the window in which the column appears. If no columns have their width set, `DataGrid` distributes all columns evenly; if some are set and others aren't, the remaining unallocated space is distributed evenly among the unspecified columns.
`wordWrap`	Special	Similar to `headerWordWrap`, but specific to the column's content. If you provide any value, content wraps; otherwise it defaults to the `wordWrap` property setting in `DataGrid`. If you enable `wordWrap`, be sure the `DataGrid`'s `variableRowHeight` property is set to `true`.

It seems like a lot of properties, but they come in handy because `DataGrid`s are among the most versatile and heavily used components.

As popular as the `DataGrid` and `List` are, their usefulness is specific to flat data. To present hierarchical data, you need to use `Tree`s.

8.4.5 *Tree*

The concept of a `Tree` goes back as far as visual operating systems and is something you've undoubtedly had experience with. A descendent of the `List`, a `Tree` becomes vital when you need to display some sort of hierarchical information (such as file-folder structure).

HIERARCHICAL DATA

Because of the nested nature of the display, it makes sense that your data needs to be structured accordingly. One form of data just happens to be structured as such—XML.

In chapter 15, we'll explore XML in depth; for now, we'll offer a cursory lesson. The snippet that follows introduces an XML object that works with a single root node (one main outer tag):

```
<mx:XML id="myXML">
  <friends>
    <friend name="Jon Hirschi"/>
    <friend name="Frank Krul"/>
    <friend name="Tariq Ahmed"/>
  </friends>
</mx:XML>
```

It has the advantage of being able to pull in data from a separate file by using the `source` attribute:

```
<mx:XML source="my.xml" id="myXML"/>
```

That works fine in many cases, but the `XMLList` (which is meant to store fragments of XML) has its own advantage in that it goes one step further and lets you have multiple root nodes:

```
<mx:XMLList id="myXML">
  <friends label="Friends">
    <friend label="Jon Hirschi"/>
  </friends>
  <families label="Family">
    <family label="Sabina Ahmed"/>
  </families>
</mx:XMLList>
```

Either of these will work with a `Tree`—but as mentioned in section 8.2, it is all about collections. The `XMLListCollection` wraps (literally) the standard abilities of a collection around either of these XML/`XMLList` objects. Let's wrap:

```
<mx:XMLListCollection id="myXMLCollection">
  <mx:XMLList id="myXML">
    <friends label="Friends">
      <friend label="Jon Hirschi"/>
    </friends>
    <families label="Family">
      <family label="Sabina Ahmed"/>
    </families>
  </mx:XMLList>
</mx:XMLListCollection>
```

You'll want to use collections if you're expecting the data to change, because doing so signals any component to whose `dataProvider` the collection is bound that it needs to refresh its display.

INVOKING A TREE

Creating a `Tree` is simple once you have the data that drives it. Let's start with the basics of invoking a `Tree`; listing 8.12 creates a folder structure of contacts.

Listing 8.12 Feeding the `Tree` XML data

```
<?xml version="1.0"?>
<mx:Application xmlns:mx="http://www.adobe.com/2006/mxml">
<mx:XMLListCollection id="myXMLCollection">
  <mx:XMLList id="myXML">
    <friends label="Friends">
      <friend label="Jon Hirschi"/>
      <friend label="Frank Krul"/>
      <friend label="Ryan Stewart"/>
    </friends>
    <families label="Family">
      <family label="Sabina Ahmed"/>
      <family label="Shiraz Ahmed"/>
    </families>
  </mx:XMLList>
</mx:XMLListCollection>

<mx:Tree dataProvider="{myXMLCollection}" labelField="@label"
      width="300" height="200"/>

</mx:Application>
```

Top-level nodes turn into top-level folders

Tells Tree to look for XML attribute called label to use for display

The compiled application in figure 8.8 shows the output. The top-level nodes are represented by folders, and final nodes display a file icon. Any item that has child nodes also includes an expand/collapse icon that can be toggled to show the hierarchy.

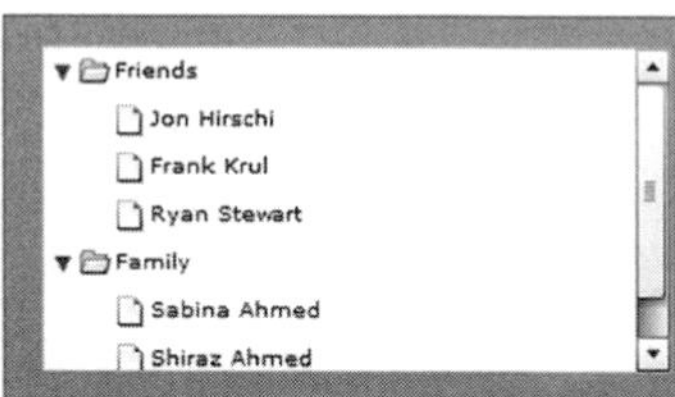

Figure 8.8 The output of a `Tree` component is reminiscent of an OS's file-folder display.

The `Tree` has no idea what field or attribute needs to be displayed. As it relates to XML data, you need to tell the `Tree` which attribute among the XML nodes contains the display field by specifying `@label` (or whatever the appropriate attribute is).

USING A SINGLE ROOT XML DOCUMENT

If you use an external XML document as a source, by definition it can have only a single root. You may think you'll waste display space with that initial folder (see figure 8.9).

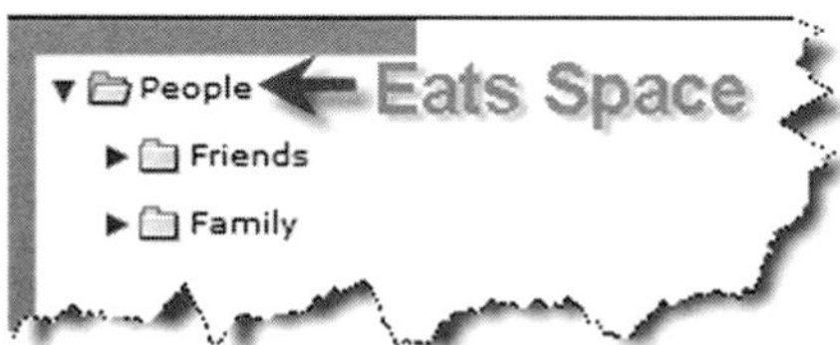

Figure 8.9 If you provide a `Tree` with an XML document for a data source, you get a single root folder at the top because there's only a single root node in the XML document.

You can achieve the same result as `XMLList`'s multiroot ability by setting the `Tree`'s `showRoot` property to `false` (see listing 8.13).

Listing 8.13 Using the `showRoot` property to start the display from the second level

```
<?xml version="1.0"?>
<mx:Application xmlns:mx="http://www.adobe.com/2006/mxml">
  <mx:XML id="myXML">
    <people label="People">
      <friends label="Friends">
        <friend label="Jon Hirschi"/>
      </friends>
      <families label="Family">
        <family label="Shiraz Ahmed"/>
      </families>
    </people>
  </mx:XML>
  <mx:Tree dataProvider="{myXML}" showRoot="false" labelField="@label"/>
</mx:Application>
```

Just like `Lists`, `Trees` aren't difficult to implement, particularly with helpful properties like `showRoot` and `labelField` to configure the display properly.

The one limitation of `Trees` is they show only that single label. What if you have multiple fields to show at each level? You need the combined strengths of a `DataGrid` and a `Tree`, which Flex conveniently offers in a component called the `AdvancedDataGrid`.

8.4.6 AdvancedDataGrid

Meet `DataGrid`'s big brother, the `AdvancedDataGrid` (ADG). This new feature (introduced with Flex 3) adds a lot of handy capabilities that could only be carried out in Flex 2 by extremely advanced developers using heavy-duty extensions on the `DataGrid`. (You may wonder why we didn't talk about the ADG immediately following the `DataGrid`. We covered the `Tree` first because the ADG combines the power of the `DataGrid` and a `Tree`.)

You get all these features:

- *Multicolumn sorting*—The DataGrid only allows single-column sorting. In the ADG, you can sort an unlimited number of columns.
- *Styling of rows and columns*—In DataGrid, you can only style the component as a whole.
- *Column groups*—This feature allows you to link multiple columns under a single header.
- *Expanded item renderer capabilities*—We don't get to this until chapter 9, but item renderers are used to add custom display logic in a cell. With the ADG, those item renderers can span an entire row (versus a single cell), and a single cell can employ multiple item renderers (the DataGrid allows only one).

With such extra capabilities, you can correctly assume that many more properties are needed to support them. Table 8.6 presents these properties and their descriptions.

Table 8.6 Additional properties that the `AdvancedDataGrid` supports

Property	Type	Description
`resizeableColumns`	Boolean	Setting that determines whether the user is allowed to resize the column. Applies to all columns. Options are `true` (default) and `false`.
`sortableColumns`	Boolean	Setting that determines whether the user is allowed to sort columns. Applies to all columns. Options are `true` (default) and `false`.
`displayDisclosureIcon`	Boolean	Disclosure icon: the drill-down toggle icon that expands and collapses the tree with which it is associated. If you turn it off, you disable the user's ability to expand/collapse the tree. Options are `true` (default) and `false`.
`displayItemsExpanded`	Boolean	Setting that displays the data fully expanded when set to `true`. Options are `true` and `false` (default).
`groupedColumns`	Array	Groups columns under a single header.
`groupIconFunction`	Function	Function to determine what icon you want to display in the `Tree` of the ADG. If you don't specify one, it uses the standard icons.
`groupLabelFunction`	Function	Similar to any other `List`'s `labelFunction`. A function you'd like to call for a basic custom display in the `Tree` of an ADG.
`groupRowHeight`	Number	Height of the row in the `Tree` group.
`itemIcons`	Object	Object that specifies which icon to use for items in the grid.
`selectedCells`	Array	Information about which cells (row and column positions) are currently selected.
`sortExpertMode`	Boolean	Setting that determines how users conduct multicolumn sorting. If `true`, the user uses the Ctrl key to execute this; otherwise she uses a sort-control box at top right in each column. Options are `true` and `false` (default).

Using these properties affords you a lot of control over the types of interactions your users are permitted. Now, let's create one of these components to see how it works.

INVOKING AN ADVANCEDDATAGRID

An ADG does whatever a `DataGrid` can do, and more. Invoking it on a basic level is as simple as putting the word `Advanced` in front of any occurrence of `DataGrid`.

As demonstrated in listing 8.14, you can easily modify one of the earlier `DataGrid` examples to use an `AdvancedDataGrid`.

Listing 8.14 Setting up the AdvancedDataGrid

```
<?xml version="1.0"?>
<mx:Application xmlns:mx="http://www.adobe.com/2006/mxml">
<mx:Script>
 <![CDATA[
  import mx.collections.ArrayCollection;
  public var myAC:ArrayCollection  = new ArrayCollection([
  {category:"Fruits", food:"Apple"},
  {category:"Fruits", food:"Avocado"},
  {category:"Vegetables",  food:"Carrot"}]);
 ]]>
</mx:Script>
<mx:AdvancedDataGrid id="adg" width="500" dataProvider="{myAC}" >
 <mx:columns>
  <mx:AdvancedDataGridColumn dataField="category"
                        headerText="Category" width="300" />
  <mx:AdvancedDataGridColumn dataField="food"
                        headerText="Food" width="200"/>
 </mx:columns>
</mx:AdvancedDataGrid>
</mx:Application>
```

Figure 8.10 shows the results after you compile and run the application. Notice that the header columns look slightly different, with each one including a small icon at the top right. This is used to indicate how each of the rows is sorted.

USING MULTICOLUMN SORTING

You can accomplish multicolumn sorting two ways, both of which are based on a property called `sortExpertMode`. This property accepts the Boolean arguments `true` and `false` to determine how the sort order is selected:

- `false` *(default)*—Click the first column by which you want to sort, and then click the top-right box in each subsequent column's header to add additional sorting. This approach is advantageous in that it is purely mouse-activated, but it forces the user to position the mouse on the small hit area.
- `true`—Click the first column by which you want to sort; then, holding down the Ctrl key, click anywhere on other column headers to add additional sorting. The advantage here is that you can click anywhere on the column header to add multicolumn sorting. The drawback is that you must hold down the Ctrl key when doing so.

You can enable or disable column sorting for the entire ADG by setting the `sortableColumns` property to `true` or `false`. If you want to set it on a column-by-column basis, set the `sortable` property on the `AdvancedDataGridColumn` to `true` or `false` as needed.

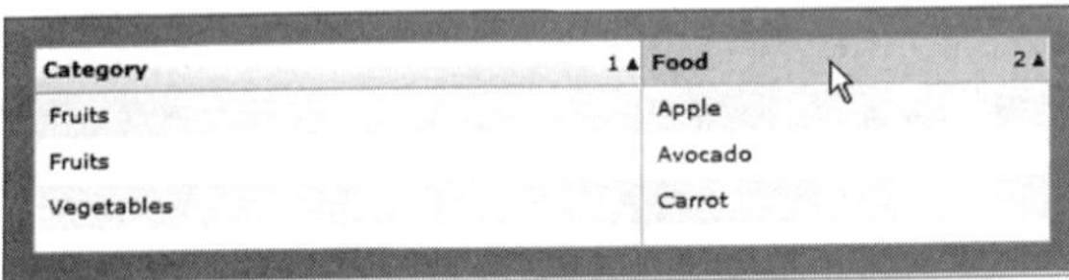

Figure 8.10 The `AdvancedDataGrid` looks similar to a `DataGrid`, with one noticeable difference: you can sort on multiple columns at the same time.

DISPLAYING HIERARCHICAL DATA

The premise behind this approach is that the data you intend to display is structured in some kind of hierarchical format. XML's structured nature works well as a source for this kind of data.

You'll use the following procedure:

- Data is created in the form of an `XMLList`.
- By default, the ADG doesn't know that your data has structure to it—even when it is XML. You need to use a middleman, the `HierarchicalData` component, to convert the `XMLList` for you.
- Setting this approach in motion, listing 8.15 implements an ADG to display hierarchical data.

Listing 8.15 Using the `AdvancedDataGrid` to show hierarchical data

```
<?xml version="1.0"?>
<mx:Application xmlns:mx="http://www.adobe.com/2006/mxml">
                                                     Raw XML data
<mx:XMLList id="myXML">
  <friends name="Friends">
    <friend name="Jon Hirschi" email="j_hirschi@domain.com"/>
    <friend name="Frank Krul" email="f_krul@domain.com"/>
    <friend name="Ryan Stewart" email="r_stewart@domain.com"/>
  </friends>
  <families name="Family">
    <family name="Zafira Ahmed" email="z_ahmed@domain.com"/>
    <family name="Shiraz Ahmed" email="s_ahmed@domain.com"/>
  </families>                                  Transforms XML data
</mx:XMLList>                                  into HierarchicalData

<mx:HierarchicalData source="{myXML}" id="myHD"/>        Creates display
                                                          using
<mx:AdvancedDataGrid dataProvider="{myHD}" width="300">   HierarchicalData
  <mx:columns>
    <mx:AdvancedDataGridColumn dataField="@name" headerText="Contacts"/>
    <mx:AdvancedDataGridColumn dataField="@email" headerText="Email"/>
  </mx:columns>
</mx:AdvancedDataGrid>

</mx:Application>
```

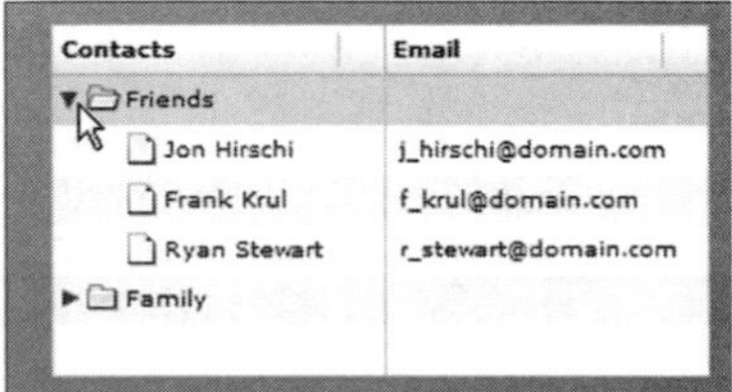

Figure 8.11 The `AdvancedDataGrid` being used to display tabular and hierarchical data

You configure the `HierarchicalData` component to bind to the `XMLList` and the `AdvancedDataGrid` in turn to bind to the `HierarchicalData`.

Figure 8.11 shows the hierarchical data is displayed similar to a `Tree` while at the same time multiple columns are displayed in `DataGrid` fashion.

USING HIERARCHICAL ARRAYCOLLECTIONS

Although XML works great for a scenario like the previous one (as long as the data is nested in this manner), it usually can be converted to work in a hierarchical environment. For example, ArrayCollections can store anything: numbers, text, and even other ArrayCollections.

As demonstrated in listing 8.16, you can use an ArrayCollection in ActionScript to accomplish the same thing.

Listing 8.16 Using nested data in an ArrayCollection to display hierarchically

```
<?xml version="1.0"?>
<mx:Application xmlns:mx="http://www.adobe.com/2006/mxml">

<mx:Script>
  <![CDATA[
  import mx.collections.ArrayCollection;
  [Bindable]
  public var myAC:ArrayCollection = new ArrayCollection([
  {
    name:'Friends',
      children:[
        {name:'Jon Hirschi',  email:'j_hirschi@domain.com'},
        {name:'Frank Krul',   email:'f_krul@domain.com'},
        {name:'Ryan Stewart', email:'r_stewart'}]
  },
  {
    name:'Family',
      children:[
        {name:'Zafira Ahmed', email:'z_ahmed@domain.com'},
        {name:'Shiraz Ahmed', email:'s_ahmed@domain.com'}]
  }]);
  ]]>
</mx:Script>

<mx:HierarchicalData source="{myAC}" id="myHD"/>

<mx:AdvancedDataGrid dataProvider="{myHD}" width="300">
  <mx:columns>
    <mx:AdvancedDataGridColumn dataField="name" headerText="Contacts"/>
    <mx:AdvancedDataGridColumn dataField="email" headerText="Email"/>
  </mx:columns>
</mx:AdvancedDataGrid>

</mx:Application>
```

ArrayCollection with nested data

Uses keyword children to delineate new data level

With ActionScript, you can create a new level of nested data by constructing a node called children. Driving hierarchical displays with hierarchical data is a natural fit, and in Flex it is possible to transform flat data into hierarchical data as well.

USING FLAT DATA FOR HIERARCHY

If you're connecting into a back-end system such as a web service, over which you have no control, the odds are the data won't be as conveniently structured as it was in the previous example. You could write a bunch of code to convert this data into a new structured format, but Flex can save you the trouble automatically.

Another new feature included in Flex 3 is the GroupingCollection component, which you can use to convert flat data into a structured format. Listing 8.17 transforms a flat tabular set of data into one that is hierarchical, by grouping the category field together into folders.

Listing 8.17 Using the GroupingCollection component

```
<?xml version="1.0"?>
<mx:Application xmlns:mx="http://www.adobe.com/2006/mxml">

<mx:Script>
  <![CDATA[
    import mx.collections.ArrayCollection;
    [Bindable]
    public var myAC:ArrayCollection = new ArrayCollection([
   {category:'Friends', name:'Jon Hirschi', email:'j_hirschi@domain.com'},
   {category:'Friends', name:'Frank Krul',  email:'f_krul@domain.com'},
   {category:'Friends', name:'Ryan Stewart', email:'r_stewart'},
   {category:'Family', name:'Zafira Ahmed', email:'z_ahmed@domain.com'},
   {category:'Family', name:'Shiraz Ahmed', email:'s_ahmed@domain.com'}]);
  ]]>
</mx:Script>

<mx:GroupingCollection id="myGC" source="{myAC}">
  <mx:Grouping>
    <mx:GroupingField name="category"/>
  </mx:Grouping>
</mx:GroupingCollection>

<mx:AdvancedDataGrid dataProvider="{myGC}" initialize="myGC.refresh()"
   width="300">
  <mx:columns>
    <mx:AdvancedDataGridColumn dataField="name" headerText="Contacts"/>
    <mx:AdvancedDataGridColumn dataField="email" headerText="Email"/>
  </mx:columns>
</mx:AdvancedDataGrid>

</mx:Application>
```

Nothing but flat data

Creates hierarchy by grouping on category column

The cool part is that the ADG's code requires no modifications; it has no idea whether the data came from a hierarchical source or a flat source (as in this case). Figure 8.12 illustrates how this tabular data was transformed to show folders on the column that was grouped on.

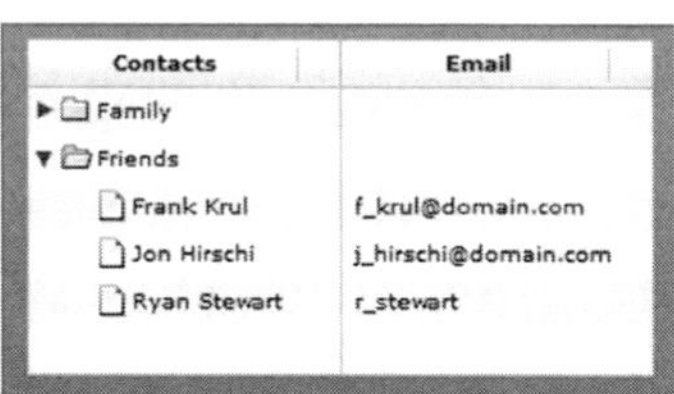

Contacts
Email
Family
Friends
Frank Krul
f_krul@domain.com
Jon Hirschi
j_hirschi@domain.com
Ryan Stewart
r_stewart

Figure 8.12 Flat tabular data was made hierarchical by grouping the contacts category.

There's one slight catch. You may have noticed the code initialize="myGC.refresh()". Remember that you must call the GroupingCollection's refresh function whenever you initially set or update properties to the GroupingCollection to trigger its processing of the data; it won't do this automatically. To be sure this happens, call the refresh function when the ADG is being initialized (out of convenience).

GROUPING COLUMNS

Another nifty thing you can do is group columns under a single header. You begin by using <mx:groupedColumns> instead of <mx:columns> to designate the columns, and then wrapping an <mx:AdvancedDataGridColumnGroup> tag around the columns you want grouped.

Let's set up the following scenario for listing 8.18: A client would like to have a tool that tracks the length of a person's commute time based on destination. You'll group the minimum and maximum commute times into a single column.

Listing 8.18 Use the groupedColumns component to group columns together

```
<?xml version="1.0"?>
<mx:Application xmlns:mx="http://www.adobe.com/2006/mxml">

<mx:Script>
  <![CDATA[
    import mx.collections.ArrayCollection;
    public var myAC:ArrayCollection = new ArrayCollection([
      {dest:'San Jose, CA',      min:'45 mins', max:'90 mins'},
      {dest:'San Francisco, CA', min:'60 mins', max:'120 mins'},
      {dest:'San Ramon, CA',     min:'25 mins', max:'60 mins'}]);
    ]]>
</mx:Script>

<mx:AdvancedDataGrid dataProvider="{myAC}" width="300">
  <mx:groupedColumns>
    <mx:AdvancedDataGridColumn dataField="dest" headerText="Destination"/>
    <mx:AdvancedDataGridColumnGroup headerText="Commute Time">
      <mx:AdvancedDataGridColumn dataField="min" headerText="Min"/>
      <mx:AdvancedDataGridColumn dataField="max" headerText="Max"/>
    </mx:AdvancedDataGridColumnGroup>
  </mx:groupedColumns>
</mx:AdvancedDataGrid>

</mx:Application>
```

Columns to be grouped

Figure 8.13 shows how the Min and Max columns were grouped using the `AdvancedDataGridColumnGroup` component to combine two regular columns under one master heading.

Up to this point, we've covered the various types of `List`-based components and how to drive their displays. The next area to explore is how to handle user interactions with them.

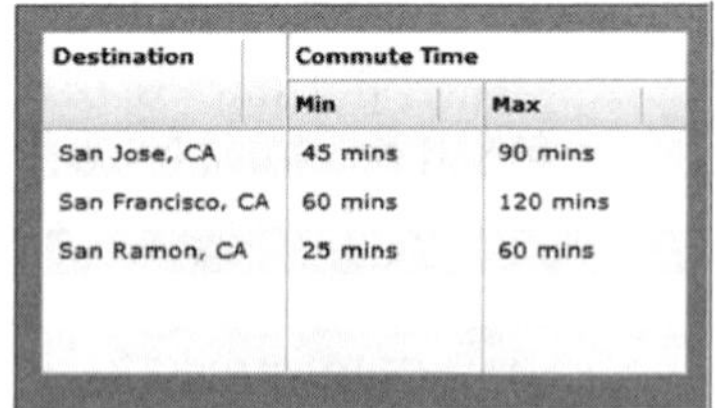

Figure 8.13 The Min and Max columns were grouped in this `AdvancedDataGrid`.

8.5 Interacting with lists

In Flex, lists—ordered sets of data, not `List` components—are versatile, and applications rarely use them strictly for display purposes. The other role lists play is furnishing the user with a means to interact with your application.

By default, when you click a cell, you're clicking the entire row. This isn't as noticeable in a `List`, because it comprises only one cell; but in a `DataGrid`, you'll notice that when you mouse over a row, the entire row becomes highlighted. This highlight is the result of an event, and as you're about to see, events are at the core of list interaction.

8.5.1 List events

Events are the driver behind Flex's interactivity; actions trigger events, and event handlers execute a response to those actions. Not all events are relevant to `Lists`, but those with which you need to concern yourself are listed in table 8.7.

Table 8.7 Table Events that can be used to handle interaction with `List`-based components

Event	Description
`click`	Occurs when the user clicks a component. This is a high-level event that is universal to many applications in Flex.
`doubleClick`	Fires when the mouse button is pressed twice.
`itemClick`	Indicates which row and column were clicked.
`change`	Occurs when the user clicks on a different row from the current selection.

Implementation of these events is similar to the techniques described in previous chapters. You can leverage them several ways. Some methods are quicker to put into use, others result in greater code reusability by decoupling the dependent logic.

8.5.2 Passing the event to a function

Listing 8.19 instructs the `DataGrid` to call some ActionScript (in this case, a function) that passes along the event object that is created as part of the process.

Listing 8.19 Handling a user interaction by passing the event object to a function

```
<?xml version="1.0"?>
<mx:Application xmlns:mx="http://www.adobe.com/2006/mxml">

<mx:Script>
 <![CDATA[
  import mx.collections.ArrayCollection;
  import mx.events.ListEvent;
  import mx.controls.Alert;

  public var myAC:ArrayCollection  = new ArrayCollection([
  {name:"Jon Hirschi", email:"j_hirschi@domain.com"},
  {name:"Frank Krul",  email:"f_krul@domain.com"}]);

  public function handleClick(evt:ListEvent):void
  {
    Alert.show("You clicked on row:" + evt.rowIndex + " and col:" +
             evt.columnIndex + "." +
               "Which is for " + evt.currentTarget.selectedItem.name);
```

```
  }
 ]]>
</mx:Script>

<mx:DataGrid id="dg" width="500" height="150" dataProvider="{myAC}"
        itemClick="handleClick(event)">
  <mx:columns>
    <mx:DataGridColumn dataField="name"
                headerText="Contact Name" width="300" />
    <mx:DataGridColumn dataField="email" headerText="E-Mail" width="200"/>
  </mx:columns>
</mx:DataGrid>

</mx:Application>
```

Figure 8.14 illustrates what happens when a row in the DataGrid is clicked. As you instructed it to do, the function displays information pertaining to the selected row—but what's particularly cool is the fact that the handleClick function doesn't know specifically which DataGrid sent the event. This is an important characteristic of a reusable function.

The DataGrid is used in this example; but you can just as easily use another component, as shown in the following snippet:

```
<mx:List dataProvider="{myAC}" labelField="name"
   itemClick="handleClick(event)"/>
```

To break it down, let's focus on this piece:

```
itemClick="handleClick(event)"
```

Here, you instruct the DataGrid to run a function called handleClick if the user triggers the itemClick event, and then to pass along the event object that is created as part of the transaction.

This function in turn accepts the event object as its parameter and accesses various properties pertaining to it. When you use this approach, the main property in which you're interested is currentTarget.selectedItem.

The currentTarget property is a reference, or pointer, to whatever item the event is related to. From an advanced perspective, it is a little more complicated than that; but from a new developer's viewpoint, it is the thing you clicked. In this case, it means currentTarget points to your DataGrid.

Going one level deeper, now that you have a reference to the DataGrid, you access the selectedItem property, which contains a reference to the data in the row with

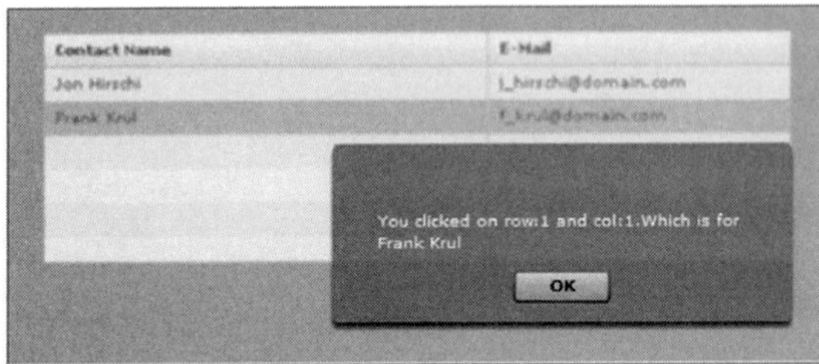

Figure 8.14 A function displaying details about the row on which a mouse click occurred

which it is associated. By continuing to drill down, you can access the specific data fields on that row:

```
evt.currentTarget.selectedItem.name
```

Mind you, you're not limited to accessing displayed data; you can access any field that is providing the data. You can do so even if you have many more fields:

```
{name:"Tariq Ahmed", email:"tariq@domain.com", domain:"www.dopejam.com"}
```

And for the moment, you're only displaying the name and email fields. You still have access to the domain field in the selectedItem:

```
evt.currentTarget.selectedItem.domain
```

Similar to selectedItem is selectedIndex. It is a number that informs you which row was clicked (0 is the first row).

8.5.3 Passing data to a function

Another approach is to pass only the event in which you're interested, versus the entire event object. This technique offers a slight advantage in that it makes the recipient function more reusable: the function doesn't need to know that the data is part of an event's payload, or need to rely on making assumptions regarding the source of the event.

In some circumstances, you may want your function to have specific knowledge about the event. But let's say you want to add a bit of abstraction. Listing 8.20 shows how you can do this.

Listing 8.20 Handling a user interaction and passing only data to a function

```
<mx:DataGrid id="dg" width="500" height="150" dataProvider="{myAC}"
          itemClick="handleClick(event.currentTarget.selectedItem)">
  <mx:columns>
    <mx:DataGridColumn dataField="name"
                 headerText="Contact Name" width="300" />
    <mx:DataGridColumn dataField="email" headerText="E-Mail" width="200"/>
  </mx:columns>
</mx:DataGrid>
```

When you click an item, your function is invoked along with a reference to the item clicked. This lets you access the various properties of the object:

```
public function handleClick(data:Object):void
{
  Alert.show("Name:" + data.name + ",Email:" + data.email);
}
```

The drawback to this approach is that the function has no reference to the component that caused the event. Without this information, the function can't carry out chores such as changing the component's color to red if a problem occurs.

8.5.4 Accessing the selected row directly

A more straightforward approach is to access the component directly. The advantage of this approach (other than it being simpler to implement) is that you can easily access any of the properties specific to that type of component (in this case, a DataGrid):

```
<mx:DataGrid id="dg" dataProvider="{myAC}" itemClick="handleClick()">
```

Notice that you don't pass anything in your itemClick handler. The function then accesses the values directly:

```
public function handleClick():void
{
  Alert.show("Name:" + dg.selectedItem.name + ", Email:" +
          dg.selectedItem.email);
}
```

It is a simple technique, but it does the job and you benefit from ease of maintenance with respect to the function—it doesn't care who called it or why it was called.

8.5.5 Binding to a selected row

This is the simplest approach. By using Flex's binding feature, you can display or store the selected item without having to use event handlers. Listing 8.21 shows how to use this technique without a function, by binding the current selection to an item that calls for the value.

Listing 8.21 Using binding to capture the selection of a List-based component

```
<mx:DataGrid id="dg" width="500" height="150" dataProvider="{myAC}">
  <mx:columns>
    <mx:DataGridColumn dataField="name"
                  headerText="Contact Name" width="300" />
    <mx:DataGridColumn dataField="email"
                  headerText="E-Mail" width="200"/>
  </mx:columns>
</mx:DataGrid>
<mx:Label text="The selected person is {dg.selectedItem.name}
   ({dg.selectedItem.email})" fontSize="16"/>
```

Figure 8.15 shows the output of this code. The information for the selected person is displayed at the bottom of the window.

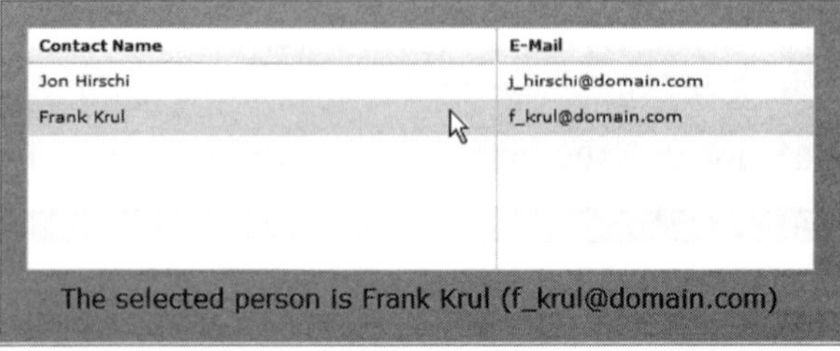

Figure 8.15 The selected person's information is displayed at the bottom using Flex's binding mechanism.

If you need nothing more than the value, binding is the easiest way to go. The drawback to this approach is that you're not adding any business logic or post-selection processing.

8.5.6 Using a different event as a trigger

As a final note to handling user interactions, we'd like to point out that these examples use the `itemClick` event, but you can use the other events mentioned just as easily. For example, if you want to use the `change` event, specify `change` instead of `itemClick`—it is that simple. You can even use both; you may want to execute some logic every time a click occurs, along with the separate logic needed to signal a move from a previously selected row.

8.6 Summary

`List`-based components are undoubtedly the visual workhorse of Flex applications. Part of this is due to lists being a common UI paradigm. At the same time, many of the Flex applications you'll build will interact with a back-end database one way or the other. Visually representing rows of data is a tailor-made job for `List`-based components.

If you have data to display, using `Lists` is the way to go. `Lists` support information ranging from simple arrays to XML for hierarchical data. Using one of the collection components/classes is the best practice because of their advanced capabilities.

Most `List`-based components are flat in nature, meaning they display content items one after the other in a sequential manner. When it comes to structured data, you can also use hierarchical-based components; the `AdvancedDataGrid` can work with both.

Once the data is displayed, the last piece of the puzzle is handling user interactions. You have many options to accomplish this—you can pass entire event objects to an event-handler function, you can pass only the data, or the data can be retrieved by the function directly. For simple cases, you can take advantage of data binding.

In the next chapter, we'll continue with `Lists` and discuss how they can be customized.

9 List customization

This chapter covers:

- Label functions
- Item renderers and editors
- Combined item editor and item renderer
- Advanced item renderers
- Filter functions

`Lists` (the component variety) are the workhorses of a Flex application. Consequently, a large portion of your development in Flex will focus on the presentation of, and interaction with, `Lists`.

Beyond the aesthetics of page formatting (discussed in previous chapters), you're likely to want a granular level of control over content presentation within the rows and cells of `List`-based components. This includes adding interactive capabilities that enable the user to work with that content. This process is called `List` customization. You'll begin learning about it by looking at the label function, which is the easiest path to customizing a `List`.

9.1 Label functions

Let's take a minute to set the stage. You've received data from a hypothetical source (probably a database), and you've reached a point at which you need to do more than present the data in its current form. You may need to format raw data into something more comfortable for users to absorb, you may need to translate a Boolean value into a human-friendly format, or you may want to take multiple data fields and join them in a single legible column.

This is where a label function can help you. Label functions operate by instructing a column in a `List` (and any relative of the `List`, including components such as the `DataGrid` and `TileList`) to call a function on each row of data. Whatever that function returns will be the value to display.

9.1.1 Types of label functions

You have the option to select from two types of label functions: one is intended for `Lists` made up of a single column, such as `Lists`, `HorizontalLists`, `TileLists`, and `Trees`; the other is designed for multicolumn `Lists` including `DataGrids`, `AdvancedDataGrids`, `PrintDataGrids`, `FileSystemDataGrids`, and `OLAPDataGrids`.

The only difference between the two types of label functions is the form of their arguments.

SINGLE-COLUMN LABEL FUNCTION

In a single-column label function, you accept one parameter—a reference to the current record (or row) of information within your data. You access whatever data fields you need and return a String, as shown in listing 9.1.

Listing 9.1 Using a label function with one-column `List`-based components

```
public function fullName(rowItem:Object):String
{
   return rowItem.firstName + ' ' + rowItem.lastName;
}
```

Conversely, if you're presenting a component made up of more than one column, you need a multicolumn label function.

MULTICOLUMN LABEL FUNCTION

Multicolumn label functions perform like their single-column stablemates, with the exception of taking an additional parameter—a reference to the column (to determine which column you're pointing to). Listing 9.2 shows what this looks like.

Listing 9.2 Using a label function with multicolumn `List`-based components

```
public function formatDate(rowItem:Object,column:DataGridColumn):String
{
   var retVal:String = "";
   if(column.dataField == "dtJoined")
     retVal = dFmt.format(rowItem.dtJoined);
   else if(column.dataField == "dtLogin")
     retVal = dFmt.format(rowItem.dtLogin);
   return retVal;
}
```

In this case, components such as the DataGrid use these label functions.

THEY'RE NOT JUST FOR LISTS

Many elements support label functions, such as charting components and even form controls like ComboBox and DateField. Keep in mind as we progress that even though the specific focus of this chapter is customizing Lists, as it relates to label functions, the same operating principles apply to these non-List components as well.

We've presented a brief overview of the two types of label functions, but we don't want to go much further without showing you examples of how to use them.

9.1.2 Using a single-column label function

In this scenario, you have a data file containing contact information for business associates. There's a problem, though: the first and last names of your contacts are stored in two separate fields, but you want to display the full names in a List component.

The List component consists of a single column; but as mentioned, the data is in two fields. You can solve this problem by using a label function to show two fields in one column.

In listing 9.3, the label function extracts the data from the first- and last-name fields and joins it to form a new String, which is then returned to the List component for display.

Listing 9.3 Using a label function to support a single-column List component

```
<?xml version="1.0"?>
<mx:Application xmlns:mx="http://www.adobe.com/2006/mxml"
  backgroundColor="white">
<mx:Script>
   <![CDATA[
      import mx.collections.ArrayCollection;
      [Bindable]
      public var myAC:ArrayCollection  = new ArrayCollection([     <- Data used to populate List
      {firstName:"Jon",lastName:"Hirschi"},
      {firstName:"Tariq",lastName:"Ahmed"}
      ]);
      public function fullName(rowItem:Object):String     <- Label function called by List to process items
      {
         return rowItem.firstName + ' ' + rowItem.lastName;     <- Merges two fields and returns them to List
      }
   ]]>
</mx:Script>
<mx:List dataProvider="{myAC}" labelFunction="fullName"/>     <- Label function requested by List
</mx:Application>
```

You have to appreciate the simplicity here. The execution is transparent, and you get the results you want, as shown in figure 9.1.

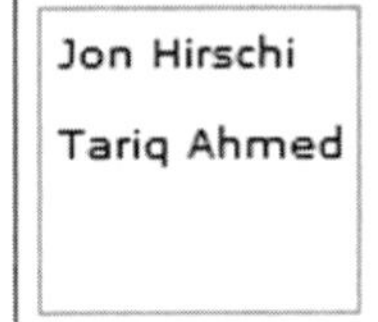

Figure 9.1 First and last names—originally stored in separate data fields—are merged into a single column by a label function.

In this case, you use a single-column

label function because the `List` component has only one column. If you're using a multicolumn `List`-based component such as a `DataGrid`, which can be made up of more than one column, you need to use a multicolumn label function.

9.1.3 Using a multicolumn label function

In this next example, you have data files that contain information regarding members of a hypothetical organization—perhaps an online forum or a blog. The data includes date and time fields that maintain information about when each member joined, as well as a field for when they last logged in. For the moment, we're not interested in the time portion, only the date, so you'll use a label function to pass that raw data through a formatter (listing 9.4) and display the result.

Listing 9.4 Using a label function to support a multicolumn `DataGrid`

```
<?xml version="1.0"?>
<mx:Application xmlns:mx="http://www.adobe.com/2006/mxml"
  backgroundColor="white">
<mx:Script>
   <![CDATA[
      import mx.collections.ArrayCollection;
      [Bindable]
      public var myAC:ArrayCollection =
         new ArrayCollection([
      {name:"Jon Hirschi", username:"jhirschi",dtJoined:"01/02/2005
         12:32:55",dtLogin:"05/20/2008 13:33:22" },
      {name:"Tariq Ahmed", username:"tahmed",dtJoined:"03/12/2005
         05:44:32",dtLogin:"07/09/2008 14:44:23"},
      ]);

      public function
   formatDate(rowItem:Object,column:DataGridColumn):String
      {
         var retVal:String = "";
         if(column.dataField == "dtJoined")
            retVal = dFmt.format(rowItem.dtJoined);
         else if(column.dataField == "dtLogin")
            retVal = dFmt.format(rowItem.dtLogin);
         return retVal;
      }
   ]]>
</mx:Script>

<mx:DateFormatter id="dFmt" formatString="MM/DD/YY"/>

<mx:DataGrid id="dg" width="500" height="100" dataProvider="{myAC}">

   <mx:columns>
      <mx:DataGridColumn dataField="name" headerText="Name"/>
      <mx:DataGridColumn dataField="username" headerText="Username"/>
      <mx:DataGridColumn dataField="dtJoined" headerText="Joined"
                  labelFunction="formatDate"/>
      <mx:DataGridColumn dataField="dtLogin" headerText="Last Login"
                  labelFunction="formatDate"/>
```

Callouts:
- Data has date with time fields
- If this is date joined field, return just date portion
- If this is date login field, return just date portion
- Formatter used to format date-only format
- Two columns use label function

```
    </mx:columns>
  </mx:DataGrid>

  </mx:Application>
```

After the application is run, figure 9.2 shows how the two date-related fields, which are supplied with raw date and time information, are nicely formatted to show only the date and ignore the time.

Name	Username	Joined	Last Login
Jon Hirschi	jhirschi	01/02/05	05/20/08
Tariq Ahmed	tahmed	03/12/05	07/09/08

Figure 9.2 The `Joined` and `Last Login` fields display a formatted date and nothing more, thanks to a label function.

Keep in mind the following points about this example:

- You can't pass parameters to the label function—Flex automatically passes a reference of the row and column.
- You use the column data to determine which column is being used, to ensure you're formatting the appropriate value.

This label function is a little more involved compared to the less complex single-column label function.

9.1.4 *Ideas for label functions*

The following are some common uses for label functions:

- Joining multiple data columns to create a single String for a single column
- Formatting raw data
- Converting raw data to human-readable format

Here's another idea you might want to try: run conditional logic to evaluate data within a row, but instead of displaying the data, display some custom information. You can present a Past Due message if a payment due date has been exceeded.

In the next section, we'll transition to item renderers, which go beyond the limitations of label functions.

9.2 *Item renderers*

Label functions are easy to use, but that ease comes with the inherent limitation of not being able to do much more than you did in the previous pair of examples. What if you needed to do more than just return and display formatted text?

This is where item renderers come into play. They give you fine-grained control over what a cell looks like. With item renderers, you can define the color of the cell's background, add images and interactive UI components.

By default, Flex uses the <mx:Text> component as its item renderer. This doesn't do much other than render text that has been provided to it. When you specify an item renderer, you're simply overriding this default.

9.2.1 Types of renderers

Flex offers three types of item renderers:

- *Regular*—Normally referred to as an item renderer. The logic for this is contained in a separate file that you reference.
- *Inline*—Identical to a regular item renderer, but the logic is inline with the rest of your code for your convenience.
- *Drop-in*—A general-use component (such as a `Button` or a `DateField`) that happens to be used as an item renderer.

Let's begin by looking at how to create all three renderers. Then, you'll add your own custom logic.

9.2.2 Creating a (regular) item renderer

Here is an overview of the steps you'll follow:

1. Create a separate MXML file called myRenderer.mxml. This will be your item renderer.
2. Use the `dataProvider`'s related row record to pull whatever fields you need.
3. Wrap everything inside a container, such as an `HBox`, for display.

You'll use the two files presented in listings 9.5 and 9.6 as sources for the examples that follow. Listing 9.5 represents the item renderer, and 9.6 is the main application file.

Listing 9.5 myRenderer.mxml: item renderer

```
<?xml version="1.0" encoding="utf-8"?>
<mx:HBox xmlns:mx="http://www.adobe.com/2006/mxml" width="100%"
   height="110">
   <mx:Image source="{data.thumbnail}"/>
   <mx:Text text="{data.firstName} {data.lastName}" fontSize="16"
      fontWeight="bold"/>
</mx:HBox>
```

Listing 9.6 HelloWorld.mxml: main application that uses an item renderer

```
<?xml version="1.0"?>
<mx:Application xmlns:mx="http://www.adobe.com/2006/mxml"
   backgroundColor="white">
<mx:Script>
   <![CDATA[
      import mx.collections.ArrayCollection;
      [Bindable]
      public var myAC:ArrayCollection  = new ArrayCollection([
      {firstName:"Jon",lastName:"Hirschi",thumbnail:"assets/jon.jpg"},
      {firstName:"Tariq",lastName:"Ahmed",thumbnail:"assets/tariq.jpg"}
      ]);
   ]]>
</mx:Script>

<mx:List dataProvider="{myAC}" itemRenderer="myRenderer" height="230"
```

```
    width="220"/>
</mx:Application>
```

Figure 9.3 shows the impressive results (of the code, of course—what did you think we were referring to?). As you can see, this presentation goes far beyond label functions by embedding images and adding some font styling.

Figure 9.3 An item renderer is used to display complex content in a single column.

Keep in mind the following points about this example:

- MXML files are based on the XML standard, which dictates that the item renderer file must include the declaration `<?xml version="1.0" encoding="utf-8"?>`.
- You'll notice that the `HBox` includes the syntax `xmlns`. This is a namespace declaration that tells the Flex compiler the `HBox` we're using is the `HBox` that comes from Adobe Flex, and not a third-party component of the same name.

This approach provides instant gratification, but it won't be long before you need to add conditional logic.

9.2.3 *Adding logic to an item renderer*

The previous example does nothing more than takes the targeted information as is and displays it. But you'll eventually arrive at a point in your Flex adventures where you need to add business logic to determine what to display in a cell.

In the next examples (listings 9.7 and 9.8), you'll build a three-column list of contacts. The third column includes a button the user can click to send an email to the corresponding contact—but only if you have email information available for that person. If no email data is available, a button isn't displayed.

Listing 9.7 myRenderer.mxml: conditional item renderer

```
<?xml version="1.0" encoding="utf-8"?>
<mx:HBox xmlns:mx="http://www.adobe.com/2006/mxml" width="100%"
   creationComplete="checkEmail()">
   <mx:Script>
      <![CDATA[
      import flash.net.*;
      private function checkEmail():void
      {
         if(data.email.length > 0)
         {
            emailButton.visible = true;
         }
      }

      public function sendMail():void
      {
```

Shows button only if email value is present

```
        var u:URLRequest = new URLRequest("mailto:" + data.email);
        navigateToURL(u,"_self");
      }
      ]]>
   </mx:Script>
   <mx:Button id="emailButton" visible="false" label="Send Email"
   click="sendMail()"/>
</mx:HBox>
```

Opens email editor when button is clicked

Listing 9.8 HelloWorld.mxml: main application file that uses an item renderer

```
<?xml version="1.0"?>
<mx:Application xmlns:mx="http://www.adobe.com/2006/mxml"
   backgroundColor="white">
<mx:Script>
   <![CDATA[
      import mx.collections.ArrayCollection;
      [Bindable]
      public var myAC:ArrayCollection  = new ArrayCollection([
      {firstName:"Jon",lastName:"Hirschi",email:""},
      {firstName:"Tariq",lastName:"Ahmed",email:"tariq@dopejam.com"},
      {firstName:"Faisal",lastName:"Abid",email:""},
      {firstName:"Tom",lastName:"Ortega",email:""},
      {firstName:"Ryan",lastName:"Stewart",email:"ryan@isreallycool.com"}
      ]);
   ]]>
</mx:Script>

<mx:DataGrid id="dg" width="500" height="100" dataProvider="{myAC}">
   <mx:columns>
      <mx:DataGridColumn dataField="firstName"  headerText="First Name"/>
      <mx:DataGridColumn dataField="lastName"  headerText="Last Name"/>
      <mx:DataGridColumn headerText="Email" itemRenderer="myRenderer"/>
   </mx:columns>
</mx:DataGrid>

</mx:Application>
```

As shown in figure 9.4, the logic-infused code produces the expected results.

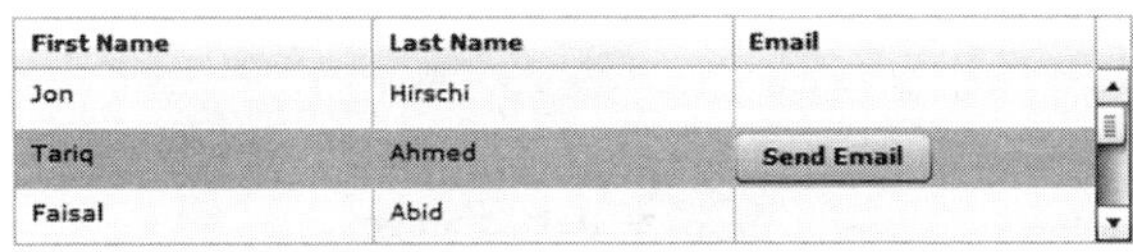

Figure 9.4 The item renderer presents a button only if email information is available.

Let's look at how this is accomplished:

- Flex creates instances of `myRenderer` as needed.
- As each `myRenderer` is created, the `creationComplete` event is triggered and runs the `checkEmail` function.
- If the email field is populated (with any characters at all—there is no validation for format), `checkEmail` changes the `visible` property from its default value of `false`, to `true`. This makes the button—which was always there—visible.

Yes, it is that simple, although there is one slight catch.

ONE SLIGHT GOTCHA

For performance reasons, Flex reuses existing rows—if you have 1,000 objects to display, it won't generate 1,000 rows; instead, it will generate the number rows that would be visible plus a few extra off screen. This means if you had 10 or so records in this example, and you scrolled up and down, you'd be likely to see the button appear in a seemingly random and inconsistent manner. Flex would reuse rows that were previously set to display the button.

To avoid this problem, do the following:

- Continue to use the `creationComplete` event to initialize the renderer. For example, the myAC `ArrayCollection` may not be populated yet.
- Use the `dataChange` event to check whether you need to display the button.
- When checking the display, configure the visible or not visible setting depending on whether the email field is blank or populated.

Listing 9.9 shows the improved item renderer.

Listing 9.9 More robust item render that resets itself as the data changes

```
<?xml version="1.0" encoding="utf-8"?>
<mx:HBox xmlns:mx="http://www.adobe.com/2006/mxml" width="100%"
   creationComplete="initDisplay()"
   dataChange="checkEmail()">
   <mx:Script>
      <![CDATA[
      import flash.net.*;
      private function initDisplay():void
      {
         emailButton.visible = false;
      }

      private function checkEmail():void
      {
         if(data.email.length > 0)
            emailButton.visible = true;
         else
            emailButton.visible = false;
      }
      public function sendMail():void
      {
         var u:URLRequest = new URLRequest("mailto:" + data.email);
         navigateToURL(u,"_self");
      }
      ]]>
   </mx:Script>
   <mx:Button id="emailButton" visible="false" label="Send Email"
   click="sendMail()"/>
</mx:HBox>
```

When item renderer is created, calls function to initialize itself

If data changes, calls function to reset display

Initializes button to be invisible

Adjusts visibility as data changes

This approach is the most commonly used because it lets you easily reuse your item renderer elsewhere in your application. But for convenience purposes, we'll discuss two other approaches, starting with an inline item renderer.

9.2.4 Creating an inline item renderer

An inline item renderer moves the logic from a separate file to the point in your code where you need it. It is definitely a convenience when you're prototyping an application, but there's a gaping drawback: you can't use that logic anywhere else in your application. Compare that to a regular item renderer, which you can use across many `Lists`, in many files.

Listing 9.10 shows how to set up an inline item renderer, which involves nothing more than copying the logic directly into your code and nesting it within the appropriate tags.

Listing 9.10 `DataGrid` column with an inline item renderer

```
<mx:DataGrid id="dg" width="500" height="100" dataProvider="{myAC}">
   <mx:columns>
      <mx:DataGridColumn headerText="Name">
         <mx:itemRenderer>
            <mx:Component>
               <mx:Text text="{data.firstName} {data.lastName}"/>
            </mx:Component>
         </mx:itemRenderer>
      </mx:DataGridColumn>
      <mx:DataGridColumn headerText="Email" itemRenderer="myRenderer"/>
   </mx:columns>
</mx:DataGrid>
```

As promised, this method is convenient. But if you think it is simple, the drop-in item renderer takes even less effort.

9.2.5 Using drop-in item renderers

Flex provides a number of components that can be used as drop-in renderers. Let's look at how you can use one of them—the `Image` component—to perform the same tasks as an item renderer, but with less effort.

Borrowing from the previous examples in which you created custom item renderers to display an image, you'll create another application to display images and text—this time using the `Image` component (listing 9.11).

Listing 9.11 Drop-in item renderer that renders an image in a column

```
<?xml version="1.0"?>
<mx:Application xmlns:mx="http://www.adobe.com/2006/mxml"
   backgroundColor="white">
<mx:Script>
   <![CDATA[
      import mx.collections.ArrayCollection;
```

```
        [Bindable]
        public var myAC:ArrayCollection  = new ArrayCollection([
        {name:"Jon Hirschi",thumbnail:"assets/jon.jpg"},
        {name:"Tariq Ahmed",thumbnail:"assets/tariq.jpg"}
        ]);

    ]]>
</mx:Script>

<mx:DataGrid id="dg" width="250" height="100" dataProvider="{myAC}">
    <mx:columns>
        <mx:DataGridColumn headerText="Name" dataField="name"/>
        <mx:DataGridColumn headerText="Picture" dataField="thumbnail"
                    itemRenderer="mx.controls.Image"/>     <-- Calls drop-in item renderer
    </mx:columns>
</mx:DataGrid>
</mx:Application>
```

Figure 9.5 shows how, with minimal effort, the Image component is used to display the images as thumbnails in the DataGrid.

TIP If you want the images to be larger, you need to set the rowHeight property for the DataGrid to the specific size. If you want it to scale to the full size of the image, set variableRowHeight="true".

Figure 9.5 The Image component used as a drop-in item renderer

Table 9.1 contains the full list of the components you can use as drop-in item renderers.

Table 9.1 Components that support the drop-in item renderer

Component	Default property	Notes
bButton	selected	Displays a button. Unfortunately, you can't control the button's associated label.
CheckBox	selected	
DateField	selectedDate	
Image	source	Use the List-based component's rowHeight or variableRowHeight property if you want the image to be larger than the default height of the row.
Label	text	
NumericStepper	value	
Text	text	By default, you're already using this.
TextArea	text	
TextInput	text	

Be aware of the default properties for these components because this is the field those components look for in your dataProvider. For example, consider what would happen if your DataGrid were configured as follows:

```
<mx:DataGridColumn headerText="Picture" itemRenderer="mx.controls.Image"/>
```

The Image component will assume you have a field in your data called source. Listing 9.12 follows this scenario through.

Listing 9.12 Image component assumes field should be labeled source

```
public var myAC:ArrayCollection  = new ArrayCollection([
      {name:"Jon Hirschi",source:"assets/jon.jpg"},
      {name:"Tariq Ahmed",source:"assets/tariq.jpg"}]);
```

Referring to listing 9.11, notice that the field was called thumbnail. This means you explicitly specified the dataField as a target for the component. Setting this instructs the component to use your setting instead of the default value.

The item renderer provides a high degree of control and logic over the display of information in a cell. But if you need a way to provide editing capabilities to your users, you can use a similar feature called an *item editor.*

9.3 Item editors

Item editors temporarily turn a cell in a List-based component into a form component, allowing you to edit its value. From a technical perspective, a form is the same thing as an item renderer—the only difference is context:

- *Item renderer*—Used to generate the default display, which is usually the read view
- *Item editor*—Temporarily invoked when the edit context is engaged

We'll start by explaining how to enable the editing process that causes an item editor, as well as any events associated with it, to capture data the user provides.

9.3.1 Enabling item editing

The components that support item renderers are the same ones that support item editors, but by default the editing feature is disabled for item renderers. To begin the process, you enable the editing feature, which then allows the user to click a cell and alter the data within it.

Here's an overview of the process:

1. Set the component to be editable. This setting can apply to the entire component, just a cell, or just a column.
2. When the user focuses on a cell that can be edited—via mouse click, or by pressing the Tab or Enter key—the item editor temporarily replaces the item renderer.
3. The item editor interacts with the user to capture certain data. It then self-terminates on certain user actions, such as pressing Enter or Tab, or clicking out of the cell.

4 As the item editor terminates, it passes the value captured from the edited cell to a `List`-based component to use for display. More important, the original variable that provided the data (the property to which the `dataProvider` is pointing) is also updated with the new value.

Listing 9.13 presents a minimalist approach.

Listing 9.13 Simple way to leverage item editors

```
<?xml version="1.0"?>
<mx:Application xmlns:mx="http://www.adobe.com/2006/mxml"
   backgroundColor="white">
<mx:Script>
   <![CDATA[
      import mx.collections.ArrayCollection;
      [Bindable]
      public var myAC:ArrayCollection  = new ArrayCollection([
      {name:"Jon Hirschi", email:"jon@iscool.com"},
      {name:"Tariq Ahmed", email:"tariq@iscool.com"}]);
   ]]>
</mx:Script>

<mx:DataGrid id="dg" width="150" height="100" dataProvider="{myAC}"
   editable="true">      <-- Defaults all columns to be editable
   <mx:columns>
      <mx:DataGridColumn headerText="Name" dataField="name"/>
      <mx:DataGridColumn headerText="EMail" dataField="email"
   editable="false"/>      <-- Overrides DataGrid's editable setting; forces column to be read only
   </mx:columns>
</mx:DataGrid>

</mx:Application>
```

When the user clicks an individual's name (figure 9.6), the cell becomes editable, and the user can change the value.

Recall that in earlier examples, you used the `Text` component as the default item renderer. Would you care to guess what the default item editor is? If you said `TextInput`, you're right. But you're by no means restricted to its use only; you're free to change it and create your own item editor.

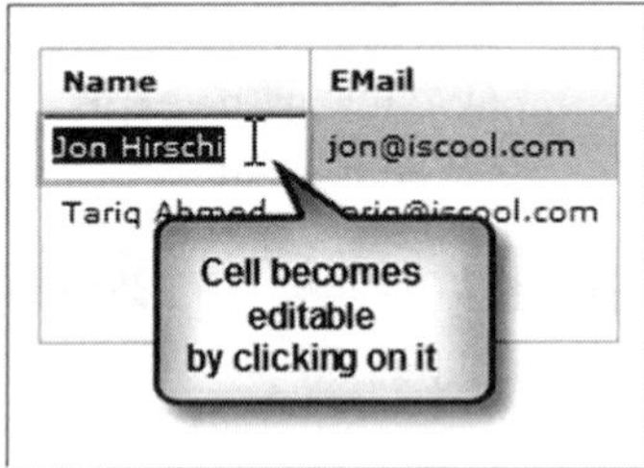

Figure 9.6 Setting the editable field allows the user to edit data in this cell.

9.3.2 Creating an item editor

Creating an item editor is similar to creating its sibling, an item renderer, but you may want to configure additional features:

- You can create a separate MXML file that can be invoked by anything that wants to use it.
- You can create a public variable that can be used by the `List`-based component to know where the new value is stored. Be sure this variable is a data type com-

patible with the original data (numbers to numbers, strings to strings, dates to dates, and so on).

- When the item editor is initiated, you should default your form input to whatever the current value is (along with the public variable).

Listing 9.14 puts this into play with a custom item editor; listing 9.15 is a consumer of this item editor.

Listing 9.14 myEditor.mxml: custom item editor

```
<?xml version="1.0" encoding="utf-8"?>
<mx:HBox xmlns:mx="http://www.adobe.com/2006/mxml"
   creationComplete="initMe()">
   <mx:Script>
      <![CDATA[
      import mx.collections.ArrayCollection;

      Bindable]
      public var newEmployeeType:String = "";         <-- Variable read by List-
                                                          based component
      [Bindable]
      private var typeAC:ArrayCollection =
            new ArrayCollection([{type:"Employee"},
               {type:"Customer"}]);

      private function initMe():void
      {                                               Initializes return variable to
         newEmployeeType = data.type;         <--     that of current value

         for(var i:int = 0; i<typeAC.length;i++)      Loops through
            if(typeAC[i].type == data.type)           ComboBox's values and
               myCB.selectedIndex = i;                defaults to current value
      }

      private function selectionChange():void         User changed option;
      {                                               update return variable
         newEmployeeType = myCB.selectedItem.type;  <-- to new value
      }

      ]]>
   </mx:Script>
   <mx:ComboBox id="myCB" dataProvider="{typeAC}"
            labelField="type" change="selectionChange()"/>
</mx:HBox>
```

Listing 9.15 HelloWorld.mxml: uses the custom item editor for a column

```
<?xml version="1.0"?>
<mx:Application xmlns:mx="http://www.adobe.com/2006/mxml"
   backgroundColor="white">
<mx:Script>
   <![CDATA[
      import mx.collections.ArrayCollection;
      [Bindable]
      public var myAC:ArrayCollection = new ArrayCollection([
      {name:"Jon Hirschi", email:"jon@iscool.com", type:"Employee"},
```

```
        {name:"Tariq Ahmed", email:"tariq@iscool.com", type:"Customer"}]);
    ]]>
</mx:Script>

<mx:DataGrid id="dg" width="350" height="200" dataProvider="{myAC}"
    editable="true">
    <mx:columns>
        <mx:DataGridColumn headerText="Name" dataField="name"/>
        <mx:DataGridColumn headerText="EMail" dataField="email"
    editable="false"/>
        <mx:DataGridColumn headerText="Type" dataField="type"
                    editorDataField="newEmployeeType"
                    itemEditor="myEditor"/>
    </mx:columns>
</mx:DataGrid>

</mx:Application>
```

Identifies which variable in item editor contains new value

Instructs column to use custom item editor

All of this boils down to two simple things: first, you initialize the item editor to make sure it is displaying the right data type; second, you pass the result of the user's selection (figure 9.7). Note how the `editorDataField` property is used to indicate which variable in the item editor should be used to populate the `DataGrid` when the user finishes editing.

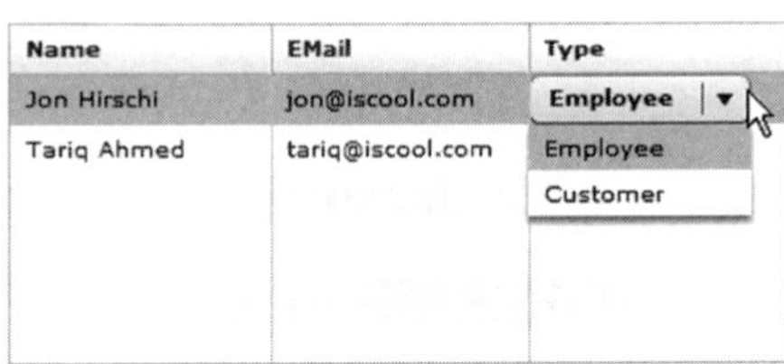

Figure 9.7 A custom item editor, used to create a `ComboBox` when editing

Although the process can be reduced to those two steps, you can leverage a number of events that are triggered along the way.

9.3.3 *Item-editing events*

Flex fires off a number of events during the editing process, which you can intercept in order to add business logic or parameters, clean up routines, or add checkpoints. These events include the following:

- `itemEditBeginning`—Dispatched as the item-editing process is about to begin. It occurs as a result of the user clicking the mouse button on a cell, pressing Enter while over a cell, or pressing the Tab key to move from one cell to the next. Typically, this is used to add business logic to determine if you're going to begin cell editing.
- `itemEditBegin`—Occurs directly after `itemEditBeginning`, when the data is about to be passed to the item editor. As a result, it is an opportunity to manipulate the data if you need to.
- `itemEditEnd`—Occurs when the user has triggered the end of the item-editing process. The item editor still exists but is about to be destroyed. This is a point at which you can compare the original value with the new value, as well as conduct any additional validation.

You can handle any of these events in the `List`-based component, as we'll demonstrate shortly. But first, let's get the lowdown on the event object that's generated when these events occur.

Depending on the type of List-based component you're using, you get its related List-based event:

- ListEvent is used by the simpler List components, such as List and Tree.
- DataGridEvent is used by the DataGrid.
- AdvancedDataGridEvent is used by the AdvancedDataGrid.

When writing your function to handle the event, you use the syntax shown in listing 9.16.

Listing 9.16 Three examples of handling item-editing events based on component

```
import mx.events.ListEvent;
public function handleListEvent(event:ListEvent):void
{
   //logic...
}

import mx.events.DataGridEvent;
public function handleDGEvent(event:DataGridEvent):void
{
   //logic...
}

import mx.events.AdvancedDataGridEvent;
public function handleADGEvent(event:AdvancedDataGridEvent):void
{
   //logic...
}
```

Each event object has some unique properties; but they have many things in common, particularly those listed in table 9.2.

Table 9.2 Properties of the event objects generated during item editing

Property	Type	Description
columnIndex	Number	Index of the column, starting at 0.
currentTarget	Object	Reference to the component that generated the event. For example, if you had a HorizontalList named myHList from which the cell-editing process was initiated, the currentTarget would link back to myHList.
itemRenderer	Object	Reference to the itemRenderer used in the cell currently being edited. You can use this to determine the current value of the cell (before editing began, that is).
reason	String	Read only. Action that caused the itemEditEnd to occur (if it occurred at all). Values include cancelled (user canceled editing), newRow (user moved onto a new row), newColumn (user moved to the next column on the same row), and other.

Table 9.2 Properties of the event objects generated during item editing *(continued)*

Property	Type	Description
`rowIndex`	Number	Related row of the cell being edited.
`type`	String	Type of event that occurred.
`dataField`	String	Data field related to the column being edited. Specific to `DataGrid/AdvancedDataGrid`.
`preventDefault`	Function	Function you can call to interrupt the chain of events.

Keep in mind that you don't need to handle any of these events—you can let them pass through as is. Alternatively, you can pick and choose which events you want to handle. We'll now look at how to use each of them individually.

USING ITEMEDITBEGINNING

The `itemEditBeginning` event occurs when the user focuses on an editable cell by clicking the cell directly, moving from one cell to another using the Tab key, or pressing the Enter key while the mouse is over a cell. Cell editing isn't yet enabled, so this is an opportunity to check whether you want to permit editing at all.

Listing 9.17 verifies that the record on which you're focused is a user record and, if so, makes sure the record is active. Otherwise, you prevent the editing process from continuing.

Listing 9.17 Intercepting the `itemEditBeginning` event to add custom logic

```
<?xml version="1.0"?>
<mx:Application xmlns:mx="http://www.adobe.com/2006/mxml"
  backgroundColor="white">
<mx:Script>
   <![CDATA[
      import mx.collections.ArrayCollection;
      import mx.events.DataGridEvent;
      [Bindable]
      public var myAC:ArrayCollection  = new ArrayCollection([
      {name:"Jon Hirschi", email:"jon@iscool.com", type:"Employee",
         isactive:true},
      {name:"Tariq Ahmed", email:"tariq@iscool.com", type:"Customer",
         isactive:false}]);

      private function checkIfAllowed(event:DataGridEvent):void
     {
           var dataItem:Object = event.itemRenderer.data;
         if(event.dataField == "type" && dataItem.isactive == false)
            event.preventDefault();
     }
   ]]>
</mx:Script>

<mx:DataGrid id="dg" width="350" height="150" dataProvider="{myAC}"
```

❶ Handles itemEditBeginning event

❷ Checks whether type field exists and record is active

❸ Stops item editing

```
    itemEditBeginning="checkIfAllowed(event)" editable="true">
    <mx:columns>
       <mx:DataGridColumn headerText="Name" dataField="name"/>
       <mx:DataGridColumn headerText="EMail" dataField="email"
          editable="false"/>
       <mx:DataGridColumn headerText="Type" dataField="type"
                    editorDataField="newEmployeeType"
                       itemEditor="myEditor"/>
    </mx:columns>
 </mx:DataGrid>

 </mx:Application>
```

Uses event handler for itemEditBeginning

The DataGrid in listing 9.17 is configured to call a function when the editing process is about to begin ❹. The checkIfAllowed function ❶ looks to see if there's a field called type ❷ and verifies that the record is active. If either of these tests fails, the event's preventDefault function is invoked to interrupt the process at that point ❸.

If the checkIfAllowed function determines that conditions have been met successfully, the process is allowed to continue with the next event in the queue, itemEditBegin.

USING ITEMEDITBEGIN

If the events are allowed to continue past the itemEditBeginning stage, you enter the itemEditBegin event. At this point, cell editing is enabled and the item editor is about to be created—but before that happens, you can do things like manipulate the data or, depending on conditions, dynamically invoke one item editor or another.

The itemEditBegin event isn't commonly used, and it is an advanced topic. You need to reproduce the default behavior, then add your own logic. We're skipping quite a bit of detail for the moment, but here's the gist of what you can do:

- Call preventDefault() on the event object to prevent Flex from executing the default chain of events.
- Call the createItemEditor function on the List-based component to create an item editor in the target cell.
- Point the data property from the item renderer to the item editor.
- Manipulate the data as needed.

Listing 9.18 manipulates the type field when a user tries to edit it by setting the field to Deactivated when isactive returns false.

Listing 9.18 Using the itemEditBegin event

```
 <mx:Script>
    <![CDATA[
       import mx.collections.ArrayCollection;
       import mx.events.DataGridEvent;
       [Bindable]
       public var myAC:ArrayCollection  = new ArrayCollection([
       {name:"Jon Hirschi", email:"jon@iscool.com", type:"Employee",
          isactive:true},
```

```
        {name:"Tariq Ahmed", email:"tariq@iscool.com", type:"Customer",
          isactive:false}]);

        private function modifyIfNecessary(event:DataGridEvent):void
        {
          if(dg.columns[event.columnIndex].dataField=="type")
          {
            event.preventDefault();

            dg.createItemEditor(event.columnIndex,event.rowIndex);

            dg.itemEditorInstance.data = dg.editedItemRenderer.data;

            if(dg.editedItemRenderer.data.isactive == false)
              dg.itemEditorInstance.data.type = "Deactivated";
          }
        }
    ]]>
  </mx:Script>

  <mx:DataGrid id="dg" width="350" height="150" dataProvider="{myAC}"
    itemEditBegin="modifyIfNecessary(event)" editable="true">
    <mx:columns>
      <mx:DataGridColumn headerText="Name" dataField="name"/>
      <mx:DataGridColumn headerText="EMail" dataField="email"
        editable="false"/>
      <mx:DataGridColumn headerText="Type" dataField="type"
                  editorDataField="newEmployeeType"
                    itemEditor="myEditor"/>
    </mx:columns>
  </mx:DataGrid>
```

Is column named type?

Prevents default itemEditBegin functionality

Creates item editor in cell

Gets cell's value; assigns it to item

If account inactive, forces type field value

Upon this event's completion, the user begins to edit the value until he commits the value, which then triggers the `itemEditEnd` event.

USING ITEMEDITEND

This is the last stage of the process. It occurs when the user has completed making changes to the data, and it presents an opportunity for you to do postedit processing. Common scenarios for using `itemEditEnd` include the following:

- Validating that the data entered is compliant with any defined parameters
- Formatting the data
- Propagating any edits to other parts of your application
- Pushing those changes permanently to a back-end database
- Forcing the cell to remain edited
- Preventing the Enter/Tab key from moving to the next cell after editing the current cell

The first thing you need to do is check what action terminated the editing process. You can do this by looking at the `event.reason` property, as described earlier. If the reason was set to `cancelled`, there's nothing more to do.

If you need to maintain focus on the cell, you'll need to use a function named `callLater`, which lets you specify a function to call after the current function has exited.

Listing 9.19 uses `itemEditEnd` to check the email field. If data within it doesn't pass as a valid email address, you maintain edit mode until the user enters the correct data.

Listing 9.19 Using the `itemEditEnd` event to validate the new value

```
<?xml version="1.0"?>
<mx:Application xmlns:mx="http://www.adobe.com/2006/mxml"
  backgroundColor="white">
<mx:Script>
  <![CDATA[
    import mx.collections.ArrayCollection;
    import mx.events.DataGridEvent;
    import mx.validators.EmailValidator;
    import mx.controls.TextInput;
    [Bindable]
    public var myAC:ArrayCollection  = new ArrayCollection([
    {name:"Jon Hirschi", email:"jon@iscool.com"},
    {name:"Tariq Ahmed", email:"tariq@iscool.com"}]);

    private function onEditEnd(event:DataGridEvent):void
    {
      //if you needed to validate different cells differently...
      if(event.dataField == 'email')            ❶ Email field?
      {
        var fCell:Array=[event.columnIndex,event.rowIndex];
        var newData:String =      ❷ Tells you user's new value
          TextInput(event.currentTarget.itemEditorInstance).text;

        var emailVal:EmailValidator =                ❸ Creates instance of
          new EmailValidator();                        EmailValidator;
        var valResult:* = emailVal.validate(newData);  validates new value
        if(valResult.type == "invalid")      ❹ Checks if validation failed
        {
          event.preventDefault();        ❺ Prevents event propagation
          callLater(maintainEdit,fCell);
        }                                      Maintains editing on
      }                                     ❻ field after current event
    }
    private function maintainEdit(colIndex:int,rowIndex:int):void
    {
      var editCell:Object = {columnIndex:colIndex, rowIndex:
        rowIndex};
      //This will invoke the datagrid's itemEditBegin
        dg.editedItemPosition = editCell;
    }                                        Makes cell stay
                                           ❼ in edit mode
  ]]>
</mx:Script>

<mx:DataGrid id="dg" width="350" height="150" dataProvider="{myAC}"
  itemEditEnd="onEditEnd(event)" editable="true">
  <mx:columns>
    <mx:DataGridColumn headerText="Name" dataField="name"/>
    <mx:DataGridColumn headerText="EMail" dataField="email"/>
  </mx:columns>
```

```
</mx:DataGrid>

</mx:Application>
```

NOTE You can find a much more complex version of this example on CFLEX.Net at http://www.cflex.net/showFileDetails.cfm?ObjectID=723.

In the listing, you define a function to handle the `itemEditEnd` event. The function's first order of business is to verify that the `email` field is being edited ❶; if not, you branch to the default behavior and move on.

If it is the email field, you capture and compare the new value that came from the user ❷. Keep in mind that this value is still uncommitted, which makes it easy to use an `EmailValidator` to verify that it is a proper email address ❸. If it is not ❹, you need to stop the event propagation ❺. You'll let this current event end but instruct Flex to call a `maintainEdit` function upon its completion ❻, which triggers the editing process to start again on the same cell ❼ to compel the user to enter something valid.

Thus far, you've treated item renderers and item editors as two separate components. But they have a lot in common, which lets you create a component that is both item renderer *and* editor.

9.4 Combining an item editor and item renderer

It is possible to create a hybrid component from the item renderer and item editor. You may want to do this if you need to employ a single component that handles switching from a read view to an edit view—or you want to stay in edit mode for a certain field.

For example, it is common for many web mail programs to display a check box beside each mail item to let users select all the email they want to bulk process. This is a good approach when you need to make many updates quickly.

Let's borrow from an earlier example (listing 9.14), in which you used a `ComboBox` to change the user type, and create an always-on edit field. Using listing 9.14 as your starting point, look for the following code segment:

```
<mx:DataGridColumn headerText="Type" dataField="type"
          editorDataField="newEmployeeType" itemEditor="myEditor"/>
```

Change those lines to the following:

```
<mx:DataGridColumn headerText="Type" dataField="type"
   rendererIsEditor="true" editorDataField="newEmployeeType"
   itemRenderer="myEditor"/>
```

The result of these changes causes the `ComboBox` to be activated and remain on for all rows, as shown in figure 9.8.

This technique is useful for data entry in applications in which you're always in edit mode, or if there's no difference between rendering and editing—that is, you're always in a state of editing.

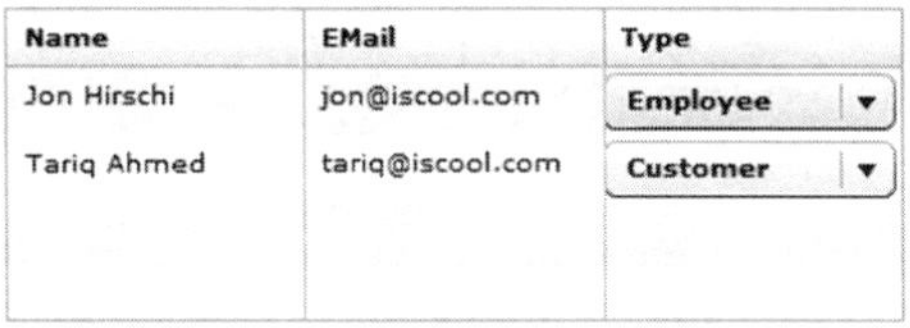

Name	EMail	Type
Jon Hirschi	jon@iscool.com	Employee ▼
Tariq Ahmed	tariq@iscool.com	Customer ▼

Figure 9.8 The `ComboBox` is used as a renderer and editor at the same time.

These item renderers and editors serve well for general purposes, but an advanced version caters specifically to the `AdvancedDataGrid`.

9.5 Advanced item renderers

The `AdvancedDataGrid` supports item renderers as any other `List`-based component does, but it takes rendering to a higher level. The `AdvancedDataGrid` can work with item renderers that can span multiple columns and use multiple item renderers on the same column, as well as item renderers that can insert rows—the latter being used if you need to summarize or categorize sequences of data.

You can do an amazing variety of things based on those capabilities. Let's take a basic look at how to use them.

9.5.1 The AdvancedDataGridRendererProvider

`AdvancedDataGridRendererProvider` is probably the longest-named component in Flex! It makes custom item rendering possible in an `AdvancedDataGrid`. Table 9.3 lists its properties.

Table 9.3 Properties of the `AdvancedDataGridRendererProvider`

Property	Type	Description
`column`	Object	References an `AdvancedDataGridColumn`. Using binding, you specify the `id` of the column to which this advanced renderer refers. For example, you can use the field `{myCol}` instead of `columnIndex`. This property lets you reference a column by its name.
`columnIndex`	Number	Similar to `Column`, but you can reference columns numerically. The first column starts at `0`.
`columnSpan`	Number	Similar to the `colSpan` property of an HTML table; specifies the number of columns you wish to span. This is an optional property that carries a default value of `1`. Setting to `0` spans all columns.
`dataField`	String	Determines which field in your data provider should be used by this item renderer (if any). An optional property.
`renderer`	Component	Name of the item renderer to be invoked. Required.
`rowSpan`	Number	Similar to the `rowSpan` property of an HTML table; specifies the number of rows you wish to span. An optional property. Default value is `1`.

You furnish AdvancedDataGridRendererProviders with these properties as part of the <rendererProviders> tag, which is nested beneath AdvancedDataGrid. Listing 9.20 shows an example of this structure.

Listing 9.20 Advanced renderers nested at the same level as columns

```
<mx:AdvancedDataGrid>
   <mx:columns>
      <mx:AdvancedDataGridColumn dataField="col1"/>
      <mx:AdvancedDataGridColumn dataField="col2"/>
     Etc...
   </mx:columns>

   <mx:rendererProviders>
      <mx:AdvancedDataGridRendererProvider [properties]/>
      <mx:AdvancedDataGridRendererProvider [properties]/>
     Etc...
   </mx:rendererProviders>
</mx:AdvancedDataGrid>
```

Listing 9.20 is a high-level overview of the concept. In terms of implementation, it is all about referencing the column to which an advanced item renderer is applied.

9.5.2 Referencing the column

You can reference a column two ways: using the column's id property, or specifying the column's position.

BY ID

Use the column property if you want to use a named approach to specify the column to which the renderer applies. Listing 9.21 binds on the column called nameCol.

Listing 9.21 Applying an advanced item renderer using a column name

```
<mx:AdvancedDataGrid dataProvider="{myAC}">
   <mx:columns>
      <mx:DataGridColumn id="nameCol" headerText="Name"
         dataField="name"/>
   </mx:columns>

   <mx:rendererProviders>
      <mx:AdvancedDataGridRendererProvider column="{nameCol}"
        renderer="myRenderer"/>
   </mx:rendererProviders>
</mx:AdvancedDataGrid>
```

This is the way to go if you feel you may reposition a particular column; the item renderer will continue to work regardless of where you move its target column.

BY INDEX

If you want to reference by the position of the column, use the columnIndex property instead. For example, listing 9.22 instructs the AdvancedDataGridRendererProvider to apply itself to the first column.

Listing 9.22 Applying an advanced item renderer to the first column

```
<mx:AdvancedDataGrid dataProvider="{myAC}">
   <mx:columns>
      <mx:DataGridColumn id="nameCol" headerText="Name"
         dataField="name"/>
   </mx:columns>

   <mx:rendererProviders>
      <mx:AdvancedDataGridRendererProvider columnIndex="0"
         renderer="myRenderer"/>
   </mx:rendererProviders>
</mx:AdvancedDataGrid>
```

The advantage of this approach becomes clear if you need to have an item renderer that's based on the position of the column. For example, an item renderer may be used for column two, regardless of that column's content. Or, you can dynamically set a variable and use it to set the `columnIndex`.

Identifying which column an advanced item renderer is linked to is the basic use case, but you can also use it to span multiple columns.

9.5.3 Spanning columns

To span columns, use the `columnSpan` property. You can use `columnSpan` in much the same way as you would the HTML `<td>` tag, which has a similar property named `colspan`. Listing 9.23 demonstrates how to use `columnSpan` by instructing an advanced item renderer to span two columns, starting at the second column.

Listing 9.23 Using an advanced item renderer to span two columns

```
<?xml version="1.0"?>
<mx:Application xmlns:mx="http://www.adobe.com/2006/mxml"
   backgroundColor="white">
<mx:Script>
   <![CDATA[
      import mx.collections.ArrayCollection;
      [Bindable]
      public var myAC:ArrayCollection  = new ArrayCollection([
      {name:"Jon Hirschi", email:"jon@iscool.com", type:"Employee"},
      {name:"Tariq Ahmed", email:"tariq@iscool.com", type:"Customer"}]);
   ]]>
</mx:Script>

<mx:AdvancedDataGrid width="350" height="120" dataProvider="{myAC}">
   <mx:columns>
      <mx:AdvancedDataGridColumn headerText="Name" dataField="name"/>
      <mx:AdvancedDataGridColumn headerText="Email" dataField="email"/>
      <mx:AdvancedDataGridColumn headerText="Type" dataField="type"/>
   </mx:columns>
   <mx:rendererProviders>
      <mx:AdvancedDataGridRendererProvider columnIndex="1"
         columnSpan="2" renderer="myRenderer"/>
   </mx:rendererProviders>
</mx:AdvancedDataGrid>
</mx:Application>
```

Name	Email	Type
Jon Hirschi	jon@iscool.com	
Tariq Ahmed	tariq@iscool.com	

Figure 9.9 The email data spans two columns using an advanced item renderer.

When you run this application, the email column for each person continues into the adjacent column, as shown in figure 9.9.

Now, the question is, what if you have to span an entire row?

9.5.4 *Spanning an entire row*

To span an entire row, set the `columnIndex` to `0`. This technique isn't particularly useful if you're working with flat data, because you're effectively creating a single column. But it can come in handy if you have hierarchical data to which you want to add a summary row, as demonstrated in listings 9.24 and 9.25.

Listing 9.24 HelloWorld.mxml: spanning rows with hierarchical data

```
<?xml version="1.0"?>
<mx:Application xmlns:mx="http://www.adobe.com/2006/mxml">

<mx:XMLList id="myXML">
   <friends name="Friends">
      <friend name="Jon Hirschi" email="j_hirschi@domain.com">
         <info>
            <summary>
               47 emails sent in the last 24hrs
            </summary>
         </info>
      </friend>
      <friend name="Tariq Ahmed" email="t_ahmed@domain.com">
         <info>
            <summary>
               12 emails sent in the last 24hrs
            </summary>
         </info>
      </friend>
   </friends>
</mx:XMLList>

<mx:HierarchicalData source="{myXML}" id="myHD"/>

<mx:AdvancedDataGrid dataProvider="{myHD}" width="300">
   <mx:columns>
      <mx:AdvancedDataGridColumn dataField="@name"
         headerText="Contacts"/>
      <mx:AdvancedDataGridColumn dataField="@email" headerText="Email"/>
   </mx:columns>
   <mx:rendererProviders>
      <mx:AdvancedDataGridRendererProvider dataField="summary"
         columnIndex="0" columnSpan="0" renderer="myRenderer"/>
   </mx:rendererProviders>
```

```
</mx:AdvancedDataGrid>

</mx:Application>
```

Listing 9.25 myRenderer.mxml: item renderer used to display a summary

```
<?xml version="1.0" encoding="utf-8"?>
<mx:Label xmlns:mx="http://www.adobe.com/2006/mxml" width="100%"
   text="{data.summary}"/>
```

As you can see in figure 9.10, this solution works well when paired with hierarchical data.

Keep in mind that the renderer itself is exactly the same, whether it is used as a normal item renderer, or as an advanced item renderer.

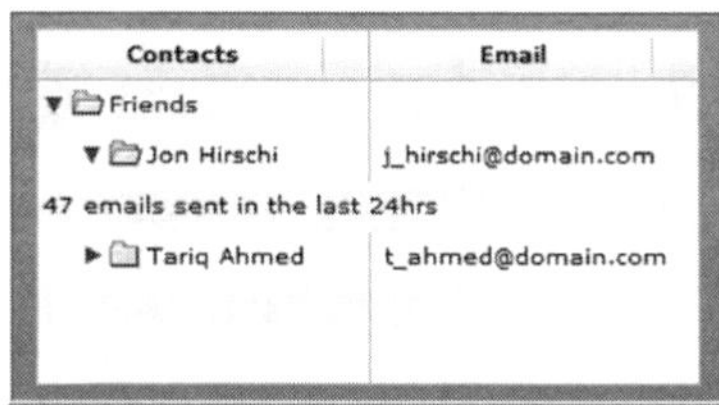

Figure 9.10 Spanning an entire row is useful with hierarchical data.

New Flex developers eventually encounter the following challenge when working with List-based components: sometimes you want to show only a subset of your data, depending on specific conditions. This is where filter functions come into play.

9.6 Filter functions

Filter functions aren't specific to Lists; they're a capability of collections. Filter functions let you filter out a subset of the information contained in the collection. One of the most common uses is in conjunction with List-based components. Instead of laboriously creating temporary arrays to hold subsets of data, you can let the collection do all the work for you.

Let's assume you're building a dashboard and want to allow the user to control what is displayed based on specified criteria. Listing 9.26 uses a filter function to provide that capability.

Listing 9.26 Controlling a dashboard display with a filter function

```
<?xml version="1.0"?>
<mx:Application xmlns:mx="http://www.adobe.com/2006/mxml"
   backgroundColor="white">
   <mx:Script>
      <![CDATA[
         import mx.collections.ArrayCollection;
         [Bindable]
         public var salesAC:ArrayCollection = new ArrayCollection([
         {name:"Canada",revenue:295323},
         {name:"United States",revenue:982832},
         {name:"England",revenue:109283},
         {name:"Brazil",revenue:12495},
         {name:"India",revenue:597232},
         {name:"China",revenue:682011}
         ]);

         public function filterFunc(item:Object):Boolean    ❶ Does record match criteria?
         {
```

```
            if(item.revenue >= salesRange.values[0] && item.revenue <=
               salesRange.values[1])
               return true;          <-- Record matches
            else
               return false; <-- Record doesn't match
         }

         public function filterSales():void      ❷ Applies filter
         {
            salesAC.filterFunction=filterFunc;        <-- ❸ Sets ArrayCollection's filterFunction property
            salesAC.refresh(); <-- ❹ Applies records that match on filter function
         }
      ]]>
   </mx:Script>

   <mx:Panel width="400" height="300" title="Sales Dashboard">
      <mx:HSlider change="filterSales()" id="salesRange" width="100%"
         thumbCount="2"
            labels="['0','250000','500000','750000','1000000']"
            tickInterval="50000" height="50"
               maximum="1000000"/>               <-- ❺ Let user filter range of values
      <mx:DataGrid id="dg" width="100%" height="100%"
         dataProvider="{salesAC}">
         <mx:columns>
            <mx:DataGridColumn headerText="Country" dataField="name"/>
            <mx:DataGridColumn headerText="Revenue" dataField="revenue"/>
         </mx:columns>
      </mx:DataGrid>
   </mx:Panel>
</mx:Application>
```

Here are the main features of listing 9.26:

- The `HSlider` ❺ is used to capture the range of values to filter via the user.
- When the `HSlider`'s values change, the `filterSales` function ❷ is called.
- `filterSales` tells the `salesAC` `ArrayCollection` to use filterFunc ❸ as its filter function.
- `filterSales` then calls `salesAC.refresh` ❹, which signals `salesAC` to check every record with `filterFunc`.
- `filterFunc` checks ❶ whether the record currently being evaluated is within the value range of the `HSlider`.

You can see how this works in figure 9.11, where only the sales revenue from countries that are within the specified slide range are displayed.

You could also use a `ComboBox` component for the values, or even a plain `TextInput` control. You can choose whatever is most convenient for you; all the action takes place in the function you designate for the `filterFunction` property on the `ArrayCollection`.

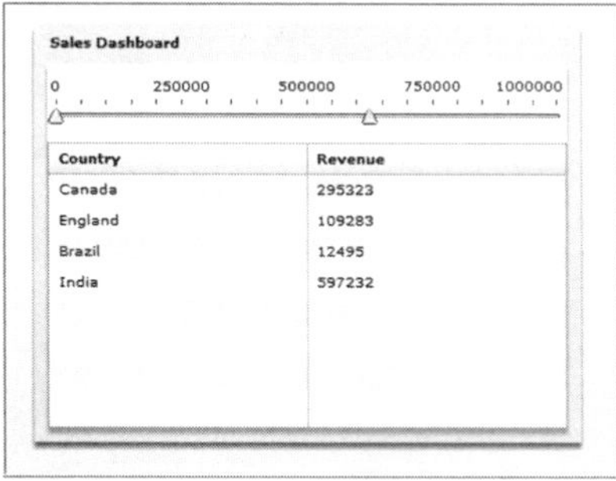

Figure 9.11 As the user moves the sliders, the content in the `DataGrid` changes in response, using a filter function.

9.7 Summary

When you begin working with `List`-based components, you get instant gratification because you can throw a lot of data at them, which is then displayed with little effort on your part. But one enhancement request can make things considerably more complicated. This chapter corralled all the independent pieces you'll need to confidently begin taking on that challenge using customized `Lists`.

You first learned to use a label function to customize the display in a `List`-based component. Label functions are easy to initialize and work well when combined with a formatter, but they're limited in what you can do with them.

Your main tool is the item renderer, which gives you maximum flexibility over display logic. Complementary to item renderers are item editors, which let users perform inline editing. Both item renderers and editors come with a number of events that let you tap into the editing process to further inject your own business logic and checkpoints.

Flex 3 comes with advanced `List`-based components (such as the `AdvancedDataGrid`), which support all the same item renderers but in more advanced ways (for instance, spanning multiple columns).

In the traditional web application world, when a user changes the selection criteria (such as date ranges, sales figures, and geographical regions), the web application requeries the back-end database for an updated set of data. With Flex, you can spare unnecessary round trips to the database by loading all the data up front (if this is logistically reasonable), and then use filter functions to parse your information on the client side.

We've used events to support various interactions; in this chapter, we looked at events that accompany item editors. We've also been reminding you regularly that Flex is an event-driven application framework. Now that you've been introduced to various cases demonstrating how events are used, it is time to look further into the mechanics of how they work.

Part 2

Application flow and structure

Part 1 focused on putting together the core blocks of an application. Part 2 moves forward with the application's wiring and structure.

Flex is an event-based environment. Although part 1 discussed the basic mechanics of using events, the next nine chapters go into much more depth about how the event model works and how you can make your own events. You'll use the power of events to add navigation and interactivity to your Flex applications.

A Flex application isn't much use without a back-end system to exchange data with. As part of application flow, you'll learn about the mechanisms available to transfer data back and forth.

That data may come in the form of XML, which Flex is adept at handling. With Flex's support for ECMAScript for XML (E4X) you can use ActionScript to work with XML as if it were a native ActionScript data type.

Having both the building blocks and the flow of an application under your belt, the application structure will be the key to making your code manageable, maintainable, and reusable. Flex supports a number of ways to achieve this, so we'll end this part of the book by discussing how to encapsulate logic into modular pieces.

10 Events

This chapter covers:

- Working with events
- Listening for events
- Dispatching events
- Creating custom events

Events are central to understanding how to work with Flex and how to create compelling, well-designed applications. Events are a powerful tool and one of the main features of the Flex framework.

Events are deceptively simple, but at the same time, they're an extremely powerful communication mechanism for your applications. We've mentioned several times up to this point that Flex is built around an event-driven framework. Events are the central nervous system within your applications, with information flowing in and out of them, up and down, and side to side. We don't mean to be melodramatic, but to understand events is to understand Flex.

Let's begin by introducing the event system and describe its all-important role in a Flex application.

10.1 The event system

If you've worked with web technologies such as ColdFusion, .Net, ASP, PHP, PERL, and Python, you already know that information is transmitted on a *request* and *response* basis. In this model, remote servers wait for requests from clients (users), then gather and process information relevant to the request. They build the appropriate response and send the data back to the client, at which point the transaction is over—until the client requests the next transaction.

The Flex framework employs a different paradigm. Instead of sending out requests and receiving responses, Flex designates components to patiently wait and *listen* for events. When a component hears an event, it performs the task it was designed to do, then waits again for the next event to occur.

In the Flex framework, events are constantly being fired off in response to a variety of user inputs. The main instigator for all these events is the user. By clicking a button, moving the mouse, or selecting an item from a drop-down menu, the user is unwittingly setting off events, which trigger the application to respond accordingly.

To the user, Flex's approach is indistinguishable from the standard request/response model—when a website link is clicked, a web server responds by sending a new page. With Flex, the difference is in the user-transparent operations that take place in the background. This gives you the ability to fire off tasks in parallel, none of which are dependent on each other, allowing for transparent activities to go on behind the scenes while your application interacts with and provides feedback to the user in real time (versus having code execute sequentially while the user waits for it to complete).

In addition, when requests for new information are made, they're sent to the target server asynchronously—the request is sent, and the application carries on with other tasks. The response will be processed whenever it comes back, whether that happens to be in five seconds or five minutes.

In contrast, when making a request to a web server, an HTML page viewed using a traditional client application (such as Internet Explorer or Firefox) waits until the complete response is received before showing any results or allowing you to move on with other interactions.

Inside the Flex application, execution is more similar to programming designed for client-side applications. We'll get into how this works in a moment; before we do, let's look at how the Flex event system is similar to another system you already know well: the Postal Service.

10.1.1 Event system—the Postal Service

Pieces, components, and classes need to communicate and pass data to each other through the event system. To illustrate this more clearly, we can draw a parallel between the event system and the Postal Service, which also passes data (in the form of letters and packages) between people, companies, and organizations.

In the Postal Service, a mail carrier makes scheduled trips to your mailbox to pick up and deliver letters and packages. Going back to an application, events are the *packages* that are picked up and delivered, or passed, to other elements within the program. Similar to their postal counterparts, events inform the addressee about what is currently happening.

Continuing with our analogy, when you prepare a package to be sent through the Postal Service, you box it up and apply a label that tells any interested parties where the package comes from, where it should be delivered, and, sometimes, what the package contains.

Events in the Flex application act in much the same way, and the local mail carrier is like the event-transportation system. Along the way, events pass by components that may be on the alert—or *listening*—for specific events. When an event passes by a component that is set to listen for it, the component is given an opportunity to inspect the package contents and see where the package is from and whether the package is of the type it was instructed to listen for.

The similarities to the Postal Service are instructive, but there are differences as well.

10.1.2 Event-delivery system

The event-delivery system differs from the Postal Service in the way it goes about sending events to each component. It's important to know the pathway events take within a Flex application, because this pathway determines which components receive the events and which don't.

All is not what it seems, though. Working strictly from the postal analogy, you may expect that if a component triggers and dispatches an event, that component must be the origin of the event. But the opposite is true: events originate from the application *root* (the upper level of a Flex application), are sent out to the component to be delivered, and are sent back to the application root, as shown in figure 10.1.

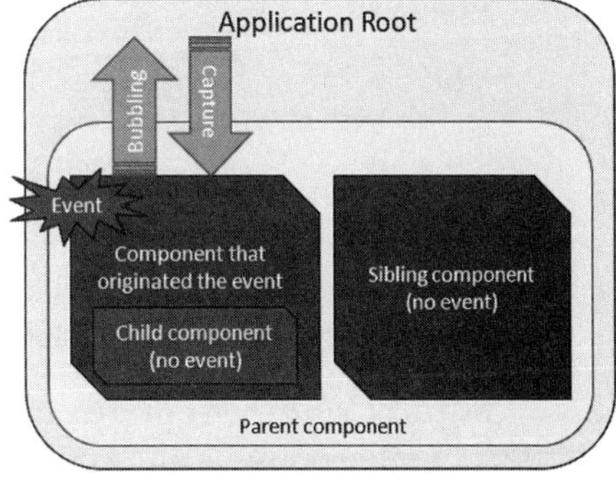

Figure 10.1 The parent/child relationship of Flex application events

When an alert event needs to be broadcast, it travels down the parent tree (start from the outermost level) toward the component that issued the alert. The event only goes through the parent tree (and any components that are specifically listening to it), which has implications for which components receive notifications about events. For example, as shown in figure 10.1, a component's parent typically receives event notifications; children and siblings don't receive notifications.

From an application perspective, when a component dispatches an event, that event can either *bubble* or not bubble. If the event bubbles, it traverses up the parent chain to the application root, passing by every parent in the chain. Each parent can listen for application events at its own level and rebroadcast those events as needed, or call methods within those child components to prompt them to take action.

This is the real power behind the Flex event system: the ability to create custom events and pass them around. Tying into the custom event system allows for maximum decoupling of logic and maximizes the components that can use that logic, which in turn affords maximum code reuse.

Now that you've learned a bit about how the application passes events around, let's break down the event's journey from start to finish by separating it into phases.

10.1.3 Set your phases on stun

Each portion of the journey—from application root to dispatching components and back again—can be divided into phases. Events have only three phases, depending on where they are in the process:

- *Capture*—Portion of the event that is sent to the dispatcher from the application
- *Bubbling*—Portion of the event that makes the trip back down to the application
- *Target*—Occurs only when the event has reached its target (the dispatcher)

You'll use the bubbling phase most often. The capture phase isn't used much, except in cases where you need to inspect an event and preempt it.

You can determine which phase you're in by using the event object's `Event.eventPhase` property. This property contains an integer that represents one of the following object constants:

- `Event.CAPTURING_PHASE:uint = 1`
- `Event.AT_TARGET:uint = 2`
- `Event.BUBBLING_PHASE:uint = 3`

When you're referring to or monitoring these phases, you can use either the number or the constant, although it's considered best practice to use the object constant wherever possible to make your code easier to read.

NOTE Using the capture phase is slower than using the bubbling phase to listen to events. Your application can slow down if you're doing too much listening in the capture phase. In general, most event listeners you create will be done on the bubbling phase.

You can think of these event phases as being along the lines of *before*, *during*, and *after*. The capture phase happens *before* the event reaches the object. Because most objects check for events during the bubbling, or *after*, phase, you can, in essence, stop events from occurring by listening for the event during the capture phase and discontinuing its propagation at that point. We'll explain this further in section 10.3.3.

For now, let's talk about what the event structure looks like and how you send events.

10.2 Sending and receiving events

A Flex event is made up of the following pieces of information:

- `Event.target`—The dispatching component.
- `Event.currentTarget`—The component that currently contains and is inspecting the event.
- `Event.type`—A string name that identifies the type of event, such as a click event (clicking a button), a mouse event (moving the mouse), or a select event (selecting an item). Events come in many types, and each type includes its own unique items; but each event has the generic types mentioned here.
- `Event.eventPhase`—The current phase of the event.

The package can contain other pieces of information as well, but at minimum it includes these items.

Let's examine what happens with a simple click event generated by pressing a mouse button, as shown in listing 10.1.

Listing 10.1 Click event example (MXML)

```
<?xml version="1.0" encoding="utf-8"?>
<mx:Application xmlns:mx="http://www.adobe.com/2006/mxml"
  layout="absolute">

  <mx:Button label="Click button!"                 Click
    click="clickFunction(event)"/>                 event
  <mx:Script>
      <![CDATA[
        import mx.controls.Alert;

        public function clickFunction(event:Event):void
        {
          var message:String = "you clicked me! ";
          message += event.target.label;                 Calls
          Alert.show(message,"Event Test");              clickFunction
        }
      ]]>
   </mx:Script>
</mx:Application>
```

When the user clicks the button, a click event is generated that calls `clickFunction()`. Each type of object carries its own set of events, which it can dispatch on cue. As seen in listing 10.1, when a user clicks the button, it dispatches the click event.

Although the example does the event listening in MXML, that doesn't mean you must work in that environment. You can do the same thing in ActionScript by using the `addEventListener()` function.

10.2.1 Adding event listeners

Using the ActionScript `addEventListener()` function provides more fine-grained control over the events and is the only way to listen for an event dispatched by components in your ActionScript code. You remove event listeners added to components when using ActionScript, but you can't remove them using MXML.

In certain circumstances, you need to use the `addEventListener()` method. For example, if you create an object at runtime in ActionScript, you must add the event listeners afterward at runtime as well.

If you need to listen for an event in any phase other than the bubbling phase, you must add the listener using the ActionScript method. As a handy reference guide, we've included the main attributes of an event listener in table 10.1.

Table 10.1 Event listener properties and method arguments

Property	Type	Description
`event_type`	`String`	(Required) Type of event for which the component will listen. You can define the event type directly or go with the more practical approach and use the event type constant defined on every event object.
`event_listener`	Function	(Required) Reference/name of a function that will respond to the event.
`use_capture`	`Boolean`	(Optional) Phase in which the component listens. If `true`, the component listens for the event during the capture phase. The default value is `false` (uses the bubbling phase).
`priority`	`Integer`	(Optional) When the listener is called. The higher the number, the sooner it's called. The value can be negative; the default value is `1`.
`weakRef`	`Boolean`	(Optional) How quickly the event listener object is picked up and destroyed by the garbage collector. `true` means it's discarded sooner. The default value is `false`, which prevents garbage collection from destroying the listener (performance at the cost of memory).

Let's look at a simple `eventListener` in listing 10.2. The code shows how you add an event listener on a previously instantiated display object using ActionScript.

Listing 10.2 Click event example using ActionScript

```
<?xml version="1.0" encoding="utf-8"?>
<mx:Application xmlns:mx="http://www.adobe.com/2006/mxml"
   layout="absolute" creationComplete="initFunc()">

  <mx:Button id="thisButton" label="Click button!"/>
  <mx:Script>
    <![CDATA[
      import mx.controls.Alert;

      public function initFunc():void
      {
       thisButton.addEventListener("click",clickFunction);
      }

      public function clickFunction(event:Event):void
```

Sets clickFunction to run when click event occurs

```
        {
          var message:String = "you clicked me! " +
            event.target.label;
          Alert.show(message,"Event Test");
        }
      ]]>
    </mx:Script>
  </mx:Application>
```

As demonstrated in listings 10.1 and 10.2, the main difference between the MXML and ActionScript methods for adding a simple event listener involves the use of `addEventListener()`.

When the button is clicked, it dispatches a click event which activates and passes the click event to `clickFunction()`. With the ActionScript method, you need an intermediary function to add the event listener to the button.

In listing 10.2, this is handled by `initFunc()`, which is called when the application issues the `creationComplete` event. This event is dispatched when every MXML item on the page has been created and is ready for display.

NOTE When you add an event listener, it listens during only one phase. For example, if you add an event listener for the capture phase of a button's click event, it listens only during the capture phase. If you need to listen to both the capture phase and the bubbling phase, you must add a second event listener for that phase specifically.

You've probably already gathered this, but most actions in Flex have corresponding events for which you can listen by using the event listeners; you can then respond as needed. This is the communication and nervous system of your Flex application. Even setting variables can cause events to be broadcast. This type of event dispatch is called *binding*.

10.2.2 Keying into binding events

Binding in Flex is carried out in the event system. When you bind a variable, you're establishing a dedicated listener that picks up on data change events issued from the variable or object to which it's bound (for more about binding, refer to chapter 3).

Whenever you create a binding to a variable, you register an event listener to respond to any changes that occur in that variable. When binding in MXML, the updating takes place behind the scenes, as demonstrated in listing 10.3.

Listing 10.3 MXML binding

```
<mx:Application xmlns:mx="http://www.adobe.com/2006/mxml"
  layout="vertical">
  <mx:Script>
    <![CDATA[
     [Bindable]
     public var labelText:String = "Label before event";
    ]]>
```

[Bindable] metadata means watch this variable

```
  </mx:Script>

  <mx:Button id="myButton" label="Change Label!"
     click="labelText='my label has changed';"/>
  <mx:Label id="myLabel" text="{labelText}"/>
</mx:Application>
```

Compare the code in listing 10.3 to what is required to accomplish the same thing in ActionScript (listing 10.4). The ActionScript version relies on an object called the `ChangeWatcher`, which monitors any changes in the value of a property to which you have it bound. If a change occurs, `ChangeWatcher` triggers the necessary events to watch that value. It's much like an event listener object in that it listens for specific events from a property.

Listing 10.4 ActionScript binding

```
<mx:Application xmlns:mx="http://www.adobe.com/2006/mxml"
  layout="vertical" creationComplete="initFunc()">
  <mx:Script>
    <![CDATA[
      import mx.Events.PropertyChangeEvent;
      import mx.Binding.utils.*;
      import mx.Events.FlexEvent;

      public var thisWatcher:ChangeWatcher;

      public function initFunc():void
      {
        watchIt();
      }

      public function watchIt():void
      {
        thisWatcher = ChangeWatcher.watch(
              someTextInput,"text",doTheBind);
      }

      public function stopIt():void
      {
        if (thisWatcher.isWatching())
        {
          thisWatcher.unwatch();
        }
      }

      public function doTheBind(e:Event):void
      {
        myLabel.text = someTextInput.text;
      }

    ]]>
  </mx:Script>
  <mx:Button id="watchButton" label="Watch Text" click="watchIt()"/>
  <mx:Button id="stopButton" label="Stop Watching"
     click="stopIt()"/>
  <mx:TextInput id="someTextInput" text="start text"/>
```

Imports are necessary to dynamically bind variables

Tells changeWatcher to detect changes

Checks list of watched variables

Removes watched variable

```
  <mx:Label id="myLabel" text=""/>
</mx:Application>
```

This method isn't as easy, but it's more flexible. Upon receipt of the creationComplete event from the application, you set the binding on the someTextInput object to let you watch or bind to its text value. This is done with the ChangeWatcher.watch() method, which acts as the constructor method for ChangeWatcher; an instantiated ChangeWatcher object is returned when you call the watch() method.

This method takes inputs for the object you want to watch and a property of the watched object that is listened to (in this case, you're watching the text property of someTextInput). The third property specifies which function to call when this event is triggered—in this case, doTheBind().

If you look back at the addEventListener() method, you'll see this approach acts in a similar manner. With the addEventListener() method, you're listening to the entire object; with the method presented in listing 10.4, you're watching a specific object property.

When you type anything in the text input, ChangeWatcher automatically listens for those updates and executes the event. Each time you press a key, you send out an event that is monitored by the ChangeWatcher. As demonstrated in listing 10.4, your binding event can be as simple as copying the user input value, or it can be as complex as you need it to be.

Another benefit of this implementation is the ability to remove a binding from an object. You can't remove the binding in MXML. As shown in listing 10.4, using ActionScript, you can click the Stop Watching button to remove the bind event as if it had never been bound at all.

If you look at the stopIt() function, you'll notice that the isWatching() function checks whether the particular watcher you identified is monitoring anything. If it's watching, you can call the unwatch() method to remove the watcher and discontinue the binding.

10.2.3 Removing event listeners

You've just seen the unwatch() method in action, which lets you stop monitoring a variable for changes. When using event listeners, you have the same type of capability. But if an event listener was added at runtime in ActionScript, you're only able to remove it using the addEventListener() method.

Listing 10.5 shows how to test an object to determine if a particular event listener is monitoring it (defined by the combination of eventType, phase, and responding function).

Listing 10.5 Example of click events

```
<?xml version="1.0" encoding="utf-8"?>
<mx:Application xmlns:mx="http://www.adobe.com/2006/mxml"
  width="100%" height="100%" layout="vertical">
```

```
<mx:Script>
  <![CDATA[
    import mx.controls.Alert;

    [Bindable]
    public var labelText:String = "Label before event";
    public var myCounter:Number = 0;

    public function clickFunction(event:Event):void
    {
      var message:String = "you clicked me! " +
         event.target.label;
      Alert.show(message,"Event Test");
    }

    public function addMyEvent():void
    {
      if (myButton.hasEventListener(MouseEvent.MOUSE_OVER))
      {
         myButton.removeEventListener(
            MouseEvent.MOUSE_OVER,changeLabel);
         myInput.text = "Event was Removed";
         addEventButton.label =
            "Click this button to add event";
         myLabel.text = "Mouse over Event listener removed";
         myCounter = 0;
      }
      else
      {
         myButton.addEventListener(
           MouseEvent.MOUSE_OVER,changeLabel);
         myInput.text = "Event was added";
         addEventButton.label =
            "Click this button to remove event";
      }
    }

    public function changeLabel(event:MouseEvent):void
    {
       myCounter++;
       myLabel.text = "Mouse over Event listener listened! - "
       myLabel.text += myCounter + " times";
     }

  ]]>
</mx:Script>

<mx:Button id="addEventButton"
    label="click this button to add listener"
    click="addMyEvent()"/>
<mx:Button id="myButton" label="Click button!"
     click="clickFunction(event)"/>
<mx:TextInput id="myInput" />
<mx:Label id="myLabel" text="{labelText}"/>
</mx:Application>
```

MXML binding watcher (can't be removed)

Removes event listener

Adds event listener

Events are happening throughout listing 10.5. Compile and run the code, and you'll see that what's going on is pretty simple.

When you click the first button, `addEventButton`, you add a `MouseOver` event to `myButton`. You check the button to see if it lists a registered `MouseOver` event. As shown in listing 10.6, if an event listener isn't listed, you create one.

Listing 10.6 Adding an event listener if one isn't present

```
public function addMyEvent():void {
     if (myButton.hasEventListener(MouseEvent.MOUSE_OVER)) {
       ...
     } else {
      myButton.addEventListener(MouseEvent.MOUSE_OVER,changeLabel);
       ...
    }
  }
```

Now, moving your mouse over `myButton` calls the `changeLabel()` function, which increments each time you pass over the button. Clicking the first button again removes the event listener, as illustrated in listing 10.7.

Listing 10.7 Removing an event listener if it exists

```
public function addMyEvent():void {
     if (myButton.hasEventListener(MouseEvent.MOUSE_OVER)) {
      myButton.removeEventListener(MouseEvent.MOUSE_OVER,changeLabel);
      ...
```

Again, it's important to note that removing event listeners works only on events that were added using the ActionScript method of defining an event listener; listener functions added using the MXML format are permanently attached to the object. For example, you can't remove an event listener added using the MXML script shown in the following snippet:

```
<mx:Button id="myButton" label="Click button!"
  click="clickFunction(event)"/>
```

If you think you might need to remove the event listener at some point, use the `addEventListener()` method.

When you click the Click Button! button, it calls `clickFunction(event)`. If you're familiar with HTML and JavaScript, you can see that the functionality is similar. If you want to pass the event to the function, you need to specifically enter the event in the function syntax; doing so passes the event as a parameter. When defined in this manner, you're not limited to passing events to your functions. You can also pass custom parameters to which you might want to respond:

```
<mx:Button id="myButton" label="Click button!"
  click="clickFunction(event, "newparam1 ", someVar) "/>
```

This gives you an incredible amount of flexibility when defining events and enables you to create your handlers to react in whatever manner you need.

In the next section, we'll cover dispatching and creating custom events. This will give you ultimate control over events and enable you to dynamically determine when events are sent out and what data these events should carry.

10.3 Custom events

Part of what makes Flex events so powerful is the ability to create your own custom alerts and use them to communicate within your application. By sending out events when data changes or when the user initiates some action, you decouple an application's logic from the objects that use it. This is critical because it creates a more modular structure that allows a component to change without affecting other parts of your application.

10.3.1 Using the dispatcher to send an event

To send a custom event, you use the `dispatchEvent()` method on the object issuing the event. Only objects in the display list can dispatch events into the event stream.

In general, this means the object dispatching the event needs to be shown in the application somewhere, at some point. Most objects that can be expressed in MXML have the ability to dispatch events.

Consider the following snippet:

```
myButton.dispatchEvent( new Event("newCustomEvent"));
```

It performs two distinct operations:

1. A new event class is instantiated to handle and hold the information.
2. The event is injected into the event stream using the `dispatchEvent()` function call.

Listing 10.8 shows this simple way of dispatching custom alerts.

Listing 10.8 Custom event

```
<mx:Application xmlns:mx="http://www.adobe.com/2006/mxml"
   layout="vertical" creationComplete="initFunc()">

  <mx:Script>
    <![CDATA[
      import flash.Events.Event;
      import mx.controls.Alert;

      public function initFunc():void
      {
        myButton.addEventListener("newCustomEvent",
           respondToEvent);

      public function doEvent():void
      {
       myButton.dispatchEvent( new Event("newCustomEvent"));
      }

      public function respondToEvent(e:Event):void
```

Dispatches custom event of type newCustomEvent

```
        {
          Alert.show("got the Event and it is of type " + e.type,
            "got the event");
        }
      ]]>
    </mx:Script>
    <mx:Button id="myButton" label="Fire off Event" click="doEvent()"/>
  </mx:Application>
```

As demonstrated in listing 10.8, the simplest way to use a custom event is to send it out by dispatching a new event and changing its event type. The event type is a text property within the event that is monitored by the `eventListener`.

To listen to that event, you must add an event listener and instruct it to focus on the particular event type of the issuing object. You do this in the `initFunc()` that's called after the `creationComplete` event is triggered. When working in an application setting, you can listen for events coming from components and respond with your own custom actions as the events occur. In this way, components can be unaware of the presence or location of other components, yet still react to events that take place in those other components.

The instantiation of an event can also happen separately from the dispatch:

```
Var myEvent:Event = new Event("eventname",false);
 myButton.dispatchEvent(myEvent);
```

This approach lets you add items and more fully customize your events. For example, you can create a custom event class that allows you to add extra information or a payload to deliver to any event listener.

In addition to sending your own custom events, you can fake events. In other words, you can create an event that impersonates an authentic Flex event normally generated by the Flex system, which you can dispatch dynamically at any time.

You can use imposters such as these to send out your own click events to simulate a button being clicked:

```
myButton.dispatchEvent(new MouseEvent(MouseEvent.Click,false));
```

This snippet instantiates a new `MouseEvent` and inserts it into the event stream as if it had been generated by the button. Anything that's listening for this mouse event will react and respond as it would to an authentic event.

Now that we've covered how to send out events, we'll spend some time explaining how to create custom events by *subclassing* the event object.

10.3.2 Creating custom events

Creating a custom event type on the fly is easy, but sometimes it doesn't get the job done. As you progress, you'll discover drawbacks to generating quick and simple custom events. For example, if you have a syntax error in either your event dispatcher code or in the event listener code, you must isolate and fix the problem at runtime.

If you're working with a large application, you can lose valuable time and effort tracking down errors. If you instead use a custom event, you can check for those errors at compile time to ensure they don't find their way into your application.

Using the New ActionScript Class wizard, you can automatically create nearly everything you need in a custom event. Figure 10.2 shows the creation of a custom event called `MyCustomEvent`, derived from the `flash.Events.Event` base class. (For more information on extending classes, see chapters 16 and 17.)

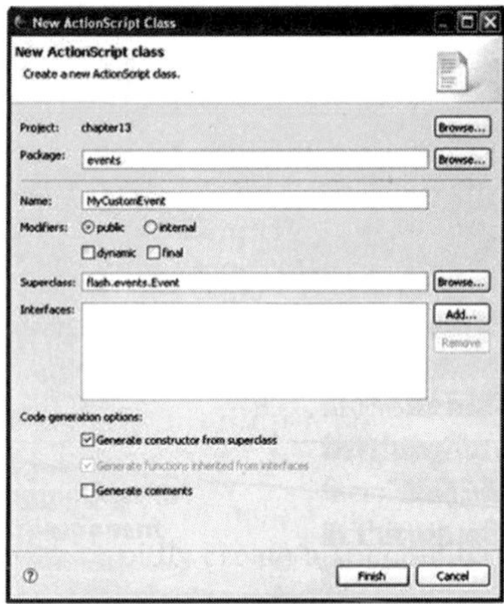

Figure 10.2 Use the New ActionScript Class wizard to create a custom event.

The wizard automatically generates most of the code for your custom event along with the majority of information populated for the class. In this case, we've made only a couple of modifications to create the `MyCustomEvent` class.

Listing 10.9 shows the code for the custom event we created and modified using the wizard. Most of this code was generated by the wizard after we indicated we wanted it to generate the constructor from the *superclass*. By using the superclass, the application can establish most of what is necessary, because the base class has a set of information it needs to create an event.

Listing 10.9 Creating a custom event

```
package Events
{
  import flash.Events.Event;

  public class MyCustomEvent extends Event
  {
    public static
    var CUSTOMEVENTTYPE:String = "CustomEventType";

    public var info:String;

     public function MyCustomEvent(type:String,
       info:String, bubbles:Boolean=false,
       cancelable:Boolean=false)
    {
      super(type, bubbles, cancelable);
      this.info = info;
    }
  }

}
```

- **Extends Event object**
- **Defines custom event type**
- **Uses multiple inputs or none**
- **Calls Event object constructor**

If you try using the wizard to create a custom event, you'll see that the code looks similar to this; we've added only a couple of items.

In this case, we added two variables to the event. One is the public static variable `CUSTOMEVENTTYPE`, which designates the event type. This variable won't change; it's a convenience variable that lets us use code hinting for the event type.

The other variable, `info`, is a `String` that stores a message to be communicated to the user. When the monitoring object receives this event, not only does it have the event properties available that it normally has from the base event class, but it also has the `info` property.

Listing 10.10 presents a simple example of how you can use custom events to communicate in an application. This code doesn't get into a lot of depth in terms of custom components and other objects, but the interactions that take place here can also take place at the macro level of intercomponent communications.

Listing 10.10 Using a custom event

```
<mx:Application xmlns:mx="http://www.adobe.com/2006/mxml"
   layout="vertical" creationComplete="initFunc()">

   <mx:Script>
    <![CDATA[
      import mx.controls.Alert;
      import Events.MyCustomEvent;

      public function initFunc():void                 Initializes function
      {
        myButton.addEventListener( MyCustomEvent.CUSTOMEVENTTYPE,
             respondToEvent);
      }                                                         Triggers custom
      public function doEvent(info:String):void  <----         event
      {
        myButton.dispatchEvent( new                                   Uses custom
         MyCustomEvent(MyCustomEvent.CUSTOMEVENTTYPE,info));          event
      }

      public function respondToEvent(e:MyCustomEvent):void   <----  Responds to
      {                                                               MyCustomEvent
        var msg:String = "got the Event and it is of type  " +
           e.type;

        msg += " and here is the message  "+ e.info;            info is variable in
        msg += " and here is some info from the button  "       MyCustomEvent

        msg += e.target.label;                       target is
       Alert.show(msg,"got the event");              myButton
     }
    ]]>
   </mx:Script>
   <mx:Button id="myButton" label="Fire off Event"
     click="doEvent('buttons are really great!')"/>
</mx:Application>
```

As listing 10.10 shows, when the application creation phase is finished, `initFunc()` is called; it sets up the event listener on the button to listen for the custom event you defined. When the button is clicked, it calls the doEvent() function that creates and dispatches the custom event, which can be received by any object designated to listen for it.

Finally, the respondToEvent() function takes all the parts of the event and uses them to create the message that is sent back to the user in the form of an alert.

When the code dispatches the custom event, it injects it into the application's event stream, where it's handled like any other event. The custom aspect of this setup is what the event can carry along with it and how you can subclass the event to be whatever kind of object you want.

Now that you've seen how to send out custom events, let's look at how to stop event propagation.

10.3.3 Stopping event propagation

During any event phase (capture, target, or bubbling), you can use the event's stopPropagation() and stopImmediatePropagation() methods to discontinue the event from broadcasting to any other components. The two methods are virtually identical, differing only in whether other event listeners on the same component are allowed to receive the event.

For example, if the event.stopPropagation() method is used on an event, it discontinues propagation after all other event listeners on a given component have completed responding to the event. If you were to use the event.stopImmediatePropagation() method, event propagation would be terminated before it was delivered to any other events, even if they were listening on the same component.

When used in conjunction with the priority attribute of the event listener (set when adding the event listener), you can set up a function to be the first responder to the event. This can be an effective gating mechanism to evaluate an event and cease propagation if necessary to any other event listener on a given component (see listing 10.11).

Listing 10.11 Stopping propagation

```
<mx:Application xmlns:mx="http://www.adobe.com/2006/mxml" layout="vertical"
   creationComplete="initFunc()">

  <mx:Script>
    <![CDATA[
      import mx.controls.Alert;

      public function initFunc():void
      {
        myButton.addEventListener("click",
          respondToEvent,false,100);        // Adds event listener with high priority

        myParentHBox.addEventListener("click",
          parentEventResponse, false,0);    // Listens for bubbling events on parent
      }

    public function respondToEvent(e:Event):void
```

```
{
  var msg:String = "This is the first responder, "
  msg += " and now the Event will be stopped ";
  Alert.show(msg,"First Event Listener");

    e.stopPropagation();        <--  Stops propagation—
  }                                   second event fires

  public function respondToEventClick(e:Event):void
  {
    Alert.show("this is the mxml click Event
        and this will fire second ",
        "Second Event Listener");
  }

  public function parentEventResponse(e:Event):void    Event never
  {                                                     reaches
    Alert.show("You should never see this alert",      parent
    "Parent Event Response");
  }

]]>
</mx:Script>
  <mx:HBox id="myParentHBox">
  <mx:Button id="myButton" label="Fire off Event"
   click="respondToEventClick(event)"/>
</mx:HBox>

</mx:Application>
```

You interrupt the propagation of the event at the button level. Normally, this event would travel through all the functions, triggering all three alerts. But after the first event, you call the `stopPropagation()` method. When you run the example, the first two events—those listening directly to the button—will run, but the parent event that is listening to `myParentHBox` won't receive the event and therefore won't run.

If you change the `stopPropagation()` method to `stopImmediatePropagation()`, you'll see only the first alert. The `stopImmediatePropagation()` method terminates any and all delivery of the event beyond the first event listener. Discontinuing the propagation of events is an effective way to handle your event flow, depending on the circumstances. This is true when you have custom components sending out custom events.

Now that we've dealt with stopping propagation and creating custom events, we'll discuss adding event metadata to components.

10.3.4 Adding event metadata to components

An important part of completing the dispatch of events—particularly when using custom components and classes—is adding metadata to components involved with dispatch events, to take advantage of code hinting in Flex Builder.

It's not absolutely necessary to add metadata to components, but doing so adds convenience by giving you the ability to see events as properties of a component. Listing 10.12 shows how to add metadata to your components.

Listing 10.12 Event metadata in an MXML component

```
<mx:Metadata>
      [Event(name="customButtonClick", type="flash.Events.Event")]
</mx:Metadata>
```

The earlier code listings include examples of how to use metadata when communicating with events from components. In the snippet that follows, the component dispatches the `customButtonClick` event by executing this dispatch event code:

```
this.dispatchEvent(new Event("customButtonClick",true));
```

This dispatch command sends an event into the parent application with the event type of `customButtonClick`. The metadata tag in the component provides hints to the main parent component and the compiler that the component will be firing off the custom event and the parent can listen to it. In the parent, the following code picks up on the event and directs it to the correct function:

```
<comp:CustomEventMeta customButtonClick="doAlert(event)"/>
```

Using events with custom components as we've presented in this chapter lets you retain loose coupling. Your components don't need to know about each other, and the parent windows can control their behavior and manage interactions.

You'll find out more about custom components in chapters 16 and 17.

10.4 Summary

This chapter focused on the events system and how this system is used in Flex. The events system is arguably the most important aspect of the Flex framework because of its permeation throughout all components of the system.

If you're coming from a web development background, learning Flex is a paradigm shift from the standard request/response model of creating web applications. The events system is the core of this shift. Everything you do through Flex in some way touches upon the events system. When you key into an application's events, you can free your objects to behave independently, to the point where they don't need awareness of the application.

Now that you've tackled the events system, we'll move on to discuss application navigation.

11 Application navigation

This chapter covers:

- Components that facilitate navigation
- Assembling data to drive navigation components
- Interacting with navigation components

You usually don't get far into the process of developing an application before you discover you need to begin separating it into distinct functional areas and purposes and enable the user to move to and from these areas. We call this *navigation*. In this chapter, we'll look at the following components that you'll use to add navigational features to your application:

- `Menu`
- `MenuBar`
- `TabBar`
- `TabNavigator`
- `Accordion`

Before we can delve into how to use each of these components, we need to prepare the data they will use. Like so many tasks, this can be done many ways; we'll explore the options along with their pros and cons.

11.1 Feeding the data provider for menus and menu bars

Drop-down menus have been a part of basic navigation since the innovation of the GUI; they add an easy way to display an application's features and selection lists without taking up a lot of your window's valuable real estate—they remain conveniently hidden until you need them. Drop-downs also reduce user fatigue and effort because the menu appears at the location where the user clicks a button, tab, or heading.

Using HTML to create drop-down menus from scratch is tricky because you need to deal with layering, *Z*-indices, overlapping form elements, cross-browser compatibility issues, and quite a bit of JavaScript and DHTML (particularly if you want context-driven menus). Many third-party products are available that abstract the complexity of implementing drop-downs in HTML, but the complexity is still there in the background. Fortunately, Flex offers easier solutions.

Putting aside the issues surrounding ease of use, we need to address how to prepare the data you intend to present in your menus. The information that populates cascading menus is usually hierarchical in nature, so your data needs to reflect this.

You can provide data to menus in many ways, each with advantages and disadvantages. Let's look at the options at your disposal.

11.1.1 Nested arrays

Nested arrays are made up of one or more levels of arrays. They simulate a tree-like structure of data, which you can program in ActionScript.

Nested arrays offer economical memory usage. But their syntax is complicated; and changes in the underlying data aren't automatically reflected visually, because nested arrays aren't collection-based objects.

Listing 11.1 demonstrates how you can set up and use a nested array.

Listing 11.1 Using a nested array to drive a menu

```
public var myMenuData:Array =          <-- Instantiates array
 [
  {
   label:'New',
    children: [{label:'Task'},{label:'Request'},{label:'Person'}]   <-- Nested array (1)
  },
  {
   label:'Import',
    children: [{label:'Image'},{label:'Document'},{label:'Project'}]  <-- (1)
  }
 ];
```

In listing 11.1, a couple of lines of code (1) start with the declaration `children:`. These lines define two nested arrays inside the primary `myMenuData` array. This declaration instructs a

Menu object to treat the data contained in these subarrays as nested information.

TIP By default, menus look for nested arrays named children.

The problem with using arrays is they're a simple type of object; and because they aren't members of the collection family, changes to the underlying data aren't automatically broadcast to other objects designated to listen. This is where upgrading to a collection-based object can be more advantageous—particularly the ArrayCollection.

11.1.2 Nested array collections

Nested array collections function nearly the same as nested arrays, except that you employ the ArrayCollection class. These array collections automatically broadcast data changes; but like arrays, they have a complicated syntax.

As listing 11.2 illustrates, there's not much difference between the nested array-collection approach and the simpler nested array.

Listing 11.2 Using a nested array collection to drive a menu

```
import mx.collections.ArrayCollection;

public var myMenuData:ArrayCollection = new ArrayCollection(
  [
   {
    label:'New',
    children: [{label:'Task'},{label:'Request'},{label:'Person'}]
   },
   {
    label:'Import',
    children: [{label:'Image'},{label:'Document'},{label:'Project'}]
   }
  ]);
```

❶ Imports ArrayCollection class

Instantiates ArrayCollection

❷ Nested array data

Listings 11.1 and 11.2 are similar, but in listing 11.2 you import the ArrayCollection ❶ class and call its constructor to initialize an instance of it. As with an array, you specify the children: declaration ❷ to create a new level.

Arrays and array collections work well in the ActionScript environment, but the syntax can be challenging to visualize when multiple levels are involved. You may prefer the easier model- or XML-based approach.

11.1.3 Models

Models are a type of data that bear a striking resemblance to XML but are actually nested low-level objects. They can be used as a parking lot to hold data that needs to be processed later. For example, you can use models to temporarily hold the values for a form.

Models offer several advantages:

- Although a model appears similar to XML, behind the scenes Flex converts the data into nested low-level objects. This provides some convenience with respect to syntax, because you're working with native ActionScript objects.

- You can easily script and visualize the code structure due to its XML-like nature.
- You can implement binding with little effort.
- Models contribute minimally to application overhead (they're low-level objects).
- You can pull in data from a separate file using the `source` property.

On the down side, models must conform to a specific syntax to be compatible with components that display hierarchical data in nested structures, such as menus.

Listing 11.3 shows an example of using a model:

Listing 11.3 Creating a model that a menu uses to drive its display

```
<mx:Model id="myMenuData">
  <menuinfo>
    <menuitem label="Task">
      <children label="Request"/>
      <children label="Person"/>
    </menuitem>
    <menuitem label="Import">
      <children label="Image"/>
      <children label="Document"/>
      <children label="Project"/>
    </menuitem>
  </menuinfo>
</mx:Model>
```

You can change the node names—`menuinfo` and `menuitem`—to whatever you prefer; but if you want to create deeper node levels, you must declare them as `children`.

Models let you benefit from XML-like convenience, but they're not actually XML. You'll come across circumstances in which there is no substitute for the real thing. For instance, if your application requires server-side data storage, it's time to bring XML into the game.

11.1.4 XML component and class

Flex's XML capabilities are rooted in the `XML` component and class; as you'll see in chapter 15, XML in Flex is an extremely powerful tool. The tree-like nature of the data needed to drive menus is a natural for XML.

Using XML offers several benefits:

- This approach is similar to using models in terms of ease of writing and reading.
- `XML` is available as a component (`<mx:XML>`) and an ActionScript class.
- Unlike models, you can name all your nodes whatever you want—you're not restricted to the top levels.
- The `XML` component is a more intelligent object that provides supporting functions for manipulating the XML.
- You can pull in data from a separate file using the `source` property.

As with a nested array, an XML component isn't a collection-based object, so changes in underlying data aren't automatically propagated throughout the event system.

In listing 11.4, the model from listing 11.3 is converted into an XML component.

Listing 11.4 Using the XML component to create menu data

```
<mx:XML id="myMenuData">
  <menuinfo>
    <menuitem label="Task">
      <submenu label="Request"/>
      <submenu label="Person"/>
  </menuitem>
  <menuitem label="Import">
    <submenu label="Image"/>
    <submenu label="Document"/>
    <submenu label="Project"/>
    </menuitem>
  </menuinfo>
</mx:XML>
```

You use the arbitrary submenu instead of the children node name required by other types of data.

Similarly, you can code this in ActionScript, as listing 11.5 demonstrates.

Listing 11.5 Using the XML ActionScript class to create menu data

```
<mx:Script>
<![CDATA[
  public var myMenuData:XML=
    <menuinfo>
      <menuitem label="Task">
        <submenu label="Request"/>
        <submenu label="Person"/>
      </menuitem>
      <menuitem label="Import">
        <submenu label="Image"/>
        <submenu label="Document"/>
        <submenu label="Project"/>
      </menuitem>
    </menuinfo>
]]>
</mx:Script>
```

XML is a great match for driving menus with tree-structured data. But you need to factor in the overarching XML rule that all XML documents must have a single root node.

Fortunately, you have options to get around this. In Menu components, you can indicate a starting point, or you can use an XMLList component instead.

11.1.5 XMLList component

An XMLList component is much like an XML component, but its primary purpose is to store fragments or sections of data extracted from an XML-based document. When you use XMLLists with menus, they offer all the advantages of XML—and you can work with multiple roots. XMLLists also provide more supporting functions for working with and manipulating data.

On the other hand, because an XMLList component isn't a collection-based object, changes in the underlying data aren't automatically propagated.

Let's try an XMLList component by modifying the menu data from listing 11.5; see listing 11.6.

Listing 11.6 Using an XMLList component to configure menu data

```
<mx:XMLList id="myMenuData">
  <menuitem label="Task">
    <submenu label="Request"/>
    <submenu label="Person"/>
  </menuitem>
  <menuitem label="Import">
    <submenu label="Image"/>
    <submenu label="Document"/>
    <submenu label="Project"/>
  </menuitem>
</mx:XMLList>
```

Listing 11.6 demonstrates there are multiple root nodes. This isn't a monumental difference, but it's another option available to you.

We continue to mention the disadvantage of not being a collection. Recall that arrays suffer from this limitation, but array collections can be used as alternatives. Likewise, the XML component/class has an alternative XMLListCollection component and class.

11.1.6 XMLListCollection component and class

The XMLListCollection acts like a wrapper by encapsulating existing XML and adding the capabilities of a collection. It offers all the benefits of XML but is collection-based so changes to underlying data are automatically transmitted to components designated to listen—in this scenario, the Menu component. XMLListCollection is available in component and ActionScript class varieties, and it can be used to wrap existing XML. It's a powerful object, so it's heavier than the lightweight objects mentioned earlier—but well worth it.

You can use the XMLListCollection a variety of ways, all of which have it act as a wrapper around existing XML data. Let's explore some of these variations. Listing 11.7 shows how the XMLListCollection is used to wrap an existing XMLList in order to populate itself with data.

Listing 11.7 XMLListCollection component wrapped around an XMLList

```
<mx:XMLListCollection id="myMenuData">
  <mx:XMLList>
    <menuitem label="Task">
```

```
      <submenu label="Request"/>
      <submenu label="Person"/>
    </menuitem>
  </mx:XMLList>
</mx:XMLListCollection>
```

Listing 11.8 takes a different approach by indirectly wrapping an existing XML component via the source property.

Listing 11.8 XMLListCollection component sourcing XML

```
<mx:XML id="config">
  <configData>
    <appData>
      <appName name="My Application"/>
    </appData>
    <menuData>
      <menuitem label="Task">
        <submenu label="Request"/>
        <submenu label="Person"/>
      </menuitem>
    </menuData>
  </configData>
</mx:XML>

<mx:XMLListCollection id="myMenuData"
                     source="{config.menuData.menuitem}"/>
```

The beauty of listing 11.8 is that the XML can be stored in a separate XML configuration file, which pares down your XMLListCollection to only the data needed to drive your menu:

```
<mx:XML id="config" source="config.xml">
<mx:XMLListCollection id="myMenuData" source="{config.menuData.menuitem}"/>
```

In listing 11.9, we switch to an XMLListCollection class instead of the component.

Listing 11.9 XMLListCollection class used to source XML

```
<mx:XML id="config" source="config.xml">
<mx:Script>
<![CDATA[
  import mx.collections.XMLListCollection;
  public var myMenuData:XMLListCollection = new XMLListCollection();
  public function setup():void
  {
    myMenuData.source = config.menuData.menuitem;
  }
]]>
</mx:Script>
```

Using ActionScript, you can declare an instance of the XMLListCollection and set up the source to point to the source of the XML information. The source can be an instance of the XML and XMLList components and classes.

11.1.7 *Choosing a data type for the data provider*

As you can see, you have several options available to configure the data for your menus and menu bars. But if you have to choose one method, use the `XMLList-Collection` because it furnishes all the benefits you'll need to develop applications quickly. This argument is so compelling we're going use the `XMLListCollection` for the remaining examples in this chapter as you learn how to use the Menu component.

11.2 *Working with menus*

A menu creates a single-column window of user-selectable choices or options. Menus can contain other menus (to any number of levels), each opening, or *cascading*, to reveal yet more choices to the user.

The main points we'll be exploring as you learn how to work with menus are:

- Creating menus
- Positioning menus
- Customizing menus
- Interacting with menus

We'll begin with the most essential step: creating a basic menu.

11.2.1 *Creating a menu*

Flex often has MXML components and ActionScript equivalents, but in this case there's no MXML component version of a menu: you have to use ActionScript to set up and display the menu (listing 11.10).

Listing 11.10 Creating a menu from scratch

```
<?xml version="1.0"?>
<mx:Application xmlns:mx="http://www.adobe.com/2006/mxml"
   backgroundColor="#FFFFFF" >

  <mx:XMLListCollection id="myMenuData">          <-- Data to drive menu
  <mx:XMLList>
    <menuitem label="Tasks">
      <submenu label="Add Request"/>
      <submenu label="Add Person">
      <submenu label="Customer"/>
        <submenu label="Employee"/>
      </submenu>
    </menuitem>
  </mx:XMLList>
  </mx:XMLListCollection>                         Imports Menu ActionScript class

  <mx:Script>
    <![CDATA[
      import mx.controls.Menu;                    <--
      public var myMenu:Menu;     <-- (1) Menu instance

      private function InitializeMenu():void      <-- (2) Initializes menu
      {
```

```
        myMenu = Menu.createMenu(null, myMenuData,true);
        myMenu.labelField="@label";       <-- ❸ @ means attribute of XML node
      }
    ]]>
  </mx:Script>

  <mx:Button id="myButton" creationComplete="InitializeMenu()"    <-- ❹ Runs when Flex creates button
          label="Display Menu" click="myMenu.show()"/>
</mx:Application>
```

After Flex creates the button, it runs the `InitializeMenu()` function (via the `creationComplete` event ❹.

`InitializeMenu()` ❷ uses the `Menu` class's `createMenu()` function to create an instance of a `Menu` and assigns the associated data to it.

You notify the `Menu` instance (`myMenu`) ❶ that the display field is named `label`. This is specified as `@label` ❸ because it's an attribute of an XML node. If instead you were using an array collection, you wouldn't use the `@` declarative.

The `InitializeMenu()` function can be run anywhere. For example, you could have run this script instead:

```
<mx:Application xmlns:mx="http://www.adobe.com/2006/mxml"
   creationComplete="InitializeMenu()">
```

If you want to expend the least amount of coding effort, you can use the approach presented in listing 11.11 and get everything done in one shot.

Listing 11.11 Compact way to initialize and display the menu all at once

```
<mx:Script>
<![CDATA[
  import mx.controls.Menu;
  private function showMenu():void
  {
    var myMenu:Menu = Menu.createMenu(null, myMenuData,true);
    myMenu.labelField="@label";
    myMenu.show();
  }
]]>
</mx:Script>
<mx:Button id="myButton" label="Display Menu" click="showMenu()"/>
```

The only drawback of taking this path is that you're constantly creating new menus. In reality, this isn't much of a problem, because Flex throws the old menu away. It's more an issue of trying to avoid unnecessary overhead.

When you click the Display Menu button, a menu appears in the upper-left corner of the window (see figure 11.1).

Although it takes quite a bit of code to generate this simple menu, it boils down to one key function: `createMenu()`. Let's take a second look at this function, which you call using the following script:

```
var myMenu:Menu = Menu.createMenu(null, myMenuData,true);
```

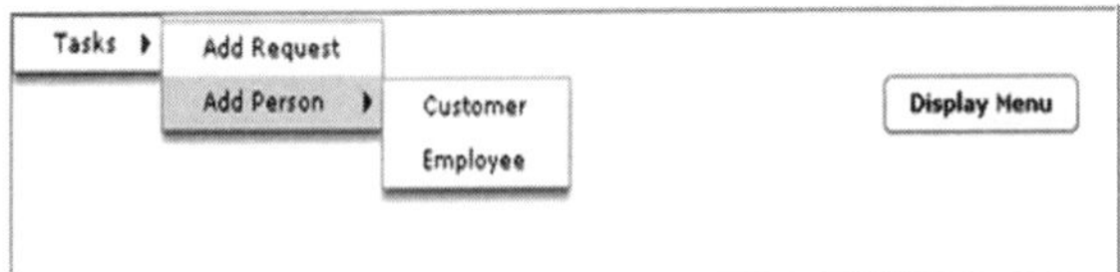

Figure 11.1 A hierarchical menu appears when you click the Display Menu button.

The `createMenu()` function takes three parameters, which are described in table 11.1.

Table 11.1 Parameters to the `Menu.createMenu()` function

Parameter	Type	Description
`parent`	`DisplayObjectContainer`	(Optional) Specifies the container with which the menu is associated. If you set `parent` to `null`, the menu is associated with the application itself.
`mdp`	`Object`	The variable containing the data.
`showRoot`	`Boolean`	If you're using `XMLList` and want to display each root value in your XML variable, select `true`. Conversely, if you're using a single-root variable in which the target information is contained in nodes below the root level, set this value to `false`. The default value is `true`.

Listing 11.11 configured your menu to open by default in the upper-left corner. Now that you know how to generate a basic menu, the next thing we'll look at is how to position it.

11.2.2 Positioning the menu

You can explicitly control the positioning of your menu by supplying *x* and *y* coordinates to the `show()` function, as follows:

```
myMenu.show(10,20);
```

Recall from chapter 4 that coordinates are defined relative to the upper-left corner of the current window. In this snippet, by specifying 10 for the *x* coordinate and 20 for the *y* coordinate, you define a position 10 pixels to the right of the left edge of the window and 20 pixels down from its top edge.

11.2.3 Customizing menu items

The data driving your menu items can contain additional display instructions for the menu. Table 11.2 lists these attributes along with their descriptions.

Table 11.2 Additional attributes embedded that instruct a menu how to display the data

Attribute	Type	Description
`enabled`	`Boolean`	Determines whether a menu item can be selected. When set to `true`, the user can select the item. When set to `false`, the menu item is displayed at half intensity (grayed out) and can't be selected. The default value is `true`.
`type`	`String`	Specifies the type of selection device (if any) that accompanies a menu item. Valid values are ■ `normal`—The user selects the menu item (default). ■ `separator`—A solid black line is placed below the menu item. ■ `check`—A check box appears beside the menu item, with which the user makes the selection. ■ `radio`—A radio button appears beside the menu item, with which the user makes the selection.
`groupName`	`String`	Links radio buttons. This is a required attribute when `type` is set to `radio`.
`toggled`	`Boolean`	When `type` is set to either `radio` or `check`, sets the menu item as selected.
`icon`	`Class`	An image variable to use as an icon. See chapter 19 to learn more about icons.
`label`	`String`	The display value in the menu item.

Listing 11.12 gives you a grand tour by demonstrating how to use everything at once.

Listing 11.12 Customizing a menu's display

```
<?xml version="1.0"?>
<mx:Application xmlns:mx="http://www.adobe.com/2006/mxml"
          backgroundColor="#FFFFFF">

  <mx:XMLListCollection id="myMenuData">          <- Menu data
  <mx:XMLList>
    <menuitem label="Tasks">
      <submenu label="Add Request" enabled="false"/>
      <submenu label="" type="separator"/>         <- Adds menu separator

      <submenu label="Add Person" icon="addPerson">     <- Displays icon beside item

      <submenu label="Customer" type="radio" groupName="personGroup"/>   <- Displays radio button

      <submenu label="Employee" type="radio" groupName="personGroup"   <- Displays toggled radio button
            toggled="true"/>
      </submenu>
      <submenu label="Auto Update" type="check" toggled="true"/>   <- Displays check box
    </menuitem>
  </mx:XMLList>
  </mx:XMLListCollection>

  <mx:Script>
```

```
<![CDATA[
 [Bindable]
 [Embed(source="addPerson.gif")]         Image to be used as
 public var addPerson:Class;             icon in menu

 import mx.controls.Menu;
 private function showMenu():void
 {
  var myMenu:Menu = Menu.createMenu(myButton, myMenuData);
  myMenu.labelField="@label";                  Indicates @label
  myMenu.iconField="@icon";                    attribute has label
  myMenu.show();            Indicates which
 }                           attribute has
]]>                          optional icon
</mx:Script>
<mx:Button id="myButton" label="Display Menu" click="showMenu()"/>
</mx:Application>
```

Figure 11.2 shows the results when you run listing 11.12.

As you can see, it's relatively painless to customize the display. Now, you need to Handling user interactions with menus

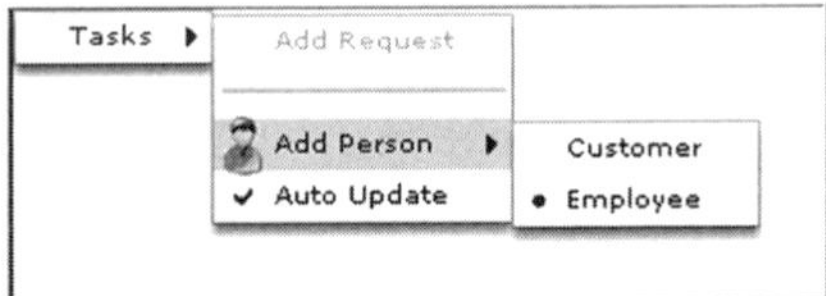

Figure 11.2 Using the additional display-control attributes, you can customize a menu's appearance.

Displaying a menu is only half the picture (pardon the irresistible pun). Just as important is how you handle all the events generated when a user interacts with the menu. Table 11.3 lists events that can be triggered by a user opening a menu and making a selection

Table 11.3 Events that can be triggered when working with menus

Event	Description
`change`	The user changed the current selection.
`itemClick`	The user clicked an enabled menu item.
`itemRollOut`	The mouse pointer moved off a menu item.
`itemRollOver`	The mouse pointer moved over a menu item.
`menuHide`	A menu or submenu closed.
`menuShow`	A menu or submenu opened.

When any of these events occur, they create an event object of the type `MenuEvent`, as defined by the `MenuEvent` ActionScript class. `MenuEvents` can carry a number of properties and information. Table 11.4 lists these properties.

Table 11.4 Properties of the `MenuEvent`

Property	Type	Description
`item`	`Object`	The row of data with which the menu item is associated.
`index`	`Number`	The index of the menu/submenu item.
`label`	`String`	The data field that contains the label to display. If the field is an attribute of an XML node, prepend it with the @ declarative.
`menu`	`Object`	A reference to the menu that created the event. Not applicable in the case of a menu bar.
`menuBar`	`Object`	A reference to the menu bar that created the event. Not applicable in the case of a menu.

Listing 11.13 combines these properties and passes the event to a function, which can then use the data.

Listing 11.13 Handling user interactions with a menu

```
<?xml version="1.0"?>
<mx:Application xmlns:mx="http://www.adobe.com/2006/mxml"
            backgroundColor="#FFFFFF">

  <mx:XMLListCollection id="myMenuData">
    <mx:XMLList>
      <menuitem label="Tasks">
        <submenu label="Add Request"/>
        <submenu label="Add Person">
        <submenu label="Customer" personType="32"/>
        <submenu label="Employee" personType="57" toggled="true"/>
        </submenu>
      </menuitem>
    </mx:XMLList>
  </mx:XMLListCollection>

  <mx:Script>
    <![CDATA[
    import mx.controls.Alert;
    import mx.controls.Menu;
    import mx.events.MenuEvent;

    private function showMenu():void
    {
      var myMenu:Menu = Menu.createMenu(myButton, myMenuData);
      myMenu.labelField="@label";
      myMenu.addEventListener("itemClick",handleMenuClick);      ❶
      myMenu.show();
    }
    private function handleMenuClick(evt:MenuEvent):void
    {
      mx.controls.Alert.show("The user just clicked on " +
                        evt.item.@label);                        ❷
      lastEvent.text = "Selection:" + evt.item.@label +
```

❶ Tells Flex to call handleMenuClick when user clicks menu item

❷ Alert window to display menu event information

```
                        ", Position: " + evt.index +          <-- 3 Position in menu
                        " Type:" + evt.item.@personType;    <-- 4 Accesses data related to menu item
    }
    ]]>
  </mx:Script>

  <mx:Button id="myButton" label="Display Menu" click="showMenu()"/>
  <mx:Label id="lastEvent"/>
</mx:Application>
```

After you click a menu item, the `itemClick` event ❶ fires and calls the `handleMenuClick()` function. Using the event payload (`evt:MenuEvent`), you can determine where the item came from, what position ❸ in the menu the item occupied, and all the data ❹ behind that item. An alert window ❷ is displayed, indicating the label for the menu item, and a `Label` field is set to display additional data the menu item carries.

Figure 11.3 Clicking the button and selecting a menu item outputs information extracted from the `MenuEvent` object.

Compile and run the example. You should see something similar to figure 11.3.

NOTE Because the extracted data is XML, to access any of the attributes you must use the @ attribute syntax (for example, `evt.item.@personType`). If you used nested objects, arrays, or array collections, you wouldn't need to use this syntax.

Using the `MenuEvent` object allows you to create reusable functions that can handle any number of menus in your application.

The `Menu` component does have a limitation: when processing XML data, it can handle only a single root node. But fear not; its cousin, the menu bar, takes matters to the next level.

11.3 Using a menu bar

The menu bar expands upon the menu by allowing for multiple top-level cascading. Menus are positioned side by side, a common layout in most applications. It's a non-intrusive mechanism that lets users navigate the features and capabilities of your application while maintaining their existing page.

Aside from the obvious visual distinctions, the primary difference between a menu and a menu bar is that a menu bar isn't meant to be a pop-up mechanism. It's designed to allow your Flex applications to offer the same kind of menu functionality common to desktop applications.

`MenuBar` is available as a component (unlike `Menu`, which is an ActionScript-only class). Table 11.5 describes the properties available for `MenuBar`.

Now, let's create a menu bar.

Table 11.5 Properties of `MenuBar`

Property	Type	Description
`dataProvider`	`Object`	The data with which to populate the menu bar. See section 11.1 for more information about providing data.
`iconField`	`String`	The name of the field that indicates which image variable to use as an icon. By default, it looks for a field labeled `icon`. If the field exists, it's used.
`labelField`	`String`	The name of the field that indicates the display value for the menu item. Defaults to `label`. If your data is XML-based, be sure to use the @ declarative to indicate which attribute of the XML node to use (for example, `@label`).
`labelFunction`	`String`	A function to call to customize the label's display (see chapter 9 for more about label functions).
`selectedIndex`	`Number (int)`	Indicates the position of the selected menu item.
`showRoot`	`Boolean`	When set to `true`, displays the top-level node of your XML structure as part of the menu. When set to `false`, skips to the next level as the starting point. The default value is `true`.

11.3.1 Creating a menu bar

Listing 11.14 creates a simple menu bar. Note the top-level placement of each top-level node.

Listing 11.14 Creating a simple menu bar

```
<?xml version="1.0"?>
<mx:Application xmlns:mx="http://www.adobe.com/2006/mxml">

  <mx:XMLListCollection id="myMenuData">
  <mx:XMLList>
    <menuitem label="File">
      <submenu label="New">
        <submenu label="Project"/>
        <submenu label="Request"/>
      </submenu>
      <submenu label="Print"/>
    </menuitem>
    <menuitem label="View">
      <submenu label="Users"/>
      <submenu label="Reports"/>
    </menuitem>
  </mx:XMLList>
  </mx:XMLListCollection>
  <mx:MenuBar id="myMBar" dataProvider="{myMenuData}"
          labelField="@label"/>
</mx:Application>
```

After compiling and running the code in listing 11.14, you'll see a rudimentary menu bar resembling figure 11.4.

As you did with the menu, let's fine-tune the menu bar's position.

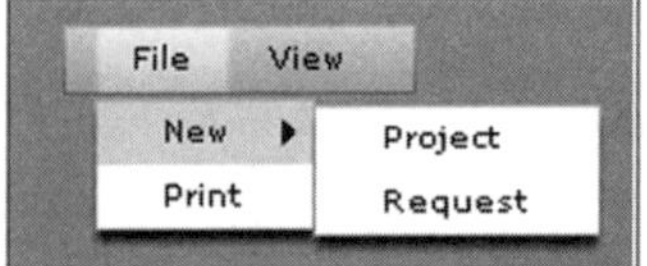

Figure 11.4 A rudimentary menu bar in action

11.3.2 Positioning the menu bar

Because a menu bar is a component inside a container (in this example, `<mx:Application>`), positioning the menu bar follows the rules of containers. By default, the `Application` container uses automatic layout, so the menu bar appears centered in your application.

If you want to position the menu bar in the upper-left corner of the browser window, you need to set the `layout` property of the `Application` container to `absolute` and then set both the `x` and `y` properties of the menu bar to 0,0. The following code snippet shows how to set the `layout` property to `absolute`:

```
<mx:Application xmlns:mx="http://www.adobe.com/2006/mxml"
   layout="absolute">
```

Similarly, if the menu bar is inside a `Panel` container, the default behavior is to lay out the container's child components vertically; for this example, there's nothing more you need to do. But if you want more fine-grained control, you need to set the `Panel` container's `layout` property to `absolute`:

```
<mx:Panel title="My Application" layout="absolute">
  <mx:MenuBar id="myMBar" dataProvider="{myMenuData}"
          labelField="@label" />
</mx:Panel>
```

Using a `Panel` container, your menu bar should look similar to figure 11.5.

Figure 11.5 Using `absolute` layout allows you to control the exact positioning of the menu bar.

In figure 11.5, the menu bar is positioned in the upper-left corner as a result defining its position to 0,0. If you want to locate it 5 pixels to the right, set the `x` property of the menu bar to 5.

As with menus, you have the option to customize your menu bars.

11.3.3 Customizing items in the menu bar

The items in menus and menu bars follow the same rules and access the same properties, which means you can add separators, radio buttons, check boxes, and icons to a menu bar exactly the same way you do a menu.

Listing 11.15 uses an XML structure to customize the output, similar to the earlier menu example.

Listing 11.15 Using special attributes in XML data to customize a menu bar

```
<?xml version="1.0"?>
<mx:Application xmlns:mx="http://www.adobe.com/2006/mxml">

  <mx:XMLListCollection id="myMenuData">
    <mx:XMLList>
      <menuitem label="Edit">
        <submenu label="Users" icon="addPerson" />
        <submenu type="separator"/>
        <submenu label="Reports" type="check"/>
      </menuitem>
      <menuitem label="Mode">
        <submenu label="Basic"   type="radio" groupName="grpMode"
              toggled="true"/>
        <submenu label="Advanced" type="radio" groupName="grpMode"/>
      </menuitem>
    </mx:XMLList>
  </mx:XMLListCollection>

  <mx:Script>
    <![CDATA[
      [Bindable]
      [Embed(source="addPerson.gif")]
      public var addPerson:Class;
    ]]>
  </mx:Script>

  <mx:MenuBar id="myMBar" dataProvider="{myMenuData}" labelField="@label"
          iconField="@icon"/>
</mx:Application>
```

After compiling and running the application, you'll see a customized menu bar, as shown in figure 11.6.

As with the earlier menu example, you now need to add the ability for the menu bar to interact with the user.

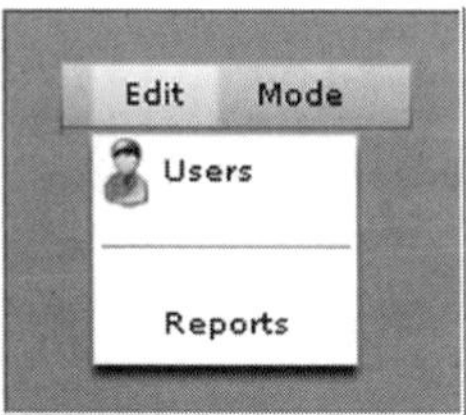

Figure 11.6 This menu bar's display is partially controlled by properties contained in the XML data.

11.3.4 Handling user interactions with menu bars

The same events that apply to menus also apply to menu bars. For your convenience, table 11.6 lists those events again.

Table 11.6 Menu bars share the same events as menus.

Event	Description
change	The user changed the current selection.

Table 11.6 Menu bars share the same events as menus. *(continued)*

Event	Description
itemClick	The user clicked an enabled menu item.
itemRollOut	The mouse pointer moved off a menu item.
itemRollOver	The mouse pointer moved over a menu item.
menuHide	A menu or submenu closed.
menuShow	A menu or submenu opened.

The events listed in table 11.6 (of the MenuEvent ActionScript class) have the same properties and values as their menu counterparts. Those properties appear again in table 11.7.

Table 11.7 The properties of a MenuEvent in a menu bar

Property	Type	Description
item	Object	The row of data with which the menu item is associated.
index	Number	The index of the menu/sub menu item.
label	String	The field in the data that contains the label to display. If the field is an attribute of an XML node prepend it with the @ declarative.
menu	Object	A reference to the menu that created the event. Not applicable in the case of a menu bar.
menuBar	Object	A reference to the menu bar that created the event. Not applicable in the case of a menu.

Listing 11.16 shows how to handle the selection and display of a menu item.

Listing 11.16 Handling a user's selection of a menu item

```
<?xml version="1.0"?>
<mx:Application xmlns:mx="http://www.adobe.com/2006/mxml"
        backgroundColor="white">

  <mx:XMLListCollection id="myMenuData">
    <mx:XMLList>
      <menuitem label="File">
        <submenu label="New">
          <submenu label="Project"/>
          <submenu label="Request"/>
        </submenu>
        <submenu label="Print"/>
      </menuitem>
      <menuitem label="View">
        <submenu label="Users"/>
        <submenu label="Reports"/>
      </menuitem>
```

```
    </mx:XMLList>
  </mx:XMLListCollection>

  <mx:Script>
    <![CDATA[
      import mx.events.MenuEvent;
      private function handleMenuClick(evt:MenuEvent):void
      {
        mx.controls.Alert.show("The user just clicked on " +
                               evt.item.@label);
        lastEvent.text = "Selection:" + evt.item.@label +
                         ", Position: " + evt.index;
      }
    ]]>
  </mx:Script>

  <mx:MenuBar id="myMBar" itemClick="handleMenuClick(event)"
          dataProvider="{myMenuData}" labelField="@label"/>
  <mx:Text id="lastEvent"/>
</mx:Application>
```

Compile and run the application, and you'll see something similar to figure 11.7. Clicking items in the menu bar causes the display to be updated with information about the item that was clicked.

Menu bars are similar to menus, but a menu bar comes as an MXML component, allowing you to populate it with multiple top-level items.

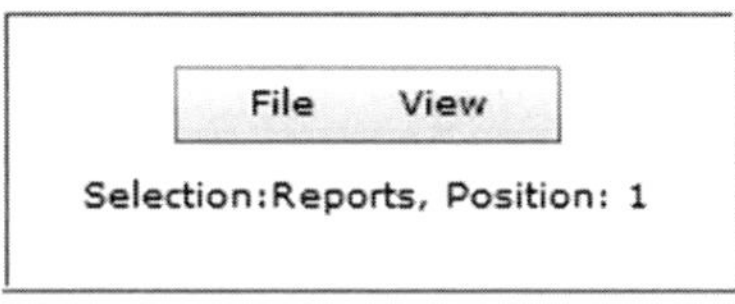

Figure 11.7 Using the `MenuEvent` object in a menu bar lets you determine which menu item was selected and display data related to that position.

11.4 Using view stacks

A view stack is an interesting mechanism for navigating within your application. A view stack operates by layering each of its child containers on top of each other. Think of a view stack like a deck of playing cards; you can select one card from the deck at any given point in time.

A view stack is a relatively uncomplicated mechanism compared to Flex's other navigation containers. This simplicity can come in handy if you need to produce innovative displays that need to easily swap containers in place of each other.

The downside is that a view stack doesn't possess any built-in UI controls to facilitate navigation. This is something you'll need to include in your code.

11.4.1 Creating a view stack

A view stack is a container that holds other containers. When you invoke a view stack, you specify all the containers that reside within it, as shown in listing 11.17.

Listing 11.17 Creating a view stack using a Canvas for each layer

```
<?xml version="1.0"?>
<mx:Application xmlns:mx="http://www.adobe.com/2006/mxml">
  <mx:ViewStack id="myViewStack" width="100%" height="100%">
    <mx:Canvas id="TVs" width="100%" height="100%"/>
```

```
    <mx:Canvas id="Cameras" width="100%" height="100%"/>
    <mx:Canvas id="Computers" width="100%" height="100%"/>
  </mx:ViewStack>
</mx:Application>
```

Containers don't need to be of a single type; listing 11.18 illustrates how you can mix and match different container types as required by your application.

Listing 11.18 Mixing and matching containers in a view stack

```
<mx:ViewStack id="myViewStack" width="100%" height="100%">
  <mx:Canvas id="TVs" width="100%" height="100%"/>
  <mx:HBox id="Cameras" width="100%" height="100%"/>
  <mx:VBox id="Computers" width="100%" height="100%"/>
</mx:ViewStack>
```

For the sake of demonstration, the inner containers in listings 11.18 and 11.19 have no content; but in the real world your containers will, of course, display information. Next, you'll begin populating your containers.

You can break an application into smaller segments called *custom components*. At the core of this technique, each container in a view stack is saved as a discrete MXML component file. Listing 11.19 shows how this is configured (chapter 17 goes into this method in detail).

Listing 11.19 Using a component as a container in a view stack

```
<?xml version="1.0" encoding="utf-8"?>
<mx:Canvas xmlns:mx="http://www.adobe.com/2006/mxml"
        width="100%" height="100%">
  <mx:Panel title="TVs" width="100%" height="100%">
    <mx:TextInput id="myTI"/>
    <mx:Button label="Search for TVs"/>
  </mx:Panel>
</mx:Canvas>
```

As listing 11.20 shows, from the application, you assign the subdirectory that contains your custom components an *alias* (formally known as a *namespace*), and you're good to go.

Listing 11.20 Using tvs.mxml as a container in the view stack

```
<?xml version="1.0"?>
<mx:Application xmlns:mx="http://www.adobe.com/2006/mxml"
           xmlns:stax="stacks.*">                           <- Maps stacks subdirectory to alias
  <mx:ViewStack id="myViewStack" width="100%" height="100%">
    <stax:tvs id="tvs"/>                                    | Invokes custom
    <stax:computers id="computers"/>                        | components
  </mx:ViewStack>
</mx:Application>
```

To recap, you've generated three files, two of which are custom components residing in a subdirectory called stacks, as shown in figure 11.8.

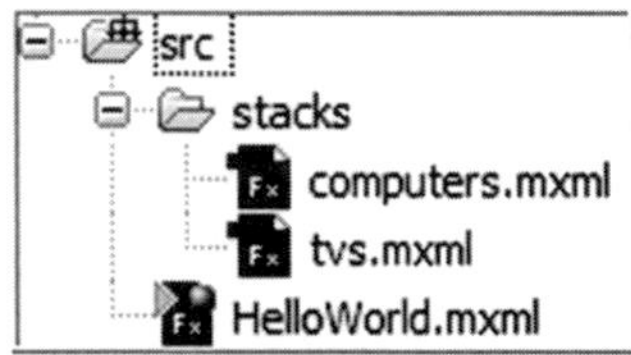

Figure 11.8 HelloWorld.mxml contains a view stack that invokes the custom components resident in the stacks subfolder.

This last approach makes things easier to read and, more important, lets you conveniently separate your components' functionality into their own set of files in a modular fashion. Compare this approach to the tightly coupled structure of the previous examples.

You still need to add the ability to switch between stacks.

11.4.2 *Adding navigation to the view stack*

Navigation isn't automatic—you need to include instructions that manage which container in the view stack is currently visible.

The following components have sufficient built-in functionality to handle this for you:

- `LinkBar`
- `ButtonBar`
- `TabBar`

To make proper use of these components, set the `dataProvider` property to the `id` value of your view stack, as shown in listing 11.21.

Listing 11.21 Adding navigation in a view stack

```
<?xml version="1.0"?>
<mx:Application xmlns:mx="http://www.adobe.com/2006/mxml"
        backgroundColor="white" xmlns:stax="stacks.*">
  <mx:ButtonBar id="myButtonBar" dataProvider="{myViewStack}"/>

  <mx:ViewStack id="myViewStack" width="100%" height="100%">
    <stax:tvs id="tvs" label="TVs"/>
    <stax:computers id="computers" label="Computers"/>
  </mx:ViewStack>

</mx:Application>
```

dataProvider is name of view stack

Navigation provided by ButtonBar

Now that you've added navigational capabilities to the view stack, you can switch between stacks with the click of a mouse, as illustrated in figure 11.9.

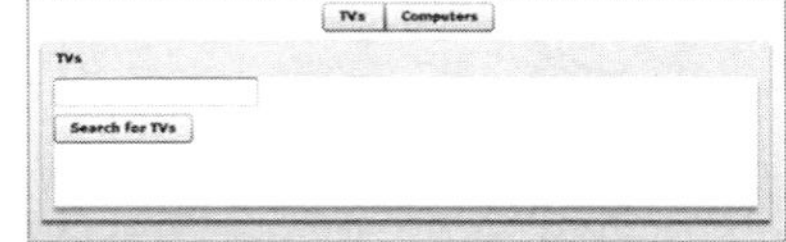

Figure 11.9 A `ButtonBar` is used to switch between stacks in a view stack.

NOTE The `LinkBar`, `ButtonBar`, and `TabBar` display their button names based on the label property of each stack.

Using the default properties of display components allows you to easily assemble a stack, but you always have the option to take control of component attributes if you prefer.

DO-IT-YOURSELF

If you need more component control, adding custom navigation features isn't much more difficult than using default attributes. Two key properties furnish this control:

- `selectedIndex`—The numeric position of a container in the view stack, where the first position is index 0
- `selectedChild`—The `id` property of a given container in the view stack

Listing 11.22 creates two buttons that let you switch views.

Listing 11.22 Programmatically controlling which stack is visible

```
<mx:Button label="Look at TVs"     click="myViewStack.selectedIndex=0"/>
<mx:Button label="Look at Computers" click="myViewStack.selectedIndex=1"/>

 <mx:ViewStack id="myViewStack" width="100%" height="100%">
  <stax:tvs id="tvs" label="TVs"/>
  <stax:computers id="computers" label="Computers"/>
</mx:ViewStack>
```

Similarly, if you want to employ a named approach, you can instead use this code:

```
<mx:Button label="Look at TVs" click="myViewStack.selectedChild=tvs"/>
<mx:Button label="Look at Computers"
      click="myViewStack.selectedChild=computers"/>
```

Keep in mind that the `selectedChild` property is associated with the `id` of the container, not its label.

TIP Be creative: there are many ways you can add custom navigation beyond the customary gang of buttons. For example, you can use images, radio buttons, combo boxes, text links—whatever you can imagine.

Flex makes it easy to take control and add your own custom navigation to a view stack. This comes in particularly handy when you integrate custom logic into your application to create context-sensitive stacks.

Being able to control which stack is selected is one form of control. Another is reacting to a selection, or finding out which stack is currently selected.

11.4.3 Determining which stack is selected

The `selectedIndex` and `selectedChild` properties can also be used to indicate which container is currently selected. Listing 11.23 shows how to display the index of the currently visible container along with its label property.

Listing 11.23 Using `selectedIndex` to check which stack is selected

```
<mx:Script>
 <![CDATA[
  import mx.controls.Alert;
  private function checkSelection():void     <-- Retrieves info on selected stack
  {
   Alert.show("Current Index:" +
```

```
                myViewStack.selectedIndex.toString() +
                " Which has a label of " +
                myViewStack.selectedChild.label);
        }
    ]]>
</mx:Script>

<mx:Button label="Check which Container is Selected"
    click="checkSelection()"/>
```

Displays selected stack

Displays title of selected stack

Calls function that leverages selected stack

Running this code yields output similar to figure 11.10.

You're leveraging the same properties that were used to set the current selection. But this time, you're using it to retrieve information about the current selection. The last thing you need to do to tie it all together is handle when such a selection occurs.

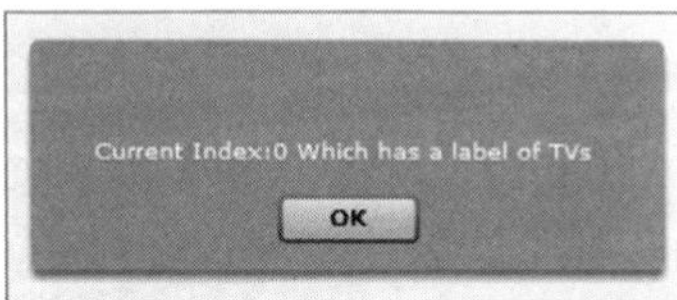

Figure 11.10 Using the `selectedIndex` and `selectedChild` to retrieve information about the currently selected stack

11.4.4 *Handling user interactions with view stacks*

A view stack is a child component of the container class, and as such it inherits all the properties of the container. But because you don't interact with the view stack directly, only one event is of any interest: `change`, which detects changes in the view-stack selection.

The `change` event generates an event (of the `IndexChangedEvent` class variety) with the properties listed in table 11.8.

Table 11.8 Properties of `IndexChangedEvent`

Property	Type	Description
`newIndex`	`Number`	Specifies the index number of the new `selectedIndex`
`oldIndex`	`Number`	Indicates the previous index number of the `selectedIndex`
`relatedObject`	`Object`	A reference to the container to which the `newIndex` is pointed

Listing 11.24 shows the old and new indexes as well as the new index's container label.

Listing 11.24 Working with the view stack's index property

```
<?xml version="1.0"?>
<mx:Application xmlns:mx="http://www.adobe.com/2006/mxml"
        backgroundColor="white" xmlns:stax="stacks.*">

  <mx:TabBar id="myBar" dataProvider="{myViewStack}"/>

  <mx:ViewStack id="myViewStack" change="checkSelection(event)">
    <stax:tvs id="tvs" label="TVs"/>
    <stax:computers id="computers" label="Computers"/>
  </mx:ViewStack>
```

checkSelection called when selection changes

```
  <mx:Script>
    <![CDATA[
      import mx.events.IndexChangedEvent;
      private function checkSelection(evt:IndexChangedEvent):void
      {
        var newObj:Object = evt.relatedObject;
        mx.controls.Alert.show(
                  " Old Index:" + evt.oldIndex.toString() +
                  " New Index:" + evt.newIndex.toString() +
                  " Label of new Selection:" + newObj.label) ;
      }
    ]]>
  </mx:Script>

</mx:Application>
```

Imports event class

Receives IndexChangedEvent object

Any further interactions would be with the component used to control the view stack—which in this example, happens to be the tab bar. But whether you use the tab bar, ButtonBar, or LinkBar (collectively called *navigation components*), they all support the `itemClick` event, which carries the properties detailed in table 11.9.

Table 11.9 Properties of the `itemClick` event

Property	Type	Description
`currentTarget`	`Object`	A reference to the object related to the event. As it relates to listing 11.24, this is a reference to the navigation component. If you pass the event to a function, the function doesn't need to know the specific ID of the component, which produces a more reusable function.
`index`	`Number`	The position of the current selection (starting at 0). For example, the second button in a `ButtonBar` has an index of 1.
`label`	`String`	The `label` property of the related navigation component button. In the examples, these are the same as the labels on the containers in the view stack because the navigation component by default sets its `label` to that of the container.
`item`	`Object`	A reference to the data item (from the `dataProvider`) to which the selection in the navigation component is related.
`relatedObject`	`Object`	Similar to `currentTarget`; but instead of a reference to the entire navigation component, you receive a reference to specific subcomponent in the navigation component (the button or tab).

Listing 11.25 presents an example of the `itemClick` in action. You call the function as a result of the `itemClick` event. Depending on the event, you can determine the index and label of the selected item, and at the same time change the color of the selection to red.

Listing 11.25 Responding to interactions on a navigation component

```
<?xml version="1.0"?>
<mx:Application xmlns:mx="http://www.adobe.com/2006/mxml"
          backgroundColor="white" xmlns:stax="stacks.*">
  <mx:Script>
    <![CDATA[
      import mx.controls.Alert;
      import mx.events.ItemClickEvent;
      private function handleClick(evt:ItemClickEvent):void    <-- Indicates what was clicked
      {
        Alert.show(" Tab Index:" + evt.index +                 <-- Displays what was clicked
                  " Label:" + evt.label);
        var myObj:Object = evt.relatedObject;                  <-- Reference to what was clicked
        myObj.setStyle("backgroundColor","red");               <-- Changes color of clicked button
          }
        ]]>
    </mx:Script>

  <mx:TabBar id="myBar" dataProvider="{myViewStack}"
        itemClick="handleClick(event)"/>

  <mx:ViewStack id="myViewStack" width="100%" height="150">
    <stax:tvs id="tvs" label="TVs"/>
    <stax:computers id="computers" label="Computers"/>
  </mx:ViewStack>

</mx:Application>
```

Figure 11.11 shows the code in action. When you click one of the tabs, the pop-up indicates the index of the tab that was clicked, along with the label of that tab.

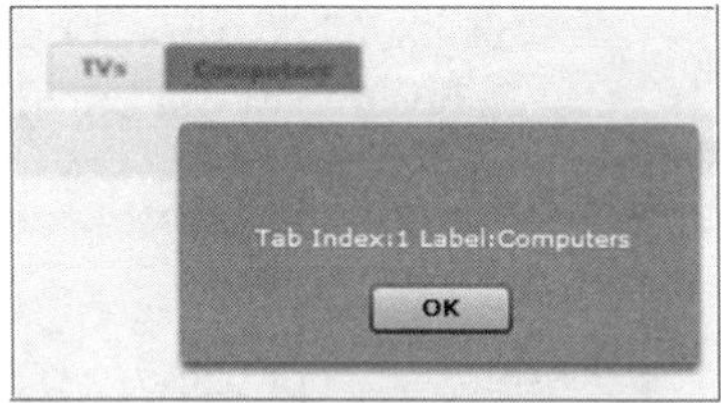

Figure 11.11 Using the itemClick event on the navigation component instead of the view stack, you can easily interact directly with navigation components.

Although the view stack has a `change` event with which you can manipulate the view stack itself, you can also leverage the `itemClick` on a navigation component directly for fine-grained control.

The view stack combined with a tab bar provides *tabbed* navigation. Not surprisingly, tabbed navigation also comes as an out-of-the-box implementation in Flex.

11.5 TabNavigator

Tabbed navigation has always been a part of GUI navigation and has survived the test of time as a navigational paradigm in all types of applications. Tabbed navigation makes efficient use of limited screen space by allowing users to choose what's currently visible in that space.

In listing 11.25, you accomplished this task using a tab bar to control a view stack. But you can achieve the same result using the `TabNavigator` component. The `TabNavigator` component is a descendent of a view stack with a tab bar incorporated directly into it.

11.5.1 Creating a tab navigator

A tab navigator works by making a tab out of each container within it. Listing 11.26 demonstrates how easily you can generate tabs using the TabNavigator component.

Listing 11.26 Using a tab navigator to created tabbed navigation

```
<?xml version="1.0"?>
<mx:Application xmlns:mx="http://www.adobe.com/2006/mxml"
          backgroundColor="white">

  <mx:TabNavigator width="300" height="100">
    <mx:Canvas label="Tab 1"/>
    <mx:VBox   label="Tab 2"/>      Tab titles
    <mx:HBox   label="Tab 3"/>
  </mx:TabNavigator>

</mx:Application>
```

The compact bit of code in listing 11.26 produces the results shown in figure 11.12.

NOTE: The title for each tab is specified via the label property of each child container.

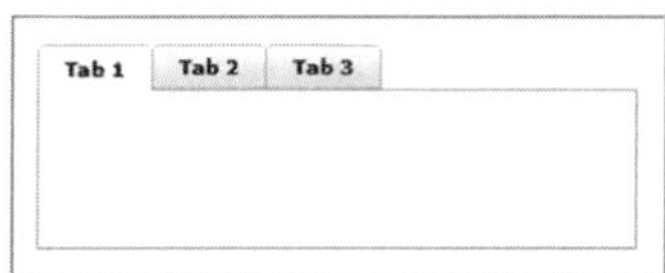

Figure 11.12 A tab navigator creates a tab for each container within it.

Just as with the view stack, you have the option to mix and match containers. This is because TabNavigator is a child object of ViewStack, so it inherits ViewStack's properties, then goes on to offer even more functionality.

Because of this lineage, handling user interactions is similar to doing so in a view stack.

11.5.2 Handling user interactions with a tab navigator

Because TabNavigator is a child object of ViewStack, you borrow upon the view stack's properties:

- selectedIndex–The position of the selected tab (starting from 0)
- selectedChild—The id of the selected tab

Likewise, the change event is the same as that for a view stack (for example, the IndexChangedEvent event): it fires when the tab selection changes (see listing 11.27).

Listing 11.27 Responding to tab changes in a tab navigator

```
<?xml version="1.0"?>
<mx:Application xmlns:mx="http://www.adobe.com/2006/mxml"
   backgroundColor="white">
  <mx:Script>
   <![CDATA[
     import mx.controls.Alert;
     private function handleChange():void
     {
      Alert.show("Changed to Tab Index " + myTabNav.selectedIndex +
```

```
                "Label: " + myTabNav.selectedChild.label);
      }
    ]]>
     </mx:Script>
     <mx:TabNavigator width="200" height="100" id="myTabNav"
                  change="handleChange()">
    <mx:Canvas  label="Tab 1"/>
    <mx:VBox    label="Tab 2"/>
    <mx:HBox    label="Tab 3"/>
  </mx:TabNavigator>
</mx:Application>
```

Compiling and running the application displays an alert window (figure 11.13) whenever the tab selection changes. The alert also posts which index is selected and the associated label for the tab.

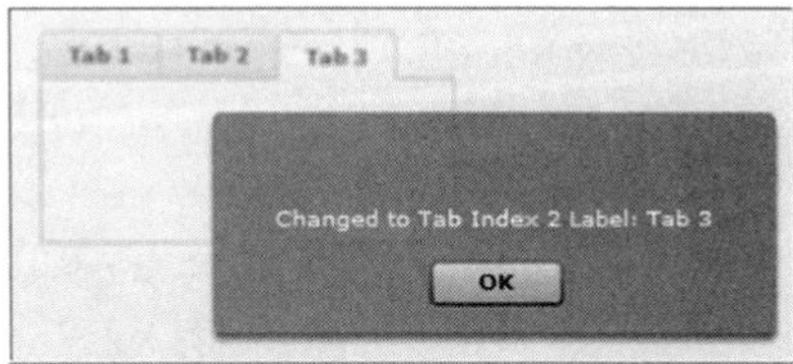

Figure 11.13 Using the `change` event, you can tell which tab was selected.

This is the same process you executed with the view stack, which also used its `change` event. The problem with this approach is that the function is explicitly told which tab navigator is involved. As we continue our never-ending quest for code reusability, we're driven to employ a more modular technique.

PASSING THE EVENT TO A FUNCTION

The previous example requires the function to have explicit knowledge of the name of the tab navigator (`myTabNav`) it needs to access. If you want to make your function more flexible and permit multiple tab navigators to use it, you need to pass the navigation component event to the function and access the `currentTarget` property of the event to reference the associated tab navigator. Listing 11.28 shows how to configure this.

Listing 11.28 Using an event object to pass information about the selected tab

```
<mx:Script>
  <![CDATA[
    import mx.controls.Alert;
    import mx.events.IndexChangedEvent;
    private function handleChange(evt:IndexChangedEvent):void
    {
     Alert.show("Changed to Tab Index "
            + evt.currentTarget.selectedIndex +
            " Label: "
            + evt.currentTarget.selectedChild.label);
    }
  ]]>
</mx:Script>
<mx:TabNavigator width="200" height="100" id="myTabNav"
            change="handleChange(event)">
    ...
</mx:TabNavigator>
```

Accepts event object from any tab navigator

Passes event to function

Listing 11.28 produces the same end result as listing 11.27, but in the background you abstract the need for the function to know the id of the tab navigator.

If you look back to the IndexChangedEvent in table 11.9, you'll see that it has a newIndex property you can use (and oldIndex), as well as relatedObject:

```
private function handleChange(evt:IndexChangedEvent):void
{
  var selectedContainer:Object = evt.relatedObject;
  Alert.show("Changed to Tab Index " + evt.newIndex +
           " Label: " + selectedContainer.label);
}
```

Although you can benefit from the extra convenience of configuring the IndexChangedEvent this way, it doesn't matter one way or the other—it's more a function of personal preference.

Tabs and menus have their purpose and are proven stalwarts of the common UI paradigm. But if you want to try something more innovative, check out the accordion navigator.

11.6 Accordion

When Flex and its implementation of the Accordion component first appeared, the web-application world was taken aback, because it was such a fresh approach to navigating an application. Although Flex wasn't the first to introduce this type of navigation (Outlook 2003 had it before Flex), it was unheard of in the traditional web application scene.

Today, the accordion has become an accepted option thanks to AJAX toolkits that make implementation so easy, such as Adobe's Spry. But Flex's version of the accordion is among the best.

11.6.1 Creating an accordion

Creating an accordion is much like creating a tab navigator; but instead of each child container displaying as a tab, it displays a section divider. Coding an accordion is similarly easy, as listing 11.29 illustrates.

Listing 11.29 Creating an accordion navigator

```
<?xml version="1.0"?>
<mx:Application xmlns:mx="http://www.adobe.com/2006/mxml"
            backgroundColor="white">
  <mx:Accordion width="150" height="150" id="myAccord">
    <mx:Canvas  label="Section 1"/>
    <mx:VBox    label="Section 2"/>
    <mx:HBox    label="Section 3"/>
  </mx:Accordion>
</mx:Application>
```

After compiling and running the application, you'll see a simple accordion displaying three sections, as shown in figure 11.14.

Accordions follow the same construction pattern as view stacks and tab navigators by placing containers within them. But what you produced in listing 11.30 is a bit boring—you need to populate it with some interactive content.

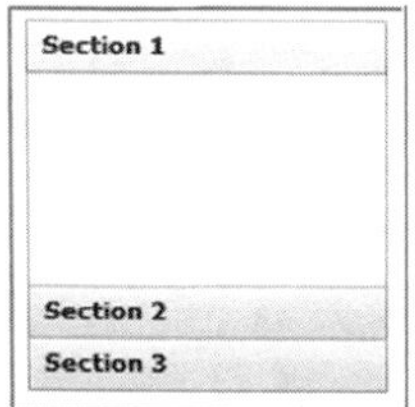

Figure 11.14 Accordion navigator with three sections.

11.6.2 *Populating an accordion*

Whatever you can put inside a container, you can use to populate an accordion. For example, you can display thumbnails in each section as part of photo album application.

BREAKING DOWN A FORM

If you need to format a large form, using an accordion is a great way to break it into smaller, more digestible pieces. For example, a loan application may look similar to that shown in figure 11.15.

Figure 11.15 An accordion used to break up a large form into sections

To keep the code manageable, see figure 11.16, which contains a code snippet showing how the accordion breaks up the form.

This accordion example employs a `VBox` to create a section/panel, within which you can place anything—in this case, a portion of a master form. You continue repeating this pattern of configuring a container to create each accordion panel.

But don't limit yourself to forms: you can put anything you want inside an accordion, including lists.

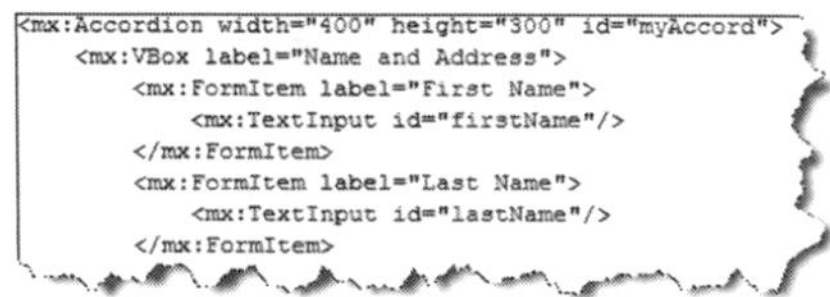

```
<mx:Accordion width="400" height="300" id="myAccord">
    <mx:VBox label="Name and Address">
        <mx:FormItem label="First Name">
            <mx:TextInput id="firstName"/>
        </mx:FormItem>
        <mx:FormItem label="Last Name">
            <mx:TextInput id="lastName"/>
        </mx:FormItem>
```

Figure 11.16 The accordion has containers inside of it, with each container representing a section of the form.

USING A LIST IN AN ACCORDION

Lists are another popular content choice for accordion sections. You can embed a `DataGrid`, a `List`, or even a `Tree` component within an individual section (see figure 11.17).

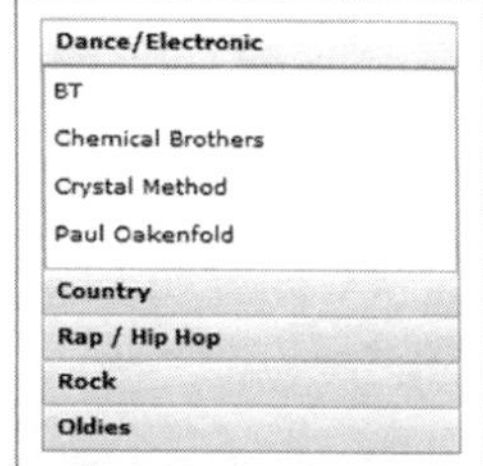

Figure 11.17 Each accordion section is a `VBox` containing a list.

Figure 11.18 shows the `VBox` and `List` components for the visible accordion section in figure 11.17.

Forms and lists are two of the most common uses for accordions, but you can add any other mechanisms you can think of. For example, if you have a complex directory structure, you can use a tree inside each accordion section to separate the directory into smaller, more easily read subsections.

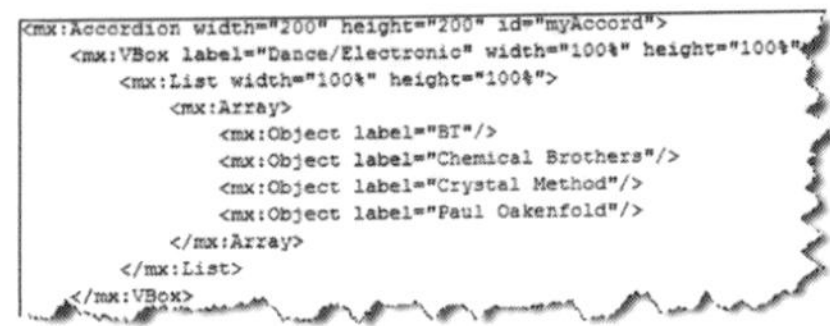

```
<mx:Accordion width="200" height="200" id="myAccord">
    <mx:VBox label="Dance/Electronic" width="100%" height="100%"
        <mx:List width="100%" height="100%">
            <mx:Array>
                <mx:Object label="BT"/>
                <mx:Object label="Chemical Brothers"/>
                <mx:Object label="Crystal Method"/>
                <mx:Object label="Paul Oakenfold"/>
            </mx:Array>
        </mx:List>
    </mx:VBox>
```

Figure 11.18 Each section of the accordion has a container with a `List` component in it.

The only thing left to consider is how to handle user interactions with an accordion.

11.6.3 *Handling user interactions with an accordion*

We're going to give your eyes a rest: everything we wrote about handling user interactions with the tab navigator applies to the accordion as well—you already know what to do. But as a quick reminder, you use `selectedIndex` or `selectedChild` to set or determine which accordion section is selected and then react to the user via the `change` event.

In most cases, the majority of user interactions are with components within containers versus the accordion (or the tab navigator) itself.

11.7 *Summary*

You have many options to provide navigation to your user, and the best part is that all these options are all easy! No complicated DHTML or complex JavaScript is required to create desktop-like experiences. For the most part, it's all out-of-the-box functionality.

Flex provides the common UI navigation paradigms with which most users are familiar, particularly drop-down menus and tab navigation. But to mix things up a bit, you can get serious and use the tab navigator's father, the view stack, and use buttons (or any other graphic) to switch from one stack to another. To experience unique navigation, explore the accordion navigation component.

Except for menus, which follow their own model, all other navigation components follow the paradigm of placing containers inside each other for each item to display or navigate. Menus tend to represent tree-like (hierarchical) data, and there are many ways you can assemble the data to drive a menu. For the most part, you'll want to stick with XML, because it lends itself to hierarchical data structures.

You can be creative with navigation components, using different components interchangeably, or customizing them with images.

Continuing with the theme of application navigation, chapter 12 teaches you how to provide pop-up windows. This includes how to exchange data with pop-ups and how to customize the experience.

12 Introduction to pop-ups

This chapter covers:

- Creating a pop-up window
- Sizing and positioning pop-ups
- Communicating with a pop-up window
- Closing pop-up windows
- Using alerts

When you construct an application, your design will likely often call for a pop-up or editing window. Flex offers a convenient mechanism in the *pop-up manager* to help you create, delete, position, close, and destroy windows. When you're choosing the type of pop-up window to add to your application, it's a good idea to plan ahead and first determine what the purpose of the pop-up will be and what you'll need to do in the pop-up window.

12.1 Creating your first pop-up

Every pop-up window is created and manipulated through the pop-up manager. The pop-up manager is the class that handles the initialization of the window and manages window layering within the application, which relieves you of the responsibility of avoiding placement conflicts. The pop-up manager is simple to use and doesn't carry a lot of properties to configure. Let's look at an example of how to create your first pop-up window.

12.1.1 First things first: create your title window

Several options are available to you for creating a pop-up. Each option requires at least one window file that is used for the display of the window. The pop-up manager calls this window and renders it in a layer above any existing layers. Additional new pop-up windows are created similarly and placed above other open pop-up or alert windows. When the top window layer is closed, the next highest window regains prominence. This continues until the last pop-up is closed, leaving the main layer, which is your parent application layer.

Listing 12.1 introduces the `TitleWindow` component, which enables all this to take place.

Listing 12.1 SimplePopupWindow.mxml: `TitleWindow` component in action

```
<?xml version="1.0" encoding="utf-8"?>
<mx:TitleWindow xmlns:mx="http://www.adobe.com/2006/mxml"
layout="vertical" width="400" height="100">
  <mx:Text text="Hello there!  I'm a simple popup window.
             I don't do much.">
  </mx:Text>
</mx:TitleWindow>
```

When creating a pop-up window, you have a choice of the container component on which to base the pop-up (a.k.a. a *base tag*). One of the most common—and easiest to use—tags is `TitleWindow`. Only certain tags can act as the main base tag; tags you would normally use, such as `<Application>`, `<VBox>`, and `<HBox>`, aren't available for use as the base tag of a pop-up window.

Once you've configured `TitleWindow` as your base component window tag, you can add any other MXML or ActionScript tags. Listing 12.1 uses the `mx:Text` tag, which lets you display a simple text message on the screen. This is a bare-bones example of a user interaction message. As you progress, you'll see that you can do much more with it.

Now, let's look at how to present this window to the user via the `PopUpManager`.

12.1.2 Using PopUpManager to open the window

With your pop-up window text complete, let's put it to work by creating the code to use it. Follow these steps:

1. Create a project in Flex Builder called CH12.
2. Create a subfolder called windows under CH12's src folder.
3. Copy SimplePopupWindow.mxml from listing 12.1 into the src/windows folder.
4. Create a testSimplePopup.mxml file in the src folder, and copy the contents of listing 12.2 into it.

Listing 12.2 generates the pop-up window shown in figure 12.1, which opens the pop-up as soon as the application loads.

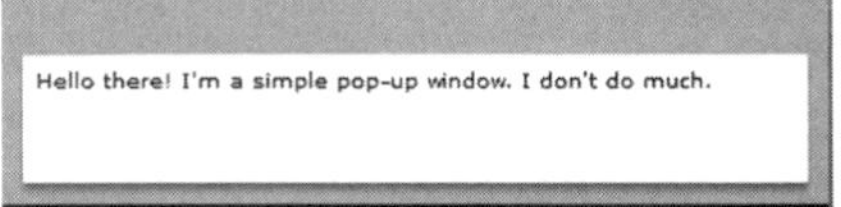
Hello there! I'm a simple pop-up window. I don't do much.

Figure 12.1 A basic pop-up window

Listing 12.2 testSimplePopup.mxml: showing a pop-up window

```
<?xml version="1.0" encoding="utf-8"?>
<mx:Application xmlns:mx="http://www.adobe.com/2006/mxml"
   creationComplete="openSimpleWindow()">
<mx:Script>
  <![CDATA[
    import mx.managers.PopUpManager;
    import windows.SimplePopupWindow;        <-- Looks in windows folder

    private var simpleWindow:Object;
    private function openSimpleWindow():void
    {
        simpleWindow =
      PopUpManager.createPopUp(this,windows.SimplePopupWindow,false);
    }
  ]]>
</mx:Script>
</mx:Application>
```

This is the most commonly used and simplest mechanism for calling a new pop-up window. The keyword `this` (the first option in the `createPopUp()` method) indicates that the parent of the pop-up is the component that launched the window.

The next option is the class, or file name, you're using to create the pop-up window. The final option determines whether the window should be *modal*. Modal windows constrain the user to clicking only within the confines of the pop-up window. Modal windows don't permit clicks beyond the borders of the window itself. Attempts to click back to the main application window (or anywhere outside the pop-up) are ignored.

Notice that in listing 12.2 you assigned the result of the `createPopUp()` method call to a variable. This is because `createPopUp()` returns an initialized window object that represents the component you created in listing 12.1. If you save the returned object to a variable, you'll be able to interact with it, which we'll show you how to do a little later in this chapter.

Pay attention to the scope, which you learned about in previous chapters. In listing 12.2, the result is saved to a private function scope that won't allow access from outside the function. If you wish to access the pop-up window from outside the function, you need to make the variable available as a class- or component-scoped variable.

Now that you've seen how to create a pop-up, you need to know how to close it when the user is finished with it.

12.1.3 Closing the pop-up

In figure 12.2, you'll notice an X in the upper-right corner of the pop-up window. As you already know, this is the universally recognized *close* button used by the vast majority of web and desktop applications.

Figure 12.2 Notice the close button in the upper-right corner of the pop-up window.

The close button is available as an option when you use a `TitleWindow` tag. You can access this option through `TitleWindow`'s `showCloseButton` property, which accepts either `true` or `false` as a value. Setting `showCloseButton` to `true` displays the X button in the corner of the pop-up. When the button is clicked, `TitleWindow` dispatches a `close` event that can be used as a trigger by components designated to listen for it.

It doesn't do all of the work for you, but it gets you close. Listing 12.3 illustrates how the `closeMe()` function is used to remove the pop-up from view.

Listing 12.3 Closing a pop-up window

```
private function closeMe():void
{
  PopUpManager.removePopUp(this);
}
```

After closing the window, the next thing to look at is controlling the position of the pop-up.

12.2 Controlling the window location

When you first launch a window, you may see that it's not automatically positioned in the middle of the screen. You need to give your pop-up layout instructions, or it will appear in the upper-left corner of the parent object in which it was created.

12.2.1 Using the centerPopUp() method

`PopUpManager` contains a `centerPopUp()` method to center (to no surprise) the location of a pop-up window. The `centerPopUp()` method takes a single argument of type `IFlexDisplayObject`, which is any visual component—in other words, it's the name of a pop-up window, as the following line describes:

```
PopUpManager.centerPopUp(IFlexDisplayObject);
```

The `IFlexDisplayObject` can be any pop-up window variable you define. For example, when you create the window, if you set the result of the create function call to a variable, you can use that in the parent application to center the pop-up. To apply this to the previous example, you could do something like this:

```
simpleWindow =
   PopUpManager.createPopUp(this,windows.SimplePopupWindow,false);
PopUpManager.centerPopUp(simpleWindow as IFlexDisplayObject);
```

Because `simpleWindow` is declared as a generic object, Flex Builder doesn't know if `simpleWindow` is an `IFlexDisplayObject`. In the `centerPopUp()` method, you convince Flex to believe all is well by using casting.

NOTE The `centerPopUp()` method centers a pop-up relative to its parent container, not the center of the page.

The centering method operates somewhat counter-intuitively. Initially, most Flex coders assume that centering a pop-up means it will display in the center of the browser window. This isn't the case. Centering a pop-up window establishes a position over the center of the parent object in which you created the pop-up. If your parent object occupies a small area in the upper-right corner of the browser window, the `centerPopUp()` method will center the pop-up over that window, not the middle of the screen as defined by the main browser window.

The easiest strategy to deal with the placement issue is to name a parent as close to the application root as possible and define this parent with the largest view possible within the window space. Or, have your main application perform all the window openings (for example, you can have a global function that components can call to ask the main application to create pop-ups).

In most cases, using `centerPopUp()` will work fine for noncritical window positioning. In the majority of circumstances, it's all you'll need to manage the placement of your windows.

12.2.2 Calculating window placement

Centering a window is easy, but you can get fancy with manipulating the position and dimensions of a pop-up. Let's demonstrate by creating another pop-up in your src/windows directory called MoveWindow.mxml. In this project (see figure 12.3), the pop-up has buttons that, when clicked, move the pop-up to each corner of the window; another button toggles visibility properties.

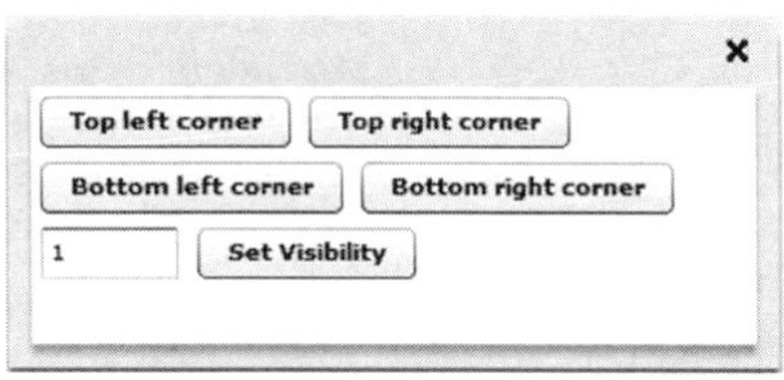

Figure 12.3 MoveWindow.mxml: clicking the buttons manipulates the *x* and *y* coordinates to reposition this pop-up.

Although the manual method of placing windows on a screen gives you more control over the exact location of the window, it requires more calculation and greater attention to where you position the window. Listing 12.4 presents the code snippet used to determine where the window is currently located and its dimensions (which you'll later manipulate to move the pop-up to each of the four window corners). The variables `this.x` and `this.y` correspond to the horizontal and vertical coordinates, respectively.

Listing 12.4 Accessing a pop-up's position and dimensions

```
var currentX:Number = this.x;
var currentY:Number = this.y;
var currentWidth:Number = this.width;
var currentHeight:Number = this.height;
```

Imagine that the window is a grid with lines that run up and across the window, as illustrated in figure 12.4. *X* and *y* are points on that grid for the window or whatever object it is that you're measuring. In listing 12.4, `this.x` and `this.y` are points on the grid.

X and *y* are points that are available in every object that can be displayed on the screen, and they match up to the current location of the object on the screen. Thus the *x* and *y* values let you identify any single pixel on the screen.

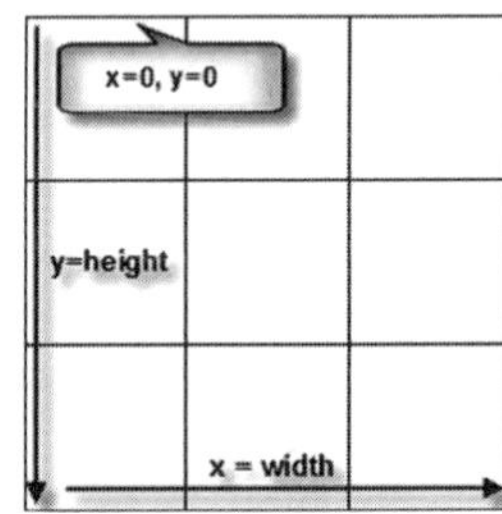

Figure 12.4 Visualizing the positioning parameters of a pop-up

If you evaluate the *x* and y properties of a newly created window that doesn't have any positioning applied to it, you'll see that the window has an *x* value of zero (0) and a *y* value of zero (0) (see the upper left corner of figure 12.4). If you combine that with the height and width of the window, you can arrive at the placement of the object on the screen.

Leveraging that as the premise for moving a pop-up window, listing 12.5 shows how to use the dimensions of the pop-up against the dimensions of the parent component (which is the main application in this case) to calculate a new position for the window. To make it more interesting, you add a 10-pixel *buffer* from the edges.

Listing 12.5 MoveWindow.mxml: manipulating the pop-up's position

```
<?xml version="1.0" encoding="utf-8"?>
<mx:TitleWindow xmlns:mx="http://www.adobe.com/2006/mxml"
    layout="vertical" width="340" height="150"
   showCloseButton="true" close="closeMe()">

  <mx:Script>
  <![CDATA[
   import mx.managers.PopUpManager;

   private function moveWindow(where:String):void
   {
     var newX:Number = 0;
     var newY:Number = 0;
     var buffer:Number = 10;
     switch (where)
     {
       case "toprightcorner" :
         newY = buffer;
         newX = (parent.width - this.width)-buffer;
```

```
            break;
          case "topleftcorner"  :
            newY = buffer;
            newX = buffer;
            break;
          case "bottomrightcorner" :
            newY = (parent.height - this.height)-buffer;
            newX = (parent.width - this.width)-buffer;
            break;
          case "bottomleftcorner"  :
            newY = (parent.height - this.height)-buffer;
              newX = buffer;
            break;
        }
        this.move(newX,newY);
      }

      private function closeMe():void
      {
        PopUpManager.removePopUp(this);
      }
    ]]>
      </mx:Script>

    <mx:HBox>
      <mx:Button label="Top left corner"
              click="moveWindow('topleftcorner');"/>
      <mx:Button label="Top right corner"
              click="moveWindow('toprightcorner');"/>
     </mx:HBox>
     <mx:HBox>
       <mx:Button label="Bottom left corner"
               click="moveWindow('bottomleftcorner');"/>
     <mx:Button label="Bottom right corner"
             click="moveWindow('bottomrightcorner');"/>
    </mx:HBox>
  </mx:TitleWindow>
```

Calculates x and y coordinates based on window dimensions

As we mentioned earlier, when you're calculating and setting window placement by coordinates, it's particularly important to remember that when centering a pop-up, all coordinate calculations are relative to the size and location of the parent object—not the coordinates of the main window.

The issues surrounding window location become important when you're dealing with modal windows. When you define a modal window, the user is forced to work within that window only and is unable to click any items outside the modal window's boundaries without first closing that window. As a worst-case scenario, if you define a modal window that appears outside of the visible screen, it renders the application unusable because the user can't close the window or click anywhere else on the screen to release the modal window's control of the application.

Specifying the location of pop-up windows in your application is a critical visual and functional responsibility. Flex provides several more ways to control pop-up attributes, to help simplify your programming burden and help with your design's visual appearance. The next aspect we'll look at is setting the window's transparency level by managing the alpha property.

12.3 Setting window transparency

One of the nice features of pop-up windows is that you can give your application some high-end pizzazz and set varying levels of window transparency. You set transparency by changing the `alpha` property of the pop-up window. This property is available for all visible objects, but it's particularly noticeable and useful when employed on pop-up windows.

The `alpha` property is defined using a numeric value between 0 and 1 that varies the opacity of your window. A value of zero (0) renders the window invisible, whereas a value of 1 makes it fully visible. Transparency settings apply only to the window itself, not necessarily to the items contained within it.

From within the window, you can set the window's transparency along the lines of this code snippet:

```
this.alpha = 0.4;
```

From outside the window (for example, from the component that created the pop-up), the code is similar. It references the name of the pop-up window instance:

```
moveWindow.alpha = 0.4;
```

To add the ability to control transparency in your sample application, let's add a `TextInput` that accepts a number for the `alpha` and a function that sets the value. Add the following MXML components to the previous code:

```
<mx:HBox>
  <mx:TextInput id="visibilityText" text="{this.alpha}" restrict="0-9\."
          width="60" />
  <mx:Button label="Set Visibility" click="setVisibility();"/>
</mx:HBox>
```

Then, add the following ActionScript function to provide the logic:

```
private function setVisibility():void
{
  this.alpha = Number(visibilityText.text);
}
```

As illustrated in figures 12.5 and 12.6, varying the transparency of a window allows for unique pop-up designs and gives you flexibility in how you manage the look and feel of your application.

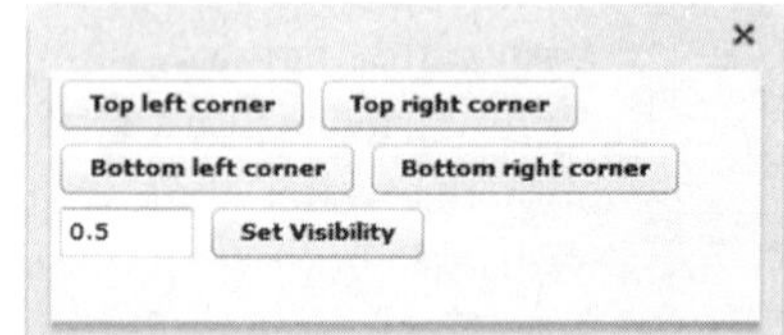

Figure 12.5 A pop-up window with transparency set to 0 (completely invisible border)

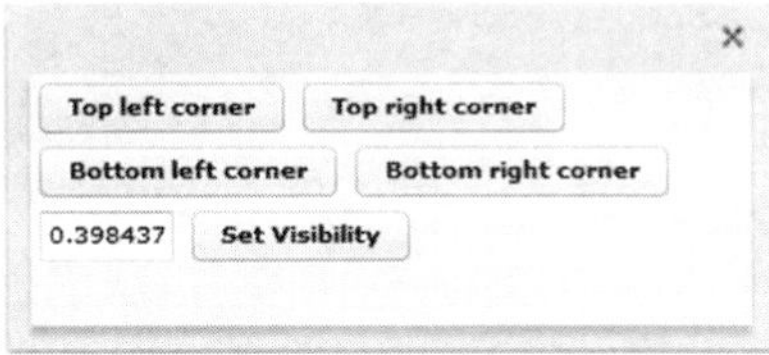

Figure 12.6 The same pop-up with its transparency set to a value of 0.5, which renders the window 50% opaque

Now that we've dealt with the visual aspects of creating and displaying a pop-up window, we'll look at one of the more common use cases: the pop-up form.

12.4 Data integration with pop-ups

In this section, you'll take your knowledge of pop-ups one step further by learning how to retrieve data inside the pop-up (usually, information the user enters on a form) or send information to a pop-up. To set up the example, you'll create a pop-up with a text input that will continually append text to a variable, as shown in figure 12.7.

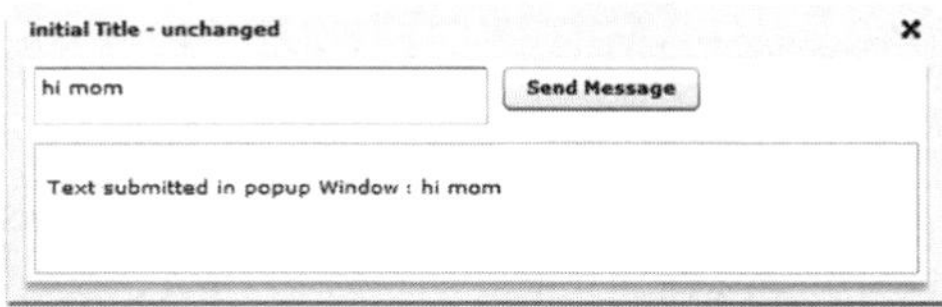

Figure 12.7 This pop-up window accepts user input and saves it to a variable that will be retrieved later.

Let's start by creating a new MXML file called AdvancedPopupWindow.mxml in the src/windows folder. Enter the code shown in listing 12.6.

Listing 12.6 AdvancedPopupWindow.mxml: pop-up that captures user input

```
<?xml version="1.0" encoding="utf-8"?>
<mx:TitleWindow xmlns:mx="http://www.adobe.com/2006/mxml" layout="vertical"
            width="500" height="300" showCloseButton="true"
            close="closeMe()" title="initial Title - unchanged"   >

  <mx:Script>
  <![CDATA[

   import mx.managers.PopUpManager;

   [Bindable] public var myPopUpVar:String = "";
   [Bindable] public var myPopupLog:String = "";

   private function closeMe():void
   {
    PopUpManager.removePopUp(this);
   }

   public function setTitle(title:String):void
   {
    this.title = title;
   }

   private function sendMessage():void
   {
    var outgoingEvent:Event = new Event("popupMessage",false);
    myPopUpVar = windowInput.text;
```

```
        myPopupLog += "\n Text submitted in popup Window : " +
                windowInput.text;
    }
  ]]>
  </mx:Script>
  <mx:HBox width="100%" height="40%">
    <mx:TextInput id="windowInput" name="windowInput" height="30"
             width="240" text=""/>
    <mx:Button id="sendMessageButton" label="Send Message"
           click="sendMessage()"/>
  </mx:HBox>
  <mx:TextArea id="pageDescription" name="pageDescription"
           text="{myPopupLog}" width="100%" height="60%"/>
</mx:TitleWindow>
```

One of the greatest advantages of using a component object to open a window is that the object can be reused and retains all of its state values.

In the example presented in listing 12.7, you open the window, make changes to it, and close the window and open it again. The window retains the changes entered by a user, because the object is never erased or reinitialized.

Listing 12.7 Using a component object as a window

```
import windows.AdvancedPopupWindow;

[Bindable]
public var advancedWindow:AdvancedPopupWindow =
new AdvancedPopupWindow();
```

Windows that aren't generated within a component object are re-created and initialized every time the window is opened. This approach can be both good and bad, depending on how you intend to use the window. On one hand, your application can benefit from the object maintaining its state if it's to be displayed often; on the other hand, storing the window and its constituent data can be a drain on memory resources—particularly if the window is used only once.

To launch and use an existing object as a pop-up window, you only need to add the pop-up to the list managed by the pop-up manager:

```
PopUpManager.addPopUp(advancedWindow,this,false);
```

The script in listing 12.7 creates a component object as a variable that you can access from within the scope of the component, class, or application. Once the object has been created in the main application or component scope, it's available outside the calling function.

As listing 12.7 demonstrates, you use the `PopUpManager.addPopUp()` method to create your pop-up window. The `addPopUp()` method lets you add an existing object or component to the display list. In more technical terms, the `createPopUp()` method creates an object and initializes it, whereas `addPopUp()` expects to receive a previously initialized object, which it adds to its display list.

If you have a previously initialized object, the process of reinitializing it wipes out any stored data. Using the `addPopUp()` method, you can display and hide the window repeatedly without affecting the data inside. This is an important distinction, particularly as you get into extracting user-edited data from a window.

12.4.1 Getting data out of your pop-up window

Half the effort involved in manipulating pop-ups is creating them; the other half is the extraction of the information they contain. A popular way of working with pop-ups is to add a form with which users can interact. A number of different ways exist for you to construct a form and manage the information entered into it.

When you're first getting started with Flex, most developers have the impulse to include a data-services tag, such as WebService, RemoteObject, or HTTPService, to communicate user-entered form data directly to a server. This approach is easy to manage but not reusable and can quickly become a maintenance headache if your back-end web service changes.

A better way to capture form data is to present it as public variables, then send out an event to notify the parent application that information is available to process. In the following sections, we'll show you how to do this; but first, we need to revisit events.

12.4.2 Sending events

When sending events from your pop-up window, remember that they aren't dispatched in exactly the same manner as with other components.

In general, events work much as you would expect, with one variation: events from pop-ups don't travel down the inheritance chain to the main application root. Instead, events dispatched from pop-up windows are terminated at the window root.

This is because the pop-up manager is the parent of the pop-up window. As a result, events launched in the pop-up don't bubble up to the main application page, which is the eventual parent of any object in the main application.

Any events launched from within the pop-up window start and end with the <mx:TitleWindow/> tag. In practical terms, this means in order to receive events from the pop-up window, you need to register any object you intend to designate as a listener.

Event listeners are objects that respond to events generated by the window (see listing 12.8). These events can be either custom events or system-type events generated by the application. For more information about events and how to use them, we recommend reviewing chapter 10. Listing 12.8 shows event listeners registered on the advanced window object.

Listing 12.8 Registering events on a window

```
advancedWindow.addEventListener("popupMessage",getWindowData);
advancedWindow.addEventListener(CloseEvent.CLOSE,windowClose);
```

In this scenario, two event listeners are configured for the `advancedWindow` object. These event listeners will monitor for the custom events to be dispatched and react to them by gathering user-supplied information from the window (listing 12.9).

Listing 12.9 Dispatching events from a window

```
private function closeMe():void
{
  PopUpManager.removePopUp(this);
  dispatchEvent(new Event("popupClose",false) );
}
private function sendMessage():void
{
  var outgoingEvent:Event = new Event("popupMessage",false);
  myPopUpVar = windowInput.text;
  myPopupLog += "\n Text submitted in popup Window : " + windowInput.text;
  dispatchEvent( outgoingEvent);
}
```

Dispatches close event to simulate closing window

Signals message update

In this case, when a user types in data and clicks the button to commit the information, whatever has been entered in the text box is copied to a public variable, after which an event is dispatched. This custom event can be monitored by other components, which can then repeat the dispatch or process the data it contains.

Listing 12.9 dispatches a custom event and uses the event as a trigger to get data from the window, as we'll explain in more detail in the next section.

12.4.3 Getting data out

To extract data from the parent, you can access the object's public properties, or you can access the object's public functions. For example, referring back to section 12.4.2, you can see when the object arrives, you can access the target's properties and public functions. Listing 12.10 sets up the event listener in the main window and calls the function when the `popupMessage` event is received.

Listing 12.10 Responding to event from the window

```
advancedWindow.addEventListener("popupMessage",getWindowData);

public function getWindowData(event:Event):void
{
 mainWindowText.text += "\n Window submitted: " +
 advancedWindow.myPopUpVar;
}
```

After the event is received, you can read the public property on the window and retrieve the necessary data. This can just as easily be a function that returns the correct data. Once you've extracted the data from the system, you can then proceed to do whatever you need with it. The full example provided with this book appends a log to show what transpired in the window.

When many first-time coders arrive at the point where they are extracting data from a pop-up window, the temptation exists to pull the data directly from the source form object. We strenuously caution against taking this approach: it violates best-practice object-coding principles by potentially forcing you to rescript your calling code in several spots if you need to update your form.

The better way to pull your data out of a window is via a user-triggered event. When the event is fired, you can copy the data from the form element into a window object property and extract the data from the property. The other approach is to include the information in an event object dispatched from the window when editing is complete.

Employing either of these approaches lets you reuse your window component to a much greater extent and also insulates your application from excessive changes. These techniques also reduce the amount of time spent testing, debugging, and recoding. These approaches can be used reciprocally to send data into your window as well.

12.4.4 Sending data to the window

You have several options available for getting data into or out of a window. First, when the window is treated as an object, all the public properties of the window can be accessed from the parent. In addition, any public functions defined on the window can be accessed from the parent. In listing 12.11, notice places where the parent application is accessing the window for the purpose of extracting or placing data.

To send data in, generally the easiest and most simple method is to call a public function on the window to which to pass the data. For example, look how the title is set for the window in listing 12.11.

Listing 12.11 Sending data to a pop-up window

```
public function launchSimplePopup():void          <-- Function lives in
{                                                     main application
  var simpleWindow:Object =
  PopUpManager.createPopUp(this,windows.SimplePopupWindow,false);
  simpleWindow.setTitle("How about a snazzy new title?");
}

public function setTitle(newTitle:String):void     <-- Function lives
{                                                      in window
  pageTitle = newTitle;
}
```

This is a simple example, but you can pass more complex variables, such as classes, arrays, or even objects, then use them to arrange your pop-up window.

One thing to remember about the example in listing 12.11 is that if you scope the window object to the function this way, you'll only be able to access the object within that specific function. In this case, you can only access the `launchSimplePopup()` function.

If you wish to access the window from anywhere other than the creation function, you need to make your variable a component or declare it an application-visible variable in the main component body, as shown in listing 12.12.

Listing 12.12 Creating a pop-up window object for use outside a function

```
Private var simpleWindow:Object;

public function launchSimplePopup():void
{
```

```
    simpleWindow =
    PopUpManager.createPopUp(this,windows.SimplePopupWindow,false);
    simpleWindow.setTitle("How about a snazzy new title?");
}
```

The object in listing 12.12 combines both methods of accessing an object outside the caller function while allowing you to have the flexibility of creating the object on the fly whenever you need it.

Now that you have a good understanding of pop-up windows as well as how to work with windows using PopUpManager, we'll move on to another type of pop-up window you've most likely already seen and used: alerts.

12.5 Using alerts

The Alert class is a specialized type of class designed to rapidly create a specific type of pop-up window. You've already had some exposure to alerts by going through the examples in the book. Alerts let you quickly advise users about important information (generally errors), but they can also serve as great tools for debugging your code and messaging back values. If you're familiar with JavaScript, you'll be intimately familiar with this method of debugging.

12.5.1 Creating a simple alert

Creating an alert is as easy as pie. Listing 12.13 constructs an alert with code you've likely already used by now.

Listing 12.13 Creating a simple alert

```
import mx.controls.Alert;

Alert.show("Hello World!");
```

Undoubtedly, that is a simple alert. The only item required to make an alert pop up is the message to be communicated to the user. Figure 12.8 shows the output of this code.

Figure 12.8 An alert issuing a simple "Hello World!" message. Click OK to close the window.

The alert in figure 12.8 and listing 12.13 performs only one action; you can't do much more with it except click OK to close the window.

This limited interactivity is sufficient for communicating an error and directing a user to some other location to address the problem, but the user can't interact with the alert. This isn't the end of the story; you can do much more with alerts.

12.5.2 Doing more with alerts

Alerts in general are like pop-up windows. You can perform most of the same tricks with them: listen to and move events, change transparency, and so on.

But alerts are more specialized entities than pop-ups—you can only add or remove buttons. In addition to providing a message for the alert, the following properties can also be manipulated:

- Title
- Buttons (Yes, No, OK, Cancel)
- Owning object
- Custom handler method

Any of these properties can be specified or omitted. If you use more than one button, you'll need to include the custom handler method.

12.5.3 A more advanced alert

A one-button-fits-all approach to alerts doesn't work for every occasion. Consider the scenario in which you want to prompt a quick agreement from the user, perhaps to confirm that she wants to save a file or configuration before moving to a new screen.

To do this, you may want to display a small confirmation dialog asking her if she wants to save changes before closing a window. Listing 12.14 creates an alert containing multiple buttons.

Listing 12.14 Setting up a more advanced alert

```
import mx.controls.Alert;
import mx.events.CloseEvent;

private function simpleAlert(event:Event):void {
   Alert.show("Do you want to save your changes?", "Save Changes",
   Alert.YES|Alert.NO, this, simpleAlertHandler);
}
```

In this case, the pop-up is created with the `Alert.show()` method, in which you can include message and title information. To add more buttons, you can use the `Alert` static variables to indicate which buttons to show. In listing 12.14, `Alert.Yes` presents a Yes button and `Alert.No` displays a No button.

You can code the button callouts in any order, but it won't affect the order in which the buttons are displayed in the alert. The alert buttons always appear in the following order: OK, Yes, No, Cancel. Figure 12.9 shows the output of the code from listing 12.14.

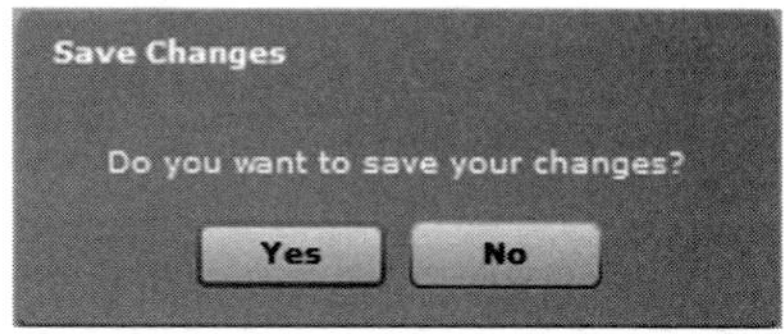

Figure 12.9 An alert message showing Yes and No buttons. You have your choice of what to do.

In listing 12.14, the alert handler, `simpleAlertHandler`, will be the called function when the user clicks a button. With alert windows, clicking a button automatically closes the window and fires a `CloseEvent`.

You can respond to this event by comparing the `event.detail` value against the static values on the alert object. For example, listing 12.15 tests whether the event.detail value is equal to Alert.YES. This listing shows the alert handler code for figure 12.9.

Listing 12.15 Alert handler

```
private function simpleAlertHandler(event:CloseEvent):void {
  if (event.detail==Alert.YES)
     status.text="You answered Yes";
  else
     status.text="You answered No";
}
```

NOTE It's considered good practice to use the object static variables whenever possible, because doing so makes your code easier to read and understand. Also, should those values ever change, you'll need to change them in only one place. For example, consider which is easier to understand: Alert.YES or 1. Intrinsically, they mean the same thing; but Alert.YES is much easier to read.

In listing 12.15, you respond to the close event that's fired from the alert window. The way you respond to an alert won't change much with any other event. For instance, to respond to an alert window, you always listen for CloseEvent and evaluate the result of the close event to determine which button was clicked.

What can and does frequently change is the appearance of the alert window, which lends itself to a fair amount of rework.

12.5.4 Pimp this alert

You can select from a variety of appearance options for your alert window. You can resize it, change the labels on the buttons, and include an icon in the alert window. Listing 12.16 combines all these options in one tricked-out message.

Listing 12.16 Launching the pimped-out alert

```
import mx.core.IFlexDisplayObject;
   import mx.controls.Alert;
   import mx.events.CloseEvent;
   import mx.managers.PopUpManager;

   [Embed(source="assets/warning.gif")]
   [Bindable]
   public var iconWarning:Class;

   private function customAlert(event:Event):void {
    var AlertObj:Alert;
    Alert.buttonWidth = 150;
    Alert.okLabel = "Disneyland";
    Alert.yesLabel = "Kennedy Space Port";       Assigns custom
    Alert.noLabel = "Six Flags";                 button labels
    Alert.cancelLabel = "Marine World";

    AlertObj = Alert.show("Where do you want to go today?", "Destination"
      ,Alert.OK|Alert.YES|Alert.NO|Alert.CANCEL,
```

```
        this,customAlertHandler,iconWarning,Alert.YES);   <-- Uses imported image
        AlertObj.height = 150;
        AlertObj.width = 700;
        PopUpManager.centerPopUp(AlertObj as
            IFlexDisplayObject);          <-- Centers alert
    }
```

You can set the labels for each of the buttons by using the `buttonLabel` property (one for each button). Setting the `buttonWidth` property allows you to determine the size of the buttons. Unfortunately, it's a one-size-fits-all situation; whatever size you choose in `Alert.buttonWidth` applies to all the buttons in that window.

In listing 12.16, you also import an image and use the image as the icon in the pop-up. The `Alert` class lets you set an icon to the right side of the alert message. In addition, you can designate which button displays as the default selection. In this example, you set `Alert.YES` (the last argument in the `Alert.show` call) as the default button. You can see what the pimped-out alert looks like in figure 12.10.

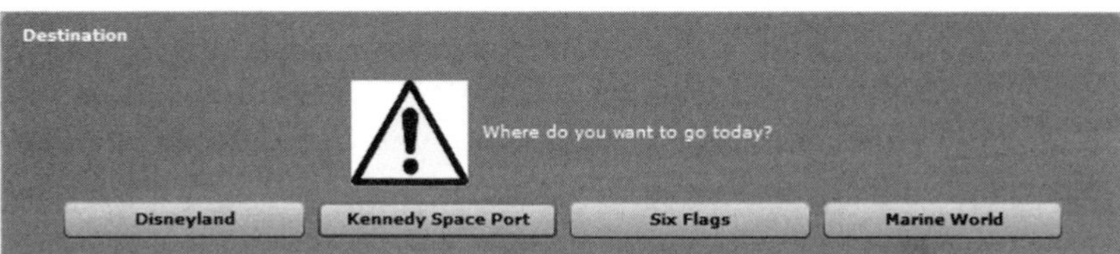

Figure 12.10 Pimped-out alert with a custom icon, custom button labels, and a default button

Listing 12.16 also sets the returned result from the `Alert.show` function to an object. This object is an initialized `Alert` object. Once the alert has opened, it acts similarly to a standard pop-up. You can do nearly everything to an alert window that you can do with a normal pop-up window, including changing its height, width, position, and transparency.

To establish which button was clicked, listen for the close event and trap the value using the `event.detail` value, as in listing 12.15.

It's also important to remember to change the button labels back to their original values if you've changed them, as shown in listing 12.17. If you don't restore the `buttonLabel` values, any other alert will display the same labels.

Listing 12.17 Pimped-out alert handler

```
private function customAlertHandler(event:CloseEvent):void {
  var message:String = "Woohoo!  Looks like we're going to ";
  switch (event.detail)   {
      case Alert.YES :
            status.text = message + Alert.yesLabel;
               break;
            case Alert.NO :
              status.text = message + Alert.noLabel;
               break;
            case Alert.OK :
               status.text = message + Alert.okLabel;
```

```
                    break;
                case Alert.CANCEL :
                  status.text = message + Alert.cancelLabel;
          }
        Alert.okLabel = "OK";
        Alert.yesLabel = "Yes";                    Resets
        Alert.noLabel = "No";                      labels
        Alert.cancelLabel = "Cancel";
      }
```

Changing the look and feel of the alert is one way you can furnish your application with a little extra sophistication. But it's not strictly necessary to change the alert function much at all. In most cases, programmers show a Yes/No type of alert because it's quick and easy and a modal way of interacting with the user. Now that you've seen how you can modify alert messages, you can include some of these extras to give your application polish.

12.6 Summary

Many applications use pop-up windows in some form or another. Pop-up windows can be easy to manage if you remember a few things:

- Creating a pop-up can be done with or without a companion MXML file, but it's most often easier using an MXML component.
- Events broadcast from a pop-up window always terminate at the pop-up window root. Events aren't broadcast through the parent up to the application root.
- Using a public-level object is an effective way of maintaining window state even when the window is closed. Creating this object often makes it easier to access the window in case you need to send data.
- A window can have public properties and public functions, which can both be used to set and retrieve data from the window.
- Pop-up placement in the application depends on the location and placement of the parent that generated the pop-up. In most cases, you should try to use a parent as close to the root as possible, or at least a component that has the widest visible range on the screen.
- You can modify alerts to include an icon image and up to four buttons. The button labels can be changed. Using `closeEvent` along with the `event.detail` item lets you tell which button was clicked.
- Alert windows act like pop-up windows. Most of the actions you expect on a pop-up window can also be done on an alert, including moving, resizing, and varying the transparency.

You've made it through another chapter, and we're happy you've stuck with us this far. The next chapter builds on the component functionality we presented here and adds view states, which allow you to modify the visual look of your components (including pop-up windows).

13 View states

This chapter covers:

- Understanding and using view states
- View states in Flex
- Transitions in view states

In previous chapters, you learned about controls, containers, layouts, and various other features incorporated within Adobe Flex, and how you can use these tools to build RIAs.

In this chapter, we'll explore another important feature: view states. With view states, you can build RIAs that impart a polished and satisfying user-experience. Before we jump into Flex-specific view state features, let's learn about the concept of view states in general.

13.1 Understanding view states

An RIA's UI consists of different views. Traditional web applications consist of stateless, or static, pages (such as HTML pages).

Views can take on different visual appearances and representations depending on the conditions in which they're presented. An example of a condition is a user input, such as picking an item from a drop-down list or clicking a button. Other examples include your application responding to a request sent to a server, or the result of an algorithm. A simple application may have only one view with some states, whereas complex applications may have several views, each with different states.

A *view state* can be defined as a particular visual appearance, behavior, and representation for a view (UI).

Views have at least one state, which is known as the *default* or *base* state of the view. You can define any number of additional states depending on your requirements.

To illustrate the concept further, let's look at a real-world example. Figure 13.1 shows the login form for Buzzword, an online word processor developed using Adobe Flex. The illustration shows the default (base) state of the login form (view).

Figure 13.1 Default view state of a login form on Buzzword.com, an online document editor

Figure 13.2 shows a different state of the Buzzword login form that displays when the user clicks the Forgot Your Password link in figure 13.1.

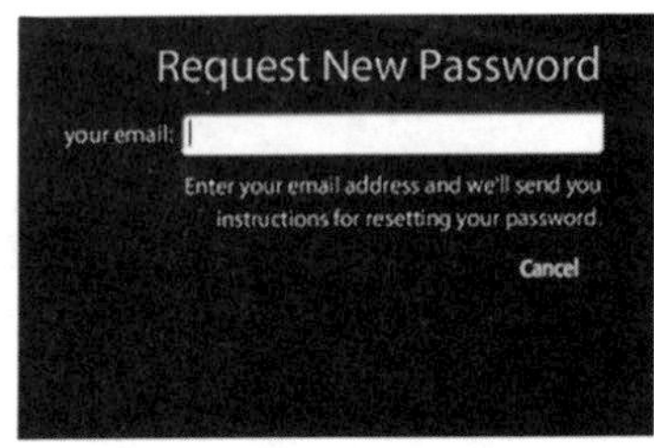

Figure 13.2 A different view state for the login form on Buzzword.com

View states can be used for many other scenarios, such as these:

- A search view that shows results in a different state than the search form
- A layout-personalization view that lets users customize their application's appearance by defining different layouts as different states
- A view that shows user data in one state, then allows editing in different states

This is a basic introduction to view states. In the remainder of the chapter, we'll explore view states in detail and their related features in Adobe Flex.

13.2 View states in Flex

In Flex, each application, custom component, or view has at least one state, which is known as the *base* or *default* view state. You can define additional states by setting the value of the `states` property.

The base or default state is the original state of the components you code into your application. Other states modify that original state by setting properties or removing or adding child objects. Listing 13.1 demonstrates how you can define two additional states.

Listing 13.1 View defining two states

```
<mx:states>
   <mx:State name="ViewState1">
      <mx:SetProperty />
      <mx:SetProperty />
```

```
        <mx:RemoveChild />
        <mx:RemoveChild />
    </mx:State>
    <mx:State name="ViewState2">
    </mx:State>
</mx:states>
```

Listing 13.1 defines two states named `ViewState1` and `ViewState2`. Only one view state is active, or displayed, at a time. The active state is set using the value of the `currentState` property of the view (the view being the application or custom component). The default value of `currentState` is an empty string (`''`), which means the base view state has no name.

Table 13.1 shows view state–related properties for `mx.core.UIComponent`.

Table 13.1 View states-related properties of the `mx.core.UIComponent` class

Property	Type	Description
`states`	`Array`	An array of state objects. This is populated to create more view states or read from to find available states.
`currentState`	`String`	The view state name. The default value is `''` (base or default view state).

To change the view's state, you set the value of the application's `currentState` property the name of the new state. In listing 13.1, the state names are `ViewState1` and `ViewState2`.

Views also automatically send out events to notify listening components that the state of the view has changed, as well as before the view state changes. Table 13.2 lists the generated events when the view changes state. By listening for these events, your components can respond accordingly. For more information about listening for events, see chapter 10.

Table 13.2 View state-related events of the `mx.core.UIComponent` class

Property	Type	Description
`currentStateChanging`	`StateChangeEvent`	This event is dispatched after the `currentState` property has been changed, but before the view state changes. This event can be used to validate the change request or to perform actions before the state changes. It can also be used to prevent the state from changing.
`currentStateChange`	`StateChangeEvent`	This event is dispatched when view's state has been changed.

13.2.1 *View states classes*

We introduced view state-related code in listing 13.1. Table 13.3 looks at this code in more detail and lists all the classes in the `mx.states` package along with a brief description for each class and interface. This package can be used in ActionScript or declarative MXML.

Table 13.3 Different view state classes in the `mx.states` package

Class/interface	Description
`State` (`<mx:State />`)	Defines a view state. This class has an `overrides` instance property that expects an array of objects that implement the `mx.states.IOverride` interface.
`IOverride` (interface)	Implemented by all the override classes. The `state` class implements the `IOverride` class. Flex framework comes with overrides, such as `AddChild`, `RemoveChild`, `SetProperty`, `SetStyle` and `SetEventHandler`, as explained in this table. Custom override classes are written by implementing this interface.
`AddChild` (`<mx:AddChild />`)	Adds a component to the view as a part of the view state change. Both view and component should be either the implementer of the `mx.core.IUIComponent` interface or a subclass of `mx.core.UIComponent`. Most Flex components are subclasses of `mx.core.UIComponent`.
`RemoveChild` (`<mx:RemoveChild />`)	Removes a component from the view as part of a view state change. Both view and component should be either the implementer of the `mx.core.IUIComponent` interface or a subclass of `mx.core.UIComponent`. Most Flex components are subclasses of `mx.core.UIComponent`.
`SetProperty` (`<mx:SetProperty />`)	Sets or overrides an object property value, which is only effective in the current view state.
`SetStyle` `<mx:SetStyle />`)	Sets the value of a component's style. This value is only effective in the current view state.
`SetEventHandler` (`mx:SetEventHandler />`)	This function lets you make an event handler change that is active only for the current view state. This allows you to set custom actions on elements that may be defined only for specific view states.
`Transition`	Lets you define a transition effect that should happen when changing from one view state to another (see section 13.4).

The classes listed in table 13.3 enable you to work with other Flex classes and objects to add them to or remove them from a state. This lets you manage how a component or application transitions from one state to the next, and even the appearance of those states. To more effectively explain how to use these classes in creating a view state, the next section will show a simple real-world example.

13.2.2 View-state example

Let's look at the classic example of a login form, as illustrated by figure 13.3. This is a continuation of the Buzzword application's login, in which an additional state is displayed when the user has forgotten his password and wants to request a new password. Figure 13.3 shows the base state, and figure 13.4 shows an additional state for requesting a new password.

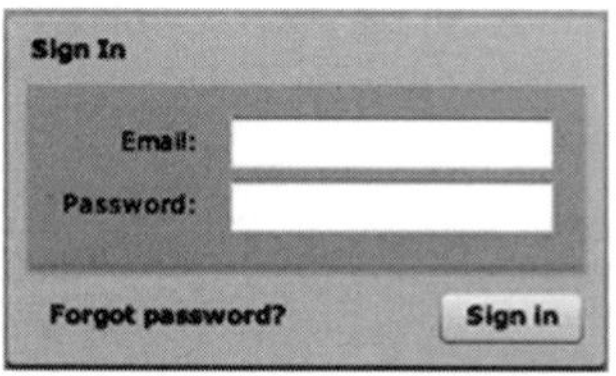

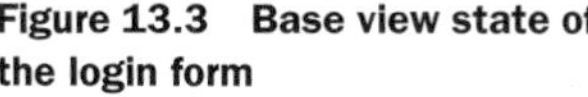

Figure 13.3 Base view state of the login form

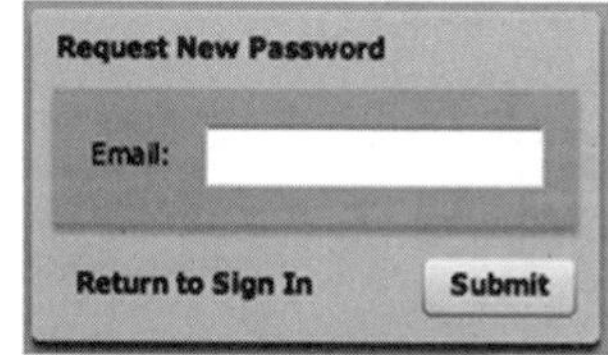

Figure 3.4 Request New Password view state, in which some controls have been removed and others have been modified

The code required to produce figure 13.3 is shown in listing 13.2. You can see how each additional state is defined.

Listing 13.2 Login form view-state code

```
<mx:Application xmlns:mx="http://www.adobe.com/2006/mxml">
  <mx:Panel title="Sign In" id="signinPanel" fontSize="12"
        backgroundAlpha="0.0">
    <mx:Form id="loginForm" backgroundAlpha="0.0">
      <mx:FormItem label="Email:"
              id="emailItem" backgroundAlpha="0.0">
        <mx:TextInput id="emailText"/>
      </mx:FormItem>
        <mx:FormItem label="Password:"
                id="passwordItem">
        <mx:TextInput id="passwordText" displayAsPassword="true"/>
      </mx:FormItem>
    </mx:Form>
    <mx:ControlBar>
      <mx:LinkButton id="forgotPasswordLink"
                label="Forgot password?"
                  click="currentState='RequestPassword'" />
      <mx:Spacer width="100%" id="spacer"/>
      <mx:Button label="Sign in" id="signinButton"/>
    </mx:ControlBar>
  </mx:Panel>

    <mx:states>
    <mx:State name="RequestPassword">
```

Interface elements in base state

RequestPassword defined in view

```
        <mx:SetProperty target="{signinPanel}" name="title"
                value="Request New Password"/>
        <mx:SetProperty target="{signinButton}" name="label"
                  value="Submit"/>
        <mx:RemoveChild target="{forgotPasswordLink}"/>
        <mx:AddChild relativeTo="{spacer}"
                position="before">
          <mx:target>
            <mx:LinkButton id="signInLink"
                      label="Return to Sign In"
                      click="currentState=''"/>
          </mx:target>
        </mx:AddChild>
        <mx:RemoveChild target="{passwordItem}"/>
      </mx:State>
    </mx:states>
</mx:Application>
```

Additional view states

As the code makes clear, the application has a view with user elements in the base (default) state. An additional state is defined to bring up the different user interface when the user clicks the Forgot Password button.

The state of the application is changed to `RequestPassword` by changing the value of the application's `currentState` property. Similarly, when the Return to Sign In button is clicked, the `currentState` property is assigned an empty string; and as you learned earlier, if the `currentState` property has an empty string as a value, the base view state is shown.

Changes in a view's state are effective only when that state is shown. For example, in the `RequestPassword` state, the password input field is removed; but if the state reverts to the default, the input field and label are automatically returned to the form.

Let's deconstruct listing 13.1 a little further. The base state of this application has a panel with two form items: a control bar with a button and a link button. You define another view state which is used to request a new password.

The `RequestPassword` state requires a different UI; accordingly, it applies changes to the base state to fulfill the requirements of the changed `RequestPassword` state. Changes are applied using override classes: `RemoveChild` to remove a form item (the password input field); `SetProperty` to change the title and label of the panel and button, respectively; `RemoveChild` to remove the Forgot Password button; and `AddChild` to add a button labeled Return to Sign In.

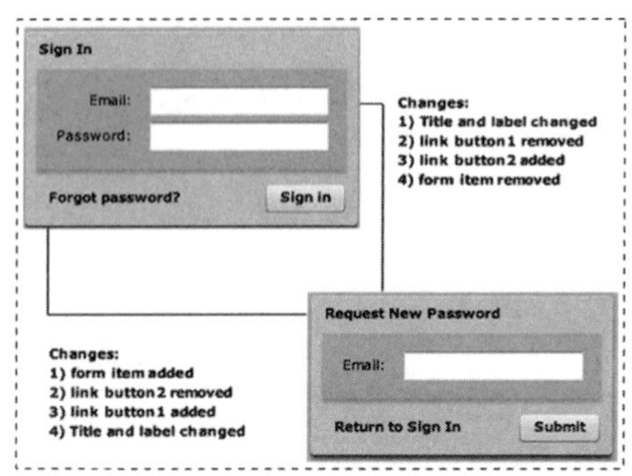

Figure 13.5 Order of view-state changes

Figure 13.5 shows the list of changes to the user interface during the view-state changes.

The changes are applied in the following order when the view's state is changed to `RequestPassword (currentState = 'RequestPassword')`:

1 The panel's title is changed to Request New Password.
2 The button's label is changed to Submit.
3 The button associated with `forgotPasswordLink` is removed.
4 The button associated with `signLink` is added just before the spacer.
5 The form item related to the password input field (`passwordItem`) is removed.

The following changes are applied in reverse order from the previous changes when the view state reverts to the base view state from the `RequestPassword` view state (`currentState=''`):

1 The form item for the password input field (`passwordItem`) is restored.
2 The button associated with `signLink` is removed.
3 The button associated with `forgotPasswordLink` is added before the spacer.
4 The button's label is changed to Sign In.
5 The Panel's title is changed back to Sign In.

As you can see, changes made by view-state overrides are effective only during that view or state's life. As soon as the state is changed, changes revert to the base view state in reverse order.

To achieve a better understanding of view states, let's look each state class individually.

13.2.3 *Defining a view state (<mx:State />)*

You can define the different states of a view by creating an instance of the `mx.states.State` class. In MXML, you do this using the `<mx:State />` tag. Table 13.4 shows key properties of the `State` class, which are used while defining a view state.

Table 13.4 Different view state classes in the `mx.states` package

Properties	Type	Description
`name`	`String`	A required property. `name` must to be set to a unique value. State names should be unique within the scope of a view. As we discussed earlier, a view's states can be defined at the root level of an application or a custom component, and the state name needs to be unique in the scope where it's defined.
`overrides`	`Array`	An array of objects implementing the `IOverride` interface. These objects are used to apply changes when moving from one view state to another. Effectively, this is a list of all the changes that will be made to the base view when making a transition from one view to another.
`basedOn`	`String`	State on which a view's states are based; must be an instance of the State class. The default value is null, which means the state is based on the default (or base) state of an application or custom component.

A view's state—that is, an instance of the `state` class—should have a name that can be set using the `name` property of the `state` class. The view-state name should be unique within the scope of its definition. In Figure 13.6, `MyView` defines an additional four states; therefore, it's the scope where state names should be unique.

A view's state can specify changes to available objects, ranging from the state it's based on to override classes. You do this by setting the `overrides` property, which we'll look at once we're finished with the `basedOn` property.

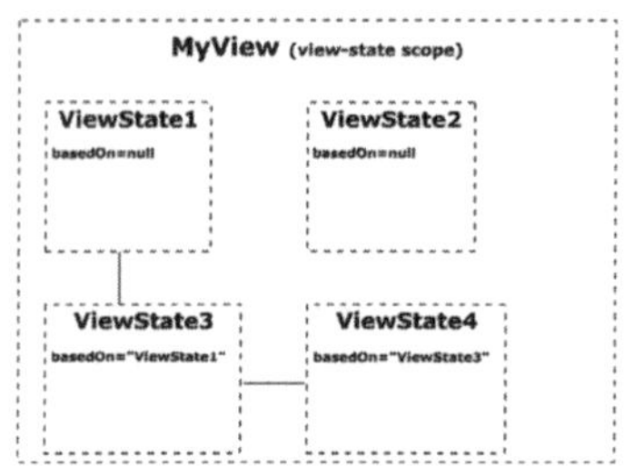

Figure 13.6 View-state scope and the `basedOn` property

View states can be nested—that is, one view's state can be based on another state. Figure 13.6 shows a view (`MyView`) with four additional states, which means there are five states including the base view state.

`ViewState1` and `ViewState2` are founded on the base view state because the `basedOn` property has a default value of `null`. `ViewState3` is based on `ViewState1`, which means all UI objects from `ViewState1` are also available in `ViewState3`.

Similarly, `ViewState4` has access to all objects from `ViewState3`. You can also define overrides to `ViewState3` and `ViewState4` to apply changes to all available objects. Phew—try saying that four times, fast!

To put it another way, when a state (state C) is based on another state (state B) other than the base state (state A), all the changes in the first state (state B) are made first; then, once those changes have been made, the changes from the second (state C) are applied. In this way, you can build states that have been built on other states and minimize the amount of work needed to create different yet similar states.

Let's look at an example to learn more about the `basedOn` property. In listing 13.3, you create two view states where one of the states is based on another.

Listing 13.3 View state overrides with the `basedOn` property

```
<mx:states>
      <mx:State name="RequestPassword">
         <mx:SetProperty target="{signinPanel}" name="title"
            value="Request New Password"/>
         <mx:SetProperty target="{signinButton}" name="label"
             value="Submit"/>
         <mx:RemoveChild target="{forgotPasswordLink}"/>
         <mx:AddChild relativeTo="{spacer}" position="before">
            <mx:target>
               <mx:LinkButton id="signInLink"
            label="Return to Sign In"
         click="currentState=''"/>
            </mx:target>
         </mx:AddChild>
      </mx:State>
      <mx:State name="NewPassword" basedOn="RequestPassword" >
          <mx:RemoveChild target="{passwordItem}"/>
```

```
    </mx:State>
</mx:states>
```

The easiest method to create view states is to use MXML, but you can also create them using ActionScript; doing so affords you the additional flexibility to manage the application as you need. Listing 13.4 shows an example of how to create view states using ActionScript.

Listing 13.4 Creating view states in ActionScript

```
import mx.states.*;
import mx.controls.LinkButton;

private var signInLink:LinkButton = new LinkButton();

private function initFunc():void   {
  var thisState:State = new State();
  thisState.name = "RequestPassword";
  thisState.overrides.push(new SetProperty(signinPanel,
     "title","Request New Password"));
  thisState.overrides.push(new SetProperty(signinButton,"label","submit"));
  thisState.overrides.push(new RemoveChild(forgotPasswordLink) );
  thisState.overrides.push(new RemoveChild(passwordItem) );

     signInLink.label = "Return to Sign In";
     signInLink.addEventListener("click",resetCurrentState);
     thisState.overrides.push(new AddChild(spacer,signInLink,"before"));
     this.states.push(thisState);
}

private function resetCurrentState(e:Event):void   {
  this.currentState='';
}
```

As listing 13.3 demonstrates, it's possible to create view states in ActionScript by piggybacking on the `creationComplete` event from the component. When all the items have been created, you can prepare the links for each state.

Components that belong to the view stack or that descend from `UIComponent` have the `states` property available. Remember that although the `states` property is available on most `UIComponents`, you can only modify the states when you're creating a custom component. If you try to add or modify states for an object that isn't a custom component, the Flex compiler will throw an error.

The `states` property is an array that accepts any number of state objects. All you need to do is to push state objects onto the `states` array to add states to the component or application. Each state object also has any number of overrides that are added to the overrides array.

13.2.4 View-state transitions

View states are primarily used to affect visual changes to your application. When you're working with the visual portions of the application, it's important to note that the Flex system will queue up the changes to the UI and generally redraw the interface all at once, such that the user will see a jump from one state to another.

Referring to the login form in which you remove or add a form field, the user will perceive a flicker in the interface as a different set of elements appears. This clearly isn't the preferred way to move from one visual queue to another.

You can smooth out the move from one view to another by adding a transition. The transition uses effects to produce a smooth flow to your view state changes. Adding in transitions is an easy trick to make your application look and feel more professional.

Transitions use Flex effects and are one of a series of effects that are grouped together to play when a change occurs in the view state. To learn more about effects, see chapter 20.

Listing 13.5 employs a simple transition.

Listing 13.5 A simple transition

```
<mx:Panel title="Sign In" id="signinPanel" fontSize="12"
      backgroundAlpha="0.0">
      <mx:Form id="loginForm" backgroundAlpha="0.0">
         <mx:FormItem label="Email:"
              id="emailItem"
              backgroundAlpha="0.0">
            <mx:TextInput id="emailText"/>
         </mx:FormItem>
         <mx:FormItem label="Password:"
                id="passwordItem">
            <mx:TextInput id="passwordText"
              displayAsPassword="true"/>
         </mx:FormItem>
      </mx:Form>
      <mx:ControlBar>
         <mx:LinkButton id="forgotPasswordLink"
           label="Forgot password?"
           click="currentState='RequestPassword'" />
         <mx:Spacer width="100%" id="spacer"/>
         <mx:Button label="Sign in" id="signinButton"/>
      </mx:ControlBar>
</mx:Panel>

<mx:states>
   <mx:State name="RequestPassword">
      <mx:SetProperty target="{signinPanel}" name="title"
          value="Request New Password"/>
      <mx:SetProperty target="{signinButton}" name="label"
        value="Submit"/>
       <mx:RemoveChild target="{forgotPasswordLink}"/>
       <mx:AddChild relativeTo="{spacer}" position="before">
         <mx:target>
           <mx:LinkButton id="signInLink"
              label="Return to Sign In" click="currentState=''"/>
         </mx:target>
       </mx:AddChild>
       <mx:RemoveChild target="{passwordItem}"/>
```

```
    </mx:State>
  </mx:states>

  <mx:transitions>
    <mx:Transition fromState="*" toState="*">
      <mx:Parallel id="t1" targets="{[signinPanel,loginForm,passwordItem]}">
        <mx:WipeLeft />
      </mx:Parallel>
    </mx:Transition>
  </mx:transitions>
```

Most transitions use either the <mx:Parallel> or <mx:Sequence> tags to control how and when the transitions are used. The targets are defined in the `targets` array, and each of these targets implements the `wipeLeft` effect when the state changes. You'll notice that `fromState` and `toState` both have an asterisk (*) for their value. This means the transition will play on all states. You can change this value to the name of a specific view state to apply, or filter, transitions selectively.

Filters allow you to specify an effect is played only on specific components. For example, using the login form from earlier in the chapter, you could prepare a transition with effects that apply only to the dynamic form elements (the password input field, for instance). Or you could apply different effects based on specific state changes. This is useful when you have several large components and those components handle their own state changes.

13.2.5 States in components

Up to this point, we've shown you how to work with view states in the main application file. You can also define states that work only within a particular component. As an example, you can make a subcomponent that includes several states and has the ability to individually change its state apart from the main application.

This process is nearly the same as changing and setting up state changes within the main application, but with the additional benefit that you can change the state from the parent application by setting the component's `currentState` property.

This is what makes view states an important and useful tool in the development of RIAs. All you need to do is change the state of your component—which can be done from outside the component—to change the way your component appears. Using this method, the parent component doesn't need to know every item in your custom component; it only needs to know the available states, which are much easier to monitor and change. Listing 13.6 shows an example of incorporating a view state into a component.

Listing 13.6 `component.passwordBox`: Custom view-state component

```
<?xml version="1.0" encoding="utf-8"?>
<mx:Panel title="Sign In" fontSize="12"
   backgroundAlpha="0.0" xmlns:mx="http://www.adobe.com/2006/mxml" >
   <mx:Form id="loginForm" backgroundAlpha="0.0">
      <mx:FormItem label="Email:" id="emailItem"
```

```
        backgroundAlpha="0.0">
        <mx:TextInput id="emailText"/>
    </mx:FormItem>
    <mx:FormItem label="Password:" id="passwordItem">
        <mx:TextInput id="passwordText"
          displayAsPassword="true"/>
    </mx:FormItem>
</mx:Form>
<mx:ControlBar id="forgotControl">
    <mx:LinkButton id="forgotPasswordLink"
        label="Forgot password?"
        click="currentState='RequestPassword'" />
    <mx:Spacer width="100%" id="spacer"/>
    <mx:Button label="Sign in" id="signinButton"/>
</mx:ControlBar>

<mx:states>
    <mx:State name="RequestPassword">
        <mx:SetProperty target="{this}" name="title"
            value="Request New Password"/>
        <mx:SetProperty target="{signinButton}" name="label"
             value="Submit"/>
        <mx:RemoveChild target="{forgotPasswordLink}"/>
        <mx:AddChild relativeTo="{spacer}" position="before">
            <mx:target>
                <mx:LinkButton id="signInLink"
                    label="Return to Sign In" click="currentState=''"/>
            </mx:target>
        </mx:AddChild>
        <mx:RemoveChild target="{passwordItem}"/>
    </mx:State>
</mx:states>

<mx:transitions>
     <mx:Transition fromState="*" toState="*">
          <mx:Parallel id="t1"
targets="{[this,loginForm,forgotControl,emailItem,passwordItem]}">
            <mx:WipeLeft />
          </mx:Parallel>
      </mx:Transition>
 </mx:transitions>
</mx:Panel>
```

When you've saved the component file in listing 13.6, you can create the main component that references your custom component (see listing 13.7).

Listing 13.7 Component that contains a view state

```
<mx:Application xmlns:mx="http://www.adobe.com/2006/mxml"
    layout="absolute" xmlns:comp="component.*"
    creationComplete="initFunc()">
   <mx:Script>
     <![CDATA[
     import mx.collections.ArrayCollection;
     import mx.states.State;

     [bindable] private var possibleStates:Array= new Array();
```

```
private function initFunc():void   {
  var i:Number;
  possibleStates.push('');
  for (i=0; i < myPasswordView.states.length; i++)   {
    possibleStates.push(myPasswordView.states[i].name);
  }
  viewSwitch.dataProvider = possibleStates;
}

  private function resetState():void   {
  myPasswordView.currentState = '';
   }

  private function newPasswordState(e:Event):void   {
 myPasswordView.currentState = possibleStates[e.target.selectedIndex];
}
]]>
</mx:Script>
<mx:ComboBox id="viewSwitch" change="newPasswordState(event)"/>

 <comp:passwordBox id="myPasswordView" x="20" y="40" />
</mx:Application>
```

From here, all you need to do from the parent application is change the component's `currentState` property to affect a state change. The component itself manages and maintains its own list of states.

Listing 13.5 also loops through the `states` property, extracting names to grant users the choice of the state to which they want to go. The names of the component states are the same as the login-window examples used throughout this chapter. You can see this example in action by looking at the example code files that are available at www.flexinaction.com.

13.3 Summary

Using view states is a powerful technique for changing your application's appearance. When used throughout your application, view states give you an easy method for quickly switching between views. Here are a few key thoughts to take away from this chapter:

- To change the view state, set the `currentState` property on your component or application.
- Using the `basedOn` property, you can easily build states from other states, and reuse the source state's properties.
- Transitions let you group effects and queue them to play on specific objects when the state of a component changes. This ensures that your effects and transitions play in the correct order and at the necessary time.

This chapter introduced view states and explained how to manipulate the visual state of your components in a configurable way. The next chapter will be a bit of a departure from the visual aspects, focusing instead on how to get data into your application from the server side of web services.

14 Working with data services

This chapter covers:

- The major elements of a WSDL document and learning how to read one
- Connecting to web services
- Retrieving data files with the `URLLoader`
- Handling `ResultEvents`
- Handling `FaultEvents`
- Passing information using `AsyncTokens`
- Using the new Flex Import Web Service wizard

For many Flex applications, most of your data sources will be web services that have been built for the purpose of delivering information to web applications. Several types of web services are available that encompass many different methods of transporting information. This chapter won't be able to go into a full discussion of each of these methods or a cost/benefit analysis of the various web services.

Instead, we'll focus on how to get data into your application using each of the different methods and objects offered by Flex, which include `RemoteObject`, `WebService`, `HTTPService`, and `URLLoader` objects.

Implicit in understanding each of these objects is the ability to read and understand the documents that describe the web services. A document called the WSDL (we'll untangle this in a moment) is your primary source of information when working with web services. In general, each type of web service you use will maintain and publish a WSDL document. If you already have a solid familiarity of WSDLs, you can safely bypass the next section and jump directly to the data objects portion.

14.1 What the heck is a WSDL document?

Let's begin with some definitions of some common terms in the world of web services. *Simple Object Access Protocol* (SOAP) is a *protocol*, or method, for transferring complex objects from one server to another or to a client application. SOAP passes information as XML tagged data, which is read on the client side and can be used to re-create the objects.

Next is *Web Services Definition Language* (WSDL). A WSDL document describes web services—a collection of methods used to retrieve documentation from a server. For our purposes, the Flex application reads in the WSDL and parses the methods and objects WSDL returns, then it uses that information to connect to the web service. Flex does a lot of the groundwork for you by reading in the web service and using it to manage the transfer of data types.

Before we start digging into the Flex code, we need to discuss how to read and decipher WSDL. The WSDL document contains information regarding the data that needs to be sent to a server, the methods available to send it, and the characteristics of the object returned by the server.

14.2 Reading WSDL

In this section, we'll pick through the WSDL document and glean the important aspects. The WSDL document has different sections to describe the way you should interact with a web service. The principle sections we'll work with are as follows:

- Methods and operations you can call
- What you need to send to the server
- What you'll receive back

For this example, you'll work with a simple WSDL document that can be found at http://www.webservicex.net/WeatherForecast.asmx?WSDL. We've selected this web service because the WSDL document isn't complicated, with only two operations and minimal input necessary. We'll start with the most important aspect: locating the operations, or methods.

14.2.1 Reading the WSDL document: operations

Toward the middle of the WSDL document, you'll find the operation definitions. This is the part that names all the methods available through this web service. Listing 14.1 shows what the operation definition looks like.

Listing 14.1 WSDL operations example

```
<wsdl:portType name="WeatherForecastSoap">
   <wsdl:operation name="GetWeatherByZipCode">
      <documentation xmlns="http://schemas.xmlSOAP.org/wsdl/">
            Get one week weather forecast for a valid Zip Code(USA)
      </documentation>
      <wsdl:input message="tns:GetWeatherByZipCodeSoapIn" />
      <wsdl:output message="tns:GetWeatherByZipCodeSoapOut" />
   </wsdl:operation>
   <wsdl:operation name="GetWeatherByPlaceName">
      <documentation xmlns="http://schemas.xmlSOAP.org/wsdl/">
       Get one week weather forecast for a place name(USA)
      </documentation>
     <wsdl:input message="tns:GetWeatherByPlaceNameSoapIn" />
     <wsdl:output message="tns:GetWeatherByPlaceNameSoapOut" />
   </wsdl:operation>
</wsdl:portType>
```

The `<wsdl:portType>` tag contains the definition for the methods you need to call to initiate an action on the server. In listing 14.1, two methods are defined: `getWeatherByZipcode` and `getWeatherByPlaceName`. These methods are defined by the `<wsdl:operation>` tag, followed by the documentation and notes below the definition.

Once you've located the operations, you have all the information you need to move on to the input and output types. Make a mental note of where this is (or perhaps make a real note), because we'll refer back to it several times. Now that you know what operations you can use, let's extract the information you need to send to them.

14.2.2 Reading the WSDL: input types

In the object definition from listing 14.1, you'll notice a tag named `<wsdl:input>`. This tag contains a pointer to another portion of the documentation that details what the system expects to receive as input parameters. These are the variables, or pieces of information, it expects to receive in order to process your request and return a result. As you can see in listing 14.2, the `<wsdl:message>` tag contains a message portion `"tns:GetWeatherByZipCodeSoapIn"` that matches the code in listing 14.1, which appears earlier in the WSDL document.

Listing 14.2 WSDL document input message

```
<wsdl:message name="GetWeatherByZipCodeSoapIn">
  <wsdl:part name="parameters" element="tns:GetWeatherByZipCode"/>
</wsdl:message>
```

Listing 14.3 illustrates that the `GetWeatherByZipCode` element from the types section of the WSDL document—the same name as the method definition—contains what you need to know. The `GetWeatherByZipCode` method takes one string argument: `ZipCode`.

Listing 14.3 WSDL document input

```
<s:element name="GetWeatherByZipCode">
```

```
    <s:complexType>
      <s:sequence>
        <s:element minOccurs="0" maxOccurs="1" name="ZipCode"
           type="s:string" />
      </s:sequence>
    </s:complexType>
  </s:element>
```

You'll do a considerable amount of jumping around in the WSDL document to find everything you need, but once you have the operation name, you can follow it throughout the document.

Now that you've established the input parameters, let's move on to the output objects.

14.2.3 Reading the WSDL document: output

As with most web services, the return values are more complicated than the data you send in. To locate the definition, you'll begin at the same point as in listing 14.1. In the operation definition, you can see that the <wsdl:output> tag directs you to the snippet presented in listing 14.4, by way of the `message` property.

Listing 14.4 WSDL document output section

```
<wsdl:message name="GetWeatherByZipCodeSoapOut">
  <wsdl:part name="parameters" element="tns:GetWeatherByZipCodeResponse" />
</wsdl:message>
```

If you follow the path to the types definitions (listing 14.5), you'll see a response with elements set up to define what the web service will return.

Listing 14.5 WSDL document element definition

```
<s:element name="GetWeatherByZipCodeResponse">
  <s:complexType>
    <s:sequence>
      <s:element name="GetWeatherByZipCodeResult"
         type="tns:WeatherForecasts" />
    </s:sequence>
  </s:complexType>
</s:element>
```

According to the WSDL document, the response from the `GetWeatherByZipCode()` method will contain a `WeatherForecasts` item. As depicted in listing 14.6, this is shown in the `type="tns:WeatherForecasts"` definition, which points to the `complexType` with the name `WeatherForecasts`.

Listing 14.6 WSDL object definition for `WeatherForecasts`

```
<s:complexType name="WeatherForecasts">
  <s:sequence>
    <s:element name="Latitude" type="s:float" />
    <s:element name="Longitude" type="s:float" />
    <s:element name="AllocationFactor" type="s:float" />
```

```
        <s:element name="FipsCode" type="s:string" />
        <s:element name="PlaceName" type="s:string" />
        <s:element name="StateCode" type="s:string" />
        <s:element name="Status" type="s:string" />
        <s:element name="Details" type="tns:ArrayOfWeatherData" />
    </s:sequence>
</s:complexType>
```

The WeatherForecasts object contains all of the detailed information for the zip-code you identified, including tidbits such as latitude, longitude, and the name of the location represented by the ZIP Code. It also contains the element type="tns:ArrayOfWeatherData", which is an array of WeatherData objects (see listing 14.7).

Listing 14.7 WSDL document output definition

```
<s:complexType name="ArrayOfWeatherData">
    <s:sequence>
        <s:element name="WeatherData" type="tns:WeatherData" />
    </s:sequence>
</s:complexType>
<s:complexType name="WeatherData">
    <s:sequence>
        <s:element name="Day" type="s:string" />
        <s:element name="WeatherImage" type="s:string" />
        <s:element name="MaxTemperatureF" type="s:string" />
        <s:element name="MinTemperatureF" type="s:string" />
        <s:element name="MaxTemperatureC" type="s:string" />
        <s:element name="MinTemperatureC" type="s:string" />
    </s:sequence>
</s:complexType>
```

Based on listing 14.7, you can expect to receive an array of weather objects back from the web service. The array contains an image and maximum and minimum temperatures for each day of the forecast, in both Fahrenheit and Celsius.

TIP Some great products exist that can help you with debugging when you're working with web services. Products such as Charles and ServiceCapture make identifying and working with web services easy because they show you exactly what your requests and responses look like. These products are invaluable when you need to debug a persistent connection issue.

In day-to-day operations, you shouldn't need to parse through the WSDL document yourself to gather this information. Most organizations that publish a web service usually have documentation that describes what you need to send in and what you'll receive back, as well as what methods are available to call. The authors of this book have, on occasion, had to slog through a WSDL document to find the appropriate methods.

14.3 Using WebService components

Once you know what methods the web service maintains, you can set up the corresponding code in the application to call the web service and parse the results. You can choose from several methods to communicate with an external web service, and we'll go through each of them, including SOAP web service, HTTP REST web service, and Remote Objects. Each has unique advantages and disadvantages.

To begin, we'll concentrate on the SOAP web services object. When connecting to a SOAP web service, the typical scenario involves each of the systems (your client application and the server application) exchanging bits of XML that contain the data and explain what the data is. The WSDL document we examined in section 14.2 is a good example of the kind of XML that is transferred.

Setting up web-service integration in Flex is easy and takes only a few lines of code. For example, if you wanted to use the `<mx:WebService>` tag to connect to the weather web service, it would look like the code in listing 14.8.

Listing 14.8 `mx:WebService` entry

```
<mx:WebService id="weatherService" wsdl="http://www.webservicex.net/
WeatherForecast.asmx?WSDL" fault="wsdlFault(event)">
<mx:operation name="GetWeatherByZipCode" result="weatherResponse(event)"
   fault="weatherFault(event)"/>
<mx:operation name="GetWeatherByPlaceName"
   result="weatherResponse(event)" fault="weatherFault(event)"/>
</mx:WebService>
```

The `<mx:WebService>` tag contains the necessary information to point the Flex application to the WSDL document. When the `mx:WebService` tag is initialized, it parses the WSDL document and extracts the information it needs to generate Flex objects with which you can interact with the web service.

The operation tags define the various operations that are used with this web service. In this case, the `GetWeatherByZipCode` and `GetWeatherByPlaceName` operations are defined and ready for you to use. Each of these items creates a handle that lets you specify which method to call. The operations also set out guidelines pertaining to the destination for the result returned by the server.

As mentioned earlier, the Flex client and the server communicate by transferring packets of XML information back and forth. The XML is only marginally useful and would place a considerable burden on your development efforts if you had to parse the XML data each application communicated with the server. Flex removes this responsibility by translating those XML packets into usable objects, such as arrays and collections that integrate seamlessly into the Flex environment.

Once Flex has completed the processing, it delivers the final object to the function as assigned by the `result` property of `ResultEvent`. In this example, you're telling Flex that you want to have the result delivered to the `weatherResponse()` function. Referring back to listing 14.8, the event is designated in the result function (`result="weatherResponse(event)"`).

A result event is generated from the `<mx:WebService>` tag after the web service and operation are called. The event contains the data you requested from the server as well as specific information about that event, such as the elapsed transfer time. Now that you've created a WebService object in MXML, we'll show you how to do the same thing in ActionScript.

14.3.1 Creating a WebService component with ActionScript

You aren't limited to creating a WebService component using MXML—although often it's much easier. You can achieve the same result through ActionScript, which affords you more flexibility when working with a web service. Listing 14.9 presents the ActionScript code needed to configure a WebService object.

Listing 14.9 Creating a WebService object in ActionScript

```
private var ws:WebService;

public function createWS(wsdl:String):void   {
  ws = new WebService();
  ws.requestTimeout = 300;
  ws.wsdl = wsdl;
  ws.addEventListener(FaultEvent.FAULT,wsdlFault);
  ws.GetWeatherByZipCode.addEventListener(ResultEvent.RESULT,
     weatherResponse);
  ws.GetWeatherByZipCode.addEventListener(FaultEvent.FAULT,weatherFault);
  ws.GetWeatherByPlaceName.addEventListener(ResultEvent.RESULT,
     weatherResponse);
  ws.GetWeatherByPlaceName.addEventListener(FaultEvent.FAULT,
     weatherFault);
  ws.addEventListener(LoadEvent.LOAD,wsdlLoaded);
  if (ws.canLoadWSDL())    {
    ws.loadWSDL();
  }
}
```

If you add the web service using ActionScript instead of MXML, you need to define the result handler on each operation separately.

TIP In some cases, a web service to which you would like to connect may use methods that are reserved words in Flex. In these situations, you can use the WebService.getOperation("nameOfOperation") function to get a handle for the operation.

Now that you know how to create a WebService using both MXML and AutoScript, it's time to give it a whirl by calling it into action.

14.3.2 Calling the WebService component

To call <mx:WebService>, you need only call the web service using webserviceID.operationname(parameters). You can see how this is implemented in listing in 14.10.

Listing 14.10 ActionScript to call WebService

```
public function getWeather():void   {
```

```
    if ( zipcode.text.length > 0 )   {
      weatherService.GetWeatherByZipCode(zipcode.text);
    } else if ( placeName.text.length > 0   )   {
      weatherService.GetWeatherByPlaceName(placeName.text);
    }
  }
```

In listing 14.10, you call the function and pass it the appropriate text—for this example, either the zipcode or the placeName. The request is prepared as a SOAP packet and then transmitted to the server. While waiting for the server's response, the Flex client is free to perform other tasks.

This is a good point in the discussion to note that web service requests from Flex are communicated *asynchronously*, which means the request and the response can occur independently, at separate times. As a result, the application doesn't wait for the server to respond, idling valuable processor resources. The downside to asynchronous transmission is that you can't be assured of the order in which requests will be returned.

14.3.3 Handling the result

Responses from the server are returned to the function named in the result option of the WebService declaration:

```
<mx:operation name="GetWeatherByZipCode"  result="weatherResponse(event)"
  fault="weatherFault(event)"/>
```

In this snippet, the weatherResponse function is called. The results of the request are passed in the form of a ResultEvent to the getWeatherResponse() function. At this point, additional processing can take place and the result can be formatted for display (review chapter 4 for more information on formatting data).

14.3.4 The ResultEvent

The ResultEvent is triggered when a successful result has been returned from a web service. The ResultEvent (mx.rpc.events.ResultEvent) is unique in that it possesses additional properties—result, token, and headers—not found in standard events. These properties have been added specifically to help manage web services and the information returned from a method call. ResultEvents are structured the same for all web service calls—<mx:WebService>, <mx:HTTPService>, and <mx:RemoteObject>.

ResultEvents behave like any other events in the Flex framework. They can be ignored, or they can be bubbled up to the parent for handling. You can also register ResultEvents and listen for them with any Flex module or component.

In addition, you can access the returned result from the web-service operation by acquiring the last result:

```
weatherService.GetWeatherByZipcode.lastResult;
```

The `WebService` operation component stores the last result retrieved by a request until either a new result is received or the result is cleared. You can clear a result using the `clearResult()` function, as follows:

```
weatherService.GetWeatherByZipcode.clearResult();
```

To retrieve the results returned by the `ResultEvent`, you pull the contents of the `ResultEvent.results` object. The data it contains reflects the exact format and structure of the return value from the web service. Flex handles the task of converting whatever format you receive—XML, remote objects, or name-value pairs—into variables you can use. The variables have the same names (case sensitive) as the XML named items. For example, if you call the `GetWeatherByZipcode()` method, a structure is returned like that shown in listing 14.6.

14.3.5 Working with the result

By default, the result returned from the SOAP packet is passed to either ActionScript objects or simple values, depending on what was sent. Each object is translated according to the SOAP object type and the information contained in the SOAP packet.

This means you should have a fully functioning set of objects you can use directly upon the web service response. Referring back to the web service you set up for the `GetWeatherByZipcode()` function, once the result has been received, you can access the values as you would any other ActionScript object. Looking at the WSDL segment in listing 14.11, you can see exactly what the object will look like.

Listing 14.11 Handling a response returned from the web service

```
[Bindable] public var longitude:String;
[Bindable] public var placeName:String;
[Bindable] public var arrDetails:ArrayCollection;

public function weatherResponse(e:ResultEvent):void        {
  longitude = e.result.WeatherForecasts.Longitude;
  placeName = e.result.WeatherForecasts.PlaceName;
  arrDetails = e.result.WeatherForecasts.Details;
}
```

NOTE It's not uncommon to receive an array of items as part of the data returned by a web service. In fact, the web service you've connected to in the example includes an array as part of the data. Arrays are easy to manipulate, but in one instance they can cause a problem. When an array is returned with one element, Flex doesn't interpret this result as an array because it appears to be a plain object. In this case, you need be aware of the contents of the array and possibly handle the situation manually. When an array is returned from the web service, it's a good idea to cast it as an array, as follows:

```
arrDetails = e.result.WeatherForecast.details.toArray();
```

Each server-side language is translated into ActionScript variable types.

The variable types in ActionScript don't change, but the different server-side types change depending on what server technology you're using. Table 14.1 lists the variable types for the ColdFusion server-side language.

Table 14.1 ColdFusion data types

ColdFusion type	ActionScript type
`String`	`String`
`Number`	`Int`, `uint`, `Number`
`Boolean`	`Boolean`
`Date`	`Date`
`Array`	`Array` or `ArrayCollection`
`Struct`	`Object` (untyped)
`Query`	`ArrayCollection` (array of objects)
`Binary`	`ByteArray`
`CFC`	`Object` (untyped, unless you use the Import Web Service wizard)

Refer to the online Flex documentation to see what ActionScript types are created for other server-side languages. In general, the main data types will remain unchanged; number types will be translated into number types, Booleans to Booleans, and so on.

`ResultEvents` can indicate the connection was successful and the web service returned an acceptable result. But even if a `ResultEvent is fired`, you still need to check the content for correct feedback, because some web services return erroneous information encapsulated in the response. Some web services return faults to alert you to potential errors. We'll examine these next.

14.3.6 Fault events

Web services can't be expected to always return perfect values. Sometimes, things don't go right—errors can occur when connecting to the web service, or maybe your values aren't correct. This is when you'll encounter the `FaultEvent`.

The `FaultEvent` contains much of the same information as a `ResultEvent`. And as with the `ResultEvent`, `FaultEvent` is used by <mx:WebService>, <mx:HTTPService>, and <mx:RemoteObject> tags. This is the method by which a general fault is communicated in the Flex system. The `FaultEvent` is the main wrapper you receive when an error is generated by the web service. This event object contains the target (the source of the fault—`WebService`, `RemoteObject`, or `HTTPService`) and any returned headers. It also includes a message from either the web service or from the Flex client, depending on which item generated the error.

In most cases, FaultEvents are generated from either the WebService operation or the RemoteObject method. RemoteObject issues a fault when the web service needs to alert you to an error within your request. You'll also find the main service object throws this fault when it's unable to connect to the web service, or when there is a problem reading the WSDL.

Generally, handling a fault is a matter of communicating to the user that a problem exists, or possibly attempting to reacquire the data. In either case, as shown in listing 14.12, you can manage the faults and catch the error without interfering with the user experience.

Listing 14.12 Handling a fault

```
public function weatherFault(e:FaultEvent):void      {
  Alert.show("an error was encountered  /n" + e.fault.faultString +
   "/n/n here are the details: /n" + e.fault.faultDetail,
   "There was an error in retrieving the weather");
}
```

When you first begin handling faults, you'll likely be predisposed to using alert popups (see listing 14.7). But the mechanism for handling the fault is an application call, which allows for greater flexibility in your fault management. For instance, you can use it to time out your sessions.

The methods you use to handle faults and results can be extended to cover the other data services. RemoteObject, WebService, and HTTPService all employ the same methods to handle faults and results returned from a data web service. You'll continue by learning how to create each of the data-service components, but the method for handling the result won't change.

14.3.7 Using asynchronous tokens

Sometimes you need to keep track of a result and attach further information to a request to make sure the response is parsed correctly. For example, if you have a set of operations you need to execute, but you need to ensure that you receive the correct result from the proper source, or if you need to make several requests for information from the same operation, you need to know what to do with the information transferred back to you.

In both of these scenarios, you can use the asynchronous token to store data and then retrieve it when the request returns. Every web-service request generates a unique asynchronous token (AsyncToken) that is used to keep track of the request and handle the response when it returns.

The AsyncToken is a dynamic object, which means you can add additional parameters or variables to the object (dynamic objects will be covered in more depth in chapter 16). Listing 14.13 illustrates how you can add further processing directives to the AsyncToken.

Listing 14.13 Using an `AsyncToken`

```
public function getWeather():void    {
  var wASync:AsyncToken;

  if ( zipcode.text.length > 0 )    {
    wASync = weatherService.GetWeatherByZipCode(zipcode.text);
   wASync.zipCode = zipcode.text;

  }

}
```

You can put any kind of object on an `AsyncToken` and then retrieve it when the result comes back, as shown in listing 14.14.

Listing 14.14 Extracting a value from an `AsyncToken`

```
public function weatherResponse(e:ResultEvent):void      {
  var myZip:String;
  Alert. show("looks like we got a good result","s'all good");
  myZip = e.token.zipCode;
}
```

The `ResultEvent.token` is the asynchronous token you filled out earlier when initiating the request. In this manner, you can keep track of which result belongs with a particular request and then handle the response appropriately. This is a useful technique because many times, when you're forming the web-service request, you have a different set of information than when the result is returned.

For example, you can't control the lag time between sending a request to a web service and receiving a response. During the interim, the application can continue to function and react to other user inputs. A user can easily change the `zipcode` in the text box before the result arrives. Or, if the web server takes too long to return a result, the user may submit a second request while your application is waiting for the first result to return. In these circumstances, it's easy to present the wrong results to the user. Using the `AsyncToken` allows you to keep track of which `zipcode` was used for the request and determine if the result being returned is valid.

14.4 Using HTTPService to retrieve results

Sometimes the service to which you need to connect isn't using a SOAP-style service. Other common frameworks are available that integrate using common HTTP get and post responses to return data. Using the <mx:HTTPService> tag allows you to work with these types of web services.

Web services that operate using HTTP post and get methods are sometimes known as Representational State Transfer (REST) services. In many cases, using an HTTP post makes the most sense for your application. This kind of service is used with large applications from large companies, such as Yahoo web services and Google web services.

A big advantage to using HTTP web services is that you'll often transfer less data than you'd otherwise transfer with SOAP web services. With SOAP, much more ancillary text is sent back to the client. SOAP contains a considerable amount of metadata in the results. This benefits data transfer, but it creates more overhead and requires more effort to parse the information. Another advantage of HTTP web services is that they're more widely accessible by a broader range of clients than SOAP.

14.4.1 Connecting to an HTTP web service

Using the `<mx:HTTPService>` tag is easy. For demonstration purposes, you'll connect to Yahoo! to perform a web search. The `<mx:HTTPService>` tag has options similar to those of the `<mx:WebService>` and `<mx:RemoteObject>` tags. Like those tags, `<mx:HTTPService>` possesses fault and result events you can listen for, as shown here:

```
<mx:HTTPService id="yahooHTTPService"
   url="http://search.yahooapis.com/WebSearchService/V1/webSearch"
   method="GET"
   makeObjectsBindable="true" result="httpServiceResult(event)"
   fault="httpServiceFault(event)" showBusyCursor="true">
</mx:HTTPService>
```

Unlike with the `<mx:WebService>` tag, you don't need to define operations. All variables sent to the server for processing are sent as name-value pairs to whatever URL is defined in the `url` field. If you have had experience with HTML and web processing, you'll be in familiar territory. This tag behaves and acts in the same fashion as HTML forms do with get and post behaviors. HTML form posts send variables to the server using a name and value-pair scenario. The `HTTPService` component works in exactly the same way. To communicate data to the server, you need only send an object with variables; Flex wraps the variables in the correct format. Listing 14.15 shows the code needed to handle the `HTTPService` component.

Listing 14.15 Working with the `HTTPService` object

```
public function httpServiceResult(e:ResultEvent):void    {
  Alert.show("received a result");
}

public function httpServiceFault(e:FaultEvent):void     {
  Alert.show("received a Fault");
}

public function sendHttpRequest():void   {
  var requestObj:Object = new Object();
  requestObj.appid = new String("YahooDemo");
  requestObj.query = new String("persimmon");
  requestObj.results = new int(2);
  yahooHTTPService. request = requestObj;
  httpAsyncToken = yahooHTTPService.send();
}
```

The function `sendHTTPRequest()` creates the `HTTPService` object, populates it with the name and value pairs, and then sends the request using the `send()` method. The response is returned in a format determined by the web service. As with the `WebService` tag, the result is automatically parsed into variables returned to you through the result function you defined on the `HTTPService` tag. Any faults are directed to the fault function you've defined.

NOTE REST services aren't without their challenges when working with Flex. For example, some web services communicate the type of error using HTTP response codes (for example, 500 for a server error). Unfortunately, the browser traps these errors and doesn't communicate any message included from a 500-error response to Flex. This can sometimes result in incomplete communications from some web services.

As with most Flex tags, you can generate an `HTTPService` object on the fly using ActionScript in much the same way you can with other types of tags. Listing 14.16 demonstrates.

Listing 14.16 Creating an `HTTPService` object in ActionScript

```
public function createHS():void   {
  yahooHTTPService = new HTTPService();
  yahooHTTPService.url =
     "http://search.yahooapis.com/WebSearchService/V1/webSearch";
  yahooHTTPService.requestTimeout;
  yahooHTTPService.request = "GET";
  yahooHTTPService.showBusyCursor = true;
   yahooHTTPService.addEventListener(ResultEvent.
     RESULT,httpServiceResult);
  yahooHTTPService.addEventListener(FaultEvent.FAULT,httpServiceFault);
}
```

In the above examples we passed parameters to the service, but you can harness Flex's binding feature to automatically do this for you.

14.4.2 Explicit parameter binding

Another way of sending information to a server is to employ parameter binding in combination with `HTTPService`. For example, see listing 14.17.

Listing 14.17 Using explicit parameter binding with MXML

```
<mx:HTTPService id="yahooHTTPService2"
   url="http://search.yahooapis.com/WebSearchService/V1/webSearch"
   method="GET"
   makeObjectsBindable="true" result="httpServiceResult(event)"
   fault="httpServiceFault(event)" showBusyCursor="true">

  <mx:request xmlns="">
    <appid>{yahooAppID}</appid>
    <query>{queryText}</query>
    <results>{numYahooResults}</results>
  </mx:request>
</mx:HTTPService>
```

Parameter binding is one way of making validation easier by allowing you to copy data from user-interface controls to request parameters. You can apply validators to the values before sending them to the server. For example, in listing 14.17, it's possible to link the results of the values with validators to validate that the data being passed back to the server is correct. For more information on working with validators, see chapter 6.

Explicit parameter binding works with variable binding to provide easy access to variables and ensure your variables are always bound correctly. The drawback to using parameter binding is that your options are hard-coded, which means that sending back any extra variables requires you to enter the variable name in the same type of structure, as shown in listing 14.17. This method of using parameter binding can also only be done in XML and can't be modeled in pure ActionScript.

14.5 Using the RemoteObject tag

The `RemoteObject` tag is different from the other web-service tags previously introduced, in that it transmits and receives data using a binary connection socket. The `HTTPService`, `WebService`, and `URLLoader` tags all work by translating your objects directly into flat text, then sending that text to the server.

The `RemoteObject` method maintains your objects in binary format, transmitting them in Adobe's proprietary AMF format. This makes it easier to translate and create objects from the data sent back by the server.

For example, to communicate back and forth between the Flex client and the server, both parties need to accept ordinary variables and objects in their native formats and translate them into a format that can be read by the receiving device. This involves some overhead. Translating objects into XML or SOAP can be a costly procedure and can consume quite a bit of processing on both sides.

In most cases, translating objects into text equivalents takes more effort and processing power than does translating those same objects into the AMF binary format. Creating objects from text carries the same inherent costs. In addition, the size of AMF-formatted objects is less than that of SOAP- or XML-encoded variables.

It's not all peaches and cream, though. AMF is a proprietary format, which means in many cases you need to supply a script to the server side to enable it to understand and translate AMF into whatever programming language you're using. Several products are available that allow the native use of `RemoteObjects`, but all these options require your web service to be explicitly configured for them.

The following list presents some of the products you can use to support communicating with Flex using `RemoteObjects`:

- Adobe LiveCycle Data Services (Java)
- Adobe ColdFusion
- AMFPHP (http://amfphp.sourceforge.net/)
- SabreAMF (http://www.osflash.org/sabreamf)
- Midnight Coders WebORB (http://www.themidnightcoders.com/)

If you're working with ColdFusion, you're in luck. ColdFusion 7 includes support for the native use of `RemoteObjects` as well as a streamlined Flex Data Services component. ColdFusion 8 offers an option in its administrator to enable or disable `RemoteObject` support.

If you want to put together a web service using Java and have that web service support `RemoteObject`, you should acquire LiveCycle Data Services (LCDS). It boasts well-integrated communication with Flex and enables you to do much more than we can show here. LCDS also lets you implement messaging, which *pushes* information to the client. This permits you to maintain your connection to the server and eliminates the need for client-side polling. As of this printing, you can download LCDS Express from the Adobe website free of charge. Whichever server-side technology you use, it must have the ability to communicate with the AMF protocol if you want to use the `RemoteObject` component. You can set up a `RemoteObject` connection in much the same way as other web-service tags. But you need to take the extra step of creating a channel object, as in listing 14.18, and specify the URL in the `channelSet`.

Listing 14.18 Creating a `ChannelSet` while using the `RemoteObject`

```
import mx.messaging.ChannelSet;
import mx.messaging.channels.AMFChannel;
import mx.messaging.Channel;

private function initFunc():void
{
  var cs:ChannelSet = new ChannelSet();                     <-- Create ChannelSet

  var customChannel:Channel = new AMFChannel("my-cfamf",    <-- Create Channel
     "http://meatwad/Flex2gateway/");

  cs.addChannel(customChannel);                             <-- Add Channel to ChannelSet

  roTest.channelSet = cs;                                   <-- Assign ChannelSet to RemoteObject
}
public function roTestHelloResult(e:ResultEvent):void
{
  Alert.show("received a result from remote services");
}

public function roTestFault(e:FaultEvent):void
{
  Alert.show("received a Fault from remote services");
}

public function sendRORequest():void
{
  roAsyncToken = roTest.hello();
}

<mx:RemoteObject id="roTest" destination="ColdFusion"
  source="helloWorld" fault="roTestFault(event)" requestTimeout="500">
   <mx:method name="hello" fault="roTestFault(event)"
      result="roTestHelloResult(event)" />
</mx:RemoteObject>
```

The channelSet in the RemoteObject declaration describes how to interact with the service, specifying that it should use the AMF protocol to the specific URL (http://www.cFlex.net/Flex2gateway/).

You should be able to get this designation from the web service provider. In listing 14.18, you're trying to connect to the server at CFlex.net. The web service source object refers to the location of the file on the web server. In this case, the file on the web server is located at http://www.CFlex.net/helloworld.cfc. If the URL of the web service were located at http://www.CFlex.net/webservice/helloworld.cfc, then by extension the source parameter would be webservice.helloworld, which is essentially a path to the object that needs to be called.

The code snippet that follows refers to the method in the server-side web-service object—a ColdFusion component (CFC)—named hello.cfc. Once again, a FaultEvent will be issued if anything goes wrong, or a ResultEvent will be fired off if a successful response is received:

```
<mx:method name="hello" fault="roTestFault(event)"
        result="roTestHelloResult(event)" />
```

If you're using ColdFusion or LCDS and you control the web service, you can simplify this by adding in a named service. The named service (which is optional) lets you specify the location of the service object on the server side, eliminating location knowledge from your Flex application.

14.6 Using the URLLoader

When you're working with Flex, at times you only need to download a file such as an image from the server or a file with XML properties that can be stored on the server. To do that, you can use the URLLoader.

The URLLoader is useful for loading HTML pages for display to the user as well as bringing in images on the fly. Another popular use for the URLLoader is to download a configuration page that can be changed on a per-server basis (for development, staging, and production). Listing 14.19 shows how to create a URLLoader to retrieve an XML list of properties from the server. This set of properties can be used to set environment variables by some form of configuration file on a deployment server. This method can also be used to load in files from a different server—for example, HTML files from a different website or an HTML file from the originating server.

Listing 14.19 Creating a URLLoader

```
public function createLoader():void   {
  var XML_URL:String = "http://www.cflex.net/urlLoaderTest.xml";
  var myXMLURL:URLRequest = new URLRequest(XML_URL);
  var myLoader:URLLoader = new URLLoader(myXMLURL);
  myLoader.dataFormat = URLLoaderDataFormat.TEXT;
  myLoader.addEventListener(Event.COMPLETE,xmlLoaded);
  myLoader.addEventListener(IOErrorEvent.IO_ERROR,loaderError);
  myLoader.addEventListener(SecurityErrorEvent.SECURITY_ERROR,
```

```
                        loaderError);
    }
    public function xmlLoaded(event:Event):void    {
      var myXML:XML = new XML();
      myXML = XML(myLoader.data);
      trace("Data loaded. ");
    }
    public function loaderError(e:FaultEvent)    {
      Alert.show("received a Fault from remote services "+
              e.fault.message);
    }
```

The `URLLoader` is the last web service tag we'll cover in this chapter. Each tag works best for some methods but not for others. You'll probably use the `HTTPService` tag or the `WebService` tag for the majority of your data loading. Flex Builder 3 includes a wizard to help you with data loading and reduce your use of SOAP web services.

14.7 Using the Flex Import Web Service wizard

Adobe Flex Builder 3 includes an Import Web Service wizard that automates the process of reading a web service and creating companion typed objects in your Flex application.

In the examples you've seen thus far, most of the data has been received as an untyped object. Untyped objects don't correlate to any of the existing objects in the Flex system. This is usually the result of Flex not having information about the return, which renders it unable to match internal objects with the external objects sent from the web service. You can go through the laborious process of manually creating these objects to maintain the linkage from the server to the client, or you can use the Import Web Service wizard to create the objects.

It's not mandatory that you create discrete objects from the web service result, but it's a best practice to create the transfer objects you're using. Doing so affords you benefits when putting your application together:

- *Code hinting*—If you're creating and using objects in your code, you can take advantage of code hinting (Flex Builder shows you the properties available on a specific class).
- *Code validation*—If you use typed classes to hold your values, Flex validates that the object is indeed what it's supposed to be and warns you if you're accessing a nonvalid property for a specific class. The benefit is you can isolate problems during application coding.

Having classes and objects creates an explicit agreement within your application so each portion that uses these objects knows exactly what is available every step of the way. This saves you time and potential headaches further down the road.

14.7.1 Using the Import Web Service wizard

To use the Import Web Service wizard in Flex Builder 3, you only need to choose Data > Import Web Service (WSDL).

This launches the Import Web Service wizard, which asks you for the URL of the WSDL you wish to import. In the example, we'll show what the Import Web Service wizard looks like when importing the web service for the `zipcode` weather generator.

As illustrated in figure 14.1, the wizard asks you to specify where to import the web service from. The web service needs to contain a valid WSDL in order to create the correct objects, or the wizard needs to connect to an LCDS. From here, the wizard downloads the WSDL and parses it in much the same way as you parsed through the WSDL earlier in section 14.1—only much faster and with little effort on your part.

Figure 14.1 First screen of the Import Web Service wizard

The wizard comes back with all the correct methods available from this web service. In this case, the methods are `GetWeatherByZipcode` and `GetWeatherByPlaceName`. In other situations, you may want to work with only one method from a particular web service, which is configurable at this point.

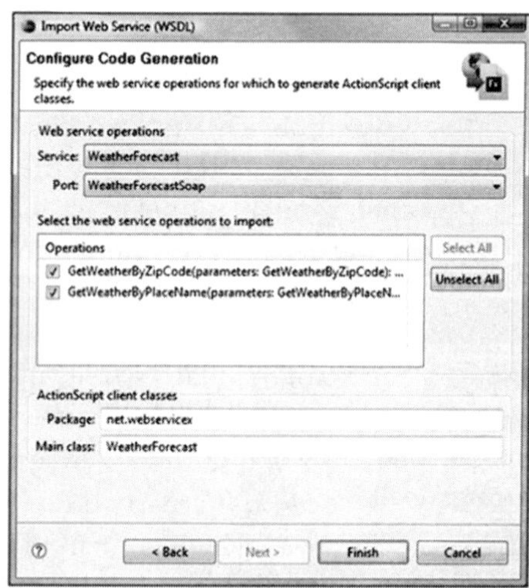

Figure 14.2 The second window of the Import Web Service wizard

Because this web service is available using different methods (HTTP `GET`, HTTP `POST`, and SOAP), you can choose which version to import. For the purposes of the example, you'll import the SOAP version. Each of the selections depicted in figure 14.2 should look the same as the other methods; with other web services, they may appear differently.

As shown in figure 14.3, you can configure where the code will be placed and what the directory structure will look like by changing the package path. All generated web-service classes will be part of the same object package in Flex. To read more about packages, go to chapter 18, which explains how to work with custom classes.

ActionScript files are automatically created for you in the net\webservicex\ folder. These objects can now be used to interact with the web service. The value of using these web services is that you'll have your internal objects as named classes.

14.7.2 Working with generated web-service code

Working with the generated web-service code is similar to how you work with the regular web services, with some minor exceptions. First, you don't use the `<mx:Webservices>` tag. Instead, you use the generated web-service code, which handles the connections and translates the code into objects for you.

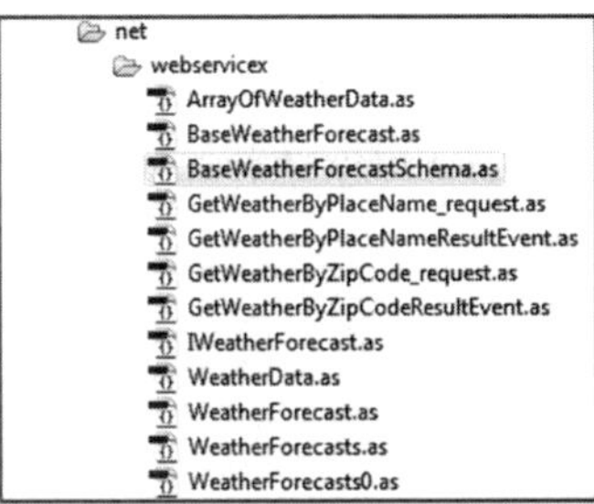

Figure 14.3 Files created on the file system

To work with the generated code, you need to create a link to it so Flex knows where to find it. You can do so by adding the following code to the application tag:

```
<mx:Application xmlns:mx="http://www.adobe.com/2006/mxml"
   layout="vertical"
   xmlns:srv="net.webservicex.*" creationComplete="initFunc()">
```

The syntax `xmlns:srv="net.webservicex.*"` instructs Flex Builder where to find the files you want to use. In this example, the files are located in the <FlexProjectRoot>\net\webservicex\ directory on your system. If you change the location of the files, it's only necessary to update the `xmlns` property to reflect the new location.

Once you've added that to the application bar, you can reference the generated objects using the `srv:` extension. As you can see in listing 14.20, in the MXML, you reference the files created by the wizard directly. The main file is identified by the name given in the WSDL `porttype` tag (in this case, `porttype="WeatherForecastSoap"`).

Listing 14.20 `WebService` object using wizard-generated code

```
<srv:WeatherForecast id="myService"
   GetWeatherByPlaceName_result="placeResponse(event)"
   GetWeatherByZipCode_result="zipResponse(event)"
   fault="weatherFault(event)">
  <srv:getWeatherByZipCode_request_var>
    <srv:GetWeatherByZipCode_request ZipCode="{zipcode.text}" />
  </srv:getWeatherByZipCode_request_var>
    <srv:getWeatherByPlaceName_request_var>
   <srv:GetWeatherByPlaceName_request PlaceName="{wPlaceName.text}"/>
 </srv:getWeatherByPlaceName_request_var>
</srv:WeatherForecast>
```

When you look at the files the wizard creates, you'll see that it has created objects for the request, `ResultEvent` objects, and data objects, as well as a couple of base objects. You can determine the file type by looking at the suffix of each filename. Request objects have the suffix `_request`, base objects have a prefix of `Base`, and result events have the suffix `ResultEvent`. Data objects have no prefix or suffix.

The main object includes properties that are close to the `<mx:WebService>` object. It includes properties to indicate the function designated to handle any response, as well as functions to handle any faults that arise in the request.

Looking more closely at listing 14.20, you may wonder where the file for the

<srv:getWeatherByZipCode_request_var> is. The file system doesn't include it. It's important to note that it isn't a separate object or file by itself; it's a property of the main web-service object that defines which request object to use. You aren't forced to use the generated request object, and it's possible to swap the request object generated by Flex Builder for another request object, if it's appropriate to your situation.

Creating the same web-service request element in straight ActionScript is as easy as using the MXML format. When you're creating the web service, it's necessary to set up the result functions slightly differently by calling the main object's custom add-event listener function. This event listener adds all the objects and ensures that when the result is created, the properly typed objects are returned, not anonymous objects.

Calling your new custom web service is remarkably similar to how you call the anonymous variety, as shown in listing 14.21. The biggest change is what gets called.

Listing 14.21 Setting up event listeners for wizard-generated code

```
private var myASService:WeatherForecast = new WeatherForecast();

private function initFunc():void   {
  myASService.addgetWeatherByZipCodeEventListener(zipResponse);
  myASService.addgetWeatherByPlaceNameEventListener(placeResponse);
  myASService.addEventListener(FaultEvent.FAULT,weatherFault);
}
```

Using the response object is where things really become interesting (see listing 14.22). It doesn't appear drastically different from the anonymous web-service object, but the way you're able to work with it has changed. Instead of receiving plain objects back from a server, you get strongly typed objects. This means Flex Builder tells you what values are available and makes sure you're calling the correct values at compile time. When you save your file, Flex alerts you to misspelled properties and lets you know where you may have tried to access a property that doesn't exist. These features will save you time and headaches.

Listing 14.22 Handling the web-service response

```
public function zipResponse(e:GetWeatherByZipCodeResultEvent):void
{
  Alert.show("looks like we got a good result by zipcode",
     "s'all good");
  longitude = e.result.Longitude;
  sPlaceName = e.result.PlaceName;
  arrDetails = e.result.Details;
}

public function placeResponse(e:GetWeatherByPlaceNameResultEvent):void
{
  Alert.show("looks like we got a good result by place name",
     "s'all good");
  longitude = e.result.Longitude;
  sPlaceName = e.result.PlaceName;
  arrDetails = e.result.Details;
}
```

As you may have noticed, the response functions in listings 14.20 and 14.21 appear remarkably similar. Two different events are being generated for each method resident on the web-service system. The Import Web Service wizard automatically generates files for each response separately, essentially duplicating files because the response structure is the same. On first looking at the wizard's results, you may think you need to call each response separately, but that's not the case. You can consolidate the code to look something like that in listing 14.23.

Listing 14.23 Handling responses in consolidated fashion

```
public function zipResponse(e:Event):void
{
  Alert.show("looks like we got a good result by zipcode","s'all good");
  Var myEvent = e as GetWeatherByZipCodeResultEvent;
  longitude = myEvent.result.Longitude;
  sPlaceName = myEvent.result.PlaceName;
  arrDetails = myEvent.result.Details;
}
```

From a coding maintenance perspective, having a consolidated function makes life easier by having less code to maintain.

14.8 Summary

Adobe Flex incorporates multiple methods for interacting with web services. From the `HTTPService` component to the `RemoteObject` and `WebService` components, Flex furnishes you the necessary tools to interact with an expanded set of web services. Each of the different types of components carries its own unique sets of properties and uses.

Reading the WSDL document can provide clues as to which methods and calls are available for a given web service and what you can expect them to return when requests are made. In particular, pay attention to the <wsdl:portType> and <wsdl:operation> tags. These tags help you determine which methods to call on the web service.

In general, each component works similarly. First, you initialize the component by passing the location (or URL) of the web service; then you set the variables and call the operation name or the `send()` function to execute the command. The last step is to wait for the `ResultEvent`—or, if things don't go as planned, the `FaultEvent`—to determine whether the request was completed successfully. From there, you can assign the returned result to the components in your application.

As an added bonus, Adobe includes the Import Web Service wizard, which lets you maintain your strong object typing by automatically transferring the returned result into created components. These custom classes are then populated with the results of the web-service call.

Now that you've mastered the art of getting data into your application, you'll continue working from the data perspective. Chapter 15 deals with XML and how to parse through XML trees in your Flex application.

15 Working with XML

This chapter covers:

- XML fundamentals
- XML-related components and ActionScript classes
- Binding to XML data
- Using E4X to work with XML

In terms of adoption, XML has achieved a level of success that rivals that of HTML. But HTML's presence has been primarily on the client side of internet-based applications, whereas XML is now ubiquitous in nearly every aspect of computing.

With its MXML language based on XML, Flex is no stranger to the format. In this chapter, we'll demonstrate Flex's robust XML support, from its ability to use XML as a source of data, to how you can use Flex to directly manipulate XML code.

15.1 XML primer

If you're knowledgeable about the workings of XML, you can skip to the next section; but for those of you who don't have a solid understanding, it's worth taking the time to read on to be sure you develop a decent operational foundation. You need not become anxious about how much XML you should know; you don't need to be a guru to be effective with it, but knowing its rules and constructs will help you when it comes to filtering and manipulating XML data.

15.1.1 What is XML?

XML stands for Extensible Markup Language. As common as it has become, views on the exact definition of XML vary. XML, in its most broadly accepted definition, is a language that serves as a flexible mechanism to describe information. But many people view it as a platform-neutral data structure. Each description is technically correct.

Functionally speaking, XML is a hybrid of both; XML's ability to describe information results in it being a neutral data-structure syntax. But it's more than that. Because it serves to describe information, it's known as a *meta-language* and is therefore more of a standard than a language.

Putting aside the debate between data-structure neutrality and data description, anything that complies with the XML syntax and rules is automatically compatible and can be considered XML. For example, Really Simple Syndication (RSS) blog and news feeds, as well as Business Process Execution Language (BPEL)) are languages defined using XML.

Unlike HTML, XML doesn't maintain predefined tags. Rather, it allows you to define your own tags and describe their relationships—hence the *Extensible* in Extensible Markup Language. These tags can be consumed and processed by other applications. For example, web services use XML to describe supporting functions as well as what the functions accept and return. This includes the definitions of complex data types.

15.1.2 Benefits of XML

We mentioned neutrality as one of the benefits of XML. This means XML-tagged data can be consumed from one system to another, regardless of hardware, programming language, or operating system.

The term *system-to-system* can mean many different things; it can apply locally to an application running on your laptop that transmits XML across APIs within the application, or it can apply broadly over the internet, as in the case of web services. The end result fosters greater reuse and facilitates interoperability.

Because of XML's structured nature, it lends itself to being a good mechanism for representing tree-structured data. Most languages don't have a native tree-structured data type. Typically, we represent hierarchical data through the cumbersome task of creating linked lists using structures. But because XML is text, you can save the tree as is.

Other benefits of XML include the following:

- Simplified data sharing
- Simplified data transfer
- Increased data availability
- Custom language creation

For reasons unknown, few people acknowledge the limitations of XML. But as we've said throughout this book, there are pros and cons to anything—and that includes XML. Let's acknowledge that up front and look at what they are.

15.1.3 Drawbacks

Making something so generic and so agnostic comes at the price. XML is all-purpose, but it isn't optimized for anything.

Specifically, this manifests itself in the form of verbosity—XML is extremely inefficient at transferring large volumes of information. Although you can use compression technologies to speed up the transfer of data, many programming languages also require significant overhead in processing all that text, because XML isn't a native data type for most languages.

Fortunately, Flex can use *E4X* to process large amounts of XML data as a native data type, as we'll explain later in this chapter.

15.1.4 Syntax and rules

In order for XML to maintain interoperability, it relies on strict adherence to a tightly defined set of rules. Fortunately, there's aren't too many rules, so it's not difficult to abide by them.

THE ROOT TAG

All XML structures must be contained inside one master root tag known as a *document element*:

```
<root>
  <node/>
  <node/>
</root>
```

In this example, `root` is the top-level tag; no other tags can reside at the same level.

WELL-FORMEDNESS

Here is a brief description of some of the basic syntactical rules from which you can't deviate. All tags must be enclosed using the open angle bracket (<) and close angle bracket (>) characters. Each tag must have a corresponding end tag, which includes the forward slash (/) character just ahead of the tag name. HTML is somewhat forgiving in this aspect; XML isn't. You must nest tags properly—a nested tag set must be ended before any higher-level tags are closed.

The following code snippets demonstrate. This code uses proper nesting:

```
<root>
  <people>
    <person>…</person>
  </people>
</root>
```

And this snippet uses incorrect nesting:

```
<root>
  <people>
    <person>
```

```
    </people>
  </person>
</root>
```

Even if you removed the closing </person> tag from the second example, the code wouldn't be valid because the opening <person> tag would still be active.

XML DECLARATION

Optionally, you can include as the first line the XML declaration statement. In addition to specifying that the content of the data is XML, this statement also reports which version of XML is being used and what type of character encoding (which character set) is employed.

In Flex, your MXML documents will all use this declaration at the top:

```
<?xml version="1.0" encoding="utf-8"?>
```

Next, we'll look at entities.

ENTITIES

Entity is a technical term for a character shortcut or the equivalent. Entities included by default in all XML documents are those that replace characters that have meaning in XML itself. In particular, they include the list presented in table 15.1.

Table 15.1 XML entities and their character equivalents

Character	Description	XML entity equivalent
&	Ampersand	`&`
<	Less than	`<`
>	Greater than	`>`
'	Apostrophe	`'`
"	Double quote	`"`

If these seem familiar to you, they probably are; they're the same entities used in HTML.

STORING DATA

You have a choice of two techniques for storing data: between opening and closing tags, or as the attribute of the tag. When using attributes, be sure to surround the value with a matched pair of quote characters (either single or double).

The following data is encapsulated within tags:

```
<person>Tariq Ahmed</person>
```

And here's the same data as an attribute:

```
<person name="Tariq Ahmed"/>
```

Neither method enjoys any particularly distinctive advantage, but slightly less text is involved using the attribute method. This can become a deciding factor when you're transmitting thousands of records, because your goal should always be to reduce the amount of data that needs to be transmitted.

Based on our earlier exercises using MXML, you know that certain characters have special meaning to XML parsers. As presented in table 15.1, characters such as the ampersand (&) and angle brackets (< and >) will pose a problem if they occur in your data. The ampersand is used to reference entity characters, and the angle brackets are an integral part of XML tag syntax. If your data contains angle brackets, the XML parser will treat them programmatically, not as data.

In these circumstances, you use a `CDATA` block to encapsulate your data. `CDATA` tells the parser to ignore syntactic characters contained within the `CDATA` block and let them pass along with the rest of the data. Listing 15.1 demonstrates how information containing XML syntax characters (in this example, the characters `-->`) in the node can cause a problem.

Listing 15.1 A script that will cause an error

```
<root>
  <people>
    <person>
      John & Mary Smith Email -->jmsmith@jmsith.com
    </person>
  </people>
</root>
```

This problem is easily solved in listing 15.2 using a `CDATA` block.

Listing 15.2 Using `CDATA` to solve the problem

```
<root>
  <people>
    <person>
     <![CDATA[
      John & Mary Smith --> jmsmith@jmsith.com
     ]]>
    </person>
  </people>
</root>
```

Alternatively, you can *escape* the right angle bracket with the entity character equivalent, as listing 15.3 shows.

Listing 15.3 Using character entities

```
<root>
  <people>
    <person>
     <![CDATA[
      John &amp; Mary Smith --&gt; jmsmith@jmsith.com
     ]]>
    </person>
  </people>
```

```
</root>
```

We recommend using the CDATA approach because your data is likely to exist in a database in its natural state, with many special characters embedded throughout. CDATA eliminates your concerns (and the labor) of trying to catch and convert each of these characters.

CASE SENSITIVITY

XML employs a case-sensitive architecture. Uppercase and lowercase characters aren't treated equally, so you must be careful when using mixed-case content. In the following example, the content is valid:

```
<root>
<someData>...</someData>
<SomeData>...</SomeData>
</root>
```

But if you're parsing it to look for one naming convention, you're likely to miss the other.

15.1.5 DTDs and XML Schema

XML documents are governed by a collection of rules known as a Document Type Definition (DTD). A DTD describes the structure of the document based on elements and attributes.

You can write your own custom DTD and then provide it to other systems to transfer information about your data structure as well as how to validate the data. Listing 15.4 provides a brief look at a DTD.

Listing 15.4 DTD describing elements and attributes of a document

```
<?xml version="1.0"?>
<!DOCTYPE root [
  <!ELEMENT root (people)>
  <!ELEMENT people  (person+)>
  <!ELEMENT person  (#PCDATA)>
  <!ATTLIST person age CDATA #REQUIRED>
]>
```

In this DTD, root has an element called people. The people element can have one or more person elements. The person element contains data that will be parsed by the XML parser. The DTD also includes a required attribute called age.

Listing 15.5 shows a document that conforms to the DTD from listing 15.4. This would be considered a well-formed XML document.

Listing 15.5 XML document that complies with the DTD from listing 15.4

```
<root>
  <people>
    <person age="35">Tariq Ahmed</person>
    <person age="34">Jon Hirschi</person>
  </people>
```

```
</root>
```

DTDs have incorporated into XML since its inception, but they're being supplanted by a newer mechanism known as XML Schema (XSD). XSD aims to be more robust by adding an object-oriented approach to document structures and supporting the ability to describe data types and the relationship between structures. Listing 15.6 shows an example.

Listing 15.6 `person.xsd`: using XML Schema to define a structure

```
<xs:schema
 xmlns:xs="http://www.w3.org/2001/XMLSchema">
  <xs:element name="person" type="Person"/>
   <xs:complexType name="Person">
    <xs:sequence>
      <xs:element name="firstname " type="xs:string"/>
      <xs:element name="lastname" type="xs:string "/>
    </xs:sequence>
  </xs:complexType>
</xs:schema>
```

To use an XML Schema, you save it to a .xsd file and then reference that file from within your XML document, as shown in listing 15.7.

Listing 15.7 Putting an XML Schema to work

```
<person
 xmlns:xsi="http://www.w3.org/2001/XMLSchema-instance"
 xsi:noNamespaceSchemaLocation="person.xsd">
  <firstname>Tariq</firstname>
  <lastname>Ahmed</lastname >
</person>
```

15.1.6 Namespaces

What if multiple systems all maintain their own set of definitions for an XML document, and each definition describes the same elements and attributes differently? This is where namespaces come into play. Namespaces use an attribute called `xmlns` to specify a prefix for a given context. This allows you to add the necessary context for a given element via the prefix. Listing 15.8 illustrates how you can avoid conflicts through the use of namespaces.

Listing 15.8 Using namespaces to add context

```
<root
xmlns:cflex="http://www.cflex.net " xmlns:dopejam="http://www.dopejam.com">
<cflex:people>
  <cflex:person username="tahmed">
  <cflex:person username="jhirschi">
</cflex:people>
<dopejam:people>
  <dopejam:person>
   <dopejam:firstname>Faisal</dopejam:firstname>
```

```
    <dopejam:lastname>Abid</dopejam:lastname>
  </dopejam:person>
</dopejam:people>
</root>
```

You can see how the tags <people> and <person> are used in each structure. Variations exist between them, but it's no problem from a parsing perspective because the namespace identifies which data is related to which definition.

15.2 XML components and classes

Flex has a number of built-in components and classes that you can use to store XML data. In this section, we'll explore them and learn how they fit into your workflow.

To begin, let's review the available XML-related components and ActionScript classes, shown in table 15.2.

Table 15.2 XML-related components and classes

MXML component	ActionScript class	Description
`<mx:XML>`	`XML`	Stores standard XML with a single root node.
`<mx:XMLList>`	`XMLList`	Stores XML containing multiple root nodes.
`<mx:XMLListCollection>`	`XMLListCollection`	A version of `XMLList` that has the power of a collection. For example, `XMLListCollection` can dispatch notification events when a change has occurred in its status. These dispatches can be used by components configured to listen for them.

Recall that chapter 11 presented a synopsis of these components and classes in which you learned how to use them to feed navigation components. Now, we'll take things further by examining their functions and properties.

15.2.1 The XML component

The `XML` component is a fundamental mechanism for interacting with XML data. It allows you to embed your XML inline with your application code, or reference an external XML source file. But because `XML` isn't a collection component, it lacks advanced data synchronization and automatic awareness of data change.

INVOKING THE XML COMPONENT

To implement the `XML` component, you can explicitly embed the XML or source it from an external file. Listing 15.9 presents an inline example.

Listing 15.9 Using the XML component to embed XML

```
<mx:Application xmlns:mx="http://www.adobe.com/2006/mxml">
<mx:XML id="usersXML">
  <users>
    <user id="1">Tariq Ahmed</user>
    <user id="2">Jon Hirschi</user>
  </users>
</mx:XML>
</mx:Application>
```

This approach is often used to store an application's configuration embedded in the code or as a variable to store structured data. But referencing external data or configurations is the more commonly utilized method. To include an external source into your application file, you use XML's source property (see listing 15.10).

Listing 15.10 Use the source property to reference an external file.

```
<mx:Application xmlns:mx="http://www.adobe.com/2006/mxml">
  <mx:XML id="usersXML" source="users.xml"/>      <- Source can be relative
</mx:Application>                                    path or fixed path
```

It's important to note that Flex will incorporate the XML file during compile time, which means any changes to the XML file won't be reflected in your application until the next time you perform a compile.

15.2.2 The XML class

The XML class is similar to its sibling, the XML component, except you can instantiate instances of it using pure ActionScript. One key difference, though, is you can't instruct an XML class to embed an XML file at compile time.

INVOKING THE XML CLASS

As listing 15.11 demonstrates, you can use the ActionScript class in much the same way as the component.

Listing 15.11 Using the XML class to embed XML

```
<mx:Application xmlns:mx="http://www.adobe.com/2006/mxml">
<mx:Script>
  <![CDATA[
    public var usersXML:XML=
      <users>
        <user id="1">Tariq Ahmed</user>
        <user id="2">Jon Hirschi</user>
      </users>
  ]]>
</mx:Script>
</mx:Application>
```

This isn't much different from the component approach, but ActionScript lends the convenience of saving the ActionScript to another file and then including it back into the MXML file (which is something you can't do using MXML code).

For example, if you rip out the ActionScript code to a loadUsersVariable.as file, it's easy to pull it in, as shown in the following code snippet:

```
<mx:Script source="loadUsersVariable.as"/>
```

A positive byproduct is that your ActionScript code can be used by multiple files, which offers you some reusability.

CONVERTING OBJECTS TO XML

Another technique available to you takes advantage of the `XML` class-initializing function (the constructor) to convert objects containing XML into a true `XML` object, such as in the following:

```
public var simpleString:String = "<users><user>Tariq Ahmed</user></users>";
public var usersXML:XML = new XML(simpleString);
```

You can't load an external file because the `XML` class lacks a `source` property (unlike its component counterpart). But if you know what the XML file is at the time of compiling, you may as well use the `XML` component anyway. Otherwise, if you're going to dynamically load an external file, you can pair up the class with other functionality specifically designed to retrieve data like this, such as the `HTTPService` (see chapter 14 for more information about retrieval of remote information) or another mechanism called a `URLLoader`, which we'll explore in detail in section 15.3.

XML CLASS PROPERTIES

The `XML` class has a handful of *static* properties (see table 15.3). These are properties with fixed, global settings that you can't control on a per-instance basis. When a property is modified, the change applies to all instances of an XML object.

Table 15.3 XML class global (static) properties

Property	Type	Description
`ignoreComments`	`Boolean`	Specifies whether comments incorporated in the XML source are filtered out. You may think there's no reason for this option; but you may want to include the raw XML to display the user/log, or to work with the comments when you're processing the XML. Default value is `true`.
`ignoreProcessing-Instructions`	`Boolean`	Specifies whether processing instructions (in the form of `<?PROC_INSTR fooBar?>`) can accompany XML. Setting this property to `false` lets you access this information; `true` filters out the instructions. Default value is `true`.
`ignoreWhiteSpace`	`Boolean`	Determines whether whitespace at the start and end of the text is maintained or stripped out. Leaving whitespace in can be handy for visual purposes. Default value is `true` (strip out whitespace).

Table 15.3 XML class global (static) properties *(continued)*

Property	Type	Description
`prettyIndent`	`int (integer)`	Specifies the number of spaces for each level of indentation (utilized when `prettyPrinting` is set to `true`). Default value is 2
`prettyPrinting`	`Boolean`	Presents XML in a structured visual manner when outputting via the `toString()` and `toXMLString()` functions. Default value is `true`.

To see how these properties work, consider the example in listing 15.12, which toggles the static `prettyPrinting` property.

Listing 15.12 Using the `XML` class's static properties

```
<mx:Application xmlns:mx="http://www.adobe.com/2006/mxml">
  <mx:Script>
  <![CDATA[
   public var usersXML:XML=
     <users>
       <user id="1">Tariq Ahmed</user>
       <user id="2">Jon Hirschi</user>
     </users>

  public function togglePretty():void
   {
      XML.prettyPrinting = !XML.prettyPrinting;      <-- Static property doesn't need specific instance
      myTextArea.text = usersXML.toString();
   }
  ]]>
  </mx:Script>

  <mx:TextArea id="myTextArea" width="200" height="100"/>
  <mx:Button label="Toggle Pretty Printing" click="togglePretty()"/>
</mx:Application>
```

The result of listing 15.12 is shown in figures 15.1 and 15.2. The XML output formatting is displayed in both structured and unstructured modes.

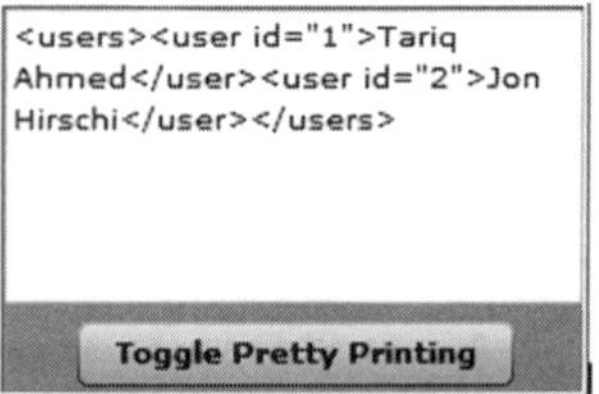

Figure 15.1 When XML `prettyPrinting` is set to `false`, the result is an unstructured display.

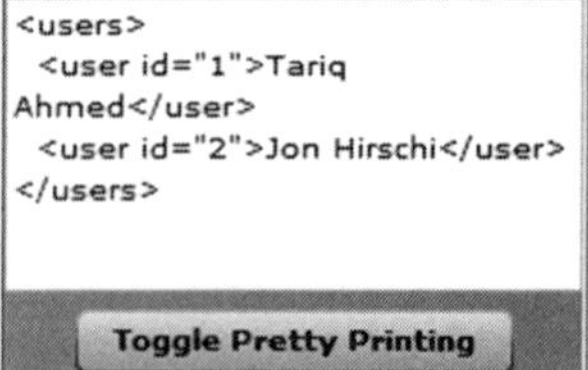

Figure 15.2 Setting `prettyPrinting` to true organizes and structures the display.

Similarly, if you were to experiment with the other properties, you'd see the display change accordingly. The premise here is that you can set properties to specify how XML should be presented on an application-wide basis.

XML CLASS FUNCTIONS/METHODS

A large number of functions are at your disposal. Those that will likely be of greatest use to you fall into the following categories:

- Acquiring and manipulating structure
- Acquiring and manipulating attributes and properties
- Manipulating the content and display

Tables 15.4 through 15.6 present all the XML-related functions, grouped by category.

Table 15.4 Functions related to XML structure

Function	Description	Returns
`appendChild`	Add a node after the last child node of a given node.	`XML`
`child`	Acquires a list of all child nodes under a given node.	`XMLList`
`childIndex`	Acquires the position of a child node.	`int`
`children`	Acquires all the child nodes from an `XML` object.	`XMLList`
`comments`	Acquires the comments in an `XML` object.	`XMLList`
`descendants`	Acquires all children of nodes that match on a given name.	`XMLList`
`elements`	Acquires the elements of an `XML` object.	`XMLList`
`insertChildAfter`	Inserts a child node after the specified node.	`Dynamic`
`insertChildBefore`	Inserts a child node before the specified node.	`Dynamic`
`parent`	Acquires the parent node of a given node.	`XMLList`
`prependChild`	Inserts a child node into a given node just before any other children.	`XML`
`processing-Instructions`	Acquires the instructions in an `XML` object.	`XMLList`
`contains`	Acts like a search function to determine if the XML contains a match.	`Boolean`
`copy`	Creates a duplicate of the existing `XML` object.	`XML`
`length`	Determines the size of the `XML` object. This property is used when looping over the XML content to calculate how many iterations you need to perform.	`int`

Table 15.5 XML functions related to attributes and properties

Function	Description	Returns
`attribute`	Acquires a specific attribute value	`XMLList`
`attributes`	Acquires all attribute values	`XMLList`

Table 15.5 XML functions related to attributes and properties *(continued)*

Function	Description	Returns
`hasOwnProperty`	Determines if a property exists	`Boolean`
`propertyIsEnumerable`	Determines if you can loop over the property	`Boolean`
`replace`	Replaces the value of a property	`XML`
`setChildren`	Replaces the values of properties of a child	`XML`

Table 15.6 XML functions related to content

Function	Description	Returns
`hasComplexContent`	Establishes whether the XML structure is deeper than one level.	`Boolean`
`hasSimpleContent`	Establishes whether the XML structure is only one level.	`Boolean`
`nodeKind`	Returns the type of node. This can be used when iterating over an XML structure. Values include `text`, `comment`, `processing-instruction`, `attribute`, and `element`.	`String`
`Text`	Acquires only the text portions of an XML document; comments, processing instructions, and attributes are filtered out. You receive only the text within the elements.	`XMLList`
`defaultSettings`	Shows what your XML would look like with the default settings, if you've overridden the XML properties (see table 15.3).	`Object`
`setSettings`	Sets other properties indirectly, including `ignoreComments`, `ignoreProcessingInstructions`, `ignoreWhitespace`, `prettyIndent`, and `prettyPrinting`.	`void`
`Settings`	Retrieves the values of XML the properties (see table 15.3).	`Object`
`Normalize`	Cleans up an XML document by combining nearby nodes and empty nodes.	`XML`
`toString`	Attempts to return the XML content as a simple `String`, unless the content is too complex, in which case it's returned as is (tags and all).	`String`
`toXMLString`	Returns the XML content as is.	`String`

That's a lot of functions! But this should give you a good idea of what tools are available in your Flex XML arsenal. You'll use some of these in moment; but first, we have a few details to cover.

15.2.3 The XMLList component

The XMLList component/class is similar to a helper object in that it can only execute a subset of what XML can do. Its purpose is to store fragments of an XML structure—much like a database view in which you're given a filtered subset.

Because of that, it doesn't need a top root node. On the downside, XMLList doesn't support referencing an external file.

INVOKING THE XMLLIST COMPONENT

Working with the XMLList component is fairly similar to using the XML component; but as you can see in listing 15.13, you can omit a root node.

Listing 15.13 Creating an XMLList component to drive a List component

```
<mx:Application xmlns:mx="http://www.adobe.com/2006/mxml">
   <mx:XMLList id="myXMLList">
      <user id="1">Tariq Ahmed</user>
      <user id="2">Jon Hirschi</user>
   </mx:XMLList>
   <mx:List dataProvider="{myXMLList}"/>
</mx:Application>
```

When you compile and run listing 15.13, you should see something similar to figure 15.3.

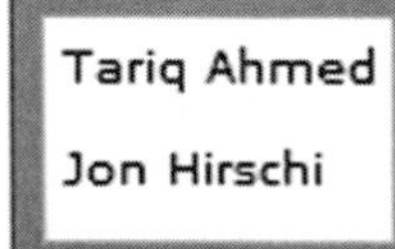

Figure 15.3 This List component is driven by data in an XMLList component.

15.2.4 The XMLList class

The XMLList class is utilitarian in nature. You probably wouldn't create one from scratch; rather, you'll use it as the result returned from one of the XML class's functions.

Consider the code in listing 15.14, which uses these two concepts.

Listing 15.14 Using XMLList

```
<mx:Application xmlns:mx="http://www.adobe.com/2006/mxml">
  <mx:Script>
     <![CDATA[
   public function displayIt():void
   {
    var admins:XMLList = myXML.children();
    myTextArea.text = admins.toXMLString();
   }
    ]]>
  </mx:Script>
  <mx:XML id="myXML">
    <users>
      <administrators>
        <user id="1">Tariq Ahmed</user>
        <user id="2">Jon Hirschi</user>
      </administrators>
    </users>
```

```
  </mx:XML>
  <mx:TextArea id="myTextArea" width="200" height="100"/>
  <mx:Button click="displayIt()" label="Try It"/>
</mx:Application>
```

If you click the button labeled Try It, you'll see something similar to figure 15.4.

Figure 15.4 Dumping an `XMLList` structure as a result of using the XML object's `children` function.

You should notice something interesting here: the root node isn't displayed because these are all the children of the root. If you want to go one level deeper, modify listing 15.14 to use this line of code:

```
var admins:XMLList =
  myXML.administrators.children();
```

This causes the display to show only the two user nodes.

15.2.5 The XMLListCollection component and class

The `XMLListCollection` is a wrapper object you can wrap around an existing `XMLList` object. By using this technique, you beef up `XML` with the powers of a collection. This comes in handy when you're using data-driven components for their display. If the underlying data is altered, the display components are notified of the change and update themselves accordingly.

WRAPPING AROUND AN XMLLIST—LITERALLY

As shown in listing 15.15, an easy way to turn an `XMLList` into a collection is to literally wrap an `XMLListCollection` around the `XMLList`.

Listing 15.15 Wrapping an `XMLListCollection` around an `XMLList`

```
<mx:XMLListCollection id="myXLC" >
<mx:XMLList id="myXML">
  <users>
    <administrators>
      <user id="1">Tariq Ahmed</user>
      <user id="2">Jon Hirschi</user>
    </administrators>
  </users>
</mx:XMLList>
</mx:XMLListCollection>
```

If you find this technique too rigid, there's an alternative approach using the `source` property of the `XMLListCollection`.

USING THE SOURCE PROPERTY TO POINT TO XML AND XMLLIST SOURCES

Not to be confused with the XML class's `source` property, this `source` is used to point to an existing `XMLList` or `XML` object. The benefit is that you decouple the dependency, affording you the flexibility to change which source of XML you want to target.

This approach also makes it easy to filter down to specific nodes, as listing 15.16 illustrates.

Listing 15.16 Using the `source` property to filter and bind to XML data

```
<mx:XMLList id="myXML">
  <users>
    <administrators>
      <user id="1">Tariq Ahmed</user>
      <user id="2">Jon Hirschi</user>
    </administrators>
  </users>
</mx:XMLList>
<mx:XMLListCollection id="myXLC" source="{myXML.administrators.user}"/>
```

This approach would also work if `myXML` was an <mx:XML> object instead of <mx:XMList>.

15.3 Loading external XML source data

As we mentioned earlier, the `XML` class lacks the `source` property to reference and load external XML source data. If you need to load XML data on demand, you can do so a number of ways using data services (see chapter 14); but a simple technique uses the `URLLoader` class, as shown in listing 15.17.

Listing 15.17 Using a `URLLoader` to reference an external XML source file

```
<mx:Application xmlns:mx="http://www.adobe.com/2006/mxml" >
<mx:Script>
  <![CDATA[
  import flash.events.Event;
  import flash.net.URLLoader;
  import flash.net.URLRequest;

  public function loadXML():void          <- Initializes request
  {
    var xmlLoader:URLLoader   = new URLLoader();       <- Creates URLLoader instance

    xmlLoader.load(new URLRequest("users.xml"));       <- Tells what URL to use

    xmlLoader.addEventListener(Event.COMPLETE,
        handleLoad);      <- Identifies function to call when URLLoader is finished
  }
  public function handleLoad(event:Event):void        <- Called when URLLoader completes
  {
    var usersXML:XML = new XML(event.target.data);     <- Converts data to XML object

    myTextArea.text = usersXML.toXMLString();          <- Displays results
  }
  ]]>
</mx:Script>
<mx:TextArea id="myTextArea" width="250" height="100"/>
<mx:Button click="loadXML()" label="Load in XML"/>
</mx:Application>
```

After compiling and running listing 15.17, you should see the results as shown in figure 15.5.

Flex fires off the URL as an event. You use the `addEventListener function` to instruct the application to call the function if a result is returned.

```
<root>
  <users>
    <user id="1">Tariq Ahmed</user>
    <user id="2">Jon Hirschi</user>
  </users>
</root>
```

Load in XML

Figure 15.5 This XML has been loaded externally via the `URLLoader`.

15.4 Binding in XML

Although binding is transparent to the end user, employing it in general is an enormous time saver. And as it relates specifically to XML, binding can simplify your coding task considerably.

15.4.1 Binding from XML

Using listing 15.18, let's first look at how you can bind from XML to some other destination.

Listing 15.18 Binding against XML data to drive a display

```
<mx:Application xmlns:mx="http://www.adobe.com/2006/mxml">
  <mx:XML source="users.xml" id="usersXML"/>
  <mx:List id="myList" dataProvider="{usersXML.users.user}"/>
</mx:Application>
```

This code gets you the text inside the XML's `<user>...</user>` tags. But if you want to acquire any of the tag's attributes (in this case, the `<user>...</user>` tag), use the `@` character. For example, if you want the `id` attribute, use the code shown here:

```
<user id="1">Tariq Ahmed</user>
```

Then, in listing 15.18, you adjust the code to look like the following snippet:

```
<mx:List id="myList" dataProvider="{usersXML.users.user}"
   labelField="@id"/>
```

If you didn't use binding, you'd need to create functions that looped over the data and build an appropriate data structure which could then be used by a display component to output the value.

15.4.2 Binding to XML

By this point in the book, binding data *from* a source is no longer a mystical technique. But binding from external sources *to* XML—well, that's genuinely cool. Let's demonstrate by looking at listing 15.19.

Listing 15.19 Populating XML by binding external data

```
<mx:Application xmlns:mx="http://www.adobe.com/2006/mxml"
          backgroundColor="white">
  <mx:Script>
    [Bindable]
    public var userid:int=0;
```

Binds variable into XML

```
  </mx:Script>
  <mx:XML id="usersXML">                                  Binds dynamic value
   <root>                                                  from TextInput
    <users>
     <user userid="{userid}">{myTextInput.text}</user>   <-
    </users>
   </root>
  </mx:XML>                                                  Updates TextArea
  <mx:Label text="Name:"/>                                whenever input changes
  <mx:TextInput id="myTextInput"
         change="myTextArea.text=usersXML.toXMLString()"/>   <-
  <mx:TextArea id="myTextArea" width="250" height="100"/>
</mx:Application>
```

Figure 15.6 shows how the value entered by a user in the Name `TextInput` input field is dynamically copied into the `<user>` tag of the XML document using binding.

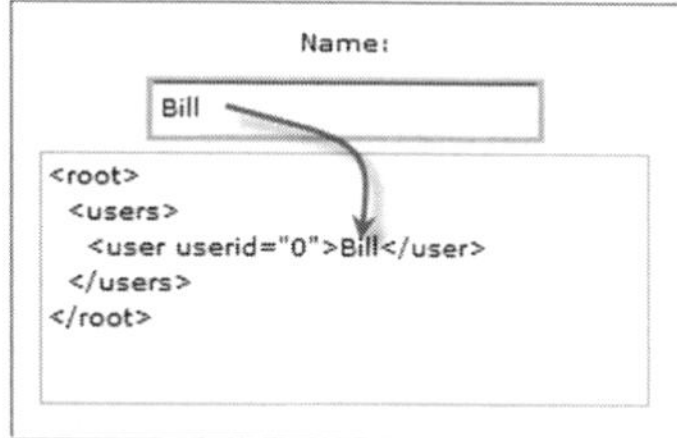

Figure 15.6 The value from the `TextInput` is copied to the XML via binding.

Listing 15.19 configures a simple variable to be `Bindable`. You also have a dynamic value coming from `TextInput`, both of which have their values bound into the XML.

In the real world, you can use this feature to save time when you're building an XML document. For example, you can build small XML objects that model the value of a form; as the user continues to add items, those XML objects will be added to a master XML object.

15.5 ECMAScript for XML (E4X)

Flex's ActionScript language follows the conventions, structure, and rules of the ECMAScript standard. An extension to that standard is a specification called ECMA-357, known as ECMAScript for XML, or E4X for short.

NOTE ECMA is the European Computer Manufacturers Association. Their ECMAScript, ECMA-262 specification, is also utilized by JavaScript, Jscript, and DMDScript.

Being based on a standard has its advantages, because knowledge regarding E4X can be ported from one language to another. But in the context of ActionScript, Flex treats E4X and XML as a native data type, which offers two key benefits to you:

- *Speed*—If it's not a native data type, the language burns a lot of resources converting data to a usable native data type.
- *Simplified syntax for accessing and working with information*—You use the same syntax you would with any other Flex object.

Without realizing it, you've already been using E4X in Flex. Everything you've done throughout the book that involves XML has been based on Flex's support for E4X—from the syntax, to the `XML` and `XMLList` objects.

15.5.1 E4X syntax

An easy way to look at XML is to view each level as an array of objects—for you ColdFusion folks, it's like a nested array of structures.

The easiest way to learn what can be done is through examples. Listing 15.20 sets up some sample XML content that you'll use as the basis for these examples.

Listing 15.20 XML used for E4X examples

```
<mx:XML id="usersXML">
  <root>
    <users>
      <user id="1" lovesDonuts="Yes">
        <firstname>Tariq</firstname>
        <lastname>Ahmed</lastname>
      </user>
      <user id="2" lovesDonuts="Yes">
        <firstname>Jon</firstname>
        <lastname>Hirschi</lastname>
      </user>
    </users>
  </root>
</mx:XML>
```

EXAMPLE 1: ACCESSING A PARTICULAR VALUE BY POSITION (INDEX)

This first example extracts the second user's first name (Jon).

```
usersXML.users.user[1].firstname
```

This works well if you know the position where the element is located. You can use this technique to loop over each user (or whatever the node represents) using an index counter to retrieve the values needed. You can also use the binding syntax for convenience (because you can bind on any E4X expression). Here's an example:

```
<mx:TextArea text="{usersXML.users.user[1].firstname}"/>
```

Let's look at another example.

EXAMPLE 2: ACCESSING A PARTICULAR NODE BY A PROPERTY VALUE

Similar to the previous example, if you don't know the node's position but you do know its value based on a property, you can do the following to access user Jon:

```
usersXML.users.user.(@id==2).firstname
```

Because you're keying off a property, you need to include the `@` character to reference the property.

EXAMPLE 3: ACCESSING A NODE BY AN ADJACENT NODES VALUE

In this scenario, you want to extract Jon's last name, which is adjacent to his first name. You could loop over the XML—in E4X it's relatively easy—but in this case, all you need to do is match on an adjacent node's value:

```
usersXML.users.user.(firstname=='Jon').lastname
```

You can also access a node's properties, as the next example shows.

EXAMPLE 4: ACCESSING A PROPERTY OF A NODE

Remember to always use the @ character when you're accessing the value of a property:

```
usersXML.users.user.(firstname=='Jon').@id
```

The final example shows how to assign values.

EXAMPLE 5: ASSIGNING VALUES

The notation you use to access XML information is the same notation you can use to assign information. The following are various snippets that illustrate how you can do this:

```
usersXML.users.user.(@id==2).firstname = 'Faisal'
usersXML.users.user.(firstname=='Faisal').lastname = 'Abid'
usersXML.users.user[1].firstname = 'Mike'
usersXML.users.user[1].@id = 3
```

Next, let's see how you can work with the XML structure.

15.5.2 *Working with XML structure*

In this section, we'll continue to expand on E4X by branching out into the XML structure in order to iterate over it as well as modify it. You'll incorporate the functions of XML to assist you in accomplishing that.

We'll continue our copious use of examples, so if you're ready, let's jump in.

EXAMPLE 1: LOOPING OVER XML STRUCTURE USING ITS INDEX

Because you can view XML as an array, you can employ the same approach used with the array to loop over the XML. For this scenario, if you want to loop over all the users and display their names, the code needs to look like listing 15.21.

Listing 15.21 Looping over an XML structure using its index

```
<mx:Application xmlns:mx="http://www.adobe.com/2006/mxml"
            backgroundColor="white"
            creationComplete="tryme()">          <- Calls function when Flex creates application
<mx:XML id="usersXML" source="users.xml"/>       <- Loads example XML; creates XML object

<mx:Script>
  <![CDATA[
    [Bindable]
    public var infoString:String = "";
    public function tryme():void
    {
      for(var i:int=0; i<usersXML.users.user.length(); i++)   <- Checks number of items
      {
        infoString = infoString + usersXML.users.user[i].firstname;
        infoString = infoString + usersXML.users.user[i].lastname;
      }
    }
  ]]>
</mx:Script>
  <mx:TextArea text="{infoString}" width="250" height="100"/>
</mx:Application>
```

Notice how the `length()` function is used to determine how many items are available to loop over. Figure 15.7 shows the results of running listing 15.21.

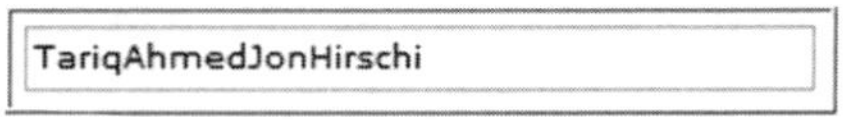

TariqAhmedJonHirschi

Figure 15.7 String populated by looping over an XML structure, keying off the index

EXAMPLE 2: LOOPING OVER NODES AS KEYS

A variation of the previous example employs our friend, the `for...each` loop and iterates over each node. Let's modify the previous example to reflect the changes shown in listing 15.22.

Listing 15.22 Looping over nodes as keys

```
public function tryme():void
{
  for each(var node:XML in usersXML.users.user)
  {
    infoString = infoString + node.firstname;
    infoString = infoString + node.lastname;
  }
}
```

In ColdFusion, this is similar to using the `StructKeyList()` function and looping over each key.

EXAMPLE 3: LOOPING OVER NODES IN AN XML FRAGMENT

Let's assume your function was designed to be more reusable. You'll configure the function to understand only the fragment of XML that contains the `users` structure. As such, it doesn't know what the overall XML document looks like.

Listing 15.23 shows how E4X syntax is used to access a fragment of XML.

Listing 15.23 Looping over an XML fragment

```
var xmlFragment:XMLList = usersXML.users.user;
for each(var node:XML in xmlFragment)
{
  infoString = infoString + node.firstname;
  infoString = infoString + node.lastname;
 }
```

The code assigns the XML fragment to a variable of type `XMLList`—precisely what `XMLList` is optimized to do.

EXAMPLE 4: ACQUIRING DESCENDENTS

E4X has a *descendant* operator, which is written out as two dots in a row (`..`). It's a quick catch-all notation to retrieve all nodes based on their tag name, regardless of where they are in the structure.

For example, this line of code acquires all `<firstname>` nodes:

```
usersXML..user.firstname
```

The output from this snippet is as follows:

```
<firstname>Tariq</firstname>
```

```
<firstname>Jon</firstname>
```

Next, let's look at how you can use a wildcard.

EXAMPLE 5: ACQUIRING NODES AND ATTRIBUTES BY WILDCARD

If you need to acquire only child nodes from a target level, E4X supports the asterisks (*) character to accomplish this. The asterisk is known as a *wildcard* character, and here's how you employ it.

This code line extracts the entire XML fragment, where user is like an array of user structures:

```
<mx:TextArea text="{usersXML.users.user}" width="250" height="200"/>
```

This code produces the results shown in figure 15.8.

```
<user id="1" lovesDonuts="Yes">
  <firstname>Tariq</firstname>
  <lastname>Ahmed</lastname>
</user>
<user id="2" lovesDonuts="Yes">
  <firstname>Jon</firstname>
  <lastname>Hirschi</lastname>
</user>
```

Figure 15.8 Acquiring nodes without the wildcard

Whereas when you use the wildcard, it extracts only nodes beneath the <user> level:

```
<mx:TextArea
  text="{usersXML.users.user.*}"
  width="250" height="200"/>
```

Figure 15.9 shows how only <firstname> and <lastname> nodes are extracted using the wildcard.

```
<firstname>Tariq</firstname>
<lastname>Ahmed</lastname>
<firstname>Jon</firstname>
<lastname>Hirschi</lastname>
```

Figure 15.9 Getting nodes with the wildcard

You can also combine the wildcard with the @ character to acquire attributes, as demonstrated in the following snippet:

```
usersXML.users.user.@*
```

This extracts the values of all the attributes of the user nodes.

EXAMPLE 6: PREPENDING AND APPENDING NODES

If you want to prepend a node before an existing node, or append a node after another node, two eponymously named functions are available to you (see table 15.4):

- prependChild(newChild)—Prepends a child at the start of a structure
- appendChild(newChild)—Appends a child at the end of a structure

Let's see what effect these functions have by adding a new user to the example usersXML object in listing 15.24.

Listing 15.24 Adding a child XML node at the end

```
var newUser:XML =
  <user id="3" lovesDonuts="no">
    <firstname>Faisal</firstname>
    <lastname>Abid</lastname>
  </user>
usersXML.users.appendChild(newUser);
```

This code adds a new user node under the users parent node. The resulting XML structure now looks like that in listing 15.25.

Listing 15.25 Adding the third user programmatically

```
<root>
  <users>
    <user id="1" lovesDonuts="Yes">
      <firstname>Tariq</firstname>
      <lastname>Ahmed</lastname>
    </user>
    <user id="2" lovesDonuts="Yes">
      <firstname>Jon</firstname>
      <lastname>Hirschi</lastname>
    </user>
    <user id="3" lovesDonuts="no">
      <firstname>Faisal</firstname>
      <lastname>Abid</lastname>
    </user>
  </users>
</root>
```

Conversely, if you used `prependChild()` instead, that third user would appear at the beginning of the list.

EXAMPLE 7: INSERTING NODES IN BETWEEN EXISTING NODES

Inserting a node is similar to appending a node, except you specify where within existing nodes you want the new node inserted. You do this by identifying the node adjacent to the position in which you wish to insert the new node. You'll insert a child node beside another child.

Referring back to the list of functions, two are available to help you do this:

- `insertChildAfter(existingChild,newChild)`—Inserts the new child after the existing one
- `insertChildBefore(existingChild,newChild)`—Inserts the new child before the existing one

The code in listing 15.26 inserts a new user between the first and second users.

Listing 15.26 Inserting a node after an existing one

```
var newUser:XML =
  <user id="3" lovesDonuts="no">
    <firstname>Faisal</firstname>
    <lastname>Abid</lastname>
  </user>
usersXML.users.insertChildAfter(usersXML.users.user[0],newUser);
```

Likewise, you can add that user before the second user by choosing the `insertChildBefore()` function:

```
usersXML.users.insertChildBefore(usersXML.users.user[1],newUser);
```

Because you're starting out with only two items, this has the same result as `insertChildAfter()` from listing 15.26.

EXAMPLE 8: COPYING A NODE

Again, referring back to table 15.4, you can use a function called `copy()` to make a duplicate of existing XML. As with any of the functions from table 15.4, you can call copy from any level, which lets you extract a copy of any node structure from anywhere within the entire `XML` object.

Because all it does is extract, you must use the other functions that add or insert nodes to physically make the copy (for instance, `appendChild()`, `insertChildBefore()`, and so on):

```
var copiedUser:XML = usersXML.users.user[1].copy();
usersXML.appendChild(copiedUser);
```

The first line extracts a chunk of XML and assigns it to a new `XML` variable. This new variable is then appended back to the original `XML` object.

EXAMPLE 9: DELETING A NODE

Deleting a node is easy; you need only use Flex's `delete` keyword to destroy an object.

If you want to delete the second user (sorry, Jon), it's as simple as this:

```
delete usersXML.users.user[1];
```

This completes our walkthrough of using E4X within the XML structure.

15.6 Summary

XML is a method for describing and structuring data. We used a considerable amount of XML in previous chapters as sample data to drive many of the components that, in turn, use data to drive their displays. This chapter went into detail about how you can fully leverage this kind of data moving forward.

Considering how complex XML documents can become, with their depth of structure, it's amazing how relatively straightforward they are to work with. This ease of use is made possible by the E4X standard, which treats XML the same as arrays of objects. The other facet is the two supporting classes (and their component variants) that go along with E4X—`XML` and `XMLList`.

The `XML` class comprises an enormous number of functions that can help you accomplish almost anything. The one drawback of having so many functions is many are only subtly different from their stablemates (many even have similar names); it may not be entirely clear what the differences are, and when you should choose one function over another. We hope that with the range of examples provided in this chapter, you have enough information to experiment on your own with those functions not demonstrated explicitly in the sample material.

16 Objects and classes

This chapter covers:

- OO concepts
- Implementing OO concepts using ActionScript classes
- Creating your own classes
- Packages

You should now be equipped with enough knowledge of ActionScript to use it to respond to events, add user interactivity to your application, and manipulate properties. Now it's time to take those skills to the next level.

In this chapter, we'll explore a fundamental feature of Flex: objects and classes. We'll also delve into some OO theory. What you'll learn will save you considerable development time and render your software easier to maintain.

By the end of this chapter, you'll have learned how to create objects and classes, invoke and destroy them, and extend those that already exist. This may seem like we're putting a lot on your plate, but it won't take more than 30 minutes to learn, and upon completion, you'll have created a fully functional OO program.

16.1 OO theory in 5 minutes

Flex is an OO-based application. As such, having some understanding of OO programming will be tremendously beneficial toward taking Flex and your designs to a higher plane and resolving issues more quickly. Most important, expanding your knowledge of OO programming will provide the foundation for creating reusable code.

In the following sections, we'll explore the basic concepts of programming using objects and classes. This is arguably the most important branch of computer programming in which you'll engage. Understanding objects and classes will help you quickly learn many other programming languages, such as C#, C++, and Java.

16.1.1 The relationship between objects and classes

To help you clearly understand objects, we'll set up a brief mental exercise. For the exercise to be effective, you need to consider objects not as an abstract concept but instead as something with which you're familiar.

Stop for a moment and look around. You'll notice that your surroundings are full of objects: a car, a television, a computer—even this book. Each object has a certain function or role to fulfill. Objects also have characteristics, such as their color or size.

Some objects rely on other objects—a computer relies on a CPU object—while other objects are independent. For example, your computer isn't dependent on this book. If you understand this analogy, that's half of the battle. The rest is implementation.

An object is a self-contained widget. It knows about itself and is aware of its capabilities. Objects display a bipolar personality in that

- They generally care only about themselves (how rude!).
- They make it easy for others to use them by doing the hard work behind the scenes (how nice!).

Now you have a cursory idea of what an object is, but what about a class?

WHAT ARE CLASSES?

In pure OO theory, only objects exist. But throughout this book, you've probably noticed we've been using the terms *objects* and *classes* interchangeably. OO theory is just theory: it has no notion of implementation. Flex has to turn that theory into reality; so, like most OO languages, Flex implements the concepts by using classes as a template (a blueprint, if you will) with which to create objects. More succinctly, objects are *instances* of classes.

For example, if you had a class called `Human`, and an instance of that human named Derek Douville, then `Derek Douville` would be an object.

16.1.2 Objects have properties and methods

An object knows about itself and its capabilities through two features:

- Properties
- Methods (or, as they're also known, functions)

Going back to the Human class, figure 16.1 shows how a human possesses various properties. Some of the properties in an instance of Human are set only once—`Place of Birth`, for example—whereas other properties can change constantly, such as `Mood`. Likewise, your human is capable of various functions, including eating and sleeping.

Human Class	
Properties	Functions/Methods
- Age	- Eat
- Height	- Sleep
- Place of Birth	- Code
- Mood	- Laugh

Figure 16.1 The `Human` class has properties that define it and various functions of which it's capable.

PROPERTIES AND METHODS HAVE SCOPE

The purpose of *scope* is to control who has access to what. For example, your human needs to keep its Social Security number (SSN) property closely guarded to avoid the number becoming publicly known. But in certain circumstances, a method may need to be provided to make use of the number, such as a method to apply for credit. Using scope, you can keep this SSN private from the outside world and use methods within that class to work with it.

Similarly, this scope applies to methods. A human can provide public methods such as a function to do work, which an external boss object can invoke. There may also be private methods that the human wants to use internally and that no one else is allowed to use (for example, a method to pick one's nose). Flex supports the following scopes for properties and methods.

- *Private*—Methods and properties are available only to this class.
- *Public*—Methods and properties are available everywhere.
- *Protected*—Methods and properties are available in the same class or any class that extends from it.
- *Internal*—The default. Methods and properties are available to classes in the same package.
- *Static*—Methods and properties can be used without an actual instance of a class.

What if you want to make an object that does everything a human does, and more? You can copy all the methods and properties and then add the additional properties and methods. A problem arises when you have to make a change common to both: you'll need to make that same change in two places. Fortunately a mechanism called *inheritance* solves this problem.

16.1.3 Inheritance

An object can inherit attributes and characteristics from another object. This allows the properties and methods of one class—also known as the *base* or *parent* class—to be passed on to the child object. You can continue to add more properties and methods to those inherited from the parent.

In Flex, a well-known custom component called `promptingTextInput` is available in the FlexLib package (http://code.google.com/p/flexlib/). This is a child of the `TextInput` component that has been extended to provide not only the native abilities of TextInput but also the additional ability to prompt the user for input by means of a message, such as *please enter a value.*

Some OO languages (including Flex) refer to this action as *extending a class.* Building on the analogy, you could take the Human class and extend it to make Male and Female subclasses (see Figure 16.2). Each of those subclasses can have unique properties and functions of their own. More significantly, they can have the same functions but implement them differently.

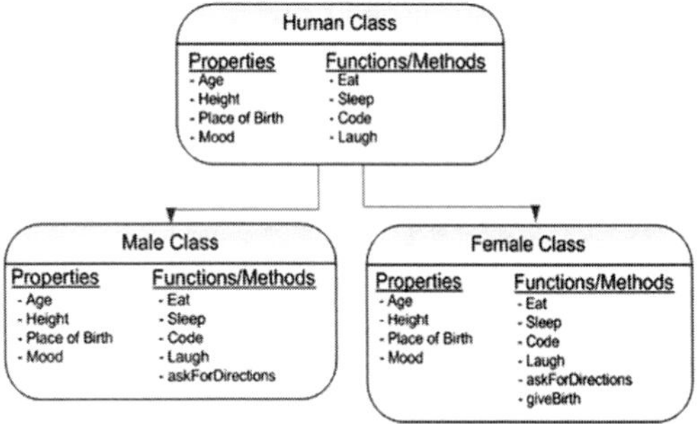

Figure 16.2 Subclasses inherit all of the parent's attributes, but you can add more.

For example, if both Female and Male have an askForDirections function, Female's version of that function will return a sequence of instructions that can be used to successfully navigate to the desired location, whereas the Male class will return nothing (asking for directions isn't something it supports).

Using inheritance, you can save a lot of time by eliminating the need to define properties and attributes in each child object you create. Ironically, though, now that you've learned about inheritance, it's time to learn how to keep your objects independent of each other. This process is called *encapsulation,* and it's useful for reusing code.

16.1.4 Encapsulation and coupling

The principle of encapsulation is key to reusable code. Encapsulation defines an object that exists in a self-contained environment, or *module.* The object doesn't need to know about the workings of the overall application in which it resides. Likewise, the application doesn't need to know how the object works.

The more you adhere to that rule, the more reusable your code will be, because the elements that form your application aren't dependent on the *knowledge* of how each other works. An object's goal is to tend to its own tasks within its self-contained world.

If you want other code elements to be able to work with your object, you need to expose methods and properties that abstract the object's inner workings from the calling code. This way, you can change aspects of the object, but the calling code still works unperturbed, and vice versa.

As an illustration, let's assume you have an object that needs a piece of information from elsewhere in the application in order to perform its task—for this example, we'll assume the information to be UserID. If your object were to reach outside itself directly into the main application to gather UserID, it would need to know what UserID is, what it looks like, and where to find it. You could provide that information to your object by giving it explicit instructions (hardcoding), but then any changes to UserID or the object would render those instructions useless and require you to update them manually.

Your object is now dependent on knowing specifically how and where to acquire a value. This breaks the object's encapsulation (it can no longer ignore the outside world) and makes it *tightly coupled* to the application around it.

The better approach is to make your objects *loosely coupled* by passing values between them in such a way that your object (and everything else with which it interacts) doesn't know or care where `UserID` came from. It knows to take the information passed to it and process it according to instructions.

16.1.5 Objects: they're everywhere!

In the world of ActionScript 3/Flex 3, everything is an object. From panels, to formatters, to user input components, everything follows the concept of OO programming.

This is true for both MXML components (for example, `<mx:Panel/>`) and ActionScript classes, such as `ArrayCollection`. More important, anything you create in MXML is converted to ActionScript classes.

To be accurate, that statement is only 99% true. The primitive data types, such as `int` and `Boolean`, aren't objects in the true sense of the term, but aside from primitive data types, everything is an object.

Enough with the theory: let's dive in and play with some objects!

16.2 Playing with objects

We've always espoused the premise that you won't learn something until you physically use it. You've been introduced to most of this material throughout the previous chapters, but let's look into the mechanics behind it. Time to roll up your sleeves and get your hands dirty.

16.2.1 A closer look at objects

To begin, you'll create a generic starting point by performing the following steps:

1. Create a Flex project called `ObjectsandClasses`.
2. Open the file ObjectsandClasses.mxml.
3. Create an `<mx:Script>` block in which to place your ActionScript code.

With these steps complete, your code should resemble that of listing 16.1.

Listing 16.1 Shell application

```
<?xml version="1.0" encoding="utf-8"?>
<mx:Application xmlns:mx="http://www.adobe.com/2006/mxml"
  layout="absolute">
  <mx:Script>
    <![CDATA[

     ]]>
  </mx:Script>
</mx:Application>
```

You're under way. Next, let's add a simple object.

ADDING A PRIMITIVE OBJECT

You'll create an instance of an object through which you can explore the process of adding an object—in this case, a primitive. A *primitive* object is an object that possesses only rudimentary capabilities.

Between the `<mx:Script>` block, add the line shown in figure 16.3.

You've now created a *new* object called `myObj`. The `new` operator following the variable definition, `myObj:Object`, informs the ActionScript compiler that you're creating a new *instance* of this object class.

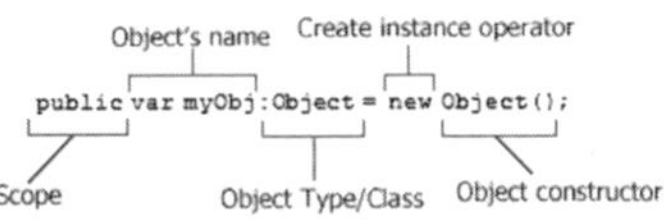

Figure 16.3 Creating an instance of an object

Now that you've created an object, let's open it up and see what's inside.

TAKING A PEEK

An easy way to view the makeup of this object is to type `myObj` on a new line and add a period directly after it. Flex Builder displays a list of associated properties and methods, as shown in figure 16.4.

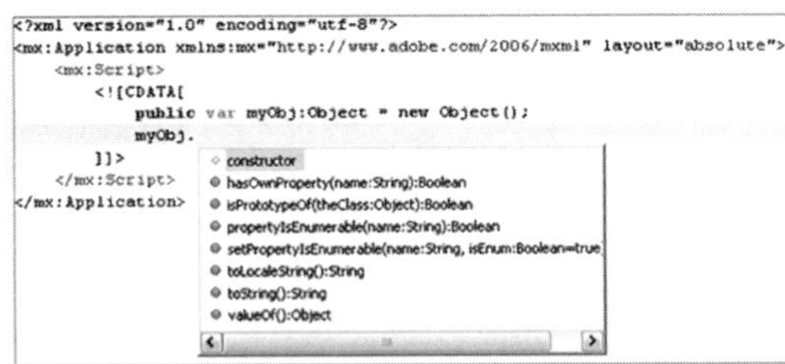

Figure 16.4 Inserting a period after an instance prompts Flex Builder to list the known public properties and methods associated with the object.

16.2.2 Methods of objects

Each ActionScript class includes methods. Methods are the workforce of objects. They perform the actions defined for them by programmers and developers. Let's spend a few moments looking at some of the methods associated with an `Array` class.

As you did earlier with a simple object, create a new array variable called `myArr`:

```
var myArr:Array = new Array();
```

Again, by using the `new` operator, you create a new instance of the `Array` class. On the next line, type `myArr.` (remember to add the period). You should see something similar to figure 16.5.

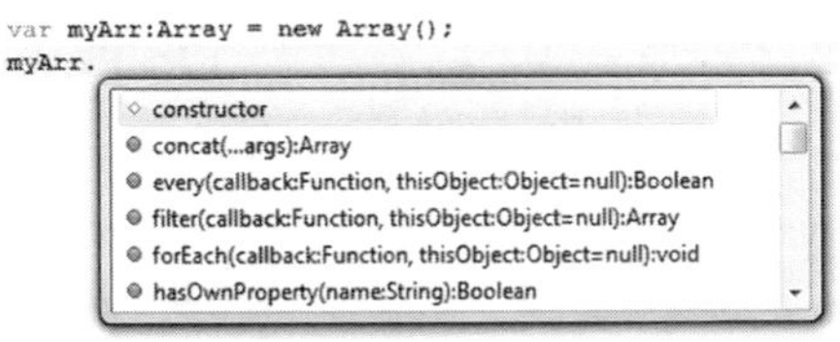

Figure 16.5 Flex Builder's auto-suggest feature displays a number of methods.

Flex Builder displays a list of methods and properties associated with `myArr`. The items followed by parentheses are the methods. Included among them are `concat()`, `every()`, and `forEach()`.

The primary mission of an object is to make programming easier. If you glance down the list, you'll notice some useful methods that help carry out that mission.

These are methods the Flex team wrote specifically for interacting with the `Array` object. For example, the array methods, `split()` and `push()`, do the following:

- `split()`—Splits an array into smaller pieces
- `push()`—Adds onto the array

Remember, objects don't concern themselves with the world around them. As a result, their methods don't know much about that environment either. To communicate with methods and give them the information to perform their tasks, you need to pass them parameters.

16.2.3 *Method parameters*

You can communicate with methods via *arguments*, or as they're also known, *parameters*. Look again at the list of methods for `Array`. Notice the text within the parentheses that follows the structure: `text:ObjectName`.

When you enter data in the parentheses, you're passing parameters, or arguments, to the method. If you want to add a new value to an array, you supply it as follows:

```
myArr.push("some Value");
```

The data, `"some Value"`, is passed to the method, which does with it whatever it has been instructed to do—remember, in OO, what the object does, and how it does it, is irrelevant to other parts of the code. As it relates to this example, `"some Value"` is added as the parameter to the `Array`.

16.2.4 *Methods return information*

Methods can also communicate information or data back to the object that sent it via a mechanism known as a *return* value. Referring back to the Flex Builder auto-suggest feature, you'll see that along with presenting the parameters each method takes, the list also indicates what is returned from the method. For example, you can see back in figure 16.5 that the method `concat()` returns another array.

16.2.5 *Objects have properties*

Properties act as another form of communication with an object. They can be used both to configure an object and to ascertain its attributes (its current state). In the `Array` example, a property known as `length` indicates how many items are currently in the array.

Objects are the fundamental building blocks behind a class. Let's take the information you've learned about objects and apply it to creating a class of your own.

16.3 *Creating a class*

We'll begin the study of classes by creating a simple math program that calculates the area of a given shape. The shapes will be drawn using your own class. You'll also create the methods to perform the area computation.

16.3.1 Creating the class file

For this example, create a dedicated project by following these steps:

1. Select File > New > Project.
2. Name the project `Shapes`.
3. Click Finish.

Next, following these steps, create an ActionScript class file:

1. Select File > New > Create New ActionScript Class.
2. Fill out the fields in the dialog box to match the information shown in figure 16.6, but don't click Finish yet. First, let's take a few moments to learn more about the New ActionScript Class wizard.

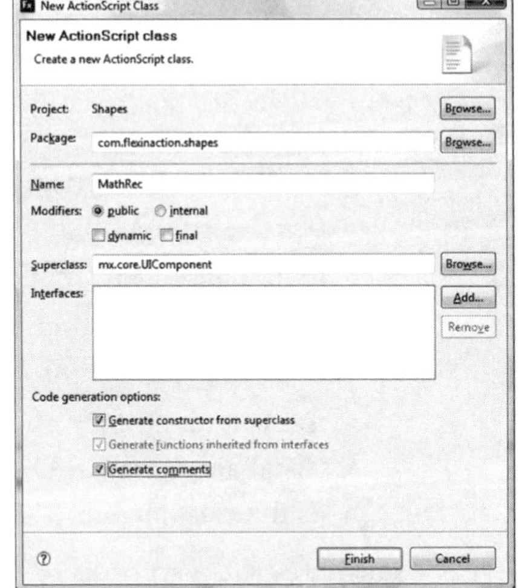

Figure 16.6 Flex Builder's class wizard

You've created the project and a simple class. Let's look in detail at what you entered in the dialog box.

16.3.2 Specifying a package

The first field you filled in defines the class package. A *package* organizes similar classes into folders. This is a more effective strategy than placing your classes in the top-level source folder. A package helps you develop applications faster and more efficiently by providing a mechanism to keep your elements organized.

Everyone has personal preferences regarding the package name, but most developers adopt reverse-domain notation, which is the domain name in reverse (for example, `com.mycompany`) and any further identifiers you deem necessary.

For example, a package named `com.mycompany.sales.management` indicates a folder structure of com/mycompany/sales/management.

This exercise uses `com.flexinaction.shapes`. You use `shapes` as the group name because this folder contains all the shape classes you create.

16.3.3 Naming classes

The next input is self-explanatory: the name of the class. You can choose any name you like, but we recommend the name be relative to the *purpose* of the class. In this case, you're creating a rectangle, so you use the name `MathRec`. When you create class names, it's always best practice not to use the same name as another class in your project.

16.3.4 Class modifiers

Class modifiers let you control what other application elements can access the class.

You set the class modifiers using a pair of radio buttons (located below the Name field) labeled Public and Internal.

Modifiers determine how *sociable* a class is with other classes in the application. If you choose the Public modifier, this permits the class to be accessed by other classes and your application. If you set the class to Internal, it can be accessed only by other classes from within the same package. You can use these four scope modifiers:

- *Public*—Any code can use this class.
- *Internal*—The default. Other classes within the same package are allowed to use this class.
- *Dynamic*—An optional modifier that you can use with the public or internal modifier, which lets you add properties during runtime.
- *Final*—An optional modifier that you can use with the public or internal modifier, which prevents other classes from extending this class.

Why choose one over another? This is an architectural decision you must make when designing your application. Some factors that can influence your decision:

- Do you want other classes accessing this class?
- What are the security implications of exposing the class?
- Is the class meant to support only other classes of which it's aware?

This gives you a synopsis of classes and how to create objects to do your bidding. But how can you incorporate a pre-existing object into your application? The next section will show you how to *extend* classes.

16.3.5 Superclasses: extending a class

No, a superclass isn't a class from the planet Krypton. A superclass is a way to extend the methods and properties of one class by including those of another class. For example, let's assume your application has two classes: class `A` and class `B`. Class `A` has 20 methods, and class `B` has 10. By instructing class `B` to extend class `A`, you make class `B` incorporate the methods from class `A` but keep those it possessed prior to extension. The extended class `B` has 30 methods.

You'll use the `mx.core.UIComponent` class to extend your area-calculating class because it's part of the Flex core and is related to visual objects on the screen—a great match for what you want to do (make shapes). You'll see shortly how to change or extend the class programmatically, not by means of the wizard.

TIP Superclasses are also known as *parent* or *base* classes.

An interface is similar to a class but not as robust.

16.3.6 Interfaces

Without being too technical, an *interface* is a predefined template that catalogues the necessary methods and properties that a class must implement in order to comply with the interface. For example, if you're making a collection of shape classes (square, circle, triangle, and so on), all of which have formulas for calculating the area or perimeter, you can use an interface to enforce that they all have methods to support each formula.

An interface serves as a contract with a class—a contract stating that the class will implement the methods defined by the interface. You could try making a `Shape` superclass with `area` and `perimeter` methods that are overridden by specific subclasses (such as a `Circle` class), but this may not be the best approach. This is because the area formula for a circle varies from that of a square, so the `Shape`'s `area` method is of little value at the cost of overhead.

The problem you're trying to solve is making sure all types of shapes employ certain methods. Interfaces work great because they solve this problem and are lightweight in the process (they carry no implementation).

Let's put some of this theory into action by creating a class and using it.

16.3.7 Looking at your class

For those of you who follow directions to the letter, you can now click the Finish button in the New ActionScript Class wizard and watch Flex Builder create the code shown in listing 16.2.

Listing 16.2 Basic class structure

```
package com.flexinaction.shapes      ❶
{
  import mx.core.UIComponent;
  public class MathRec extends UIComponent      ❷
  {         ❸
    public function MathRec()
    {
       super();
    }
  }
}
```

Much of what you see is probably familiar to you by now:

- The `package` identifier ❶ is followed by the name of the package you entered.
- The `public` modifier ❷ is assigned the class so it can be accessed by other classes and the application itself.
- The `UIComponent` ❸ class is extended by the `MathRec` class.

NOTE Throughout this chapter, we've been talking about methods, yet the code in listing 16.2 presents functions. Confused? Don't be. *Function* is another name for a method. *Method* is the term used by those in the programming and development community, but both terms refer to the same thing.

In listing 16.2, you create a function called `MathRec()`. Coincidentally, this happens to be the name of the class as well. Whenever an instance of a class is created, ActionScript automatically generates a default method for that class (hence, the same name). The mechanism that executes this is known as a *constructor*.

Within this method resides another method named `super()`, which is a way to call the parent's (superclass) constructor. In this example, because you extend from `UIComponent`, `super()` calls the `UIComponent`'s constructor (which initializes the object). You don't need to have a constructor, and you can realize a slight performance boost by omitting it, but it's best practice to include one.

In the next section, you'll learn how to impart unique characteristics to your class by adding properties.

16.4 Adding properties

Now that you've created your class, you need to get down to the business of drawing the shape. But before you do, we need to consider a few user cases. For instance, what if the user prefers a red rectangle instead of blue? Or, what if the user wants a big rectangle rather than a small one? It's easy for the user to input values to effect the changes, but how will the class know about these modifications, and how will it accommodate them?

Returning to an earlier analogy, in the real world you can change aspects of the environment around you by passing instructions, or information, to the appropriate resource. For example, you can instruct a builder to create a rectangular shape of a specific length and width, and further instruct that the rectangle be painted red.

You can do the same thing with classes by creating variables to hold the specification data. In the line beneath the class identifier, create these three private variables:

- `_color` of type `uint`
- `_height` of type `int`
- `_length` of type `int`

The underscore character at the beginning of each variable is a common industry convention for naming private variables. You don't need to do this, but it helps to visually identify privately scoped variables in your code.

After you add your new variables, the code should appear as shown in listing 16.3.

Listing 16.3 A class with private properties defined

```
package com.flexinaction.shapes
{
  import mx.core.UIComponent;
  public class MathRec extends UIComponent
  {
    private var _color:uint = 0x000000;
    private var _length:int = 10;
    private var _height:int = 20;
    public function MathRec()
    {
      super();
```

```
        }
    }
}
```

NOTE Why wasn't the whole new `Object()` thing done with these `int` and `uint` variables? These are primitive data types, so there's no object instantiation to go around. Refer to chapter 3 for a refresher.

These variables are the *properties* of the class.

16.5 Adding getter/setter methods

You could have taken the easy way out and defined our new properties as public, allowing the outside world to access and manipulate them. There would be nothing wrong with doing this, but to properly and efficiently program with Flex, it's best to use an alternate mechanism to provide access to those variables: *getter* and *setter* methods.

These are special methods that have only one role: access the variable and change it. This approach provides a controlled way to access variables and change them internally without interfering with the calling code.

First, you'll create setter methods to set the three variables. The setter method follows a simple pattern:

```
public function set yourPropertyname(value:DataTypeOfProperty):void{
    this._propertyname = value; }
```

You use the `public` identifier at the beginning of the line to define the setter method as accessible to the other classes and the main application. You use the `function` identifier to create the method, then add the special keyword `set` to indicate this is a setter method.

The property name should be assigned with an eye toward avoiding confusion about what you're setting and getting. The name can be whatever you prefer, but it's best to use the same name as your private variables. Next, the value and data type of the parameter you want to pass are specified within parentheses. The `:void` designation indicates that this function won't return a value. Finally, code within the curly braces will be executed. Listing 16.4 shows some examples.

Listing 16.4 Examples of setter functions

```
public function set color(value:uint):void
{
  this._color = value;
}

public function set Reclength(value:int):void
{
  this._length = value;
}

public function set Recheight(value:int):void
{
```

```
    this._height = value;
}
```

The syntax `this.` that precedes the variable name is an option you can use when referring to variables in the class. Like the underscore character, it makes the code easier to read and clearly identifies where that variable is coming from (in this case, the class).

Next, you'll configure the three getter functions so you can provide access to the variable. The syntax is similar, except you use the keyword `get` instead of `set`, as shown in listing 16.5.

Listing 16.5 Examples of getter functions

```
public function get color():uint
{
  return this._color;
}

public function get Reclength():int
{
  return this._length;
}

public function get Recheight():int
{
  return this._height;
}
```

Of course, the key difference between a getter function and a setter function is that instead of passing values, a getter function returns values.

16.6 Creating methods for your class

With the getter and setter methods in place, it's time to draw the rectangle and add the required methods to calculate the area and perimeter. ActionScript comes with a number of drawing classes; among them is a rectangle class you can easily employ in the application.

Create a new method called `DrawRectangle()`, and enter the code from listing 16.6.

Listing 16.6 Method to draw a rectangle

```
public function DrawRectangle():void
{
  this.graphics.clear();      ❶
  this.graphics.lineStyle(1,_color);      ❷
  this.graphics.drawRect(120,120 ,_length,_height);      ❸
}
```

Whenever you call this method, it will do the following:

- Clear the stage ❶ of any other rectangles.

- Set the line color ❷ to the color specified via the private variable `_color` (defaulted to black in the class definition).
- Draw the rectangle ❸ at coordinate `120,120` on the screen using the `_length` and `_height` variables.

Using the constructor-generated default method, you call the `DrawRectangle` function. This causes a default rectangle to be created when an instance of this class is created. Your code should look as shown in the following snippet:

```
public function MathRec()
{
  super();
  DrawRectangle();
}
```

Now that you have the shape drawn, you'll create helper methods to calculate the area and perimeter. Listing 16.7 presents the functions needed to perform the calculations.

Listing 16.7 Supporting methods

```
public function getArea():int
{
  return (this._length * this._height);        <-- Area = base * height
}

public function getPerim():int
{
  return ((2*(this._height)) + (2*(this._length)));     <-- Calculates perimeter
}
```

Let's put the application to work. Try entering values in the height and length input fields, and watch the results, as illustrated in figure 16.7.

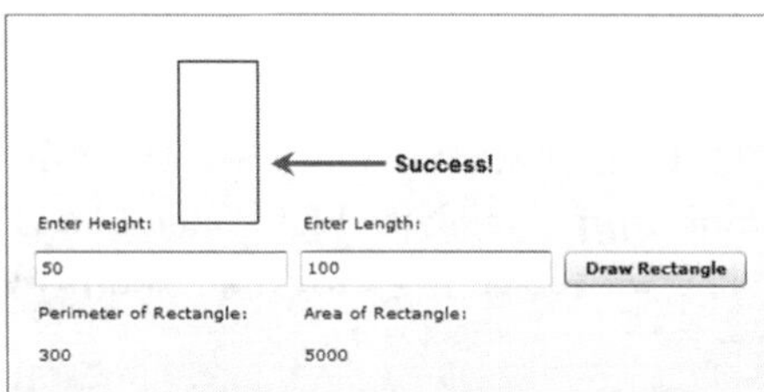

Figure 16.7 The `Rectangle` class in action

Listing 16.8 presents the complete code for the class.

Listing 16.8 CH16.mxml: using the class you created

```
<?xml version="1.0" encoding="utf-8"?>
<mx:Application xmlns:mx="http://www.adobe.com/2006/mxml"
             layout="absolute" backgroundColor="white"
             initialize="addChild(myRectangle);" >      <-- Adds myRectangle to application
  <mx:Script>
    <![CDATA[
     import com.flexinaction.shapes.MathRec;      <-- Imports class
```

```
    public var myRectangle:MathRec = new MathRec();

    private function drawMyRectangle():void
    {
      myRectangle.Recheight = Number(inputHeight.text);
      myRectangle.Reclength = Number(inputLength.text) ;
      myRectangle.DrawRectangle();
      outputArea.text = myRectangle.getArea().toString();
      outputPerim.text = myRectangle.getPerim().toString();
    }
  ]]>
</mx:Script>

<mx:Button x="365" y="207" label="Draw Rectangle"
 click="drawMyRectangle()"/>
<mx:Label text="Enter Length:" x="197" y="181"/>
<mx:TextInput x="29" y="207" id="inputLength"/>
<mx:Label text="Enter Height:" x="29" y="181"/>
<mx:TextInput x="197" y="207" id="inputHeight"/>

<mx:Label text="Area of Rectangle:" x="197" y="237"/>
<mx:Label id="outputArea" x="197" y="263"/>
<mx:Label text="Perimeter of Rectangle:" x="29" y="237"/>
<mx:Label id="outputPerim" x="29" y="263"/>
</mx:Application>
```

Creates instances of MathRec

Setter functions

Getter functions

Invokes public method

As you learned earlier, when you want to use an object, you must first import the class. This is what you do when you import the `MathRec` class using the `import` statement, as shown in the following extract from listing 16.8:

```
import com.flexinaction.MathRec
```

The `drawMyRectangle()` method converts the height and length values specified by the user to numbers, then sets the parameters in the `MathRec` class using the setter functions.

16.7 Summary

Regardless of what you do in Flex, it all boils down to ActionScript. It may not be something you're used to if you're coming from a tag-based language like HTML, but over time you'll become more comfortable with it. Along with that comfort will come the power to harness ActionScript classes.

You can spend months learning about OO programming, only to find yourself struggling with its vast number of theories and advanced techniques. But in the time it took for you to read this chapter, you successfully learned the ins and outs of basic OO programming, which will dramatically extend your Flex development skills.

This knowledge will form the foundations that will enable you to create well-designed applications that have self-contained, reusable objects. In the next chapter, we'll continue to enhance your understanding of reusability through the use of custom components.

17 Custom components

This chapter covers

- Making your own custom components
- Using existing components as a base
- Passing parameters to custom components
- Retrieving values from custom components
- Employing getter and setter functions
- Broadcasting events from a custom component
- Creating ActionScript components

You've come a long way in a short amount of time in your journey through Flex. In fact, you now know enough to create a standard Flex application.

You can capture and validate input from the user, interact with back-end data services to get and transmit data, and format and display information. This is fine and dandy, but unless you like having all your code in one huge file, you'll need to know how to break your application into smaller, reusable pieces.

This is where custom components come into play. Although they're not the only option for making code reusable, they're the most popular due to their ease of implementation.

NOTE In this chapter, we'll teach you the thought process involved in building applications in Flex. Instead of giving you the final answer, we'd rather show you how to arrive at the solution.

This chapter covers the basics of creating and utilizing custom components and tackles ways to get information into and out of them. As with many programming languages, you can approach things many ways, each of which has its pros and cons. We'll look in depth at how you can overcome these challenges. But first, we'll explain what custom components are.

17.1 What are custom components?

You've used components since the start of this book. They range from visual components like the `Button` (`<mx:Button>`) that accept input from the user, to layout components like the `VBox`.

Custom components are those you make on your own versus the ones that come with Flex. With practice, you may reach a point where your custom components are so reusable, it's as if they came with the Flex product.

TIP Here's a parallel for ColdFusion developers. Although there's no direct match to ColdFusion, we can argue that a Flex custom component is similar to a ColdFusion custom tag containing user-defined functions (UDF)s. But behind the scenes, Flex implements the custom component much like the way it would a CFC.

Why didn't Adobe include components that you feel are obvious? The Flex engineering team's stated goal was to build a framework that enabled the Flex developer community to build components for themselves. Had the team focused on building more components, less time would have been spent on Flex's overall capabilities.

17.1.1 A custom component example

Let's walk through a simple example. Say your application is geocentric, meaning that pieces of information tend to carry location data. As a result, a few forms require the user to specify an address of some sort. To help your users, you want to provide a drop-down menu of U.S. states, as figure 17.1 demonstrates.

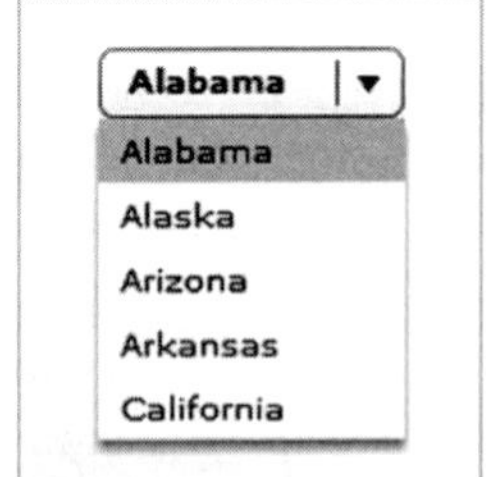

Figure 17.1 This custom component uses a `ComboBox` to present a list of U.S. states.

Wouldn't it be awesome if any part of your application could display this list by calling a single line of code? OK, that's a loaded statement, but the example is as simple as this:

```
<local:cbStates/>
```

The full code is shown in listings 17.1 and 17.2. When it comes to making custom components, your goal should be to make it simple for other developers to use your component (even if it's complicated inside).

Later, we'll give you tips on how to achieve this goal. Now that you have some perspective on what we're talking about, the rest of the chapter will be easier to relate to.

17.2 How custom components work

The general game plan for building a custom component is to base it on an existing Flex component and add the capabilities and business logic you need.

The U.S. state selector is based on the ComboBox component, similar to this block of code:

```
<?xml version="1.0" encoding="utf-8"?>
<mx:ComboBox xmlns:mx="http://www.adobe.com/2006/mxml"/>
```

If you saved these two lines to a file, you could use them as a fully functional ComboBox component; if you're thinking it sounds like object-oriented inheritance, you're right! Creating a custom component is exactly that: creating a component that extends from an existing one. When you do this, you inherit

- Properties
- Functions
- Events
- Styles

With components inheriting from components, the amount of stuff that's inherited can add up. And that's the general strategy: to incrementally add more capabilities with each new tier of the lineage. The children become progressively more powerful, but the differences from one generation to another aren't too drastic, allowing you to inherit from any necessary level to add that extra bit of functionality.

Public domain components

If you're looking for a general component, it probably already exists. Popular places to find public domain components include:

- *CFLEX.Net*—http://www.cflex.net
- *FlexLib*—http://code.google.com/p/flexlib/
- *FlexBox*—http://flexbox.mrinalwadhwa.com/
- *RIAForge*—http://www.riaforge.org

Contribute to the community; if you come up with nifty components, share them!

The fun doesn't stop there. For even greater flexibility, you can create components that group disparate components in what's called a composite component.

17.2.1 Simple and composite types

There are two major types of custom components: simple and composite. A simple custom component is based on a single component, just like the example state-selector ComboBox. A composite custom component is based on a container and includes one or more components inside it.

You have choices about the types of components you create, and you can also choose how you store them as part of your application.

17.2.2 Implementation choices

A few implementation approaches are available to you, each of which has advantages and limitations. Don't forget: when the Flex compiler is building your application, it converts all custom components into pure ActionScript classes.

JUST MXML

This approach is the easiest to get started with. Your custom components exist as MXML files that declare at the top which Flex component they derive from.

Imagine taking your main MXML application file and changing the word *Application* in <mx:Application> to another container like a Canvas. If you did that, you'd have your first custom component.

This approach is convenient because it's straightforward and leverages your existing skills (thus far). Layout is also easier because you use visual components. But you can't override functions of the component you're basing the custom component on.

JUST ACTIONSCRIPT

A pure ActionScript custom component lives as an ActionScript .as file and works by extending the ActionScript version of a Flex component (known as the *component class*). This technique is more advanced because it requires stronger ActionScript skills. You can override the functions of the component class you're extending from, and you have fine-grained control. On the other hand, this way you can't lay out a custom component visually in Flex Builder.

CODE-BEHIND

This approach marries the previous two techniques by using ActionScript to create an extended component class, then using an MXML file that bases itself on your ActionScript class to lay out the component visually.

Although this technique provides the advantages of both an MXML and an ActionScript component, more work is involved, and it requires slightly more overhead due to the double extending.

17.3 Simple custom components

Enough theory. Let's get into the fun stuff. Listings 17.1 and 17.2 show how to reproduce the example we showed you earlier in the chapter.

Listing 17.1 cbStates.mxml: ComboBox-based custom component

```
<?xml version="1.0" encoding="utf-8"?>
<mx:ComboBox xmlns:mx="http://www.adobe.com/2006/mxml">
    <mx:dataProvider>
      <mx:Object stateCode="AK" label="Alaska"/>
      <mx:Object stateCode="AL" label="Alabama"/>
```

```
        ...
      </mx:dataProvider>
</mx:ComboBox>
```

Continue for all U.S. states

Listing 17.2 HelloWorld.mxml: Main application file

```
<?xml version="1.0"?>
<mx:Application xmlns:mx="http://www.adobe.com/2006/mxml"
            backgroundColor="white" xmlns:local="*">
   <local:cbStates/>
</mx:Application>
```

If you save the two files to the same directory (see figure 17.2) in Flex Builder and then run the application, you should end up with a drop-down combo box listing all the U.S. states, as shown earlier in figure 17.1.

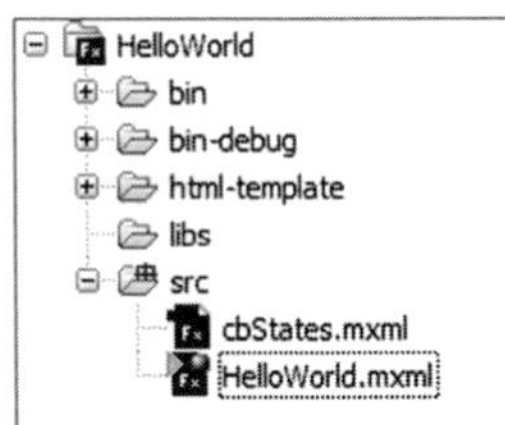

Figure 17.2 The location of the main application file and a custom component

One nice thing about basing the component on a noncontainer is that people who use your component will know its general properties and behaviors as a result of inheritance. In this case, if they know your simple custom component is based on a ComboBox, then they also know your component supports the same properties, events, styles, and functions as a ComboBox.

Now that you know how to create a custom component, you'll want to communicate with it by passing it information in the form of parameters.

17.4 Passing parameters

Let's keep working on the example custom component. Next, you'll pass values to it—particularly a parameter that specifies the U.S. state that's displayed by default. (In the real world, if you were pulling an existing record from a database into an edit form, you'd default all the values based on that data.)

Flex provides mechanisms to support doing this, each of which has pros and cons. The nice thing is that you're not forced to make a choice; you can employ combinations of these options.

17.4.1 Using a function to pass a value

One simple way to specify the default value would be to call a function that sets the value. In applying that concept, listing 17.3 enhances the custom component by providing a public function that the calling code can use to set the default U.S. state. Listing 17.4 shows how the calling code uses that function.

Listing 17.3 cbStates.mxml: Component with a function to set a default

```
<?xml version="1.0" encoding="utf-8"?>
<mx:ComboBox xmlns:mx="http://www.adobe.com/2006/mxml">
  <mx:Script>
    <![CDATA[
```

```
        public function setDefaultState(stateCode:String):void
        {
            for(var x:int=0;x<this.dataProvider.length;x++)
              if(this.dataProvider[x].stateCode == stateCode)
                this.selectedIndex = x;
        }
      ]]>
    </mx:Script>
        <mx:dataProvider>
          <mx:Object stateCode="AK" label="Alaska"/>
          <mx:Object stateCode="AL" label="Alabama"/>
          ...
        </mx:dataProvider>
  </mx:ComboBox>
```

Listing 17.4 HelloWorld.mxml: Main application file that calls `setDefaultState`

```
<?xml version="1.0"?>
<mx:Application xmlns:mx="http://www.adobe.com/2006/mxml"
creationComplete="initApp()" backgroundColor="white" xmlns:local="*">
  <mx:Script>
    <![CDATA[
      public function initApp():void
      {
        myStates.setDefaultState('CA');
      }
        ]]>
        </mx:Script>
      <local:cbStates id="myStates"/>
</mx:Application>
```

This custom component is useable and ready to go. One advantage of providing a public function like this is that if the calling application needs to go through a complicated initialization routine and call functions that set things up, you can support that process.

Although you can use a public function to pass information along, such a function is also a vehicle by which the custom component can support people who use it. You can provide functions that do all kinds of things, such as resetting the custom component.

17.4.2 *Passing a value as a property*

Because you're a nice coder and you like to make life easier for those who use your stuff, it would be good to be able to set the value as a property:

```
<local:cbStates id="myStates" defaultValue="AZ"/>
```

That's doable using the conventional method you probably already have in mind. Let's use the case of a custom component that's based on a `TextInput` (as shown in figure 17.3).

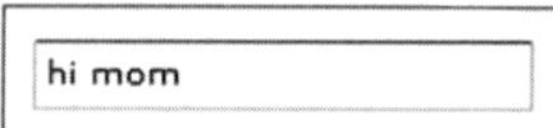

Figure 17.3 `TextInput` custom component displaying a value via property assignment

The code uses a simple approach. In listing 17.5, you can see that what the calling application file (listing 17.6) thinks is a property is a public variable internal to myTextInput.mxml.

Listing 17.5 myTextInput.mxml: Sets itself to the value of a public variable

```
<?xml version="1.0" encoding="utf-8"?>
<mx:TextInput xmlns:mx="http://www.adobe.com/2006/mxml"
          text="{defaultValue}">
  <mx:Script>
    <![CDATA[
        [Bindable]
          public var defaultValue:String = "";
      ]]>
    </mx:Script>
</mx:TextInput>
```

Listing 17.6 HelloWorld.mxml: Sets a property on the custom component

```
<?xml version="1.0"?>
<mx:Application xmlns:mx="http://www.adobe.com/2006/mxml"
            backgroundColor="white" xmlns:local="*">
     <local:myTextInput defaultValue="hi mom"/>
</mx:Application>
```

How easy is that? This solution works great in some cases, but will it work for the custom ComboBox?

SOMETIMES YOU NEED LOGIC

Consider the code in listing 17.7, which uses the same approach. How could you use the defaultValue in this case?

Listing 17.7 cbStates.mxml with a public variable: Would this work?

```
<?xml version="1.0" encoding="utf-8"?>
<mx:ComboBox xmlns:mx="http://www.adobe.com/2006/mxml">
  <mx:Script>
    <![CDATA[
      [Bindable]
      public var defaultValue:String = "";
    ]]>
    </mx:Script>
    <mx:dataProvider>
      <mx:Object stateCode="AK" label="Alaska"/>
      <mx:Object stateCode="AL" label="Alabama"/>
      ...
    </mx:dataProvider>
</mx:ComboBox>
```

You don't have a simple text field to display the value as is. What if you set it via the component's creationComplete event? This way, when Flex is done creating the component, that function runs and sets the default U.S. state properly:

```
<mx:ComboBox xmlns:mx="http://www.adobe.com/2006/mxml"
         creationComplete="setDefaultState()">
```

This approach works only if you're setting defaultValue up front all the time:

```
<local:cbStates defaultValue="AZ"/>
```

What if the calling code changes the `defaultValue`? If that occurs, you won't know about it. You need to know the value it has changed, then apply logic to determine which value to use for the `ComboBox`'s `selectedIndex` property.

LEVERAGING BINDING EVENTS TO TRACK CHANGES

One solution taps into Flex's binding mechanism and catches when a binding event occurs—which happens when the value changes.

The new strategy is as follows:

- Use the `creationComplete` idea mentioned previously to initially set the value.
- Use Flex's `ChangeWatcher` object to watch for data binding occurring on your `defaultValue` property. When that happens, update the selected U.S. state.

Listings 17.8 and 17.9 put those two ideas to work by adding the automatic mechanism to intercept changes and handle them.

Listing 17.8 cbStates.mxml: Enhanced to auto-detect changes to defaultValue

```
<?xml version="1.0" encoding="utf-8"?>
<mx:ComboBox xmlns:mx="http://www.adobe.com/2006/mxml"
        creationComplete="initComponent()">
  <mx:Script>
   <![CDATA[
    import mx.binding.utils.*;
    [Bindable]
    public var defaultValue:String = "";

    private function initComponent():void
    {
     setDefaultState(null);                          <-- Sets default if specified
     ChangeWatcher.watch(this, "defaultValue", setDefaultState);   <-- Watches for binding events on default
    }

    public function setDefaultState(evt:Event):void
    {
     for(var x:int=0;x<this.dataProvider.length;x++)
      if(this.dataProvider[x].stateCode == defaultValue)
       this.selectedIndex = x;
    }
   ]]>
  </mx:Script>
  <mx:dataProvider>
   <mx:Object stateCode="AK" label="Alaska"/>
   <mx:Object stateCode="AL" label="Alabama"/>
   ...
  </mx:dataProvider>
</mx:ComboBox>
```

Listing 17.9 HelloWorld.mxml: Set up to change defaultValue

```
<?xml version="1.0"?>
<mx:Application xmlns:mx="http://www.adobe.com/2006/mxml"
          backgroundColor="white" xmlns:local="*">
```

```
  <local:cbStates id="stateSelect" defaultValue="AZ"/>
  <mx:Button click="stateSelect.defaultValue='AL'" label="Change State"/>
</mx:Application>
```

The result of all this hard work is a custom component that can accept an initial property setting and track changes to the settings as well (see figure 17.4). Nice!

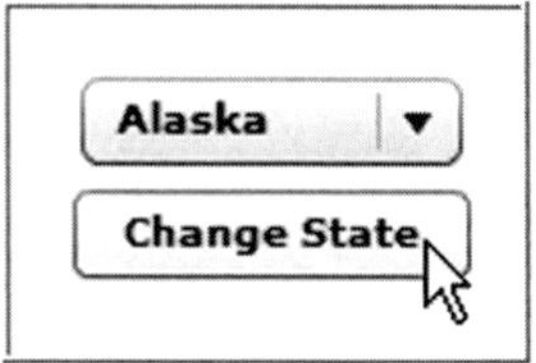

Figure 17.4 The custom component in action with the default U.S. state. When you click the button, the state changes.

Although we could have demonstrated the final code, we wanted to teach you the thought process you'll tend to follow when developing Flex applications and, at the same time, continue to show you different ways of accomplishing results.

You can use a few more tricks to set values. The next is called a *setter function*, which is a neat way of making a function behave like a property to the outside world.

17.4.3 Using a setter function as a property proxy

Flex supports *setter functions*. From the calling code's perspective, the code seems to be setting a regular property, but in reality, it's calling a function.

Using this approach is advantageous because it gives you the best of both worlds:

- The convenience of setting a property
- The ability to apply functional logic when the property is set
- The ability to abstract from the outside world how things are handled internally
- Simplicity from an implementation perspective

NOTE Why bother with the other methods mentioned? It's about knowing your options, so when you come across challenges that are unique to your project, you can leverage the technique that best solves those challenges.

When you use a setter function, the function is declared in a certain way that sets an internal private variable. Converting the previous example (listing 17.8) to use a setter function, you end up with the code shown in listing 17.10.

Listing 17.10 cbStates.mxml: Updated to use a setter function

```
<?xml version="1.0" encoding="utf-8"?>
<mx:ComboBox xmlns:mx="http://www.adobe.com/2006/mxml">
  <mx:Script>
    <![CDATA[
      private var _defaultValue:String="";          <-- Real property, made private
      public function set defaultValue(statecode:String):void   <-- set keyword indicates setter function
      {
        _defaultValue = statecode;
        for(var x:int=0;x<this.dataProvider.length;x++)
          if(this.dataProvider[x].stateCode == _defaultValue)
            this.selectedIndex = x;
      }
    ]]>
```

```
      </mx:Script>
      <mx:dataProvider>
        <mx:Object stateCode="AK" label="Alaska"/>
          <mx:Object stateCode="AL" label="Alabama"/>
        ...
      </mx:dataProvider>
    </mx:ComboBox>
```

Going forward, anything that thinks it's setting a property called `defaultValue` is actually running a function called `defaultValue`, which then sets an internal variable accordingly:

```
<local:cbStates id="stateSelect" defaultValue="AZ"/>
```

TIP Using the underscore prefix (for example, `_defaultValue`) on a variable related to a setter function is an industry convention. It makes no functional difference.

As you can see, setter functions make life easier for the caller and the implementer; they're yet another tool to add to your arsenal as a Flex developer. Now imagine being able to pair setters with binding—you'd have a winning combo.

17.4.4 Using bound parameters

Keep in mind that calling code can pass a bound value rather than set a static property value. Similarly to how you use binding for the `dataProvider` of many `List`-based components, you can support it in your own components:

```
<mx:List dataProvider="{myArrayCollection}"/>
```

Continuing with the U.S. states selector, say you want to support passing in the set of states, because you've decided the only purpose of this component is to present data: it's not this component's job to know where to get the data (which is a plausible scenario if you have an international application and the list of states depends on the related country).

Listing 17.11 passes bound values to listing 17.12, which accepts them.

Listing 17.11 HelloWorld.mxml: Passes a bound property to a custom component

```
<?xml version="1.0"?>
<mx:Application xmlns:mx="http://www.adobe.com/2006/mxml"
  backgroundColor="white" xmlns:local="*">
  <mx:Script>
    <![CDATA[
      import mx.collections.ArrayCollection;
      [Bindable]
      public var myAC:ArrayCollection  = new ArrayCollection([
      {label:"Alaska", stateCode:"AK"},
      {label:"Alabama", stateCode:"AL"},
      {label:"Arizona", stateCode:"AZ"}]);
      ]]>
  </mx:Script>
```

```
  <local:cbStates id="stateSelect" useThisData="{myAC}"/>    <— Propagates changes to myAC
</mx:Application>
```

Listing 17.12 cbStates.mxml: Uses the bound property

```
<?xml version="1.0" encoding="utf-8"?>
<mx:ComboBox xmlns:mx="http://www.adobe.com/2006/mxml"
  dataProvider="{useThisData}">    <— List changes as this value changes
  <mx:Script>
    <![CDATA[
      import mx.collections.ArrayCollection;
      [Bindable]
      public var useThisData:ArrayCollection;
    ]]>
  </mx:Script>
</mx:ComboBox>
```

The binding feature is so universal throughout Flex that you shouldn't overlook it; it can save you a lot of time.

You can see that whether or not you're using binding, there are many ways to get information to the custom component. The next logical step is to get information *from* the custom component. This generally follows the same plan of attack, but the other way around.

17.5 Retrieving values

Setting and passing values is one thing. The other half of that story is being able to get the values. In this chapter's example, once the user has selected a U.S. state, the calling code needs to retrieve the user's current selection (in a real-world application, the code would commit that value to a database at some point).

Similar to passing values, there are a number of ways to accomplish this, and some are more complicated than others. We'll save the best (in this case) for last, but it's worth knowing what your options are. Those options include using functions and properties to retrieve data.

17.5.1 Using a function to retrieve a value

You can use a function not only to set a value but to retrieve one as well. The benefit of providing a function like this is that it lets you perform any necessary logic before you return data. This approach isolates and abstracts the logic used to determine what to send back; you can add custom business logic as necessary, so the calling code doesn't need to worry about it. More work is involved on the custom component side, but it's worth it. You must also keep in mind that no `Bindable` property is available.

Consider a shopping-cart example where items are added, those items have prices, and the user has selected the quantity. Internally, you may not have a variable that keeps track of the total price, but because you're nice to those who use your custom components, you provide a function that calculates the total on the fly.

In this case, you'll send the value back by adding the following function to the cbStates.mxml custom component from listing 17.10:

```
public function getValue():String
{
  return this.selectedItem.stateCode;
}
```

Because the function is public, you can access it with relative ease, as listing 17.13 shows.

Listing 17.13 HelloWorld.mxml: Uses a function to check the current value

```
<?xml version="1.0"?>
<mx:Application xmlns:mx="http://www.adobe.com/2006/mxml"
            backgroundColor="white" xmlns:local="*">
  <mx:Script>
    <![CDATA[
      import mx.controls.Alert;
      public function checkValue():void
      {
        Alert.show(stateSelect.getValue(),"Current U.S. state");
      }
      ]]>
  </mx:Script>
  <local:cbStates id="stateSelect" defaultValue="AZ"/>
  <mx:Button click="checkValue()" label="Check which state is selected"/>
</mx:Application>
```

After compiling and running the application, you'll end up with something that resembles figure 17.5, which is a simple way of retrieving a value from a custom component.

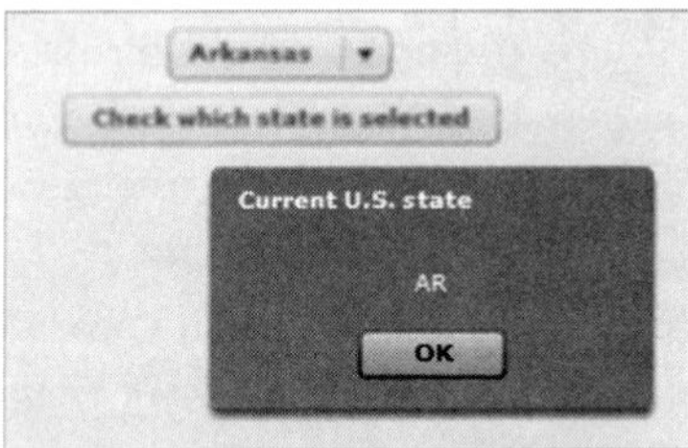

Figure 17.5 Viewing the currently selected U.S. state by accessing the custom component's public function

Now you have the inverse problem that you had with using functions to send information: what if you want to use the convenience of a property? In particular, suppose you want to bind the current value:

```
<mx:Label text="The current state is:
   {stateSelect.getValue()}"/>
```

Unfortunately, the code in listing 17.13 won't work, because you can't bind like that. But never fear; a solution is coming up. Let's see what a property has to offer.

17.5.2 *Using a property to retrieve a value*

No one likes limitations. Why not expose a public variable and let the calling code access it that way? This is achievable—and because your custom component is based on a ComboBox, you can already access a number of common properties like selecte-dIndex and selectedItem (see listing 17.14).

Listing 17.14 HelloWorld.mxml: Accesses existing public properties

```
<?xml version="1.0"?>
<mx:Application xmlns:mx="http://www.adobe.com/2006/mxml"
   backgroundColor="white" xmlns:local="*">
  <mx:Script>
    <![CDATA[
      import mx.controls.Alert;
      public function checkValue():void
      {
        Alert.show(stateSelect.selectedItem.stateCode,"Current State");
      }
      ]]>
  </mx:Script>
  <local:cbStates id="stateSelect"/>
  <mx:Button click="checkValue()" label="Check which state is selected"/>
</mx:Application>
```

After running the code in listing 17.14, you'll end up with the result shown in figure 17.6.

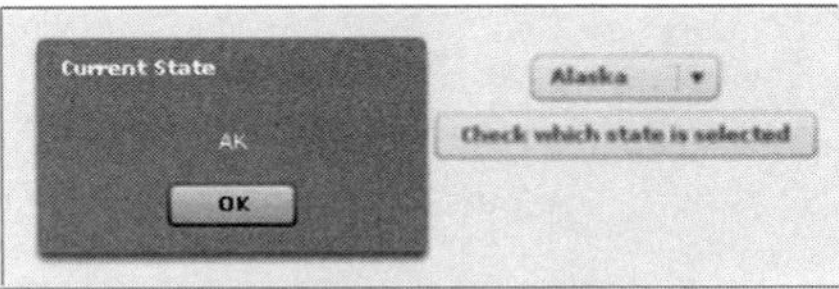

Figure 17.6 The same information can be accessed as a property.

At this point, you need to ask yourself whether you want your application to be designed this way. Although it sounds like a good idea, there's one key problem: you're forcing the calling application to have to know how to get the U.S. state.

You may like it this way, but it breaks the rules of encapsulation. This matters because if you make a change in your custom component that requires the calling code to update how it works with the component, you must make those changes in all the places where the custom component is used (which could be across many applications).

Let's improve on this approach by using a property that the custom component sets based on its internal business rules and by accessing the property from the outside. The first step is to create a `Bindable` and public property that the outside world can use:

```
[Bindable]
public var selectedValue:String="";
```

You then default the property to the initial value (which could be the first item in the list, or it could be passed in via the calling code). In order to support that, you use the `creationComplete` event as follows:

```
creationComplete="selectedValue=selectedItem.stateCode"
```

The last thing you need to do is make sure you update `selectedValue` whenever the user changes to a different U.S. state, using the `Change` event:

```
change="selectedValue=selectedItem.stateCode"
```

TIP In the real world, you'd probably have the `Change` event call a function (such as `setValue`) whose purpose would be to apply any necessary logic as it sets the applicable value. That logic could do more than determine the right value; it could gray out the component visually or reset to a fresh state to start the process over.

Putting it all together, the custom component is coming along nicely, as you can see in listing 17.15.

Listing 17.15 cbStates.mxml: Component updated with a bindable public property

```
<?xml version="1.0" encoding="utf-8"?>
<mx:ComboBox xmlns:mx="http://www.adobe.com/2006/mxml"
       creationComplete="selectedValue=selectedItem.stateCode"
       change="selectedValue=selectedItem.stateCode">
<mx:Script>
 <![CDATA[
  private var _defaultValue:String="";


  [Bindable]                                        Component users
  public var selectedValue:String="";               can bind to this

  public function getValue():String
  {                                                 Updates function
   return selectedValue;                            to return value
  }

  public function set defaultValue(statecode:String):void
  {
    _defaultValue = statecode;
    for(var x:int=0;x<this.dataProvider.length;x++)
     if(this.dataProvider[x].stateCode == _defaultValue)
      this.selectedIndex = x;
  }
 ]]>
 </mx:Script>
 <mx:dataProvider>
  <mx:Object stateCode="AK" label="Alaska"/>
  <mx:Object stateCode="AL" label="Alabama"/>
  . . .
 </mx:dataProvider>
</mx:ComboBox>
```

You update the previous section's `getValue` function to make use of `selectedValue` by returning it as is.

The calling code also uses a new feature: data binding. It can continue to access the value on an as-needed basis, or it can use binding to get the value in real time, as listing 17.16 shows.

Listing 17.16 Taking advantage of the bindable public property

```
<?xml version="1.0"?>
<mx:Application xmlns:mx="http://www.adobe.com/2006/mxml"
  backgroundColor="white" xmlns:local="*">
 <mx:Script>
```

```
  <![CDATA[
    import mx.controls.Alert;
    public function checkValue():void
    {
      Alert.show(stateSelect.selectedValue,"Current State");
    }
    ]]>
  </mx:Script>
  <local:cbStates id="stateSelect" defaultValue="AZ"/>
  <mx:Button click="checkValue()" label="Check which state is selected"/>
  <mx:Label text="The current state is: {stateSelect.selectedValue}"/>
</mx:Application>
```

Binds on component's property

Figure 17.7 shows how the currently selected U.S. state is displayed in real time using data binding.

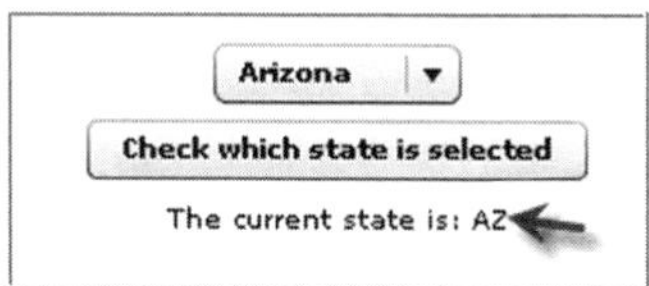

Figure 17.7 Binding on a custom component's public property

Your custom component encapsulates business logic and provides the convenience of a `Bindable` public property. The component is even more work to implement—but it's worth it.

If you hadn't implemented your own `Bindable` property, the glaring disadvantage would be that you'd force users of your component to have to know how to determine the current value based on existing public properties. In this case, that wouldn't be a big deal, because we all know `ComboBoxes` have a `selectedItem` property, but here are some things to consider:

- What if you need to add custom logic?
- Do you want the calling code to have to know how to evaluate the value?

Functions have their strengths, and properties have their conveniences; but combining them in what's known as a *getter function* gives you the best of both worlds.

17.5.3 Using a getter function as a property proxy

You probably saw this coming: If there's a setter function, there's probably a getter function, right?

Absolutely! The getter function lets you combine a function and a property. Using the same approach as with a setter, let's try this by doing the following:

1. Switch `selectedValue` to a `private` variable and rename all occurrences of `selectedValue` in `cbStates.mxml` to `_selectedValue`.
2. Create a public get-property function:

```
[Bindable]
private var _selectedValue:String="";

public function get selectedValue():String
{
  return _selectedValue;
}
```

Without any changes to the calling code, you should be able to run it as is and see the output shown in figure 17.8.

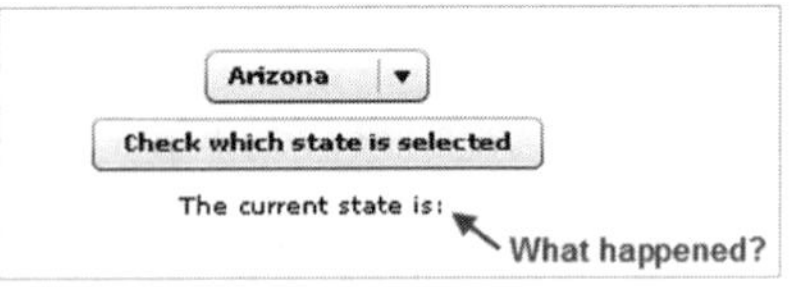

Figure 17.8 Binding doesn't seem to work with this approach.

Houston, we have a problem! The data binding on the `_selectedValue` property doesn't seem to be propagating to the calling code. That's because the calling code is binding to the property and not the function. The next step is to bind to the function itself:

```
[Bindable]
public function get selectedValue():String
{
  return _selectedValue;
}
```

NOTE Normally you can't bind to a function—it works only with getter and setter functions.

If you save at this point, you'll get an error from Flex Builder stating: *[Bindable] on read-only getter is unnecessary and will be ignored.* This occurs when a getter doesn't have a corresponding setter. As far as Flex knows, that property will never change (without a setter), so why bother trying to bind to it?

Obviously the property can change, just not through a setter in this case. This is another one of those implementation decisions that gives you choices:

- Create a real setter function that allows you to set `_selectedValue`. You may want to let the calling code arbitrarily change the selection, or you may not want to allow the variable to be set directly.
- Create a fake setter function that doesn't do anything other than make Flex Builder happy.

In most cases, you're fine with the first option—the setter function still lets you add any logic you need to act as a guardian in front of the property. You can also use this approach as an opportunity to convert the `defaultValue` setter to one that handles `selectedValue` instead; this way, the solution needs only one setter instead of (potentially) two.

The final version of cbStates.mxml is shown in listing 17.17.

Listing 17.17 cbStates.mxml: Getter and setter functions for a single property

```
<?xml version="1.0" encoding="utf-8"?>
<mx:ComboBox xmlns:mx="http://www.adobe.com/2006/mxml"
    creationComplete="selectedValue=selectedItem.stateCode"
    change="selectedValue=selectedItem.stateCode">
  <mx:Script>
    <![CDATA[
      [Bindable]
      private var _selectedValue:String="";
```

Updated to implicitly use setter function

```
      [Bindable]
      public function get selectedValue():String
      {
        return _selectedValue;
      }

      public function set selectedValue(statecode:String):void
      {
        _selectedValue = statecode;
        for(var x:int=0;x<this.dataProvider.length;x++)
          if(this.dataProvider[x].stateCode == _selectedValue)
            this.selectedIndex = x;
      }
    ]]>
  </mx:Script>
  <mx:dataProvider>
    <mx:Object stateCode="AK" label="Alaska"/>
    <mx:Object stateCode="AL" label="Alabama"/>
    . . .
  </mx:dataProvider>
</mx:ComboBox>
```

To wrap it up, you make a final change in the calling code to use the getter and setter functions by setting and binding on what the custom component thinks is a property:

```
<local:cbStates id="stateSelect" selectedValue="AZ"/>
<mx:Label text="The current state is: {stateSelect.selectedValue}"/>
```

You've got encapsulation going on, you're providing convenience to the calling function, and you know what your options are if you need to expose more or control more.

Now that you've conquered the world of creating simple custom components and can send and receive data, let's branch out into composite components.

17.6 Creating composite components

You now know how to make a simple custom component with the ability to pass information and get that information back. This is the bulk of what making a custom component is all about; the remainder of the chapter explains the rest of the picture.

Next up are composite components, which sound complicated but aren't. The term implies that you're basing your component on a container rather than another type of component. By basing your component on a container, you can fit multiple components inside it; it's almost like including a small application.

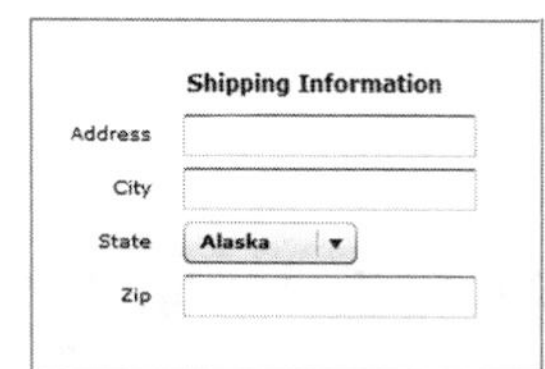

Figure 17.9 Shipping information in a composite component

Let's take the example we've been working with (the state selector) and expand it by making a composite component that captures a shipping address (see figure 17.9).

Listing 17.18 shows the code that produces this composite component. It uses a container to house a number of routine Flex components. The component is then invoked by the application in listing 17.19.

Listing 17.18 shippingAddress.mxml: Composite custom component

```
<?xml version="1.0" encoding="utf-8"?>
<mx:VBox xmlns:mx="http://www.adobe.com/2006/mxml" xmlns:local="*">
  <mx:Form>
    <mx:FormHeading label="Shipping Information"/>
    <mx:FormItem label="Address">
      <mx:TextInput id="frmAddress"/>
        </mx:FormItem>
    <mx:FormItem label="City">
      <mx:TextInput id="frmCity"/>
    </mx:FormItem>
        <mx:FormItem label="State">
      <local:cbStates/>                    <-- Custom component in
     </mx:FormItem>                            a custom component
     <mx:FormItem label="Zip">
       <mx:TextInput id="frmZip"/>
     </mx:FormItem>
  </mx:Form>
</mx:VBox>
```

Listing 17.19 HelloWorld.mxml: Uses a composite custom component

```
<?xml version="1.0"?>
<mx:Application xmlns:mx="http://www.adobe.com/2006/mxml"
    backgroundColor="white" xmlns:local="*">
  <local:shippingAddress id="shipping"/>
</mx:Application>
```

Notice anything cool? You have a custom component inside a custom component! Being able to break things into small reusable pieces is the key to success with custom components.

Everything else mentioned thus far applies to composite custom components, including providing functions to the calling code and passing and retrieving values.

One advantage of composites is that you have more control over layout and positioning (in addition to being able to put many things inside them), but the onus is on you to provide enough functions and properties that the calling code can work with your composite component. Because the component is based on a container, users have no ability to expect or predict anything other than what the root container provides.

Until now, our discussion has been all about Flex MXML custom components. But don't count out ActionScript, because it too can be used to create custom components.

17.7 Creating ActionScript components

As we mentioned previously, everything we've shown you so far can also be done through ActionScript. Those of you coming from tag-based languages (like ColdFusion and HTML) will naturally want to stick to the MXML route, and that's perfectly all right.

But as you progress in your Flex skills and become more comfortable, you'll find that ActionScript can be your friend. Let's see if we can begin that process by examining the state-selector custom component in ActionScript (see listing 17.20).

Listing 17.20 cbStatesScripted.as: ActionScript version of cbStates.mxml

```
package
{
  import flash.events.Event;

  import mx.controls.ComboBox;
  public class cbStatesScripted extends ComboBox
  {
    [Bindable]
    private var _selectedValue:String="";

    public function cbStatesScripted()
    {
      super();
      dataProvider = [{label:"Alaska", stateCode:"AK"},
                 {label:"Alabama", stateCode:"AL"},
                 {label:"Arizona", stateCode:"AZ"}];
       addEventListener("creationComplete", setItem);
       addEventListener("change", setItem);
    }

    public function setItem(evt:Event):void
    {
      selectedValue=selectedItem.stateCode;
        }

    [Bindable]
    public function get selectedValue():String
    {
      return _selectedValue;
    }

    public function set selectedValue(statecode:String):void
    {
        _selectedValue = statecode;
        for(var x:int=0;x<this.dataProvider.length;x++)
          if(this.dataProvider[x].stateCode == _selectedValue)
            this.selectedIndex = x;
    }
  }
}
```

❶ Package declaration

❷ Import and extend class

❸ Create constructor

❹ Call super function

❺ Import and extend class

Here's how it works:

1. Create a file called cbStatesScripted.as.
2. The main block is encapsulated by a `package` declaration ❶. A `package` indicates a directory and is a way to group multiple ActionScript classes together. You're using the same directory as the main MXML file; later we'll talk about how you can structure custom components.
3. Import the ActionScript class you're basing the component on (in this case, a `ComboBox`), and create a class of your own that extends it ❷.
4. The constructor function ❸ has the same name as the class. It's called automatically by Flex when it creates instances of this class.

5 The `super` function is called to make sure the constructor of the parent class is executed ❹ (the `ComboBox`'s class constructor).
6 Register to listen for the `creationComplete` and `change` events ❺.
7 Everything else remains the same, except that in order to invoke it you would use `<local:cbStatesScripted/>` instead of `<local:cbStates>`.

This technique is a little more work; but one of the advantages is you can override the functions from the parent class. This comes with an expense: You can't work with the component visually in Flex Builder.

At this point, you may feel that your back is against the wall, because you have to make a decision regarding using MXML versus ActionScript. But a little trick can get you the best of both: the *code-behind* technique.

Using the code-behind technique

MXML custom components can't override their parent class's functions, and ActionScript components aren't visually represented in Flex Builder. But using a technique called code behind lets you get the benefits of both approaches.

You begin by creating a typical ActionScript custom component (as in section 17.8). Then you create an MXML custom component that extends from that the ActionScript component (as it would from anything else).

Listing 17.21 shows how to base an MXML custom component on cbStatesScripted.as from listing 17.20, using the code-behind technique.

Listing 17.21 cbStatesFromScripted.mxml: Uses the code-behind technique

```
<?xml version="1.0" encoding="utf-8"?>
<local:cbStatesScripted xmlns:mx="http://www.adobe.com/2006/mxml"
   xmlns:local="*"/>
```

That's it! You could add more stuff to the MXML component if you wanted (some styling, for example), but it's up to you where you want to implement certain logic.

Now that you can create custom components, structure them, and pass data back and forth, there's one piece you don't want to overlook: the form of events. Flex is an event-driven environment, and you'll want to tap into events as a communication vehicle for your custom components.

17.8 Custom events

Because a custom component inherits from another component, all events from the parent are present (`creationComplete`, `change`, and so on). But a custom component can dispatch its own events, which implies that other things can listen for it.

Listings 17.22 and 17.23 put this to a test by defining an event called `invalidState`, which is dispatched if the calling code tries to set the custom component to a U.S. state that doesn't exist.

Listing 17.22 cbStates.mxml: Dispatches an `invalidState` event

```
<?xml version="1.0" encoding="utf-8"?>
<mx:ComboBox xmlns:mx="http://www.adobe.com/2006/mxml"
        creationComplete="selectedValue=selectedItem.stateCode"
        change="selectedValue=selectedItem.stateCode">
 <mx:Metadata>                                   <-- ❶ Define event
  [Event(name="invalidState")]
 </mx:Metadata>

<mx:Script>
   <![CDATA[
   [Bindable]
   private var _selectedValue:String="";

   [Bindable]
   public function get selectedValue():String
   {
     return _selectedValue;
   }

   public function set selectedValue(statecode:String):void
   {
      var isFound:Boolean=false;
      _selectedValue = statecode;
      for(var x:int=0;x<this.dataProvider.length;x++)
       if(this.dataProvider[x].stateCode == _selectedValue)
       {
         this.selectedIndex = x;
         isFound=true;
       }
      if(!isFound)
         dispatchEvent(new Event("invalidState"));   <-- ❷ Dispatch event
    }
   ]]>
  </mx:Script>
  <mx:dataProvider>
    <mx:Object stateCode="AK" label="Alaska"/>
    <mx:Object stateCode="AL" label="Alabama"/>
    . . .
  </mx:dataProvider>
</mx:ComboBox>
```

You define the event using the `Metadata` tag ❶. It tells the Flex compiler and Flex Builder that this component potentially dispatches this event. Then you dispatch the event using the `dispatchEvent` function ❷.

Listing 17.23 HelloWorld.mxml: Captures the `invalidState` event

```
<?xml version="1.0"?>
<mx:Application xmlns:mx="http://www.adobe.com/2006/mxml"
```

```
  backgroundColor="white" xmlns:local="*">
 <mx:Script>
   <![CDATA[
   import mx.controls.Alert;
   public function invalidStateHandler():void
   {
     mx.controls.Alert.show("Invalid State Specified");      Function to    ❶
   }                                                         handle event
   ]]>
 </mx:Script>
 <local:cbStates id="myStates" invalidState="invalidStateHandler()"/>
 <mx:Button click="myStates.selectedValue='BB'"
       label="Set to fake State"/>
</mx:Application>
```

In the calling code, you set up a function to handle the event ❶.

If you execute this code, you should see a pop-up, as shown in figure 17.10.

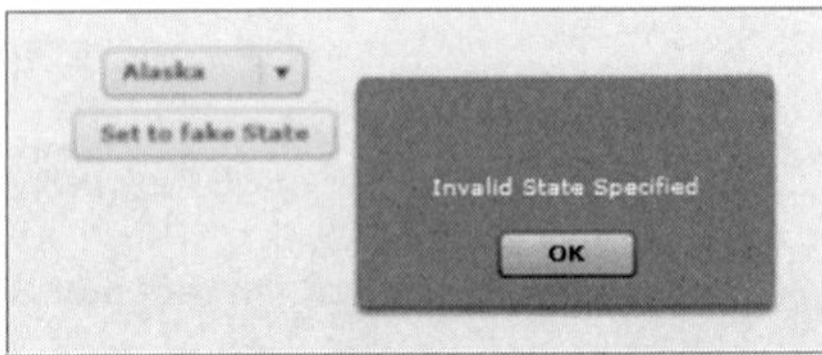

Figure 17.10 Pop-up called as the result of a custom event being caught

That's pretty cool; you don't have to explicitly check a property or a function to find out that this event occurred. You just tell the component, "I care when this happens," and Flex's event mechanism takes care of the rest.

17.8.1 Passing along the event object

Optionally, you can also pass along the event object that gets generated when you dispatch the event. To do so, modify the `Metadata` tag as follows:

```
<mx:Metadata>
[Event(name="invalidState", type="flash.events.Event")]
</mx:Metadata>
```

Then, to take advantage of the event object, you can pass that along in your calling code's event handler:

```
<mx:Script>
  <![CDATA[
   import mx.controls.Alert;
   public function invalidStateHandler(evt:Event):void
   {
    mx.controls.Alert.show("Invalid State Specified");
   }
  ]]>
</mx:Script>
<local:cbStates id="myStates" invalidState="invalidStateHandler(event)"/>
```

We've kept everything in one directory to keep things simple, but in the real world you'll want to organize your custom components in some kind of folder structure, and to do this you'll want to use something called a namespace to make it easy to reference your components.

17.9 Namespaces and structure

The last thing we'll talk about in this chapter is where your custom components live. The examples have kept everything in the same directory for simplicity, but many examples on the web use a subdirectory named components. As you build real-life applications, you'll want to come up with a folder structure that makes sense for you.

This section discusses key considerations in developing that folder structure as well as the related mechanisms Flex provides to support you.

17.9.1 The MX namespace

Namespaces are a simple mechanism that tells Flex which component you're talking about. For example, all out-of-the-box components have a namespace as specified by the following code:

```
<mx:Application xmlns:mx="http://www.adobe.com/2006/mxml"/>
```

`xmlns` tells the Flex compiler that whenever you prefix something with `mx` (for example, `<mx:VBox/>`), you're talking about the component that comes with Flex. Why does that matter? Because nothing prevents you from making your own `VBox` component, and Flex needs to know which one you're referring to.

17.9.2 The local namespace

In the examples thus far, when we referred to a custom component it was prefixed with a label called `local`. For example:

```
<mx:Application xmlns:mx="http://www.adobe.com/2006/mxml" xmlns:local="*">
  <local:cbStates/>
</mx:Application>
```

The `local` moniker is a namespace, and the `xmlns:local="*"` instructs Flex that when you prefix any component with `local`, the component you're referring to is in the same directory. You don't have to use the `local` label, but that's what Flex Builder defaults to if you reference a component in the same directory.

17.9.3 Directory structure and namespaces

Many examples on the web place custom components in a subdirectory called components, as shown in figure 17.11.

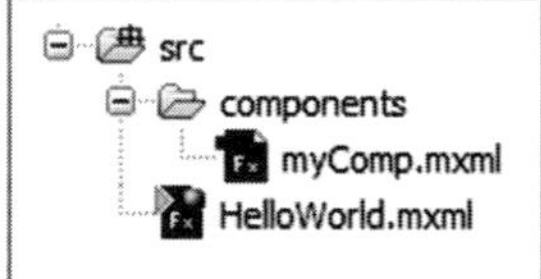

Figure 17.11 Placing your components in a folder structure is a good idea.

You can, for example, map a `comp` namespace to that folder and invoke the custom components inside it, as listing 17.24 shows.

Listing 17.24 Using a component subdirectory namespace

```
<?xml version="1.0"?>
<mx:Application xmlns:mx="http://www.adobe.com/2006/mxml"
   xmlns:comp="components.*">
 <comp:myComp/>
```

```
</mx:Application>
```

You can go as deep as necessary in your folder structure, separating subdirectories with dots. For example, components/userinterface/widgets maps to `components.userinterface.widgets`.

Use your folder structure to organize your components, but use namespaces to map and reference them. This poses one key challenge: What if someone uses the exact same naming structure that you have? An industry-accepted standard called *reverse-domain syntax* aims to solve this problem.

REVERSE-DOMAIN SYNTAX

Because you can download other component packages or make your own, the potential exists for many people to create the same directory structure or component names and thus cause a conflict.

To avoid this conflict, the reverse-domain syntax is generally adopted and recommended. You use your organization's domain as a folder structure—but in reverse.

Suppose you have a collection of UI components for dopejam.com. You can package that collection as `com.dopejam.components.ui`. Other popular nomenclatures include the application's name as part of the path (that way, if the organization has multiple applications that tend to have a common structure, you can differentiate).

This works great for setting things up in MXML, but you can apply it to ActionScript as well as part of its package feature.

17.9.4 Namespace in ActionScript

In ActionScript, you incorporate the directory structure as part of the `package` declaration—if you don't specify a namespace, it's the same as a local namespace, but if you throw an ActionScript custom component into your components subdirectory, you update the package name as follows:

```
package components
{
  import mx.controls.ComboBox;
  public class widget extends ComboBox
  {
    . . .
  }
}
```

This code exists as the widget.as file, as shown in figure 17.12.

Note that the package naming must match the directory structure, or Flex Builder won't be able to find it.

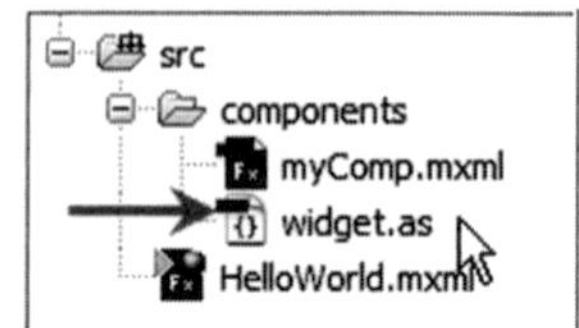

Figure 17.12 Widget.as uses a package components namespace.

17.10 Summary

Making custom components is where you'll spend a good portion of your time as you scale out your Flex applications, so it's worth getting as solid a foundation as possible.

All visual components inherit from a top-level interface object called `UIComponent`; when you make a custom component, one way or another you're inheriting from `UIComponent`. You get all the events, styles, properties, and functions that come with the parent you're inheriting from.

Focus on encapsulation, and try to make your components reusable by limiting their understanding of how your application works; then they should be able to stand as independent widgets that many applications can use. If your custom component doesn't care who is calling it and what the caller does, and if the caller doesn't care how the custom component works, you've done a good job.

Chapter 18 takes what you've learned here and continues on the path of reducing duplication by exploring the ability to share things like custom components across multiple applications.

18 Advanced reusability in Flex

This chapter covers:

- Runtime shared libraries
- Shared reusability
- The Module API
- Adding patches
- Refactoring

So far, you've learned the basics of OOP and how to make custom classes. We've also looked at how to develop cool components that spit out pieces of functionality. In this chapter, we'll give you an overview of some of Flex's advanced reusability features.

What is *reusability*? We use the term loosely to mean ways you can reuse chunks of code either in the same application or across multiple applications. The concept of reusability isn't unique to Flex; each language provides mechanisms to achieve it. The more you're able to reuse, the faster you can develop new applications by leveraging existing code. From a maintenance perspective, you can achieve faster turnaround time when implementing changes. With Flex, reusability can also result in improved performance.

Previous chapters have covered common reusability techniques, including using custom classes and custom components. One of the advanced reusability features is the *runtime shared library* (RSL). By the end of this chapter, you'll have a strong starting point to understanding what RSLs are as well as Flex's additional reuse capabilities.

A Flex application (which is compiled to a SWF file) can include several kinds of advanced elements: SWC files, RSLs, and modules.

Leveraging these pieces will enable your applications to load quickly and will make them easy to maintain in the long run. You'll learn what each of these elements means for you and how to utilize them in your Flex 3 development.

Let's first explore the primary element: the SWC file.

18.1 SWC files

SWC (pronounced "swick") files aren't to be confused with SWF (pronounced "swiff") files. To use a Java analogy, the SWF file is like the .class file (the executable); a SWC is like a .jar file (an archive containing supporting items).

SWC files are containers that can house all the classes, assets, and components that you want to put in them and reuse. Most of the third-party components and libraries you'll use will come in SWC files because they're much easier to distribute than many .as files.

If you open a SWC file with WinZip or any compression program, you'll see a library.swf file and a catalog.xml file. The SWF file contains all your code/assets, and catalog.xml tells the compiler where to look for a class or asset.

Most often, SWC files are used for themes and code you want to share during runtime. Let's briefly explore the benefits of using a SWC file for theme development.

Let's look at how to use SWC files for runtime shared libraries.

18.2 Runtime shared libraries

RSLs are code that is loaded during runtime by multiple applications and domains (for domains, some restrictions apply). Suppose you create a new class that you'll use in 20 applications. Instead of having this class be compiled in all 20 applications and take up an extra 300 KB, you can trim those 300 KB by having the applications load the class during runtime.

This is also a neat way to deploy patches to your application until you release the next major version, as we'll discuss this later. You'll see a big performance increase only when you're developing really large Flex applications, which require the same components and classes.

We'll explore three different types of RSLs:

- *Standard*—Cached in the browser and only available to a single domain
- *Cross-domain*—Cached by the browser; can be accessed by another domain
- *Framework*—Cached by the Flash Player

Learning about RSLs may seem daunting when you're faced with terms like standard, cross-domain, and framework RSLs, but in reality they're simple concepts. Let's start by learning about standard RSLs.

18.2.1 Standard RSLs

To understand how to use a standard RSL, you'll create a simple class and make it into an RSL for use in other applications from the same domain. The first step is to create a new Flex library project:

1. In Flex Builder, create a new Flex library project by choosing File > New > Flex Library Project.
2. Name the project `MyRSL`.
3. Click Finish.

You now have an empty library project. If you already have classes that you want to convert into a SWC file, all you have to do is drag them into the library folder; Flex Builder will compile them into a SWC file for you.

In this case, you'll create a class to use:

1. Right-click the project folder, and create a new class.
2. Give the class a package of `com.gunix.myrsl` and a class name of `MyClass`.
3. Extend the `Button` class by specifying `Button` for the superclass.

NOTE Because you learned about objects and classes previously, you should be fairly comfortable with creating a new class. If you need a refresher, see chapter 16.

In this class, you'll add a simple label to the button; listing 18.1 shows the full code for the class.

Listing 18.1 Simple class to use in an RSL

```
package com.gunix.myrsl
{
  import mx.controls.Button;

  public class MyClass extends Button
  {
    public function MyClass()
    {
      super();
      this.label = 'Hey Look, I am Dynamically Loaded';
    }
  }
}
```

Creates a new label for the button

After you've done this, it's always good practice to clean your project. You do this in Flex Builder via the following steps:

1. Click the Project menu item on the Flex Builder toolbar.
2. Select the Clean option.
3. Clean recompiles your project and creates a new SWC file in the /bin folder, ready to be deployed.

There you have it; you've created your first SWC file. Next, you'll learn how you use this file in multiple projects.

18.2.2 *Making your Flex application use RSL*

What we've done so far is to create a class and compile it into a SWC file. This now gives us the convenience of being able to access the SWC and the classes inside it from any application we're building.

When working on multiple projects that use shared classes like these, it can be useful to store the SWCs in a centralized folder such as C:\Flex\SWC\. This would include not only SWCs that you've made but also others that you've downloaded.

A SWC is a shared library, and it can be linked either statically or dynamically. In the static approach you're embedding everything inside the SWC into the final SWF, which from an application development perspective is convenient if you have classes and assets (for example, images) that you use across multiple applications. However, this still results in a large SWF file.

Dynamic linkage is what makes a SWC an RSL (and thus the cooler approach) in that it's loading the classes as needed during runtime. Let's leave our SWC file where it is and create a project that can make use of it.

CREATING A PROJECT TO USE THE RSL

For now, leave the SWC file where it is. You'll create a Flex project and then configure it to use the RSL. Follow these steps:

1. In Flex Builder, create a new project called `RSLTest`.
2. In the project navigator, right-click the `RSLTest` project and select Properties.
3. Select Flex Build Path (see figure 18.1).
4. Click the Library Path tab to see the external libraries loaded into the Flex application.
5. One of the first things you should always do when you want to use an RSL is to make the entire Flex framework an RSL. To do this, change the Framework Linkage option in the Properties for RSLTest dialog box to Runtime Shared Library.

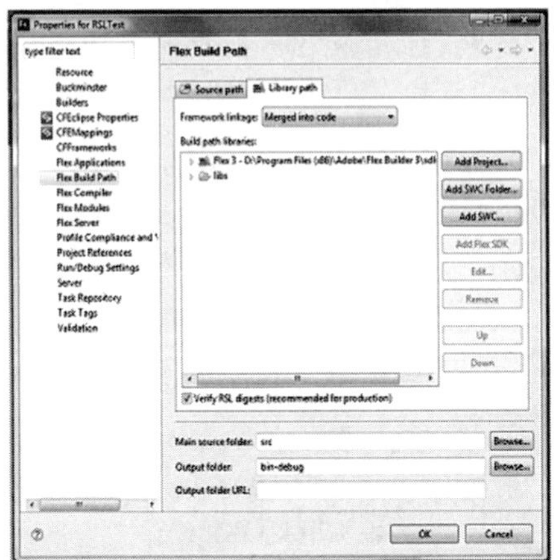

Figure 18.1 Select Flex Build Path in the SWC build dialog box.

Doing so creates a SWZ file and a SWF file containing the Flex framework. A SWZ file is a digitally signed Adobe SWF file that can be cached into the Flash Player. The next time the end user views your Flex application, the load time will be drastically shorter because Flash Player won't have to reload the Flex framework.

But why does Flex Builder create a SWF file when it already has a SWZ file? Framework caching became available in version r115 of the Flash Player. By the time you read this, r115 will be installed on 90% of computers; but Flex also creates the SWF file so that if the end user doesn't have r115, the SWF file will be cached in the browser and will act like a standard RSL or a cross-domain RSL. One thing to be aware of is that the browser cache is easily cleared by the user, which would require caching the framework again.

Next up is turning the `myRSL` project into an RSL.

CREATING THE RSL

Now that you've made your Flex framework an RSL, you have to also make `MyRSL` an RSL. First, you must import it into the library:

1. Click Add SWC in the Properties for RSLTest dialog box.
2. Browse to the path of your SWC file.
3. Click OK.

You'll see the `MyRSL` SWC file added to the application library. But you still haven't made it an RSL: if you expand the `MyRSL` tree node, you'll see that the link type is merged to code. Merged to code isn't what you want, because it's the same thing as having `MyRSL` compiled in the application (via static linkage).

Instead, you want to make the SWC an RSL by dynamically linking to it. To do so, continue from the last step and follow these steps:

1. Click the link type, and click Edit (see figure 18.2).
2. In the resulting Edit dialog box, select the Use Same Linkage as Framework check box. This option gives `MyRSL` the same linkage as the Flex framework, which we've made dynamic and thus would make `MyRSL` dynamic as well and ergo an RSL.
3. The Deployment Path/URL is now MyRSL.swf. This is the file that will be cached by the browser and will be shared by all applications that use this class.
4. Click OK.
5. Click OK in the Library dialog box. Flex Builder will compile the application with the new properties.

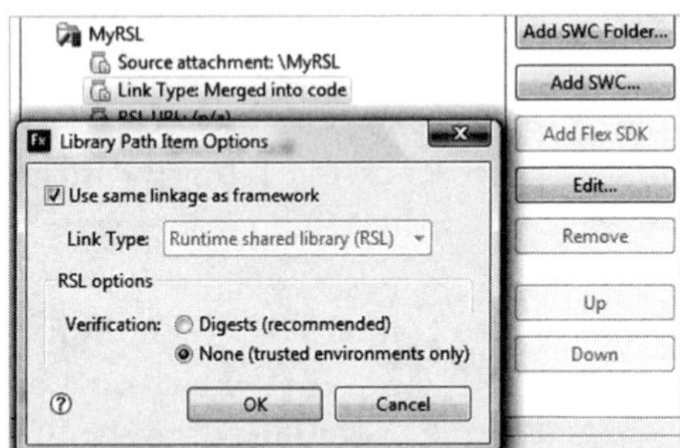

Figure 18.2 Select the Link Type option, then click the Edit button to change the linkage of a SWC library.

You've linked your custom class and made it so that it will be cached by the browser and used in all applications that use this class in your domain.

You'll need to perform these steps for every application you want to be able to share this class. But when you upload your application to your domain, you'll need only:

- One MyRSL.swf file
- One Framework.swz file
- One Framwork.swf file per domain

Make sure the path of the RSL is the same throughout your applications, so the Flash Player knows where to check whether the file is cached in order to load it. You'll see a significant difference in application load times, because the Flash Player won't have to load the 200–300 KB Flex framework or your custom classes each time you view the application.

In the next section, you'll learn about the next element of making a good SWF file: the module.

18.3 Modular Flex application development

One of the neat new features in Flex 3 is that you can develop Flex applications using modules. By using modules, you encapsulate the different parts of your application. A key benefit is modules being independent of one another. If the application has a bug, it's much easier to locate and fix.

The primary difference in using modular programming rather than component-driven programming is that modules are loaded and unloaded at runtime rather than being compiled in the SWF file. This means your SWF file size is greatly decreased, your Flex application is structured much better, and you can reuse the modules in other applications if you wish.

18.3.1 Components vs. modules

As we stated earlier, the main difference between components and modules is the fact that components are compiled in the Flex application and modules aren't. But you can still do the same things with modules that you're able to do with components.

They consist of essentially the same code, except that a module starts with the <mx:Module/> tag and a component starts with a tag of the class it's extending. Following the <mx:Module/> tag, you're free to copy and paste your component code, making the module behave exactly like your component.

Modules are loaded when the Flex display list sees that the module needs to be shown. For example, if your module is on a different view state (see chapter 13), it isn't loaded from an external SWF file until the view state is shown.

On the other hand, if you're using a component, it's embedded in the Flex application. Regardless of whether or not it's shown, it takes up space in the SWF file.

18.3.2 Creating a simple module

Let's create a simple module that holds a button. Create a new Flex application project, or use the one you previously created, and follow these steps:

1 On the Flex Builder menu bar, choose File > New > MXML Module to open the dialog box shown in figure 18.3.

2 Type the name of the module you're creating, and specify whether you want to be able to use this module in other applications.

If you indicate that you want to use this module only for this Flex application, Flex removes unnecessary classes from the module and optimizes it by making it smaller in size and faster to load. If you specify that you want to be able to use the module in other applications, Flex gives the module the functionality of being independent of the application; you'll be able to use it in other projects.

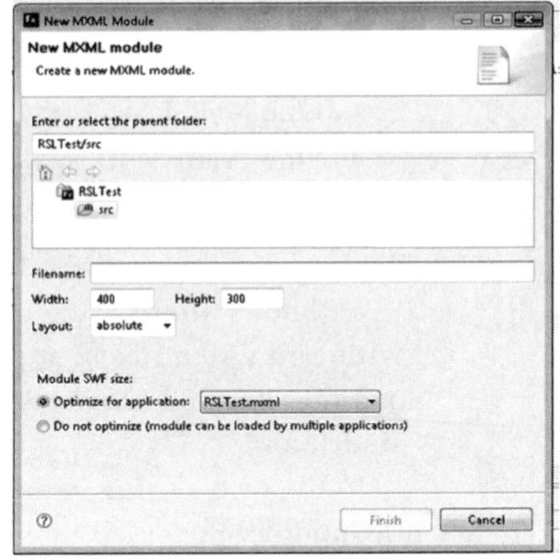

Figure 18.3 Creating a new MXML module

For this example, select the Optimize for Application option.

3 Click Finish.

After you've created your module, you're free to add things like buttons, panels, and canvases—anything you need to create the features or user interface you want.

You may wonder how you'll access data from the module in your application. Flex has a solution called the *Module API*.

18.3.3 Loading modules the MXML way with the Module API

Now that you've created your module, how do you use it in your Flex application? Your first instinct might be to go to the component library in Flex Builder, find your module in the Custom folder, and add it.

That approach will work. But doing so is the same as using components and doesn't have any impact on your application load times or size. So how do you load a module in Flex?

You can do so two ways. The easier one uses the `<mx:ModuleLoader/>` tag and passes the `url` parameter the path of your module:

```
<mx:ModuleLoader url="MyModule.swf" x="100" y="100" width="356"
   height="274" />
```

This creates a new instance of the `MyModule.swf` module and loads it in Flex when the `<ModuleLoader/>` tag is called. This is a good solution for beginners who are just scratching the power of modules, but if you want greater control and the ability to unload modules when you don't need them, you're going to get your hands wet in ActionScript.

18.3.4 Loading and unloading modules with ActionScript

Before you learn how to load and unload modules using ActionScript, you need to learn how the Module API works. It's located in the `mx.modules` package, and it has one interface and four classes. You don't have to know the ins and outs of the classes and interfaces, but table 18.1 covers them briefly.

Table 18.1 The Module API package

Name	Type	Description
`IModuleInfo`	Interface	Handler for the module being used
`Module`	Class	Base class for an MXML module
`ModuleBase`	Class	Base class for an ActionScript 3 module
`ModuleLoader`	Class	Similar to `SWFLoader` but can interact with the module
`ModuleManager`	Class	Manages the loading and unloading of modules in the Flex application

To load and unload modules, you use the `ModuleManager` class to manage the `ModuleLoader` tag. First, create a new `ModuleLoader` tag in your Flex application and give its `id` property the value `MyModule` (see listing 18.2).

Listing 18.2 New module using MXML

```
<?xml version="1.0" encoding="utf-8"?>
<mx:Application xmlns:mx="http://www.adobe.com/2006/mxml"
          layout="absolute">
   <mx:ModuleLoader id="MyModule" url="MyModule.swf" x="100" y="100"
      width="356" height="274" />
</mx:Application>
```

Run the application, and make sure the module is being loaded; you may see a one-second delay in loading the module, depending on how big it is and what its contents are.

Next, create a new button named `unloadBtn`, and title it appropriately using the label property, as shown in listing 18.3.

Listing 18.3 Unloading a module using MXML

```
<mx:Application xmlns:mx="http://www.adobe.com/2006/mxml"
   layout="absolute" >
   <mx:ModuleLoader id="MyModule" url="MyModule.swf" x="100"
      y="100" width="356" height="274" />
   <mx:Button x="348" y="382" label="Unload Module" id="unloadBtn"/>
</mx:Application>
```

Now, create a <mx:Script/> tag in which to put your ActionScript, and create a function called `unloadMyModule()`.

In this function, call MyModule's `unloadModule()` function (which is a function of `ModuleLoader`). See listing 18.4.

Listing 18.4 Unloading a module using ActionScript

```
<?xml version="1.0" encoding="utf-8"?>
<mx:Application xmlns:mx="http://www.adobe.com/2006/mxml"
          layout="absolute" >
<mx:Script>
  <![CDATA[
   private function unloadMyModule():void
   {
     MyModule.unloadModule();
   }
  ]]>
</mx:Script>
 <mx:ModuleLoader url="MyModule.swf" x="100" y="100" width="356"
           height="274"  id="MyModule"/>
  <mx:Button x="348" y="382" label="Unload Module" id="unloadBtn"
         click="unloadMyModule()"/>
</mx:Application>
```

When you call the `unloadModule()` function, it tells the Flex display list to remove the module from the Flash Player render list and to remove it completely from memory. Loading the module again is easy: you call `MyModule.loadModule()`, and Flex loads the module for you.

Modules are the most effective way to develop large-scale and small-scale applications. They're effective in the long run when you need to add new features or remove features because they aren't dependent on the code in the application and won't cause bugs.

18.3.5 Pros and cons of modules

Modules sound almost too good to be true. Unfortunately, like anything in life, modules have their pros and cons. Figure 18.4 shows some of them and which ones have more impact.

As you can see, the benefits of using modules greatly outnumber the consequences of using them. In the next section, we'll explore how to use the ideas you've learned and make patches for your application.

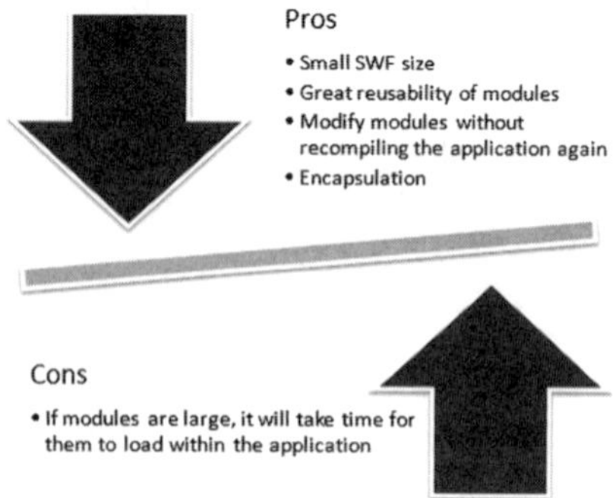

Pros
• Small SWF size
• Great reusability of modules
• Modify modules without recompiling the application again
• Encapsulation
Cons
• If modules are large, it will take time for them to load within the application

Figure 18.4 Pros and cons of a module

18.4 Adding patches in your Flex application lifecycle

As a programmer developing large-scale applications, sometimes you'll have to patch your application before the next major release. Instead of compiling the application and redeploying the entire application onto your servers, a quick and easy way to apply patches is to leverage the power of RSLs.

Recall that an RSL is loaded during runtime in the form of a SWF, cached into the browser, and cached again only if the browser cache was cleared or the file was updated. You can use this to your advantage and have a SWC file called patches that the application checks for updates during runtime. But when you patch something, it usually replaces or updates a class, which isn't an explicit capability of using SWCs, but there is a neat trick to effectively get the same end result, which we'll explain next.

18.4.1 Using a SWC to update and replace a class

One of the neat features of the Flex compiler is that it will prioritize RSLs to load from top to bottom. Say you have a class in your application that has two functions, and you want to add a third function while updating the other two to take advantage of the new function. You can copy and paste the class in your Flex library project, modify it to meet your needs, and have it create a patches.swc file.

Then you can go to your application, pull up the Properties window, and edit the Flex Build Path dialog box (see figure 18.5) to add the patches.swc file. Now you move this file to the top of the list and build your application.

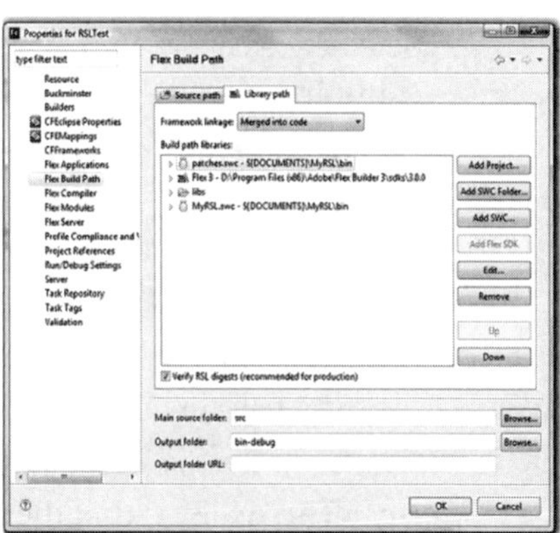

Figure 18.5 Adding a patches.swc RSL to the Flex Build Path

By moving it to the top, you make the Flex compiler load the classes in patches.swc and drop any duplicate classes it finds later. This is a good way to get those temporary fixes out before your next major release.

During your development process, you'll sometimes encounter situations where you'll want to rename parts of your code. In the next section, you'll learn how to do this without copying and pasting or rewriting.

18.5 Refactoring

Refactoring was a major feature added to the new Flex Builder version 3. It's a good way to reuse code throughout your applications.

It happens to all of us: you start with a small proof of concept, or what was initially scoped as a quick-'n'-dirty application that over time exploded in scope. It results in functions that were named poorly, or that have changed in purpose, and now you want to clean it up.

You could hunt down every instance and fix it, which would be time-consuming and inefficient. A global search and replace may work, but that approach isn't bulletproof and may cause you more grief than it cures.

The solution? Refactor! Let Flex Builder do the work: it will rename everything for you, and all will be well.

Consider the poorly named function in listing 18.5.

Listing 18.5 Bad method name

```
package com.a.b.c
{
 public class Alphabet
 {
  public function Alphabet()
  {}
  public function badMethodName():void
  {}

    }
}
```

The function is called more than 100 times throughout the application. If this were Flex Builder 2, you'd have to go through your code and rename `badMethodName()` to `goodMethodName()` for each occurrence.

But by using the power of refactoring, you can do the following:

1. Highlight the function, right-click it, and choose Refactor.
2. Flex Builder displays a refactor prompt. Type a new name for the function.
3. Click Preview. Flex Builder scans your code and shows you all the references it will update, so you can make sure Flex Builder will do the job correctly.
4. Click OK. Flex Builder looks through your code and renames the function and the calls being made to it.

If you've never heard the term *refactoring* before, it may sound amorphous and complicated. The reality is that there's not much to it; it's one of the easiest tools you can use in Flex.

18.6 Summary

When you're developing large-scale applications, the size of your SWF file can quickly go from a few hundred KB to one or two MB. You can reduce the size of your SWF file and make your code much more reusable in other applications by using techniques like RSL and modules.

You've learned how to reuse your code and make your application perform at its best. But even with increased speed, you'll also want to make your application look good. The next chapter will teach you how to make your application look sexy.

Part 3

The finishing touches

Technically, by the end of part 2 you have what you need to make full-fledged Flex applications. Part 3 takes you beyond making vanilla applications and shows you how to create customized experiences.

For starters, you have not only stylesheets that are similar to HTML's CSS but also the ability to create themes that package a complete look and feel for a Flex application, including skins that transform the look of any Flex component.

In this part of the book, you'll learn how to add pizzazz with jaw-dropping effects that will wow your users. Enabling these effects is ridiculously simple but has a powerful impact.

It's all about the experience. Although it has a major cool factor, you'll leverage Flex's drag-and-drop feature to add usability to your applications.

Last but not least in the coolness bag, you'll have management eating from the palm of your hand when you give them a dose of Flex's charting abilities, which let you visualize data in a variety of ways.

As part 3 wraps up, your Flex projects are near the end of their development lifecycle. This is the point at which you'll learn how to test, debug, and prepare your applications for prime time.

19 Customizing the experience

This chapter covers:

- Using styles to control an application's look and feel
- Making use of fonts
- Embedding images and icons
- Skinning Flex components

A cool thing about developing applications in Flex is that it's hard to make them look bad. Many developers don't come from a design background, but the default look and feel that Flex comes with makes you appear to be a design hero.

This saves you time and lets you focus on features and functionality, but there's one slight problem: by default, everyone's Flex applications look the same! In this chapter, we'll explore features that will let you add that personal touch and customize the experience per your or your user's tastes.

We start by reviewing styles in Flex.

19.1 Styles

Here's some good news: what you're used to with CSS translates to the Flex side of things. Flex follows the CSS 2.0 syntax and supports many of the common properties, but it goes far beyond font sizes and background colors by allowing you to control things like how rounded corners are, transparency, and even the angle of drop shadows.

You can define styles and style properties three ways:

- *Inline styles*—You set style attributes on the component.
- *Local style*—Style definitions are grouped in a common area.
- *External stylesheets*—You import an external file that has all the style settings.

Because of these similarities, you'll be able to whip through this chapter quickly. Let's first compare how each of these approaches works in Flex versus HTML/CSS.

19.1.1 Inline styles

Inline styles involve applying style properties directly on a specific component. You've probably used HTML, so this is something you've done from time to time:

```
<span style="font-size:14px;font-family:Tahoma;color:#AE0000">
   Inline Style</span>
<textarea style="background-color:#CC0033">Text Area</textarea>
```

In Flex, you can accomplish the same thing via the style properties on a component:

```
<mx:Text text="Inline Style" fontFamily="Tahoma" fontSize="14"
   color="#AE0000"/>
<mx:TextArea backgroundColor="#CC0033" text="Text Area"/>
```

Figure 19.1 shows the HTML version versus the Flex version. Basically they're the same, although not identical.

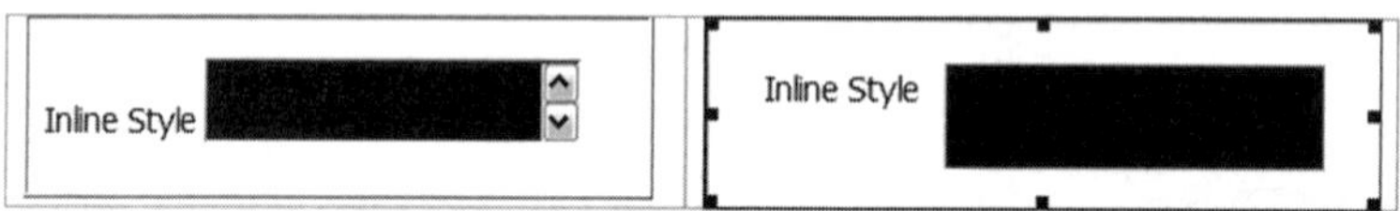

Figure 19.1 Using the same style properties in HTML (left) versus Flex to see the differences

Not much to it, right? Next, to determine what style properties are available, you can use three quick techniques.

USING FLEX BUILDER'S PROPERTY-SUGGEST

The first way is to begin typing a component name into Flex Builder. As you do this, Flex will auto-suggest all properties, as shown in figure 19.2.

Flex will do this for all the properties of a component, so you won't get a list of just style-related properties. Look for the ones that have the style icon ( ) beside the name.

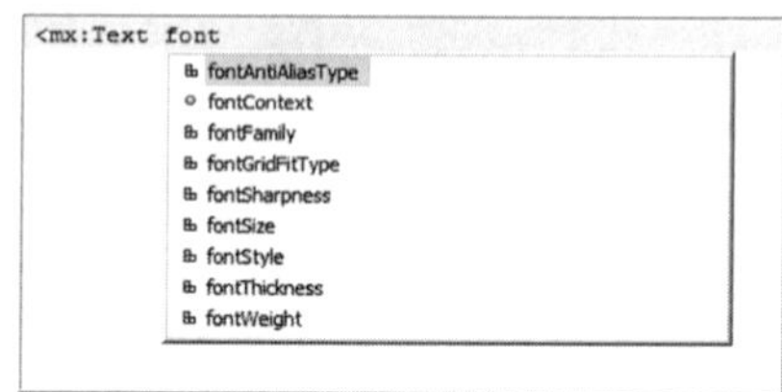

Figure 19.2 Save time by using Flex Builder's auto-suggest feature to find properties.

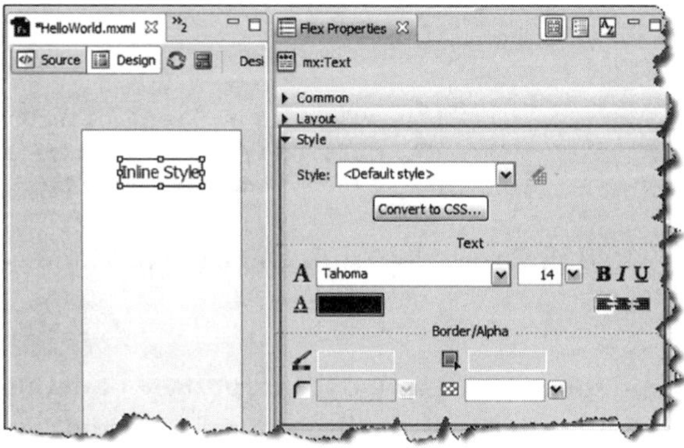

Figure 19.3 Flex Builder's Design View lets you adjust style properties visually.

USING DESIGN VIEW

Near the top of your editing window in Flex Builder are two buttons labeled Source and Design. Click the Design button to switch to Design View, and then click the component you want to style.

On the right, the Flex Properties section displays all the properties of the selected component. The Style subsection lets you adjust some of the style properties (figure 19.3).

To adjust all possible properties, click the Category View button at upper right (see figure 19.4) to display a list of all the properties available (most important, the style properties).

This method of adjusting styles works well when you're starting out in Flex, but once you get into it, you'll find that leveraging the API Language Reference will become a habit.

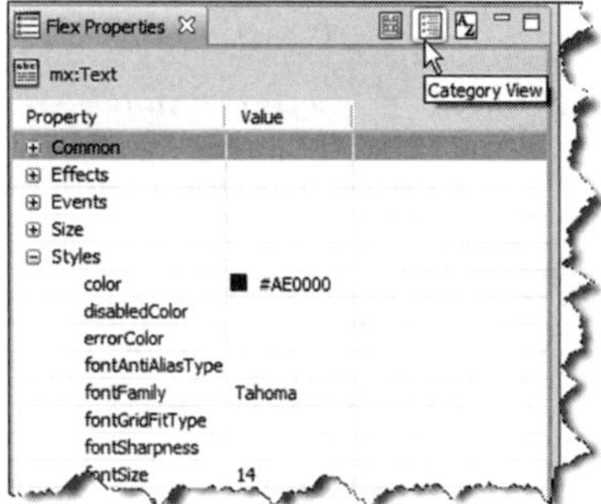

Figure 19.4 Category View provides a catalog of all style properties you can tinker with.

USING THE LANGUAGE REFERENCE

Some properties suggest the type of value they expect; for example, `fontSize` sounds like it takes a number. But if you ever need clarification, do the following:

1. Click the name of the component in Flex Builder, and press Shift+F2. Doing so displays the Language Reference for that component, as shown in Figure 19.5.
2. Scroll down to the section titled Styles.
3. Click the link under Show Inherited Styles. Doing so brings up a full list of all the styles you can set on a component and what each of those properties expects (see figure 19.6).

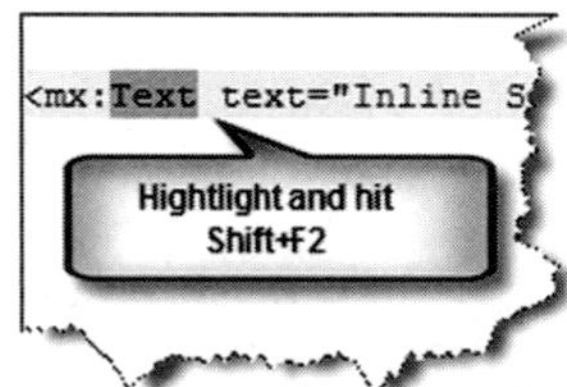

Figure 19.5 Click a component and press Shift+F2 to open the API Language Reference.

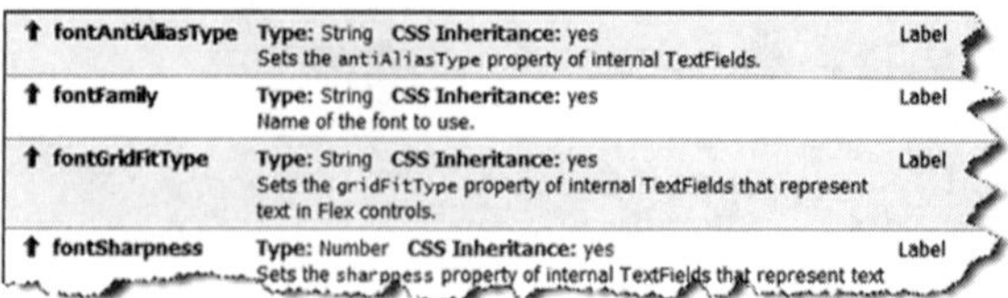

fontAntiAliasType	**Type:** String **CSS Inheritance:** yes Sets the antiAliasType property of internal TextFields.	Label
fontFamily	**Type:** String **CSS Inheritance:** yes Name of the font to use.	Label
fontGridFitType	**Type:** String **CSS Inheritance:** yes Sets the gridFitType property of internal TextFields that represent text in Flex controls.	Label
fontSharpness	**Type:** Number **CSS Inheritance:** yes Sets the sharpness property of internal TextFields that represent text	Label

Figure 19.6 The Styles section of the API Language Reference lists the available style properties.

Regardless of which way you find the style properties, there are pros and cons to using inline styles.

WHEN TO USE INLINE STYLES

Overall, this approach is good during the proof-of-concept stage of developing a Flex application, when you quickly want to tweak the display, or if a specific component has a unique set of style properties. The drawback of using this approach excessively is that you run the risk of having to go through a lot of work in a large application to update all the settings if you decide to change the design.

19.1.2 Local style definitions

Local style definitions are a lot more practical than inline styles because they decouple the formatting from specific components to a more reusable format. This approach uses two types of definitions:

- *Type definition*—The style applies to all components of that type.
- *Class definition*—Individual components specify which style class they are to use.

Let's take a closer look at each type.

TYPE DEFINITION

Type definition is a good choice when you want all instances of a component to adhere to a common style. In HTML, you'd use the <style> tags in your page to specify CSS type definitions (see listing 19.1).

Listing 19.1 Using a type definition in HTML CSS to define text input boxes

```
<style>
   input
   {
      font-family:Tahoma;
      font-size:14px;
      color:#AA4400;
      background:#CCCCFF;
   }
</style>
<input value="Input 1">
<input value="Input 2">
```

As you can see in figure 19.7, all instances of the text input box follow the style definition without your having to tell each input to use the definition.

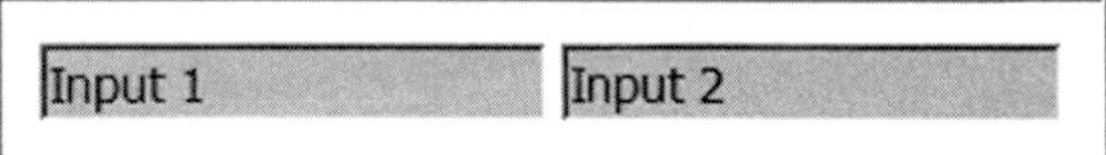

Figure 19.7 Both HTML text input boxes look the same because of a CSS type definition.

With Flex, it's almost the same, as listing 19.2 shows.

Listing 19.2 Flex's type definitions, which are almost identical to HTML's CSS

```
<mx:Style>
   TextInput
   {
      fontFamily:Tahoma;
      fontSize:14px;
      color:#AA4400;
      backgroundColor:#CCCCFF;
   }
</mx:Style>
<mx:TextInput text="Input 1" />
<mx:TextInput text="Input 2"/>
```

Figure 19.8 shows that using CSS type definitions has the same effect as using HTML CSS type definitions—all instances of the `TextInput` look the same.

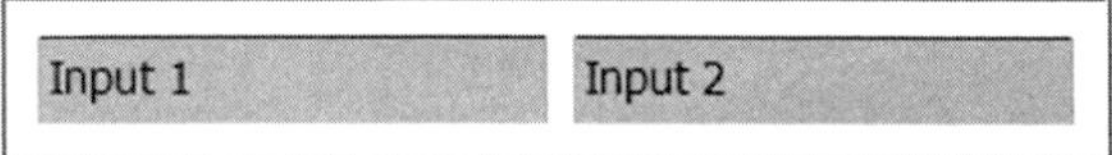

Figure 19.8 Both of Flex's `TextInput` components look the same as a CSS type definition.

If you want a style to apply on an arbitrary basis, you should use a class definition.

CLASS DEFINITION

Class definitions are higher level and aren't specific to a component. They're a good choice when you have styles that are context-specific—for example, you want all inputs on an address search form to use one style and all inputs on a user profile form to use another style. They also have the advantage that they can be used arbitrarily by components of different types (assuming that CSS style properties are supported).

In HTML, you use class definitions as shown in listing 19.3.

Listing 19.3 HTML CSS: class definitions that can be used on an at-will basis

```
<style>
   .coolStuff
   {
      font-family:Tahoma;
      font-size:14px;
      color:#AA4400;
      background:#CCCCFF;
   }
</style>
<!-- Style reused on multiple HTML tags -->
<input  class="coolStuff" value="Input 1">
<textarea class="coolStuff" rows="2" cols="40">Input 2</textarea>
```

```
<!-- Same tag, but no style -->
<input value="Input 3">
```

In figure 19.9 you see that the class definition is used on only some of the HTML elements; more important, it can be used on different types.

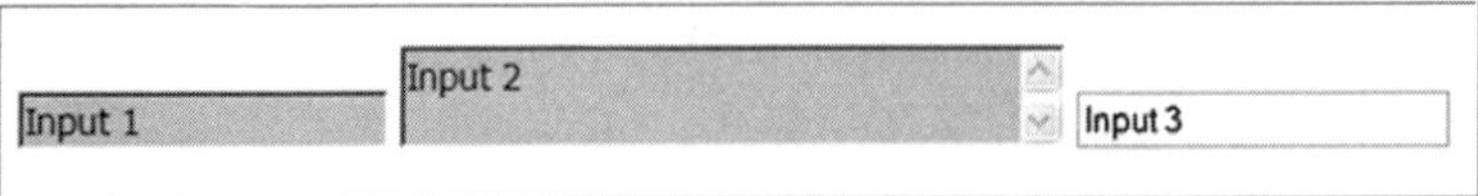

Figure 19.9 The HTML CSS class definition can be used arbitrarily.

Flex follows the same convention with the use of the decimal point and class name (see listing 19.4).

Listing 19.4 Flex CSS: class definitions that work the same way as HTML CSS

```
<mx:Style>
   .coolStuff
   {
      fontFamily:Tahoma;
      font-Size:14px;
      color:#AA4400;
      backgroundColor:#CCCCFF;
   }
</mx:Style>
<mx:TextInput text="Input 1" styleName="coolStuff"/>
<mx:TextArea  text="Input 2" styleName="coolStuff"/>
<mx:TextInput text="Input 3"/>
```

The result is the same with Flex, as shown in figure 19.10. The class-definition approach gives you the flexibility to apply the style to components as needed and to different types of components.

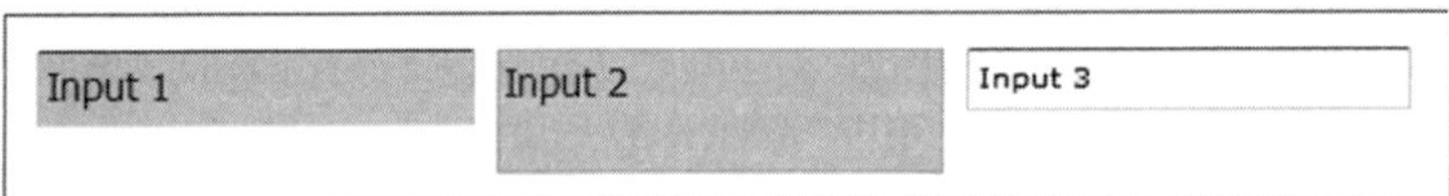

Figure 19.10 Using a CSS class definition, you can apply a style to various components in Flex.

To make the transition to Flex's CSS as transparent as possible, Flex supports some of the same style property names.

FINDING OUT WHAT CSSPROPERTIES ARE AVAILABLE

To determine property names, you can use the techniques described earlier: Flex Builder's auto-suggest feature, Design View, or the Language Reference. But there's a slight catch. Flex supports many of the common CSS style properties that are common in HTML. For example, you can use `font-Family` instead of `fontFamily` or `font-Size` instead of `fontSize`:

```
TextInput
{
   font-Family:Tahoma;
   font-Size:18px;
}
```

Although this is somewhat convenient when you're converting an HTML-based application to Flex, you can almost copy your CSS as is—but in practicality it's too confusing to try keeping track of which literal HTML CSS properties are supported versus the native Flex CSS properties. The HTML CSS that Flex supports is only a small subset of all the Flex-specific CSS properties that are available, and when you use the help techniques, they show you only the native Flex properties.

To give you an idea, listing 19.5 shows a full-blown set of style definitions that could be used on a `Panel` component.

Listing 19.5 Controlling characteristics using CSS in Flex

```
Panel {
  borderColor: #33cc33;
  borderAlpha: 0.27;
  borderThicknessLeft: 15;
  borderThicknessTop: 6;
  borderThicknessBottom: 21;
  borderThicknessRight: 19;
  roundedBottomCorners: true;
  cornerRadius: 27;
  headerHeight: 26;
  backgroundAlpha: 0.5;
  highlightAlphas: 0.19, 0.52;
  headerColors: #990033, #ccff99;
  footerColors: #000000, #ccff33;
  backgroundColor: #ffcccc;
  shadowDistance: 8;
  shadowDirection: center;
  dropShadowColor: #9933ff;
  titleStyleName: "mypanelTitle";
}

.mypanelTitle {
  color: #000099;
  textAlign: center;
  fontFamily: Palatino;
  fontSize: 14;
  fontWeight: bold;
}
```

This approach works well, but like anything else, it has its place. Let's review when to use local styles.

WHEN TO USE LOCAL STYLES

When you know your app is destined for prime time, you also know that you'll eventually need a reusable mechanism to manage the styles. Local styles are a great staging area for doing that. They also come in handy when you have one-off styles that are unlikely to be reused.

19.1.3 External stylesheets

With this approach, you store your style definitions in a dedicated file that is then referenced by your application. This technique is nearly identical to using local styles; the only difference is that you save the CSS in a file.

Using the previous HTML example, you can separate out the style portion into its own file, as shown in listing 19.6.

Listing 19.6 my.css—Separating the HTML CSS into a separate file

```
.coolStuff
{
   font-family:Tahoma;
   font-size:14px;
   color:#AA4400;
   background:#CCCCFF;
}
```

Using the `<link>` tag in HTML, you can source the CSS back in, as shown in listing 19.7.

Listing 19.7 HelloWorld.html—Sourcing the CSS back in

```
<link rel=stylesheet type="text/css" href="my.css">

<input   class="coolStuff" value="Input 1">
<textarea class="coolStuff" rows="2" cols="40">Input 2</textarea>
```

Flex-wise, you continue to use the `style` tag, but you specify the file accordingly (listing 19.8).

Listing 19.8 my.css—Separating the Flex CSS into a separate file

```
.coolStuff
{
   fontFamily:Tahoma;
   font-Size:14px;
   color:#AA4400;
   backgroundColor:#CCCCFF;
}
```

With Flex we can use the HTML technique of sourcing in CSS, except we use the `<mx:Style>` tag instead of the `<Style>` tag, as listing 19.9 highlights.

Listing 19.9 HelloWorld.mxml—Using the `Style` tag to source in the CSS

```
<mx:Style source="my.css"/>

<mx:TextInput text="Input 1" styleName="coolStuff"/>
```

This technique is easy and convenient. Let's review when to use external stylesheets.

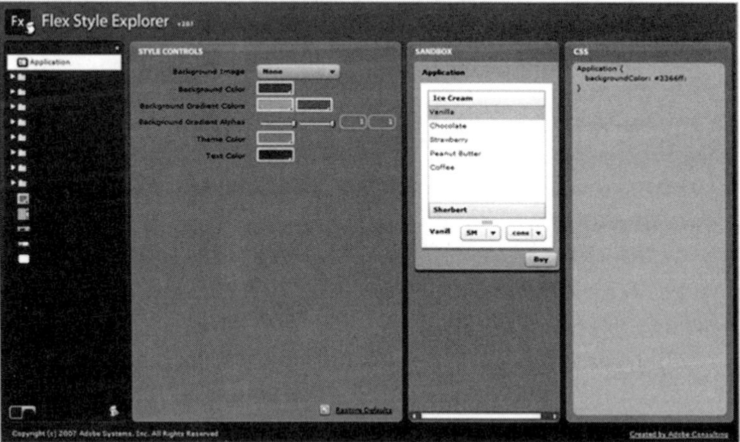

Figure 19.11 The Flex Style Explorer speeds up the process of styling.

WHEN TO USE EXTERNAL STYLESHEETS

Ideally, you should use external stylesheets as much as possible. Doing so makes it easier to change the design elements of your application without having to edit the Flex MXML files. This is advantageous because another developer or designer can focus on working on the CSS definitions without needing access to your MXML files. In addition, you can reuse the same CSS file in other applications.

19.1.4 The Style Explorer

The Style Explorer, shown in figure 19.11, is a great resource from Adobe. It's an interactive tool that lets you tinker with properties of common visual components and generates the corresponding CSS on the fly: http://www.adobe.com/devnet/flex/samples/style_explorer/.

This is useful when you want to come up with a color and design scheme for your application. It's as simple as copying and pasting the CSS that the Style Explorer generates into your application.

19.1.5 Working with color

Color can be specified in a few different formats, the most common of which are named colors (what Flex calls VGA color names) and RGB values specified in hexadecimal format. Both of these formats are supported by HTML's CSS.

NAMED COLORS

Named colors are the plain-text versions of several key colors. Compared to HTML's CSS, fewer named colors are available on the Flex side.

These named colors are aqua, black, blue, fuchsia, gray, green, lime, maroon, navy, olive, purple, red, silver, teal, white, and yellow. You can use them in any form of a style (see listing 19.10).

Listing 19.10 Using named colors in CSS style definitions

```
<mx:Style>
.myTeal
   {
      backgroundColor:teal;
   }
</mx:Style>
<mx:TextInput text="Input 1" styleName="myTeal"/>
<mx:TextArea text="Input 2" backgroundColor="Teal"/>
```

Alternatively, you can use numeric colors for a fine level of control.

NUMERIC COLORS

The common method when specifying colors in any domain is to use their numeric representation: the RGB values (a combination of red, green, and blue). Each color has a range of 0 to 255, and mixing these values results in millions of combinations of colors.

Flex has two ways to do this, the first of which is the popular *hexadecimal* format. Instead of using the base 10 (decimal) number system (where digits range from 0 to 9), in hexadecimal you use a base 16 with digits ranging from 0 to F (where F is 15).

In either HTML's or Flex's CSS, you can specify colors in such a format:

```
.coolStuff
{
   color:#FF0000;
}
```

This example specifies a full red (FF in hexadecimal is 255 in decimal). You can do this in the style definition or via the inline format.

A disclaimer: when you're using stylesheets, the `#FF0000` notation is fine, but when you're using inline styles, Adobe recommends the `0xFF0000` type of notation (use `0x` instead of #).

Here are two ways you can use hexadecimal colors:

```
<mx:TextArea backgroundColor="0xAEAEAE" text="Text Area 1"/>
<mx:TextArea backgroundColor="#AEAEAE" text="Text Area 2"/>
```

The bottom line is, use whatever you're more comfortable with.

The second method involving numeric colors uses an RGB saturation paradigm to specify on a percentage basis the color intensity from 0% to 100% (see listing 19.11).

Listing 19.11 Defining colors using RGB saturation values

```
<mx:Style>
   TextArea
   {
      backgroundColor: rgb(100%,0%,0%);
   }
</mx:Style>
```

This is another way of doing the same thing. This isn't a popular way of expressing colors, because most design and color tools don't give color values in such a format.

19.1.6 Transparency

As you layer things (containers inside of containers, and what not) you can control the transparency of each component. You do so by setting the `Alpha` level, which ranges from 0.00 (full transparency) to 1.00 (no transparency).

Any `Alpha` property has *Alpha* in its name, but a few of the color properties have a corresponding `Alpha` property to go with them. Some of these are listed in table 19.1.

Table 19.1 Many color properties support a corresponding Alpha property.

Color property	Alpha property
`borderColor`	`borderAlpha`
`backgroundColor`	`backgroundAlpha`
`fillColors`	`fillAlphas`

A base-level `Alpha` property controls the transparency for the entire component. Listings 19.12 and 19.13 show examples of a fairly transparent component versus one that's fairly opaque. The results appear in figures 19.12 and 19.13.

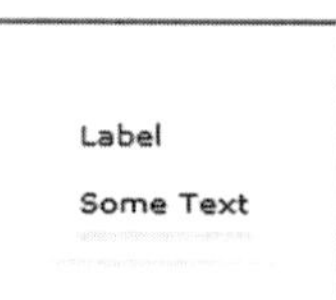

Figure 19.12 The panel is barely visible.

Figure 19.13 The panel is almost but not quite fully opaque.

Listing 19.12 A panel that is almost transparent

```
<mx:Panel alpha="0.16" >
   <mx:Label text="Label"/>
   <mx:Text text="Some Text"/>
</mx:Panel>
```

Listing 19.13 A panel that is nearly opaque

```
<mx:Panel alpha="0.90" >
   <mx:Label text="Label"/>
   <mx:Text text="Some Text"/>
</mx:Panel>
```

To make full use of this capability, you can try something like listing 19.14.

Listing 19.14 Using various `Alpha` properties

```
<mx:Panel alpha="0.80" borderColor="#33ff99" borderAlpha="0.37"
  backgroundAlpha="0.29" backgroundColor="#ff0000">
   <mx:Label text="Label"/>
   <mx:Text text="Some Text"/>
</mx:Panel>
```

This code controls not only the overall `Alpha` but also the `Alpha` of the border and the background. Controlling `Alpha` is something you can't do explicitly in HTML's CSS; gradients are another of those powerful assets.

19.1.7 Using gradients

A *gradient* is a range of colors starting from one color value and ending with another, transitioning evenly across the range. This isn't easily implemented in HTML's CSS; you have to employ some tricks to accomplish it (either by stretching an image of a gradient or by using many `span/div` tags to specify each change in the color transition).

Fortunately, in Flex it's easy as pie. It's similar to the solid-color style properties, except that you specify two color values instead of one. Many of the solid-color properties (such as `backgroundColor`) have a gradient equivalent. These properties are plural: `fillColors`, `headerColors`, and so on.

TIP A great resource for ideas as well as entire themes is a site called Scale Nine, at http://www.scalenine.com.

The Flex Style Explorer is the easiest way to experiment with what gradients are available. You can also look at the style properties in the Language Reference.

Note that gradients are arrays, usually consisting of two values. By using the array shorthand notation, you can specify a gradient using the inline approach:

```
<mx:Panel headerColors="[0x4D0808, 0x7A93B8]"/>
```

But using a style definition is simpler, because you specify just the two values:

```
<mx:Style>
   Panel {headerColors: #4D0808,#7A93B8}
</mx:Style>
<mx:Panel label="My Panel"/>
```

In some cases, gradient properties can take up to four values, to accommodate the regular fill gradient as well as the gradient to use when the user mouses over the component. Here's an example:

```
Button {fillColors: #000000, #006666, #00ff99, #cccc00}
```

And last but not least, there are `Alphas` that go along with these gradients so you can control the gradients' transparency:

```
Button
{
  fillAlphas: 0.33, 0.67, 0.75, 0.65;
  fillColors: #000000, #006666, #00ff99, #cccc00;
}
```

All the styling you've done so far has used hardcoded values. But if your application requires dynamic manipulation of styles, you can do this programmatically.

19.1.8 *Working with styles programmatically*

Instead of using static stylesheets, you can use ActionScript to programmatically set styles during runtime.

To do this, use the `setStyle()` function, available on any component. It takes two parameters: the style property you want to set and the value to set the property to.

For example, you've been using CSS to change the background color of `TextAreas`; now let's use the ActionScript approach to do that (see listing 19.15).

Listing 19.15 Using `setStyle` to programmatically manipulate a style property

```
<?xml version="1.0" encoding="utf-8"?>
<mx:Application xmlns:mx="http://www.adobe.com/2006/mxml"
   backgroundColor="0xFFFFFF">

<mx:Script>
   <![CDATA[
      public function changeColor():void
      {
         myTextArea.setStyle("backgroundColor",0xFF0000);
      }
   ]]>
</mx:Script>
<mx:TextArea text="Text Area" id="myTextArea"/>
<mx:Button click="changeColor()" label="Try Me"/>

</mx:Application>
```

Figure 19.14 shows the text area before and after the style change.

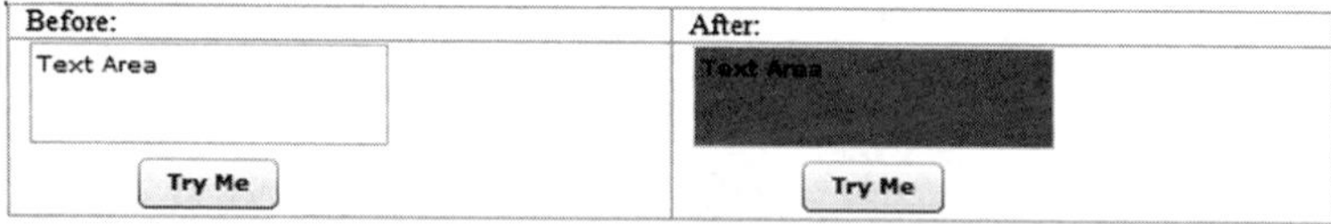

Figure 19.14 This `TextArea`'s background color was changed programmatically.

That's straightforward: you find the style you want to manipulate and set it to the value needed. Let's review guidelines for using the `setStyle()` function, which point out performance implications.

GUIDELINES ON USING SETSTYLE()

If you have a large application that uses `setStyle()` frequently, keep in mind the performance impact. Part of this is due to the fact that styles are inherited, so if you set up something at the top, a ripple effect occurs all the way down.

The biggest key to mitigating this issue is to minimize calling this function:

- Use the regular CSS stylesheets to define the base style for your application, as opposed to trying to define everything through the `setStyle()` function.
- Use `setStyle()` to alter just the changes that your CSS doesn't set.

- When an application or component initializes itself, and you need to use `setStyle()`, use the `preinitialize` event instead of other events (such as `creationComplete`):

```
<mx:TextArea text="Text Area" id="myTextArea"
   preinitialize="changeColor()"/>
```

To complement setting styles programmatically, you can also get the current value of a style using ActionScript.

GETTING STYLES

The sibling to `setStyle()` is `getStyle()`, which obviously gets a component's style information. This function takes one parameter: the name of the style property for which you want information. Depending on the property type, you'll get different variable types (usually a `String`, but some properties are numbers).

Listing 19.16 demonstrates how to retrieve the background color of the `TextArea` using the `getStyle()` property.

Listing 19.16 Retrieving the current color of the `TextArea` programmatically

```
<?xml version="1.0" encoding="utf-8"?>
<mx:Application xmlns:mx="http://www.adobe.com/2006/mxml"
   backgroundColor="0xFFFFFF">
   <mx:Script>
      <![CDATA[
         [Bindable]
         public var currentColor:Number;

         public function changeColor():void
         {
            myTextArea.setStyle("backgroundColor",myCP.selectedColor);
            currentColor= myTextArea.getStyle("backgroundColor");
         }

      ]]>
   </mx:Script>

   <mx:TextArea id="myTextArea" text="My Color is {currentColor}"/>

   <mx:Label text="Change the Text Area's color:"/>
   <mx:ColorPicker id="myCP" change="changeColor()"/>
</mx:Application>
```

Figure 19.15 shows the result. Although colors are normally expressed in hexadecimal, the number here is displayed in decimal because it's assigned to a `Number`.

As long as you know the style property, you're in business, because that's the only property the `getStyle()` function needs.

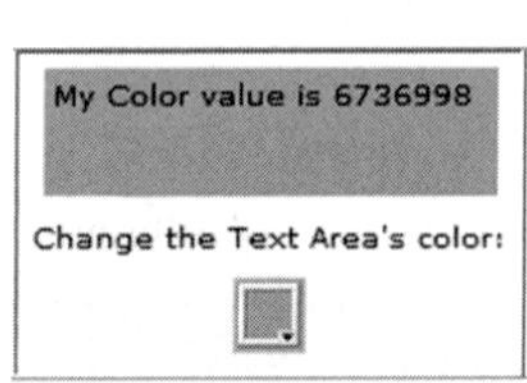

Figure 19.15 You can get the current style property programmatically.

19.2 Embedding fonts

One of the limitations of traditional HTML web pages is that if you use a font that users don't have installed, they won't experience your application as you intended. The same is true with Flex, but if you know you're using a nonstandard font, you can embed it into the application.

You use styles to accomplish this via the `@font-face` CSS definition. Its properties are listed in table 19.2.

Table 19.2 Properties of the `@font-face` declaration

Property	Description
`src:url`	Path to a font file (True Type or Open Type). Required if `src:local` isn't specified. You can use relative paths (such as myfonts/dope-jam.ttf) and absolute paths (such as c:\windows\fonts\cflex.otf).
`src:local`	Name of the font as per the system. For example: Tahoma.
`fontFamily`	A name you want to use to refer to the font.
`fontStyle`	`normal` (default), `italic`, or `oblique`.
`fontWeight`	`normal` (default), `bold`, or `heavy`. Keep in mind that certain components default to using the bold version of a font, so you either have to specify the bold face or set the font weight on the component to `normal`.
`advancedAntiAliasing`	`true` (default) or `false`. Makes the edges smooth.

After making a CSS style definition, set the `fontFamily` property of the component (directly or via CSS) to use the alias you defined for the font.

19.2.1 Embedding via the font's system name

You can embed a font using the font's name as it's known in the system, as the example in listing 19.17 shows.

Listing 19.17 Embedding a font via its system name

```
<mx:Style>
   @font-face
   {
     src:local("Tahoma");
      fontFamily: localFont;
      fontWeight: bold;
   }
</mx:Style>
<mx:Button fontFamily="localFont" label="Try Me"/>
```

The advantage of using this approach is that you don't need to care where the font is located, but it relies on the font being installed on the computer. The font-file approach doesn't have that dependency.

19.2.2 Embedding using a font file

Alternatively, you can reference a file. Remember, True Type and Open Type fonts only, please! In listing 19.18, the Tahoma font file is located in an assets subfolder under the project.

Listing 19.18 Embedding a font by specifying a filename

```
<mx:Style>
   @font-face
   {
     src:url("assets/tahoma.ttf");
      fontFamily: localFont;
      fontWeight: bold;
   }
</mx:Style>
<mx:Button fontFamily="localFont" label="Try Me"/>
```

The advantage is that you can place the font file in a location that's part of the application build. Whether it's installed on the system is irrelevant.

19.2.3 Leveraging CSS

You can use CSS as normal to create entire style definitions that use the font (see listing 19.19). That way, the component doesn't need to know which font alias to use.

Listing 19.19 Reuse the embedded font inside other style definitions

```
<mx:Style>
   @font-face
   {
      src:url("assets/Abduction.ttf");
      fontWeight: normal;
      fontFamily: localFont;

   }
   .coolStyle
   {
      fontFamily: localFont;
      fontWeight: normal;
   }
</mx:Style>
<mx:Button styleName="coolStyle" label="Try Me"/>
```

Listing 19.19 employs this idea by embedding the font as a local style definition. Then that definition is used as if it's an actual font name.

19.3 Images and icons

Images in Flex are often referred to as a type of *media asset*, which is a term that comes from the design world. Adding images is straightforward, but there are few ways to do it, and each approach has pros and cons.

19.3.1 Image types

Flex supports the following types:

- JPG
- GIF
- PNG
- SVG (Scalable Vector Graphic)
- SWF (Flash animation)

You can embed these types of images right into the application, as you did with fonts, or you can load them after the application is running.

19.3.2 To embed or not to embed

Because Flex applications are compiled, you have the option of embedding the image into the application or loading it during runtime.

EMBEDDED IMAGES

The advantage of embedding an image is that it appears instantaneously. One drawback is that whatever the size of the image, that's how much bigger you'll be making your Flex application. This may adversely impact how long it takes for your application to load (but once it's loaded, you're good to go). The other drawback is that if the image changes, you'll need to recompile the application.

You embed an image using the `@Embed` directive, which tells Flex to make the image part of the file:

```
<mx:Image id="myImage" source="@Embed(source='image.jpg')"/>
```

Keep the following in mind:

- You can use absolute or relative paths:
  - Relative path example: `source='../../image.jpg'` (relative to your application's Flex Builder src directory for the project)
  - Absolute path example: `source='c:/Documents/Images/myImage.png'`
- Make sure your paths use forward slashes (/) instead of backslashes (\).
- You can't use a URL as part of the source.

On the flip side, you can load images, which offers some unique advantages.

LOADED IMAGES

Loading an image during runtime keeps the file size down so your application loads faster; but when the application needs the image, there will be a delay as it pulls in the graphic. The other advantage is that changing the image is fairly easy because images are decoupled from the application.

In this case, let's get rid of the @Embed directive and specify a relative or absolute URL instead:

```
<mx:Image id="myImage" source="assets/myImage.png')"/>
```

Keep in mind:

- Flex uses a sandbox security model: by default, your Flex application can access only the server from which it came. To get around this, you'll want to read up on configuring a crossdomain.xml file.
- Relative paths are relative to the location from which the application is loaded.
- Absolute paths can be in the form of the absolute position from the root (such as /images/myImage.png) or can be a full URL (such as http://myserver/images/myImage.png).
- You can't load in SVG images at runtime.

Evaluate the pros and cons of embedding versus loading images, and determine which is most advantageous for your application. Another component of that decision is the ability to use images as variables in Flex.

19.3.3 Images as variables

Imagine that you're embedding an image throughout your application based on a particular file, and you decide to use a new file. It would be a pain in the neck to have to search your code to find all the places where you need to make that update.

Fortunately, in Flex you can loosen that tight coupling by assigning the image to a variable and then referencing the variable. If you need to point to a new file, you need to change only the one spot where you assign the image to the variable. Listing 19.20 shows what we're talking about.

Listing 19.20 Assigning an image to a variable to decouple its location

```
<?xml version="1.0" encoding="utf-8"?>
<mx:Application xmlns:mx="http://www.adobe.com/2006/mxml"
   backgroundColor="white">

   <mx:Script>
      <![CDATA[
         [Bindable]
         [Embed(source="assets/star.gif")]
         public var imgStar:Class;
      ]]>
   </mx:Script>
   <mx:Image source="{imgStar}"/>
</mx:Application>
```

The Image component binds to the variable; if you ever need to point to a different graphic, you do so in one spot.

Similar to images are icons, which are images used in particular contexts.

19.3.4 Icons

Some visual components in Flex have a dedicated property called `icon`. Many components support icon properties for different contexts (for example, an icon for when the user has clicked the component versus a default icon).

Icons are a nice feature that let you quickly add personalization to your application. Listing 19.21 uses the `@Embed` directive because icons must be embedded images.

Listing 19.21 Adding an icon to the button

```
<?xml version="1.0" encoding="utf-8"?>
<mx:Application xmlns:mx="http://www.adobe.com/2006/mxml">
    <mx:Button label="my button" icon="@Embed(source='assets/star.gif')"/>
</mx:Application>
```

Figure 19.16 shows how the icon appears, and figure 19.17 shows where the file is physically stored in this example.

Figure 19.16 Buttons support an `icon` property.

The button is an interesting candidate for the icon because you can specify several different icons for different purposes:

- `downIcon`
- `overIcon`
- `selectedDisabledIcon`
- `selectedDownIcon`
- `selectedOverIcon`
- `selectedUpIcon`
- `upIcon`

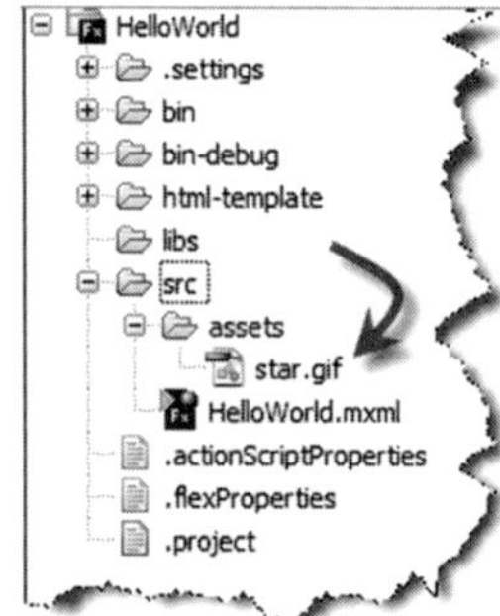

Figure 19.17 This icon is located in a subfolder in the project.

The previous example uses a non-data-driven component, in that a button is a `Button`. But when you're using data-driven components, you may want to display icons dynamically based on the data.

ICONS IN DYNAMIC LISTS

Components that dynamically list items have a convenient feature that allows an icon to be displayed beside each item. These components include `Lists`, `DataGrids`, `Trees`, and even input controls like the `ComboBox`.

The technique is to create variables for your images and, in your data, have a field that declares which image variable it should use. Listing 19.22 uses that idea.

Listing 19.22 List component that displays icons specified in the data

```
<?xml version="1.0" encoding="utf-8"?>
<mx:Application xmlns:mx="http://www.adobe.com/2006/mxml"
   backgroundColor="white">
   <mx:Script>
```

```
    <![CDATA[
       import mx.collections.ArrayCollection;

       [Bindable]
       public var myData:ArrayCollection = new ArrayCollection([
       {label:"Jeff", icon:"imgYellow"},
          {label:"Mike",icon:"imgRed"}]);          ❶

       [Bindable]
       [Embed(source="assets/yellowstar.gif")]
       public var imgYellow:Class;                  ❷

       [Bindable]
       [Embed(source="assets/redstar.gif")]
       public var imgRed:Class;
    ]]>
  </mx:Script>

  <mx:List labelField="label" iconField="icon"
     dataProvider="{myData}" height="50"/>          ❸
</mx:Application>
```

❶ Icon field contains text of variable name

❷ Sets up variables to embed images for icons

❸ List looks for specified iconField

The data stores simple Strings ❶ containing the name of the image icon, and Bindable images are set up for each possible icon name ❷. The List component then goes through each data item, and the iconField ❸ looks for the specified field and uses that to determine which icon image to use (see figure 19.18).

Figure 19.18 List component displaying icons dynamically, based on data

Although it isn't a list-based component, the ComboBox works in a similar way because it's also a data-driven component. It uses an internal list to manage its list of items. Although the ComboBox component doesn't have an iconField, it has a subcomponent called dropdown, which is of the List family (see figure 19.19)—and hence supports an icon.

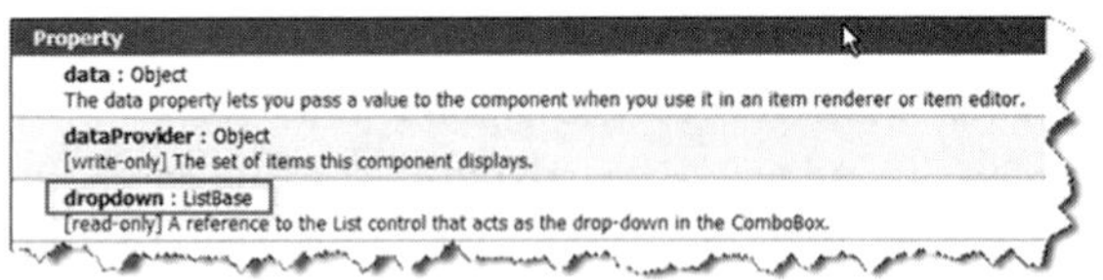

Property
data : Object The data property lets you pass a value to the component when you use it in an item renderer or item editor.
dataProvider : Object [write-only] The set of items this component displays.
dropdown : ListBase [read-only] A reference to the List control that acts as the drop-down in the ComboBox.

Figure 19.19 The Flex API Language Reference shows that a ComboBox has a List inside it.

You can replace the previous example's <mx:List> with the following ComboBox:

```
<mx:ComboBox id="myCB" labelField="label"
   creationComplete="myCB.dropdown.iconField='icon'"
   dataProvider="{myData}"/>
```

The point is that even if a component doesn't have obvious support for icons, there's a chance that one of its properties is a type that does.

The question to ask, then, is where you find icon properties in the first place.

WHERE TO FIND ICON PROPERTIES

When you look at a component in the Flex Language Reference, expand the Styles section to show all inherited styles. Because icons are part of the style family, you'll see any of the icon properties available (see figure 19.20).

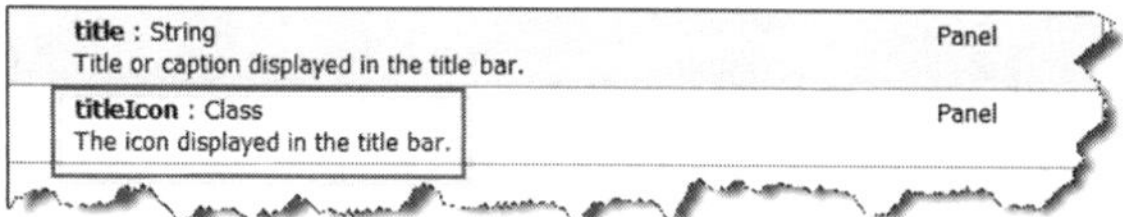

Figure 19.20 Using the Flex API Language Reference, you can find icon-related properties in the Styles section.

Along the lines of images and icons is the concept of a *skin*, which is like a configured package of interface assets.

19.4 Skins

If you're an avid user of applications like WinAmp and Firefox, you'll have seen how skins are used to transform the way the application looks. Stylesheets go a long way, but skins can take you even further.

19.4.1 Types of skins

There are two ways to skin:

- *Graphical skins*—Images are used to replace portions of the component.
- *Programmatic skins*—You use code to script how a component looks and behaves.

Skins are styles, so to use them is to use all the stuff you've already learned about styles in Flex. But because they're graphical, you also use what you learned about images earlier in this chapter.

19.4.2 19.4.2 Graphical skins with images

Graphical skins can use the JPG, PNG, and GIF image types.

TIP You'll probably want to stick with PNGs and GIFs because they support transparent backgrounds.

You can employ these skins' Flex stylesheet definitions either inline or externally—it's up to you, although we recommend that you stick with local styles or preferably the external CSS stylesheet.

Because the `Button` component is an excellent example when it comes to UI customization, we'll continue to use it as our test bed for skins. The API Language Reference (table 19.3) includes style properties that contain the word *skin*.

Table 19.3 Skin properties of the `Button` component

Property	Type	Description
`disabledSkin`	`Class`	The image to use when the `Button` component's `enabled` property is set to `false`.
`downSkin`	`Class`	The image when the mouse button is pressed down on the `Button`.
`overSkin`	`Class`	The image when the mouse is hovering over the `Button`.
`upSkin`	`Class`	The image when the mouse isn't over the `Button`.
`selectedDisabledSkin`	`Class`	The image to use when the `Button` is selected and disabled at the same time (`enabled` is `false`, and `selected` is `true`).
`selectedDownSkin`	`Class`	The image to use when the `Button` is selected and the mouse button is down.
`selectedUpSkin`	`Class`	The image to use when the `Button` is selected but the mouse isn't hovering over it.
`selectedOverSkin`	`Class`	The image to use when the `Button` is selected and the mouse is still hovering over the `Button`.

Having these skin properties, you can now go about skinning the button. One way to do that is via an inline style.

SKINNING VIA INLINE STYLES

Using the inline style syntax, you can set the properties directly on the component. In listing 19.23, you skin the common cases: a button's default state, when the mouse hovers over the button, and when the mouse button is down.

Listing 19.23 Skinning a `Button` component using inline styles

```
<?xml version="1.0" encoding="utf-8"?>
<mx:Application xmlns:mx="http://www.adobe.com/2006/mxml"
   backgroundColor="white">
<mx:Button label="My Skinned Button"
   upSkin="@Embed(source='assets/ButtonUp.png')"
   overSkin="@Embed(source='assets/ButtonOver.png')"
   downSkin="@Embed(source='assets/ButtonDown.png')"/>
</mx:Application>
```

Figures 19.21 through 19.23 show how each skin comes into play depending on the conditions.

Although it's convenient to style inline that way, it won't be convenient for long if you have 50 instances of that button. Once you move past the prototyping stage, you should use a local or external stylesheet.

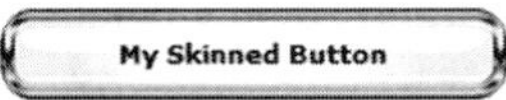

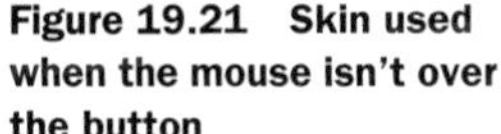

Figure 19.21 Skin used when the mouse isn't over the button

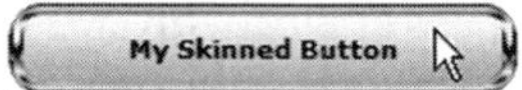

Figure 19.22 Skin used when the mouse is hovering over the button

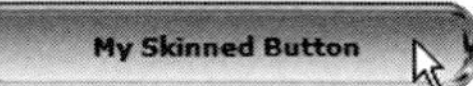

Figure 19.23 Skin used when the mouse button is down on the button

SKINNING VIA LOCAL OR EXTERNAL STYLES

Listing 19.24 takes the previous example's definitions and moves them into a local style definition using a class definition so that a component can choose to use the skin (via the style) if it wants.

Listing 19.24 Using a local stylesheet to decouple the style implementation

```
<?xml version="1.0" encoding="utf-8"?>
<mx:Application xmlns:mx="http://www.adobe.com/2006/mxml"
   backgroundColor="white">
<mx:Style>
   .styledButton
   {
      upSkin: Embed("assets/ButtonUp.png");
      downSkin: Embed("assets/ButtonDown.png");
      overSkin: Embed("assets/ButtonOver.png");
   }
</mx:Style>
<mx:Button label="My Skinned Button" styleName="styledButton"/>
</mx:Application>
```

If you want the style to apply to all buttons, you can rename `.styledButton` to `Button`. And if you want to make this an external style, copy the definition to a separate CSS file.

Graphical skins aren't limited to traditional images. In Flex, because skins run inside the Flash Player, they can use Flash animations.

19.4.3 Graphical skins with SWFs

SWFs are compiled Flash applications (so are Flex applications), but they can be used to package media assets such as fonts, sound files, and images. Using this capability, you can create static SWF files that contain the image assets you want to use as skins.

You must adhere to a few rules to make this work, all of which come from the Flash side:

- All images must exist as symbols.
- All images you want to use as skins must be on the stage.
- When exporting, you use the Export for ActionScript feature. When you do this, be sure a linkage name is provided (this is what you'll refer to in Flex).
- No ActionScript is allowed in the Flash (FLA) source file.
- All exported symbols must have an upper-left registration point.

Unless you're familiar with Flash, you probably won't want to go into Flash to do this—as a Flex developer, you'll work with SWFs only if a designer on your team is providing graphical assets in SWF form.

The main thing from your perspective is that you can think of a SWF file in this context as a zip file, and because it can contain many images, you need to know which one to use for each case. This is where symbols come into play; by using the same examples as in listing 19.24, you can add one extra parameter to the `Embed` directive, which lets you specify which image symbol to use (see listing 19.25).

Listing 19.25 Using a Flash SWF file as a skin

```
<mx:Style>
   .styledButton
   {
      upSkin: Embed("assets/ButtonSkin.swf",symbol="up");
      downSkin: Embed("assets/ButtonSkin.swf",symbol="down");
      overSkin: Embed("assets/ButtonSkin.swf",symbol="over");
   }
</mx:Style>
```

Now your button has been skinned, and it doesn't even know it!

This skinning business can be time-consuming if you really get into it, but fortunately the Adobe suite of tools makes that transition more seamless.

19.4.4 Flex skin design extensions (SDE)

Currently the CS3 versions of Photoshop, Illustrator, Flash, and Fireworks already have the design side of the integration piece built in. Its usage is fairly simple and works like this:

1. In the CS3 tool (such as Photoshop), select File > Scripts > New Flex skin. You're prompted to select which component you'd like to skin; you can choose to skin all instances of that component or only components that use a style name.
2. A single image with the default skin is loaded and ready for editing. Make the necessary changes for each state (mouse over, mouse down, and so on).
3. Hide the first layer, which hides the stuff used to visually guide you but isn't part of the skin.
4. Select File > Scripts > Export Flex Skins, and select the location where you'd like to store the skin. The skin images are stored in the target location as a directory called assets.
5. In Flex, select File > Import > Skin Artwork, and locate the assets folder created in step 4.
6. You're prompted with the available skins. Select the ones you want, and click Continue.
7. Flex Builder creates the style definitions for you.

NOTE At the time this book is being written, Adobe's CS4 hasn't been released.

> However, it's worth noting some changes. The steps described in section 19.4.4 remain relatively the same, except that in Illustrator CS4 you'll find the Create Skins dialog under File > Scripts > Flex Skins. Fireworks CS4 places the option under Commands > Flex Skinning.

The goal is to allow designers to produce artwork that you can apply to your application with little effort.

19.4.5 Image slicing

There's one problem when it comes to using images for skins: if you try to change the dimension of the component, the image becomes distorted because Flex scales the image linearly. For example, this line of code takes the image used in figure 19.21 and increases its height:

```
<mx:Button label="My Skinned Button" styleName="styledButton" height="75"
   width="140"/>
```

This result is shown in figure 19.24. The top and bottom of the image are stretched. Although Flex scaled the image proportionally, that's not how the designer would like it to be resized.

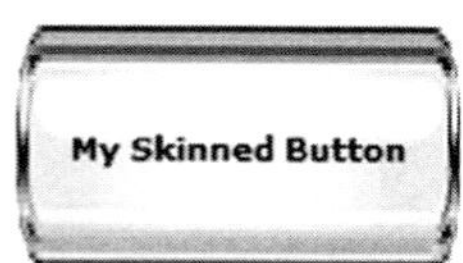

Figure 19.24 Notice the top of the image: it's stretched due to scaling.

Fortunately, there's a remedy for this problem, called 9-slice scaling. It's sort of how tables are used in HTML to slice an image and put it back together so it can accommodate varying dimensions.

In HTML, you might use a repeating table-cell background for the parts that adjust in size, while you have columns that are fixed width and never change in size. In Flex, the mechanism is different: you're defining a perimeter around the image that results in the corners not scaling while the inner part of the image does scale.

You can append four 9-slice properties to the `Embed` function, as listed in table 19.4.

Table 19.4 9-slice properties you can append to the `Embed` function

Property	Type	Description
`scaleGridLeft`	`Number`	Pixels in from the left
`scaleGridRight`	`Number`	Pixels in from the right
`scaleGridTop`	`Number`	Pixels in from the top
`scaleGridBottom`	`Number`	Pixels in from the bottom

All the numbers are relative from the upper-left coordinates, as shown in figure 19.25.

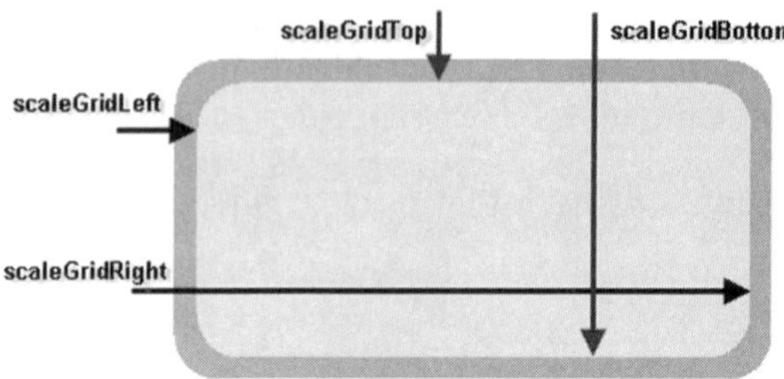

Figure 19.25 9-slicing protects how the edges of an image scale.

To use these properties, you put them in the Embed function, as shown in listing 19.26.

Listing 19.26 Using 9-slice properties

```
<mx:Style>
   .styledButton
   {
      upSkin: Embed("assets/ButtonUp.png",
         scaleGridLeft="5",scaleGridRight="194",scaleGridTop="5",
            scaleGridBottom="31");
      downSkin: Embed("assets/ButtonDown.png",

         scaleGridLeft="5",scaleGridRight="194",
            scaleGridTop="5",scaleGridBottom="31");
      overSkin: Embed("assets/ButtonOver.png",
         scaleGridLeft="5",scaleGridRight="194",scaleGridTop="5",
            scaleGridBottom="31");
   }
</mx:Style>
```

Now the edges stretch in a controlled manner (see figure 19.26). The top and bottom are significantly cleaned up by remaining 5 pixels in height, as they should be.

This 9-slice feature isn't particular to skins; you can use it anywhere the Embed function is used, including on a regular image:

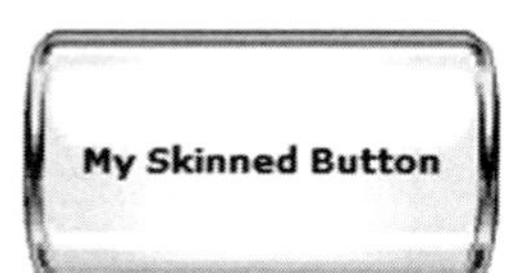

Figure 19.26 As a result of 9-slicing, the image scales cleanly.

```
<mx:Image width="100" height="50" id="myImage"
   source="@Embed(source='assets/
  ButtonUp.png',scaleGridLeft='5',
   scaleGridRight='194',scaleGridTop='5',scaleGridBottom='31')"/>
```

But 9-slicing and skinning go hand in hand for components that are continually reused.

Note that although 9-slices are cool, they have a limitation: they rely on the images being "rectangularish," where only the corners don't stretch.

19.4.6 Programmatic skins

Programmatic skins are an advanced topic that is out of the scope for this book, but we do want to give you a heads-up about them. Basically, for a programmatic skin to work, you use pure ActionScript to create skin classes that implement at a minimum a certain set of functions. You import other classes to help out, in particular a `Graphics` class that lets you draw shapes, manipulate colors, and do all that graphical goodness.

When you start making a programmatic skin, you can go about it in three primary ways:

- *Extend an existing one skin.*

  This is a good choice because an existing skin will provide all the functionality and behavior, ready to go—you're building on top of that.
- *Modify an existing skin.*

  This is similar to extending a skin, but you're not adding on, you're altering an existing skin. Flex's default skin is called Halo, and you can copy it and modify it to make it your own.
- *Build a skin from scratch.*

  This is the hardest approach, but if you needed to make a totally unique skin, you can go this route.

Not many developers venture down this road because the time investment factor is significant. Although the results can be fruitful and interesting, from a business perspective the odds are that the return on investment isn't there unless the application's business model revolves around a particular interface look.

19.5 Summary

This chapter has presented an impressive amount of content, but it shouldn't have been much of a stretch from what you already know (if you come from a web background, that is). You should have a strong feel for how you can make your Flex application unique in look by using stylesheets (CSS) to define style definitions, embedding custom fonts, leveraging images and icons, and skinning your application.

Continuing on the theme of interface customization, we'll get into Flex's effects capability in the next chapter. Most people love effects for the wow factor, but if used correctly, they also offer usability.

20 Working with effects

This chapter covers:

- Defining and invoking effects
- Types of effects
- Easing functions
- Using fonts in effects

Effects set Flex applications apart. Because Flex is based on the Flash platform, it draws on a long history of delivering engaging animated UIs, which gives it a powerful base on which to create effects.

In this chapter, we'll start by explaining effects and how they're invoked, then we'll describe the types of effects that come with Flex out of the box. Having conquered some heavy topics up to this point in the book, we're going to keep this chapter light.

20.1 What is an effect?

An *effect* modifies visual properties of a component over a period of time. These properties include a component's position, transparency, and size. For example, you can transition one of these properties over a period of 5 seconds.

20.1.1 Cause and effect

You can make an effect run two ways:

- *With a trigger*—The effect is automatically kicked off when a certain event occurs. You can trigger an effect from an event such as a mouse moving over a component or the component changing from a visible state to an invisible state.
- *Programmatically*—You can create an effect on the fly and run it as desired. For example, you could programmatically determine whether an account is overdue and make the Date Due date field glow red.

You can use either of these approaches on the out-of-the-box effects that come with Flex.

20.1.2 Out-of-the-box effects

Flex comes with an assortment of effects that are ready to go out of the box:

- AnimateProperty
- Blur
- Dissolve
- Fade
- Glow
- Iris
- Move
- Pause
- Resize
- Rotate
- SoundEffect
- WipeLeft, WipeRight, WipeUp, WipeDown
- Zoom

You can also combine effects into a *composite effect.*

20.1.3 Composite effects

To do some cool stuff, you can combine effects using either of these approaches:

- *Sequence*—Plays one effect after another
- *Parallel*—Plays all the effects in parallel, at once

Now that we've introduced effects at a high level, let's cover each area in more detail, starting with triggered effects.

20.2 Triggered effects

As we mentioned earlier, a triggered effect occurs as a result of an event. All visual components support a set of properties that let you specify which effect you want to use for a corresponding event.

For example, you can specify which effect to use when a mouse rolls over a component, as follows:

```
<mx:SomeComponent rollOverEffect="{idOfEffect}"... />
```

The visual components that come with Flex support, at a minimum, the effect triggers listed in table 20.1.

Table 20.1 Effect-trigger properties of all visual components

Property	Type	Caused by
`addedEffect`	Effect object	The component being added to a container
`creationCompleteEffect`	Effect object	Flex finishing creating the component
`focusInEffect`	Effect object	The keyboard focusing on the component
`focusOutEffect`	Effect object	The keyboard focusing off the component
`hideEffect`	Effect object	The component's `visible` property changing to `false`
`mouseDownEffect`	Effect object	The mouse button being pressed down on the component
`mouseUpEffect`	Effect object	The mouse button going up after being pressed down on the component
`moveEffect`	Effect object	The component changing position
`removedEffect`	Effect object	The component being removed from the container it was in
`resizeEffect`	Effect object	The component being resized
`rollOutEffect`	Effect object	The mouse moving off the component
`rollOverEffect`	Effect object	The mouse moving over the component

Let's use this information in a practical example. A popular effect for photo albums is to make the thumbnail grow in size as you mouse over the item; listing 20.1 does this using a Resize effect.

Listing 20.1 Using the Resize effect to enlarge an image on mouse-over

```
<?xml version="1.0" encoding="utf-8"?>
<mx:Application xmlns:mx="http://www.adobe.com/2006/mxml"
   backgroundColor="white">
  <mx:Resize id="fxEnlarge" widthTo="300" heightTo="176"/>
  <mx:Resize id="fxShrink"  widthTo="150" heightTo="88"/>
  <mx:Image  id="thumbnail"
         rollOverEffect="{fxEnlarge}"
         rollOutEffect="{fxShrink}"
         source="assets/bmw.jpg"/>
</mx:Application>
```

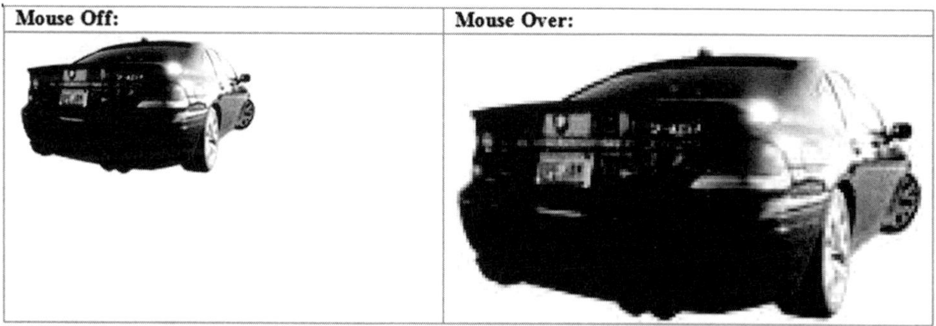

Figure 20.1 Mousing over the image triggers the image to enlarge using the Resize effect.

Could it be any easier? The image applies various effects when the mouse moves over and off the graphic, as shown in figure 20.1.

TIP When you match a trigger with an effect, it's referred to as a *behavior.*

Triggered effects are easy to create but are limited to the known triggers supported by components. If you need an effect to occur due to business logic, you must programmatically apply the effect.

20.3 Programmatically applying an effect

With triggered events, you leverage canned scenarios that the Flex product considers "the usual." But your applications will include unique scenarios to which you may want to apply an effect.

20.3.1 Creating effects with ActionScript

Suppose you have a reminder feature, and if something becomes overdue you want to make the reminder glow red. Listing 20.2 demonstrates this concept by counting down the seconds; if a threshold is crossed, the message glows each time the threshold is checked.

Listing 20.2 Playing an effect when certain business rules kick in

```
<?xml version="1.0"?>
<mx:Application xmlns:mx="http://www.adobe.com/2006/mxml"
   backgroundColor="white" initialize="initMe()">
  <mx:Script>
  <![CDATA[
   import flash.utils.Timer;
   [Bindable]
   public var secondsTillDue:int=120;
   public var myTimer:Timer;

   public function initMe():void
   {                                               Sets up timer to
    myTimer = new Timer(1000);                     check every second
    myTimer.addEventListener('timer',warnIfClose);
```

```
      myTimer.start();
    }

    public function warnIfClose(event:TimerEvent):void
    {
      secondsTillDue=secondsTillDue-1;
      if(secondsTillDue<90)
      {
        myEffect.target = idDueLabel;
        myEffect.play();
      }
    }
      ]]>
  </mx:Script>
  <mx:Glow id="myEffect" duration="750"
      alphaFrom="1.0" alphaTo="0.3"
      blurXFrom="0.0" blurXTo="50.0"
      blurYFrom="0.0" blurYTo="50.0"
      color="0xFF0000"/>

   <mx:Label text="This is due in {secondsTillDue} seconds"
        id="idDueLabel"/>

</mx:Application>
```

Animates if Due is less than 90 seconds

Assign label as component to apply effect to

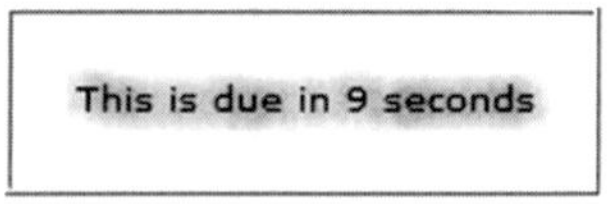

When you run the application, you'll see a message that begins to glow when the countdown gets to be less than 90 seconds, as shown in figure 20.2.

This is due in 9 seconds

Figure 20.2 Glow effect engaged using programmatic

In this case, you use an instance of an MXML `Effect` component (`myEffect`), which has the key advantage of being able to change the effect without having to change what goes on in your function. If you want to use something other than a Glow effect, as long as the `id` property stays the same, the `myEffect.play()` portion will work the same.

20.3.2 Using just ActionScript

You can go all out on ActionScript if you want to. Instead of using a component, listing 20.3 adapts the previous example to use the class version of an effect (versus the MXML component).

Listing 20.3 Creating an instance of an effect using pure ActionScript

```
<?xml version="1.0"?>
<mx:Application xmlns:mx="http://www.adobe.com/2006/mxml"
    backgroundColor="white" initialize="initMe()">
  <mx:Script>
  <![CDATA[
    import flash.utils.Timer;
    import mx.effects.Glow;
    [Bindable]
    public var secondsTillDue:int=120;
    public var myTimer:Timer;
```

```
    public var myEffect:Glow;

    public function initMe():void
    {
      myTimer = new Timer(1000);
      myTimer.addEventListener('timer',warnIfClose);
      myTimer.start();
      myEffect = new Glow();
      myEffect.alphaFrom=1.0;
      myEffect.alphaTo=0.3;
      myEffect.blurXFrom=0.0;
      myEffect.blurXTo=50.0;
      myEffect.blurYFrom=0.0;
      myEffect.blurYTo=50.0;
      myEffect.color=0xFF0000;
      myEffect.duration=750;
    }

    public function warnIfClose(event:TimerEvent):void
    {
      secondsTillDue=secondsTillDue-1;
      if(secondsTillDue<90)
      {
        myEffect.target = idDueLabel;
        myEffect.play();
      }
    }
  ]]>
  </mx:Script>

  <mx:Label text="This is due in {secondsTillDue} seconds"
         id="idDueLabel"/>

</mx:Application>
```

Sets up timer to check every second (annotation for `myTimer = new Timer(1000);`)

Animates if Due is less than 90 seconds (annotation for `if(secondsTillDue<90)`)

Assign label as component to apply effect to (annotation for `myEffect.target = idDueLabel;`)

Note how the `Glow` class is imported near the start so that Flex knows which glow you're talking about.

Remember the advantage of the previous example, where it's relatively easy to switch to a different effect? You can also do that using this approach, but the real advantage of creating an effect this way is the ability to create `Effect` objects dynamically on the fly. For example, if you wanted to go to town, you could store configuration information about what effect you want to play based on certain circumstances.

20.4 Creating composite effects

It's possible to group independent effects into a collection called a *composite effect*. You can do so in either a parallel or a serial manner.

20.4.1 Sequential effects

To make one effect come after another, group them using the `<mx:Sequence>` tag, as shown in listing 20.4.

Listing 20.4 Grouping effects and playing them one after another

```
<?xml version="1.0"?>
<mx:Application xmlns:mx="http://www.adobe.com/2006/mxml">
   <mx:Sequence id="sequenceEffect">
      <mx:Fade alphaFrom="0.0" alphaTo="1.0"/>
      <mx:Zoom zoomWidthFrom="0.5" zoomWidthTo="1.0"
         zoomHeightFrom="0.5" zoomHeightTo="1.0"/>
   </mx:Sequence>
   <mx:Button id="myButton" label="Mouse Over To Play Effect"
      rollOverEffect="{sequenceEffect}"/>
</mx:Application>
```

When you mouse over the button, the Fade effect begins. After that effect has finished, a Zoom effect takes place.

Alternatively, if you want to play all the effects at the same time, you can use a parallel effect.

20.4.2 *Parallel effects*

To make a group of effects begin at the same time, use the <mx:Parallel> tag. Listing 20.5 alters the previous example to apply the effects in parallel.

Listing 20.5 Playing multiple effects at the same time

```
<?xml version="1.0"?>
<mx:Application xmlns:mx="http://www.adobe.com/2006/mxml">
  <mx:Parallel id="parallelEffect">
  <mx:Fade alphaFrom="0.0" alphaTo="1.0"/>
  <mx:Zoom zoomWidthFrom="0.5" zoomWidthTo="1.0"
        zoomHeightFrom="0.5" zoomHeightTo="1.0"/>
  </mx:Parallel>
  <mx:Button id="myButton" label="Mouse Over To Play Effect"
          rollOverEffect="{parallelEffect}"/>
</mx:Application>
```

What if you want to do a bit of both? Flex lets you combine composites.

20.4.3 *Composite composites*

The fun doesn't stop there. You can mix and match these approaches in any way you can imagine. For example, you can play two sets of parallel effects one after the other, as shown in listing 20.6.

Listing 20.6 Nesting two parallel composites in a sequence

```
<mx:Sequence id="compositeEffect">
  <mx:Parallel>
    <mx:Fade alphaFrom="0.0" alphaTo="1.0"/>
    <mx:Zoom zoomWidthFrom="0.5" zoomWidthTo="1.0" zoomHeightFrom="0.5"
          zoomHeightTo="1.0"/>
  </mx:Parallel>
  <mx:Parallel>
    <mx:Zoom zoomWidthFrom="1.0" zoomWidthTo="0.5" zoomHeightFrom="1.0"
```

```
        zoomHeightTo="0.5"/>
    <mx:Fade alphaFrom="1.0" alphaTo="0.0"/>
  </mx:Parallel>
</mx:Sequence>
```

Theoretically, there's no limit to how deep you can nest composite effects, but from a usability perspective, you don't need to go overboard with effects in order to communicate change.

Now that you know how to create and instantiate effects, let's move on to the types of effects that are available.

20.5 Using out-of-the-box effects

As we mentioned earlier, Flex comes a nice set of effects that are ready to go. They all have certain unique properties but also share (as a result of inheritance) a number of properties. These are listed in table 20.2.

Table 20.2 Properties that all effects support

Property	Type	Description
`duration`	`Number`	Time, in milliseconds, over which the effect transpires. For example, a value of `5000` results in an effect taking 5 seconds to complete.
`easingFunction`	`Function`	Name of an easing function. Default is to use `none`. We discuss easing functions in section 20.6.
`repeatCount`	`Number`	Number of times you want the effect to repeat. Default is `1`. To loop indefinitely, use `0`.
`repeatDelay`	`Number`	If you're repeating the effect, the delay in milliseconds before the effect plays again. Default is `0` (no delay).
`startDelay`	`Number`	Time, in milliseconds, before the effect begins.
`id`	`String`	Name by which components can reference the effect.

These properties let you control the primary configuration of an effect; they focus on runtime. Using these common properties, in the following sections we'll examine the effects that come with Flex, starting with AnimateProperty.

20.5.1 The AnimateProperty effect

This is a general-purpose effect that lets you change a component property from one value to another. For example, you can use an AnimateProperty effect to change the width of something to a specific value or use it to alter a component's `alpha` property and make the component disappear.

That sounds like some of the other effects, you say. Yes, some effects are effectively preselected property manipulations that use AnimateProperty. But if you needed fine-grained control, AnimateProperty can do the job. Listing 20.7 alters a button's `transparency` property (alpha) from fully opaque to fully transparent over a period of 3 seconds.

Listing 20.7 Using the AnimateProperty effect to fade a button

```
<?xml version="1.0"?>
<mx:Application xmlns:mx="http://www.adobe.com/2006/mxml">
  <mx:AnimateProperty id="myEffect" property="alpha"
                  fromValue="1.0" toValue="0.0" duration="3000"/>
  <mx:Button label="Click me" mouseDownEffect="{myEffect}"/>
</mx:Application>
```

TIP The duration property is an inherited property that all effects share.

The Fade effect (discussed in section 20.5.4) causes the same behavior.

20.5.2 The Blur effect

A Blur effect does what you'd expect: it make things blurry. You have control over two directions: horizontal (X) and vertical (Y). Table 20.3 lists the properties used to manipulate them.

Table 20.3 Properties specific to the Blur effect

Property	Type	Description
blurXFrom	Number	Starting value for the horizontal blur. 0–255.
blurXTo	Number	Ending value for the horizontal blur. 0–255.
blurYFrom	Number	Starting value for the vertical blur. 0–255.
blurYTo	Number	Ending value for the vertical blur. 0–255.

Listing 20.8 uses a Blur effect to blur in a horizontal direction when the user presses the mouse button down on the button.

Listing 20.8 Using a Blur effect on a button

```
<?xml version="1.0"?>
<mx:Application xmlns:mx="http://www.adobe.com/2006/mxml"
    backgroundColor="white">
  <mx:Blur id="myEffect" blurXFrom="0" blurXTo="255"/>
  <mx:Button label="Click me" mouseDownEffect="{myEffect}"/>
</mx:Application>
```

When you hold down the button as shown in figure 20.4, the button becomes progressively blurred.

Next, let's examine the Dissolve effect.

20.5.3 The Dissolve effect

A Dissolve effect is similar to a Fade, but it's implemented differently. It puts a transparent rectangle over the component, which then progressively becomes opaque. You

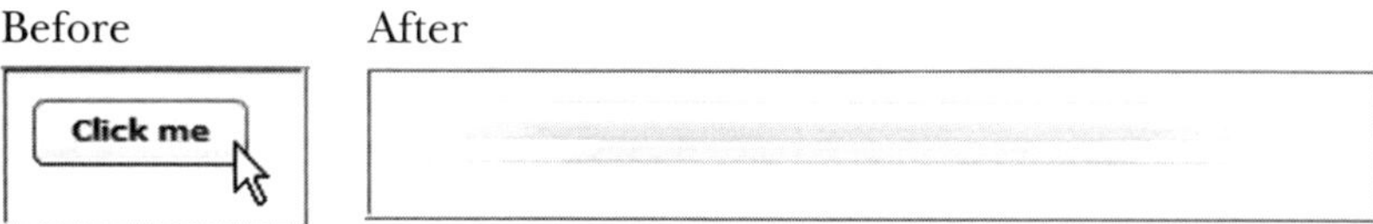

Figure 20.3 The result of a Blur effect used on a button

don't see the rectangle per se, because its color is the same as the background it hovers over. Table 20.4 lists the properties that are unique to the Dissolve effect.

Table 20.4 Properties specific to the Dissolve effect

Property	Type	Description
`alphaFrom`	`Number`	Starting transparency value. `0.0–1.0`.
`alphaTo`	`Number`	Ending transparency value. `1.0–0.0`.
`color`	`Color`	Color into which the rectangle dissolves. Defaults to the component's `backgroundColor`. (Optional.)

Listing 20.9 uses these properties by applying a Dissolve effect that transitions from fully opaque to nearly transparent.

Listing 20.9 Using a Dissolve effect on the button

```
<?xml version="1.0"?>
<mx:Application xmlns:mx="http://www.adobe.com/2006/mxml"
   backgroundColor="white">
  <mx:Dissolve id="myEffect" alphaFrom="1.0" alphaTo="0.1"/>
  <mx:Button label="Click me" mouseDownEffect="{myEffect}"/>
</mx:Application>
```

As mentioned previously, the Fade effect is similar to the Dissolve effect in its behavior.

20.5.4 *The Fade effect*

A Fade effect works by transitioning a component's `alpha` property over a period of time, which makes it identical to using an AnimateProperty effect that manipulates the `alpha`. Table 20.5 lists the properties that are specific to the Fade effect.

Table 20.5 Properties specific to the Fade effect

Property	Type	Description
`alphaFrom`	`Number`	Starting transparency value. `0.0–1.0`.
`alphaTo`	`Number`	Ending transparency value. `1.0–0.0`.

Listing 20.10 uses these properties by fading a button from fully opaque to nearly transparent.

Listing 20.10 Using the Fade effect on the button

```
<?xml version="1.0"?>
<mx:Application xmlns:mx="http://www.adobe.com/2006/mxml"
    backgroundColor="white">
  <mx:Fade id="myEffect" alphaFrom="1.0" alphaTo="0.1"/>
  <mx:Button label="Click me" mouseDownEffect="{myEffect}"/>
</mx:Application>
```

Look back at figure 20.3, which shows the button fading away; the result is the same in this case.

20.5.5 The Glow effect

Implementing a Glow effect is similar to creating a border around a component while at the same time blurring and fading the component. As a result, this effect shares the properties of a Fade and a Blur. Table 20.6 lists the properties that are unique to the Glow effect.

Table 20.6 Properties specific to the Glow effect

Property	Type	Description
blurXFrom	Number	Starting value for the horizontal blur. 0–255.
blurXTo	Number	Ending value for the horizontal blur. 0–255.
blurYFrom	Number	Starting value for the vertical blur. 0–255.
blurYTo	Number	Ending value for the vertical blur. 0–255.
alphaFrom	Number	Starting transparency value. 0.0–1.0.
alphaTo	Number	Ending transparency value. 1.0–0.0.
color	Color	Color of the glow.
inner	Boolean	true or false (default). Lets you control whether it's an inner or outer glow (the default).
knockout	Boolean	true or false (default). If true, the inner part of the component is transparent.
strength	Number	Strength of the glow. 0–255.

Listing 20.11 creates a Glow effect that glows in both horizontal and vertical directions using the color red.

Listing 20.11 Using a Glow effect on the button

```
<?xml version="1.0"?>
<mx:Application xmlns:mx="http://www.adobe.com/2006/mxml"
   backgroundColor="white">
  <mx:Glow id="myEffect" duration="750"
```

```
        alphaFrom="1.0" alphaTo="0.3"
        blurXFrom="0.0" blurXTo="50.0"
        blurYFrom="0.0" blurYTo="50.0" knockout="true"
        color="0xFF0000"/>
    <mx:Button label="With Knock Out" mouseDownEffect="{myEffect}"/>
</mx:Application>
```

Figure 20.4 shows how setting the knockout property prevents the Glow effect from overlapping the component and instead cuts out a solid inner area.

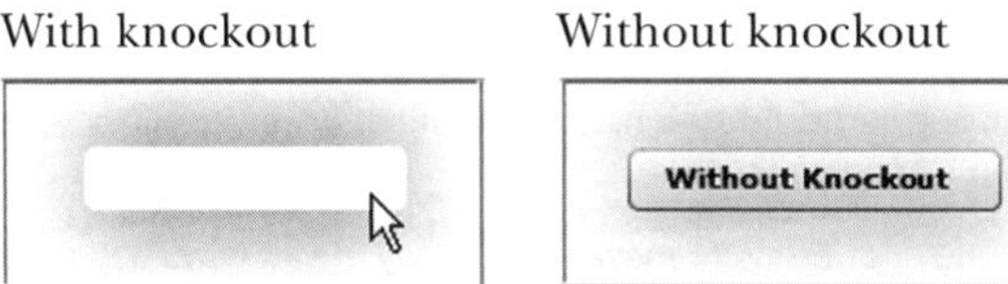

Figure 20.4 The knockout property alters how the Glow effect appears.

Next up: the Iris effect.

20.5.6 The Iris effect

The Iris effect uses a *mask*. You may have come across masks in other Adobe tools such as Flash and Photoshop; they let you create a black-and-white shape that specifies the visible area (white indicates visible, black indicates invisible).

By default, an Iris effect makes a small rectangular mask in the center of your component and expands the mask outward. As it expands, more of the component is revealed.

This effect doesn't have any unique properties—it does what it does, as shown in listing 20.12.

Listing 20.12 Using the Iris effect on the button

```
<?xml version="1.0"?>
<mx:Application xmlns:mx="http://www.adobe.com/2006/mxml"
    backgroundColor="white">
  <mx:Iris id="myEffect"/>
  <mx:Button label="Click on me" mouseDownEffect="{myEffect}"/>
</mx:Application>
```

This effect isn't used much, mostly because of its name—most people can't tell from the word *Iris* what the effect implies. But it's fun to use, because most users aren't accustomed to this effect.

20.5.7 The Move effect

The Move effect lets you transition the position of a component from one place to another. All the properties in table 20.7 are in pixels, starting from the upper-left corner relative to the container the component is in.

Table 20.7 Properties specific to the Move effect

Property	Type	Description
xFrom	Number	Starting horizontal position. If unspecified, uses the current position as the starting point.
xTo	Number	Ending horizontal position. If unspecified, uses the current position as the ending point.
yFrom	Number	Starting vertical position. If unspecified, uses the current position as the starting point.
yTo	Number	Ending vertical position. If unspecified, uses the current position as the ending point.
xBy	Number	Number of pixels to move horizontally. Negative values move to the left, positive to the right.
yBy	Number	Number of pixels to move vertically. Negative values move up, positive down.

Listing 20.13 moves the button diagonally down to the bottom right every time you click it.

Listing 20.13 Using the Move effect to move the button diagonally

```
<?xml version="1.0"?>
<mx:Application xmlns:mx="http://www.adobe.com/2006/mxml"
   backgroundColor="white">
   <mx:Move id="myEffect" xBy="50" yBy="50"/>
   <mx:Button label="Click on me" mouseDownEffect="{myEffect}"/>
</mx:Application>
```

Note that when you use this effect, the component remains in the ending position—you'll need a reverse effect if you want to move it back to its original location.

If you're thinking there's no difference between this and manipulating the X and Y properties yourself, you're somewhat correct. But don't forget that all effects share common properties, such as `repeatCount` and `duration`; plus, you can make a Move effect part of a composite effect.

20.5.8 *The Pause effect*

Although you can, you won't normally use a Pause effect on its own, because all it does is create a delay. It's useful in a composite effect, to put a delay between other effects.

Pause doesn't have any unique properties—you use the common `duration` property to control the length of the delay. Using the previous example, let's move the button down after clicking it and, 5 seconds later, move it back (see listing 20.14).

Listing 20.14 Using the Pause effect to pause between two other effects

```
<?xml version="1.0"?>
<mx:Application xmlns:mx="http://www.adobe.com/2006/mxml"
```

```
    backgroundColor="white">
  <mx:Sequence id="myEffect">
    <mx:Move xBy="50" yBy="50"/>
    <mx:Pause duration="5000"/>
    <mx:Move xBy="-50" yBy="-50"/>
  </mx:Sequence>
  <mx:Button label="Click on me" mouseDownEffect="{myEffect}"/>
</mx:Application>
```

If you try this with a parallel composite effect, the pause effect won't be noticeable because all the effects run at the same time.

20.5.9 The Resize effect

You saw the Resize effect in use when we introduced the triggered effect—it lets you control resizing both vertically and horizontally. You can resize from/to a specific size or increase/decrease size by an incremental amount. Table 20.8 lists the properties that are specific to the Resize effect.

Table 20.8 Properties specific to the Resize effect

Property	Type	Description
`heightFrom`	`Number`	Starting height. If unspecified, uses the current height (for example, if you specify only `heightTo`).
`heightTo`	`Number`	Ending height. If unspecified, uses the current height (for example, if you specify only `heightFrom`).
`widthFrom`	`Number`	Starting width. If unspecified, uses the current width (for example, if you specify only `widthTo`).
`widthTo`	`Number`	Ending width. If unspecified, uses the current width (for example, if you specify only `widthFrom`).
`heightBy`	`Number`	Number of pixels by which to change the height. Negative values decrease the height; positive values increase it.
`widthBy`	`Number`	Number of pixels by which to change the width. Negative values decrease the width; positive values increase it.

Listing 20.15 uses a button that, when clicked, will make its height grow, beginning at 0 pixels and ending at 50 pixels taller than its original height.

Listing 20.15 Resizing a button that starts small and grows bigger

```
<?xml version="1.0"?>
<mx:Application xmlns:mx="http://www.adobe.com/2006/mxml"
   backgroundColor="white">
  <mx:Resize id="myEffect" heightFrom="0" heightBy="50"/>
  <mx:Button label="Click on me" mouseDownEffect="{myEffect}"/>
</mx:Application>
```

Because you aren't manipulating the `width` property, it appears that the component starts out pancake thin and stretches vertically.

20.5.10 The Rotate effect

Make it spin! You can use the Rotate effect to rotate a component around a point of your choice. Table 20.9 lists the properties that are specific to the Rotate effect.

Table 20.9 Properties specific to the Rotate effect

Property	Type	Description
`angleFrom`	`Number`	Starting angle. If unspecified, starts from the current angle. `0–360`.
`angleTo`	`Number`	Ending angle. If unspecified, ends at the current angle. `0–360`.
`originX`	`Number`	Horizontal position relative to the center of the component. Negative values move the rotation point left; positive values move the rotation point right.
`originY`	`Number`	Vertical position relative to the center of the component. Negative values move the rotation point up; positive values move the rotation point down.

Listing 20.16 rotates the component 45 degrees clockwise.

Listing 20.16 Rotating the button 45 degrees

```
<?xml version="1.0"?>
<mx:Application xmlns:mx="http://www.adobe.com/2006/mxml"
    backgroundColor="white">
  <mx:Rotate id="myEffect" angleTo="45"/>
  <mx:Button label="Click on me" mouseDownEffect="{myEffect}"/>
</mx:Application>
```

It's possible to use ActionScript to apply your own algorithm that manipulates the button's properties to achieve the rotation, but using this effect is much easier. Don't forget to rotate the component back if you need to.

20.5.11 The SoundEffect effect

When was the last time you saw an AJAX application use sound effects as a form of communication? Using the SoundEffect effect, you can add an element of usability to your applications by communicating without the user having to read anything.

The SoundEffect employs a concept called *panning*, which lets you control the volume from left to right (if you wish). Table 20.10 lists the properties that are specific to the SoundEffect effect.

Table 20.10 Properties of the SoundEffect effect

Property	Type	Description
`autoLoad`	`Boolean`	Whether the MP3 is loaded automatically. `true` (default) or `false`.
`bufferTime`	`Number`	Number of milliseconds to buffer. Default is `1000`.
`loops`	`Number`	Number of times to repeat a loop. `0` (default) plays once.
`panEasingFunction`	`Function`	Easing function to use when panning.
`panFrom`	`Number`	Starting pan value. Default is `0` (center). `-1.0` (full left) to `1.0` (full right).
`panTo`	`Number`	Ending pan value. Default is `0` (center). `-1.0` (full left) to `1.0` (full right).
`source`	`Object`	Reference to an MP3 sound file.
`startTime`	`Number`	Milliseconds into the sound file to start. Default is `0`.
`useDuration`	`Boolean`	Whether to respect the `duration` property. `true` (default) or `false`.
`volumeEasingFunction`	`Boolean`	Easing function to use on volume changes.
`volumeFrom`	`Number`	Starting volume. `0.0`–`1.0` (default).
`volumeTo`	`Number`	Ending volume. `0.0`—`1.0` (default).

The example in listing 20.17 plays a sound when the button is clicked.

Listing 20.17 Playing a sound when the button is clicked

```
<?xml version="1.0"?>
<mx:Application xmlns:mx="http://www.adobe.com/2006/mxml"
   backgroundColor="white">
 <mx:SoundEffect id="myEffect" source="@Embed(source='assets/bing.mp3')"/>
 <mx:Button label="Click on me" mouseDownEffect="{myEffect}"/>
</mx:Application>
```

Unfortunately, sound is a dimension that isn't often utilized in RIAs, largely because developers who come from traditional web applications aren't used to leveraging sound. We encourage you to try adding this element to your applications.

20.5.12 The Wipe effects

Wipes progressively show or hide a component by sliding a rectangle onto or off of the component. The rectangle is the same color as the background, so it looks like the component itself is sliding out or in.

Although you don't have to, you should toggle the component's `visible` property to leverage the usefulness of the effect. You can use four types of Wipe effects:

- WipeLeft
- WipeRight
- WipeUp
- WipeDown

These effects have no unique properties.

Listing 20.18 makes a panel disappear and reappear using Wipe effects.

Listing 20.18 Sliding a panel in and out when the button is clicked

```
<?xml version="1.0"?>
<mx:Application xmlns:mx="http://www.adobe.com/2006/mxml"
   backgroundColor="white">
  <mx:WipeLeft id="wipeleft" />
  <mx:WipeRight id="wiperight" />
  <mx:Panel id="myPanel" label="Wipe Me"
         showEffect="{wipeleft}" hideEffect="{wiperight}"/>
  <mx:Button label="Toggle the Panel"
          click="myPanel.visible=!myPanel.visible"/>
</mx:Application>
```

When you click the button, the `visible` property is toggled on and off. This triggers the `showEffect` or the `hideEffect` event to occur, which then plays the appropriate Wipe.

20.5.13 The Zoom effect

A Zoom effect is somewhat like a Resize effect but retooled to focus on starting with a small component and zooming in to make the component bigger (as well as the other way around). Extra parameters are available to specify the zoom-origin point (by default, it zooms from the center). Table 20.11 lists properties unique to the Zoom effect.

Table 20.11 Properties specific to the Zoom effect

Property	Type	Description
`originX`	`Number`	Horizontal origin to zoom into or out of. If not specified, uses the horizontal center of the component.
`originY`	`Number`	Vertical origin to zoom into or out of. If not specified, uses the vertical center of the component.
`zoomWidthFrom`	`Number`	Starting width. Defaults to the current width if unspecified.
`zoomWidthTo`	`Number`	Ending width. Defaults to the current width if unspecified.
`zoomHeightFrom`	`Number`	Starting height. Defaults to the current height if unspecified.
`zoomHeightTo`	`Number`	Ending height. Defaults to the current height if unspecified.

In listing 20.19, after you click the button, a Zoom effect is used to grow the button from no size (width and height equal to 0) and expand it to the original size.

Listing 20.19 Using the Zoom effect to make the button zoom-in large

```
<?xml version="1.0"?>
<mx:Application xmlns:mx="http://www.adobe.com/2006/mxml"
    backgroundColor="white">
  <mx:Zoom zoomWidthFrom="0" zoomHeightFrom="0" id="myEffect"/>
  <mx:Button label="Click on me" mouseDownEffect="{myEffect}"/>
</mx:Application>
```

That's the last of the effects that come with Flex. In these examples, you'll have noticed that the motion was linear in nature, which gives it a mechanical feel. You can alter that behavior by using an *easing function.*

20.6 Easing functions

By default, when Flex plays an effect, it spaces the changes evenly over time. For example, a Move effect that moves a component 100 pixels over 100 seconds will move the component at a rate of 1 pixel per second.

Suppose you want to add a little spice to that by making the component begin by moving quickly, then gradually slow to a stop (like a car braking). That's where an easing function comes into play.

20.6.1 Out-of-the-box easing functions

Out of the box, Flex provides an Easing package (`mx.effects.easing`) that includes a number of classes with easing functions. Table 20.12 lists these classes and functions.

Table 20.12 Easing functions that come with Flex

Class	Functions	Class	Functions	Class	Functions

`Back`	`easeIn,`
	`easeOut,`
	`easeInOut`
		`Elastic`	`easeIn,`
			`easeOut,`
			`easeInOut`
				`Quartic`	`easeIn,`
					`easeOut,`
					`easeInOut`

`Bounce`	`easeIn,`
	`easeOut,`
	`easeInOut`
		`Exponential`	`easeIn,`
			`easeOut,`
			`easeInOut`
				`Quintic`	`easeIn,`
					`easeOut,`
					`easeInOut`

`Circular`	`easeIn,`
	`easeOut,`
	`easeInOut`
		`Linear`	`easeIn,`
			`easeOut,`
			`easeInOut,`
			`easeNone`
				`Sine`	`easeIn,`
					`easeOut,`
					`easeInOut`

That's quite a few options! Fortunately, using them is simple, as listing 20.20 shows.

Listing 20.20 Using easing functions with the Move effect to make motion less linear

```
<?xml version="1.0"?>
<mx:Application xmlns:mx="http://www.adobe.com/2006/mxml"
    backgroundColor="white">
  <mx:Script>
    import mx.effects.easing.*
  </mx:Script>
  <mx:Move id="myEffect" xBy="300" easingFunction="{Elastic.easeOut}"/>
  <mx:Button label="Make me move" mouseDownEffect="{myEffect}"/>
</mx:Application>
```

This example makes the button slingshot to the right, as if being catapulted by an elastic band, then bounce against the edge until it comes to a stop.

20.6.2 Making your own easing functions

You can make your own easing functions. When you specify an easing function, Flex passes you the parameters shown in table 20.13.

Table 20.13 Parameters to a custom easing function

Parameter	Type	Description
t	Number	Current point in time
b	Number	Starting position of component
c	Number	Total change in position
d	Number	Total duration of effect (in milliseconds)
s	Number	Overshoot value (default is 0); optional

Flex will keep calling your function for each time interval to find out what the current position of the component should be (a number you return). Listing 20.21 shows a rudimentary example.

Listing 20.21 Using a custom easing function

```
<?xml version="1.0"?>
<mx:Application xmlns:mx="http://www.adobe.com/2006/mxml"
  backgroundColor="white">
  <mx:Script>
  public function myEasing(t:Number, b:Number, c:Number, d:Number):Number
  {
    t/=d;
    return b+c*(t);
  }
  </mx:Script>
  <mx:Move id="myEffect" xBy="300" easingFunction="{myEasing}"/>
  <mx:Button label="Make me move" mouseDownEffect="{myEffect}"/>
</mx:Application>
```

TIP To explore this topic in more depth, check out the nifty easing function generator on the web, created by Timothee Groleau: http://timothee-groleau.com/Flash/experiments/easing_function_generator.htm. It will help you generate the code for easing functions.

Before we wrap up this chapter, we need to discuss an issue related to fonts and effects.

20.7 Fonts and effects

If you've been experimenting with various effects, you may have noticed that sometimes the text inside components doesn't seem to be affected by the effect. What's up with that?

By default, Flex uses system fonts—as a result, it's limited in its ability to manipulate them. This is particularly true with the Dissolve, Fade, and Rotate effects. But there's an easy workaround: embedding the font.

You can do this by using styles, as shown in listing 20.22.

Listing 20.22 Embedding fonts to ensure that effects work on text

```
<?xml version="1.0"?>
<mx:Application xmlns:mx="http://www.adobe.com/2006/mxml"
    backgroundColor="white">
  <mx:Style>
    @font-face
    {
      src:local("Tahoma");
      fontFamily: localFont;
      fontWeight: bold;
    }
  </mx:Style>
  <mx:Fade id="myEffect" alphaFrom="1.0" alphaTo="0.0"/>
  <mx:Button fontFamily="localFont" label="Try Me"
        mouseDownEffect="{myEffect}"/>
</mx:Application>
```

The drawback of embedding fonts is that the file size of your application will grow with the size of the font. Be careful not to go overboard and embed too many fonts.

20.8 Summary

Effects can take your applications to new levels. They can definitely get a "gee-whiz" reaction from an audience—particularly management folks whom you're trying to impress as you sell them on the idea of using Flex.

But don't limit yourself to thinking that effects are only good for the wow factor. They also play a role in adding usability by letting you draw attention to things going on in your application as well as providing a motion-driven vehicle for communication.

Another "gee-whiz" topic that raised a lot of eyebrows when Flex first came out is its drag-and-drop abilities. We'll look at this in the next chapter.

21 Drag-and-drop

This chapter covers:

- Controlling when dragging and dropping is allowed
- Supporting a multi-item drag-and-drop operation
- Building custom drag-and-drop functionality
- Customizing the drag-and-drop experience

When Flex first came out, drag-and-drop (D&D) was a key feature that set the tone for what RIAs are capable of. From a developer's perspective, Flex's D&D feature is easy to implement because many components provide a built-in mechanism to support it. At the same time, you can hook into and override any of the default behavior throughout the stages of the process.

In this book, we want to show you not just how to do something but also *why* to do something. We don't want you doing D&D just for the sake of it, or because it's cool, but because it adds usability.

Because of the restrictions of using HTML/JavaScript to make applications, functionality that has been available since the desktop GUI was introduced has unfortunately been forgotten on the web. In traditional web applications, you relied on boatloads of clicking links and buttons to move data—web developers tend to forget the D&D concept (in the web context), even though they use it every day on the desktop side of life. And because D&D is so uncommon on the web, even users forget the concept.

We urge you to consider D&D from a usability point of view rather than just because you can or because of the coolness factor. The challenge is not so much the programming effort (you'll see in this chapter that it's easy) but rather the mindset. You'll want to provide the typical data-management paradigms that are common in web applications, because that's what your users look for by default, but you should also train them to use your application's D&D capabilities.

Ultimately, the level at which your users are successful is the level at which your application is successful. We'll get the ball rolling for your success by reviewing the overall D&D process.

21.1 The drag-and-drop process

You love events, right? Well, the D&D process is nothing but events being fired off at various stages in the lifecycle of dragging and dropping.

Let's first get some definitions out of the way:

- *Drag initiator*—The component from which the drag starts.
- *Drag proxy*—The mouse icon displayed to the user during the D&D process.
- *Drag source*—The data that is being transferred between the drag initiator and the drop target. The name is somewhat misleading because it sounds like it's the source of the drag operation; that's the drag initiator.
- *Drop target*—The component that's receiving the data.

Which one is in play at certain points can be confusing, so let's go through the D&D process. It includes a number of steps, depending on what the user does. We'll go over each step in moderate detail so you can understand what the user is doing, which events are fired, and what the user experiences at each step:

1. The drag is initiated:
   - The user clicks an item in a component that allows dragging (via the `dragEnabled="true"` property setting). Event fired: `mouseDown`.
   - While holding down the mouse button on the item, the user begins the drag process. The starting component is now the drag initiator. Events fired: `mouseMove` and `dragStart`.
2. During the dragging process, a drag source object is created. It contains all the data associated with the item being dragged. For example, if you're dragging a row from a `DataGrid` component, it may show only 2 fields when the record includes 10 fields. When you drag, you're dragging the entire row record.
3. The drag proxy kicks in, giving visual indicators to the user. A red ⊗ indicates the component the mouse is over won't accept drops. A green ⊕ is used when dropping is allowed.

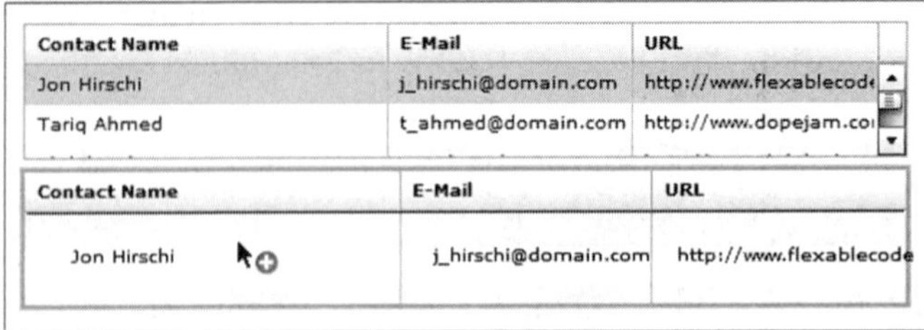

Figure 21.1 The drag proxy provides a visual indicator to the user about whether the operation is allowed.

4 The user moves to the destination component. The drag proxy continues to check with each component that is being moused over to determine whether that component will accept a drop.

The destination is a potential drop target, and the destination component examines the drag source to see if it likes what it sees (is the data of compatible type? are certain business rules in place? and so on). Events fired: `dragEnter` and `dragOver`.

The drop target's acceptance (for example, see figure 21.1) or denial is visibly communicated to the user by the drag proxy.

5 One of two things happens:
   - The user releases the mouse button over the drop target. The drop target handles the drop and does whatever it needs to do with the data item (by default, the data is added to the `dataProvider`). The user sees the data item in the drop target if the drop is successful. Events fired: `dragDrop` and `dragComplete`.
   - The user moves the mouse off the potential drop target while still holding down the mouse button. The drag proxy updates its indicator. Event fired: `dragExit`.

Events keep coming up, as you'd expect—Flex is an event-driven system. If there's ever a place for events, it's definitely in D&D.

21.2 Drag-and-drop events

We mentioned a lot of events that get fired during the D&D process. Let's flesh these out so you know what they imply. The Recipient column in table 21.1 tells what component gets the event.

Table 21.1 Drag-and-drop events

Event	Recipient	Description
`mouseDown`	Drag initiator	Occurs when the user mouses down over the data item. This is the point at which you can add business logic to determine whether you want to allow the start of a drag operation.
`mouseMove`	Drag initiator	User begins to move the data item.

Table 21.1 Drag-and-drop events *(continued)*

Event	Recipient	Description
`dragStart`	Drag initiator	Drag initiator fires an event to itself. (This event is kind of strange.)
`dragEnter`	Drop target	Drag proxy initially moves over a potential drop target. The drop target can use this as an opportunity to examine data and determine whether it will accept or deny the drop.
`dragOver`	Drop target	Occurs immediately after `dragEnter`. Can be used to do post-acceptance processing (if the drop was going to be denied, you'd do so in `dragEnter`).
`dragDrop`	Drop target	Result of the user releasing the mouse button. This is where you commit the data and finalize the operation.
`dragExit`	Drop target	Occurs if the user doesn't release the mouse button and moves off the drop target: you go from `dragOver` to `dragExit`. This is where you undo/reset things you did in the `dragOver` process.
`dragComplete`	Drag initiator	Sent to the drag initiator when the D&D process ends for whatever reason (the user drops the item or cancels the operation by letting go of the mouse button while not over a component).

So far, we've defined the process and the events that go along with it. Next, we'll discuss the components that support D&D.

21.3 Components that support drag-and-drop

The obvious usage candidates for D&D operations are components that list things. In Flex, those are the `List`-based components, particularly the following:

- `List`
- `TileList`
- `HorizontalList`
- `Tree`
- `DataGrid`
- `AdvancedDataGrid`
- `PrintDataGrid`

These components provide built-in support for D&D, but nothing prevents you from adding your own logic to support D&D from one component to another.

21.4 Enabling D&D on List-based components

To enable D&D is easy—almost too easy. `List`-based components support two properties that make this happen (see table 21.2).

Table 21.2 Drag-and-drop properties of `List`-based components

Property	Type	Description
`dragEnabled`	`Boolean`	Indicates whether the component is allowed to serve as a drag initiator. `true` or `false` (default).
`dropEnabled`	`Boolean`	Indicates whether the component is allowed to serve as a drop target. `true` or `false` (default).

Using those two properties, listing 21.1 shows the code used in figure 21.2 (D&D process).

Listing 21.1 `DataGrid` accepting dragging and dropping from another `DataGrid`

```
<?xml version="1.0"?>
<mx:Application xmlns:mx="http://www.adobe.com/2006/mxml"
   backgroundColor="white">
<mx:Script>
 <![CDATA[
  import mx.collections.ArrayCollection;
  [Bindable]
  public var myAC:ArrayCollection  = new ArrayCollection([
  {name:"Jon Hirschi", email:"j_hirschi@domain.com",
     url:"http://www.flexablecoder.com"},
  {name:"Tariq Ahmed", email:"t_ahmed@domain.com",
     url:"http://www.dopejam.com"},
  {name:"Abdul Qabiz", email:"a_qabiz@domain.com",
     url:"http://www.abdulqabiz.com"},
  {name:"Faisal Abid", email:"f_abid@domain.com",
     url:"http://www.g-unix.com"},
  {name:"Frank Krul", email:"f_krul@domain.com", url:""}
  ]);
 ]]>
</mx:Script>
<mx:DataGrid id="dgSource" dataProvider="{myAC}" dragEnabled="true" >
   <mx:columns>
      <mx:DataGridColumn dataField="name" headerText="Contact Name"
         width="300" />
      <mx:DataGridColumn dataField="email" headerText="E-Mail"
         width="200"/>
      <mx:DataGridColumn dataField="url" headerText="URL" width="200"/>
   </mx:columns>
</mx:DataGrid>
<mx:DataGrid id="dgTarget" dropEnabled="true" >
   <mx:columns>
      <mx:DataGridColumn dataField="name" headerText="Contact Name"
         width="300" />
      <mx:DataGridColumn dataField="email" headerText="E-Mail"
         width="200"/>
      <mx:DataGridColumn dataField="url" headerText="URL" width="200"/>
   </mx:columns>
</mx:DataGrid>
</mx:Application>
```

This chapter will talk more about customization and control, but this listing is real-world application material.

21.5 Moving versus copying

You may have noticed that listing 21.1 results in a copy operation instead of moving the data from one `DataGrid` to another. If you want to make it a move operation instead of a copy, the change is simple.

`List`-based components support a `dragMoveEnabled` property, which by default is set to `false` and which causes the default behavior of copying the data item. (There is one exception: the `Tree` component has the opposite default.)

All you need to do is set `dragMoveEnabled`, and the D&D performs a move instead of a copy; see listing 21.2.

Listing 21.2 Setting the `dragMoveEnabled` property to move instead of copy

```
<mx:DataGrid id="dgSource" dataProvider="{myAC}" dragEnabled="true"
          dragMoveEnabled="true" >
   <mx:columns>
      <mx:DataGridColumn dataField="name" headerText="Contact Name"
         width="300" />
      <mx:DataGridColumn dataField="email" headerText="E-Mail"
         width="200"/>
      <mx:DataGridColumn dataField="url" headerText="URL" width="200"/>
   </mx:columns>
</mx:DataGrid>
```

After making that alteration, if you were to try the example again, the item is removed from the source once the drop occurs.

This workflow is probably something you're quite familiar with, and it works well for moving a single item.

TIP Note that you can still do a copy with `dragMoveEnabled` set to `true`; to do so, hold down the Ctrl key during the dragging process.

But all this would be tedious if you needed to move many items at once. Similar to Windows, Flex also supports a multi-item drag.

21.6 Multi-item drag

If you want to let the user move many items at once, check out the `allowMultipleSelection` property. Setting it to `true` enables this ability (see listing 21.3).

Listing 21.3 Enabling the user to move many items at once

```
<mx:DataGrid id="dgSource" dataProvider="{myAC}"
   dragEnabled="true" dragMoveEnabled="true"
      allowMultipleSelection="true" >
   <mx:columns>
      <mx:DataGridColumn dataField="name" headerText="Contact Name"
         width="300" />
```

```
        <mx:DataGridColumn dataField="email" headerText="E-Mail"
          width="200"/>
        <mx:DataGridColumn dataField="url" headerText="URL" width="200"/>
    </mx:columns>
</mx:DataGrid>
```

The user can interact with this ability either of two ways: using individual selections or using a range of selections. To select items one by one, follow these steps:

1. Hold down the Ctrl key, and use the mouse to select each item that you want to drag.
2. Once all the items are selected, release the Ctrl key.
3. Click into the component, hold down the mouse button, and proceed with the D&D process.

Figure 21.2 shows what this looks like by moving every other row to the target.

Flex also supports selecting a range of items. A range selection is a quick way to select a range of items by picking a start and an end; Flex selects everything in between as well.

To do this, follow these steps:

1. Select the first item you want to include.
2. Scroll to the last item you want to include, press the Shift key, then select the last item.

   Flex highlights all the items in between.
3. Release the mouse button, click into the component, and begin the D&D process.

This UI behavior isn't unique to Flex, and it's something you've most likely experienced in a Windows application.

What we've shown so far is a one-way D&D operation, where you have a source and destination. Flex also supports going both ways.

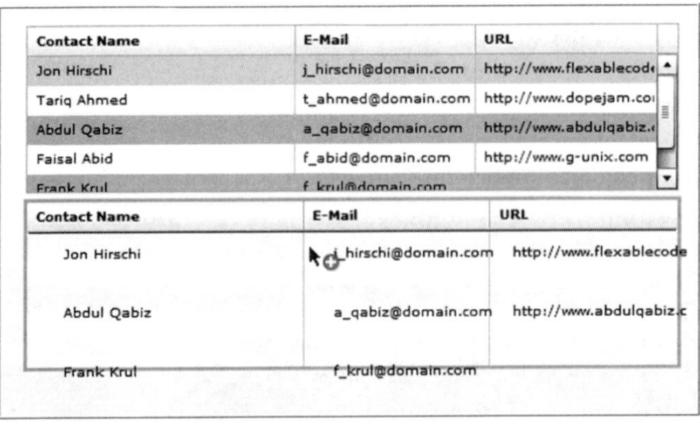

Figure 21.2 Use the Ctrl key to select multiple items to drag.

21.7 Two-way drag-and-drop

Drag-and-drop doesn't have to be limited to moving or copying items from one component to another; it's great to be able to move things back and forth. In Flex, that's not a problem, and here's how you do it.

Set the `dragEnabled` and `dropEnabled` properties to `true` for all components involved. Don't forget to set `dragMoveEnabled` to `true` as well, if you want the default behavior to be moving instead of copying.

The example in listing 21.4 shows a fictitious divorce application that lets the users divvy up their assets and determine who gets what. You can move the items back and forth across any of the three lists.

Listing 21.4 Dragging and dropping among three `List` components

```
<?xml version="1.0"?>
<mx:Application xmlns:mx="http://www.adobe.com/2006/mxml"
   backgroundColor="white">
<mx:Script>
 <![CDATA[
  import mx.collections.ArrayCollection;
  [Bindable]
  public var allAssets:ArrayCollection  = new ArrayCollection([
  {label:"House"},{label:"BMW 745i"},{label:"Lexus IS350"},{label:"Stocks"}
  ]);
 ]]>
</mx:Script>

<mx:Panel title="DivorceNET" width="300">

    <mx:Label text="Assets"/>
    <mx:List id="listAll" dataProvider="{allAssets}" width="100%"
       height="90"
            dragEnabled="true" dragMoveEnabled="true"
               dropEnabled="true"/>

    <mx:HBox width="100%">
       <mx:VBox width="50%">
          <mx:Label text="His"/>
          <mx:List id="listHis" width="100%" height="90"
               dragEnabled="true" dragMoveEnabled="true"
                  dropEnabled="true"/>
       </mx:VBox>

       <mx:VBox width="50%">
          <mx:Label text="Hers"/>
          <mx:List id="listHers" width="100%" height="90"
                dragEnabled="true" dragMoveEnabled="true"
                  dropEnabled="true"/>
       </mx:VBox>

    </mx:HBox>
</mx:Panel>

</mx:Application>
```

As you move an asset from one person to another, it's removed from the source location. You can always move it back.

The nice thing about this two-way approach is that you can use it to drag and drop something onto itself.

21.8 Using D&D for user-controlled sorting

D&D doesn't have to be about moving data from one component to another. You can also use it to reposition data within the same component. For example, have you ever developed or seen something like figure 21.3?

Movie Queue

Order	Movie	Year	Availability	Delete
1	Evan Almighty	2007	In Stock	☐
2	Death Proof	2007	Not In Stock	☐
3	Dragon Wars	2007	In Stock	☐

Number the items in the order you want them. [Update Sequence]

Figure 21.3 In standard HTML, without D&D, it can be cumbersome to let users sort a queue of items.

From a usability perspective, it becomes progressively more time-consuming to manage the ordering of content in a list as the amount of content grows. Using D&D, you can save your users a lot of time.

Set the following properties on a component to allow dragging and dropping from and to the component itself:

- `dragEnabled="true"`
- `dropEnabled="true"`
- `dragMoveEnabled="true"`

The example in listing 21.5 demonstrates by using a `DataGrid` that enables both drag and drop.

Listing 21.5 Dragging and dropping within a component, to allow ordering

```
<mx:DataGrid id="dgSource" dataProvider="{myAC}" dragEnabled="true"
                    dropEnabled="true" dragMoveEnabled="true" >
   <mx:columns>
      <mx:DataGridColumn dataField="name" headerText="Contact Name"
         width="300" />
      <mx:DataGridColumn dataField="email" headerText="E-Mail"
         width="200"/>
      <mx:DataGridColumn dataField="url" headerText="URL" width="200"/>
   </mx:columns>
</mx:DataGrid>
```

After running the application, you can do something similar to figure 21.4 and control the order of your contacts.

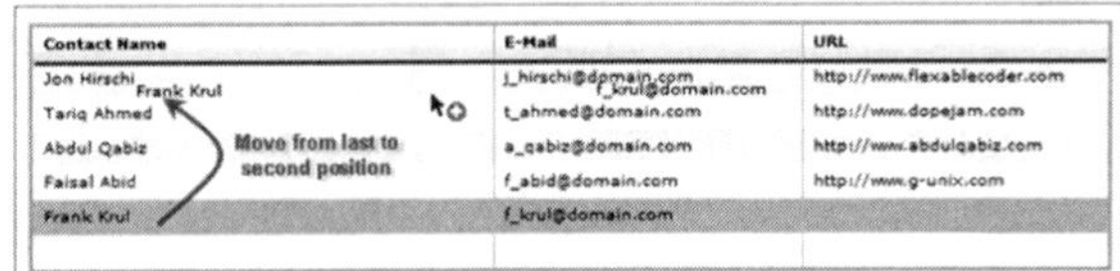

Figure 21.4 Using D&D on itself, the `DataGrid` lets the user easily control the position of items.

So far, you've been able to add D&D in an autonomous manner: components employ their built-in D&D behavior. If only life were that easy! In a real-world application, you'll need to enter business logic and business rules; this is where you can leverage the `DragManager`.

21.9 Enter the DragManager

The `DragManager` is a global object that is always there in case you need it—it does all the work behind the scenes to make D&D possible. Whenever you need to handle objects in play, you can access the DragManager to help.

To do anything custom, you must use the DragManager, as you'll see in the sections that follow. But before we get into that, it's worth summarizing a few key properties.

21.9.1 Operational values

The `DragManager` has four static values (also called *constants*, which are variables that never change in value) that can be used to evaluate what the user is doing (such as a move or a copy) and communicate back to the user visually. Those values are listed in table 21.3.

Table 21.3 Constants defined in the `DragManager`

Value	Description
`COPY`	Current action is copying the dragged item. `List`-based components assume that if you hold down the Ctrl key, you're doing a copy (if `dragMoveEnabled="true"`).
`LINK`	Current action is linking: like a copy, but instead of making a duplicate, you have multiple items linking to a single source. This action occurs when the Shift key is held down.
`MOVE`	Current action is moving the dragged item from one place to another.
`NONE`	No action allowed. Operation is denied.

These values, along with the constants, are supporting functions.

21.9.2 DragManager functions

You need to take advantage of three important functions (also known as methods) in order to perform custom D&D work:

- `doDrag()`—Kicks off the D&D process. Usually initiated in a `mouseMove` event handler.
- `acceptDragDrop()`—Lets the `DragManager` know whether it's allowed to continue the D&D process. Called in a `dragEnter` event handler.
- `showFeedback()`—Communicates to the user about the current operational value (`COPY`, `LINK`, `MOVE`, or `NONE`).

Using a combination of the DragManager's constants and its supporting functions, you have the pieces necessary to accept or deny a drop operation.

21.10 Accepting or denying a drop

All of what we've discussed is fine and dandy if you're allowing D&D in an uncontrolled manner, but in the real world, the next logical step is to add business logic to determine whether to allow a drop on a given component. A common case includes doing a check to prevent duplicates, so the user can't add another item if there's already a copy.

21.10.1 Limiting who gets into the party

The key event to facilitate adding a gatekeeper that determines whether to allow a drop is the dragEnter event. This event fires whenever the mouse moves into the component.

Let's use an example where the drop target lets the drop take place only after inspecting the item to see if the record appears to be active. Here's the game plan for the code in listing 21.6:

1. Add a dragEnter event handler to the DataGrid that will potentially accept a drop.
2. The event handler looks at the DragEvent event to see what data is being dragged.

   The data is in the form of an array of objects. Even though you may be dragging only one item, the DragManager supports multi-item drags—it's possible to receive more than one item (for example, if the initiating component has allowMultipleSelection="true").
3. Examine the data to see whether any of the items are active (via isActive being false).
4. If all is well, tell the DragManager that it can continue; otherwise, take a pass.

Listing 21.6 Allowing a drop only for items that are active

```
<?xml version="1.0"?>
<mx:Application xmlns:mx="http://www.adobe.com/2006/mxml"
   backgroundColor="white">
<mx:Script>
 <![CDATA[
  import mx.collections.ArrayCollection;
  import mx.events.DragEvent;
  import mx.managers.DragManager;

  [Bindable]
  public var myAC:ArrayCollection  = new ArrayCollection([
  {name:"Jon Hirschi", email:"j_hirschi@domain.com", isActive:true},
  {name:"Tariq Ahmed", email:"t_ahmed@domain.com", isActive:false},
  {name:"Abdul Qabiz", email:"a_qabiz@domain.com", isActive:true}]);

    public function handleDragEnter(event:DragEvent):void
    {
```

```
        var arItems:Array= event.dragSource.dataForFormat("items")
           as Array;
        var isAllowed:Boolean = true;

        for (var i:int = 0; i < arItems.length; i++)
           if(arItems[i].isActive == false)
              isAllowed = false;

        if (isAllowed)
           DragManager.acceptDragDrop(dgTarget);
        else
        {
           DragManager.showFeedback(DragManager.NONE);
           event.preventDefault();
        }
     }
  ]]>
  </mx:Script>
  <mx:DataGrid id="dgSource" dataProvider="{myAC}"
           dragEnabled="true" dragMoveEnabled="true" >
     <mx:columns>
        <mx:DataGridColumn dataField="name" headerText="Contact Name"
           width="300" />
        <mx:DataGridColumn dataField="email" headerText="E-Mail"
           width="200"/>
        <mx:DataGridColumn dataField="isActive" headerText="Active"
           width="75"/>
     </mx:columns>
  </mx:DataGrid>
  <mx:DataGrid id="dgTarget" dropEnabled="true"
     dragEnter="handleDragEnter(event)" >
     <mx:columns>
        <mx:DataGridColumn dataField="name" headerText="Contact Name"
           width="300" />
        <mx:DataGridColumn dataField="email" headerText="E-Mail"
           width="200"/>
        <mx:DataGridColumn dataField="isActive" headerText="Active"
           width="75"/>
     </mx:columns>
  </mx:DataGrid>

  </mx:Application>
```

Get an Array of items being moved over

Check each item's status

When you try this example, if you try to move the user Tariq, the second DataGrid will refuse to allow the drop to occur.

If the DragManager never sees that acceptDragDrop call, the rest of the D&D process won't occur (because the dragOver and dragDrop events won't fire).

21.10.2 Preventing event propagation

In the previous example, because you have dropEnabled="true", you ask Flex to engage its default event handlers. Even though you specify your own handler for dragEnter, after your function is run, Flex will then use its own:

```
<mx:DataGrid id="dgTarget" dropEnabled="true"
```

```
dragEnter="handleDragEnter(event)" >
```

But if you determine that you don't want to allow the drop, you need to prevent the rest of the events in the propagation chain—specifically, Flex's default event handler for these events. That's why you call the `preventDefault()` function:

```
else
{
   DragManager.showFeedback(DragManager.NONE);
   event.preventDefault();
}
```

If you didn't do this, then after your function finished (whether you accepted the drop or not), the default handler would let it go through (assuming the data was compatible).

21.10.3 Use the DragEvent object to find the drop target

When you call `acceptDragDrop()`, you tell it that the `dgTarget DataGrid` is the component to accept the drop. To make the function more reusable, you can use the `DragEvent`'s `currentTarget` property, because it's a reference to the drop target.

If you pull up the `DragManager`'s `acceptDragDrop()` function in the API reference, you'll see that it expects an object that follows the `IUIComponent` interface class (the fundamental of any UI component).

But if you just pass `currentTarget`, Flex Builder complains about an incompatibility (see figure 21.5). As far as it knows, `currentTarget` could be pointing to anything.

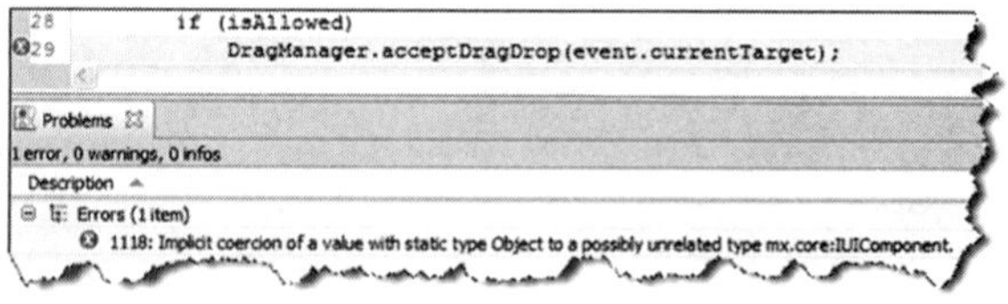

Figure 21.5 Although `currentTarget` points to a UI component during runtime, Flex Builder's compiler needs more assurance.

The remedy is simple: create an object that is the same type as the drop target. Listing 21.7 shows how to do so by creating a temporary `dropTarget` variable that is of type `DataGrid` (which is a UI component) and passing that to the `acceptDragDrop()` function.

Listing 21.7 Converting `currentTarget` to a UI component

```
public function handleDragEnter(event:DragEvent):void
{
    .
    .
    var dropTarget:DataGrid=DataGrid(event.currentTarget);
    .
    .
    if (isAllowed)
       DragManager.acceptDragDrop(dropTarget);
    else
       DragManager.showFeedback(DragManager.NONE);
}
```

This is a great solution if you want to perform a bunch of operations on that `dropTarget` object (perhaps to change its color to indicate whether you're accepting or denying the drop).

If you want a quick and simple approach, tell Flex that the object that `currentTarget` is pointing at complies with the `IUIComponent` interface:

```
DragManager.acceptDragDrop(event.currentTarget as IUIComponent);
```

Although you're still using the component's built-in abilities to process the drop, you can override that and apply your own custom approach.

21.11 Applying your own drop

The next need you're likely to encounter is to apply the drop yourself; this involves storing the data directly in the component's `dataProvider` or in a variable to which the component is bound. For example, you may want to store information in a database on the backend as it's dragged in.

To keep the code blocks short, we'll expand the previous example but show only what's added.

21.11.1 Adding to the component's dataProvider explicitly

Let's add a `dragDrop` event handler that takes the data that's being moved and copies it to the component's `dataProvider`. Because the `dataProvider` isn't set to anything, it defaults to `null`; you need to check for that and initialize the `dataProvider` if need be (see listing 21.8).

Listing 21.8 Creating a function to directly add data to a component

```
<mx:Script>
 <![CDATA[
   public function handleDrop(event:DragEvent):void
   {
     var arItems:Array= event.dragSource.dataForFormat("items")
          as Array;
     if(dgTarget.dataProvider==null)
       dgTarget.dataProvider = new ArrayCollection();

     for(var i:int=0; i<arItems.length;i++)
       dgTarget.dataProvider.addItem(arItems[i]);
   }
 ]]>
</mx:Script>
<mx:DataGrid id="dgTarget" height="100"
           dragEnter="handleDragEnter(event)"
           dragDrop="handleDrop(event)">
  <mx:columns>
   <mx:DataGridColumn dataField="name" headerText="Contact Name"
         width="200" />
   <mx:DataGridColumn dataField="email" headerText="E-Mail"
         width="200"/>
   <mx:DataGridColumn dataField="isActive" headerText="Active"
```

Access dragged data as an Array

Add to drop target's ArrayCollection

```
        width="75"/>
  </mx:columns>
</mx:DataGrid>
```

If you don't feel comfortable with manipulating the dataProvider of the source of the drag operation, you'll find the implicit approach less intrusive.

21.11.2 Adding to the component's dataProvider implicitly

An alternative is to have a variable that your List-based component is bound to and manipulate that instead. That way, you're not so tightly coupled to the component, and you have a more data-centric approach. It also makes your dragDrop event handler simpler by only having to manipulate the ArrayCollection and not having to worry about components that may use it.

Listing 21.9 does so by having the same handleDrop() function but manipulating the ArrayCollection—which could be used by any number of components, for all it knows.

Listing 21.9 Manipulating the variable that drives the component's display

```
<mx:Script>
 <![CDATA[
   [Bindable]
   public var targetAC:ArrayCollection = new ArrayCollection();

   public function handleDrop(event:DragEvent):void
   {
    var arItems:Array= event.dragSource.dataForFormat("items") as Array;
    for(var i:int=0; i<arItems.length;i++)
         targetAC.addItem(arItems[i]);
   }
 ]]>
</mx:Script>
<mx:DataGrid id="dgTarget" height="100" dataProvider="{targetAC}"
          dragEnter="handleDragEnter(event)"
          dragDrop="handleDrop(event)">
   <mx:columns>
      <mx:DataGridColumn dataField="name" headerText="Contact Name"
         width="200" />
      <mx:DataGridColumn dataField="email" headerText="E-Mail"
         width="200"/>
      <mx:DataGridColumn dataField="isActive" headerText="Active"
         width="75"/>
   </mx:columns>
</mx:DataGrid>
```

Using what you know about adding your own drop operation, plus your knowledge of the DragManager, you can take this one step further and add D&D capabilities to components that don't natively support D&D.

21.12 Adding D&D to non-List components

The List-based components do all the work when it comes to D&D. But if you want to add D&D to a non-List-based component, you're pretty much on your own and need to add the necessary logic.

To do this, you'll leverage the events from the previous sections (dragEnter and dragDrop), but you need to use a few more events as well—particularly mouseMove and dragComplete.

21.12.1 Setting up the example

This example uses a rudimentary shopping-cart concept, where you choose things to buy by dragging and dropping them into a shopping cart (see figure 21.6).

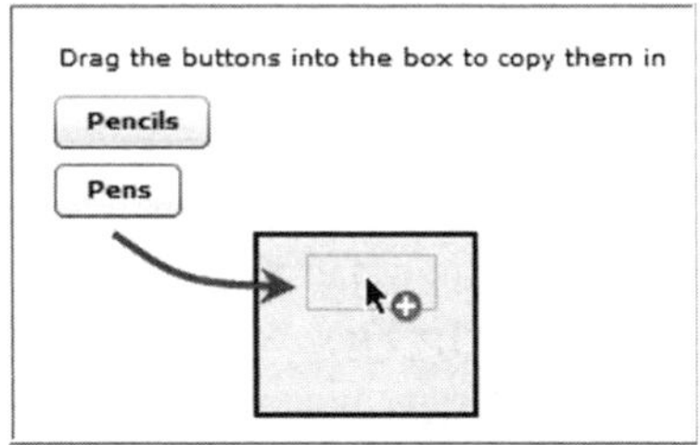

Figure 21.6 Buttons aren't D&D ready by nature, but you can easily add that functionality.

This example is *really* rudimentary, but you get the point. In the real world, you'd query a database for all the details of your catalog (price, title, description, thumbnail image, and so on) and build a list containing those details (perhaps by using a HorizontalList or a DataGrid).

You'll use Button components in this case to keep the code simple, but you could just as easily use an Image component. Knowing what you know about the process, let's begin by initiating the drag operation.

21.12.2 Initiating the drag

To kick off the D&D process, you'll use the mouseMove event and create an event handler that utilizes the DragManager to make this happen. This drag-initiator function performs three major tasks:

- Creates a reference to the drag initiator
- Creates a drag-source object containing all the data that needs to be passed along by the DragManager
- Calls the DragManager's doDrag() function and passes along the reference to the drag initiator, the drag-source object, and the mouseMove event object created by the user

Listing 21.10 shows what this looks like.

Listing 21.10 Function to support initialization of a drag

```
public function initiateDrag(event:MouseEvent):void
{
  var dragInitiator:Button=Button(event.currentTarget);
  var ds:DragSource = new DragSource();
  ds.addData(dragInitiator.label,"name");
   DragManager.doDrag(dragInitiator, ds, event);
}
```

A reference to the dragged Button

Create the drag-source object

Add data we want to pass along

Kick off the dragging

Now you're in business! Halfway, anyway: the other half is to add the logic for the drop operation. Between those two steps, you can optionally provide visual feedback to the user.

21.12.3 Adding visual feedback

You don't need to do this step, but let's add visual feedback to the user. You did this earlier, in the `dragEnter` event handler in section 21.10.1, to let the user know you're refusing the operation. In this case, you'll assume that you'll allow all drags and drops. The event that follows immediately after `dragEnter` is `dragOver`, which is an opportunity to add the visual feedback. Although the code performs a simple copy, if you're supporting various types of operations or have custom visual D&D business logic, this is the place to do it.

In Flex, a `List`-based component automatically changes its border color when a drag item is over it, thus giving the user a visual queue that the drag item is recognized by the potential drop target. The implied operation is different if you're holding down the Shift key or the Ctrl key.

Listing 21.11 replicates that kind of feedback and changes the border color of the drop target depending on what the user is doing.

Listing 21.11 Visually communicating to the user in different ways

```
public function handleDragOver(event:DragEvent):void
{
if (event.ctrlKey)
   {
      DragManager.showFeedback(DragManager.COPY);
      event.currentTarget.setStyle('borderColor', 'blue');
   }
   else if (event.shiftKey)
   {
     DragManager.showFeedback(DragManager.LINK);
      event.currentTarget.setStyle('borderColor', 'green');
   }
   else
   {
      DragManager.showFeedback(DragManager.MOVE);
      event.currentTarget.setStyle('borderColor', 'yellow');
   }
}
```

There's a subtle yet valuable reason for doing this: when you call the `showFeedback()` function, it sets the `DragEvent.action` property to that operation. This comes in handy in later event handlers that need to know what operation that was.

21.12.4 Handling the drop

You aren't using `List`-based components, so they don't have any sort of default behavior to handle a drop. In this example, you'll access the data that's pushed into the drag-source object and create a button based on that information that is then added to the shopping-cart box. Once that's done, you'll also need to change the border back to its original color.

Just to show how you can handle a move operation, you'll check to see whether a move is what the user wants to do, and you'll destroy the original if that's the case (see listing 21.12).

Listing 21.12 Adding logic to support a move D&D

```
public function handleDrop(event:DragEvent):void
{
  var newButton:Button = new Button();                          <- Create a Button
  newButton.label = event.dragSource.dataForFormat("name") as String;   <- Utilize data passed to us
  ShoppingCart.addChild(newButton);                             <- Add to the shopping
  ShoppingCart.setStyle('borderColor','black');                    cart VBox

  if(event.action == DragManager.MOVE)                          <- Nuke the source
   Catalog.removeChild(event.dragInitiator as Button);             if moving
}
```

Alternatively, another good spot to handle the remove logic is in a `dragComplete` handler function, which is an event generated from the drag initiator:

```
<mx:Button label="Pencils" mouseMove="initiateDrag(event)"
  dragComplete="handleDragComplete(event)"/>
```

This covers the bulk of what needs to be done. But in such custom scenarios it's possible that you have some cleanup work to do, and that's where you'll handle the exit.

21.12.5 Handling the exit

Finally, because you changed the color of the border on the `dragOver` event, you need to change it back in case the user decides to mouse off the drop target:

```
public function handleDragExit(event:DragEvent):void
{
  ShoppingCart.setStyle('borderColor','black');
}
```

Now you have each piece necessary to add D&D capabilities between components that don't necessarily support D&D. Next, you'll put it all together.

21.12.6 Putting it all together

It may seem like a lot of work, but that's largely due to all the supporting detail that describes how each piece works. When you combine all the information, it's not that much code, surprisingly, to make the custom D&D happen. Listing 21.13 shows the full example.

Listing 21.13 Supporting D&D between two non-`List`-based components

```
<?xml version="1.0"?>
<mx:Application xmlns:mx="http://www.adobe.com/2006/mxml"
```

```
backgroundColor="white">
<mx:Script>
 <![CDATA[

 import mx.core.DragSource;
 import mx.managers.DragManager;
 import mx.events.*;
 import mx.controls.Button;
 import mx.collections.ArrayCollection;

  [Bindable]
  public var myAC:ArrayCollection  = new ArrayCollection([
   {name:"Pencil", price:1.25},{name:"Pen", price:1.78}]);

  public function initiateDrag(event:MouseEvent):void
  {
      var dragInitiator:Button=Button(event.currentTarget);
      var ds:DragSource = new DragSource();
      ds.addData(dragInitiator.label,"name");
      DragManager.doDrag(dragInitiator, ds, event);
  }

  public function handleDragEnter(event:DragEvent):void
  {
     DragManager.acceptDragDrop(event.currentTarget as VBox);
  }

  public function handleDragOver(event:DragEvent):void
  {
   if (event.ctrlKey)
   {
       DragManager.showFeedback(DragManager.COPY);
         event.currentTarget.setStyle('borderColor', 'blue');
   }
   else if (event.shiftKey)
   {
     DragManager.showFeedback(DragManager.LINK);
         event.currentTarget.setStyle('borderColor', 'green');
   }
   else
   {
     DragManager.showFeedback(DragManager.MOVE);
     event.currentTarget.setStyle('borderColor', 'yellow');
   }
  }

   public function handleDrop(event:DragEvent):void
   {
     var newButton:Button = new Button();
     newButton.label = event.dragSource.dataForFormat("name")
         as String;
       ShoppingCart.addChild(newButton);
       ShoppingCart.setStyle('borderColor','black');
       if(event.action == DragManager.MOVE)
          Catalog.removeChild(event.dragInitiator as Button);
   }
```

Create the Drag Source Object

Create a reference to the dragged button

Add data to pass along

Kick off the dragging

```
        public function handleDragExit(event:DragEvent):void
        {
            ShoppingCart.setStyle('borderColor','black');
        }
    ]]>
</mx:Script>
<mx:VBox id="Catalog">
        <mx:Label text="Drag the buttons into the box to copy them in"/>
        <mx:Button label="Pencils"  mouseMove="initiateDrag(event)"/>
        <mx:Button label="Pens" mouseMove="initiateDrag(event)"/>
</mx:VBox>
<mx:VBox id="ShoppingCart" borderColor="black" borderThickness="2"
        dragEnter="handleDragEnter(event)"
        dragOver="handleDragOver(event)"
       dragDrop="handleDrop(event)"
       dragExit="handleDragExit(event)"
        width="94" height="76" backgroundColor="#D7FE2E"
           borderStyle="solid"/>
</mx:Application>
```

If you made it through that, give yourself a pat on the back! It's one of the larger examples in this book. If you view it as small functions that handle the various events a D&D process goes through, it's straightforward.

21.13 Customizing the drag-and-drop experience

To wrap up this chapter, we'll shift to the creative aspect of D&D. That means you can swap in your own icons for the various UI gestures to the user. First, you'll change the drag image.

21.13.1 Changing the drag image

Flex usually displays an outline of the component you're dragging. You can change it to whatever image you want. This functionality is facilitated by the `DragManager`'s `doDrag()` function—the function that begins the dragging operation. When you used it previously, you passed in only the required parameters:

```
DragManager.doDrag(dragInitiator, ds, event);
```

Looking at the `DragManager` class in the Flex API shows you can see a bunch of operational parameters—particularly one called `dragImage`. You'll use it to make this happen.

The next step is to create an image and pass it along. To demonstrate, listing 21.14 borrows snippets from the custom D&D example in listing 21.13.

Listing 21.14 Creating a custom drag image

```
<?xml version="1.0"?>
<mx:Application xmlns:mx="http://www.adobe.com/2006/mxml"
   backgroundColor="white">
   <mx:Script>
   <![CDATA[
   import mx.managers.DragManager;
   import mx.core.DragSource;
```

```
    import flash.events.MouseEvent;
    import mx.controls.Image;

    public var imgCopy:Class;
    [Embed(source='assets/dragimage.png')]
    public var imgDrag:Class;

    public function initiateDrag(event:MouseEvent):void
    {
      var dragInitiator:Button=Button(event.currentTarget);
      var ds:DragSource = new DragSource();
      var dragImage:Image = new Image();
      var xOffset:int = -5;
      var yOffset:int = -5;
      var alphaLevel:Number = 1.00;
      dragImage.source = imgDrag;
      dragImage.height=59;
      dragImage.width=57;
      DragManager.doDrag(dragInitiator, ds, event,
                    dragImage,xOffset,yOffset,alphaLevel);
    }
    ]]>
    </mx:Script>
    <mx:Button label="Pencils"  mouseMove="initiateDrag(event)"/>
</mx:Application>
```

When a user tries to drag the button (see figure 21.7), a funky icon is used instead of the typical gray box.

Here's how it works:

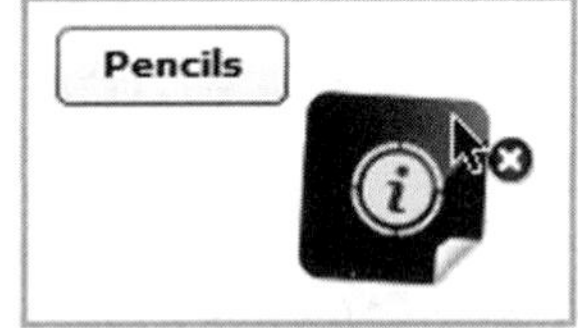

Figure 21.7 Using a custom drag image to customize the experience

1. A graphic is imported into the application as a global variable.
2. An `Image` object is created using that graphic when a drag is about to occur.
3. The `Image` object is passed in the `doDrag()` function along with additional (optional) parameters that control the X and Y offsets where the image should appear relative to the mouse pointer, as well as the transparency level.

Similarly, you can control the images used to communicate to the user about what the drag operation is (move, copy, deny, and so on).

21.13.2 Changing the drag proxy Icons

As we mentioned earlier, the drag proxy is the visual feedback that is communicated to the user during the D&D process. The easiest way to change it is to use CSS/styles (see chapter 19 for more information).

From a code perspective, listing 21.15 shows how using CSS declarations defines which images are used by the drag proxy for each scenario.

Listing 21.15 Overriding the default drag-proxy images

```
<mx:Style>
 DragManager
 {
   copyCursor: Embed(source="assets/copy.png");
   linkCursor: Embed(source="assets/link.jpg");
   moveCursor: Embed(source="assets/move.png");
   rejectCursor: Embed(source="assets/reject.jpg");
 }
</mx:Style>
```

That's obviously a lot easier than changing the drag image, and it lets you leverage your CSS skills.

21.14 Summary

Drag-and-drop is interesting because it can be as involved as you want it to be. For the most part, Flex does all the hard work for you; you just need to intercept the points at which you want to interject custom business logic.

`List`-based components come with built-in support for doing most of the work, but you can trap none, some, or all of the D&D events. For non-`List`-based components, leverage the `DragManager` as your workhorse. Flex calls your drag-related event handlers and passes you the `DragEvent` object each time, giving you the information you need to work with.

Don't forget to make your application fun by customizing the user experience. Keep usability the primary reason you're using D&D, and take advantage of its ability to save your users time.

In the next chapter, we'll shift gears to a different subject: charting. Continuing the theme of usability, just as D&D adds interface usability, charting adds usability to information.

22 Charting

This chapter covers:

- Understanding the parts of a chart
- Using chart series
- Types of charts
- Customizing charts

If you ever need a way to sell Flex to your organization, charting will help you do it. Management loves charting; give the bosses a taste of Flex's charts, and you'll soon have them addicted and begging for more.

Flex charts are so compelling because, unlike using static charts (and even some animated ones), with Flex you can create interactive and engaging dashboard experiences. This is especially true if you combine charting with effects to seal the deal.

In this chapter, we'll explore what makes up a chart, the charts that come with Flex, and how to customize them. Let's start with an introduction to charting.

22.1 Introduction to charting

Flex's charting feature comes as part of the Professional Edition. But even if you haven't paid for that version, you can still build charts—they'll just have a Flex Charting Trial watermark superimposed on the image.

Flex's charting engine is incredibly flexible from a developer's point of view. You can control what each specific data point looks like, build powerful dashboards, employ multiple axes, and support various forms of user interaction.

For example, you can handle the event when a user clicks a particular data point and use that information to drive another chart or pull up data related to that data point. Your charts can be programmed to support drag-and-drop operations and let the user draw selections around a collection of data points.

In Flex, all charts are derived from either the `Cartesian` charting class or the `PolarChart` class. Cartesian charting is premised on the Cartesian coordinate system of using X and Y coordinates to define data points on horizontal and vertical axes. The `PolarChart` class is used to define regions within a circular or radial space, although the only chart derived from this is the pie chart.

22.1.1 Chart parts

Charts comprise various pieces that make them work; those parts exist as MXML components and ActionScript class equivalents. The parts of a chart are listed in table 22.1.

Table 22.1 Parts of a chart

Chart part	Description
Chart	The chart itself, the framework to which all other parts are connected.
Series	A collection of related data points.
Axis/Axes	Horizontal and vertical axes. Flex's charts are two-dimensional only, but you can have multiple axes.
Axis renderers	A powerful mechanism to control how lines and labels are displayed.
Elements	Anything else that needs to be displayed in the chart area. For example, you can display special icons at certain points, grid lines, annotations, and so on.
Labels	Textual information about the chart's axes and series.

They may not sound like much, but with those pieces you can produce an enormous variety of charting experiences for your users.

22.1.2 Chart types overview

You want charts? We've got charts—nine types of charts, as listed in table 22.2.

Table 22.2 Types of charts in Flex 3

Type	MXML component and class	Series component and class
Area	`AreaChart`	`AreaSeries`
Bar	`BarChart`	`BarSeries`

Table 22.2 Types of charts in Flex 3 *(continued)*

Type	MXML component and class	Series component and class
Bubble	`BubbleChart`	`BubbleSeries`
Candlestick	`CandleStick`	`CandlestickSeries`
Column	`ColumnChart`	`ColumnSeries`
HLOC	`HLOCChart`	`HLOCSeries`
Line	`LineChart`	`LineSeries`
Pie	`PieChart`	`PieSeries`
Plot	`PlotChart`	`PlotSeries`

We know you're anxious to start using these. Before you do so, let's prepare by discussing a hypothetical FlexMoto exotic car company for which you'll build a sales dashboard.

22.2 Setting the stage with series and data

Let's set the stage by talking about how charts display data in the first place, and how you'll facilitate that display in the examples.

Charts display collections of related data in what's called a *series*, and each chart has at least one series. A ubiquitous usage of a series is to display financial information broken into periodic time internals—for example, sales by month or quarterly revenues.

The series is the heart of a chart, and each chart type has a corresponding series component/class to go along with it. Figure 22.1 illustrates with a line chart that has a single series with a data point at each quarter in the year.

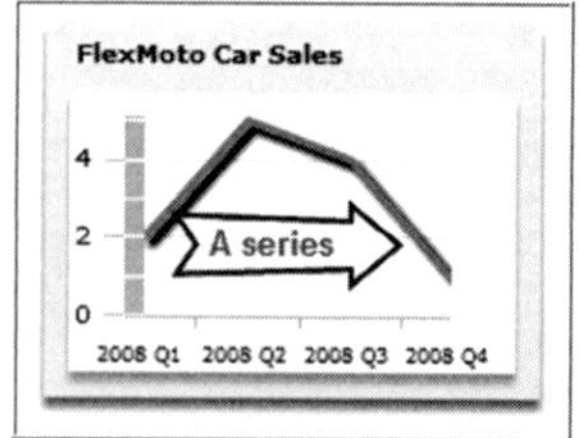

Figure 22.1 This chart has one series representing the number of cars sold per quarter.

A series is nothing without its data, and that information traditionally is in tabular form. In the FlexMoto example, let's assume the data is as shown in table 22.3.

Table 22.3 FlexMoto data that will be used for the examples

Interval	FerrariUnits	FerrariSales	PorscheUnits	PorscheSales
2008 Q1	2	2.32	2	0.180
2008 Q2	5	7.82	3	0.240
2008 Q3	4	6.92	7	0.420
2008 Q4	1	1.80	12	1.180

In the real world, you'd retrieve this data from a database using a back-end data service such as a web service or a remote object (see chapter 14) and assign that to an `ArrayCollection`. The result would be an `ArrayCollection` similar to the hardcoded example in listing 22.1 (just to give you an idea).

Listing 22.1 FlexMoto's data in the form of an `ArrayCollection`

```
salesAC:ArrayCollection = new ArrayCollection( [
{interval: "2008 Q1", ferrariUnits:2, ferrariSales:2.32, porscheUnits:2,
   porscheSales: 0.180},
{interval: "2008 Q2", ferrariUnits:5, ferrariSales:7.82, porscheUnits:3,
   porscheSales: 0.240},
{interval: "2008 Q3", ferrariUnits:4, ferrariSales:6.92, porscheUnits:7,
   porscheSales: 0.420},
{interval: "2008 Q4", ferrariUnits:1, ferrariSales:1.80, porscheUnits:12,
   porscheSales: 1.180}
]);
```

Alternatively, data in the form of XML is always a popular choice, and this is the form you'll use in the examples. Listing 22.2 contains the XML version of the data.

Listing 22.2 data.xml: FlexMoto's sales data in XML form

```
<salesdata>
  <all>
    <data interval="2008 Q1" ferrariUnits="2" ferrariSales="2.32"
                       porscheUnits="2" porscheSales="0.180"/>

    <data interval="2008 Q2" ferrariUnits="5" ferrariSales="7.82"
                       porscheUnits="3" porscheSales="0.240" />

    <data interval="2008 Q3" ferrariUnits="4" ferrariSales="6.92"
                       porscheUnits="7" porscheSales="0.420"/>

    <data interval="2008 Q4" ferrariUnits="1" ferrariSales="1.80"
                       porscheUnits="12" porscheSales="1.180"/>
  </all>
</salesdata>
```

Now that you have your data, you can move forward to create charts.

22.3 Creating charts

A convenient feature of charting is that you can create a chart, and if you don't like it, change it to a different type of chart with minimal effort. In this section, we'll show you how to create a chart and progressively add pieces to it to build it out.

22.3.1 Invoking a chart

Creating a chart involves picking the chart type you want, using its corresponding series component to plot the data points, and providing at least a horizontal axis.

TIP The chart is the foundation on which a series and other pieces build.

Using the FlexMoto sales data, let's start by using a line chart to display how many Ferraris and Porsches have been sold quarter by quarter (see listing 22.3).

Listing 22.3 Line chart displaying the number of units sold by car type

```
<?xml version="1.0"?>
<mx:Application xmlns:mx="http://www.adobe.com/2006/mxml"
   backgroundColor="white">
 <mx:XML id="salesDataXML" source="data.xml"/>
 <mx:XMLListCollection source="{salesDataXML.all.data}"
                id="salesData"/>

 <mx:Panel title="FlexMoto Car Sales" width="500" height="250">

  <mx:LineChart id="salesChart" dataProvider="{salesData}"
           height="100%" width="100%" >
   <mx:horizontalAxis>
    <mx:CategoryAxis categoryField="@interval"/>
   </mx:horizontalAxis>

   <mx:series>
    <mx:LineSeries yField="@ferrariUnits"/>
    <mx:LineSeries yField="@porscheUnits"/>
   </mx:series>
  </mx:LineChart>

  </mx:Panel>
</mx:Application>
```

Retrieve and set up data

Set up horizontal axis to display quarters

Set up series for each car manufacturer

Compiling and running the application gives you a chart with two line series on it, resembling figure 22.2.

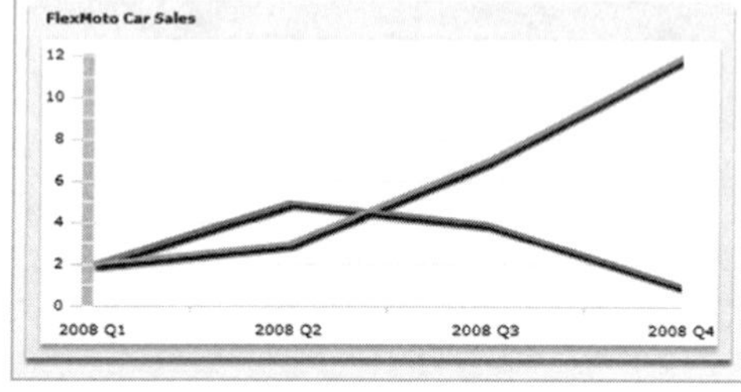

Figure 22.2 FlexMoto's car sales by units sold for each type of car, displayed using a line chart

Note a few things in this example:

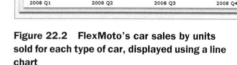

- The *Y* axis represents the value in the series. It's sometimes called the value axis.
- The *Y* axis by default starts at 0 and goes to the largest value found in the entire series.
- The *X* axis represents the category and is known as the category axis.
- The *X* axis labels by default are spread evenly across the width of the chart.

That was fairly painless, considering you created a chart in only nine lines of code. But you're missing something: how is a user to know what each line color represents? This is where a legend comes in.

22.3.2 Adding a legend

A *legend* is a visual guide whose purpose is to map each series to a context. We could have said a legend is used to map a color to a series, which is true to an extent; but a series can be differentiated by more than just a color. For example, a series may plot itself with a different transparency level, pattern (such as dashed lines), or texture (such as gradient colors).

Let's add a legend using the code in listing 22.4.

Listing 22.4 Adding a legend so users know what each line means

```
<mx:Legend dataProvider="{salesChart}"/>
<mx:LineChart id="salesChart" dataProvider="{salesData}"
          height="100%" width="100%" >
  <mx:horizontalAxis>
    <mx:CategoryAxis categoryField="@interval"/>
  </mx:horizontalAxis>
  <mx:series>
    <mx:LineSeries yField="@ferrariUnits"
              displayName="Ferrari Count"/>
    <mx:LineSeries yField="@porscheUnits"
              displayName="Porsche Count"/>
  </mx:series>
</mx:LineChart>
```

Legend uses chart as data source

displayName field tells legend to label each series

This code produces an application that has a `Legend` component at the top.

You should observe a few things:

- The `Legend` component exists outside of the chart tag.
- The legend uses the chart's `id` property as the source for its data.
- The legend that has a reference to the chart examines all of the chart's child series and extracts the design of each series (such as its color) as well as the `displayName` property used for each series.

You have a fully viable chart at this point. But if you need to change to a different type of chart, doing so isn't difficult.

22.3.3 *Changing chart types*

How easy it is to switch from one chart type to another depends on the specifics, but even in the worst case it doesn't require much effort. To cover every permutation wouldn't be of much value; all we want to do here is give you a sense of the process.

Imagine that you've taken your FlexMoto sales dashboard to your boss. He's the kind of guy who's never happy and who has a thing against line charts, and he prefers that you switch to a different type of chart. Not a problem; let's change to an area chart, as shown in listing 22.5.

Listing 22.5 FlexMoto's sales dashboard switched to an area chart

```
<mx:AreaChart id="salesChart" dataProvider="{salesData}"
          height="100%" width="100%" >
  <mx:horizontalAxis>
    <mx:CategoryAxis categoryField="@interval"/>
  </mx:horizontalAxis>
  <mx:series>
```

```
    <mx:AreaSeries yField="@ferrariUnits"
              displayName="Ferrari Count"
              alpha="0.5"/>
    <mx:AreaSeries yField="@porscheUnits"
              displayName="Porsche Count"
              alpha="0.5"/>
  </mx:series>
</mx:AreaChart>
```

Alpha property controls transparency

All you've done is change `line` to `area` in the code and called it a day. Figures 22.3 and 22.4 show how the chart looks now.

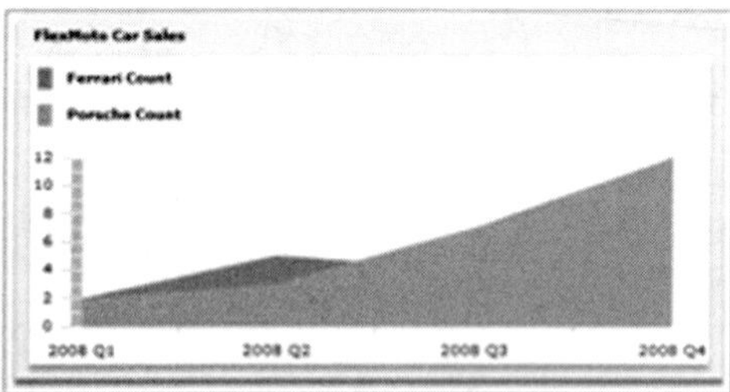

Figure 22.3 Because the area chart defaults to laying one series on top of another, you can only see where one series exceeds the other.

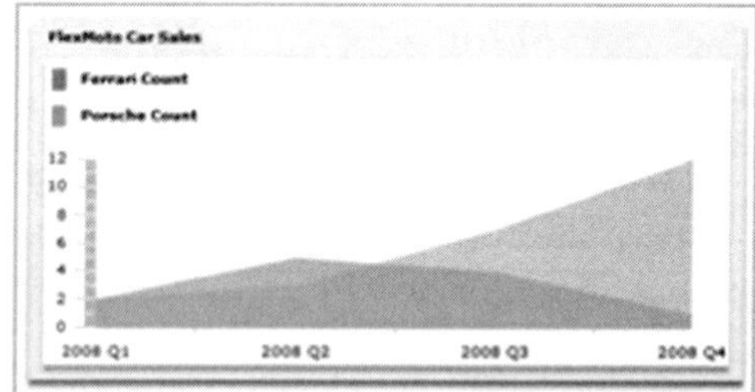

Figure 22.4 Using transparency levels lets you see where one series overlaps the other.

One problem, as you can see, is that a series can be blocked by another. Here, you solve that by customizing the chart and controlling the transparency level (using the `alpha` property). We'll get further into customization later in this chapter.

TIP The examples use the `@` character because you're accessing attributes of an XML node. You wouldn't need it if your data came from an `ArrayCollection`.

Unfortunately, your boss still isn't happy. He wants you to switch to using a bar chart—which, although still fairly easy, requires a bit more work (see listing 22.6).

Listing 22.6 A bar chart, which uses a vertical axis

```
<mx:BarChart id="salesChart" dataProvider="{salesData}"
        height="100%" width="100%" >
  <mx:verticalAxis>
     <mx:CategoryAxis categoryField="@interval"/>
  </mx:verticalAxis>
 <mx:series>
   <mx:BarSeries xField="@ferrariUnits"
            displayName="Ferrari Count"/>
   <mx:BarSeries xField="@porscheUnits"
            displayName="Porsche Count"/>
  </mx:series>
</mx:BarChart>
```

Required because bar charts use Y axis for categories

Listing 22.6 uses the same approach of using the `<BarChart>` and `<BarSeries>` where necessary, but a bar chart uses the vertical (Y) axis to display groupings. See figure 22.5.

The charts used in these examples all support a capability called *stacking*, but there are different ways charts can stack or cluster their display.

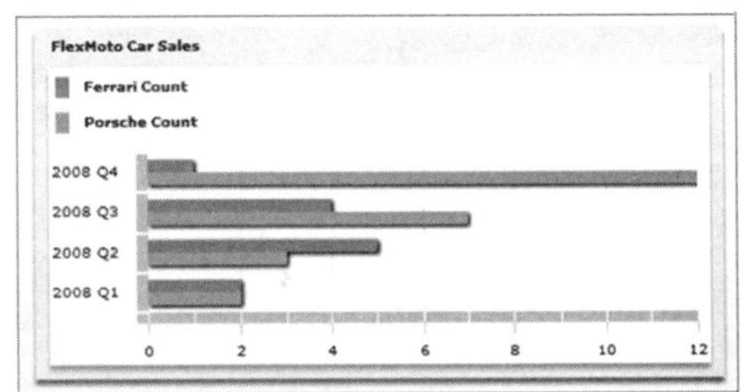

Figure 22.5 Switching to a bar chart also requires switching to using a vertical axis for the category axis.

22.4 Stacking charts

A number of charts support the ability to stack their series; stacking is useful when you need to show an accumulative visualization of data. The following charts support stacking:

- Area chart
- Bar chart
- Column chart

They support stacking through the use of their `type` property. The possible stacking options for this field are:

- `clustered`—Clusters the data points in the series by category. This is the default for the bar chart and column chart, which you saw in figure 22.4. Note that this type isn't available for the area chart.
- `overlaid`—Layers one series over another (think onion skin) in the order that the series are defined in the code. This is the default for the area chart (figure 22.3). Used to contrast one series from another.
- `stacked`—Stacks one series on top of another (think Lego blocks). Used to demonstrate how each series makes up a whole (via the cumulative effect). Each series accumulates toward the total value.
- `100%`—The same as `stacked`, but each series accumulates to 100% (similar to how a pie chart works).

Listing 22.5 used an area chart to show sales volume, but its default behavior was to use an `overlaid` display to layer one series over the other. But to show how the sales of each car accumulate to a total, you can switch the `type` property to `stacked`:

```
<mx:AreaChart type="stacked" id="salesChart"
         dataProvider="{salesData}">
. . .
</mx:AreaChart>
```

Figure 22.6 shows how the display provides a different perspective than figure 22.3, even though they're both area charts of the same data.

Similarly, if you switch the type to other values, you get different visual perspectives. Each perspective tells part of the story.

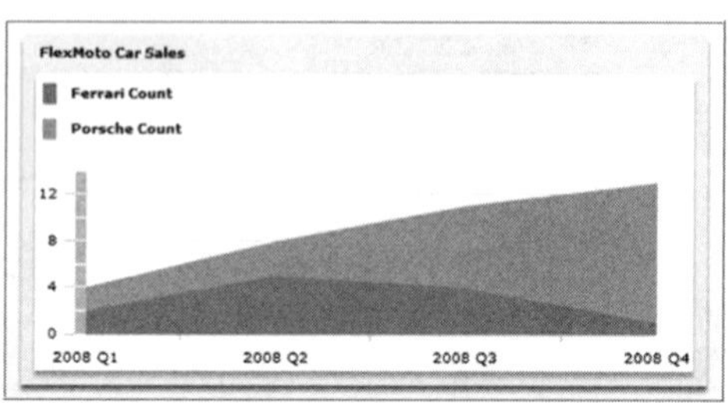

Figure 22.6 Changing the area chart to a stacked mode accumulates each series toward a whole.

Now that you have a feel for creating charts, let's take a closer look at the types of charts that come with Flex.

22.5 Exploring chart types

From what you've seen so far, there's not a drastic difference (code-wise) between using one chart or another. But you also saw a case (the bar chart) where the difference was significant enough to require additional details.

In this section, we'll discuss each of the charting types and how to create them, as well as provide tips on the business cases for which they're most useful.

22.5.1 Area charts

Area charts are like line charts, except the area under the line is filled in. By controlling transparency levels, you can make your charts appear either *layered*, where you can visually see the differences and overlap, or *stacked*, where one series appears to be stacked on top of another. Although line charts and area charts are similar, they differ in that an area chart is particularly good at representing volume trends.

Using the `AreaSeries` component, you can use a number of parameters to control the display of the series.

To show you something interesting, let's look at the `minField` property. Area charts are used to represent volume, and that volume can have a specific range of values.

NOTE The area chart supports stacking; see section 22.3.

Suppose you have temperature data specifying daily high and low values for each day. You can use an `AreaSeries` defined as follows:

```
<mx:AreaSeries yField="@high" minField="@low" displayName="Temperature"/>
```

This results in figure 22.7, where the temperate range is filled in between the low and high values.

This is an interesting way to look at data: changes to the shape tell a story without users having to look at the numbers. Where the width expands, you're able to determine that differences emerge; and as the width becomes thinner, the variance converges.

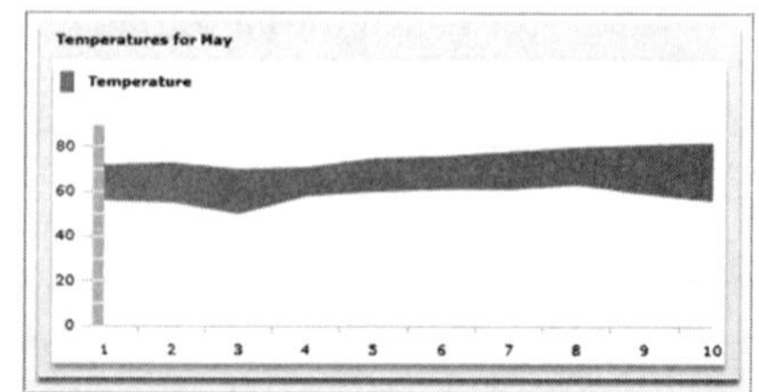

Figure 22.7 Using the `minField` property, you can start each data point from an arbitrary value.

Using the area chart's stacking abilities, you can display many types of stories that the data can tell. The `overlaid` type can highlight and contrast differences and commonalities in data, and `stacked` and `100%` show you the accumulative effect of all the series combined.

Although the area chart supports these stacking modes, it doesn't support clustered series—this is something supported by bar charts and column charts.

22.5.2 Bar charts and column charts

Bar charts and column charts are the same thing; the only difference is that a bar chart draws horizontally, whereas a column chart is vertical. Oddly enough, if you say "bar chart" to someone, the first thing they think of is what Flex calls a column chart.

Although these charts can be used to display trending information (information that changes over time), they're particularly strong displaying *clustered* information—data clumped together by some category.

NOTE Bar charts and column charts support stacking; see section 22.3.

In figure 22.5, you saw a bar chart used to show how many cars by type were sold over each given quarter. Bar charts are perfectly useful for showing this time-bound information, but consider the data in listing 22.7.

Listing 22.7 candidates.xml: support for candidates by age demographics

```
<candidates>
  <all>
    <data category="18-25" clinton="50" mccain="30" obama="20"/>
    <data category="26-35" clinton="40" mccain="20" obama="40"/>
    <data category="36+" clinton="10" mccain="60" obama="30"/>
  </all>
</candidates>
```

Listing 22.7 shows statistical information broken down by age groups (the category); the percentage of support from that demographic bracket is listed for each candidate. To visualize this information, you can employ a bar chart, as shown in listing 22.8.

Listing 22.8 Using a bar chart to show clustered information

```
<mx:Legend dataProvider="{candidateChart}"/>
<mx:BarChart  id="candidateChart" dataProvider="{tempData}"
          height="100%" width="100%" >
  <mx:verticalAxis>
    <mx:CategoryAxis categoryField="@category"/>
  </mx:verticalAxis>
  <mx:series>
    <mx:BarSeries xField="@clinton" displayName="Clinton"/>
    <mx:BarSeries xField="@mccain"  displayName="McCain"/>
    <mx:BarSeries xField="@obama"   displayName="Obama"/>
  </mx:series>
</mx:BarChart>
```

Uses xField because chart is horizontal

After compiling and running the application, you get the chart shown in figure 22.8.

No time intervals here—figure 22.8 shows the statistical breakdown for each age cluster. Bar charts and column charts support stacking, and their default mode as previously shown is to cluster each series by category.

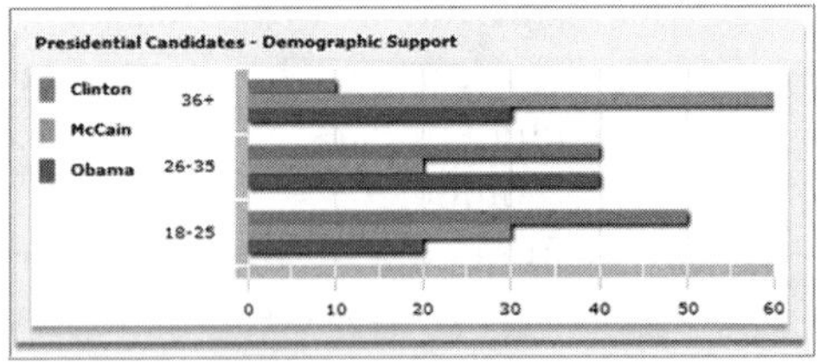

Figure 22.8 This bar chart shows statistics clustered by an age-range category.

You can change the type to use the other stacking values. To demonstrate, let's switch to a column chart and set the `type` property to `stacked` (see listing 22.9).

Listing 22.9 Using a stacked column chart

```
<mx:Panel title="Presidential Candidates - Demographic Support"
   layout="horizontal" width="500" height="200">
  <mx:Legend dataProvider="{candidateChart}"/>
   <mx:ColumnChart type="stacked"  id="candidateChart"
              dataProvider="{tempData}" height="100%" width="100%" >
     <mx:horizontalAxis>
       <mx:CategoryAxis categoryField="@category"/>
     </mx:horizontalAxis>
     <mx:series>
       <mx:ColumnSeries yField="@clinton" displayName="Clinton"/>
       <mx:ColumnSeries yField="@mccain"  displayName="McCain"/>
       <mx:ColumnSeries yField="@obama"   displayName="Obama"/>
     </mx:series>
   </mx:ColumnChart>
</mx:Panel>
```

Defines categories on X axis (annotation for the `horizontalAxis` block)

Defines values (annotation for the `ColumnSeries` lines)

Note that you have to switch to using `yField` because column charts are vertical in nature: the height of each data point requires a *Y*-axis value. Similarly, because the horizontal axis displays each category, you switch back to the `horizontalAxis`.

The values now accumulate to 100—this is because the data represents percentages. But suppose the data represented the number of delegates that each presidential hopeful has acquired; you could set `type` to `100%` to achieve the same result (Flex would automatically calculate the percentages for you).

Bar charts and column charts can show time series with no problem, and a unique advantage comes into play when you need to show clustered information using some arbitrary grouping. But if trending against time is what you're after, you want a line chart.

22.5.3 Line charts

Line charts are the classic way to display data points that represent a trend over time. Because you used a line chart back in listings 22.3 and 22.4, we've covered the primary ground already.

We have something new to show you: the `interpolateValues` property. This property lets Flex fill in the gaps for missing data points if needed.

In this example, let's purposely take out one of the data points. Flex can then only draw lines from the spot at which it has contiguous data points, as shown in figure 22.9.

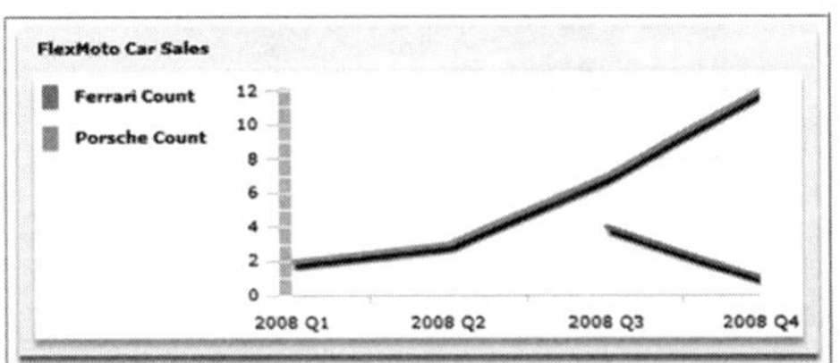

Figure 22.9 Without contiguous data points, the Ferrari series is broken.

You can fix this by setting `interpolateValues` to `true`:

```
<mx:LineSeries interpolateValues="true" yField="@ferrariUnits"
        displayName="Ferrari Count"/>
```

After rerunning the application with this setting, you can see in figure 22.9 how the line is able to continue as Flex fills in the gaps.

Odds are that you're likely to use line charts in your career as a Flex developer; they're versatile and great for historical trending. The other value of line charts, along with bar/column charts, is that people are familiar with them and are able to digest what they display. If you want to get away from the traditional charts, look no further than the bubble chart.

22.5.4 *Bubble charts*

Bubble charts have been around for a while, and you've probably seen examples; but have you seen one actively used in your workplace? They've been slowly gaining traction in the business intelligence space, but some argue that their usefulness is limited.

Bubble charts let you add a third dimension by not only plotting *X* and Y coordinates but also using the size of a bubble as a way of communicating scale (for example, volume, intensity, weight, or size). Flex supports only two-dimensional charts, so this type of chart allows you to get around that limitation.

The `BubbleChart` component supports some unique properties you'll want to be aware of (see table 22.4).

Table 22.4 Additional properties of bubble charts

Property	Type	Description
`minRadius*`	`Number`	Minimum value for a data point; defaults to 0
`maxRadius*`	`Number`	Maximum value for a data point; defaults to 50

* These values are used to calculate how to scale the bubbles.

Next, to complement the `BubbleChart` component, the `BubbleSeries` component has a unique property among the list in table 22.5.

Table 22.5 `BubbleSeries` properties

Property	Type	Description
`xField`	`String`	Optional. Field that contains the related category value. If not specified, the series looks for the category specified in the `CategoryAxis` component.
`yField`	`String`	Field that contains the category/value field.
`radiusField`	`String`	Field that contains the value for the size of the bubble.

So far, you've been plotting the number of units sold in FlexMoto's sales data (see listing 22.2). To add an extra dimension, you can include sales revenues. Listing 22.10 does so by using a `BubbleChart` component to plot units sold and using the sales revenues as a basis for the size of the bubbles.

Listing 22.10 Bubble chart that visually demonstrates sales revenues

```
<mx:Legend dataProvider="{salesChart}"/>
<mx:BubbleChart maxRadius="10" id="salesChart" dataProvider="{salesData}"
            height="100%" width="100%" >
  <mx:horizontalAxis>
    <mx:CategoryAxis categoryField="@interval"/>
  </mx:horizontalAxis>
  <mx:series>
    <mx:BubbleSeries yField="@ferrariUnits" radiusField="@ferrariSales"
                displayName="Ferrari Count"/>
    <mx:BubbleSeries yField="@porscheUnits" radiusField="@porscheSales"
                displayName="Porsche Count"/>
  </mx:series>
</mx:BubbleChart>
```

Look at how the data is visually communicated in figure 22.10.

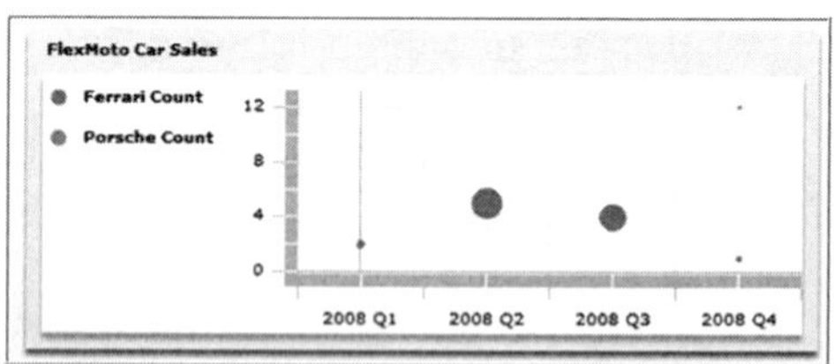

Figure 22.10 Using a bubble chart tells a different story by adding a third dimension.

Adding that third dimension helps put a different perspective on the same data. In a line chart it may look like management should focus on selling Porsches, but on a bubble chart (figure 22.10), Porsche revenues are overshadowed by the larger Ferrari sales revenues.

In going back to the question of whether bubble charts are useful, our opinion is that they definitely are, thanks to that third dimension of information. The key to business intelligence is being able to communicate the story behind the numbers, and the more dimensions you're able to leverage, the more rounded the picture.

The only real issue with bubble charts is that because they're not common, people aren't used to them and aren't immediately sure how to interpret what they're seeing.

If you use a bubble chart, be sure to provide thorough training or help information for the end user.

The bubble chart isn't alone in its learning challenge for users. Candlestick and HLOC charts share some of that challenge.

22.5.5 Candlestick and HLOC charts

You may have seen a candlestick and/or high-low-open-close (HLOC) chart in your walks through life—they're heavily used in the financial industry to illustrate granular levels of information. Without this type of chart, you'd need to use many individual charts, which would clutter the screen and be difficult to assimilate.

Candlesticks and HLOC charts are four charts in one. A user of financial information can easily interpret these four sets of data as well as examine the relationships between them.

Here's how candlesticks work:

- A vertical line represents the high and low (the top is the high, and the bottom is the low). For financial data, this line indicates the range of prices for that day (or whatever the time interval is).
- A rectangular box (a.k.a. the *body*) floats on top of the line.
- If the box is hollow, then the top of the box is the closing price and the bottom of the box is the opening price: the closing price is higher than the opening, meaning that the financial vehicle (such as a stock) appreciated.
- If the box is filled in, then the top of the box is the opening price and the bottom is the closing price: the financial vehicle depreciated.

Figure 22.11 illustrates.

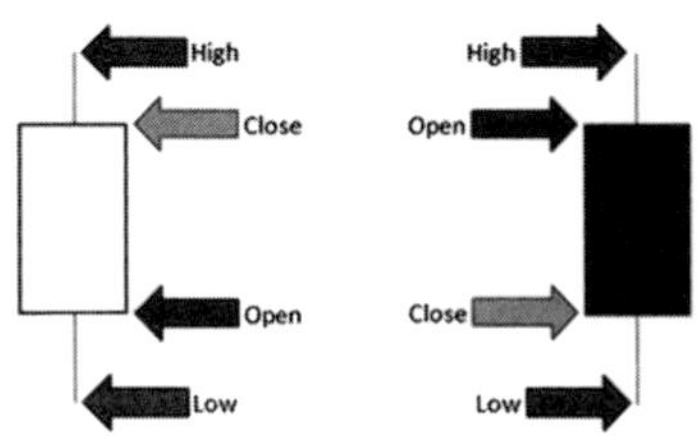

Figure 22.11 How to read a candlestick chart

The varying size of the body (the rectangle) tells the user different perspectives. For example, a longer body indicates increased buying or selling pressure; a shorter body represents consolidation. Long, hollow candlesticks indicate strong buying pressure (due to aggressive buyers); long, solid candlesticks indicate strong selling pressure (a bearish market).

HLOC charts work the same way, except that they use left and right sticks to indicate the opening and closing prices. Here's how they work:

- A vertical line represents the high and low (the top is the high, and the bottom is the low). This line indicates the range of prices for that day (or whatever the time interval is).
- A left tick indicates the opening price.
- A right tick indicates the closing price.

One key difference is that candlesticks require all four data points. Despite the HLOC's name, the open value is optional. Figure 22.12 shows how to interpret an HLOC chart.

To use these charts, you need the four data points to create the `CandlestickSeries` and `HLOCSeries`, as listed in table 22.6.

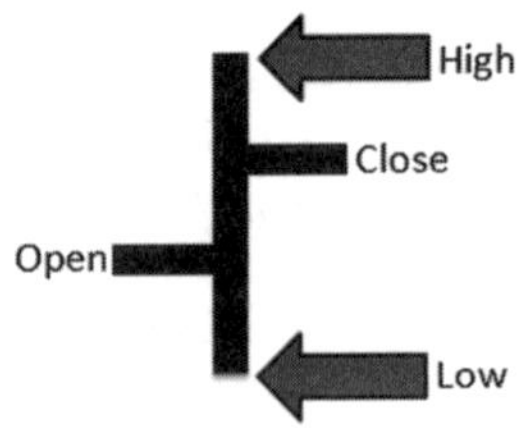

Figure 22.12 How to read an HLOC chart

Table 22.6 `CandlestickSeries` and `HLOCSeries` properties

Property	Type	Description
`highField`	`String`	Field that contains the high value
`lowField`	`String`	Field that contains the low value
`openField`	`String`	Field that contains the open value; optional for `HLOCSeries`
`closeField`	`String`	Field that contains the close value
`xField`	`String`	Field that contains the category value for the X axis; optional

Imagine that the CEO of FlexMoto wants to chart the stock price using a candlestick chart. Assume that listing 22.11 contains the historical stock price data; you can use a `CandlestickChart` as shown in listing 22.12 to plot the data.

Listing 22.11 hloc.xml: FlexMoto's stock-price history

```
<stockdata>
  <ticker>
    <data interval="09/01/2008" high="54" low="40" open="53" close="43"/>
    <data interval="09/02/2008" high="69" low="37" open="62" close="40"/>
    <data interval="09/03/2008" high="62" low="52" open="55" close="60"/>
    <data interval="09/04/2008" high="65" low="30" open="60" close="52"/>
    <data interval="09/05/2008" high="60" low="20" open="42" close="48"/>
  </ticker>
</stockdata>
```

Listing 22.12 Candlestick chart displaying stock prices

```
<mx:XML id="DataXML" source="hloc.xml"/>
<mx:XMLListCollection source="{DataXML.ticker.data}" id="stockData"/>
<mx:Panel title="FlexMoto Stock" width="500" height="200"
       layout="horizontal">
  <mx:CandlestickChart id="hlocChart" dataProvider="{stockData}"
                 height="100%" width="100%" >
    <mx:horizontalAxis>
      <mx:CategoryAxis categoryField="@interval"/>
    </mx:horizontalAxis>
```

```
    <mx:series>
      <mx:CandlestickSeries highField="@high" lowField="@low"
                     openField="@open" closeField="@close"/>
    </mx:series>
  </mx:CandlestickChart>
</mx:Panel>
```

The results of this application are shown in figure 22.13.

Similarly, if you switch from `<mx:CandlestickChart>` to `<mx:HLOCChart>` (and its related series), the result is the chart shown in figure 22.14.

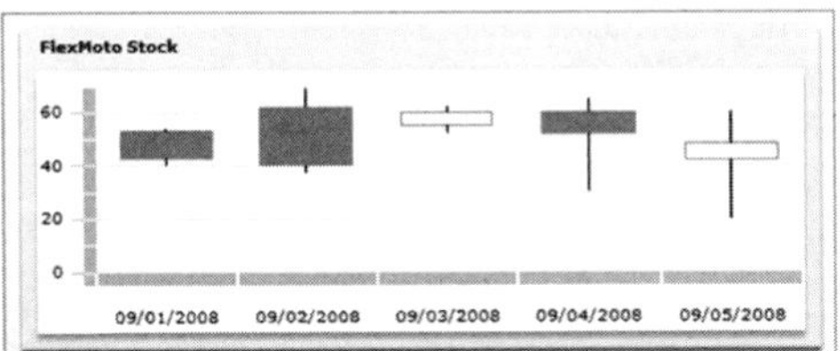

Figure 22.13 Candlestick chart used to display stock price information

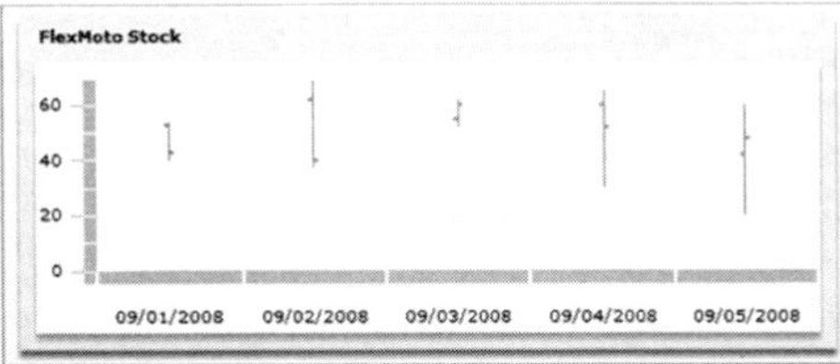

Figure 22.14 HLOC chart representing the same stock data

The financial context is the most prevalent for these types of charts, although if you're creative with your data you can supply business and management folks with nonfinancial data as well.

Moving back into the more popular charts, let's next look at pie charts.

22.5.6 *Pie charts*

This type of chart is one that everyone is familiar with—we're used to partitioned segments that make up a whole. The size of each slice is an indicator of weight, importance, or impact.

Because a pie chart represents components that make up a whole, you need data that is representative of that whole (trending data isn't much use for a pie chart). In this case, you'll use a pie chart to display the annual revenues of FlexMoto, broken down by brand sold (see listing 22.13 for the raw data).

Listing 22.13 pie.xml: annual revenues by manufacturer

```
<salesdata>
  <revenues>
    <data brand="Ferrari" rev="987265"/>
    <data brand="Porsche" rev="678293"/>
    <data brand="BMW" rev="567987"/>
    <data brand="Mercedes" rev="210697"/>
  </revenues>
</salesdata>
```

Using this data, you can use a `PieChart` component with a single `PieSeries` component that looks at the brand and revenue fields (see listing 22.14).

Listing 22.14 Pie chart displaying annual revenues by brand

```
<mx:Legend dataProvider="{salesChart}"/>
<mx:PieChart id="salesChart" dataProvider="{salesData}"
        height="100%" width="100%" >
  <mx:series>
    <mx:PieSeries field="@rev" nameField="@brand"
          labelPosition="outside"/>
  </mx:series>

</mx:PieChart>
```

The result is a pie chart that slices up each brand by revenue and provides a legend; see figure 22.15.

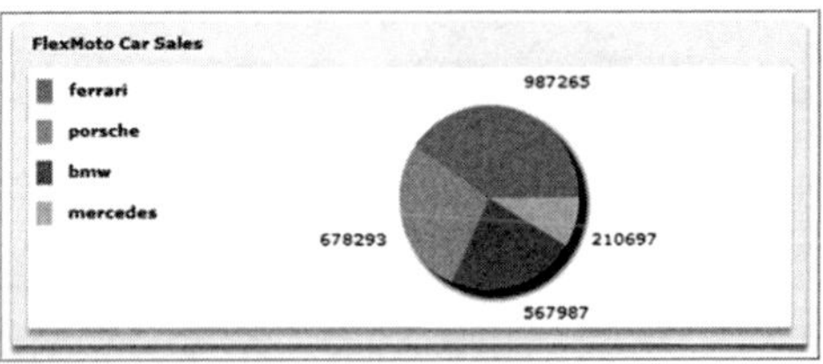

Figure 22.15 Annual revenues by brand, displayed using a pie chart

Here's something neat you can do. Normally, a pie chart has a single series (as shown in figure 22.15). But what if you try more than one pie series? Let's find out.

You'll add another set of data to represent profits; pie.xml is now as shown in listing 22.15.

Listing 22.15 pie.xml: updated to include both revenue and profit data

```
<salesdata>
  <revenues>
    <data brand="Ferrari" rev="987265"/>
    <data brand="Porsche" rev="678293"/>
    <data brand="BMW" rev="567987"/>
    <data brand="Mercedes" rev="210697"/>
  </revenues>
  <profits>
    <data brand="Ferrari" profit="87265"/>
    <data brand="Porsche" profit="78293"/>
    <data brand="BMW" profit="67987"/>
    <data brand="Mercedes" profit="10697"/>
  </profits>
</salesdata>
```

Now, let's modify listing 22.15 to include both sets of data and create a `PieSeries` component for each one (see listing 22.16).

Listing 22.16 Code extended to create a pie chart with two series

```
<mx:XML id="salesDataXML" source="pie.xml"/>
<mx:XMLListCollection source="{salesDataXML.revenues.data}"
            id="salesData"/>
<mx:XMLListCollection source="{salesDataXML.profits.data}"      Creates second set of data
            id="profitData"/>

<mx:Panel title="FlexMoto Car Sales" width="500" height="400"
      layout="horizontal">
```

```
<mx:Legend dataProvider="{salesChart}"/>
 <mx:PieChart id="salesChart" dataProvider="{salesData}"
         height="100%" width="100%" >
  <mx:series>
    <mx:PieSeries field="@rev" nameField="@brand"
              labelPosition="callout"/>
    <mx:PieSeries dataProvider="{profitData}" field="@profit"
              nameField="@brand" labelPosition="inside"/>

  </mx:series>
 </mx:PieChart>
 </mx:Panel>
```

Creates second PieSeries (note dataProvider)

Note how the second pie series specifies a `dataProvider`; it does this because otherwise it will default to the data that the pie chart is using.

There's always more than one way to do something, and listing 22.16 demonstrates how you can handle two complete sets of data. You could instead structure your data as follows:

```
<data brand="ferrari" rev="987265" profit="23424"/>
<data brand="porsche" rev="678293" profit="42323"/>
```

Then you wouldn't need to bother specifying the `dataProvider`, and the code would be as simple as this:

```
<mx:PieSeries field="@rev" nameField="@brand"
  labelPosition="callout"/>
<mx:PieSeries field="@profit" nameField="@brand"
  labelPosition="inside"/>
```

The output is a pie chart inside of a pie chart.

The biggest advantage is that you're able to save desktop space by combining pie series—and you could argue that it provides a business use case in which you're able to compare the relative portions of related data sets.

You've almost finished learning about chart types. The last one is the plot chart.

22.5.7 Plot charts

Last but not least, the plot chart is simple. Other charts calculate where to draw data points by examining the data and determining how to translate it onto the chart. A plot is just a grid—you tell it specifically where each data point goes. In this example, you'll use X and Y coordinate data to plot two different sets of data, as shown in listing 22.17.

Listing 22.17 plot.xml: data to be plotted

```
<plotdata>
 <one>
  <data x="1" y="5"/>
  <data x="3" y="8"/>
  <data x="3" y="9"/>
  <data x="5" y="9"/>
 </one>
```

```
  <two>
    <data x="2" y="1"/>
    <data x="2" y="3"/>
    <data x="4" y="7"/>
    <data x="4" y="4"/>
  </two>
</plotdata>
```

This data is consumed by a plot chart with two plot series in listing 22.18.

Listing 22.18 Plot chart used to display two series

```
<mx:XML id="plotDataXML" source="plot.xml"/>
<mx:XMLListCollection source="{plotDataXML.one.data}" id="plotData1"/>
<mx:XMLListCollection source="{plotDataXML.two.data}" id="plotData2"/>
<mx:Panel title="Plot Data" width="500" height="200"
        layout="horizontal">                              Creates two
 <mx:Legend dataProvider="{plotChart}"/>                  sets of data ❶
  <mx:PlotChart id="plotChart" height="100%" width="100%" >
   <mx:series>
     <mx:PlotSeries dataProvider="{plotData1}" displayName="One"
                 xField="@x" yField="@y" radius="4"/>
     <mx:PlotSeries dataProvider="{plotData2}" displayName="Two"
                 xField="@x" yField="@y" radius="4"/>
                                                     Each series points
   </mx:series>                                     to related data set ❷
  </mx:PlotChart>
 </mx:Panel>
```

First, you separate the data in the XML file into two separate variables ❶. Each plot series ❷ points to one of those variables. Look at the results in figure 22.16; you can see how each series is assigned a color and shape.

What is a plot chart good for? Because you can control the exact positioning by *X* and Y coordinates, you're inherently using the *X* axis and *Y* axis as a way to measure the relationship between the two. For example, if the *X* axis represented people's ages and the *Y* axis represented the average number of car accidents, you could visually see how those two related to each other.

From a statistical point of view, if you have a collection of independent data points and you're able to see how the data points clump together, this may reveal something interesting that averaging those numbers may not tell you. For example, figure 22.17

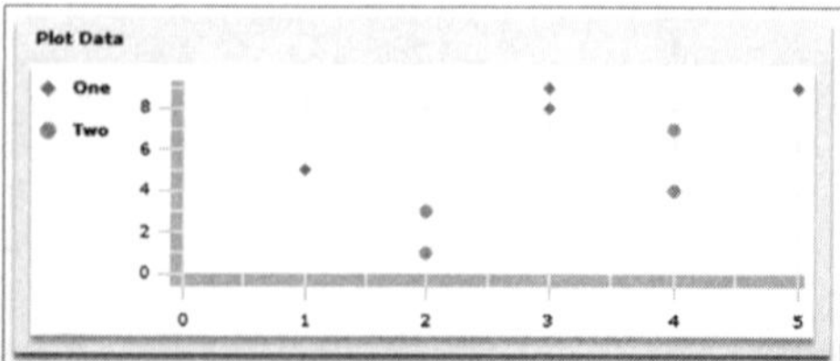

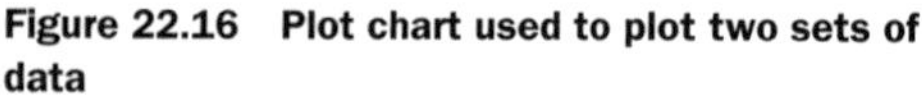

Figure 22.16 Plot chart used to plot two sets of data

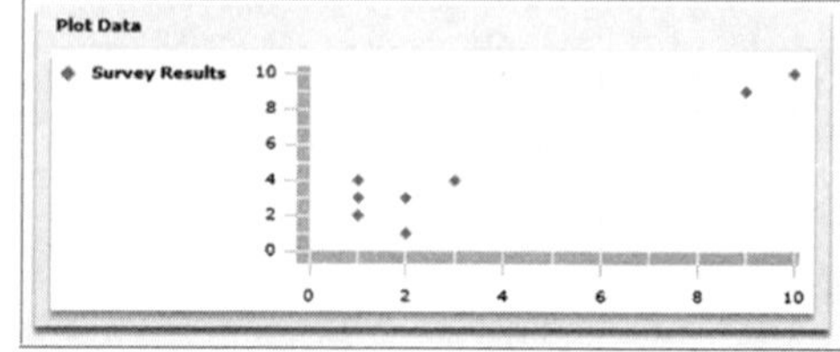

Figure 22.17 The clustering of these data points reveals more than the average of their value.

shows a clustering of data points, from the *Y* axis perspective, around the 3 mark—yet if you were to average all the values, you'd get a result of 5. Knowing this perspective gives you a better interpretation of the information.

In the next section, we'll explore how you can customize your charts.

22.6 Customizing charts

It would be boring if everyone's charts looked the same. More important, getting the right look and feel to plug into your application's overall theme is necessary for consistency. In this section, we'll give you a high-level overview of how you go about customizing your charts.

Many charts support their own unique characteristics, and we'll show you how to find out what those are by using the Flex API Reference; but we'll also introduce a few common customization features.

22.6.1 Series strokes

A *stroke* augments the display of the line or the perimeter of the series. To use a stroke, you need to find out which property to use for a given series. Let's take an area chart as an example by following these steps:

1. Pull up the related series in the Flex API Reference—in this case, the `AreaSeries` component. The quickest way is to click `<mx:AreaSeries>` in the code, then press Shift+F2.
2. Scroll down to the Styles section.
3. Look for the style that has `stroke` in it. In this case, you'll find `AreaStroke`.

Putting this into practice, let's first define a stroke:

```
<mx:Stroke id="stroke1" color="#6600CC" weight="4" alpha="0.8"/>
```

Then, you bind the stroke-related property to a particular instance:

```
<mx:AreaSeries yField="@ferrariUnits" displayName="Ferrari Count"
          areaStroke="{stroke1}"/>
```

This changes things by drawing a predominantly thick line over the area.

A stroke has no impact on the area under the line; this is where fills come into play.

22.6.2 Series fills

Fills tackle adding background color to a series. You can use them a couple of ways; the easiest way to demonstrate is to go straight into examples.

SINGLE-COLOR FILL

First, you follow the same steps you use with strokes and identify which property of the series you're using supports fills:

1. Pull up the related series in the Flex API Reference—in this case, the `AreaSeries` component. The quickest way is to click `<mx:AreaSeries>` in the code and then press Shift+F2.

2 Scroll down to the Styles section.
3 Look for the style that has `fill` in it. In this case, you'll find `areaFill`.

TIP Most charting series include `fill` and `fills` properties, but these are ignored by `AreaSeries` and `LineSeries`.

You create a solid fill by declaring an instance of a `SolidColor` component, and then you bind the `fill` property of the series to that `SolidColor`. Here's an example:

```
<mx:SolidColor id="solidcolor1" color="#33FF66" alpha="0.5"/>
```

Then in the `AreaSeries` component, you bind the `areaFill` to it as follows:

```
<mx:AreaSeries yField="@ferrariUnits" displayName="Ferrari Count"
      areaStroke="{stroke1}" areaFill="{solidcolor1}"/>
```

This creates a semi-transparent greenish fill.

This example works well for charts that show trends. But charts whose data points aren't linked together (visually) support an array of colors.

COLOR ARRAY FILLS

Charts whose behavior is to segregate each data point as if it's a series (such as bar and pie charts) use a property called `fills` that accepts an array of colors. This lets you color-code all the data items (because they're contained in one series).

For example, if you didn't want to use a pie chart's default colors, you can override them as shown in listing 22.19.

Listing 22.19 Specifying a color for each slice in a pie chart

```
<?xml version="1.0"?>
<mx:Application xmlns:mx="http://www.adobe.com/2006/mxml"
   backgroundColor="white">
  <mx:XML id="salesDataXML" source="pie.xml"/>
  <mx:XMLListCollection source="{salesDataXML.revenues.data}"
                  id="salesData"/>

  <mx:Script>
    <![CDATA[
     import mx.graphics.SolidColor;                    Imports SolidColor
     [Bindable]                                        ActionScript class
     private var clrArray:Array = new Array(
       new SolidColor(0x6666CC,0.5),
       new SolidColor(0xCC6666,0.6),                   Creates array
       new SolidColor(0x66CC66,0.7),                   of SolidColors
       new SolidColor(0xB8B83D,0.8)
     );
    ]]>
  </mx:Script>

  <mx:Panel title="FlexMoto Car Sales" width="500" height="400"
        layout="horizontal">
   <mx:Legend dataProvider="{salesChart}"/>
   <mx:PieChart id="salesChart" dataProvider="{salesData}" height="100%"
           width="100%" >
```

```
    <mx:series>
      <mx:PieSeries field="@rev" nameField="@brand"
              fills="{clrArray}"/>
    </mx:series>
  </mx:PieChart>
  </mx:Panel>
</mx:Application>
```

Binds fills property to array

The result is that each slice of the pie chart adopts those colors. If there are more slices (data points) than there are colors defined, Flex uses default colors for those additional items.

The amount of customization you can do in Flex is amazing, but customizing the series with strokes and fills is the primary thing to do.

22.7 Summary

Charting in Flex is such a powerful and popular feature that it's not uncommon to find teams that use Flex only for this purpose (particularly to build dashboards). Charts are made up of many parts; they have series, labels, axes, elements, and of course the charts themselves.

Flex comes with nine out-of-the-box charts that cater to the common needs of most businesses. Some charts, like line and area charts, are premised on trending information; others, like bar charts, focus on category comparisons.

Although we've only scratched the surface of customizing charts, it boils down to checking the API Reference for the styles that are available and leveraging them as needed. The stroke and fills features are by far the most popular form of chart customization.

This chapter is the last one that involves coding. We've covered all the programming bases. From here on out, it's all about wrapping up the development lifecycle; testing and debugging are up next.

23 Debugging and testing

- This chapter covers:
- Debugging applications using the Flex debugger as well as third-party tools
- Using test automation tools to find bugs and fix them before they go live
- Deploying your applications

This chapter's purpose is to give you a sampling of all the weaponry available both out of the box and in the form of third-party tools, to help speed up the process of developing in Flex from a tooling perspective. Flex Builder comes with a full-blown debugger that allows you to step through the code and watch the value of variables in real time. And new to Flex 3 is the Profiler, which lets you analyze how memory and resources are consumed.

Beyond what comes out of the box, the Flex and Flash ecosystem provides tools from open source and low-cost solutions to full-blown enterprise test-automation packages that will help speed up your debugging and testing. You may not get into the more advanced tooling for a while, but from the start you'll need simple ways to figure out why things aren't working. Let's begin by discussing how you can debug your Flex applications.

23.1 Debugging

You can use debugging at multiple levels. We'll review each approach, starting with the easiest.

23.1.1 Using the Flash Debug Player

When you install Flex Builder, it automatically installs the Flash Debug Player for you; this Debug Player allows for diagnostic logging, and you can connect external tools to it for debugging purposes.

You can download the latest player at Adobe's website via http://www.adobe.com/support/flashplayer/downloads.html. Look in the Debugger Versions section.

To test which version you currently have, visit http://kb.adobe.com/selfservice/viewContent.do?externalId=tn_15507. Be sure the Debug Player item says Yes.

You should already have the Debug Player, but sometimes other software you install may try to install the production version of the Flash Player as part of its installation. In any case, if you're not running the Debug Player, go ahead and get it installed.

Once you've verified that you have the Debug Player, you need to configure logging.

23.1.2 Configuring logging

To get logging going, you need to set up the Flash Debug Player's configuration file. If there isn't one, create a text file called mm.cfg and place it in the appropriate directory based on your operating system (see table 23.1).

Table 23.1 Location of the Flash Player's configuration file

Operating system	Path
MAC OS X	/Library/Application Support/Macromedia
Windows 95/98/ME	%HOMEDRIVE%\%HOMEPATH%
Windows 2000/XP	C:\Documents and Settings\[username]
Windows Vista	C:\Users\[username]
Linux	/home/username

Inside this file are three configuration properties to define, as listed in table 23.2.

Table 23.2 Flash Player's configuration-file settings

Configuration property	Type	Description
`TraceOutputFileEnable`	`Boolean`	`0` for `false` (default), `1` for `true`. Turns logging on or off.
`ErrorReportingEnable`	`Boolean`	`0` for `false` (default), `1` for `true`. Turns logging of error messages on or off.

Table 23.2 Flash Player's configuration-file settings *(continued)*

Configuration property	Type	Description
`MaxWarnings`	`Number`	Maximum number of warnings to record. Default is `100`; use `0` for unlimited.

You'll want to set up your mm.cfg file to look like this:

```
TraceOutputFileEnable=1
ErrorReportingEnable=1
MaxWarnings=500
```

With logging now enabled, details will be stored in a log file called flashlog.txt whose location is operating-system specific (see table 23.3).

Table 23.3 Output location of the Flash Player's log file

Operating system	Path
MAC OS X	/Users/[username]/Library/Preferences/Macromedia/Flash Player/Logs/
Windows 95/98/ME/2000/XP	C:\Documents and Settings\[username]\Application Data\Macromedia\Flash Player\Logs
Windows Vista	C:\Users\[username]\AppData\Roaming\Macromedia\Flash Player\Logs
Linux	/home/[username]/.macromedia/Flash_Player/Logs/

With the configuration good to go, you can now use it via the `trace()` function.

23.1.3 *Using the trace() function*

`trace()` is a simple global function that is available from anywhere in your code. It lets you record text to the flashlog.txt log file. Now that you have mm.cfg set up, you can use this function, as listing 23.1 demonstrates.

Listing 23.1 Using trace() to write information to the Flash log file

```
<mx:Label text="Type in something:"/>
<mx:TextInput id="something"/>
<mx:Button click="trace('Something is currently: ' + something.text)"
   label="Record Something"/>
```

When you type something and click the Record Something button, the text you type shows up in the flashlog.txt file (listing 23.2 shows an example).

Listing 23.2 Sample Flash log file

```
*** WARNING: Please use gotoAndPlay(1) in the last frame of your Motif
   creative if you intend to loop. ***
*** Please use 'stop();' at the end of your Motif creative if you do not
   intend for it to loop. ***
```

```
showing end copy
hiding end copy
showing end copy
Something is currently: show this please
```

This is an effective mechanism if you want to record the value of various variables and components.

Viewing this log file may seem cumbersome without the right tool; fortunately, trace-log viewers are available.

23.1.4 Trace-log viewers

It's one thing to make a log, and it's another to view the log. Using what you have so far, it would be tedious to continually reload flashlog.txt to see what it currently looks like.

Fortunately third-party tools are available that do this for you by having a viewing panel that automatically refreshes as the log file changes. You can use any generic log-viewing tool, but here are a few we like.

- *Flash Tracer*—This extension to the Firefox web browser adds a built-in panel to Firefox, which is convenient because you don't need to switch back and forth between two separate applications. Price: free. https://addons.mozilla.org/en-US/firefox/addon/3469.
- *ABLogFile Viewer*—This is an open source viewer that is actively maintained. It's generic in nature, but it remembers the last few files opened, so it's easy to get back to the log file. In Windows, the application data directory is hidden, so you may need to navigate to the directory using Explorer and drag and drop the file into the ABLogFile Viewer. Price: free. http://www.amleth.com/ablogfile/.
- *Afterthought*—This tool was developed specifically for Flash, but it hasn't been updated to reflect a modification in the current Flash Player that changed where the flashlog.txt file is stored; you'll need to edit the options to tell it where to look. This tool is nice because it makes sure the window floats at the front, can filter out warnings, and has handy Clear Screen and Clear Log buttons. Price: free. http://www.blazepdf.com/downloads/afterthought_v2_1.zip.

These log files obviously log text, but many things in Flex aren't textual in nature, so we'll need a way to convert these objects into strings.

23.1.5 Converting objects to strings

Whether you're dumping complex data types to a log file or on screen, you must transform them into text. Flex makes this easy: most objects support a `toString()` function that will do the conversion for you. Here's an example:

```
var myNumber:Number = 32;
trace(myNumber.toString());
```

But for more complex objects like ArrayCollections, the ObjectUtil ActionScript class has a toString() function that takes a reference of any other object and converts it to a string.

In listing 23.3, the ObjectUtil class is used to display all the items in an ArrayCollection.

Listing 23.3 Using ObjectUtil to dump an object's properties

```
<?xml version="1.0" encoding="utf-8"?>
<mx:Application xmlns:mx="http://www.adobe.com/2006/mxml"
   creationComplete="trace(ObjectUtil.toString(myAC))">

<mx:Script>
   <![CDATA[
      import mx.collections.ArrayCollection;
      import mx.utils.ObjectUtil;
      public var myAC:ArrayCollection  = new ArrayCollection([
      {label:"Jon Hirschi", data:"jhirschi"},
      {label:"Tariq Ahmed", data:"tahmed"},
      {label:"Frank Krul", data:"fkrul"}
      ]);
   ]]>
</mx:Script>
</mx:Application>
```

This code produces something like the log file shown in listing 23.4.

Listing 23.4 Sample output from ObjectUtil

```
(mx.collections::ArrayCollection)#0
  filterFunction = (null)
  length = 3
  list = (mx.collections::ArrayList)#1
    length = 3
    source = (Array)#2
      [0] (Object)#3
        data = "jhirschi"
        label = "Jon Hirschi"
      [1] (Object)#4
        data = "tahmed"
        label = "Tariq Ahmed"
      [2] (Object)#5
        data = "fkrul"
        label = "Frank Krul"
    uid = "70528450-89C6-9120-D5D4-847C1D8C3B70"
  sort = (null)
  source = (Array)#2
```

Another popular approach shows the value on screen via the Alert.show() function, instead of dumping it to a log file. Here's an example:

```
Alert.show(ObjectUtil.toString(myAC))
```

Using this technique and the Flash log file can get you reasonably far, but to take your game to a new level, you'll want more advanced tooling.

23.1.6 FxSpy

FxSpy (a.k.a. Flex Spy) is an open source tool that allows you to inspect your components and see what their properties and styles are set to, while allowing you to manipulate many of these items (see figure 23.1).

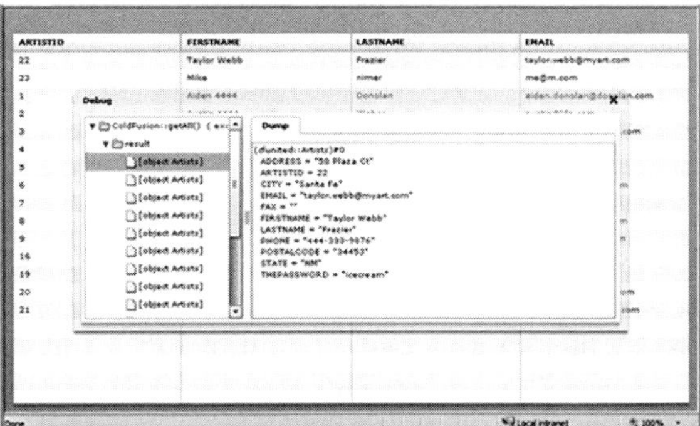

Figure 23.1 FxSpy allows you to browse and inspect components and their properties.

This tool is particularly handy when you want to tinker with properties that affect the visual aspects of the application. This can save you time compared to making changes in the code and having to recompile constantly to test those changes.

You can download this free tool at http://code.google.com/p/fxspy/.

The tools mentioned so far cater to the front end, but monitoring the back end also becomes vital when you need to know what's going over the wire.

23.1.7 Monitoring network activity

One of the most challenging things you'll encounter when developing Flex applications is trying to figure out why communications with a back-end data service (such as a web service or remote object) doesn't seem to be working. Yes, you can specify fault handlers to handle exceptions, but that may not be enough.

Flex Builder has a built-in ability to monitor network activity. This is facilitated by adding <mx:TraceTarget/> to your application, as shown in listing 23.5.

Listing 23.5 Using the TraceTarget component to monitor network activity

```
<?xml version="1.0" encoding="utf-8"?>
<mx:Application xmlns:mx="http://www.adobe.com/2006/mxml">
   <mx:TraceTarget/>
   ...
   ...
</mx:Application>
```

When you launch your application using the Debug button (see figure 23.2), all network traffic appears in the Console view.

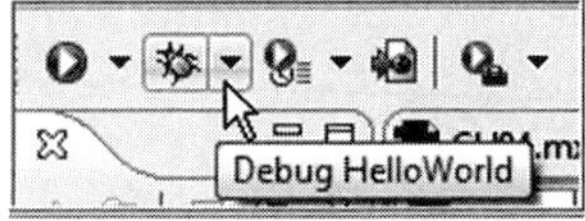

Figure 23.2 You'll find the Debug button on the Flex Builder toolbar.

This feature is considered anemic and underpowered. Fortunately, a number of third-party tools do an amazing job of speeding up the debugging process:

- *ServiceCapture*—One of the best tools out there. Not only does it understand Flash's native AMF Remote object protocol, but it deciphers web service SOAP and JSON-RPC. Its interactive nature lets you see what parameters were passed to remote functions and what the data looked like coming back in real time. Price: $35 U.S. http://kevinlangdon.com/serviceCapture/.
- *Charles Web Debugging Proxy* (CWDP)—A well-polished product loaded with features. It provides protocol support similar to ServiceCapture, but it also does bandwidth throttling to simulate network connection speed, and you can export the results to a CSV file. It's available on multiple platforms but requires the Sun Java JDK to be installed. Price: $50 U.S. http://xk72.com/charles/index.php.

Moving onto the heavyweight tool of debugging, let's look at the Debugger that comes with Flex Builder, a feature that came to maturity with Flex 3.

23.1.8 Using the Debugger

If you've reached a point where you need to see how things are changing and you also need fine-grained control, the Debugger is the way to go. It helps you isolate where issues are by allowing you to step through your code in a controlled manner and see how variables change as the code executes.

The tool works by launching in Debug mode, setting breakpoints to pause execution, then adding variables to watch.

LAUNCHING DEBUG MODE

Enabling the Debugger is similar to how you've been launching your applications thus far, except in this case you use the Debug button (refer back to figure 23.2).

Notice that along with the bin folder, there's also bin-debug—this is the folder to which Flex Builder publishes a debug version of your application. When you click the Debug button, this version is launched.

If Flex Builder hasn't done so already, switch to the Debug perspective in Flex Builder by choosing Window > Perspective > Flex Debugging. You'll see a number of views, including the following:

- *Debug*—Where you are in the application
- *Variables*—An area where you can watch the values of all the variables Flex is managing

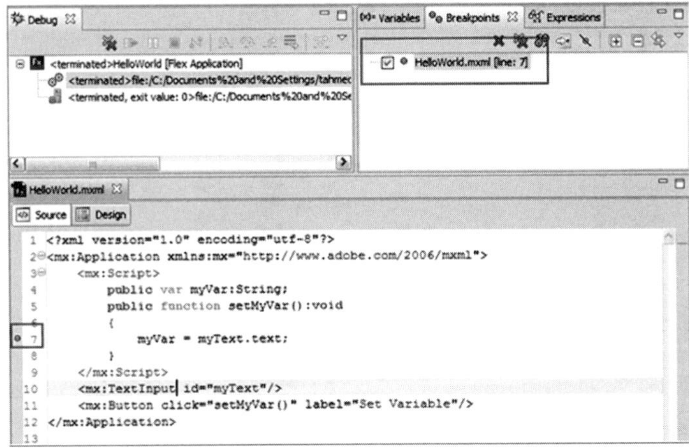

Figure 23.3 Set breakpoints show up in the Breakpoints view.

- *Breakpoints*—Points at which you want the application to stop running so you can pause and evaluate the situation.
- *Expressions*—All the variables you indicated you want to watch

With the Debugger enabled, let's proceed to working with breakpoints.

ADDING/REMOVING A BREAKPOINT

You can add a breakpoint anywhere you have ActionScript. For instance, you can add a breakpoint to inline ActionScript in an MXML tag:

```
<mx:Button click="myVar=myText.text"/>
```

You can also place a breakpoint inside an <mx:Script> block or in an ActionScript (.as) file.

To do this, follow these steps:

1. Using Flex Builder, locate a line of code on which you want to halt execution.
2. Right-click in the marker bar (where the line numbers are displayed).
3. Select Toggle Breakpoint.

To remove the breakpoint, repeat the same steps.

If all goes well, you should see your breakpoint listed in the Breakpoints view, as shown in figure 23.3.

With the Debugger launched and breakpoints set, you can control the execution of your application.

CONTROLLING EXECUTION

After you've set your breakpoints, launch your application in Debug mode. As soon as you hit the line that has a breakpoint, execution will stop and Flex Builder will want your attention.

You can use Debug view to control what happens next by using the functions outlined in table 23.4.

Table 23.4 Flex Builder's Debugger functions

Icon	Function	Description
	Resume	Resumes execution of the application
	Suspend	Pauses the application
	Terminate	Terminates the application
	Disconnect	Disconnects the Debugger from the application
	Step Into	Steps into the next line of code
	Step Over	Skips over the next line of code
	Step Return	Continues the current function until it's done

Now that you can control execution, the feature that people generally use the Debugger for is watching variables.

WATCHING VARIABLES

Watching a variable lets you track the value that the variable is assigned in real time. You can also manually manipulate the value if you want to experiment with how the application would behave using another value.

Whether you've already launched your application or are about to, you can indicate that you want to watch a variable by doing the following:

1 Right-click the variable name.
2 Select Watch.

Once the variable is added, you should see the variable listed in the Expressions view. Let's try it:

1 Set a breakpoint on the line indicated in listing 23.6.

Listing 23.6 Using a breakpoint on the line that sets the variable

```
<?xml version="1.0" encoding="utf-8"?>
<mx:Application xmlns:mx="http://www.adobe.com/2006/mxml">
   <mx:Script>
      public var myVar:String;
      public function setMyVar():void
      {
```

```
        myVar = myText.text;
    }
  </mx:Script>
  <mx:TextInput id="myText"/>
  <mx:Button click="setMyVar()" label="Set Variable"/>
</mx:Application>
```

Set breakpoint here (annotation on `myVar = myText.text;`)

2 Watch the `myVar` and `myText.text` variables.

3 Launch your application in Debug mode.

4 Type something in the text box, and click the button. The application will suspend execution.

5 Switch to Flex Builder; you should see the variables listed.

6 Keep clicking the Step Into button, and watch how the variables change (see figure 23.4).

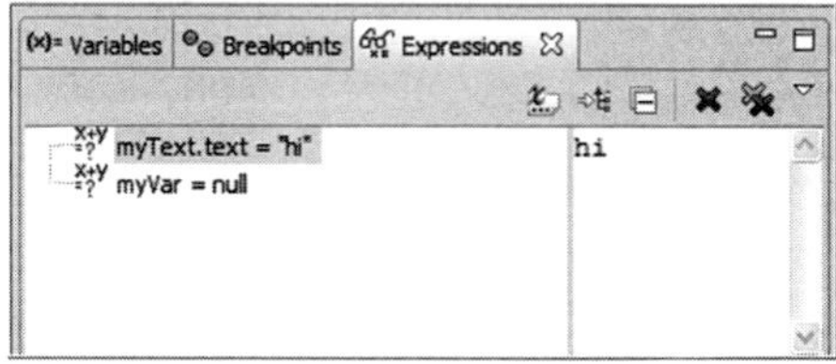

Figure 23.4 Watched variables show their values in the Expressions view.

This process of using a Debugger will be a new experience for those coming from high-level languages like ColdFusion and PHP, because the asynchronous nature of Flex lends itself to the step debugging needed in an event-driven environment. Once you do it a few times, you'll get used to it.

Similar to debugging is the process of testing. Whereas debugging is about fixing problems, testing is about making sure problems don't exist.

23.2 Testing

It's always a good idea as part of your Systems Development Life Cycle to do as much upfront testing as possible before you go live with the application. ASP, PHP, ColdFusion, and other such languages will tell you the line of code and filename when a crash occurs—this luxury doesn't exist in the land of Flex because of its compiled nature.

After you've finished the debugging phase, testing is a good idea to make sure new features work the way they're supposed to and previous features continue to function. Testing is also an opportunity to fine-tune the application.

23.2.1 Types of tests

Three main types of testing are available:

- Profiling
- Unit testing
- Functional testing

Let's define each, starting with profiling.

PROFILING

Profiling is a process whereby you're not testing for proper behavior but rather are looking to see how you can optimize the resource usage of your application. Using profiling tools, you can identify memory leaks and unnecessary processing overhead and highlight areas that could use optimization.

UNIT TESTING

Unit testing is a way to automate programmatically testing your components, functions, and classes. It's considered a back-end type of testing, because it makes sure other pieces that utilize these back-end pieces receive the proper results and behavior from a programmatic perspective.

FUNCTIONAL TESTING

Functional testing covers the other end of the QA process by focusing on the front-end experience. Functional testing simulates a user running the application and verifies that the behavior and information are accurate. This could be done manually, but that would be prone to human error as well as a potentially huge time investment.

Functional testing works by recording actual use of your application and tracking what was entered and how the application behaved. Each one of these recordings represents a test case for which you've documented the expected results.

It goes beyond checking whether the results shown are right; it also makes sure that various business rules are enforced, that things validate properly, and that the overall experience is the intended result. In addition to automating the testing of new features, you can also use functional testing to verify that existing functionality continues to work properly.

23.2.2 Flex Profiler

New to Flex 3, profiling adds the ability to see where resource bottlenecks (processing and memory utilization) in your application occur so you can isolate and address the issues.

The Profiler works by periodically sampling what's going on in your application. Kind of like time-lapse photography, it takes a snapshot of what things look like at given intervals. In doing so, it's able to determine how many objects currently exist, how much memory they're using, how many functions are being called, and how much time those functions are consuming.

Here's what you should look for:

- *Function call frequency*—How often are you calling functions? Are you making unnecessary calls? See if you can minimize how often heavy-duty functions are called or if they be broken into smaller pieces, only a portion of which are called frequently.
- *Duration of functions*—How long are functions taking to run? Hand in hand with the previous item, you can investigate particular functions to determine the average amount of time a particular function takes to run.
- *Who's calling whom*—Observing this *call stack* and observing the chain of functions calling functions may reveal interesting information.

- *Object count/object allocation*—How many objects have been instantiated? What if you have many instances of the same object? For example, if you can use fewer instances, you'll save on overhead.
- *Object size*—How big are these objects? For objects that have many instances, is their combined size a concern?
- *Garbage collection*—By default, Flex takes care of destroying objects when they're no longer needed. *Garbage collection* is the process of recovering the memory that they once held. It's possible that objects may linger for a while before this process occurs (which causes memory leaks), so you may want to add logic in these cases to explicitly destroy them.

Using the Profiler is similar to using the Debugger: you launch the tool from Flex Builder.

LAUNCHING THE PROFILER

You'll find the Profile button on the toolbar in Flex Builder, beside the Debug icon.

If you click it, the window shown in figure 23.5 opens, where you can select what you want to watch.

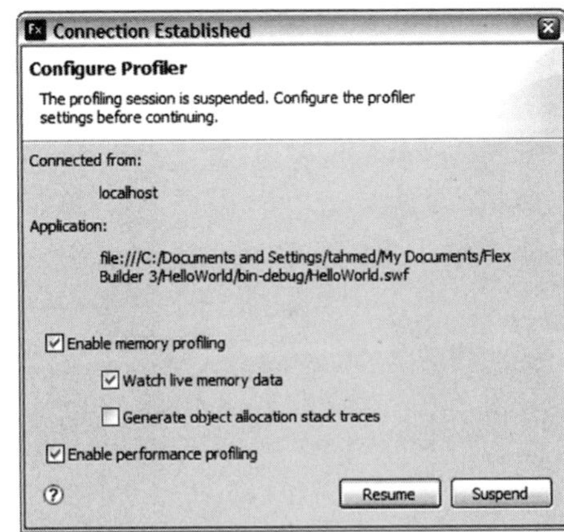

Figure 23.5 Launching the Profiler prompts you with configuration options.

The settings in the dialog box are:

- *Connected From*—The server you're connected to (or localhost, if it's the same computer).
- *Application*—Path to the Flex application's SWF file.
- *Enable Memory Profiling*—Enables the tracking of memory usage.
- *Watch Live Memory Data*—Memory tracking will occur if Enable Memory Profiling is selected. Watch Live Memory Data indicates whether you want to watch it in the Live Objects view.
- *Generate Object Allocation Stack Traces*—Lets you track how objects are created.
- *Enable Performance Profiling*—Lets you watch where processing time is spent.

You could use all of these options all the time; the only difference is how much profiling data is generated and the performance impact while profiling is running.

Launch the Profiler to see it in action, as shown in figure 23.6.

The Profiler functions similarly to the Debugger. After you've launched it, switch back to Flex Builder to control the application's execution.

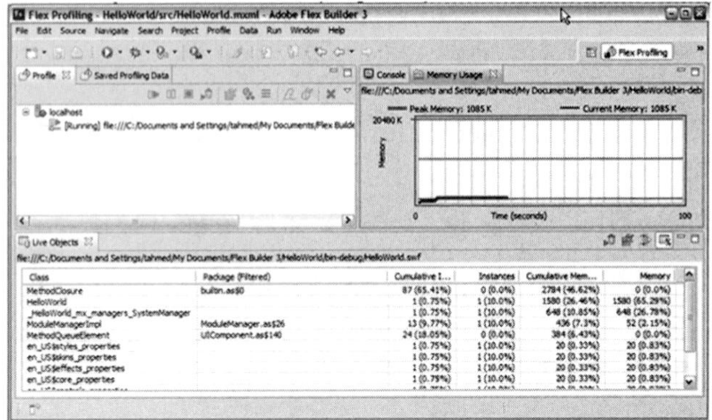

Figure 23.6 The Profiler provides aggregate statistics on memory and CPU usage.

CONTROLLING EXECUTION

Once the Profiler is running, you'll see your application listed in the Profile view. Select the application, and a bunch of icons will light up and give you options. Table 23.5 describes these options, which are execution-control functionality.

Table 23.5 Flex Builder's Profiler functions

Icon	Function	Description
	Resume	Resumes execution of the application.
	Suspend	Pauses the application.
	Terminate	Terminates the application.
	Run Garbage Collection	Forces garbage collection to run now versus waiting for it to happen. This recovers memory from objects that are no longer in use.
	Take Memory Snapshot	Takes a snapshot of your memory usage and breaks it down by how that memory is used. Use this feature to take snapshots whenever you suspect major memory operations occur, and later evaluate these snapshots.
	Find Loitering Objects	Goes hand in hand with Take Memory Snapshot in that this feature can compare the differences between snapshots.
	View Allocation Trace	Available after selecting two memory snapshots. Shows which functions were called from one snapshot to another and how much memory was utilized in the process.
	Reset Performance Data	Resets the recorded information.

Table 23.5 Flex Builder's Profiler functions *(continued)*

Icon	Function	Description
	Capture Performance Profile	Used in conjunction with Reset Performance Data. After clicking Reset Performance Data, click this button to snapshot a number of function calls and how long they took to run. You can repeat this process as often as you like.
	Delete	Deletes an item you've selected (for example, a memory snapshot).

The Profiler is the only tool available for Flex that allows this kind of testing, and it does a great job. It gives you deep insight into how much memory and resources are being consumed and where that consumption occurs.

Next we'll discuss unit testing, which automates the testing of objects in order to verify that they behave as expected. The Flex community has produced a number of unit-testing frameworks that can assist you.

23.2.3 *FlexUnit (unit testing)*

If you're familiar with Java, you may have encountered a tool called JUnit—FlexUnit is a Flex spin on that. It's a unit-testing framework for Flex and ActionScript 3, created collaboratively by a few Adobe and non-Adobe developers. This tool is free and is available at http://opensource.adobe.com/wiki/display/flexunit/.

You create an application called a *test runner*, which executes ActionScript functions you create to conduct tests on various functions and classes. Although the project has documentation, we'll give you a crash course on it, starting with setting it up.

SETTING UP FOR FLEXUNIT

A test runner is a small application that uses FlexUnit's `TestSuite` class to run through all your tests. You could add it to your main project MXML file, but because a GUI component is involved it's easier to make it a simple application on its own. This can be a new project or an auxiliary application to your main one. Follow these steps:

1. Download the latest zip file from the FlexUnit site: http://opensource.adobe.com/wiki/display/flexunit/.
2. Unzip the file to a location such as c:\flexunit.
3. Open your project in Flex Builder.
4. Right-click the project's top-level folder, and select Properties.
5. Click the Library Path tab.
6. Click the Add SWC button.
7. Navigate to the FlexUnit directory, and under bin, select the flexunit.swc file.
8. The next step is to create a test-runner application to execute your tests.

CREATING A TEST RUNNER

A test runner can add any number of test-case collections and run through them.

FlexUnit calls these test-case collections a *test suite*, which adds a level of convenience when you're working with a lot of test cases. Listing 23.7 shows an example of a test-runner application.

Listing 23.7 Setting up a FlexUnit test runner

```
<?xml version="1.0" encoding="utf-8"?>
<mx:Application xmlns:mx="http://www.adobe.com/2006/mxml" xmlns="*"
        xmlns:flexunit="flexunit.flexui.*" >          Add FlexUnit namespace

   <mx:Script>
     <![CDATA[
        import flexunit.framework.TestSuite;          Import TestSuite class

        private function runTests():void
        {
           var ts:TestSuite = new TestSuite();
           ts.addTest( myTest.suite() );              Call addTest() function as
                                                      needed to add TestSuites
           testRunner.test = ts;
           testRunner.startTest();                    Execute tests
        }

     ]]>
   </mx:Script>
   <mx:Button label="Begin Tests" click="runTests()"/>
   <flexunit:TestRunnerBase id="testRunner"           Add FlexUnit MXML
     width="100%" height="100%" />                    visual component
</mx:Application>
```

Now all you need to do is create the test cases.

CREATING A TEST CASE

The last piece involves scripting your test cases by creating ActionScript classes that return a test suite containing all the necessary tests. You can make one big test suite with many test cases, or you can make many test suites with fewer test cases—whatever is easier for you.

In this test-runner example, you invoke a test suite called `myTest`, shown in listing 23.8.

Listing 23.8 myTest.as: Sample FlexUnit test suite with a number of test cases

```
package {

   import flexunit.framework.TestCase;
   import flexunit.framework.TestSuite;

   public class myTest extends TestCase {

      public function myTest( methodName:String ) {
         super( methodName );
      }

      public static function suite():TestSuite {
         var ts:TestSuite = new TestSuite();
```

```
            ts.addTest( new myTest( "testMilesToKm" ) );
            ts.addTest( new myTest( "testKmToMiles" ) );
            return ts;
        }

        public function testMilesToKm():void {
            var mph:Number = 65;
            var kmh:Number = speedConverter.toKmh( mph );
            assertTrue( "We want to see 104km/h", kmh == 104 );
        }

        public function testKmToMiles():void {
            var kmh:Number =104;
            var mph:Number = speedConverter.toMph( kmh );
            assertTrue( "We want to see 65mph", mph==65 );
        }

    }
}
```

This code tests an ActionScript class called speedConverter (see listing 23.9), whose purpose is to convert speed values from km/h to mph and vice versa.

Listing 23.9 speedConverter.as: the test suite tests this code

```
package
{
   public class speedConverter
   {
      public static function toKmh(i:Number):Number
      {
         return (i*1.6);
      }
      public static function toMph(i:Number):Number
      {
         return (i/1.6);
      }
   }
}
```

The test runner application has been created, and the test cases are ready to go. All that's left is to execute them.

EXECUTING THE TESTS

A number of files are involved, so let's recap by looking at figure 23.7.

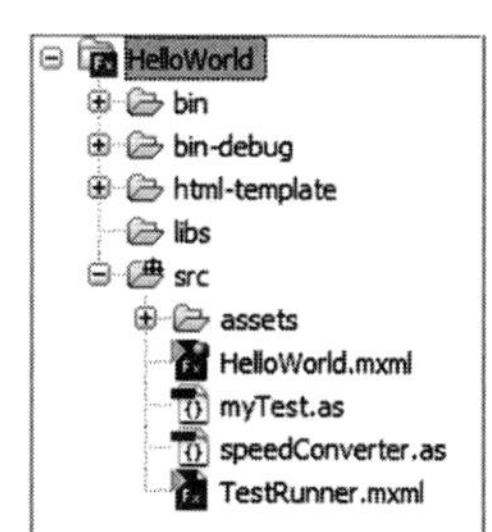

Figure 23.7 Files involved in the FlexUnit test case

The test runner won't run automatically because it's not the project's main MXML file. Don't fret! You can easily work around this by loading the TestRunner.mxml file, then clicking the Run/Launch application button.

In this example, you begin the tests with the click of a button.

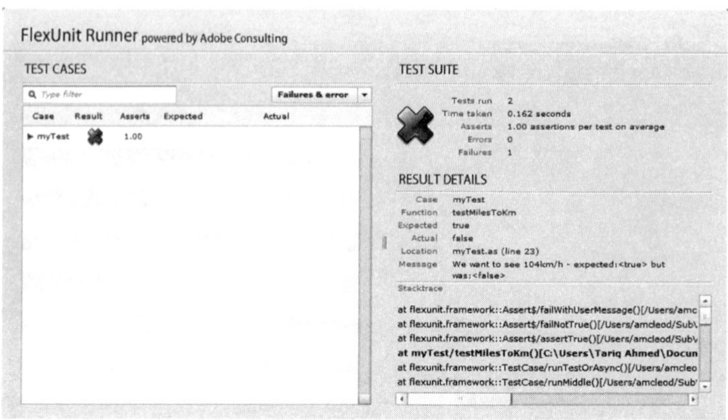

Figure 23.8 FlexUnit's display outputs all issues it encounters.

But if things don't go well, the items that failed appear on the right with a dump of the diagnostics to go with them (see figure 23.8). Clicking a failure shows a stack trace that describes the situation when the test failed.

Another unit-testing framework available to Flex is Fluint, which works in the same manner.

23.2.4 Fluint (unit testing)

Originally known as the oddly named dpUInt (that's not a typo), Fluint is the relative newcomer on the block; it was created by Digital Primates (www.digitalprimates.net) and released as an open source project. It's free and available at http://code.google.com/p/fluint.

It's similar to FlexUnit, but it's considered a unit and integration test framework (which explains the name). It goes beyond what FlexUnit can do by adding robust asynchronous support, test sequencing, XML output, test UI components, and Adobe Integrated Runtime (AIR) support.

Test methods are the functions that actually perform a test. They're contained in test cases, which in turn are used by test suites.

Like FlexUnit, Fluint has documentation, but we'll briefly run down how to use it.

SETTING UP FOR FLUINT

Fluint also uses a test runner to execute tests—you can make a separate project to facilitate this or run it as a secondary application to your main project. In this example, you'll run it from an existing project:

1. Download the latest SWC file from http://code.google.com/p/fluint/downloads.
2. Open your project in Flex Builder.
3. Right-click the project's top-level folder, and select Properties.
4. Click the Library Path tab.
5. Click the Add SWC button.
6. Navigate to the directory to which you downloaded the SWC file, and select the file.

With Fluint installed, let's look at how to create the test runner.

CREATING A TEST RUNNER

The test runner is a mini Flex application that loads all the test cases and runs through them. Here are the steps to create Fluint test runner:

1. Download the sample test runner from http://code.google.com/p/Fluint/downloads/list.
2. Save the SampleTestRunnerFlex.mxml file to your project's folder.
3. Open it, and modify the line that calls `suiteArray.push()`, as shown in listing 23.10.

Listing 23.10 Setting up a Fluint test runner

```
<?xml version="1.0" encoding="utf-8"?>
<mx:Application
  xmlns:mx="http://www.adobe.com/2006/mxml"
  xmlns:fluint="http://www.digitalprimates.net/2008/fluint"
  layout="absolute"
  creationComplete="startTestProcess(event)"
  width="100%" height="100%">

  <mx:Script>
    <![CDATA[
    import
    net.digitalprimates.fluint.unitTests.frameworkSuite.FrameworkSuite;

   protected function startTestProcess( event:Event ) : void
    {
      var suiteArray:Array = new Array();
      suiteArray.push( new testSuite() );        <-- Add test
      testRunner.startTests( suiteArray );           suites
    }
    ]]>
  </mx:Script>

  <fluint:TestResultDisplay width="100%" height="100%" />
  <fluint:TestRunner id="testRunner"/>
</mx:Application>
```

Now the test runner needs the actual tests to execute against.

CREATING TEST CASES

You can create as many test-case files as you want; these are ActionScript classes, each of which has functions/methods that perform some kind of test. Each function's name must start with lowercase `test`.

Fluint automatically searches for all functions that start with the word `test`, so you don't need to explicitly call these functions yourself. Listing 23.11 shows an example test case that tests the `speedConverter` class from the FlexUnit example.

Listing 23.11 testCase.as: Creating Fluint test cases

```
package
{
  import net.digitalprimates.fluint.tests.TestCase;

  public class testCase
  extends net.digitalprimates.fluint.tests.TestCase
  {
    public function testMilesToKm():void
    {
      var mph:Number = 65;
      var kmh:Number = speedConverter.toKmh( mph );
      assertEquals( 104,kmh);
    }

    public function testKmToMiles():void
    {
      var kmh:Number =104;
      var mph:Number = speedConverter.toMph( kmh );
      assertEquals( 65,mph);
    }
  }
}
```

Create all test cases

You have the test runner, which is the foundation; you have the test cases coded; and now you just need to add the test cases to test suites.

CREATING TEST SUITES

A Fluint test suite does one simple thing: it adds all the test cases that are needed as part of the test suite. It too is an ActionScript class.

If you look back at listing 23.10, when creating the test runner, you added a test suite called `testSuite`:

```
suiteArray.push( new testSuite() );
```

That file looks something like listing 23.12.

Listing 23.12 testSuite.as: Adding test cases to the Fluint test suite

```
package
{
  import net.digitalprimates.fluint.tests.TestSuite;

  public class testSuite
  extends net.digitalprimates.fluint.tests.TestSuite
  {
    public function testSuite()
    {
      addTestCase( new testCase() );
    }
  }
}
```

Add all cases to test (annotation on `addTestCase( new testCase() );`)

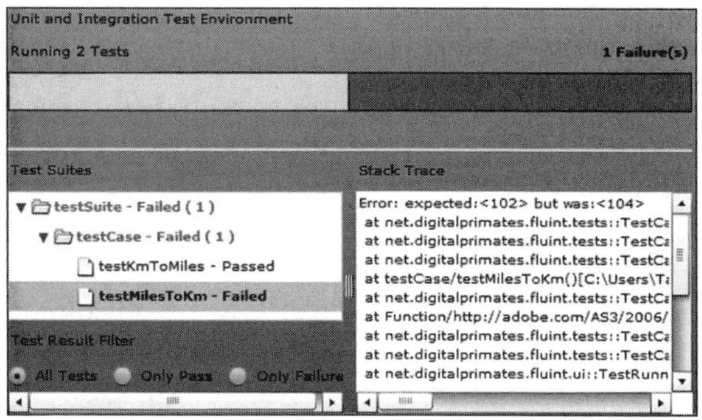

Figure 23.9 Fluint's output highlights cases that passed and failed.

Now you're ready to rock. Test cases are grouped into test suites, and the test runner executes the test suites.

EXECUTING THE TESTS

A number of files and pieces were mentioned in setting up this example.

All you have to do is launch the SampleTestRunnerFlex application. Its output is shown in figure 23.9.

At the top is a color chart representing each test—green for pass and red for fail. On the left is a folder structure of your test suites and each of their test cases. On the right is diagnostic information about any failures. And at the bottom left is a filter to display only passes, only failures, or all the tests.

We've covered profiling and unit testing so far, which help you evaluate the inner workings of your application. The last type of test we'll discuss is functional testing, which focuses on testing the interface from a user's perspective.

23.2.5 *FunFX (functional testing)*

FunFX is an open source initiative to make functional testing available to all. It's closer to a framework (which lets people make test-automation tools) than a functional test automation tool in itself. It's free; the initiative's website is http://funfx.rubyforge.org/, and you can download FunFX from http://files.rubyforge.vm.bytemark.co.uk/funfx/.

FunFX has the potential to save you time in your functional testing endeavors. It's written in Ruby for its scripting abilities, but buyer beware—this is a new project, so it isn't a simple plug-and-play situation.

23.2.6 *RIATest (functional testing)*

Considering the competition, whose prices are in the thousands, RIATest is a low-cost solution that can save you a lot of time in your QA cycle. The product works by embedding an agent during compile time or by using a runtime loader. It costs $499 U.S. and is available at http://www.riatest.com.

We like its simple and straightforward approach:

- Compile your application with the `RIATest` module embedded in it, or use its loader feature to dynamically wrap the agent around your application.
- Record your dry runs through the application (optionally, you can hand-write the test scripts).
- Play back your scripts to verify the results.

Key features include:

- An Action Recorder simplifies the process of recording actions into a human-readable script.
- Syntax highlighting makes those human-readable scripts even easier to read via color coding.
- The engine comes with its own scripting language, which is modeled after ActionScript. This gives you a lot of control while using a language you already know.
- A Component Inspector allows you to mouse over a UI component and inspect its properties.
- Built-in script debugging helps you figure out problems with your test scripts.

RIATest has a lot of momentum behind it. What's interesting is that it has a public mechanism for submitting enhancement requests and bug reports—making it community driven.

23.2.7 HP QuickTest Pro (functional testing)

QuickTest Pro (a.k.a. QTP) is an industrial-strength product from HP (via acquisition of Mercury Interactive). It's powerful and versatile—hence the price tag: $6,000–$9,000 U.S. (pricing may vary depending on licensing options). Go to http://www.hp.com and search for *QuickTest Professional*. QTP was the first functional-testing tool available for Flex, and for a long time it was the only choice.

Some key features are:

- Defect replication
- Keyword-driven test case development
- The ability to update multiple test scripts quickly using a shared object repository
- Easy to use, with minimal training required
- Simple interface

Test cases are in the context of business workflows (versus a purely technical perspective), which makes QTP easy for QA users to relate to.

Test-case creation is advanced: for example, contextual and conditional test cases can go down various branches depending on the results; you can query your database to find data that is in a current state, then perform tests on that data; and so on.

23.2.8 IBM Rational Functional Tester (functional testing)

Not many Flex developers are aware that Rational Functional Tester exists, and in particular that it supports Flex. This Enterprise-class product is specifically aimed at the Java and .NET communities, and it supports testing of all sorts of applications from standalone to the web-based variety. It costs $5,400–$10,500 (pricing may vary depending on licensing options) and is available via http://www-306.ibm.com/software/awdtools/tester/functional/index.html.

Some key features are:

- Data-driven as well as keyword-driven test cases
- Supports test scripts written in many languages including Java and Visual Basic
- Version control
- Dynamic data validation

The Rational Functional Tester is a world-class product that has a world-class price. It's an extremely robust piece of software that even allows for test automation of dumb terminal clients, all the way to Siebel and SAP application testing.

23.3 Summary

In Flex's relatively short life, testing and debugging used to be weak points, but the ecosystem has come a long way in a short amount of time with a variety of tooling and advanced capabilities.

When it comes to debugging, you can do simple things to get insight into what's going on. In addition, the Flex Debugger is a robust tool that gives you tactile control over isolating issues.

Ancillary to debugging is profiling, and the Flex Profiler (new to Flex 3) gives you an advanced tool for understanding the internals of your application. Use it to find out how your application is consuming memory and processing resources.

Making sure new bugs aren't introduced in the first place is what testing is all about. Testing tools range from free, open source projects to pricey, enterprise-strength tools from commercial vendors.

After you've tested and debugged your software, the last stage in the development process is polishing and wrapping up the project. The next chapter teaches you how to prepare for deployment.

24 Wrapping up a project

This chapter covers:

- Printing from your application
- Loading applications with wrappers
- Deploying applications

Look at you, Mr./Mrs./Ms. fancy Flex developer: you've come a long way in a short time. You've conquered things like using data services to hook into databases, you know how to lay out an application, you can address usability with up-front validation, and you can deliver an engaging user experience with effects.

You have the power to have managers beg you for cool business intelligence charts, and your AJAX friends are secretly jealous of you. Now it's just a matter of tying up loose ends and getting the project out the door.

24.1 Printing

Try to contain your excitement! Let's not kid ourselves; printing isn't exactly the most glamorous portion of developing a Flex application (especially when you can do fancy interactive drill-down charts), but it's important to the user.

In chapter 1, we talked about the differences between RIAs and RWAs and how the origin of the browser and the web is that of a disparate document-delivery mechanism. As a result, web browsers are inheritably limited in their ability to function as full-blown platform-agnostic application environments—but the flipside is that they're inherently good at document rendering, and printing is strong as a result (got a doc, print a doc).

The inverse is true for Flex. It's an amazing application framework, but to be honest, printing isn't a strength (got a live application, print a live application?).

We'll show you how to make the best of it.

24.1.1 Flex's approach to printing

Flex isn't working with a document (it's a live application), so printing is facilitated by creating an object for printing and associating all the things that you want printed to that object. Flex renders what that would look like; it then screen-caps it internally to create a print image, which it sends to the printer.

24.1.2 Tools of the trade

A bunch of ActionScript classes make this process work. The core classes come from the `mx.printing` package:

- `FlexPrintJob`—The workhorse of Flex printing. You feed it things to print, and it handles the rest.
- `FlexPrintJobScaleType`—A companion class to `FlexPrintJob` that assists in scaling and sizing.

To make printing manageable, specialized versions of the list-based classes are optimized to support printing: they do away with scrollbars and instead have additional logic to support sizing themselves for print purposes. Those classes are also a part of the `mx.printing` package and include:

- `PrintDataGrid`—A version of the `DataGrid` that is optimized to support printing.
- `PrintAdvancedDataGrid`—A version of the `AdvancedDataGrid` that is optimized to support printing.
- `PrintOLAPDataGrid`—A version of the `OLAPDataGrid` that is optimized for printing.

Let's put these classes to work by using them to print something.

24.1.3 Printing things

Now that you have your tools, let's print something by putting the `FlexPrintJob` to work. Here's the game plan:

1. Create an instance of `FlexPrintJob`.
2. Start the print process. This causes the OS's print dialog box to kick in and lets the user specify which printer to use, page orientation, which pages to print, and all that.

3 You now have a stream open to the print spooler, so the next step is to add objects to the spool for printing.
4 Complete the process by sending the spool to the printer.

NOTE You can only print visual components (that is, anything that is a descendent of the `UIComponent` class).

Putting this game plan in effect, look at listing 24.1, which shows how it appears put together.

Listing 24.1 Printing some stuff, literally

```
<?xml version="1.0" encoding="utf-8"?>
<mx:Application xmlns:mx="http://www.adobe.com/2006/mxml"
   layout="vertical" backgroundColor="white">
  <mx:Script>
      <![CDATA[
    import mx.printing.*;
    public function printStuff():void
    {
      var printJob:FlexPrintJob = new FlexPrintJob();
      printJob.start();
      printJob.addObject(stuff);
      printJob.send();
    }
   ]]>
  </mx:Script>
  <mx:TextArea text="This is some Stuff." id="stuff"/>
  <mx:Button click="printStuff()" label="Print Stuff"/>
</mx:Application>
```

Don't forget to import classes

Instantiate FlexPrintJob object, start print spool, add objects, fire away

After compiling and running, click the button and see what happens—does it come out the way you expected?

To cut to the chase, you'll be surprised because the result isn't the small text you were expecting. By default, the `TextArea` component scales to the full width of the page and prints out huge.

24.1.4 Scaling things for print

Let's deal with the issue of the size not being what you want. To do so, you'll use the companion `FlexPrintJobScaleType` class, which has the properties shown in table 24.1; these properties are declared as constants (fixed values that can't change).

Table 24.1 Properties you can use to control how things are scaled with `FlexPrintJob`

Property	Value	Description
`FILL_PAGE`	`fillPage`	Instructs `FlexPrintJob` to scale the object to either `MATCH_WIDTH` or `MATCH_HEIGHT` depending on which is bigger.

Table 24.1 Properties you can use to control how things are scaled with `FlexPrintJob` *(continued)*

Property	Value	Description
MATCH_WIDTH	matchWidth	Tells `FlexPrintJob` to scale the object horizontally to the full width of the page. If this causes the height of the object to be taller than the page height, the object is printed over more than one page. This is the default that `FlexPrintJob` uses.
MATCH_HEIGHT	matchHeight	Similar to `MATCH_WIDTH`, but scales the image vertically to fill the height of the page. If that causes the width of the object to spill over the edge, the extra portion prints onto additional pages.
NONE	none	Doesn't scale at all—shows the image as is.
SHOW_ALL	showAll	The inverse of `FILL_PAGE`: scales to the smaller of either `MATCH_WIDTH` or `MATCH_HEIGHT`.

Having said that, if you want to go back to the previous example and have things print out as is, you use these properties by passing them as the optional argument to `FlexPrintJob`'s `addObject()` function:

```
printJob.addObject(stuff,FlexPrintJobScaleType.NONE);
```

As you begin adding print functionality to your application, one of the first things to determine is what type of scaling (if any) is necessary to have the desired outcome.

24.1.5 *The art of adding objects*

The second thing to determine in your quest to be a print master is how you want to add objects. You can keep calling the `addObject()` method, but each time you do that the object that gets passed along starts on a new page.

The trick is to group objects together using a container. For example, consider the code in listing 24.2.

Listing 24.2 Printing objects on separate pages

```
<mx:Script>
  . . .
  printJob.addObject(text1,FlexPrintJobScaleType.NONE);
  printJob.addObject(text2,FlexPrintJobScaleType.NONE);
  . . .
</mx:Script>

<mx:VBox id="myVBox" width="100%">
  <mx:Text id="text1" text="This is a bunch of text..."/>
  <mx:Text id="text2" text="This is more text text..."/>
</mx:VBox>
```

If you don't want each object on a separate page, you need to work off a container that wraps around both the objects you want. In this case, you can use the `VBox` to accomplish that:

```
printJob.addObject(myVBox,FlexPrintJobScaleType.NONE);
```

That container is viewed as a single object and thus is printed as a whole. You may not always have that level of control, but there is a workaround.

WHAT IF THE OBJECTS AREN'T UNDER THE SAME CONTAINER?

In the real world, you're unlikely to have all the components you want printed all under one container. And even if you do, what if you don't want to print all the components that are in there?

The next thing you need to solve is dealing with the scenario where all the objects you want printed on one page aren't conveniently wrapped by a single container. The solution is to use ActionScript to temporarily create a container and print that, as illustrated by listing 24.3.

Listing 24.3 Using ActionScript to create a temporary container to print

```
<?xml version="1.0" encoding="utf-8"?>
<mx:Application xmlns:mx="http://www.adobe.com/2006/mxml"
  layout="vertical" backgroundColor="white">
<mx:Script>
  <![CDATA[
    import mx.containers.VBox;
    import mx.printing.*;
    public function printStuff():void
    {
      var printJob:FlexPrintJob = new FlexPrintJob();
      var   tmpVBox:VBox = new VBox();            <-- Creates temporary container
      printJob.start();                  | Adds container to
      addChild(tmpVBox);                 | current view
      tmpVBox.addChild(text1);                     | Adds components
      tmpVBox.addChild(text2);                     | to be printed
      printJob.addObject(tmpVBox,FlexPrintJobScaleType.NONE);
      printJob.send();
      removeChild(tmpVBox);              <-- Destroys container
    }
  ]]>
</mx:Script>
<mx:HBox id="myHBox1" width="100%">
  <mx:Text id="text1" text="Lorem ipsum dolor sit amet"/>
  <mx:Text id="text2" text="Nunc dui purus, egestas id"/>
</mx:HBox>
<mx:HBox id="myHBox2" width="100%">
  <mx:Text id="text3" text="porttitor mi sit amet mi."/>
  <mx:Text id="text4" text="consectetuer adipiscing elit."/>
</mx:HBox>
<mx:Button click="printStuff()" label="Print Stuff"/>
</mx:Application>
```

Note that you have to add the temporary object to the current view using the application's `addChild()` function—but do so only after the user has accepted printing (by adding that code after the `FlexPrintJob`'s `start()` function); otherwise, the user will see that on the screen.

USING A PRINT CUSTOM COMPONENT

An extension of the previous idea creates a custom component that is dedicated to printing. The steps are:

1. Create a custom component whose layout is designed for print.
2. Create a temporary instance of that custom component.
3. Pass the information to the custom component.
4. Add the custom component for printing.
5. Destroy the custom component.

See listings 24.4 and 24.5.

Listing 24.4 Invoking a custom component for print layout

```
<mx:Script>
  <![CDATA[
   import mx.printing.*;                         Imports component if
   import components.*;                        <- not in root directory
   public function printStuff():void
   {
     var printJob:FlexPrintJob = new FlexPrintJob();                Creates
     var   printComp:printComponent = new printComponent();  <-    instance
     addChild(printComp);
     printComp.dAppointment = "05/07/2009";        Sets
     printComp.location = "San Jose, CA";          data
     printJob.start();
     printJob.addObject(printComp,FlexPrintJobScaleType.NONE);
     printJob.send();
     removeChild(printComp);
   }
  ]]>
</mx:Script>
```

Listing 24.5 printComponent.mxml custom component designed for print

```
<?xml version="1.0" encoding="utf-8"?>
<mx:VBox xmlns:mx="http://www.adobe.com/2006/mxml">
  <mx:Script>
   <![CDATA[
     [Bindable]
     public var dAppointment:String = "";
     [Bindable]
     public var location:String = "";
   ]]>
  </mx:Script>
  <mx:Label text="Appointment" fontSize="20" fontWeight="bold"/>
  <mx:HBox>
      <mx:Label text="Date: {dAppointment}"/>
    <mx:Label text="Location: {location}"/>
  </mx:HBox>
</mx:VBox>
```

If you put this all together, you should end up with a nicely formatted page that resembles figure 24.1.

But when it comes to list-based components, you should use the specialized print versions.

Appointment

Date: 05/07/2009 Location: San Jose, CA

Figure 24.1 The output of a custom component made for printing

24.1.6 Printing lists

Regular list-based components like the DataGrid are optimized for the on-screen experience; they invoke scrollbars when necessary and allow for sorting by header. Obviously this isn't of much use when it comes to printing, so when you need to output a list-based component, look for its print counterpart. These lists for print components are optimized for print layout, so they expand to show all rows necessary in order to print all the data you want.

To accommodate that, these print-focused list components give you the ability to control how many pages are to be printed (because list-based components can contain thousands of items), and that control comes by way of the following:

- `validNextPage`—A Boolean property that indicates if there's another page
- `nextPage()`—A function that advances to the next page of data

USING A CUSTOM COMPONENT

The easiest way to do this is to continue from the last example and employ a custom component to house the print version of the list-based control (see listings 24.6 and 24.7).

Listing 24.6 Printing using a custom component that has a `PrintDataGrid`

```
<?xml version="1.0" encoding="utf-8"?>
<mx:Application xmlns:mx="http://www.adobe.com/2006/mxml"
  layout="vertical" backgroundColor="white">
 <mx:Script>
 <![CDATA[
  import mx.printing.*;
  import components.*;
  public function printPages():void
  {
   var printJob:FlexPrintJob = new FlexPrintJob();
   var printComp:printComponent = new printComponent();

   printJob.start();
   printComp.dataProvider=myAC;                  // Passes data
   addChild(printComp);

   printJob.addObject(printComp);                // Prints first page of data
   while(printComp.validNextPage)                // Loops over and adds remaining pages (if any)
   {
    printComp.nextPage();
    printJob.addObject(printComp);
   }
   printJob.send();
```

```
      removeChild(printComp);
    }
  ]]>
  </mx:Script>

  <mx:ArrayCollection id="myAC">
    <mx:Object firstName="Jon" lastName="Hirschi"/>
    <mx:Object firstName="Faisal" lastName="Abid"/>
    <mx:Object firstName="Frank" lastName="Krul"/>
    <mx:Object firstName="Abdul" lastName="Qabiz"/>
  </mx:ArrayCollection>
  <mx:Button click="printPages()" label="Print"/>
</mx:Application>
```

Listing 24.7 printComponent.mxml: custom component based of a `PrintDataGrid`

```
<?xml version="1.0" encoding="utf-8"?>
<mx:PrintDataGrid  xmlns:mx="http://www.adobe.com/2006/mxml">
  <mx:columns>
    <mx:DataGridColumn dataField="firstName" headerText="First Name" />
    <mx:DataGridColumn dataField="lastName" headerText="Last Name"/>
  </mx:columns>
</mx:PrintDataGrid>
```

Using this approach makes it easy to lay out your columns, specify any necessary item renderers, and so on (as opposed to trying to do it all in ActionScript).

USING A COMPOSITE CUSTOM COMPONENT

Although the previous approach is the simplest way to achieve the goal, nothing prevents you from using a composite custom component instead. For example, you may want to have your company's logo displayed on every page; in that case, basing it on a container is what you want. Listing 24.8 updates the code to use this concept by using listing 24.9 as the composite custom component.

Listing 24.8 Using a composite component that contains a `PrintDataGrid`

```
public function printPages():void
{
  var printJob:FlexPrintJob = new FlexPrintJob();
  var printComp:printComponent = new printComponent();
  printJob.start();
  addChild(printComp);
  printComp.width=printJob.pageWidth;        ❶ Sets component's dimensions
  printComp.height=printJob.pageHeight;        to page dimensions
  printComp.printAC=myAC;

  printJob.addObject(printComp);

  while(printComp.pdg.validNextPage)
  {
    printComp.pdg.nextPage();
    printJob.addObject(printComp);
  }

  printJob.send();
```

```
        removeChild(printComp);
    }
```

There's something important to note when you use this approach: the container has no idea how to size itself, so it's important to set the dimensions based on the `printJob`'s `pageWidth` and `pageHeight` properties ❶.

Listing 24.9 printComponent.mxml: composite component containing a PrintDataGrid

```
<?xml version="1.0" encoding="utf-8"?>
<mx:VBox xmlns:mx="http://www.adobe.com/2006/mxml">
  <mx:Script>
    <![CDATA[
      import mx.collections.ArrayCollection;
      [Bindable]
      public var printAC:ArrayCollection;
    ]]>
  </mx:Script>
  <mx:Image source="@Embed(source='assets/cflex.png')"/>
  <mx:PrintDataGrid id="pdg" dataProvider="{printAC}">
    <mx:columns>
      <mx:DataGridColumn dataField="firstName" headerText="First Name" />
      <mx:DataGridColumn dataField="lastName" headerText="Last Name"/>
    </mx:columns>
  </mx:PrintDataGrid>
</mx:VBox>
```

Other good uses for this approach include putting conditional headers and footers on only the first and last pages. Give it a try!

24.1.7 *Catching when a user cancels*

If you need to detect when a user clicks Cancel in the print pop-up window, that's easy to do (see listing 24.10). The `FlexPrintJob`'s `start()` function returns `true` or `false` depending on the action (`true` for print, `false` for cancel), so you need to tap into that.

Listing 24.10 Differentiating a start vs. cancel selection

```
var printJob:FlexPrintJob = new FlexPrintJob();
if(printJob.start())
{
  printJob.addObject(myObj);
  printJob.send();
}
else
{
  mx.controls.Alert("User cancelled printing.");
}
```

No big surprises there; you may want to employ this technique as a good best practice (where you add objects only if you have the green light).

24.1.8 FlexReport

An open source project called FlexReport, headed by Frederico Garcia, aims to improve the printing experience—particularly from a reporting angle. The main areas of focus include these:

- Report layout
- Strong multipage support
- Print preview

FlexReport is a collection of ActionScript and MXML components that you invoke depending on what you want to do. For more information, visit http://www.kemelyon.com/bts.

24.2 Customizing the wrapper

No, not Eminem or 50 Cent! A *wrapper* is the thing that loads your Flex application.

As you've been building and launching your application, Flex Builder has been creating a wrapper for you. It's an HTML file with the necessary code to launch your Flex application (the SWF file).

The default wrapper that Flex Builder generates does the following:

- Loads in JavaScript to support back/forward JavaScript history functionality as well as the ability to bookmark a view of your application (known as *deep linking*)
- Checks to make sure the user has a minimum level of the Flash Player
- Creates the HTML to load the Flex application
- Supports Express Install, which is a mechanism that helps users stay up to date on the minimum level of the Flash Player required by making upgrades simple and painless

A wrapper is the perfect place to introduce a few things:

- Pass outside parameters to your Flex application
- Embed JavaScript functions that your Flex application needs to work with

Let's look at where these wrapper files are located and what they look like.

24.2.1 Wrapper files

Take a moment to look in the bin-debug folder of your Flex Builder projects; you may have noticed these appearing out of nowhere for some time now. Here's an explanation of those files:

- *<filename>.html*—The main wrapper file. All the action goes down here.
- *AC_OETags.js*—Supports JavaScript functions like Flash Player version checking, as well as functions to support launching your Flex application.
- *playerProductInstall.swf*—Invoked when the user's Flash Player version is less than the minimum. Has a simple mechanism of prompting the user to install the latest version.

- *history/**—Contains files necessary to support history functionality in Flex.

Fortunately you don't need to start from scratch with making these because you can use templates as a starting point.

24.2.2 Wrapper templates

If you need to customize the wrapper, one place to look for examples is the wrapper templates that come with Flex. You'll find these in the following directory:

```
<installdir>\sdks\3.0.0\templates
```

If you installed Flex Builder in the default location in Windows, you can find these specifically in

```
C:\Program Files\Adobe\Flex Builder 3\sdks\3.0.0\templates
```

The following templates are available:

- `client-side-detection`—Determines if the user has the appropriate version of the Flash Player, and loads the application only if that requirement has been met.
- `client-side-detection-with-history`—Flash Player version verification plus the ability to do browser history management.
- `express-installation`—Enables Express Install if the user needs to upgrade.
- `express-installation-with-history`—Enables Express install plus browser history management.
- `no-player-detection`—A bare-bones example.
- `no-player-detection-with-history`—Bare bones with history management.

You can switch to any of these easily by doing the following:

1. Open the desired template directory.
2. Select all the files.
3. Copy the files to the `html-template` directory in your project.

At this point, if you wish to customize further, open index.template.html.

Let's start with the bare essentials of a wrapper: the must-have pieces.

24.2.3 The bare essentials

It all boils down to two main tags:

- `<object>`—Used by Internet Explorer
- `<embed>`—Used by Mozilla-based browsers (such as FireFox)

To create an extremely bare-bones wrapper, check out listing 24.11, which includes only the essentials to launch a Flex application.

Listing 24.11 An extremely basic wrapper

```
<object classid="clsid:D27CDB6E-AE6D-11cf-96B8-444553540000"
```

```
   width="${width}" height="${height}"
  codebase="http://fpdownload.macromedia.com/get/flashplayer/
    ➥ current/swflash.cab">
 <param name="movie" value="${swf}.swf" />
   <embed src="${swf}.swf"
     width="${width}" height="${height}"
     type="application/x-shockwave-flash"
     pluginspage="http://www.adobe.com/go/getflashplayer">
    </embed>
</object>
```

NOTE Flex Builder inserts the necessary values wherever a `${...}` placeholder is specified when compiling the application.

You could pare that down even further if you knew your audience was using only one specific browser (for example, in an intranet environment where the company allows only one browser to be installed).

24.2.4 Embedding into a web application

If you're a user of web technologies like ColdFusion, PHP, and JSP, you can embed your Flex application into the web application itself. The easiest way to do that is to rename the generated wrapper (.html) file's extension to whatever extension your preferred server-side web application technology uses; doing so immediately transforms the wrapper to your web-application environment.

For example, if you're a ColdFusion person and you rename your application to a .cfm extension, it will execute like any other ColdFusion template—allowing that file to have access to various scopes (application, session, request, CGI, and so on) and enabling you to embed any necessary logic.

What kind of logic do people normally incorporate? Here are a couple of ideas:

- Pass parameters to the Flex application, such as the current `UserID` or configuration information.
- Include security code to do a precheck to see whether the user is allowed to launch the application.

You can also use this capability to embed a Flex application inside a web application.

MAKING IT A PORTLET

A *portlet* is an application that exists inside another application. To take the previous idea a bit further, your web application can do an include (or generate the wrapper launch code) that causes your Flex application to launch inside a web application.

For example, in ColdFusion, if you rename the wrapper file from MyProject.html to MyProject.cfm, you can do the following:

```
<cfinclude template="/path/to/MyProject.cfm">
```

This invokes your Flex application as part of your ColdFusion application.

24.2.5 Passing parameters in a wrapper

Whether you're launching the Flex application as a portlet inside an overall web application or your wrapper is executed by some server-side technology, you may need to pass startup parameters to the Flex application. Doing this is easy: you can do so in the wrapper template (the Flex project's html-template/index.template.html) or in the generated wrapper by adding an extra setting called `flashvars`.

Open a wrapper file, in this case MyProject.html; you'll see a section that looks similar to listing 24.12.

Listing 24.12 Code in the wrapper that invokes your application

```
} else if (hasRequestedVersion) {
  AC_FL_RunContent(
    "src", "CH24",
    "width", "100%",
    "height", "100%",
    "align", "middle",
    "id", "CH24",
    "quality", "high",
    "bgcolor", "#ffffff",
    "name", "CH24",
    "allowScriptAccess","sameDomain",
    "type", "application/x-shockwave-flash",
    "pluginspage", "http://www.adobe.com/go/getflashplayer"
);
```

This is the key JavaScript function that invokes your Flex application and is where you add the additional `flashvars` variable. If you need to pass security credentials about the user, you can do so as shown in listing 24.13.

Listing 24.13 Adding the `flashvars` property to pass info to the application

```
} else if (hasRequestedVersion) {
  AC_FL_RunContent(
    "src", "CH24",
    "width", "100%",
    "height", "100%",
    "align", "middle",
    "id", "CH24",
    "quality", "high",
    "bgcolor", "#ffffff",
    "name", "CH24",
    "allowScriptAccess","sameDomain",
    "flashvars","UserID=12321&SessionKey=BAE23424A",
    "type", "application/x-shockwave-flash",
    "pluginspage", "http://www.adobe.com/go/getflashplayer"
);
```

If you've converted the wrapper to one that can execute code, you can pass that information dynamically. For example, using ColdFusion may look like the following:

```
    "allowScriptAccess","sameDomain",
<cfoutput>
    "flashvars","UserID=#Session.UserID#&SessionKey=#Session.Key#",
</cfoutput>
    "type", "application/x-shockwave-flash",
```

On the Flex side of things, you access those two values via the following syntax:

```
Application.application.parameters.UserID;
Application.application.parameters.SessionKey;
```

A full implementation is along the lines of listing 24.14: upon initialization of the application, you retrieve all these parameters and then store them locally.

Listing 24.14 Accessing wrapper `flashvars` from Flex

```
<?xml version="1.0" encoding="utf-8"?>
<mx:Application xmlns:mx="http://www.adobe.com/2006/mxml"
        backgroundColor="white" creationComplete="initApp()">
<mx:Script>
  <![CDATA[
    import mx.controls.Alert;
    [Bindable]
    public var UserID:int;

    [Bindable]
    public var SessionKey:String;

    public function initApp():void
    {
      UserID = Application.application.parameters.UserID;
      SessionKey = Application.application.parameters.SessionKey;
         mx.controls.Alert.show("UserID="+UserID+" Key="+SessionKey);
    }
  ]]>
</mx:Script>
</mx:Application>
```

That's all there is to it; anything more is dependent on what you want to do. A possible next step in this example would be to take the `UserID` and `SessionKey` and use a back-end data service to verify that those match, to be sure the user is authentic.

24.3 Deployment

This is the last piece to wrapping up your project—getting it out the door! At this point, the application has been tested, and it passes QA and user acceptance; the next step is to push it into a production environment.

Because applications can vary drastically in implementation, there's no one-size-fits-all approach. But we'll give you general pointers and procedures.

24.3.1 Create a production build

Throughout the course of building your Flex applications, you'll have noticed that by default they're built into a bin-debug folder. Care to guess what kind of file it is?

Even though it's fairly obvious, if you said "debug," you get a prize. The debug version of your Flex application allows for the memory profiling, step debugger, and so on.

But for a production build, you don't want that overhead. To create the production version of your application, follow these steps:

1 Select File > Export > Release Build. Doing so brings up a dialog box that allows you to do a production build of any of your applications.
2 Select the desired application.
3 Choose the output folder (by default, it creates a `bin-release` folder, as shown in figure 24.2), and click Finish.

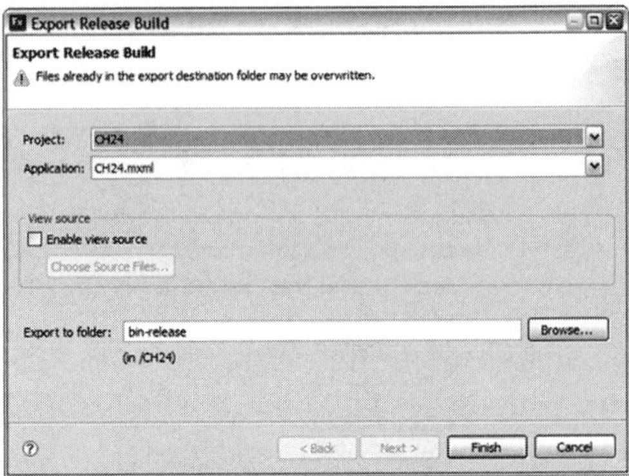

Figure 24.2 The Export Release Build dialog lets you build production versions of your applications.

You should notice that the export folder has been created and is populated with your application's various files.

NOTE Selecting the Enable View Source option allows users to view the source code of your application.

You're almost there, and now that you have a production build of your application, you need to deploy all the client files.

24.3.2 Positioning client-side files

The next stage involves copying all the client-side Flex files into place. The list of things to move is application specific, but here's a good starting point:

- Everything generated by the release build process
  - Wrapper file
  - JavaScript files (such as AC_OETags.js)
  - Lowercase is correct for "history" in the following
  - history folder
  - playerProductInstall.swf
  - SWF files
- External assets (things you didn't embed in the application)
  - Graphics and icons
  - Audio/MP3 files
  - Video files
  - Stylesheets
- Configuration
  - XML files
- Libraries
  - RSLs
  - SWCs
  - SWF modules

With the front-end pieces in place, next you need to deal with the back-end pieces that reside on the server.

24.3.3 Positioning server-side files

If your application relies on back-end pieces being in place, you need to position them into your production environment. This is technology specific, but don't forget that if you created a custom wrapper in your web technology of choice, you need to move it into place.

Other server-side pieces include:

- Remote objects, web services, and data services
- Database changes
- Server-side configuration
- Web server configuration

Now all you need to do is make sure it works.

24.3.4 Testing that it works

This may go without saying, but whether you're deploying to a staging environment or directly to production, these environments won't be the same as your local development environment. In particular, you're accessing the application via a web server, whereas locally you may have loaded it directly. For example, your URL may go from

```
file:///C:/Documents%20and%20Settings/tahmed/My%20Documents/
  Flex%20Builder%203/CH24/bin-debug/CH24.html
```

to an HTTP-based URL:

```
http://www.cflex.net/myApplication.cfm
```

Because you're going over the wire, some things may get in the way that you should be aware of:

- Network access
- Firewalls
- Web server configuration/authentication
- Flash Player not passing cookies in your browser
- If the application doesn't work immediately, these should be the first things you look into.

24.4 Summary

That's a wrap! You know all the things you need to know to be a productive Flex developer. There's always more to learn, and that can come in time; don't sweat it. The more you get comfortable with the technology, the more you'll naturally learn and expand your knowledge.

The next steps are to put your new-found Flex knowledge to work and focus on making real applications. You'll encounter hurdles, and you'll overcome them, but you're never alone.

One of the best things about being a Flex developer is the supportive community you'll be part of. See the resources which follows this chapter, be sure to join your local Flex user group, and attend Flex-based conferences.

As you become proficient, you can help grow the strength of the community by participating in discussion forums, starting a blog, and writing articles. We hope this book has given you a solid foundation to build on, and we look forward to seeing you out in the Flex ecosystem.

resources

Developer resources

- Adobe Flex Developer Center—http://www.adobe.com/devnet/flex/
- AYFABTU aggregated blogs—http://www.allyourflexarebelongtous.com/
- Community Flex—http://www.cflex.net
- Flex.org—http://www.flex.org
- Flex Developer Center—http://www.adobe.com/devnet/flex/
- JAM: Just ActionScript and MXML—http://www.onflex.org/code/
- FlexBox (Catalog of thirds-party Flex components)—
  http://flexbox.mrinalwadhwa.com/
- MyFlex.org (Commercial Flex components)—http://www.myflex.org/
- ScaleNine (Themes and skins)—http://www.scalenine.com/
- Adobe MXNA aggregated blogs—http://weblogs.macromedia.com/mxna/
- Feed-squirrel.com aggregated blogs—http://www.feed-squirrel.com/
- Flex Search—http://flexsearch.org/
- Flex Cookbook—http://www.adobe.com/go/flex_cookbook/

Discussion forums

- FlexCoders—http://www.adobe.com/go/flexcoders
- Flex Component Development—
  http://tech.groups.yahoo.com/group/flexcomponents/

- Flex Support Forums—
  http://www.adobe.com/cfusion/webforums/forum/index.cfm?forumid=60
- FlexCoders.ru (Russian)—http://www.flexcoders.ru/
- FlexForum.de (German)—http://www.flexforum.de/
- FlexComponents—http://www.adobe.com/go/flexcomponents
- House of Fusion (Flex for ColdFusion developers)—
  http://www.houseoffusion.com/groups/flex/
- European Flex Developer Forum—http://www.flexdeveloper.eu/

Open source initiatives

- FlexLib (Open source Flex 2 component library)—http://code.google.com/p/flexlib/
- Cairngorm microarchitecture (Lightweight framework)—
  http://www.adobe.com/go/cairngorm/
- eBay ActionScript 3 library—http://code.google.com/p/as3ebaylib/
- Flickr ActionScript 3 library—http://code.google.com/p/as3flickrlib/
- Mappr ActionScript 3 library—http://code.google.com/p/as3mapprlib/
- Odeo ActionScript 3 library—http://code.google.com/p/as3odeolib/
- RSS/ATOM ActionScript 3 library—http://code.google.com/p/as3syndicationlib/
- YouTube ActionScript 3 library—http://code.google.com/p/as3youtubelib/
- RIA Forge—http://www.riaforge.org/

The Flex ecosystem

- Adobe Labs (Things being experimented with)—http://labs.adobe.com/
- The Flex Show podcast—http://www.theflexshow.com/blog/
- FlexCursion (Social Networking among Flexers)—http://flexcursion.ning.com/
- Flex Authority Magazine—http://www.flex-authority.com/

User groups

North America

- Silicon Valley Flex User Group—http://www.silvafug.org
- Seattle Flex User Group—http://www.flexilicio.us

- Adobe Developers of Idaho—http://www.adidaho.org/
- Utah Flex User Group—http://www.flexusergroup.org/
- Denver RIA Developers Group—http://www.ria5280.org/
- Minnesota Flash/Flex/AIR Programmer Group—http://www.mnswf.com/
- The Michigan Flex User's Group—http://www.theflexgroup.org/
- Indianapolis Adobe Flex User Group—http://www.indyflex.com/
- Toronto Flex User Group—http://www.torontoflex.org
- New York Flex User Group—http://www.nyflex.org/
- Philadelphia Flash and Flex User Group—http://www.pfpaug.org
- Washington Capital Area Flex User Group—http://www.dc-flex.org/
- Atlanta Flash and Flex User Group—http://www.affug.com/

International

- French Adobe Flex User Group—http://fr.groups.yahoo.com/group/flexeurs/
- Italian Flex User Group—http://www.augitaly.com/
- Tokyo Flex User Group—http://www.fxug.net/
- Korea Flex User Group—http://www.fxug.co.kr/
- New Zealand Adobe Flex User Group—http://fxug.org.nz/
- Spanish Flex User Group—http://www.madeinflex.com/

index

B

C

D

E

F

G

H

I

J

K

L

Q

R

S

T

U

V

W

X

Y

Z

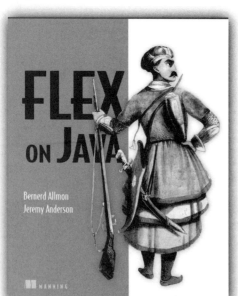